Consistent Four-Part Pedagogy

The four-part pedagogy of ZAPS clarifies the concepts behind each experiment:

1

An **Introduction** helps students connect each experiment to a concrete, real-world example.

2

An **Experiment** allows students to experience psychological phenomena in the role of subject or researcher. Where appropriate, a Data section with a detailed breakdown of results follows the experiment. Instructors can collect aggregate class data.

3

A **Theory** section allows students to read about the theoretical basis behind each experiment after completion.

4

A **Further Info** section offers students additional real-world examples or discussion of similar phenomena.

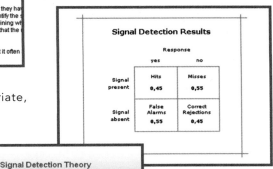

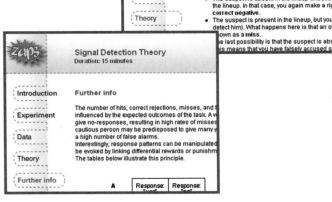

Cognition

FIFTH EDITION

FIFTH EDITION

Cognition

EXPLORING THE SCIENCE OF THE MIND

Daniel Reisberg

REED COLLEGE

W. W. Norton & Company

New York • London

W. W. Norton & Company has been independent since its founding in 1923, when William Warder Norton and Mary D. Herter Norton first published lectures delivered at the People's Institute, the adult education division of New York City's Cooper Union. The firm soon expanded its program beyond the Institute, publishing books by celebrated academics from America and abroad. By midcentury, the two major pillars of Norton's publishing program—trade books and college texts—were firmly established. In the 1950s, the Norton family transferred control of the company to its employees, and today—with a staff of four hundred and a comparable number of trade, college, and professional titles published each year—W. W. Norton & Company stands as the largest and oldest publishing house owned wholly by its employees.

Editor: Aaron Javsicas
Project Editor: Jack Borrebach
Copyeditor: Jackie Estrada
Electronic Media Editor: Callinda Taylor
Editorial Assistant: Catherine Rice
Marketing Manager, Psychology: Andrea Matter
Production Manager: Ashley Horna
Photo Editor: Mike Fodera
Permissions Manager: Megan Jackson
Permissions Clearing: Bethany Salminen
Text Design: Jillian Burr
Composition: Jouve International—Brattleboro, VT
Manufacturing: Quad/Graphics—Versailles, KY

The text of this book is composed in Gotham with the display set in Sabon MT Pro.

Library of Congress Cataloging-in-Publication Data

Reisberg, Daniel.
    Cognition : exploring the science of the mind / Daniel Reisberg. — 5th ed.
        p. cm.
    Includes bibliographical references and index.
    ISBN 978-0-393-92176-2 (hardcover)
    1. Cognitive psychology.   I. Title.
    BF201.R45 2013
    153—dc23

                                                        2012029679

W. W. Norton & Company, Inc., 500 Fifth Avenue, New York, NY 10110-0017
wwnorton.com
W. W. Norton & Company Ltd., Castle House, 75/76 Wells Street, London W1T 3QT

1 2 3 4 5 6 7 8 9 0

For my parents, with gratitude, respect,
and—above all—love

Brief Contents

Contents

PART 5 THINKING 397

Preface

I was a college sophomore when I took my first course in cognitive psychology. I was excited about the material then, and I've been excited about the field ever since. Why? First, cognitive psychologists ask terrific questions, including questions that have intrigued humanity for thousands of years. Why do we think the things we think? Why do we believe the things we believe? What is "knowledge," and how *secure* (how complete, how accurate) is our knowledge of the world around us?

Other questions asked by cognitive psychologists, though, are of a more immediate, personal, concern: How can I help myself to remember more of the material that I'm studying in my classes? Is there some better way to solve the problems I encounter? Why is it that my roommate can study with the radio on, but I can't?

And sometimes the questions have important consequences for our social or political institutions: If an eyewitness reports what he saw at a crime, should we trust him? If a newspaper raises questions about a candidate's integrity, how will voters react?

Of course, we want more than interesting questions—we also want *answers* to these questions, and this is the second reason I find cognitive psychology so exciting. In the last half-century or so, the field has made extraordinary progress on many fronts, providing us with a rich understanding of the nature of memory, the processes of thought, and the content of knowledge. There are many things still to be discovered—that's part of the fun. Even so, we already have something to say about all of the questions just posed and many more as well. We can speak to the specific questions and to the general, to the theoretical issues and to the practical. Our research has uncovered principles useful for improving the process of education and we have made discoveries of considerable importance for the courts. What I've learned as a cognitive psychologist has changed how I think about my own memory; it's changed how I make decisions; it's changed how I draw conclusions when I'm thinking about events in my life.

On top of all this, I'm also excited about the connections that cognitive psychology makes possible. In the modern academic world, intellectual disciplines are often isolated from each other, sometimes working on closely related problems without even realizing it. In the last decades, though, cognitive psychology has forged rich connections with its neighboring disciplines, and in this book we will touch on topics in philosophy, neuroscience, economics, linguistics, politics, computer science, and medicine. These connections bring obvious benefits, since insights and information can be traded back and forth between the domains. In addition, these connections highlight the importance of the material we will be examining, since these connections make it clear that the issues before us are of interest to a wide range of scholars. This provides a strong signal that we're working on questions of considerable power and scope.

I have tried in this text to convey all this excitement. I've done my best to describe the questions being asked within my field and the substantial answers we can provide for these questions, and, finally, some indications of how cognitive psychology is (and has to be) interwoven with other intellectual endeavors.

I also had other goals in writing this text. In my own teaching, I try to maintain a balance among many different elements: the nuts and bolts of how our science proceeds, the data provided by the science, the practical implications of our findings, and the theoretical framework that holds all of these pieces together. I've tried to find the same balance in this text.

In addition, I try throughout this book to "tell a good story," one that conveys how the various pieces of our field fit together into a coherent package. I certainly want the specific evidence for our claims to be in view, so that students can see how our field tests its hypotheses. And I certainly want students to see that our hypotheses *have been* tested, so that our claims must be taken seriously. But I've also put a strong emphasis on the flow of ideas—how new theories lead to new experiments, and how those experiments can lead to new theory. I've also emphasized the ways in which different forms of evidence weave together—so that, for example, the coverage of neuroscience is not just used to tell students which brain areas seem associated with which function; instead, the neuroscience is used to address the psychological questions that have long been of interest to the field.

The notion of telling a "good story" also emerges in another way: I've always been impressed by the ways in which the different parts of cognitive psychology are interlocked. Our claims about attention, for example, have immediate implications for how we can theorize about memory; our theories of object recognition are linked to our proposals for how knowledge is stored in the mind. Linkages like these are intellectually satisfying, because they ensure that the pieces of the puzzle really do fit together. But, in addition, these linkages make the material within cognitive psychology easier to learn, and easier to remember. Indeed, if I were to emphasize one crucial fact about memory, it would be that memory is best when the memorizer perceives the organization and interconnections within the material being learned. (We'll discuss this point further in Chapter 5.) With an eye on this point, I've therefore made sure to highlight the interconnections among various topics, so that students can appreciate the beauty of our field, and can also be helped in their learning by the orderly nature of our theorizing.

I've also worked hard to help students in two other ways. First, I've tried throughout the book to make sure the prose is approachable. I want students to gain a sophisticated understanding of the material in this text, but I certainly don't want students to struggle with the ideas. Therefore, I've kept the presentation as straightforward as possible, and have attempted to keep the presentation focused for students by highlighting the main themes that bind our field together. This edition also includes many more illustrations—including many new data figures—to facilitate student understanding.

Second, I've also taken steps that I hope will foster an "alliance" with readers. My strategy here grows out of the fact that, like most teachers, I value the questions I receive from students, and the discussions I have with them. In the classroom, this allows a two-way flow of information and unmistakably improves the educational process. Of course, a two-way flow is not possible in a textbook, but I've offered what I think is a good approximation: Often, the questions I hear from students, and the discussions I have with them, focus on the relevance of the material we're covering—relevance to students' own lives, or relevance to the world outside of academics. I've tried to capture that dynamic, and to present my answers to these student questions, in *The Cognition Workbook* (and I'll say more about the *Workbook* in a moment). I hope in this way to make sure that students see that the material *is* relevant to their lives— and perhaps as exciting for them as it is for me.

Have I met all of these goals? You, the readers, will need to be the judges of this. I would love to hear from you about what I have done well in the book, and what I could have done better; what I've covered (but should have omitted) and what I've left out. I'll do my best to respond to every comment. You can reach me via e-mail (reisberg@reed.edu); I've been delighted to get comments from students about previous editions, and I hope for more e-mails with this edition.

The book's thirteen chapters are designed to cover the major topics within cognitive psychology. The first section of this book lays the foundation. Chapter 1 provides the conceptual and historical background for the subsequent chapters. In addition, this chapter seeks to convey the extraordinary scope of this field and why, therefore, research on cognition is so important. This chapter also highlights the relationship between theory and evidence in cognitive psychology, and discusses the logic on which this field is built.

Chapter 2 then offers a brief introduction to the study of the brain. Most of cognitive psychology is concerned with the functions that our brains make possible, and not the brain itself. Nonetheless, our understanding of cognition has certainly been enhanced by the study of the brain, and, throughout this book, we'll use biological evidence as one means of evaluating our theories. Chapter 2 is designed to make this evidence fully accessible to the reader—by providing a quick survey of the research tools used in studying the brain, an overview of the brain's anatomy, and also an example of how we can use brain evidence as a source of insight into cognitive phenomena. New in this edition is expanded coverage of a point that sometimes confuses students—what exactly we can learn from detailed study of the brain and the localization of function.

In the second section of the book, we consider the problems of object recognition, and then the problem of attention. Chapter 3 discusses how we recognize the objects that surround us. This seems a straightforward matter—what could be easier than recognizing a telephone, or a coffee cup, or the letter Q? As we will see, however, recognition is surprisingly complex, and discussion of this complexity allows us to showcase several key themes: how *active* people are in organizing and interpreting the information they receive from the world; the degree to which people *supplement* the information by relying on prior experience; and the ways in which this knowledge can be built into a *network*. In this edition, I've said more about classic issues in Gestalt psychology, but also said more about recent (and, I think, intriguing) developments in face perception.

Chapter 4 then considers what it means to "pay attention." The first half of the chapter is concerned largely with selective attention—cases in which you seek to focus on a target while ignoring distractors. The second half of the chapter is concerned with divided attention—i.e., cases in which you seek to focus on more than one target, or more than one task, at the same time. Here, too, we will see that seemingly simple processes often turn out to be more complicated than one might suppose. In the fifth edition, this chapter has fuller discussion of key theoretical issues (the nature of the mind's executive control processes) and also applied issues (including the worrisome case of people using their phones while driving).

The third section turns to the broad problem of memory. Chapters 5, 6, and 7 start with a discussion of how information is "entered" into long-term storage, but then turn to the complex interdependence between how information is first learned and how that same information is subsequently retrieved. A recurrent theme in this section is that learning that is effective for one sort of task, one sort of use, may be quite ineffective for other uses. This theme is examined in several contexts, and leads to a discussion of current research on unconscious memories—so-called "memory without awareness." These chapters also offer a broad assessment of human memory: How accurate are our memories? How complete? How long-lasting? These issues are pursued both with regard to theoretical treatments of memory, and also the practical consequences of memory research, including the application of this research to the assessment, in the courtroom, of eyewitness testimony. These chapters—like the entire book—have expanded coverage in three major domains: fuller discussion of the relevant neuroscience; a broader exploration of theory (including working memory's role in making someone *intelligent*); and a greater emphasis on key applied issues (such as eyewitness memory).

The book's fourth section is about knowledge. Earlier chapters show over and over that humans are, in many ways, guided in their thinking and experiences by what they already know—i.e., the broad pattern of knowledge they bring into each new experience. This invites the questions posed by Chapters 8, 9, and 10: What is knowledge? How is it represented in the mind?

Chapter 8 tackles the question of how "concepts," the building blocks of our knowledge, are represented in the mind. Chapters 9 and 10 focus on two special types of knowledge. Chapter 9 examines our knowledge about language, with discussion of both *linguistic competence* and *linguistic performance*. Chapter 10 considers *visual knowledge* and examines what is known about mental imagery. These chapters now include coverage of several points that I believe were understated in previous editions—including exciting research on bilingualism, and the phenomenon of eidetic imagery (both in ordinary people and in those diagnosed with autism).

The chapters in the fifth section are concerned with the topic of thinking. Chapter 11 examines how each of us draws conclusions from evidence— including cases in which we are trying to be careful and deliberate in our judgments, and also cases of informal judgments of the sort we often make in our everyday lives. The chapter then turns to the question of how we reason from our beliefs—how we check on whether our beliefs are correct, and how we draw conclusions, based on things we already believe. The chapter also considers the pragmatic issue of how errors in thinking can be diminished through education. This chapter has updated coverage of theorizing from (Nobel Laureate) Daniel Kahneman, and expanded discussion of the role of *emotion* within decision-making.

Chapter 12 is also about thinking, but with a different perspective: This chapter considers some of the ways people differ from each other in their ability to solve problems, in their creativity, and in their intelligence. The chapter also addresses the often heated, often misunderstood debate about how different groups—men vs. women, or American Whites vs. African Americans—might (or might not) differ in their intellectual capacities.

The final chapter in the book does double service. First, it pulls together many of the strands of contemporary research relevant to the topic of consciousness—what consciousness is, and what consciousness is for. In addition, most students will reach this chapter at the end of a full semester's work, a point at which they are well served by a review of the topics already covered and ill served by the introduction of much new material. Therefore, this chapter draws many of its themes and evidence from previous chapters, and in that fashion serves as a review of points that appear earlier in the book. Chapter 13 also highlights the fact that we are using these materials to approach some of the greatest questions ever asked about the mind, and, in that way, this chapter should help to convey some of the power of the material we have been discussing throughout the book.

This basic structure of the book differs in important ways from that of the previous editions, and two changes will be especially visible: First, the book is now printed in full color, and I've done all I can to use the color intelligently—to make the artwork more instructive, and also to make the material more engaging! Second, the book has been shortened by two chapters, an evolution designed in part to mirror the evolution of cognitive psychology itself. Specifically, I have de-emphasized several issues that the field now regards as less pressing, and united certain issues that, in previous editions, had been covered separately, but which the field now regards as related. This shortening of the chapter count has allowed some streamlining throughout the book, with the ironic result that I believe I am now conveying more information via a somewhat less dense presentation. And, happily, the streamlining has also created space for a lot of new material. Some of that material involves updating through the book; some has allowed me to expand discussion of key points (for example, the mind's executive processes, or applications of memory research to eyewitness testimony). And some of the new material involves entirely new coverage—for example, coverage of the intriguing, important, but sometimes controversial research on intelligence and intelligence testing.

I have also expanded and enlarged the *Cognition Workbook*. It is, of course, common these days for textbooks to come with supplementary materials, and many are included with this book: For instructors, there is an extensive test bank; lecture-ready PowerPoint slides; Coursepacks for use in hybrid and online courses; and an instructor's resource disc. For students, there is an online StudySpace, and an available eBook version. Also available is a broad set of online labs (ZAPS) to engage students in the scientific process.

In addition to these resources, though, I wanted to do something more personal. Specifically, I wanted a supplement for the book that was fully integrated with the text, truly emphasizing themes that were already in the book, but also carefully picking up on points that the text hadn't covered. In addition, as a reader I find it jarring when a text's supplementary materials take a perspective or offer a view that doesn't line up well with the emphasis of the text itself.

For all of these reasons, I decided, for the fourth edition of this text, to create the *Cognition Workbook,* hoping to ensure that you, the reader, got ancillary materials that were completely in tune with the goals, themes, and emphases of the main text. The workbook includes two types of materials: First, in my own classroom, I include many demonstrations—usually miniature versions of experimental procedures—so that students can see for themselves what these experiments involve, and can also see just how powerful many of our effects are. The workbook contains adaptations of these classroom demonstrations, designed so that they can be used in whatever fashion an instructor (or the reader) wishes: Readers who want to run the demos for themselves as they read along certainly can, and, to facilitate this, a marginal icon (like the one shown here) will appear in the text to indicate the availability of a relevant demonstration. Instructors who want to run the demos within their classrooms (as I do) are certainly encouraged to do so. Instructors who want to use the demonstrations in discussion sections, aside from the main course, can do that

WORKBOOK DEMONSTRATION

as well. In truth, I suspect that some demos will work better in one of these venues, and that other demos will work better in others, but, in all cases, I hope the demos help bring the material to life—putting students directly in contact with both our experimental methods and our experimental results.

Second, in my own course, I often want to go beyond the information in the text itself. Part of this "going beyond" involves an emphasis on research methods, and so in the workbook I've included essays for each chapter to explore key principles involved in our research. One essay, for example, works through the question of what a "testable hypothesis" is, and why this is so important; another essay works through the power of random assignment; another discusses how we deal with confounds. In all cases, my hope is that these essays will guide students toward a sophisticated understanding of why our research is as it is, and why, therefore, our research is so persuasive. In addition, each of the essays ends with a discussion question, so that students can think about, and *apply*, the issues being considered.

My own students are also eager to know how the material we're studying *matters*—for their own lives, or for the broader world. To help them think about this issue, I often draw on my own experience in working with law enforcement and the criminal justice system. In this work, I'm sometimes called on to help juries understand how an eyewitness might be certain in his recollection, but *mistaken*. I also work with police officers, to help them determine how to draw as much information from a witness as possible, without leading the witness in any way. Based on this experience, each chapter of the workbook also includes essays that discuss how the material in that chapter might be useful for the legal system. These essays will, I hope, be immediately interesting for students, and will persuade them that the material they're studying has important real-world consequences. In turn, it's my hope that this will make it obvious to students why it's crucial that the science be done carefully and well—so that we bring only high-quality information into the legal system. And for these essays, too, I've written discussion questions (for students', instructors', *or* TAs' use) to help students think about these materials, and to explore the implications of what they're studying.

In addition, my students often seek "take-home messages" from the material that will, in a direct way, benefit them. We are, after all, talking about memory, and students obviously are engaged in an endeavor of putting lots of new information—information they're learning in their courses—into their memories! We're talking about attention, and students often struggle with the chore of keeping themselves "on task" and "on target." In light of these points of contact, I've written essays for each chapter designed to build the bridge between the course materials and the concerns that often fill students' lives. This will, I hope, make the material more useful for students, and also make it clear just how important an enterprise cognitive psychology is.

In the current edition, I've updated many of these essays but—more important—I've added a number of new demonstrations and new essays. For me, this expansion is especially fun, because the *Workbook*, by design, involves *interaction*—students interacting (via the demonstrations) with the material, and me interacting (via the essays) with the reader. On this basis, I am particularly interested in hearing from students what they think of the *Workbook*—so that I can, in effect, make it into an avenue of communication between me and my readers.

Finally, let me turn to the happiest of chores—thanking all of those who have contributed to this book. I begin with those who helped with the previous editions: Bob Crowder (Yale University) and Bob Logie (University of Aberdeen) both read the entire text of the first edition, and the book was unmistakably improved by their insights. Other colleagues read, and helped me enormously with, specific chapters: Enriqueta Canseco-Gonzalez (Reed College); Rich Carlson (Pennsylvania State University); Henry Gleitman (University of Pennsylvania); Lila Gleitman (University of Pennsylvania); Peter Graf (University of British Columbia); John Henderson (Michigan State University); Jim Hoffman (University of Delaware); Frank Keil (Cornell University); Mike McCloskey (Johns Hopkins University); Hal Pashler (UCSD); Steve Pinker (MIT); and Paul Rozin (University of Pennsylvania).

The second edition was markedly strengthened by the input and commentary provided by: Martin Conway (University of Bristol); Kathleen Eberhard (Notre Dame University); Howard Egeth (Johns Hopkins University); Bill Gehring (University of Michigan); Steve Palmer (University of California, Berkeley); Henry Roediger (Washington University); and Eldar Shafir (Princeton University).

In the third edition, I was again fortunate to have the advice, criticism, and insights provided by a number of colleagues who, together, made the book better than it otherwise could have been, and I'd like to thank: Rich Carlson (Penn State); Richard Catrambone (Georgia Tech); Randall Engle (Georgia Tech); Bill Gehring and Ellen Hamilton (University of Michigan); Nancy Kim (Rochester Institute of Technology); Steve Luck (University of Iowa); Michael Miller (University of California, Santa Barbara); Evan Palmer, Melinda Kunar, and Jeremy Wolfe (Harvard University); Chris Shunn (University of Pittsburgh); and Daniel Simons (University of Illinois).

A number of colleagues also provided their insights and counsel for the fourth edition—either for the textbook itself or for *The Cognition Workbook*. I'm therefore delighted to thank: Ed Awh (University of Oregon); Glen Bodner (University of Calgary); William Gehring (University of Michigan); Katherine Gibbs (University of California, Davis); Eliot Hazeltine (University of Iowa); William Hockley (Wilfrid Laurier University); James Hoffman (University of Delaware); Helene Intraub (University of Delaware); Vikram Jaswal (University of Virginia); Karsten Loepelmann (University of Alberta); Penny Pexman (University of Calgary); and Christy Porter (College of William and Mary).

I have even more people to thank for their help and constructive suggestions for this edition: Karin M. Butler (University of New Mexico); Mark A. Casteel (Penn State University, York); Alan Castel (University of California, Los Angeles); Robert Crutcher (University of Dayton); Kara D. Federmeier (University of Illinois, Urbana-Champaign); Jonathan Flombaum (Johns Hopkins University); Katherine Gibbs (University of California, Davis); Arturo E. Hernandez (University of Houston); James Hoeffner (University of Michigan); Timothy Jay (Massachusetts College of Liberal Arts); Timothy Justus (Pitzer College); Janet Nicol (University of Arizona); Robyn T. Oliver (Roosevelt University); Raymond Phinney (Wheaton College, and his comments were especially thoughtful!); Brad Postle (University of Wisconsin, Madison); Erik D. Reichle (University of Pittsburgh); Eric Ruthruff (University of New Mexico); Dave Sobel (Brown University); Martin van den Berg (California State University, Chico); and Daniel R. VanHorn (North Central College).

I also want to thank the people at Norton. I've had a succession of terrific editors, and I'm grateful to Jon Durbin, Sheri Snavely, and Aaron Javsicas for their support and fabulous guidance over the years. And here I get to say publicly that I resisted when Sheri urged me to make the fifth edition a full-color project, but I was wrong; she was right, and I'm thrilled that her sense prevailed. Aaron Javsicas, editor for this edition, continues to be a remarkably alert, thoughtful, and attentive reader, and I look forward to future editions with him!

I also want to thank Jack Borrebach, Michael Fodera, Catherine Rice, Elyse Rieder, Trish Marx, and Callinda Taylor for their extraordinary work in keeping the production on track, beautifully illustrated, and of the highest quality. Jackie Estrada was a fine copyeditor, and I'm grateful for her tolerance of my craziness.

This is also the chance for me to take a broader view, and acknowledge my long-term debt to a number of friends, colleagues, and mentors, people who have instructed me and inspired me. I therefore want to express my deep gratitude to several people, many still alive, but some sadly gone: Barry Schwartz, Jeff Travers, and Hans Wallach; Jon Baron, Henry Gleitman, Dick Neisser, and Liz Spelke; Arien Mack and Leon Festinger. Collectively, they played a huge role in bringing me to where I am.

Finally, in dozens of ways, Friderike makes this possible, and worthwhile. She forgives me the endless hours at the computer, tolerates the tension when I'm feeling overwhelmed by deadlines, and is always ready to read my pages and offer thoughtful, careful, instructive insights. My gratitude to, and love for, her are boundless.

Daniel Reisberg
Portland, Oregon

Cognition

FIFTH EDITION

Cognition

The Foundations of Cognitive Psychology

W hat is cognitive psychology? In Chapter 1, we'll define this discipline and offer an early sketch of what this field can teach us—through its theories and through its practical applications. We'll also provide a brief history, in order to explain why cognitive psychology takes the form that it does.

Chapter 2 has a different focus. In the last decade or two, cognitive psychology has formed a productive partnership with the field of *cognitive neuroscience*—the effort toward understanding our mental functioning by close study of the brain and nervous system. In this book, our emphasis will be on psychology, not neuroscience, but even so, we'll rely on neuroscience evidence at many points. To make sure this evidence is useful, we need to provide some background, and that's the

provide a rough mapping of what's where in the brain, and we'll describe the functioning of many of the brain's parts. We'll also discuss the broad issue of *what it means* to describe the functioning of this or that brain region, because, as we will see, each of the brain's parts is enormously specialized in what it does. As a result, mental achievements such as reading or remembering or deciding depend on the coordinated functioning of many different brain regions, with each contributing its own small bit to the overall achievement.

CHAPTER ONE

The Science of the Mind

This is a book about our broad intellectual functioning. What's at stake, though, is far more than "intellectual functioning," because, as we'll see, virtually everything that we do, and everything that we feel or say, depends on our *cognition*—what we know, what we remember, and how we think.

As one example, we will, in just a few pages, consider the way in which a person's ability to cope with grief depends on how memory functions. We'll also discuss the role that memory plays in shaping someone's self-image—and hence his or her self-esteem. As a more basic example, we'll also discuss a case in which your understanding of a simple story depends on the background knowledge that you supply. Related claims can be made for virtually every conversation you participate in and every social interaction you witness: In each of these settings, your ability to understand your world depends critically on knowledge you bring to the situation. Examples like these make it clear that cognition matters in an extraordinary range of circumstances, and it is on this basis that our focus in this book is, in a real sense, on the intellectual foundations of almost every aspect of human experience.

- The chapter begins with a sketch of the scope of cognitive psychology. The domain of this field includes activities that are obviously "intellectual" (such as remembering, or attending, or making judgments) and also a much broader range of activities that *depend on* these intellectual achievements.

- A brief review of the history of cognitive psychology highlights two essential themes. One is the idea that we cannot study the mental world by means of direct observation. The second theme is that we *must* study the mental world if we are to understand behavior, because our behavior depends in crucial ways on how we *perceive* and *understand* the world around us.

- Combining these themes, we are led to the view that we must study the mental world *indirectly*, but as we will see, the (inferential) method for doing this is the same method used by other sciences, including physics.

- Finally, we consider an example of research in cognitive psychology, to illustrate the types of data that psychologists consider and the logic they use in testing their theories.

The Scope of Cognitive Psychology

When the field of cognitive psychology was first launched, it was generally understood as the *scientific study of knowledge*, and this conception of the field led immediately to a series of questions: How is knowledge acquired? How is knowledge retained so that it's available when needed? How is knowledge used— whether as a basis for making decisions or as a means of solving problems?

These are great questions, and it's easy to see that answering them might be quite useful. For example, imagine that you're studying for next Wednesday's exam, but for some reason the material just won't "stick" in your memory. You find yourself wishing, therefore, for a better strategy to use in studying and memorizing. What would that strategy be? Is it possible to have a "better memory"?

As a different case, let's say that while you're studying, your friend is moving around in the room, and you find this to be quite distracting. Why can't you just shut out your friend's motion? Why don't you have better control over your attention and your ability to concentrate?

Here's one more example: You pick up the morning newspaper and you're horrified to learn how many people have decided to vote for candidate X. How do people decide whom to vote for? For that matter, how do people decide what college to attend, or which car to buy, or even what to have for dinner? And how can we help people make *better* decisions—so that, for example, they choose healthier foods, or vote for the candidate who (in your view!) is obviously preferable?

Before we're through, we'll consider evidence pertinent to all of these questions. Let's note, though, that in the various examples just listed, things aren't going as you might have wished: You remember less than you want to; you are

TRYING TO FOCUS

Often, you want to focus your attention on just one thing, and you want to "shut out" the other sights and sounds that are making it hard for you to concentrate. What steps should you take to promote this focus, and to avoid distraction?

unable to ignore a distraction; the voters make a choice you don't like. But what about the other side of things? What about the remarkable intellectual feats that humans achieve—brilliant deductions or creative solutions to complex problems? In this text, we'll also have a lot to say about these cases, and thus how it is that people accomplish the great things they do.

Clearly, then, there is an important set of issues in play here, but even so, the questions just catalogued risk a misunderstanding, because they make it sound like cognitive psychology is concerned only with our functioning as intellectuals—and so our ability to remember, or to pay attention, or to think through options when making a choice. As we said at the very start, though, the relevance of cognitive psychology is far broader—thanks to the fact that a huge range of our actions, thoughts, and feelings *depend on knowledge*. To illustrate this point, let's look at the study of *memory* and ask: When we investigate how memory functions, what exactly is it that we're investigating? Or, to turn this around, what tasks rely on memory?

You obviously rely on memory when you're taking an exam—memory for what you have learned during the term. Likewise, you rely on memory when you're at the supermarket and trying to remember the cheesecake recipe so that you can buy the ingredients. You also rely on memory when you're reminiscing about childhood. But what else draws on memory?

Consider this simple story (adapted from Charniak, 1972):

> *Betsy wanted to bring Jacob a present. She shook her piggy bank. It made no sound. She went to look for her mother.*

A SIMPLE STORY

What is involved in your understanding of this simple story? *Betsy wanted to bring Jacob a present. She shook her piggy bank. It made no sound. She went to look for her mother.*

This four-sentence tale is easy to understand, but *only because you provided some important bits of background yourself*. For example, you weren't at all puzzled about why Betsy was interested in her piggy bank; you weren't puzzled, specifically, about why the story's first sentence led naturally to the second. This is because you already knew (a) that the things one gives as presents are often things bought for the occasion (rather than things already owned), (b) that buying things requires money, and (c) that money is stored in piggy banks. Without these facts, you would have been bewildered as to why a desire to give a gift would lead someone to her piggy bank. (Surely you did not think she intended to give the piggy bank itself as the present!) Likewise, you immediately understood why Betsy *shook* her piggy bank. You didn't suppose that she was shaking it in frustration or trying to find out if it would make a good percussion instrument. Instead, you understood that she was trying to determine its contents. But you knew this fact only because you already knew (d) that children don't keep track of how much money is in their bank, and (e) that one cannot simply look into the bank to learn its contents. Without these facts, Betsy's shaking of the bank would make no sense. Similarly, you understood what it meant that the bank made no sound. That's because you know (f) that it's usually coins (not bills) that are kept in piggy banks, and (g) that coins make noise when they are shaken. If you didn't know these facts, you might have interpreted the bank's silence, when it was shaken, as good news, indicating perhaps that the bank was jammed full of $20 bills—an inference that would have led you to a very different expectation for how the story would unfold from there.

Of course, there's nothing special about the "Betsy and Jacob" story, and it seems likely that we'd uncover a similar reliance on background knowledge if we explored how you understand some other narrative, or how you follow a conversation, or comprehend a TV show. Our suggestion, in other words, is that many (and perhaps all) of your encounters with the world depend on your supplementing your experience with knowledge that you bring to the situation. And perhaps this *has* to be true. After all, if you didn't supply the relevant bits of background, then anyone telling the "Betsy and Jacob" story would need to spell out all the connections and all the assumptions. That is, the story would have to include all the facts that, *with* memory, are supplied by you. As a result, the story would have to be many times longer, and the telling of it much slower. The same would be true for every story you hear, every conversation you participate in. Memory is thus crucial for each of these activities.

Here is a different sort of example: In Chapter 6, we will consider various cases of clinical *amnesia*—cases in which someone, because of brain damage, has lost the ability to remember certain materials. These cases are fascinating at many levels, including the fact that they provide us with key insights into what memory is *for*: Without memory, what is disrupted?

One well-studied amnesia patient was a man identified as H.M.; his memory loss was the unanticipated by-product of brain surgery intended to control his epilepsy, and the loss was quite profound. H.M. was in his mid-20s when he had the surgery, and he survived for more than 50 years after the operation. For all of those years, H.M. had no trouble remembering events *prior to* the surgery, but he

CELEBRATING HUMAN ACHIEVEMENTS

Many of the text's examples so far have involved failures or limitations in our cognition. But we also need to explain our species' incredible intellectual achievements—the complex problems we've solved, or the extraordinary devices we've invented.

seemed completely unable to recall any event that occurred *after* his operation. If asked who the president is, or about recent events, he reported facts and events that were current at the time of the surgery. If asked questions about last week, or even an hour ago, he recalled nothing.

The memory loss, of course, had massive consequences for H.M.'s life, and some of the consequences are perhaps surprising. For example, H.M. had an uncle he was very fond of and he often asked his hospital visitors about how his uncle was doing. Unfortunately, the uncle died sometime after H.M.'s surgery, and H.M. was told this sad news. The information came as a horrible shock, triggering enormous grief, but because of his amnesia, he soon forgot about it.

Sometime later, though, because he'd *forgotten* about his uncle's death, H.M. again asked how his uncle was doing, and he was again told of the death. However, with no memory of having heard this news before, he was again hearing it "for the first time," with the shock and grief every bit as strong as it was initially. Indeed, each time he heard this news, he was hearing it "for the first time." With no memory, he had no opportunity to live with the news, to adjust to it. Hence his grief could not subside. Without memory, H.M. had no way to come to terms with his uncle's death.

A different glimpse of memory function comes from H.M.'s poignant comments about his state and about "who he is." Each of us has a conception of who we are, and of what sort of person we are, and that conception is supported by numerous memories: We know whether we're deserving of praise for our good deeds or blame for our transgressions because we remember our good deeds and our transgressions. We know whether we've kept our promises or achieved our

H.M.'S BRAIN

H.M. died in 2008, and the world then learned his full name, Henry Molaison. Throughout his life, H.M. cooperated with researchers in many studies of his memory loss. Even after his death, H.M. is contributing to science: His brain (shown here) was frozen and has now been sliced into sections for detailed anatomical study.

goals because, again, we have the relevant memories. None of this is true for people who suffer from amnesia, and H.M. sometimes commented on the fact that, in important ways, he didn't know who he was. He didn't know if he should be proud of his accomplishments or ashamed of his crimes; he didn't know if he'd been clever or stupid, honorable or dishonest, industrious or lazy. In a sense, then, without a memory, there is no self. (For broader discussion, see Conway & Pleydell-Pearce, 2000; Hilts, 1995.)

What, then, is the scope of cognitive psychology? As we mentioned earlier, this field is sometimes defined as the scientific study of the acquisition, retention, and use of knowledge. We are starting to see, though, that "knowledge," and hence the study of how we gain and use knowledge, is relevant to a huge range of concerns. Our self-concept, it seems, depends on our knowledge (and, in particular, on our episodic knowledge). Our emotional adjustments to the world, as we have seen, rely on our memories. Or, to take much more ordinary cases, our ability to understand a story we've read, or a conversation, or, presumably, any of our experiences, depends on our supplementing that experience with some knowledge.

The suggestion, then, is that cognitive psychology can help us understand capacities relevant to virtually every moment of our lives. Activities that don't, on the surface, appear intellectual would nonetheless collapse without the support of our cognitive functioning. The same is true whether we're considering our actions, our social lives, our emotions, or almost any other domain. This is the scope of cognitive psychology and, in a real sense, the scope of this book.

A Brief History

In its modern form, cognitive psychology is roughly 50 years old; the earliest textbook in cognition, for example, was published by Ulric Neisser in 1967. Despite this relative youth, though, cognitive psychology has had an enormous impact—so much so that many speak of the "cognitive revolution" within psychology. This "revolution," which took place across the 1950s and 1960s, represented a striking change in the style of research used by most psychologists. The new style was intended initially for studying problems we've already met: problems of memory, decision-making, and so on. But this new type of research, and its new approach to theorizing, was soon exported to other domains, with the consequence that, in important ways, the cognitive revolution changed the intellectual map of our field.

The Years of Introspection

To understand these historical developments, we need some context. In the late 19th century, scholars—notably Wilhelm Wundt (1832–1920) and his student Edward Bradford Titchener (1867–1927)—launched the new enterprise of research psychology, defining their field for the first time as an endeavor separate from philosophy or biology.

WILHELM WUNDT

Wilhelm Wundt (1832–1920) is shown here sitting and surrounded by his colleagues and students; Wundt is often regarded as the "father of experimental psychology."

In Wundt's and Titchener's view, psychology needed to be concerned largely with the study of conscious mental events—feelings, thoughts, perceptions, and recollections. But how should these events be studied? The early researchers started with the obvious fact that there is no way for you to experience my thoughts, or I yours. The only person who can experience or observe your thoughts is you. They concluded, therefore, that the only way to study thoughts is for each of us to **introspect**, or "look within," to observe and record the content of our own mental lives and the sequence of our own experiences.

Wundt and Titchener insisted, though, that this introspection could not be casual. Instead, introspectors had to be meticulously trained: They were given a vocabulary to describe what they observed; they were taught to be as careful and as complete as possible; and above all, they were trained simply to report on their experiences, with a minimum of interpretation.

This style of research was enormously influential for several years, but psychologists gradually became disenchanted with it, and it's easy to see why. As one concern, these investigators were soon forced to acknowledge that some thoughts are *un*conscious, and this meant that introspection was inevitably limited as a research tool. This conclusion follows from the fact that introspection, by its nature, is the study of conscious experiences and so can tell us nothing about unconscious events.

Indeed, we now know that unconscious thought plays a huge part in our mental lives. For example, what is your phone number? It's likely that the moment you read this question, the number "popped" into your thoughts without any effort, noticeable steps, or strategies on your part. But, in fact, there's good reason to think that this simple bit of remembering requires a complex series of steps. These steps take place outside of awareness; and so, if we rely on introspection as our means of studying mental events, we have no way of examining these processes.

But there is also another and deeper problem with introspection: In order for any science to proceed, there must be some way to test its claims; otherwise, we have no means of separating correct assertions from false ones, accurate descriptions of the world from fictions. Hand in hand with this requirement, science needs some way of resolving disagreements: If you claim that Earth has one moon and I insist that it has two, we need some way of determining who is right. Otherwise, we cannot locate the facts of the matter, and so our "science" will become a matter of opinion, not fact.

With introspection, though, this testability of claims is often unattainable. To see why, imagine that I insist my headaches are worse than yours. How could we ever test my claim? It might be true that I describe my headaches in extreme terms: I talk about my "unbelievable, agonizing, excruciating" headaches. But that might mean only that I'm inclined toward extravagant descriptions; it might reflect my verbal style, not my headaches. Similarly, it might be true that I need bed rest whenever one of my headaches strikes. Does that mean my headaches are truly intolerable? It might mean instead that I am self-indulgent and rest even in the face of mild pain. Perhaps our headaches are identical, but you're stoic about yours and I'm not.

How, therefore, should we test my claim about my headaches? What we need is some means of directly comparing my headaches to yours, and that would require transplanting one of my headaches into your experience, or vice versa. Then one of us could make the appropriate comparison. But (setting aside the science fiction notion of telepathy), there's no way to do this, leaving us, in the end, unable to determine whether my headache reports are exaggerated, distorted, or accurate. We're left, in other words, with the brute fact that our only information about my headaches is what comes to us through the filter of my description, and we have no way to know how (or whether) that filter is coloring the evidence.

For purposes of science, this is not acceptable. For science, we need objective observations, observations that aren't dependent on a particular point of view or a particular descriptive style. It is not enough to consider "the world as one person sees it" or "describes it." Instead, we want to consider the world as it truly is. In scientific discourse, we achieve this objectivity by making sure the raw data are out in plain view, so that you can inspect my evidence, and I yours. In that way, we can be certain that neither of us is distorting or misreporting or exaggerating the facts. And that is precisely what we cannot do with introspection.

The Years of Behaviorism

These concerns led many psychologists, particularly those in the United States, to abandon introspection as a research tool. Psychology could not be a science, they argued, if it relied on this method. Instead, psychology needed objective data, and that meant researchers needed to focus on data that were out in the open, for all to observe.

What sorts of data does this allow? First, an organism's *behaviors* are obviously observable in the right way: You can watch my actions, and so can anyone else who is appropriately positioned. Therefore, data concerned with behavior are objective data, and thus grist for the scientific mill. Likewise, *stimuli* in the world are in the same "objective" category: These are measurable, recordable, physical events.

In addition, you can arrange to record the stimuli I experience day after day after day and also the behaviors I produce each day. This means that you can record how the pattern of behaviors changes with the passage of time and with the accumulation of experience. Thus, my *learning history* can also be objectively recorded and scientifically studied.

In contrast, my *beliefs*, *wishes*, *goals*, and *expectations* are all things that cannot be directly observed, cannot be objectively recorded. Thus, we need to rule out any discussion of these "mentalistic" notions. They can be observed only via introspection (or so it was claimed), and introspection, we have suggested, is worthless as a scientific tool. Hence, a scientific psychology needs to avoid these invisible internal entities.

It was this perspective that led researchers to the **behaviorist** movement, a movement that dominated psychology in America for roughly the first half of the 20th century. This movement was a success in many ways and uncovered a range of principles concerned with how behavior changes in response to various stimuli (including the stimuli we call "rewards" and "punishments"). Many of these principles remain in place within contemporary psychology and

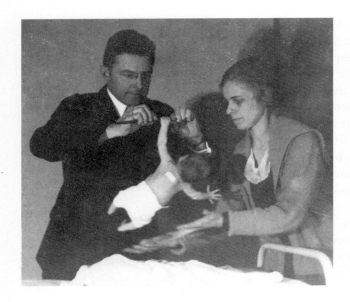

JOHN B. WATSON

John B. Watson (1878–1958) was a prominent and persuasive advocate for the behaviorist movement. Given his focus on learning *and* learning histories, *it is unsurprising that Watson was intrigued by babies' behavior and learning. Here he tests the grasp reflex displayed by all human neonates.*

provide the base for an important enterprise called "learning theory," as well as a wide range of practical applications. (For a description of these principles, see Robbins, Schwartz, & Wasserman, 2001.)

By the late 1950s, however, psychologists were convinced that a great deal of behavior could not be explained in these terms—that is, could not be explained with reference only to objective, overt events (such as stimuli and responses). The reason, to put it plainly, is that the ways people act, and the ways that they feel, are guided by how they *understand* or *interpret* the situation, and not by the objective situation itself. Therefore, if we follow the behaviorists' instruction and focus only on the objective situation, we will regularly misunderstand why people are doing what they're doing and will make the wrong predictions about how they'll behave in the future. To put this point another way, the behaviorists' perspective demands that we not talk about mental entities such as beliefs, memories, and so on, because these things cannot be studied directly, and therefore cannot be studied scientifically. Yet it seems that these subjective entities play a pivotal role in guiding behavior, and so we *must* consider these entities if we want to understand behavior!

Evidence pertinent to these assertions is threaded throughout the chapters of this book. Over and over, we will find it necessary to mention people's perceptions and strategies and understanding, as we strive to explain why (and how) they perform various tasks and accomplish various goals. Indeed, we've already seen an example of this pattern: Imagine that we present the "Betsy and Jacob" story to people and then ask them various questions: Why did Betsy shake her piggy bank? Why did she go to look for her mother? Their responses will surely reflect their understanding of the story, which in turn depends on far more than the physical stimulus—that is, the 29 syllables of the story itself. If we wanted to predict their responses, therefore, we would need to refer to the stimulus (the story itself) *and also* to the persons' knowledge and understanding of, and contribution to, this stimulus.

Here's a different example that makes the same general point: There you sit in the dining hall. A friend produces this physical stimulus: "Pass the salt, please," and you immediately produce a bit of salt-passing behavior. In this exchange, there is a physical stimulus (the words that your friend uttered) and an easily defined response (your passing of the salt), and so this simple event seems fine from the behaviorists' perspective: The elements are out in the open, for all to observe, and can easily be objectively recorded. But let's note that the event would have unfolded in the same way if your friend had offered a different stimulus. "Could I have the salt?" would have done the trick. Ditto for "Salt, please!" or "Hmm, this sure needs salt!" If your friend is both loquacious and obnoxious, the utterance might have been, "Excuse me, but after briefly contemplating the gustatory qualities of these comestibles, I have discerned that their sensory qualities would be enhanced by the addition of a number of sodium and chloride ions, delivered in roughly equal proportions and in crystalline form; could you aid me in this endeavor?" You might giggle (or snarl) at your friend, but you would still pass the salt.

Now let's work on the science of salt-passing behavior. When is this behavior produced? Since we've just observed that the behavior is evoked by all of these different stimuli, we would surely want to ask: What do these stimuli have in common? If we can answer that question, we're well on our way to understanding why all of these stimuli have the same effect.

If we focus entirely on the observable, objective aspects of these stimuli, they actually have little in common. After all, the actual sounds being produced are rather different in that long utterance about sodium and chloride ions and the utterance, "Salt, please!" And in many circumstances, *similar* sounds would not lead to salt-passing behavior. Imagine that your friend says, "Salt the pass," or "Sass the palt." These are acoustically similar to "Pass the salt" but wouldn't have the same impact. Or imagine that your friend says, "She has only a small part in the play. All she gets to say is, 'Pass the salt, please.'" In this case, exactly the right syllables were uttered, but you wouldn't pass the salt in response.

It seems, then, that our science of salt passing won't get very far if we insist on talking only about the physical stimulus. Stimuli that are physically different from each other ("Salt, please" and the bit about the ions) have similar effects. Stimuli that are physically similar to each other ("Pass the salt" and "Sass the palt") have different effects. Physical similarity, therefore, is plainly not what unites the various stimuli that evoke salt passing.

It is clear, though, that the various stimuli that evoke salt passing do have something in common with each other: *They all mean the same thing.* Sometimes this meaning derives easily from the words themselves ("Please pass the salt"). In other cases, the meaning depends on certain pragmatic rules. (For example, we pragmatically understand that the question "Could you pass the salt?" is not a question about arm strength, although, interpreted literally, it might be understood that way.) In all cases, though, it seems plain that to predict your behavior in the dining hall, we need to ask what these stimuli *mean to you.* This

PASSING THE SALT

If a friend requests the salt, your response will depend on how you understand your friend's words. This is a simple point, echoed in example after example, but is the reason why a rigid behaviorist perspective will not allow us to explain your behavior.

seems an extraordinarily simple point, but it is a point, echoed over and over by countless other examples, that indicates the impossibility of a complete behaviorist psychology.[1]

The Roots of the Cognitive Revolution

We seem to be nearing an impasse: If we wish to explain or predict behavior, we need to make reference to the mental world—the world of perceptions, understandings, and intentions. This is because how people act is shaped by how they *perceive* the situation, how they *understand* the stimuli, and so on. But how should we study the mental world? We can't employ introspection, because we've argued that introspective data are (at best) problematic.

It seems, then, that we're caught in a trap: We need to talk about the mental world if we hope to explain behavior. The only direct means of studying the mental world is introspection. And introspection is scientifically unworkable. Thus, in brief: We need to study the mental world, but we can't.

There is, however, a solution to this impasse, and it was actually suggested many years ago, by the philosopher Immanuel Kant (1724–1804). To use Kant's **transcendental method**, you begin with the observable facts and then work backward from these observations. In essence, you ask: How could these observations have come about? What must the underlying *causes* be that led to these *effects*?

This method, sometimes called "inference to best explanation," is at the heart of most modern science. Physicists, for example, routinely use this method to study objects or events that cannot be observed directly. To take just one case, no physicist has ever observed an electron, but this has not stopped physicists from learning a great deal about electrons. How do they proceed? Even though electrons themselves are not observable, their presence often leads to observable results—in essence, *visible effects* from an *invisible cause*. Thus, among other things, electrons leave observable tracks in cloud chambers, and they produce momentary fluctuations in a magnetic field. Physicists can then use these observations the same way a police detective uses clues—asking what the "crime" must have been like if it left this and that clue. (A size 11 footprint? That probably tells us what size feet the criminal has, even though no one observed his feet. A smell of tobacco smoke? That suggests the criminal was a smoker. And so on.) In the same fashion, physicists observe the clues that electrons leave behind, and from this information they form hypotheses about what exactly electrons must be like in order to have produced these specific effects.

Of course, physicists (and other scientists) have a huge advantage over a police detective: If the detective has insufficient evidence, she can't arrange for the crime to happen again in order to produce more evidence. (She can't say to the robber: "Please visit the bank again, but this time don't wear a mask.") Scientists, in

---

1. We should note that the behaviorists themselves quickly realized this point. Hence, modern behaviorism has abandoned the radical rejection of mentalistic terms; indeed, it's hard to draw a line between modern behaviorism and a field called "animal cognition," a field that often employs mentalistic language! The behaviorism being criticized here is a historically defined behaviorism, and it's this perspective that, in large measure, gave birth to modern cognitive psychology.

IMMANUEL KANT

Philosopher Immanuel Kant (1724–1804) made major contributions to many fields, and his transcendental method allowed him to ask what qualities of the mind made experience possible.

contrast, can arrange for a repeat of the "crime" they're seeking to explain. More precisely, they can arrange for new experiments, with new measures. Better still, they can set the stage in advance, to maximize the likelihood that the "culprit" (in our example, the electron) will leave useful clues behind. They can, for example, add new recording devices to the situation, or they can place various obstacles in the electron's path. In this way, the scientist can gather more and more data, including data that are crucial for testing the specific predictions of a particular theory. This prospect—of reproducing experiments and varying the experiments to test hypotheses—is what gives science its power. It's what allows scientists to assert that their hypotheses have been rigorously tested, and it's what gives scientists assurance that their theories are correct.

Psychologists work in the same fashion—and the notion that we *could* work in this fashion was one of the great contributions of the cognitive revolution. The idea, in essence, is simply this: We know that we need to study mental processes; that's what we learned from the limitations of behaviorism. But we also know that mental processes cannot be observed directly; we learned that from the downfall of introspection. Our path forward, therefore, is to study mental processes *indirectly*, relying on the fact that these processes, themselves invisible, have visible consequences: measurable delays in producing a response, performances that can be assessed for accuracy, errors that can be scrutinized and categorized. By examining these (and other) effects produced by mental processes, we can develop—and then *test*—hypotheses about what the mental processes must have been. In this fashion, we use Kant's method, just as physicists (or biologists or chemists or astronomers) do, to develop a science that does not rest on direct observation.

Research in Cognitive Psychology: An Example

In setting after setting, cognitive psychologists have applied the Kantian logic to explain how people remember, make decisions, pay attention, or solve problems. In each case, we begin with a particular performance—say, a memory task—and then hypothesize a series of unseen mental events that made the performance possible. But, crucially, we don't stop there. We also ask whether some other, perhaps simpler, sequence of events might explain the data or whether some other sequence might explain both these data and some other findings. In this fashion, we do more than ask how the data came about; we also seek the *best* way to think about the data.

For some data, the sequence of events we hypothesize resembles the processing steps that a computer might use. (For classic examples of this approach, see Broadbent, 1958; Miller, Galanter, & Pribram, 1960.) For other data, we might cast our hypotheses in terms of the strategies a person is using or the inferences she is making. No matter what the form of the hypothesis, though, the next step is crucial: The hypothesis is tested by collecting more data. Specifically, we seek to derive new predictions based on our hypothesis: "If this is the mechanism behind the original findings, then things should work differently in this circumstance or that one." If these predictions are tested and confirmed, this outcome suggests that the proposed hypothesis was correct. If the predictions are not confirmed, then a new hypothesis is needed.

How does this method work in practice? Let's explore this point with a concrete example. We will return to this example in Chapters 4 and 5, where we put it into a richer context. For now, though, our focus is on the method, rather than on the theory itself.

Working Memory: Some Initial Observations

Many of the sentences in this book—including the one you are reading right now, which consists of 23 words—are rather long. In these sentences, words that must be understood together (such as "sentences . . . are . . . long") are often widely separated (note the 16 words interposed between "sentences" and "are"). Yet you have no trouble understanding these sentences.

We begin, therefore, with a simple fact—that you are able to read, even though ordinary reading requires you to integrate words that are widely separated on the page. How should we explain this fact? What is the (unseen) cause that leads to this (easily observed) fact? The obvious suggestion is that you're relying on some form of *memory* that allows you to remember the early words in the sentence as you forge ahead. Then, once you've read enough, you can integrate what you have decoded so far. In this section's very first sentence, for example, you needed to hang on to the first seven words ("Many of the sentences in this book") while you read the interposed phrase ("including . . . of 23 words"). Then you had to bring those first seven words back into play, to integrate them with the sentence's end ("are rather long").

The form of memory proposed here is called **working memory**, to emphasize that this is the memory you use for information that you are actively working on. Working memory holds information in an easily accessible form, so that the information is, so to speak, at your fingertips, instantly available when you need it. This instant availability is promoted by several factors, including, quite simply, working memory's *size:* Working memory is hypothesized to have a small capacity, and so, with only a few items held in this store, you will never have a problem locating just the item you want. (If you have only two keys on your key ring, it's easy to find the one that unlocks your door. If you had a hundred keys on the ring, the situation would be rather different.)

Can we test this proposal? One way to measure working memory's capacity is via a **span test**. In this test, we read to someone a list of, say, four items, perhaps four letters ("A D G W"). The person has to report these back, immediately, in sequence. If she succeeds, we try it again with five letters ("Q D W U F"). If she can repeat these back correctly, we try six letters, and so on, until we find a list that the person cannot report back accurately. Generally, people start making errors with sequences of seven or eight letters. Most people's letter span, therefore, is about seven or eight. This finding not only confirms our hypothesis that working memory is limited in size but, just as important, also provides a simple example of how we can learn about this memory's properties by seeing how this (unseen) memory influences observable performance.

Working Memory: A Proposal

As it turns out, the procedure for measuring working memory's span also puts another observation into view—another "effect" for which we need to seek a "cause." Specifically, when we measure people's memory span, we find that they often make errors—they report letters that they hadn't heard at all—and these errors follow a simple pattern: When people make mistakes in this task, they generally substitute one letter for another with a similar sound. Having heard "S," they'll report back "F"; or having heard "V," they'll report back "B." The problem is not in hearing the letters in the first place: We get similar sound-alike confusions if the letters are presented visually. Thus, having *seen* "F," people are likely to report back "S"; they are not likely, in this situation, to report back the similar-looking "E."

This finding provides another clue about working memory's nature, and two British researchers—Alan Baddeley and Graham Hitch—proposed a model to explain both this finding and many other results as well. Their model (e.g., Baddeley & Hitch, 1974) starts by stipulating that working memory is not a single entity. Instead, working memory has several different parts, and so they prefer to speak of a **working-memory system**. At the heart of the system is the **central executive**. This is the part that runs the show and does the real work.

We'll say more about the executive in upcoming chapters; this turns out by itself to be an intriguing and complex topic. For now, though, let's focus on the fact that the executive is helped out by a number of low-level "assistants." These assistants are not at all sophisticated; and so, if you need to analyze or interpret some information, the assistants can't do it—the executive is needed for that. What the assistants can do, however, is provide storage, and this function, simple though it is, makes the assistants extremely useful.

Specifically, information that will soon be needed, but isn't needed right now, can be sent off to the assistants for temporary storage. As a result, the executive isn't burdened by the mere storage of this information and so is freed up to do other tasks. In effect, therefore, the assistants serve the same function as a piece of scratch paper on your desk. When you're going to need some bit of information soon (a phone number, perhaps), you write it down on the scratch paper. Of course, the scratch paper has no mind of its own, and so it can't do anything with the "stored" information; all it does is hold onto the information. But that's helpful enough: With the scratch paper "preserving" this information, you can cease thinking about it with no risk that the information will be lost. This in turn allows you to focus your attention more productively on other, more complex chores. Then, when you're ready for the stored information (perhaps just a moment later), you glance at your note, and there the information will be.

Working memory's assistants provide the same benefit, and one of the most important assistants is the **articulatory rehearsal loop**. To see how it works, try reading the next few sentences while holding onto this list of numbers: "1, 4, 6, 4, 9." Got them? Now read on. You are probably repeating the numbers over and over to yourself, rehearsing them with your inner voice. But this turns out to require very little effort, so you can continue reading while doing this rehearsal. Nonetheless, the moment you need to recall the numbers (what were they?), they are available to you. How did you do this? The numbers were maintained by working memory's rehearsal loop, and, with the numbers thus out of the way, the central executive was free to continue reading. And that is the advantage of this system: With storage handled by the helpers, the executive is available for other, more demanding tasks.

To launch the rehearsal loop, you rely on the process of **subvocalization**, or silent speech (see Figure 1.1). In other words, you quietly say the numbers to yourself. This step is easy for you, because the activity of speaking is of course immensely well practiced, and so there's no need for the executive to monitor or supervise this activity. As a result, the executive is needed to initiate this silent speech, but then it can turn to other matters, and that's exactly what we want: The chore of holding onto the numbers is now carried by the "inner voice," not the executive.

Subvocalization, in turn, produces a representation of these numbers in the **phonological buffer**. In other words, an auditory image is created in the "inner ear." This image will fade away after a second or two, but before it does, subvocalization can be used once again to create a new image, sustaining the material in this buffer.

Note, then, that the rehearsal loop requires two elements, working in tandem: subvocal speech (the "inner voice") and the phonological buffer (the "inner ear").

FIGURE 1.1 | THE WORKING-MEMORY SYSTEM

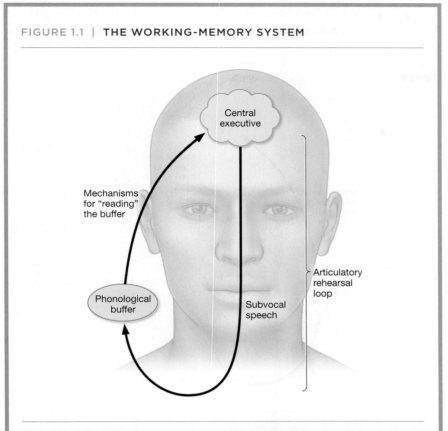

Mechanisms for "reading" the buffer

Central executive

Phonological buffer

Subvocal speech

Articulatory rehearsal loop

Working memory's central executive is supported by a number of low-level assis-tants. One assistant, the articulatory rehearsal loop, involves two components: subvocal speech (the "inner voice") and a phonological buffer (the "inner ear"). Items are rehearsed by using subvocalization to "load" the buffer. While this is going on, the executive is free to work on other matters.

These two elements can store materials you'll likely need in a moment. Thus, the executive isn't needed to maintain these materials and is free to focus on other activities.

Evidence for the Working-Memory System

Baddeley and Hitch proposed their model as an explanation for the available evi-dence; it was, in their view, the best way to explain the facts collected so far. For example, why do people make "sound-alike" errors in a span task? It's because they're relying on the rehearsal loop, which involves a mechanism (the "inner ear") ordinarily used for actual hearing. In other words, the memory items are briefly stored as (internal representations of) sounds, and so it's no surprise that errors, when they occur, are shaped by this mode of storage.

WORKBOOK DEMONSTRATION 1.2

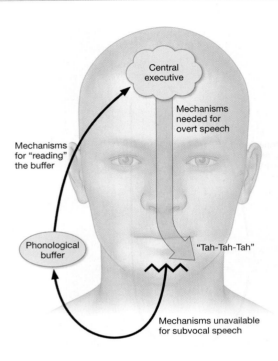

FIGURE 1.2 | THE EFFECTS OF CONCURRENT ARTICULATION

Central
executive

Mechanisms
needed for
overt speech

Mechanisms
for "reading"
the buffer

Phonological
buffer

"Tah-Tah-Tah"

Mechanisms unavailable
for subvocal speech

The mechanisms needed to control subvocal speech (the "inner voice") overlap heavily with those needed for the control and production of overt speech. Therefore, if these mechanisms are in use for actual speech, they are not available for subvocal rehearsal. Hence, many experiments block rehearsal by requiring participants to say "Tah-Tah-Tah" out loud.

Notice, then, that we're using the Kantian logic we described earlier: generating a hypothesis about unseen mechanisms (e.g., the operation of the rehearsal loop) in order to explain visible data (e.g., the pattern of the errors). Crucially, though, this hypothesis also leads to many new predictions, which allow us to test the hypothesis—by asking whether its predictions are accurate. It is this step that turns a "mere" hypothesis into solid scientific knowledge.

For example, imagine that we ask people to take the span test while simultaneously saying "Tah-Tah-Tah" over and over, out loud. This **concurrent articulation task** obviously requires the mechanisms for speech production. Therefore, these mechanisms are not available for other use, including subvocalization. (If you're directing your lips and tongue to produce the "Tah-Tah-Tah" sequence, you can't at the same time direct them to produce the sequence needed for the subvocalized materials; see Figure 1.2.)

According to the model, how will this constraint matter? First, note that our original span test measured the combined capacities of the central executive and the loop. That is, when people take a span test, they store some of the to-be-remembered items in the loop and others via the central executive. (This is a poor use of the executive, underutilizing its talents, but that's okay here, because the span task doesn't demand anything beyond mere storage.) With concurrent articulation, though, the loop isn't available for use, and so we are now measuring the capacity of working memory without the rehearsal loop. We should predict, therefore, that concurrent articulation, even though it's extremely easy, should cut memory span drastically. This prediction turns out to be correct. Span is ordinarily about seven items; with concurrent articulation, it drops by roughly a third—to four or five items (Chincotta & Underwood, 1997; see Figure 1.3).

Second, with visually presented items, concurrent articulation should eliminate the sound-alike errors. Repeatedly saying "Tah-Tah-Tah" blocks use of the articulatory loop, and it is in this loop, we've proposed, that the sound-alike errors arise. This prediction, too, is correct: With concurrent articulation and visual presentation of the items, sound-alike errors are largely eliminated.

FIGURE 1.3 | THE EFFECT OF CONCURRENT ARTICULATION ON SPAN

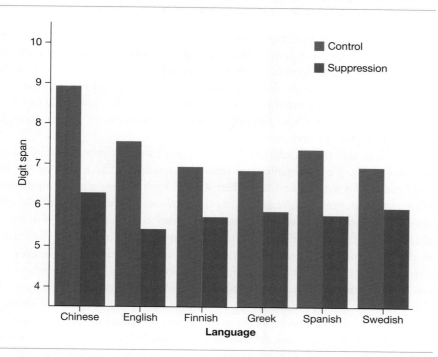

In the Control condition, people were given a normal digit-span test. In the Suppression condition, people were required to do concurrent articulation while taking the test. Concurrent articulation is easy, but blocks use of the articulatory loop, and consistently decreased memory span, from roughly seven items to four or five. And plainly this use of the articulatory loop is not an occasional strategy; instead, it can be found in a wide range of countries, and a wide range of languages. (After Chincotta & Underwood, 1997)

Third, we can also test people's memory spans by using complex visual shapes. People are shown these shapes and then must echo the sequence back by drawing what they have just seen. If we choose shapes that are not easily named, then the shapes cannot be rehearsed via the inner-voice/inner-ear combination. (What would you subvocalize to rehearse them?) With these stimuli, therefore, there should be no effect of concurrent articulation: If people aren't using the rehearsal loop, there should be no cost attached to denying them use of the loop. This prediction is also correct.

Finally, here is a different sort of prediction. We have claimed that the rehearsal loop is required only for storage; this loop (like all of working memory's assistants) is incapable of any more sophisticated operations. Therefore, these other operations should not be compromised if the loop is unavailable. This, too, turns out to be correct: Concurrent articulation blocks use of the loop but has no effect on someone's ability to read brief sentences, to do simple logic problems, and so on. (Blocking use of the loop *does* have an effect when you're reading more complex sentences or doing harder problems; that's because these harder tasks require analysis *and* the storage of interim steps and so require the entire working-memory system—the executive *and* the assistants.)

The Nature of the Working-Memory Evidence

No one has ever seen the "inner voice" or "inner ear" directly. Nonetheless, we're confident that these entities exist, because they are essential parts of our explanation for the data and—crucially—there seems to be no other way to explain the data. Moreover, our claims about the inner voice and inner ear have consistently led us to new predictions that have been confirmed by further testing. In this way, our claims have been *useful* (leading to new observations) as well as *accurate* (leading to correct predictions).

Let's note also that in supporting our account, we have many forms of data available to us. We can manipulate research participants' activities, as we did with concurrent articulation, and then we can look at how this manipulation changes their performance (e.g., the size of the measured memory span). We can also manipulate the stimuli themselves, as we did in testing memory for visual shapes, and see how this changes things. We can also look in detail at the nature of the performance, asking not just about someone's overall level of success in our tasks but also about their specific errors (sound-alike vs. look-alike). We can also measure the speed of participants' performance and ask how it is influenced by various manipulations. We do this, for example, when we ask whether problem solving is compromised by a concurrent articulation. The assumption here is that mental processes are very fast but nonetheless do take a measurable amount of time. By timing how quickly participants answer various questions or perform various tasks, we can ask what factors speed up mental processes and what factors slow them down.

We can also gather data from another source. So far, we've been concerned with people's *performance* on our tasks—for example, how much or how well they remember. There's much to learn, though, by also considering the biological mechanisms that make this performance possible. That is, we can draw evidence from the realm of **cognitive neuroscience**—the study of the biological basis for cognitive functioning.

For example, what exactly is the nature of subvocalization? Is it just like actual speech, but silent? If so, does it involve movements (perhaps tiny movements) of the tongue, the vocal cords, and so on? One way to find out would be to paralyze the relevant muscles. Would this action disrupt use of the rehearsal loop? As it turns out, we don't have to perform this experiment; nature has performed it for us. Because of specific forms of neurological damage, some individuals have no ability to move these various muscles and so suffer from **anarthria**—an inability to produce overt speech. Data indicate, however, that these individuals show sound-alike confusions in their span data, just as ordinary participants do; they also show other results (for example, something called the word-length effect) associated with the use of the rehearsal loop. These observations suggest that actual muscle movements aren't needed for subvocalization, because the results are the same *without* these movements. It seems likely, therefore, that "inner speech" relies on the brain areas responsible for *planning* and *controlling* the muscle movements of speech and not on the movements themselves. This is by itself an interesting fact, but for present purposes, note the use of yet another type of data: observations from **neuropsychology**, concerned with how various forms of brain dysfunction influence observed performance.

We can pursue related questions by examining the brain activity of people without any brain damage. Recent developments in brain-imaging technology tell us that when a participant is engaged in working-memory rehearsal, considerable activity is observed in brain areas that we know (from other evidence) are crucially involved in the production of spoken language, as well as in areas that play an important role in the perception of spoken language. These findings suggest that claims about the "inner voice" and "inner ear" are more than casual metaphors; instead, the "inner voice" uses brain mechanisms that are ordinarily used for overt speech, and the "inner ear" uses mechanisms ordinarily used for actual hearing (cf. Jonides, Lacey, & Nee, 2005; for more on the neuroscience of working memory, see Jonides et al., 2008).

We can also gain insights by comparing diverse populations—for example, by comparing people who speak different languages, or comparing people with normal hearing to people who have been deaf since birth and who communicate via sign language. It turns out, for example, that the deaf rely on a different assistant for working memory: They use an "inner hand" (and covert sign language) rather than an "inner voice" (and covert speech). As a result, they are disrupted if they are asked to wiggle their fingers during a memory task (akin to a hearing person saying "Tah-Tah-Tah"), and they also tend to make "same-hand-shape" errors in working memory (analogous to the sound-alike errors made by the hearing population). These results speak not only to the generality of the claims made here but also to the need to fine-tune these claims when we consider other groups of people.

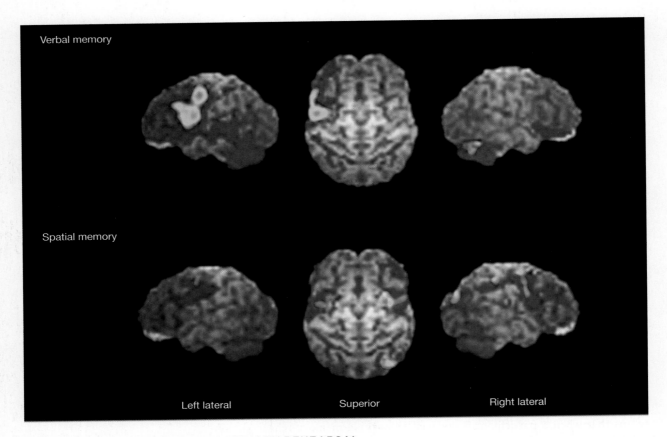

Verbal memory

Spatial memory

Left lateral   Superior   Right lateral

BRAIN ACTIVITY AND WORKING MEMORY REHEARSAL

Color is used here as an indication of increased brain activity (measured in this case by positron emission tomography). When people are engaged in a verbal memory task (and so using the articulatory loop), activation increases in areas ordinarily used for language production and perception. A very different pattern is observed when people are engaged in a task requiring memory for spatial position.

Finally, it is important that we build our argument with *multiple lines* of evidence. That's because, in most cases, no single line of evidence is decisive by itself. There are, after all, probably other ways to explain our initial observations about span, if those results were all we had to go on. There are also other ways to explain the other individual findings we have mentioned, if these likewise were considered in isolation. It's only when we take the results as a package that we can make headway, and if we have done our work well, there will be just one theoretical account that fits with the entire data pattern. At that point, with no other way to explain the data, we will conclude that we have understood the evidence and that we have correctly reconstructed what is going on in the mind, invisibly, never directly observed.

We should also emphasize that there's no reason for you, as a reader, to memorize this catalogue of different types of evidence. This is because we'll encounter

THE INNER HAND, RATHER THAN THE INNER VOICE

People who can speak and hear rely on the articulatory rehearsal loop as part of the working-memory system; as a result, errors in working memory are often "sound-alike errors." Members of the deaf community, in contrast, rely on a "signing rehearsal loop," using an "inner hand" rather than an "inner voice." Their errors often involve confusions between different words that happen to have similar hand shapes when expressed in sign language.

each of these forms of data again and again in this text. Our point for now, therefore, is not to create an intimidating memory load for you but instead to highlight—and, indeed, to celebrate—the fact that we have multiple tools with which we can test, and eventually confirm, our claims.

Working Memory in a Broader Context

Having made all of these methodological points, let us round out this section with one final comment. Why should we care about the structure of working memory? Why is working memory interesting? The memory-span task itself seems quite unnatural: How often do you need to memorize a set of unrelated numbers or letters? For that matter, how often do you need to work on a problem while simultaneously saying "Tah-Tah-Tah" over and over? In short, what does this task, or this procedure, have to do with things we care about?

The answer to these questions allows us to replay an issue we have already discussed: You rely on working memory in a vast number of circumstances; and so, if we understand working memory, we move toward an understanding of this far broader set of problems and issues. For example, bear in mind our initial comments about the role of working memory in reading or in any other task in which you must store early "products," keeping them ready for integration with later "products." One might imagine that many tasks have this character; reading, reasoning, and problem solving are a few. If you make effective use of working memory, therefore, you will have an advantage in all of these domains. Indeed, some scholars have suggested that "intelligence" in many domains amounts to nothing more than excess capacity in working memory. (We'll return to this point in Chapter 12.)

In a similar vein, the use of articulatory rehearsal seems a simple trick—a trick you use spontaneously, a trick in which you take no special pride. But it is a trick you had to learn, and young children, for example, often seem not to know it. There is some indication that this lack can be a problem for these children in learning to read: Without the option of relying on articulatory rehearsal, reading becomes much more difficult. It also appears that the rehearsal loop plays an important role when someone is learning new vocabulary, including vocabulary in a new language (Baddeley, Gathercole, & Papagno, 1998; Gathercole, Service, Hitch, Adams, & Martin, 1999). So here, too, is an important function of the working-memory system.

These examples can easily be multiplied, but by now the point should be clear: Working memory and articulatory rehearsal are relevant to a wide range of mental activities in adults and in children. Understanding working memory, therefore, may give us insight into a broad range of tasks. Similar claims can be made about many other cognitive resources: By understanding what it means to pay attention, we move toward an understanding of all the contexts in which attention plays a role. By understanding how we comprehend text, or how we use our knowledge to supplement our perceptions, we move toward an understanding of all the contexts in which these abilities play a part. And in each case, the number of such contexts is vast.

We end this chapter, therefore, by echoing a comment we have already made: The machinery of cognition is essential to virtually all of our waking activities (and perhaps some of our sleeping activities as well). The scope of cognitive psychology is broad indeed, and the relevance of our research is wide.

CHAPTER SUMMARY

- Cognitive psychology is concerned with how people remember, pay attention, and think. The importance of all these issues arises in part from the fact that most of what we do, think, and feel is guided by things we already know. One example is the comprehension of a simple story, which turns out to be heavily influenced by the knowledge we supply.

- Cognitive psychology emerged as a separate discipline in the late 1950s, and its powerful impact on the wider field of psychology has led many to speak of this emergence as the cognitive revolution. One predecessor of cognitive psychology was the 19th-century movement that emphasized introspection as the main research tool for psychology. Psychologists soon became disenchanted with this movement, however, for several reasons: Introspection cannot inform us about unconscious mental events; even with conscious events, claims rooted in introspection are often untestable, because there is no way for an independent observer to check on the accuracy or completeness of an introspective report.

- The behaviorist movement rejected introspection as a method, insisting instead that psychology speak only of mechanisms and processes that were objective and out in the open for all to observe. However, evidence suggests that our thinking, behavior, and feelings are often shaped by our perception or understanding of the events we experience. This is problematic for the behaviorists: Perception and understanding are exactly the sorts of mental processes that the behaviorists regarded as subjective and not open to scientific study.

- In order to study mental events, psychologists have turned to a method in which one focuses on observable events but then asks what (invisible) events must have taken place in order to make these (visible) effects possible.

- Research in working memory provides an example of how cognitive psychologists use evidence. One theory of working memory proposes that this memory consists of a central executive and a small number of low-level assistants, including the articulatory rehearsal loop, which stores material by means of covert speech. Many forms of evidence are used in supporting this account: measures of working memory's holding capacity in various circumstances, the nature of errors people make when using working memory, the speed of performance in working-memory tasks, evidence drawn from the study of people with brain damage, and evidence drawn from brain-imaging technology.

The Workbook Connection

See the *Cognition Workbook* for further exploration of the science of the mind:

- Demonstration 1.1: The Articulatory Rehearsal Loop
- Demonstration 1.2: Sound-Based Coding
- Research Methods: Testable Hypotheses
- Cognitive Psychology and Education: Enhancing Classroom Learning
- Cognitive Psychology and the Law: Improving the Criminal Justice System

---

NEED HELP STUDYING?

 wwnorton.com/studyspace

Visit StudySpace to access free review material such as

- Chapter study plans
- Quizzes
- Flashcards, and more

CHAPTER TWO

The Neural Basis for Cognition

Cognitive psychologists rely on many sorts of findings—response times, error rates, questionnaire responses, and more. Each type of data is important, and all contribute to the broad fabric of evidence that allows us to test our theories.

One form of evidence, however, needs its own presentation: evidence concerning the brain functioning that makes cognition possible. We'll encounter this biological evidence throughout this book, woven together with other sorts of data, as we develop and test our theories. But we need to lay the appropriate foundation—background information about the brain and the methods used to study the brain.

We'll begin with an example that shows some of the bizarre symptoms that can result from brain damage; we'll use this example to illustrate what we can learn about the mind by studying the brain, and what we can learn about the brain by studying the mind. The example will, in addition, highlight the fact that each part of the brain has its own specialized function, so that our behaviors, thoughts, and feelings almost invariably depend on the coordinated action of many brain regions. To explore this point, we'll need to consider some basic brain anatomy, and also look at the methods used to study the functioning of the brain's various parts. Then, with this broad framework in place, we will zoom in for a closer look at one part of the brain—the tissue that allows us to see, and to understand, the visual world that surrounds us.

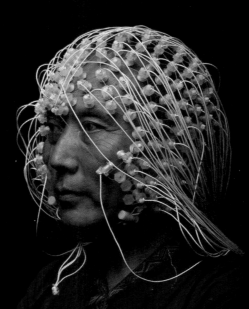

- We begin by exploring the example of *Capgras syndrome* to illustrate how seemingly simple achievements actually depend on many parts of the brain; we also highlight the ways that the study of the brain, and of brain damage, can illuminate questions about the mind.

- We then survey the brain's anatomy, emphasizing the function carried out by each region. The identification of these functions is supported by

neuroimaging data, which can assess the activity levels in different areas, and also by studies of the effects of brain damage.

- We consider the *visual system* as an illustration of what we can learn from closer scrutiny of brain function. Here we see that the analysis of the visual input begins the moment visual information enters the nervous system and depends on many highly specialized brain areas, all working in parallel with the others.

Capgras Syndrome: An Initial Example

The human brain is an extraordinarily complex organ in which the functioning of the whole is dependent on many interconnected systems. As a result, damage virtually anywhere in the brain will produce specific—and sometimes highly disruptive—symptoms. These symptoms are often deeply tragic for the afflicted persons and their families, but the symptoms can also be a rich source of insight into how the brain functions.

Consider, for example, a remarkable disorder known as **Capgras syndrome** (Capgras & Reboul-Lachaux, 1923). This disorder is rare on its own, but it seems to be one of the accompaniments to Alzheimer's syndrome and so is sometimes observed among the elderly (Harwood, Barker, Ownby, & Duara, 1999). More directly, though, the disorder can result from various injuries to the brain (Ellis & De Pauw, 1994).

Someone with Capgras syndrome is fully able to recognize the people in her world—her husband, her parents, her friends—but she is utterly convinced that these people are not who they appear to be. The real husband or the real son, the afflicted person insists, has been kidnapped (or worse). The person now on the scene, therefore, isn't the genuine article; instead, he or she must be a well-trained impostor—a fraud of some sort, impersonating the (allegedly) absent person.

Imagine what it is like to have this disorder. You turn, let's say, to your father—and exclaim, "You look like my father, sound like him, and act like him. But I can tell that you're not my father. *Who are you?*"

Often a person with Capgras syndrome insists that there are slight differences between the impostor and the person he has replaced—subtle changes in personality or tiny changes in appearance. Of course, no one else detects these (nonexistent) differences, and this can lead to all sorts of paranoid suspicions about why a loved one has been replaced and why no one is willing to acknowledge this replacement. In the extreme, these suspicions can lead the Capgras sufferer to desperate steps. In some cases, for example, patients suffering from this syndrome have murdered the supposed impostor in an attempt to end the charade and relocate the "genuine" character. Indeed, in one case, a Capgras patient was convinced his father had been replaced by a robot and so decapitated him in order to look for the batteries and microfilm in his head (Blount, 1986).

What is going on here? The answer, according to some researchers, lies in the fact that facial recognition involves two separate systems in the brain, one of which leads to a cognitive appraisal ("I know what my father looks like, and I can perceive that you closely resemble him"), and the other to a more global, emotional appraisal ("You look familiar to me and also trigger a warm response in me"). The concordance of these two appraisals then leads to the certainty of recognition ("You obviously are my father"). In Capgras syndrome, though, the latter (emotional) processing is disrupted, leading to the intellectual identification without the familiarity response (Ellis & Lewis, 2001; Ellis & Young, 1990; Ramachandran & Blakeslee, 1998): "You resemble my father but trigger no sense of familiarity, so you must be someone else."

The Neural Basis for Capgras Syndrome

Is this the right way to think about Capgras syndrome? More precisely, is this hypothesis about the disorder correct? One line of evidence comes from **neuroimaging techniques**, developed in the last few decades, that allow researchers to take high-quality, three-dimensional "pictures" of living brains, without in any way disturbing the brains' owners. We'll have more to say about neuroimaging later, but first, what do these techniques tell us about Capgras syndrome?

Some types of neuroimaging data provide portraits of the physical makeup of the brain: What's where? How are structures shaped, or connected to each other? Are there structures present (such as tumors) that shouldn't be there, or structures that are missing (perhaps because of disease, or birth defects)? These facts about structure were gained in older studies from PET scans; current studies usually rely on MRI scans (see Figure 2.1). These scans suggest a link between Capgras syndrome and abnormalities in several brain areas, indicating that our account of the syndrome will need several elements (Edelstyn & Oyebode, 1999; also see O'Connor, Walbridge, Sandson, & Alexander, 1996).

One site of damage in Capgras patients is in the temporal lobe (see Figure 2.2), particularly on the right side of the head. This damage probably disrupts circuits involving the **amygdala**, an almond-shaped structure that—in the intact brain— seems to serve as an "emotional evaluator," helping an organism to detect stimuli associated with threat or danger. The amygdala is also important for detecting positive stimuli—indicators of safety or indicators of available rewards. With *damaged* amygdalae, therefore, people with Capgras syndrome won't experience the warm sense of feeling good (and safe and secure) when looking at a loved one's familiar face. This lack of an emotional response is probably why these

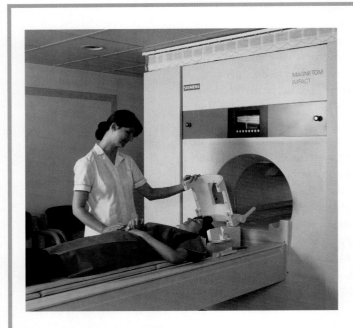

FIGURE 2.1 | NEUROIMAGING

Scanners like this one are used for both MRI and fMRI scans. MRI scans tell us about the structure of the brain; fMRI scans tell us which portions of the brain are especially active during the scan. An fMRI scan usually results in color images, with each hue indicating a particular activity level.

faces don't feel familiar to them, and is, of course, fully in line with the two-systems hypothesis we've already sketched.

Patients with Capgras syndrome also have brain abnormalities in the frontal lobe, specifically in the right **prefrontal cortex**. What is this area's normal function? To find out, we turn to a different neuroimaging technique, fMRI, which allows us to track moment-by-moment *activity levels* in different sites in a living brain. (We'll say more about fMRI in a later section.) This technique allows us to answer such questions as: When a person is reading, which brain regions are particularly active? How about when a person is listening to music? With data like these, we can ask which tasks make heavy use of a brain area, and from that base we can draw conclusions about what the brain area's function is.

Studies make it clear that the prefrontal cortex is especially active when a person is engaged in tasks that require planning, or careful analysis. Conversely, this area is less active when someone is *dreaming*. Plausibly, this latter pattern reflects the *absence* of careful analysis of the dream material, which in turn helps us understand why dreams are often illogical or bizarre.

Related, consider fMRI scans of patients suffering from schizophrenia (e.g., Silbersweig et al., 1995). Neuroimaging reveals diminished activity in the frontal lobes whenever these patients are experiencing hallucinations. One interpretation is that the diminished activity reflects a decreased ability to distinguish internal events (thoughts) from external ones (voices), or to distinguish imagined events from real ones (cf. Glisky, Polster, & Routhieaux, 1995).

How is all of this relevant to Capgras syndrome? With damage to the frontal lobe, Capgras patients may be less able to keep track of what is real and what

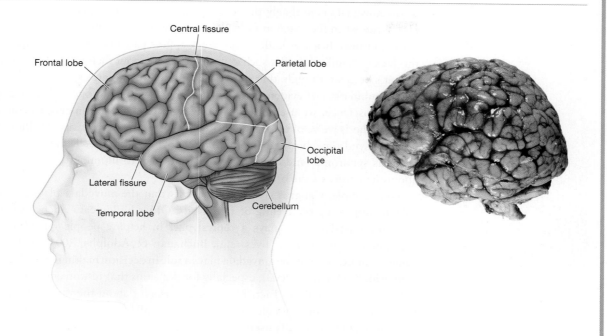

FIGURE 2.2 | THE LOBES OF THE HUMAN BRAIN

The left panel identifies the various lobes and some of the brain's prominent features. Actual brains, however, are uniformly colored, as shown in the photograph in the right panel. The four lobes of the forebrain surround (and hide from view) the midbrain and most of the hindbrain. (The cerebellum is the only part of the hindbrain that is visible, and, in fact, the temporal lobe has been pushed upward a bit in the left panel to make the cerebellum more visible.) The side view shows the left cerebral hemisphere; the structures on the right side of the brain are similar. However, the two halves of the brain have somewhat different functions, and so the results of brain injury depend on which half is damaged. The symptoms of Capgras syndrome, for example, result from damage to specific sites on the right side of the frontal and temporal lobes.

is not, what is sensible and what is not. As a result, weird beliefs can emerge unchecked, including delusions (about robots and the like) that you or I would find utterly bizarre.

What Do We Learn From Capgras Syndrome?

As it turns out, we also have other lines of evidence that help us understand the peculiar symptoms of Capgras syndrome (e.g., Ellis & Lewis, 2001; Ramachandran & Blakeslee, 1998). Some of the evidence comes from the psychology laboratory and confirms the suggestion that recognition of all stimuli (and not just faces) does involve two separate mechanisms—one that hinges on factual knowledge, and one that's more "emotional" and tied to the warm sense of familiarity (see Chapter 6). These findings join the neuroscience evidence we've just described, and the overall package of evidence fits well with our hypothesis: Specifically, the damage to the amygdala is probably the reason Capgras patients experience no sense of familiarity when they look at faces they know well. The damage to the prefrontal cortex, in turn, helps us understand why Capgras patients, when they experience this lack of familiarity, offer such crazy hypotheses about their skewed perception.

Let's be clear, though, that our understanding of Capgras syndrome depends on a combination of evidence drawn from cognitive psychology and from cognitive neuroscience; we use both perspectives to test (and, ultimately, to confirm) the hypothesis we've offered. In addition, just as both perspectives can illuminate Capgras syndrome, both can be *illuminated by* the syndrome. That is, we can use Capgras syndrome (and other biological evidence) to illuminate broader issues about the nature of the brain and of the mind.

For example, Capgras syndrome suggests that the amygdala plays a crucial role in supporting the feeling of familiarity. Other biological evidence suggests that the amygdala also plays a central part in helping people remember the emotional events of their lives (e.g., Buchanan & Adolphs, 2004). Still other evidence indicates that the amygdala plays a role in decision making (e.g., Bechara, Damasio, & Damasio, 2003), especially for decisions that rest on emotional evaluations of one's options. Facts like these tell us a lot about the various functions that make cognition possible and, more specifically, tell us that our theorizing needs to include a broadly useful "emotional evaluator," involved in many cognitive processes. Moreover, Capgras syndrome tells us that this emotional evaluator works in a fashion separate from the evaluation of factual information, providing us a way to think about the occasions in which someone's evaluation of the facts points toward one conclusion, while an emotional evaluation points toward a different conclusion. These are clues of great value as we seek to understand the processes that support ordinary remembering or decision making.

Likewise, consider what Capgras syndrome teaches us about how the parts of the brain must work together for even the simplest achievement. In order to recognize your father, for example, one part of your brain needs to store the factual memory of what your father looks like. Another part of the brain is responsible for analyzing the visual input you receive when looking at a face. Yet another brain area has the job of comparing this now-analyzed input to the factual information provided from memory, to determine whether there's a match. Another site provides the emotional evaluation of the input. A different site presumably assembles the data from all these other sites, and so registers the fact that the face being inspected does match the factual recollection of your father's face, and also produces a warm sense of familiarity.

Ordinarily, all of these brain areas work together, allowing the recognition of your father's face to go smoothly forward. If they don't work together—that is, if the coordination among these areas is disrupted—yet another area works to make sure you offer plausible hypotheses about this, and not zany ones. (Thus, if your father looks less familiar to you on some occasion, you're likely to explain this by saying, "I guess he must have gotten new glasses" rather than "I bet he's been replaced by a robot.")

Unmistakably, then, this apparently easy task—seeing your father and recognizing who he is—requires multiple brain areas. The same is true of most tasks, and in this way, Capgras syndrome illustrates this crucial aspect of brain function.

The Study of the Brain

In order to discuss Capgras syndrome, we needed to refer to different brain areas; we also had to rely on several different research techniques. Thus, the syndrome also illustrates another point—namely, that this is a domain in which we need some technical foundations before we can develop our theories. Let's start building those foundations.

The human brain weighs between 3 and 4 pounds; it's roughly the size of a small melon. Yet this structure has been estimated to contain a trillion nerve cells (that's 10^{12}), each of which is connected to 10,000 or so others—for a total of roughly 10 million billion connections. The brain also contains a huge number of *glial* cells (and, by some estimates, the glia outnumber the nerve cells by roughly 10 to 1, so there's roughly 10 trillion of these!). We'll have much more to say about nerve cells and glial cells later, but, more immediately, how should we begin our study of this densely packed, incredibly complex organ?

One place to start is with a simple fact we've already met: that different parts of the brain perform different jobs. We've known this fact about the brain for many years, thanks to clinical evidence showing that the symptoms produced by brain damage depend heavily on the location of the damage. In 1848, for example, a horrible construction accident caused Phineas Gage to suffer damage in the frontmost part of his brain (see Figure 2.3); this damage led to severe personality and emotional problems. In 1861, physician Paul Broca noted that damage in a different location, on the left side of the brain, led to a disruption of language skills. In 1911, Édouard Claparède (1911/1951) reported his observations with patients who suffered from profound memory loss, a loss produced by damage in still another part of the brain.

Clearly, therefore, we need to understand brain functioning with reference to brain anatomy. Where was the damage that Gage suffered? Where exactly was the damage in Broca's patients, or Claparède's? In this section, we fill in some basics of brain anatomy.

Hindbrain, Midbrain, Forebrain

The human brain is divided into three main structures: the hindbrain, the midbrain, and the forebrain. The **hindbrain** sits directly atop the spinal cord and includes several structures crucial for controlling key life functions. It's here, for example, that the rhythm of heartbeats and the rhythm of breathing are regulated. The hindbrain also plays an essential role in maintaining the body's overall tone; specifically, the hindbrain helps maintain the body's posture and balance, and it helps control the brain's level of alertness.

FIGURE 2.3 | **PHINEAS GAGE**

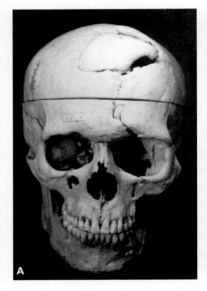
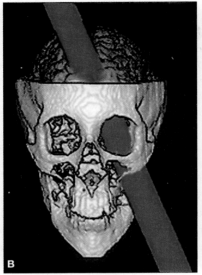

Phineas Gage was working as a construction foreman when some blasting powder misfired and launched a piece of iron into his cheek and through the front part of his brain. Remarkably, Gage survived and continued to live a more-or-less normal life, but his pattern of intellectual and emotional impairments provide valuable cues about the function of the brain's frontal lobes. Panel A is a photo of Gage's skull; the drawing in Panel B depicts the iron bar's path as it blasted through his head. Panel C is actually a photograph of Gage, and he's holding onto the bar that went through his brain!

The largest area of the hindbrain is the **cerebellum.** For many years, investigators believed this structure's main role was in the coordination of bodily movements and balance. Recent studies, however, suggest that the cerebellum also plays a diverse set of other roles, and damage to this organ can cause problems in spatial reasoning, in discriminating sounds, and in integrating the input received from various sensory systems (Bower & Parsons, 2003).

The **midbrain** has several roles. It plays an important part in coordinating your movements, including the skilled, precise movements of your eyes as you explore the visual world. Also in the midbrain are circuits that relay auditory information from the ears to the areas in the forebrain where this information is processed and interpreted. Still other structures in the midbrain help to regulate the experience of pain.

For our purposes, though, the most interesting brain region (and, in humans, the largest region) is the **forebrain.** Drawings of the brain (like the one shown in Figure 2.2) show little other than the forebrain, because this structure surrounds (and hides from view) the entire midbrain and most of the hindbrain. Of course, it is only the outer surface of the forebrain—the **cortex**—that is visible in such pictures. In general, the word *cortex* (from the Latin word for "tree bark") refers to an organ's outer surface, and many organs each have their own cortex; what's visible in the drawing, then, is the *cerebral* cortex.

The cortex is just a thin covering on the outer surface of the forebrain; on average, it is a mere 3 mm thick. Nonetheless, there's a great deal of cortical tissue; by some estimates, the cortex constitutes 80% of the human brain. This considerable volume is made possible by the fact that the cerebral cortex, thin as it is, consists of a very large sheet of tissue; if stretched out flat, it would cover more than 2 square feet. But the cortex isn't stretched flat; instead, it is all crumpled up and jammed into the limited space inside the skull. It's this crumpling that produces the brain's most obvious visual feature—the wrinkles, or **convolutions**, that cover the brain's outer surface.

Some of the "valleys" between the wrinkles are actually deep grooves that divide the brain into different sections. The deepest groove is the **longitudinal fissure**, running from the front of the brain to the back, which separates the left **cerebral hemisphere** from the right. Other fissures divide the cortex in each hemisphere into four lobes (again, look back at Figure 2.2), and these are named after the bones that cover them—bones that, as a group, make up the skull. The **frontal lobes** form the front of the brain—right behind the forehead. The **central fissure** divides the frontal lobes on each side of the brain from the **parietal lobes,** the brain's topmost part. The bottom edge of the frontal lobes is marked by the **lateral fissure,** and below it are the **temporal lobes.** Finally, at the very back of the brain, connected to the parietal and temporal lobes, are the **occipital lobes.**

Subcortical Structures

Hidden from view, underneath the cortex, are the **subcortical** parts of the forebrain. One of these parts, the **thalamus**, acts as a relay station for nearly all the sensory information going to the cortex. Directly underneath the thalamus is the **hypothalamus**, a structure that plays a crucial role in controlling motivated behaviors such as eating, drinking, and sexual activity.

Surrounding the thalamus and hypothalamus is another set of interconnected structures that together form the **limbic system**. Included here is the amygdala, and close by is the **hippocampus**, both located underneath the cortex in the temporal lobe (plurals: amygdalae and hippocampi; see Figure 2.4). These structures are essential for learning and memory, and the patient H.M., discussed in Chapter 1, developed his profound amnesia after surgeons removed these structures—a strong confirmation of their role in the formation of new memories.

We mentioned earlier that the amygdala plays a key role in emotional processing, and this role is reflected in many findings. For example, presentation of frightful faces causes high levels of activity in the amygdala (Williams et al., 2006). Likewise, people ordinarily show more complete, longer-lasting memories for emotional events, compared to similar but emotionally flat events. This memory advantage for emotional events is especially pronounced in people who showed greater activation in the amygdalae while they were witnessing the event

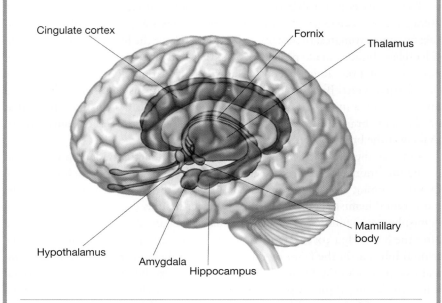

FIGURE 2.4 | THE LIMBIC SYSTEM AND THE HIPPOCAMPUS

Cingulate cortex

Fornix

Thalamus

Hypothalamus

Amygdala

Hippocampus

Mamillary body

Color is used in this drawing to help you visualize the arrangement of these brain structures. Imagine that the cortex is semi-transparent, allowing you to look into the brain, to see the (subcortical) structures highlighted here. The limbic system includes a number of subcortical structures that play a crucial role in learning and memory and in emotional processing.

in the first place. Conversely, the memory advantage for emotional events is diminished (and may not be observed at all) in people who (through sickness or injury) have suffered damage to the amygdalae.

Lateralization

Virtually all parts of the brain come in pairs, and so there is a hippocampus on the left side of the brain and another on the right, a left-side amygdala and a right one. Of course, the same is true for the cerebral cortex itself: There is a temporal cortex (i.e., a cortex of the temporal lobe) in the left hemisphere and another in the right, a left occipital cortex and a right one, and so on. In all cases, cortical and subcortical, the left and right structures in each pair have roughly the same shape and the same pattern of connections to other brain areas. Even so, there are differences in function between the left-side and right-side structures, with the left-hemisphere structure playing a somewhat different role from the corresponding right-hemisphere structure.

Let's bear in mind, though, that the two halves of the brain work together; the functioning of one side is closely integrated with that of the other side. This integration is made possible by the **commissures**, thick bundles of fibers that carry information back and forth between the two hemispheres. The largest commissure is the **corpus callosum**, but several other structures also ensure that the two brain halves work as partners in nearly all mental tasks.

In some cases, though, there are medical reasons to sever the corpus callosum and some of the other commissures. (For many years, this surgery was a last resort for extreme cases of epilepsy.) The person is then said to be a "split brain patient"—still having both brain halves, but with communication between the halves severely limited. Research with these patients has taught us a great deal about the specialized function of the brain's two hemispheres and has provided evidence, for example, that language capacities are generally lodged in the left hemisphere, while the right hemisphere seems crucial for a number of tasks involving spatial judgment (see Figure 2.5).

However, it is important not to overstate the contrast between the two brain halves, and it's misleading to claim (as some people do) that we need to silence our "left-brain thinking" in order to be more creative, or that intuitions grow out of "right-brain thinking." Instead, in people with intact commissures, the two hemispheres work together, with each hemisphere providing its own specialized skills that contribute to overall performance. Put differently, the complex, sophisticated skills we each display (including creativity, intuition, and more) depend on the whole brain. Our hemispheres are not cerebral competitors, each trying to impose its style of thinking on the other. Instead, the hemispheres pool their specialized capacities to produce a seamlessly integrated single mental self.

Data From Neuropsychology

How can we learn about these various structures—and many others that we have not named? Just as cognitive psychology relies on many types of evidence in order to study the mind, cognitive neuroscience relies on many types of evidence to study the brain and nervous system. We've already mentioned one form of evidence—the study of individuals who (tragically) have suffered brain damage, whether through accident, disease, or in some cases birth defect. The study of all these cases generally falls within the domain of *neuropsychology*: the study of the brain's structures and how they relate to brain function. Within neuropsychology, the specialty of *clinical neuropsychology* seeks (among other goals) to understand the functioning of intact, undamaged brains by careful scrutiny of cases involving brain damage.

Data drawn from clinical neuropsychology will be important for us throughout this text. For now, though, let's emphasize the fact that the symptoms resulting from brain damage depend heavily on the site of the damage. A **lesion** (a specific area of damage) in the hippocampus produces memory problems but not language disorders; a lesion in the occipital cortex produces problems in vision but spares the other sensory modalities. Likewise, the consequences of brain lesions depend on which hemisphere is damaged: Damage to the left side

FIGURE 2.5 | STUDYING SPLIT-BRAIN PATIENTS

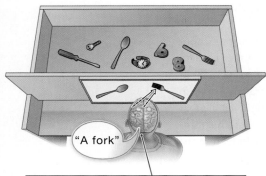
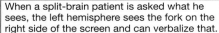
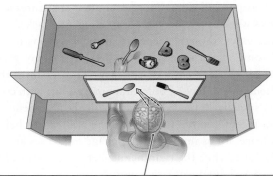

"A fork"

When a split-brain patient is asked what he sees, the left hemisphere sees the fork on the right side of the screen and can verbalize that.

The right hemisphere sees the spoon on the screen's left side, but it cannot verbalize that. However, if the patient reaches with his left hand to pick up the object, he does select the spoon.

In this experiment, the patient is shown two pictures, one of a spoon and one of a fork. If asked what he sees, his verbal response is controlled by the left hemisphere, which has seen only the fork (because it's in the right visual field). If asked to pick up the object shown in the picture, however, the patient—reaching with his left hand—picks up the spoon. That happens because the left hand is controlled by the right hemisphere, and this hemisphere receives visual information from the left-hand side of the visual world.

of the frontal lobe, for example, is likely to produce a disruption of language use; damage to the right side of the frontal lobe generally doesn't have this effect. In obvious ways, all of these patterns confirm that different brain areas perform different functions and provide a rich source of data helping us develop and test hypotheses about those functions.

Data From Neuroimaging

We can also learn a great deal from neuroimaging data. As we mentioned earlier, neuroimaging allows us to take precise three-dimensional pictures of the brain. For many years, researchers used **computerized axial tomography** (CT scans) to study the brain's structure and **positron emission tomography** (PET scans) to study the brain's activity. CT scans rely on X-rays and thus—in essence—provide a three-dimensional X-ray picture of the brain. PET scans, in contrast, start by introducing a tracer substance such as glucose into the body; the molecules of this tracer have been tagged with a low dose of radioactivity and the scan keeps track of this radio-activity, allowing us to tell which tissues are using more of the glucose (the body's main fuel) and which are using less. For both types of scan, though, the primary data (X-rays or radioactive emissions) are collected by a bank of detectors surrounding the head; a computer then compares the signals received by each of the detectors and

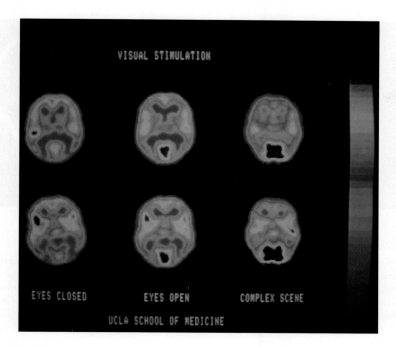

VISUAL STIMULATION

EYES CLOSED   EYES OPEN   COMPLEX SCENE

UCLA SCHOOL OF MEDICINE

PET SCANS

PET scans can measure how much glucose (the brain's fuel) is being used at specific locations within the brain; this provides a measurement of each location's activity level at a certain moment in time. In the figure, the brain is viewed from above, with the front of the head at the top and the back at the bottom. The various colors indicate relative activity levels (the brain itself is not colored!), using the ordered palette shown on the right side of the figure. As the figure shows, visual processing involves increased activity in the occipital cortex.

uses this information to pinpoint the source of each signal. In this way, the computer reconstructs a three-dimensional map of the brain. For CT scans, the map tells us the shape, size, and position of structures within the brain. For PET scans, the map tells us what regions are particularly active at any point in time.

More recent studies have turned to two newer techniques, introduced earlier in the chapter. **Magnetic resonance imaging** (MRI) relies on the magnetic properties of the atoms that make up the brain tissue, and it yields fabulously detailed pictures of the brain. A closely related technique, **functional magnetic resonance imaging** (fMRI), measures the oxygen content in the blood flowing through each region of the brain; this turns out to be an accurate index of the level of neural activity in that region. In this way, fMRI scans provide an incredibly precise picture of the brain's moment-by-moment activities.

The results of a CT or MRI scan are relatively stable, changing only if the person's brain structure changes (because of an injury, perhaps, or the growth of a tumor). The results of PET or fMRI scans, in contrast, are highly variable, because the results depend on what task the person is performing. This confirms once again the fundamental point that different brain areas perform different functions and are involved in different tasks. More ambitiously, though, we can use the neuroimaging

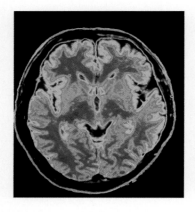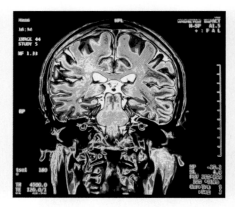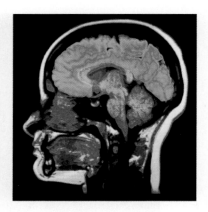

MAGNETIC RESONANCE IMAGING

Magnetic resonance imaging produces magnificently detailed pictures of the brain. The left panel shows a "slice" of the brain viewed from the top of the head (the front of the head is at the top of the image); clearly visible is the longitudinal fissure, which divides the left cerebral hemisphere from the right. The middle panel shows a slice of the brain viewed from the front; again, the separation of the two hemispheres is clearly visible, and so are some of the commissures linking the two brain halves. The right panel shows a slice of the brain viewed from the side; many of the structures in the limbic system (see Figure 2.4) are easily seen.

procedures as a means of exploring brain function—using fMRI scans, for example, to ask which brain sites are especially activated when someone is listening to Mozart or when someone is engaged in memory rehearsal. In this fashion, the neuroimaging data can provide crucial information about how these complex activities are made possible by specific brain functioning.

Data From Electrical Recording

Neuroscientists have another technique in their toolkit: electrical recording of the brain's activity. To explain this point, though, we need to say a bit about how the brain functions: As we mentioned earlier, the brain contains a trillion nerve cells—more properly called *neurons*—and it is the neurons that do the brain's main work. (We'll say more about these cells later in the chapter.) Neurons vary in their shape, size, and functioning, but for the most part they communicate with each other via chemical signals called *neurotransmitters*: Once a neuron is "activated," it releases the transmitter, and this chemical can then activate (or, in some cases, *de*-activate) other, immediately-adjacent neurons. The adjacent neurons, in other words, "receive" this chemical signal, and they, in turn, can send the signal onward to still other neurons.

This process actually requires two types of communication: One type is "between neurons" and involves the chemical signals we just described: A neuron releases the transmitter substance, and this activates (or de-activates) another neuron. The other type of communication is "within neuron" and is demanded by the fact that—to put it roughly—neurons generally have an "input" end and an "output" end. The "input" end is the portion of the neuron that's most sensitive to neurotransmitters; this is where the signal from other neurons is received. The "output" end is the portion of the neuron that releases the neurotransmitter, sending the signal on to other neurons. The question, then, is how neurons get the signal from one end of the cell to the other.

The answer involves an electrical pulse, made possible by a flow of charged atoms (ions) in and out of the neuron (again, we will say more about this process later in the chapter). The amount of electrical current involved in this ion flow is minute, but, of course, many millions of neurons are active at the same time, and the current generated by all of them together is great enough to be detected by sensitive electrodes placed on the surface of the scalp. This is the basis for **electroencephalography**—a recording of voltage changes occurring at the scalp that reflect activity in the brain underneath. The result of this procedure is an *electroencephalogram,* or EEG.

Often, EEGs are used to study broad rhythms in the brain's activities. This is, for example, how we study the various rhythms that characterize the different stages of sleep. Sometimes, though, we want to know about the brain's electrical activity over a shorter period of time—for example, how the brain responds to a specific event or a particular stimulus. In this case, we measure the changes in EEG in the brief period just before, during, and after the event; these changes are referred to as an **event-related potential** (see Figure 2.6).

The Power of Combining Techniques

Each of the research tools we have described has its own strengths and weaknesses. CT scans and MRI data tell us about the shape and size of brain structures, but they tell us nothing about the activity levels within these structures. PET scans and fMRI studies do tell us about brain activity, and they can locate the activity rather precisely (within a millimeter or two). However, these techniques are less precise about *when* the activity took place. For example, fMRI data summarize the brain's activity over a period of several seconds and cannot tell us when, within this time window, the activity took place. EEG data give us much more precise information about timing but are much weaker in telling us *where* the activity took place.

Researchers deal with these limitations by means of a strategy commonly used in science: We seek data from multiple sources, so that we can use the strengths of one technique to make up for the shortcomings of another. Thus, for example, some studies combine EEG recordings with fMRI scans, with the EEG's telling us *when* certain events took place in the brain, and the scans telling us *where* the activity took place. Likewise, some studies combine fMRI scans with CT data, so that we can link our findings about brain activation to a detailed portrait of the person's brain anatomy.

Researchers also need to deal with another limitation on their findings: the fact that many of the techniques described so far provide only *correlational data*. To understand this point, consider the finding that a brain area called the *fusiform face area* (FFA) seems to be especially active whenever a face is being perceived (see Figure 2.7). Does this mean the FFA is needed for face perception? A different

FIGURE 2.6 | RECORDING THE BRAIN'S ELECTRICAL ACTIVITY

A

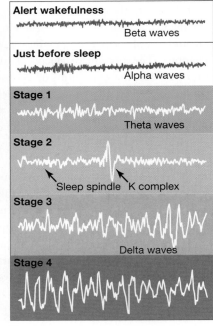

B

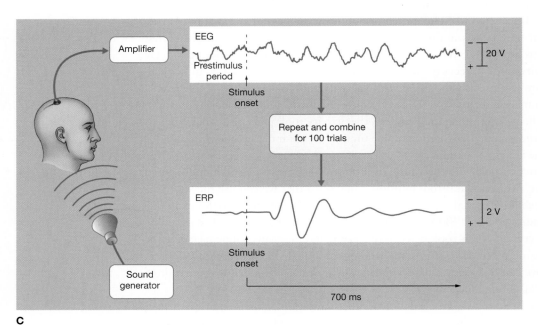

C

To record the brain's electrical signals, researchers use a cap that has electrodes attached to it. The procedure is easy and entirely safe—it can even be used to measure brain signals in a young baby (A). In some procedures, researchers measure recurrent rhythms in the brain's activity, including the rhythms that distinguish the stages of sleep (B). In other procedures, they measure the brain activity produced in response to a single event—such as the presentation of a well-defined stimulus (C).

FIGURE 2.7 | BRAIN ACTIVITY AND AWARENESS

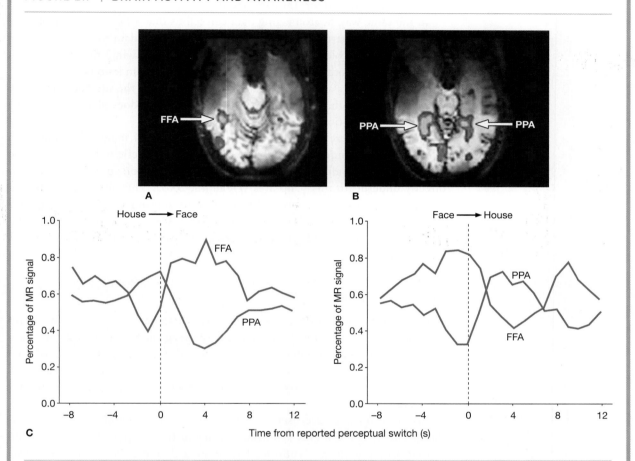

Panel A shows an fMRI scan of a subject looking at faces. Activation levels are high in the fusiform face area (FFA), an area that is apparently more responsive to faces than to other visual stimuli. Panel B shows a scan of the same subject looking at pictures of places; now activity levels are high in the parahippocampal place area (PPA). Panel C compares the activity in these two areas when the subject has a picture of a face in front of one eye, and a picture of a house in front of the other eye. When the viewer's attention shifts from the house to the face, activation increases in the FFA. When the viewer's attention shifts from the face to the house, PPA activation increases. Thus, the activation level reflects what the subject is aware of, and not just the pattern of incoming stimulation. (After Tong, Kakayma, Vaughan, & Kanwisher, 1998)

possibility is that the FFA activation may just be a by-product of face perception and does not play a crucial role. As an analogy, think about the fact that a car's speedometer becomes "more activated" (i.e., shows a higher value) whenever the car goes faster. That doesn't mean that the speedometer *causes* the speed or *is necessary* for the speed. Indeed, the car would go just as fast and would, for many purposes, perform just as well if the speedometer were removed. The speedometer's state, in other words, is *correlated* with the car's speed but in no sense causes (or promotes, or is needed for) the car's speed.

In the same way, neuroimaging data can tell us that a brain area's activity is correlated with a particular function, but we need other data to ask whether the brain site plays a role in *causing* (or supporting, or allowing) that function. In many cases, those other data come from the study of brain lesions: If damage to a brain site disrupts a function, that's an indication that the site does play some role in supporting that function. (And, in fact, the FFA does play an important role in face recognition.)

Also helpful here is a technique called **transcranial magnetic stimulation** (TMS). This technique creates a series of strong magnetic pulses at a specific location on the scalp, causing a (temporary!) disruption in the brain region directly underneath this scalp area (Helmuth, 2001). This allows us to ask, in an otherwise normal brain, what functions are compromised when a particular bit of brain tissue is temporarily "turned off." The results of a TMS procedure can therefore provide crucial information about the functional role of that brain area.

Localization of Function

Overall, then, the data make it clear that different portions of the brain each have their own jobs to do. Indeed, drawing on the techniques we have described, neuroscientists have learned a great deal about the function of specific brain structures—a research effort broadly referred to as the **localization of function**, aimed (roughly) toward figuring out what's happening where within the brain.

Localization data are useful in many ways. For example, think back to the discussion of Capgras syndrome earlier in this chapter. Brain scans told us that people with this syndrome have damaged amygdalae. To interpret this observation, though, we needed to ask about the function of the amygdalae: Yes, we can locate the brain damage in these patients, but how does the brain damage affect them? To tackle this question, we relied on localization of function—and, in particular, on data telling us that the amygdala is involved in many tasks involving emotional appraisal. This combination of points, then, helped us to build (and test) our claims about this syndrome and, more broadly, claims about the role of emotional processing within the ordinary experience of "familiarity."

As a different illustration, consider the experience of calling up a "mental picture" before the "mind's eye." We'll have more to say about this experience in Chapter 10, but we can already ask: How much does this experience have in common with ordinary seeing—i.e., placing a real picture before the actual eyes? As it turns out, localization data reveal enormous overlap between the brain structures needed for these two activities (visualizing and actual vision), telling us immediately that these activities do have a great deal in common (see Figure 2.8). Thus, again, we build on localization—this time to ask how exactly two mental activities are related to each other.

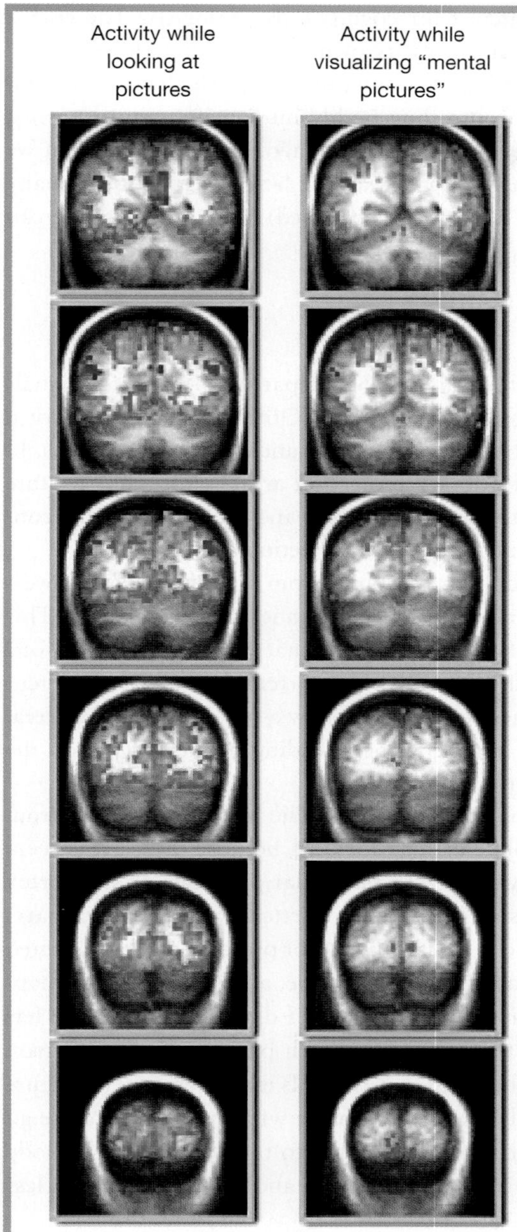

Activity while looking at pictures

Activity while visualizing "mental pictures"

FIGURE 2.8 | **A PORTRAIT OF THE BRAIN AT WORK**

These fMRI images show different "slices" through the living brain, revealing levels of activity in different brain sites. More-active regions are shown in yellow, orange, and red. The first column shows brain activity while a person is making judgments about simple pictures. The second column shows brain activity while the person is making the same sorts of judgments about "mental pictures," visualized before the "mind's eye."

The Cerebral Cortex

As we've already noted, the largest portion of the human brain is the cerebral cortex—the thin layer of tissue covering the cerebrum. This is the region in which an enormous amount of information processing takes place, and so, for many topics, is the brain region of greatest interest for cognitive psychologists. The cortex includes many distinct regions, each with its own function, but these regions are traditionally divided into three categories: *motor areas*, which contain brain tissue crucial for organizing and controlling bodily movements; *sensory areas*, which contain tissue essential for organizing and analyzing the information we receive from the senses; and *association areas*. These latter areas support many functions, including the essential (but not-well defined) human activity we call "thinking."

Motor Areas

Specific areas of the cerebral cortex serve as the "departure points" for signals leaving the cortex and controlling muscle movement. Other areas are the "arrival points" for information coming from the eyes, ears, and other sense organs. In both cases, these areas are called **primary projection areas**, with the departure points known as the **primary motor projection areas** and the arrival points contained in regions known as the **primary sensory projection areas**.

Evidence for the motor projection area comes from studies in which investigators apply mild electrical current to this area in anesthetized animals. This stimulation often produces specific movements, so that current applied to one site causes a movement of the left front leg, while current applied to a different site causes the ears to perk up. These movements show a pattern of **contralateral control**, with stimulation to the left hemisphere leading to movements on the right side of the body, and vice versa.

Why are these areas called "projection areas"? The term is borrowed from mathematics and from the discipline of map making, because these areas seem to form "maps" of the external world, with particular positions on the cortex corresponding to particular parts of the body, or particular locations in space. In the human brain, the map that constitutes the motor projection area is located on a strip of tissue toward the rear of the frontal lobe, and the pattern of mapping is illustrated in Figure 2.9; in this illustration, a drawing of a person has been overlaid on a depiction of the brain, with each part of the little person positioned on top of the area of the brain that controls its movement. The figure makes clear that areas of the body that we can move with great precision (e.g., fingers and lips) have a lot of cortical area devoted to them; areas of the body over which we have less control (e.g., the shoulder and the back) receive less cortical coverage.

Sensory Areas

Information arriving from the skin senses (your sense of touch or your sense of temperature) is projected to a region in the parietal lobe, just behind the motor projection area; this is labeled the "somatosensory" area in Figure 2.9. If a patient's brain is stimulated in this region (with electrical current or touch), the patient will typically report a tingling sensation in a specific part of the body.

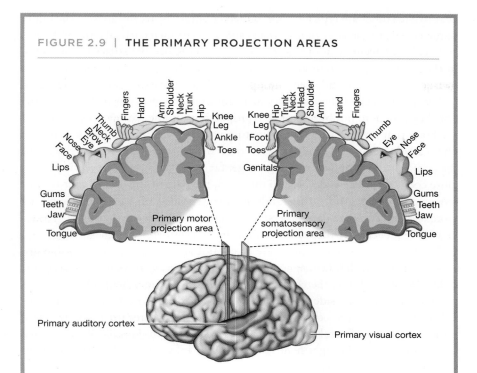

The primary motor projection area is located at the rearmost edge of the frontal lobe, and each region within this projection area controls the motion of a specific body part, as illustrated on the top left. The primary somatosensory projection area, receiving information from the skin, is at the forward edge of the parietal lobe; each region within this area receives input from a specific body part. The primary projection areas for vision and hearing are located in the occipital and temporal lobes, respectively. These two areas are also organized systematically. For example, in the visual projection area, adjacent areas of the brain receive visual inputs that come from adjacent areas in visual space.

Figure 2.9 also shows the region (in the temporal lobes) that functions as the primary projection area for hearing (the "auditory" area). If the brain is directly stimulated here, the patient will hear clicks, buzzes, and hums. An area in the occipital lobes is the primary projection area for vision; stimulation here produces the experience of seeing flashes of light or visual patterns.

The sensory projection areas differ from each other in important ways, but they also have features in common, and they're features that parallel the attributes of the motor projection area. First, each of these areas provides a "map" of the sensory environment. In the somatosensory area, each part of the body's surface is represented by its own region on the cortex; areas of the body that are near to each other are typically represented by similarly nearby areas in the brain. In the visual area, each region of visual space has its own cortical representation, and again, adjacent areas of space are usually represented by adjacent brain sites. In the auditory projection area, different frequencies of sound each have their own cortical sites, and adjacent brain sites are responsive to adjacent frequencies.

Second, in each of these sensory maps the assignment of cortical space is governed by function, not by anatomical proportions. In the parietal lobes, parts of the body that are not very discriminating with regard to touch, even if they're physically large, get relatively little cortical area. Other, more sensitive areas of the body (the lips, tongue, and fingers) get far more space. In the occipital lobes, more cortical surface is devoted to the fovea, the part of the eyeball that is most sensitive to detail. And, in the auditory areas, some frequencies of sound get more cerebral coverage than others; it's surely no coincidence that these "advantaged" frequencies are those essential for the perception of speech.

Finally, we also find evidence here of contralateral connections: The somatosensory area in the left hemisphere, for example, receives its main input from the right side of the body; the corresponding area in the right hemisphere receives its input from the left side of the body. Likewise for the visual projection areas, although here the projection is not contralateral with regard to body parts; instead, it's contralateral with regard to physical space. Specifically, the visual projection area in the right hemisphere receives information from both the left

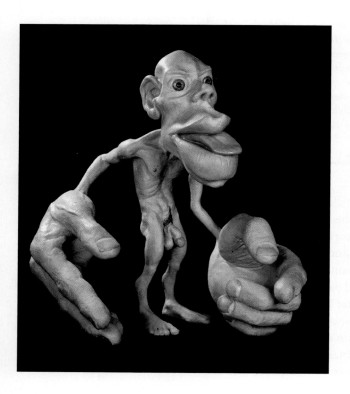

THE SENSORY HOMUNCULUS

An artist's rendition of what a man would look like if his appearance were proportional to the area allotted by the somatosensory cortex to his various body parts.

eye and the right, but the information it receives corresponds to the left half of visual space (i.e., all of the things visible to your left when you're looking straight ahead). The reverse is true for the visual area in the left hemisphere: It receives information from both eyes, but from only the right half of visual space. The pattern of contralateral organization is also evident—although not as clear-cut—for the auditory cortex, with roughly 60% of the nerve fibers from each ear sending their information to the opposite side of the brain.

Association Areas

The areas described so far—both motor and sensory—make up only a small part of the human cerebral cortex—roughly 25%. The remaining cortical areas are traditionally referred to as the **association cortex,** on the idea that these areas perform the task of associating simple ideas and sensations in order to form more complex thoughts and behaviors.

This terminology, however, is falling out of use, in part because this large volume of brain tissue can be subdivided further on both functional and anatomical grounds. These subdivisions are perhaps best revealed by the diversity of symptoms that result if the cortex is damaged in one or another specific location. For example, some lesions in the frontal lobe produce **apraxias,** disturbances in the initiation or organization of voluntary action. Other lesions (generally in the occipital cortex, or in the rearmost part of the parietal lobe) lead to **agnosias,** disruptions in the ability to identify familiar objects. Agnosias usually affect one modality only, so a patient with visual agnosia, for example, can recognize a fork by touching it but not by looking at it. A patient with auditory agnosia, by contrast, might be unable to identify familiar voices but might still recognize the face of the person speaking.

Still other lesions (usually in the parietal lobe) produce **neglect syndrome,** in which the individual seems to ignore half of the visual world. A patient afflicted with this syndrome will shave only half of his face and eat food from only half of his plate. If asked to read the word "pigpen," he will read "pen," and so on.

Damage in other areas causes still other symptoms. We mentioned earlier that lesions in areas near the lateral fissure (again, the deep groove that separates the frontal and temporal lobes) can result in disruption to language capacities, a problem referred to as **aphasia.**

Finally, damage to the frontmost part of the frontal lobe, the **prefrontal area,** causes a variety of problems. In many cases, these are problems of planning and implementing strategies. In other cases, patients with damage here show problems in inhibiting their own behaviors, relying on habit even in situations for which habit is inappropriate. Frontal lobe damage can also (as we mentioned in our discussion of Capgras syndrome) lead to a variety of confusions, such as whether a remembered episode actually happened or was simply imagined.

We will have much more to say about these diagnostic categories—aphasia, agnosia, neglect, and more—in upcoming chapters, where we'll consider these disorders in the context of other things we know about object recognition, attention, and so on. Our point for the moment, though, is a simple one: These clinical patterns make it clear that the so-called association cortex contains many subregions, each specialized for a particular function, but with all of the subregions working together in virtually all aspects of our daily lives.

Brain Cells

This brief tour has described only the large-scale structures in the brain. For many purposes, though, we need to zoom in for a closer look, in order to see how the brain's functions are actually carried out. In the remainder of the chapter, we'll illustrate this sort of closer look by considering the brain systems that allow us to see, and to recognize the objects and events that we see. Let's start, though, by saying a bit more about the individual cells that make the brain's functioning possible. We'll then build on these points when we turn to our discussion of the visual system.

Neurons and Glia

We've already mentioned that the human brain contains roughly a trillion **neurons** and a much greater number of **glia**. The glia perform many functions: They help to guide the development of the nervous system in the fetus and young infant, support repairs if the nervous system is damaged, maintain and control the flow of nutrients to the neurons, and more. Specialized glial cells also provide a layer of electrical insulation surrounding parts of the neuron; this insulation dramatically increases the speed with which neurons can send their signals. Finally, some research suggests the glia may also constitute their own signaling system within the brain, separate from the information flow provided by the neurons.

There is no question, though, that the main flow of information through the brain—from the sense organs inward, from one part of the brain to the others, and then from the brain outward—is made possible by the neurons. As we noted earlier, neurons come in many shapes and sizes, but, in general, neurons have three major parts (see Figure 2.10). The **cell body** is the portion of the cell that contains the neuron's nucleus and all the elements needed for the normal metabolic activities of the cell. The **dendrites** are usually the "input" side of the neuron, receiving signals from many other neurons. In most neurons, the dendrites are heavily branched, like a thick and tangled bush. The **axon**, finally, is the "output" side of the neuron and sends neural impulses to other neurons. Axons can vary enormously in length; if you wiggle your toes, the axon that sent this command signal from your spine to your toes is more than a meter long.

The Synapse

We've already noted that communication from one neuron to the next is generally made possible by a chemical signal: When a neuron has been sufficiently stimulated, it releases a minute quantity of a **neurotransmitter.** The molecules of this substance drift across the tiny gap between neurons and latch onto the cell wall of the adjacent

FIGURE 2.10 | NEURONS

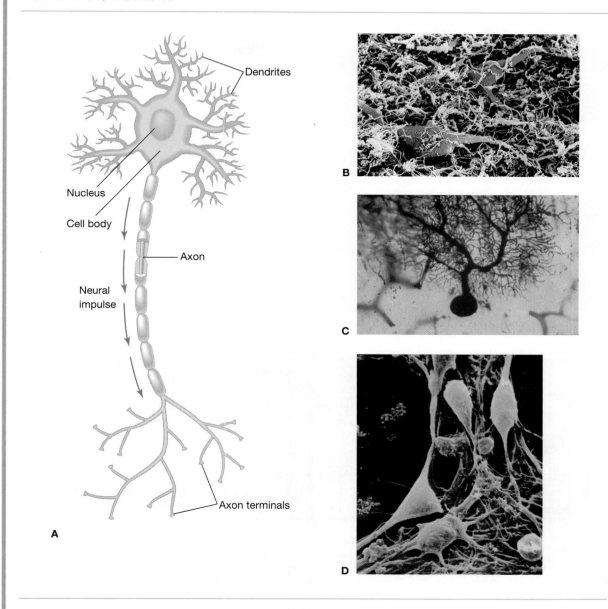

Most neurons have three identifiable regions, as shown in Panel A: The dendrites *are the part of the neuron that usually detects incoming signals. The* cell body *contains the metabolic machinery that sustains the cell. The* axon *is the part of the neuron that transmits a signal to another location. When the cell fires, neurotransmitters are released from the terminal endings at the tip of the axon. We should note, though, that neurons actually come in many shapes and sizes. Panel B shows neurons from the spinal cord (stained in red); Panel C shows neurons from the cerebellum; Panel D shows neurons from the cerebral cortex. Neurons usually have the same basic parts (dendrites, a cell body, at least one axon), but plainly the dimensions and configuration of these parts can vary widely.*

FIGURE 2.11 | SCHEMATIC VIEW OF SYNAPTIC TRANSMISSION

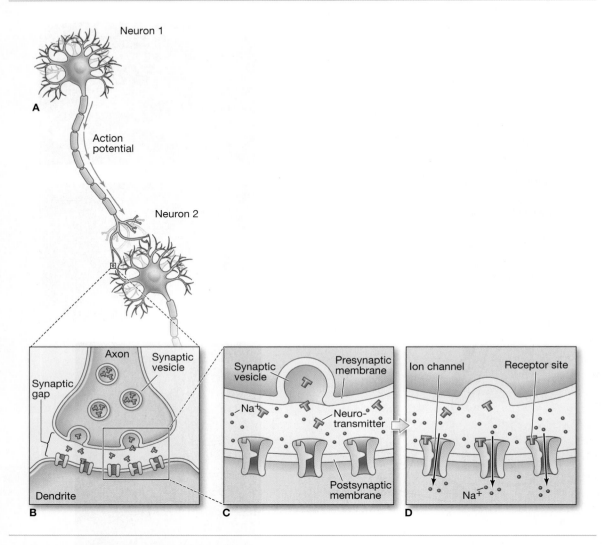

(A) Neuron 1 transmits a message across the synaptic gap to Neuron 2. (B) Synaptic vesicles in the axon terminal are stimulated. (C) The vesicle bursts, and neurotransmitter molecules are ejected toward the postsynaptic membrane. (D) Neurotransmitter molecules settle on the receptor site, an ion channel opens, and sodium (Na⁺) floods in.

dendrites. If the dendrites receive enough of this substance, the next neuron will "fire," and so the signal will be sent along to other neurons (see Figure 2.11).

Notice, then, that neurons usually don't touch each other directly. Instead, at the end of the axon, there is a tiny gap separating each neuron from the next. This site—the end of the axon, plus the gap, plus the receiving membrane of the next neuron—is called a **synapse.** The space between the neurons is called the *synaptic gap*; the bit of the neuron that releases the transmitter into this gap is called the *presynaptic membrane*, and the bit of the neuron on the other side of the gap, affected by the transmitters, is the *postsynaptic membrane.*

When the neurotransmitters arrive at the postsynaptic membrane, they cause changes in the membrane that allow certain ions to flow into and out of the postsynaptic cell. If these ionic flows are relatively small, then the postsynaptic cell quickly recovers and the ions are transported back to where they were initially. But if the ionic flows are large enough, they trigger a response in the postsynaptic cell. In formal terms, if the incoming signal reaches the postsynaptic cell's **threshold,** then the cell **fires;** that is, it produces an **action potential**—a signal that moves down its axon, which in turn causes the release of neurotransmitters at the next synapse, potentially causing the next cell to fire.

Let's emphasize several points about this sequence of events. First, recall our earlier mention that neurons depend on two different forms of information flow. Communication from one neuron to the next is (for most neurons) mediated by a chemical signal. In contrast, communication from one end of the neuron to the other (usually from the dendrites down the length of the axon) is made possible by an electrical signal, created by the flow of ions in and out of the cell.

Second, note that the postsynaptic neuron's initial response can vary in size; the incoming signal can cause a small ionic flow or a large one. Crucially, though, once these inputs reach the postsynaptic neuron's firing threshold, there's no variability in the response: Either a signal is sent down the axon or it is not; if the signal is sent, it is always of the same magnitude, a fact referred to as the **all-or-none law.** Just as pounding on a car horn won't make the horn any louder, a stronger stimulus won't produce a stronger action potential. A neuron either fires or it doesn't; there's no in between.

This does not mean, however, that neurons always send exactly the same information. A neuron can fire many times per second, or only occasionally. A neuron can fire just once and then stop, or it can keep firing for an extended span. But, even so, each individual response by the neuron is always the same size.

Third, we should note also that the brain relies on many different neurotransmitters. Roughly a hundred transmitters have been catalogued so far, and this diversity allows the brain to send a variety of different messages: Some transmitters have the effect of stimulating subsequent neurons; some do the opposite and *inhibit* other neurons. Some transmitters play an essential role in learning and memory; others play a key role in regulating the level of arousal in the brain; still others influence motivation and emotion.

Finally, let's be clear about the central role of the synapse: Transmission across the synaptic gap does slow down the neuronal signal, but this is a tiny price to pay for the *advantages* created by this mode of signaling. Each neuron receives information from (i.e., has synapses with) many other neurons, and this allows the "receiving" neuron to integrate information from many sources. Among other benefits, this pattern of many neurons feeding into one makes it possible for a neuron to "compare" signals, and to adjust its functioning in light of information received from other sources. In addition, communication at the synapse is *adjustable*: The strength of a synaptic connection can be altered by experience, and this is almost certainly the biological basis for *learning*—the storage of new knowledge and new skills within the nervous system.

The Visual System

We have now described the brain's basic anatomy, and also zoomed in for a closer look at the brain's microscopic parts—the individual neurons. But how do all of these elements, large and small, function in ways that allow us to think, remember, learn, speak, or feel? As a step toward tackling this issue, let's take a closer look at the portions of the nervous system that allow us to *see*. We'll use the visual system as our example for two important reasons. First, vision is the modality through which humans acquire a huge amount of information, whether by reading or simply by viewing the world around us. If we understand vision, therefore, we understand the processes that bring us much of our knowledge! Second, investigators have made enormous progress in mapping out the neural "wiring" of the visual system, providing us with a detailed and sophisticated portrait of how this system operates. As a result, the study of vision provides an excellent illustration of how the study of the brain can proceed and what it can teach us.

The Photoreceptors

You look around the world, and instantly, effortlessly, you recognize the objects that surround you—words on this page, objects in the room in which you're sitting, things you can view out the window. You know the identities of these objects, and you also perceive that each has a particular size, position, color, and texture. What makes all of this possible? The sequence of events begins, of course, with the eye.

Light is produced by many objects in our surroundings—the sun, lamps, candles—and this light then reflects off most other objects. It is usually this reflected light—reflected from this book page, or from a friend's face—that launches the processes of vision. Some of this light hits the front surface of the eyeball, passes through the **cornea** and the **lens**, and then hits the **retina**, the light-sensitive tissue that lines the back of the eyeball (see Figure 2.12). The cornea and lens focus the incoming light, just as a camera lens might, so that a sharp image is cast onto the retina. Adjustments in this process are made possible by the fact that the lens is surrounded by a band of muscle. When the muscle tightens, the lens bulges somewhat, creating the proper shape for focusing images cast by nearby objects; when the muscle relaxes, the lens returns to a flatter shape, allowing the proper focus for objects farther away.

On the retina, there are two types of **photoreceptors**—specialized neural cells that respond directly to the incoming light (see Figure 2.13). One type of photoreceptor, the **rods**, are sensitive to much lower levels of light and so play an essential role whenever you're moving around in semidarkness, or whenever you're trying to view a fairly dim stimulus. But the rods are also color-blind: They distinguish among different intensities of light (and so contribute to our

FIGURE 2.12 | THE HUMAN EYE

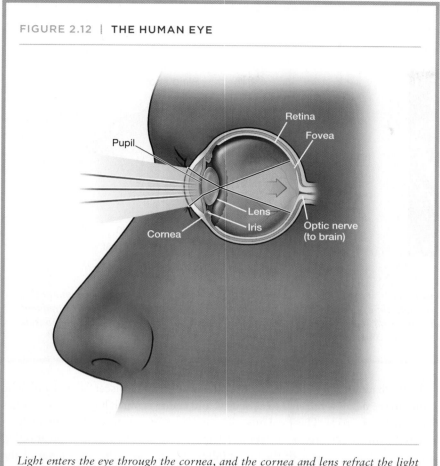

Light enters the eye through the cornea, and the cornea and lens refract the light rays to produce a sharply focused image on the retina. The iris can open or close to control the amount of light that reaches the retina. The retina is made up of three main layers: the rods and cones, which are the photoreceptors; the bipolar cells; and the ganglion cells, whose axons make up the optic nerve.

perception of brightness), but they provide no means of discriminating one hue from another.

Cones, in contrast, are less sensitive than rods and so need much more incoming light to operate at all. But cones are sensitive to color differences. More precisely, there are three different types of cones, each having its own pattern of sensitivities to different wavelengths. We perceive color, therefore, by comparing the outputs from these three cone types. Strong firing from only the cones that prefer short wavelengths, for example, accompanied by weak (or no) firing from the other cone types, signals purple. Blue is signaled by equally strong firing from the cones that prefer short wavelengths and those that prefer medium wavelengths, with only modest firing by cones that prefer long wavelengths. And so on, with other patterns of firing, across the three cone types, corresponding to different perceived hues.

FIGURE 2.13 | RODS AND CONES

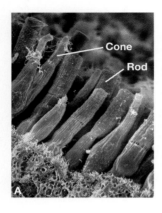

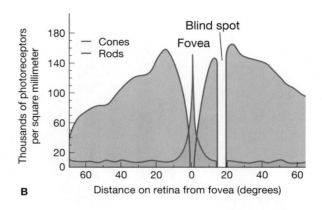

(A) Rods and cones are the light-sensitive cells at the back of the retina that launch the neural process of vision. In this (colorized) photo, cones appear green; rods appear brown. (B) Distribution of photoreceptors. Cones are most frequent at the fovea, and the number of cones drops off sharply as we move away from the fovea. In contrast, there are no rods at all on the fovea. There are neither rods nor cones at the retina's blind spot.

Cones have another crucial function: They allow us to discern fine detail. The ability to see detail is referred to as **acuity**, and acuity is much higher for the cones than it is for the rods. This explains why we point our eyes toward a target whenever we wish to perceive it in detail. What we are actually doing is positioning our eyes so that the image of the target falls onto the **fovea**, the very center of the retina. Here cones far outnumber rods (and, in fact, the center of the fovea has no rods at all). As a result, this is the region of the retina with the greatest acuity.

As we move away from the fovea and into the visual periphery, the rods predominate; well out into the periphery, there are no cones. This is why we're better able to see very dim lights out of the corner of our eyes. Sailors and astronomers have known this for years; when looking at a barely visible star, they know it's best not to look directly at the star's location. By looking slightly away from the star, they ensure that the star's image will fall outside of the fovea and onto a region of the retina dense with the more light-sensitive rods.

Lateral Inhibition

Rods and cones do not report directly to the cortex. Instead, the photoreceptors stimulate **bipolar cells**, which in turn excite **ganglion cells**. The ganglion cells are spread uniformly across the entire retina, but all of their axons converge to form the bundle of nerve fibers that we call the **optic nerve**; this is the nerve tract that leaves the eyeball and carries information to various sites in the brain. This information is sent first to an important way station in the thalamus called the

**WORKBOOK
DEMONSTRATIONS 2.1 AND 2.2**

lateral geniculate nucleus, or LGN; from there, information is transmitted to the primary projection area for vision, in the occipital lobe.

Let's be clear, though, that the optic nerve is far more than a mere cable that conducts signals from one site to another. Instead, the cells that link retina to brain are already engaged in the task of analyzing the visual input. One example lies in the phenomenon of **lateral inhibition**, a pattern in which cells, when stimulated, inhibit the activity of neighboring cells. To see why this is important, consider two cells, each receiving stimulation from a brightly lit area (see Figure 2.14). One cell (Cell B in the figure) is receiving its stimulation from the middle of the lit area. It is intensely stimulated, but so are its neighbors (including Cell A and Cell C). As a result, all of these cells are active, and therefore each one

WORKBOOK
DEMONSTRATION 2.3

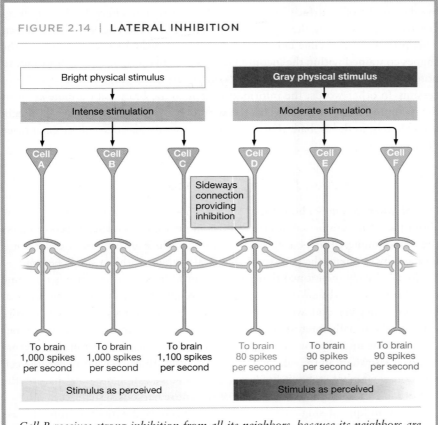

FIGURE 2.14 | **LATERAL INHIBITION**

Cell B receives strong inhibition from all its neighbors, because its neighbors are intensely stimulated. Cell C, in contrast, receives inhibition only from one side (because its neighbor on the other side, Cell D, is only moderately stimulated). As a result, cells B and C start with the same input, but C, receiving less inhibition, sends a stronger signal to the brain, emphasizing the edge in the stimulus. The same logic applies to Cells D and E, and explains why Cell D sends a weaker signal to the brain. Note, by the way, that the spikes per second numbers are hypothetical, and are intended only to illustrate lateral inhibition's effects.

is trying to inhibit its neighbors. The upshot is that the activity level of Cell B is *increased* by the stimulation, but *decreased* by the lateral inhibition it is receiving from Cells A and C. This combination leads to only a moderate level of activity in Cell B.

In contrast, another cell (Cell C in the figure) is receiving its stimulation from the edge of the lit area. It is intensely stimulated, and so are its neighbors *on one side*. Therefore, this cell will receive inhibition from one side but not from the other (in the figure: inhibition from Cell B, but *not* from Cell D), and so it will be less inhibited than Cell B (which is receiving inhibition from all sides). Thus, Cells B and C initially receive the same input, but C is less inhibited than B and will therefore end up firing more strongly than B.

The pattern of lateral inhibition, then, actually leads to stronger responses from cells detecting the edge of a surface (such as Cell C) than from cells detecting the middle of a surface (such as Cell B). This will, in effect, lead to an exaggerated response along the surface's edges, making those edges easier to detect. This process, called **edge enhancement**, helps the visual system to discern the shapes contained within the incoming visual information. And it is important to note that this edge enhancement occurs at a very early stage of the visual processing. In other words, the information sent to the brain isn't a mere copy of the incoming stimulation; instead, the steps of interpretation and analysis begin immediately, in the eyeball. (For a demonstration of this edge enhancement, see Figure 2.15.)

WORKBOOK
DEMONSTRATION 2.4

Single Neurons and Single-Cell Recording

Part of what we know about the visual system—indeed, part of what we know about the entire brain—comes from a technique called **single-cell recording**. As the name implies, this is a procedure through which investigators can record, moment by moment, the pattern of electrical changes within a single neuron.

We've already mentioned that when a neuron fires each response is the same size; this is, again, the *all-or-none law*. However, neurons can, we've said, vary in *how often* they fire, and, when investigators record the activity of a single neuron, what they're usually interested in is the cell's firing rate, measured in "spikes per second." The investigator can then vary the circumstances (either in the external world or elsewhere in the nervous system) in order to learn what makes the cell fire more, and what makes it fire less. In this way, we can figure out what job the neuron does within the broad context of the entire nervous system.

The technique of single-cell recording has been used with enormous success in the study of vision. In a typical procedure, the animal being studied is first immobilized. Then electrodes are placed just outside a neuron in the animal's optic nerve or brain. Next a computer screen is placed in front of the animal's eyes, and various patterns are flashed on the screen: circles, lines at various angles, or squares of various sizes at various positions. Researchers can then ask: Which patterns cause that neuron to fire? To what visual inputs does that cell respond?

FIGURE 2.15 | MACH BANDS

Edge enhancement, produced by lateral inhibition, helps us to perceive the outline that defines an object's shape. But the same process can produce illusions—including the so-called Mach bands. Each vertical strip is of uniform light intensity, but the strips do not appear uniform. For each strip, contrast makes the left edge (next to its darker neighbor) look brighter than the rest, while the right edge (next to its lighter neighbor) looks darker. To see that the differences are illusions, try placing some thin object (such as a toothpick or a straightened paper clip) on top of the boundary between strips. With the strips separated in this manner, the illusion disappears.

By analogy, we know that a smoke detector is a smoke detector because it "fires" (makes noise) when smoke is on the scene. We know that a motion detector is a motion detector because it "fires" when something moves nearby. But what kind of detector is a given neuron? Is it responsive to any light in any position within the field of view? In that case, we might call it a "light detector." Or is it perhaps responsive only to certain shapes at certain positions (and therefore is a "shape detector")? With this logic, we can map out precisely what it is that the cell responds to—what *kind of* detector it is. More formally, this procedure allows us to define the cell's **receptive field**—that is, the size and shape of the area in the visual world to which that cell responds.

Multiple Types of Receptive Fields

David Hubel and Torsten Wiesel were awarded the Nobel Prize for their exploration of the mammalian visual system (e.g., Hubel and Wiesel, 1959, 1968). They documented the existence of specialized neurons within the brain, each of which has a different type of receptive field, a different kind of visual trigger. For example, some neurons seem to function as "dot detectors." These cells fire at their maximum rate when light is presented in a small, roughly circular area, in a specific

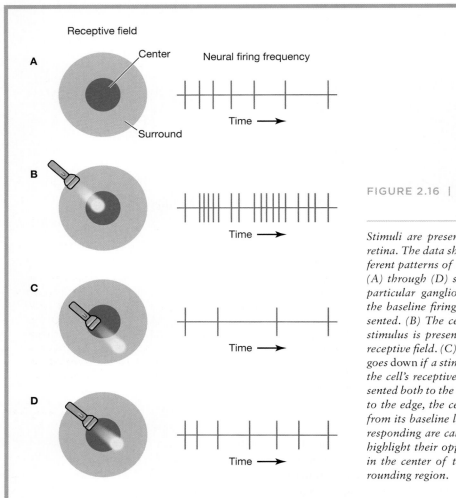

Receptive field

A

Center

Surround

Neural firing frequency

Time ⟶

B

Time ⟶

C

Time ⟶

D

Time ⟶

FIGURE 2.16 | CENTER-SURROUND CELLS

Stimuli are presented to various regions of the retina. The data show that different cells have different patterns of responding. For example, parts (A) through (D) show the firing frequency of a particular ganglion cell. (A) This graph shows the baseline firing rate when no stimulus is presented. (B) The cell's firing rate goes up when a stimulus is presented in the middle of the cell's receptive field. (C) In contrast, the cell's firing rate goes down *if a stimulus is presented at the edge of the cell's receptive field. (D) If a stimulus is presented both to the center of the receptive field and to the edge, the cell's firing rate does not change from its baseline level. Cells with this pattern of responding are called "center-surround" cells, to highlight their opposite responses to stimulation in the center of the receptive field and the surrounding region.*

position within the field of view. Presentations of light just outside of this area cause the cell to fire at *less* than its usual "resting" rate, so the input must be precisely positioned to make this cell fire. Figure 2.16 depicts such a receptive field.

These cells are often called **center-surround cells**, to mark the fact that light presented to the central region of the receptive field has one influence, while light presented to the surrounding ring has the opposite influence. If both the center and the surround are strongly stimulated, the cell will fire neither more nor less than usual; for this cell, a strong uniform stimulus is equivalent to no stimulus at all.

Other cells fire at their maximum only when a stimulus containing an edge of just the right orientation appears within their receptive fields. These cells, therefore, can be thought of as "edge detectors." Some of these cells fire at their

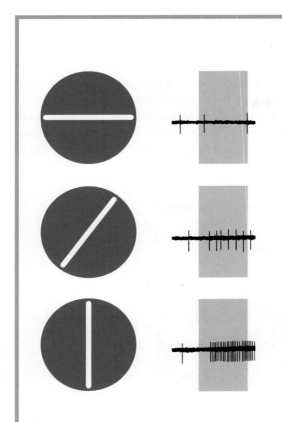

FIGURE 2.17 | **ORIENTATION-SPECIFIC VISUAL FIELDS**

Some cells in the visual system fire only when the input contains a line segment at the proper orientation. For example, one cell might fire very little in response to a horizontal line, fire only occasionally in response to a diagonal, and fire at its maximum rate only when a vertical line is present. In this figure, the circles show the stimulus that was presented. The right side shows records of neural firing. Each vertical stroke represents a firing by the cell; the left–right position reflects the passage of time. (After Hubel, 1963)

maximum rate when a horizontal edge is presented; others, when a vertical edge is in view; still others fire at their maximum to orientations in between horizontal and vertical. Note, though, that in each case, these orientations merely define the cells' "preference," because these cells are not oblivious to edges of other orientations. If a cell's preference is for, say, horizontal edges, then the cell will still respond to other orientations but will respond less strongly than it does for horizontals. Specifically, the further the edge is from the cell's preferred orientation, the weaker the firing will be, and edges sharply different from the cell's preferred orientation (say, a vertical edge for a cell that prefers horizontal) will elicit virtually no response (see Figure 2.17).

Other cells, elsewhere in the visual cortex, have receptive fields that are more specific. Some cells fire maximally only if an angle of a particular size appears in their receptive fields; others fire maximally in response to corners and notches. Still other cells appear to be "movement detectors" and will fire strongly if a stimulus moves, say, from right to left across the cell's receptive field. Other cells favor left-to-right movement, and so on through the various possible directions of movement.

Parallel Processing in the Visual System

This proliferation of cell types suggests that the visual system relies on a "divide and conquer" strategy, with different types of cells, located in slightly different areas of the cortex, each specializing in a particular kind of analysis. This pattern is plainly evident in **Area V1**, the site on the occipital lobe where axons from the LGN first reach the cortex. In this brain area, some cells fire to (say) horizontals in *this* position in the visual world, others to horizontals in *that* position, others to verticals in specific positions, and so on (see Figure 2.18). The full ensemble of

FIGURE 2.18 | **AREA V1 IN THE HUMAN BRAIN**

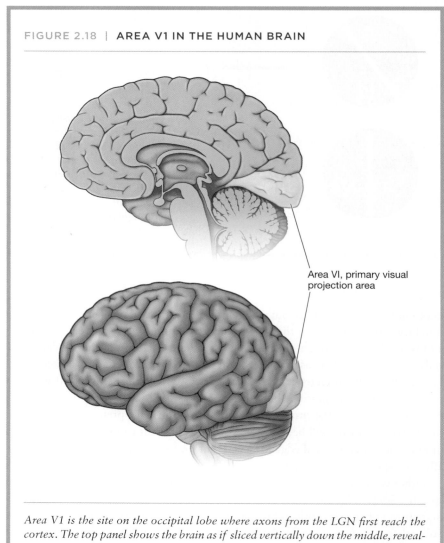

Area VI, primary visual projection area

Area V1 is the site on the occipital lobe where axons from the LGN first reach the cortex. The top panel shows the brain as if sliced vertically down the middle, revealing the "inside" surface of the brain's right hemisphere; the bottom panel shows the left hemisphere of the brain viewed from the side. As the two panels show, most of Area V1 is located on the cortical surface between the two cerebral hemispheres.

cells in this area provides a detector for every possible stimulus, making certain that no matter what the input is, or where it's located, some cell will respond to it.

The pattern of specialization becomes all the more evident as we consider other brain areas. Figure 2.19, for example, reflects one recent summary of the brain areas known to be involved in vision. The details of the figure aren't crucial, but it is noteworthy that some of these areas (V1, V2, V3, V4, PO, and MT) are in the occipital cortex; other areas are in the parietal cortex; others are in the temporal cortex (we'll have more to say in a moment about these areas outside of the occipital cortex). Most important, though, each area seems to have its own function. Neurons in Area MT, for example, are acutely sensitive to direction and speed of movement. Cells in Area V4 fire most strongly when the input is of a certain color and a certain shape.

Let's also emphasize that all of these specialized areas are active at the same time, so that (for example) cells in Area MT are detecting movement in the visual input at the same time that cells in V4 are detecting shapes. In other words, the visual system relies on **parallel processing**—a system in which many different steps

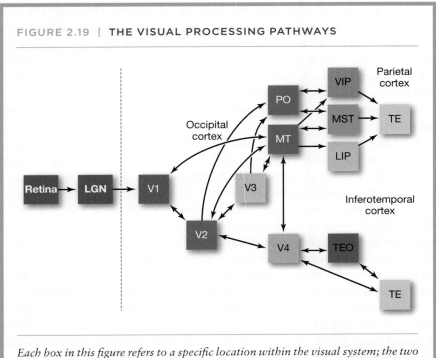

FIGURE 2.19 | THE VISUAL PROCESSING PATHWAYS

Each box in this figure refers to a specific location within the visual system; the two purple boxes at the left refer to locations outside the cortex; all other boxes refer to locations on the cortex. Notice that vision depends on many brain sites, each performing a specialized type of analysis. Note also that the flow of information is complex, so there's no strict sequence of "this step" of analysis followed by "that step." Instead, everything happens at once, with a great deal of back-and-forth communication among the various elements.

(in this case, different kinds of analysis) are going on simultaneously. (Parallel processing is usually contrasted with **serial processing**, in which steps are carried out one at a time—that is, in a series.)

One advantage of this simultaneous processing is speed: Brain areas trying to discern the shape of the incoming stimulus don't need to wait until the motion analysis or the color analysis is complete. Instead, all of the analyses go forward immediately when the input appears before your eyes, with no waiting time.

Another advantage of parallel processing is the possibility of mutual influence among multiple systems. To see why this is important, consider the fact that sometimes your interpretation of an object's motion depends on your understanding of the object's three-dimensional shape. This suggests that it might be best if the perception of shape happened first. That way, you could use the results of this processing step as a guide to later analyses. In other cases, though, it turns out that the relationship between shape and motion is reversed: In these cases, your interpretation of an object's three-dimensional shape depends on your understanding of its motion. To allow for this possibility, it might be best if the perception of motion happened first, so that it could guide the subsequent analysis of shape.

How do you deal with these contradictory demands? The answer is provided by parallel processing: Since both sorts of analysis go on simultaneously, each type of analysis can be informed by the other. Put differently, neither the shape-analyzing system nor the motion-analyzing system gets priority. Instead, the two systems work concurrently and "negotiate" a solution that satisfies both systems (Van Essen & DeYoe, 1995).

Parallel processing is easy to document throughout the visual system. As we have seen, the retina contains two types of specialized receptors (rods and cones) each doing its own job (e.g., the rods detecting stimuli in the periphery of your vision and stimuli presented at low light levels, and the cones detecting hues and detail at the center of your vision). Both types of receptors function at the same time—another case of parallel processing.

Likewise, within the optic nerve itself, there are two types of cells, **P cells** and **M cells**. The P cells provide the main input for the LGN's **parvocellular cells** and appear to be specialized for spatial analysis and the detailed analysis of form. M cells provide the input for the LGN's **magnocellular cells** and are specialized for the detection of motion and the perception of depth.[1] And, again, both of these systems are functioning at the same time—more parallel processing.

Parallel processing remains in evidence when we move beyond the occipital cortex. As Figure 2.20 indicates, some of the activation from the occipital lobe is passed along to the cortex of the temporal lobe. This pathway, often called the *what* system, plays a major role in the identification of visual objects, telling

---

1. A quick note on terminology: The names here refer to the relative sizes of the relevant cells: *parvo* derives from the Latin word for "small," and *magno* from the word for "large." To remember the function of these two types of cells, many students find it useful to think of the P cells as specialized roughly for the perception of *pattern* and M cells as specialized for the perception of *motion*. These descriptions are crude, but they're easy to remember.

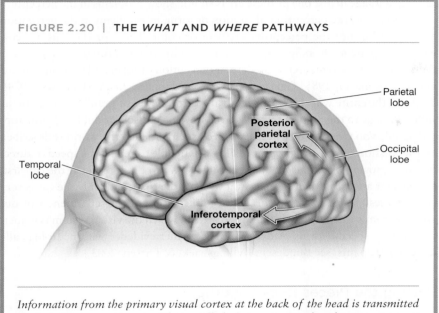

FIGURE 2.20 | THE *WHAT* AND *WHERE* PATHWAYS

Parietal
lobe

Posterior
parietal
cortex

Occipital
lobe

Temporal
lobe

Inferotemporal
cortex

Information from the primary visual cortex at the back of the head is transmitted to the inferotemporal cortex (the so-called what *system) and to the posterior parietal cortex (the* where *system). The term "inferotemporal" refers to the lower part of the temporal lobe. The term "posterior parietal cortex" refers to the rearmost portion of this cortex.*

us whether the object is a cat, an apple, or whatever. At the same time, activation from the occipital lobe is also passed along a second pathway, leading to the parietal cortex, in what is often called the ***where*** **system**. This system seems to perform the function of guiding our action, based on our perception of where an object is located—above or below us, to our right or to our left (Goodale & Milner, 2004; Ungerleider & Haxby, 1994; Ungerleider & Mishkin, 1982; for some complications, though, see Borst, Thompson & Kosslyn, 2011; deHaan & Cowey, 2011).

The contrasting roles of these two systems can be revealed in many ways, including studies of brain damage. Patients with lesions in the *what* system show visual agnosia—an inability to recognize visually presented objects, including such common things as a cup or a pencil. However, these patients show little disorder in recognizing visual orientation or in reaching. The reverse pattern is observed with patients who have suffered lesions in the *where* system: They have difficulty in reaching, but no problem in object identification (Damasio, Tranel, & Damasio, 1989; Farah, 1990; Goodale, 1995; Newcombe, Ratcliff, & Damasio, 1987).

Still other data echo this broad theme of parallel processing among separate systems. For example, we noted earlier that different brain areas are critical for the perception of color, motion, and form. If this is right, then someone who has suffered damage in just one of these areas should show problems in the perception of color but not the perception of motion or form, or problems in the perception of motion but not the perception of form or color. These predictions are correct: Some patients do suffer a specific loss of color vision through damage to the central nervous system, even though their perception of form and motion remains normal (Damasio, 1985; Gazzaniga, Ivry, & Mangun, 2002; Meadows, 1974). To them, the entire world is clothed only in "dirty shades of gray."[2] Other patients suffer damage to the motion system and so develop a disorder dubbed "akinetopsia" (Zihl, Von Cramon, & Mai, 1983). For such patients, the world is described as a succession of static photographs. They're unable to report the speed or direction of a moving object; as one patient put it, "When I'm looking at the car first, it seems far away. But then when I want to cross the road, suddenly the car is very near." Cases like these provide dramatic confirmation of the separateness of our visual system's various elements and the ways in which the visual system is vulnerable to very specific forms of damage. (For further evidence with neurologically intact participants, see Bundesen, Kyllingsbaek, & Larsen, 2003.)

Putting the Pieces Back Together

It should be clear, then, that our intellectual achievements depend on an array of different, highly specialized brain areas all working together in parallel. This was evident in our consideration of Capgras syndrome, and the same pattern has now emerged in our description of the visual system. Here, too, many brain areas must work together: the *what* system and the *where* system, areas specialized for the detection of movement and areas specialized for the identification of simple forms.

We have identified certain advantages that derive from this division of labor and the parallel processing it allows. But the division of labor also creates a problem: If multiple brain areas contribute to an overall task, how is their functioning coordinated? When you see a ballet dancer in a graceful leap, the leap itself is registered by motion-sensitive neurons, but the recognition of the ballet dancer depends on shape-sensitive neurons. How are the pieces put back together? When you reach for a coffee cup but stop midway because you see that the cup is empty, the reach itself is guided by the *where* system; the fact that the cup is empty is registered by the *what* system. How are these two streams of processing coordinated?

Investigators refer to this broad issue as the **binding problem**—the task of reuniting the various elements of a scene, elements that are initially dealt with by different systems in different parts of the brain. And obviously this problem is solved: What you perceive is not an unordered catalogue of sensory elements. Instead, you perceive a coherent, integrated perceptual world. Apparently, then, this is a case in which the various pieces of Humpty Dumpty are reassembled to form an organized whole.

2. This is different from ordinary color blindness, which is usually present from birth and results from abnormalities that are outside the brain itself—for example, abnormalities in the photoreceptors.

Visual Maps and Firing Synchrony

Look around you. Your visual system registers whiteness and blueness and brownness; it also registers a small cylindrical shape (your coffee cup), a medium-sized rectangle (this book page), and a much larger rectangle (your desk). How do you put these pieces together so that you see that it's the coffee cup, and not the book page, that's blue; the desktop, and not the cup, that's brown?

There is still debate about how the visual system solves this problem, but we can identify three elements that certainly contribute to the solution. One element is *spatial position*. The part of the brain registering the cup's shape is separate from the parts registering its color or its motion; nonetheless, these various brain areas all have something in common: They each keep track of where the target is—where the cylindrical shape was located, and where the blueness was; where the motion was detected, and where things were still. Thus, the reassembling of these pieces can be done with reference to position. In essence, you can overlay the map of *which forms are where* on top of the map of *which colors are where* to get the right colors with the right forms, and likewise for the map showing *which motion patterns are where*.

Information about spatial position is of course important for its own sake: You have a compelling reason to care whether the tiger is close to you or far away, or whether the bus is on your side of the street or the other. But in addition, location information apparently provides a frame of reference used to solve the binding problem. Given this double function, we shouldn't be surprised that spatial position is a major organizing theme within all the various brain areas concerned with vision, with each area seeming to provide its own map of the visual world.

However, spatial position, as important as it is, is not the whole story. Evidence is accumulating that the brain also uses a special *rhythm* to identify which sensory elements belong with which. Imagine two groups of neurons in the visual cortex. One group of neurons fires maximally whenever a vertical line is in view; another group fires maximally whenever a stimulus is in view moving from left to right. Let's also imagine that right now a vertical line is presented, and it is moving in the right way, and so, as a result, both groups of neurons are firing strongly. How does the brain encode the fact that these attributes are bound together, different aspects of a single object? The visual system seems to mark this fact by means of **neural synchrony**: If the neurons detecting a vertical line are firing in synchrony with those signaling movement, then these attributes are registered as belonging to the same object. If they are not in synchrony, the features are not bound together (Buzsáki & Draguhn, 2004; Csibra, Davis, Spratling, & Johnson, 2000; Elliott & Müller, 2000; Fries, Reynolds, Rorie, & Desimone, 2001).

What causes this synchrony? How do the neurons become synchronized in the first place? Here another factor appears to be crucial: *attention*. We will have more to say about attention in Chapter 4, but for now let's just note that attention plays a key role in binding together the separate features of a stimulus. (For a classic statement of this argument, see Treisman & Gelade, 1980; Treisman, Sykes, & Gelade, 1977. For a more recent and more complex view, see Quinlan, 2003; Rensink, 2012; and also Chapter 4.)

Evidence for attention's role comes from many sources, including the fact that when we overload someone's attention, she is likely to make **conjunction errors**—correctly detecting the features present in a visual display, but making mistakes about how the features are bound together (or *conjoined*). Thus, someone shown a blue *H* and a red *T* might report seeing a blue *T* and a red *H*—an error in binding. Similarly, individuals who suffer from severe attention deficits (because of brain damage in the parietal cortex) are particularly impaired in tasks that require them to judge how features are conjoined to form complex objects (e.g., Robertson, Treisman, Friedman-Hill, & Grabowecky, 1997). Finally, studies suggest that synchronized neural firing is observed in an animal's brain when the animal is attending to a specific stimulus but is not observed in neurons activated by an unattended stimulus (e.g., Buschman & Miller, 2007; Saalman, Pigarev, & Vidyasagar, 2007; Womelsdorf et al., 2007). All of these results are pointing us toward the claim that attention is indeed crucial for the binding problem and, moreover, that attention is linked to the neural synchrony that seems to unite a stimulus's features.

Let's close out the chapter, though, by highlighting some themes that have now emerged again and again: There is no question that virtually all mental achievements depend on multiple brain areas, with each area specialized for some aspect of the overall achievement, and all the areas working in parallel. To coordinate these various areas, the brain needs to bind together the various types of analysis, the various components of the overall achievement. This binding, in turns, calls our attention to the various ways in which information is represented in the brain: in terms of *which* cells are firing, *how often* they are firing, and also, it turns out, the *rhythm* in which they are firing. Finally, note that our account of vision requires discussion of "lower level" activities (such as what happens just one or two synapses into the brain) and also "higher level" activities (e.g., the influence of attention on neural activity). In a sense, then, our account of brain functioning will need to depend on an understanding of cognition at the same time that our account of cognition will rely heavily on what is known about the brain.

CHAPTER SUMMARY

* The brain is divided into several different structures, but of particular importance for cognitive psychology is the forebrain. In the forebrain, each cerebral hemisphere is divided into the frontal lobe, parietal lobe, temporal lobe, and occipital lobe. In understanding these brain areas, one important source of evidence comes from studies of brain damage, enabling us to examine what sorts of symptoms result from lesions in specific brain locations. This has allowed a localization of function, an effort that is also supported by neuro-

imaging research, which shows that the pattern of activation in the brain depends heavily on the particular task being performed.

- Different parts of the brain perform different jobs, but for virtually any mental process, different brain areas must work together in a closely integrated fashion. When this integration is lost (as it is, for example, in Capgras syndrome), bizarre symptoms can result.

- The primary motor projection areas are the departure point in the brain for nerve cells that initiate muscle movement. The primary sensory projection areas are the main points of arrival in the brain for information from the eyes, ears, and other sense organs. These projection areas generally show a pattern of contralateral control, with tissue in the left hemisphere sending or receiving its main signals from the right side of the body, and vice versa. Each projection area provides a map of the environment or the relevant body part, but the assignment of space in this map is governed by function, not by anatomical proportions.

- Most of the forebrain's cortex has traditionally been referred to as the association cortex, but this area is itself subdivided into specialized regions. This subdivision is reflected in the varying consequences of brain damage, with lesions in the occipital lobe leading to visual agnosia, damage in the temporal lobes leading to aphasia, and so on. Damage to the prefrontal area causes many different problems, but these are generally problems in the forming and implementing of strategies.

- The brain's functioning depends on neurons and glia. The glia perform many functions, but the main flow of information is carried by the neurons. Communication from one end of the neuron to the other is electrical and is governed by the flow of ions in and out of the cell. Communication from one neuron to the next is generally chemical, with a neuron releasing neurotransmitters that affect neurons on the other side of the synapse.

- One brain area that has been mapped in considerable detail is the visual system. This system takes its main input from the rods and cones on the retina. Then, information is sent via the optic nerve to the brain. An important point is that cells in the optic nerve do much more than transmit information; they also begin the analysis of the visual input. This is reflected in the phenomenon of lateral inhibition, which leads to edge enhancement.

- Part of what we know about the brain comes from single-cell recording, which can record the electrical activity of an individual neuron. In the visual system, this recording has allowed researchers to map the receptive fields for many cells, and this mapping has provided evidence for a high degree of specialization among the various parts of the visual system, with some parts specialized for the perception of motion, others for the perception of color, and so on. These various areas function in parallel, and this parallel processing allows great speed; it also allows mutual influence among multiple systems.

- Parallel processing begins in the optic nerve and continues throughout the visual system. For example, the *what* system (in the temporal lobe) appears to be specialized for the identification of visual objects; the *where* system (in the parietal lobe) seems to tell us where an object is located.

The reliance on parallel processing creates a problem of reuniting the various elements of a scene so that these elements are perceived in an integrated fashion. This is called the binding problem. One key in solving this problem, though, lies in the fact that different brain systems are organized in terms of maps, so that spatial position can be used as a framework for reuniting the separately analyzed aspects of the visual scene.

The Workbook Connection

See the *Cognition Workbook* for further exploration of the neural basis for cognition:

- Demonstration 2.1: Foveation
- Demonstration 2.2: Eye Movements
- Demonstration 2.3: The Blind Spot and the Active Nature of Vision
- Demonstration 2.4: A Brightness Illusion
- Research Methods: Control Groups
- Cognitive Psychology and Education: Food Supplements and Cognition
- Cognitive Psychology and Education: The So-Called "Smart Pills"
- Cognitive Psychology and the Law: Detecting Lies

NEED HELP STUDYING?

 wwnorton.com/studyspace

Visit StudySpace to access free review material such as

- Chapter study plans
- Quizzes
- Flashcards, and more

Go to **wwnorton.com/zaps** for these online labs:

- Split-Brain
- Synaptic Transmission
- Lateral Inhibition

Learning About the World Around Us

I n the previous section, we described some of the early steps involved in vision, but we emphasize that these are only the early steps. We begin Chapter 3, therefore, with an elaboration on the various ways the perceiver analyzes, organizes, and interprets the visual input. We then turn to the broad issue of how we recognize the various objects that surround us in the world, starting with how we recognize printed letters and then turning to the recognition of more complex (three-dimensional) objects.

In both cases, we discuss the ways in which object recognition is shaped by both "bottom-up" processes (processes driven by information in the stimulus input) and "top-down" processes (processes governed by expectations and prior knowledge). We'll describe a mechanism that is made up of very simple components but that is nonetheless sensitive to this broader pattern of knowledge, and that will lead us into a discussion of how complex knowledge can be "distributed" across an entire system.

Chapter 4 then turns to the study of attention. As we'll see, paying attention is a complex achieve-ment involving many different elements. Some of the steps needed for attention are the same no matter what a person is paying attention to; other steps depend on the particular task. In either case, paying attention requires that you commit some mental resources, and in the absence of those resources, performance drops off markedly. In addition, these resources are available only in limited quantities, and this constraint may set boundaries on human performance. Part of what's at stake in Chapter 4, therefore, is a discussion of what people can or cannot accomplish and whether there may be ways to escape the apparent limits on attention.

CHAPTER THREE

Recognizing Objects

As we saw in Chapter 2, information about the visual world is picked up by a huge array of neural detectors, each tuned to a particular aspect of the stimulus information. Some detectors specialize in horizontal line segments; others prefer vertical lines or diagonals. Still others pick out specific patterns of movement or fire only when certain angles or notches are in view. For that matter, there are even neurons (in the monkey's brain) that fire only when a monkey's hand is in view (whether the fingers are stretched out or clenched in a fist) or only when another monkey's face is in view!

However, visual perception involves far more than a simple detection of these elements. As one consideration, we've already mentioned that the input's various attributes are detected by separate brain systems, and thus a further step is required to reunite these various attributes so that we recognize that it is the squirrel that is brown and moving and the leaves that are green and still, rather than some other combination of these features. But the complexities of perception do not stop there. In this chapter, we consider some of the other steps involved in perceiving the visual world, and with that, we discuss just how large a role the perceiver plays—not just as a detector of incoming information, but as an active interpreter of that information.

Our focus in the chapter will be on the fundamental problem of how you manage to recognize the objects you encounter every day in the

- In important ways, perception goes "beyond the information given" in interpreting a stimulus. The perceiver organizes, interprets, and in some ways *supplements* the visual input, and these various steps determine what a stimulus looks like and what the stimulus is seen to resemble.

- Recognition of visual inputs begins with features, but it's not just the features that matter. How easily we recognize a pattern also depends on how frequently or recently we have viewed the pattern and on whether the pattern is well formed (such as letter sequences with "normal" spelling patterns). We explain these findings in terms of a feature net—a network of detectors, each of which is "primed" according to how often or how recently it has fired. The network relies on distributed knowledge to make inferences, and this process gives up some accuracy in order to gain efficiency.

- The feature net can be extended to other domains, including the recognition of three-dimensional objects. However, the recognition of faces requires a different sort of model, sensitive to configurations rather than to parts.

- Finally, we consider top-down influences on recognition. The existence of these influences tells us that object recognition is not a self-contained process; instead, knowledge external to object recognition is imported into and clearly shapes the process.

world around you. (We'll hold to the side the important questions of how you perceive movement or how you figure out how far away a stimulus is; these issues are covered in detail in courses on visual perception.) Even with this narrowed focus, we'll see that the processes of perception are more complex than one might expect!

Form Perception

We receive information about the world through various sensory modalities: We hear the sound of the approaching train, we smell the chocolate cake almost ready to come out of the oven, we feel the tap on our shoulder. There's no question, though, that for humans *vision* is the dominant sense. This is reflected in how much brain area is devoted to vision compared to how much is devoted to any of the other senses. It's also reflected in many aspects of our behavior. For example, if visual information conflicts with information received from other senses, we usually place our trust in vision. This is the basis for ventriloquism, in which we see the dummy's mouth moving while the sounds themselves are coming from the dummy's master. Vision wins out in this contest, and so we experience the illusion that the voice is coming from the dummy.

But how does vision operate? You open your eyes, and you see a world filled with familiar objects—chairs and desks, windows and walls, telephones and pencils. As you read this page, you can see the individual letters printed here, and they are letters that you know and can identify. The letters form words, which you also can recognize; you could say them out loud if requested, and you know the meaning of the words, so that you easily understand these sentences.

How is any of this possible? How do you manage to perceive, and then recognize, the objects you see every day? This is the problem, first, of **form perception**, the process through which you manage to see the basic shape and size of an object. Next is the problem of **object recognition**, the process through which you identify what the object is.

Why Is Object Recognition Crucial?

Form perception and object recognition seem at first like trivial achievements. Surely it's easy to recognize a shoe when you see one, or a frying pan, or a pickup truck. You've probably never met someone who has any difficulties in identifying these objects. But, easy or not, these steps of recognition are crucial. To see this, think about what would happen if you *couldn't* recognize these objects. Let's imagine that you want to put your shoes on, in order to go outdoors. You'd fail in this attempt if you couldn't recognize your shoes when you saw them. ("Gee, those are interesting sculptures, but I still need something to put on my feet.") Likewise, you know perfectly well how to use a telephone, or how to open a door, or what a chair is for, but you'd never be able to use this knowledge if you couldn't recognize these ordinary objects when you saw them.

Examples like these make it clear that object recognition is essential whenever you want to *apply* your knowledge to the world (and so to take action based on what you know about shoes or telephones or whatever). In a similar fashion, object recognition is crucial for *learning*. After all, if you learn something today about, say, your friend Jacob, it will probably be useful to combine this information with other things you know about Jacob—for example, combine it with your memory of what you saw him do yesterday. But, to do this, you need to realize that the person you saw today is the same person as the one you saw yesterday. Without this recognition, there will be no way for you to combine information bits collected on different occasions.

It seems, then, that object recognition may not be a glamorous skill, but it is essential for our interactions with the world. For our purposes, therefore, we will start our inquiry where much of knowledge starts: with the recognition and identification of objects in the world.

Beyond the Information Given

In Chapter 2, we saw how the process of object recognition begins: with the detection of simple visual features. But we've known for many years that there's more to the process than this. Early in the 20th century, for example, a group called the "Gestalt psychologists" noted that our perception of the visual world

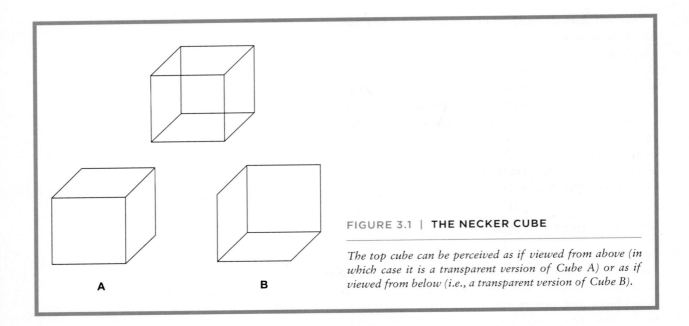

FIGURE 3.1 | THE NECKER CUBE

The top cube can be perceived as if viewed from above (in which case it is a transparent version of Cube A) or as if viewed from below (i.e., a transparent version of Cube B).

A   B

is organized in ways that the stimulus input is not.[1] They argued, therefore, that the organization must be contributed by the perceiver; this is why, they claimed, the perceptual whole is often different from the sum of its parts. Some years later, Jerome Bruner (1973) voiced similar claims and coined the phrase "beyond the information given" to describe some of the ways that our perception of a stimulus differs from (and goes beyond) the stimulus itself.

Consider the form shown in the top of Figure 3.1: the **Necker cube**. This drawing is an example of a *reversible figure*—so-called because people routinely perceive it first one way, and then another. Specifically, this form can be perceived as a drawing of a cube viewed from above (in which case it's similar to the cube marked "A" in the figure); it can also be perceived as a cube viewed from below (in which case it's similar to the cube marked "B"). Both perceptions fit perfectly well with the information received by your eyes, and so the drawing itself is fully compatible with either of these perceptions. Put differently, the lines on the page are entirely neutral with regard to the shape's configuration in depth; the lines on the page don't specify which is the "proper" interpretation. Your perception of the cube, however, is not neutral. Instead, you perceive the cube as having one configuration or the other—similar either to Cube A or to Cube B. Your perception, in other words, goes beyond the information given in the drawing, by specifying an arrangement in depth.

The same point can be made for many other stimuli. Consider Figure 3.2A, for example (after Rubin, 1915, 1921). This figure can be perceived as a vase centered

---

1. *Gestalt* is the German word for "shape" or "form." The Gestalt psychology movement was, overall, committed to the view that our theories need to emphasize the organization of the entire shape, and not just focus on the shape's parts.

FIGURE 3.2 | AMBIGUOUS FIGURES

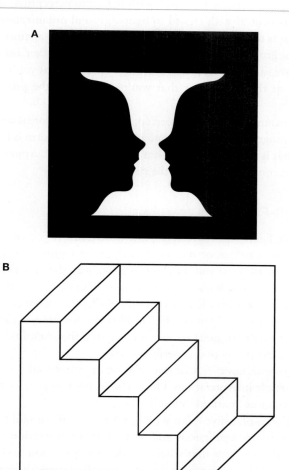

Many stimuli that you encounter can (with a bit of effort) be reinterpreted. Little effort is needed, though, for a smaller number of stimuli, which easily and naturally lend themselves to reinterpretation. These figures are often called "reversible" or "bistable," because there are two prominent and stable interpretations of the figure. The vase/profiles figure, for example, is spontaneously perceived by many people to be a white vase (or candlestick) on a black background, but perceived by other people to be two black faces, shown in profile and looking at each other. (A similar bistable form, by the way, is visible in the Canadian flag!) The Schroeder staircase, likewise, can be perceived either as a right-side-up set of stairs, or an upside-down set. Both of these figures will often "flip" from one organization to the other.

in the picture, or it can be perceived as two profiles facing each other. The drawing by itself, it seems, is fully compatible with either of these perceptions, and so, once again, the drawing is neutral with regard to perceptual organization. In particular, it is neutral with regard to **figure/ground organization**, the determination of what is the figure (the depicted object, displayed against a background) and what is the ground. Your perception of this figure, however, isn't neutral about this point. Instead, your perception somehow specifies that you're looking at the vase and not at the profiles, or that you're looking at the profiles and not at the vase.

In these examples, then, your perception contains information—about how the form is arranged in depth, or about which part of the form is figure and which is ground—that is not contained within the stimulus itself. Apparently, then, this is information contributed by you, the perceiver.

WORKBOOK
DEMONSTRATIONS 3.1, 3.2

The Gestalt Principles

With reversible figures, the perceiver's role is obvious: If you stare at the Necker cube (or the vase profiles, or the staircase figure in Figure 3.2), your perception flips back and forth: First you see the figure one way, then another, then back to the first way, and so on. With all of these figures, though, the information that's actually reaching your eyes is constant—the exact geometry of the figure is the same, no matter how you perceive it. The change, therefore, is caused by *you*—a change in how you're organizing and interpreting the stimulus—and thus your role in shaping the perception is perfectly clear.

One might argue, however, that reversible figures are special—carefully designed to support multiple interpretations. On this basis, perhaps perceivers play a smaller role with other, more "natural" stimuli.

This position is plausible—but wrong, because many stimuli (and not just the reversible figures) are ambiguous and in need of interpretation. We often don't detect this ambiguity, but that's because the interpretation is done so quickly that we don't notice it. Consider, for example, the scene shown in Figure 3.3. It's almost certain that you perceive segments B and E as being united, forming a complete apple, but notice that this information isn't provided by the stimulus; instead, it's your interpretation. (If we simply go with the information in the figure, it's possible that segments B and E are parts of entirely different fruits, with the "gap" between the two fruits hidden from view by the banana.) It's also likely that you perceive the banana as entirely banana-shaped, and thus continuing downward out of your view into the bowl, where it eventually terminates with the sort of point that's normal for a banana. Similarly, surely you perceive the horizontal stripes in the background as continuous, and merely hidden from view by the pitcher. (You'd likely be surprised if we removed the pitcher and revealed a pitcher-shaped gap in the stripes.) But, of course, the stimulus doesn't in any way "guarantee" the banana's shape or the continuity of the stripes; these points are, again, just your interpretation.

Even with this ordinary scene, therefore, your perception goes "beyond the information given," and so the unity of the two apple slices and the continuity of

FIGURE 3.3 | THE ROLE OF INTERPRETATION IN PERCEIVING AN ORDINARY SCENE

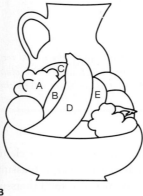

A

B

The text emphasizes that perception must go "beyond the information given" in important ways. Most of the examples in the text involve simple line drawings, but the same points apply to real-life scenes. For example, consider the still life (Panel A) and an overlay designating five different segments of the scene (Panel B). For this picture to be perceived correctly, the perceptual system must first decide what goes with what—for example, that Segment B and Segment E are different bits of the same object (even though they are separated by Segment D) and that Segment B and Segment A are different objects (even though they are adjacent and the same color).

the stripes is "in the eye of the beholder," not in the stimulus itself. Of course, you don't feel like you're "interpreting" this picture or extrapolating beyond what's on the page. But your role becomes clear the moment we start cataloguing the differences between your perception and the information that's truly present in the photograph.

Let's be clear, though, that your interpretation of the stimulus isn't careless or capricious. Instead, you're guided by a few straightforward principles, and these were catalogued by the Gestalt psychologists many years ago. For example, your perception is guided by principles of *proximity* and *similarity:* If, within

FIGURE 3.4 | GESTALT PRINCIPLES OF ORGANIZATION

    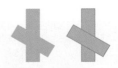

Similarity
We tend to group these dots into columns rather than rows, grouping dots of similar colors.

Proximity
We tend to perceive groups, linking dots that are close together.

Good continuation
We tend to see a continuous green bar rather than two smaller rectangles.

Closure
We tend to perceive an intact triangle, reflecting our bias toward perceiving closed figures rather than incomplete ones.

Simplicity
We tend to interpret a form in the simplest way possible. We would see the form on the left as two intersecting rectangles (as shown on the right) rather than as a single 12-sided irregular polygon.

As Figure 3.3 illustrated, your ordinary perception of the world requires that you make decisions about what goes with what—which elements are part of the same object, and which elements belong to different objects. Your decisions are guided by a few simple principles, catalogued many years ago by the Gestalt psychologists.

the visual scene, you see elements that are close to each other, or elements that resemble each other, you assume these elements are parts of the same object (Figure 3.4). You also tend to assume that contours are smooth, not jagged, and you avoid interpretations that involve coincidences (see Figure 3.5).

These perceptual principles are—as we said—quite straightforward, but they are essential if your perceptual apparatus is going to make sense of the often-ambiguous, often-incomplete information provided by your senses. In addition, it's worth mentioning that everyone's perceptions are guided by the same principles, and that's why you generally perceive the world the same way that other people do. Each of us imposes our own interpretation on the perceptual input, but we all tend to impose the *same* interpretation, because we're all governed by the same rules.

Organization and "Features"

In thinking about our discussion so far, it seems plausible that perception proceeds in two broad steps: First, we collect information about the stimulus, so that we know (for example) what corners or angle or curves are contained in the input. Then, once we've gathered the "raw data," we *interpret* this information, and that's when we "go beyond the information given"—deciding how the form is laid out in depth (as in Figure 3.1), deciding what is figure and what is ground (Figure 3.2), and so on.

However, this view is wrong, and, in fact, our interpretation of the input sometimes seems to happen *before* we start cataloguing the input's basic features, not after. Consider, for example, Figure 3.6. Initially, these shapes seem to

FIGURE 3.5 | **AVOIDING COINCIDENCES**

Most people immediately perceive this form as two lines crossing, but notice that other perceptions are possible: The form could, for example, be perceived as two V shapes, one on the top and one on the bottom, or as two V's, with one on the left and one on the right. However, the "V" interpretations would involve jagged lines and would depend on the two shapes being in exactly the right positions— just touching, with no overlap. (In any other position, the combined V's would look quite different.) Therefore, interpreting this figure as two V's would rely on a coincidence—that the forms just happen to be in exactly the right positions—and this is why other interpretations of the form seem to be preferred.

have no meaning, but after a moment, most people discover the word hidden in the figure. That is, people find a way to reorganize the figure so that the familiar letters come into view. But let's be clear about what this means. At the start, the form seems not to contain the features needed to identify the L, the I, and so on. Once the form is reorganized, though, it does contain these features, and the letters are immediately recognized. In other words, with one organization, the features are absent; with another, they're plainly present. It would seem, then, the features themselves depend on how the form is organized by the viewer, and so the features are as much "in the eye of the beholder" as they are in the figure itself.

FIGURE 3.6 | **A HIDDEN FIGURE**

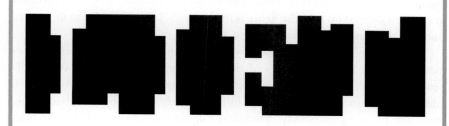

Initially, these dark shapes have no meaning, but after a moment, the hidden figure becomes clearly visible. Notice, therefore, that at the start, the figure seems not to contain the features needed to identify the various letters. Once the figure is reorganized, with the white parts making up the figure and not the dark parts, the features are easily detected. Apparently, therefore, the analysis of features depends on a prior step, in which the figure is first organized by the viewer.

FIGURE 3.7 | MISSING FEATURES

PERCEPTION

People have no trouble reading this word, despite the fact that most of the features needed for recognition are absent from the stimulus. People easily "supply" the missing features, emphasizing once again that the analysis of features depends on how the overall figure has been interpreted and organized.

As a different example, you have no difficulty reading the word printed in Figure 3.7, although most of the features needed for this recognition are absent from the figure. You easily "provide" the missing features, though, thanks to the fact that you interpret the black marks in the figure as shadows cast by solid letters. Given this interpretation and the extrapolation it entails, you can, with no trouble, "fill in" the missing features and in this way read the word.

How should we think about all of this? On one hand, your perception of a form surely has to start with the stimulus itself and must in some ways be governed by what's in that stimulus. (After all, no matter how you try to interpret Figure 3.7, it won't look to you like a photograph of Queen Elizabeth—the basic features of the queen are just not present, and your perception respects this obvious fact.) This suggests that the features must be in place *before* an interpretation is offered, because the features govern the interpretation. But, on the other hand, Figures 3.6 and 3.7 suggest that the opposite is the case: that the features you find in an input depend on how the figure is interpreted. Therefore, it's the interpretation, not the features, that must be first.

The solution to this puzzle, however, is easy, and it hinges on points we first met in Chapter 2: Many aspects of the brain's functioning depend on parallel processing, with different brain areas all doing their work at the same time. In addition, the various brain areas all influence each other, so that what's going on in one brain region is shaped by what's going on elsewhere. Thus, the brain areas that analyze a pattern's basic features do their work at the same time as the brain areas analyzing the pattern's large-scale configuration, and these brain areas interact, so that the perception of the features is guided by the configuration, and analysis of the configuration is guided by the features. In other words, neither type of processing "goes first." Neither has priority. Instead, both work together, with the result that the perception that is achieved makes sense at both the large-scale and fine-grained levels.

Object Recognition

So far, we've been discussing the processes of form perception—processes that tell us the shapes, sizes, and positions of the objects in front of our eyes. But, of course, our perception provides us with more information than this. We're also able to *identify* the objects we encounter—and thus to recognize a shape as a truck, a tree, or a character in a video game. Let's turn, therefore, to the steps involved in this identification. Our goal in this chapter is to describe how we recognize the huge variety of objects we encounter in our day-to-day world. We'll start, though, with a narrower focus: examining how we recognize the letters and words that make up printed language. Later in the chapter, we'll return to a discussion of visual targets other than print.

Recognition: Some Early Considerations

You are obviously able to recognize a huge number of different patterns—different objects (cats, cups, coats), various actions (running, jumping, falling), and different sorts of situations (crises, comedies). You can also recognize many variations of each of these things. You recognize cats standing up and cats sitting down, cats running and cats asleep. And the same is true for your recognition of pigs, stepladders, and the many other patterns in your recognition repertoire.

You also recognize objects even when your information is partial. For example, you can still recognize a cat if only its head and one paw are visible behind a tree. You recognize a chair even when someone is sitting on it, despite the fact that the person blocks much of the chair from view.

All of this is true for print as well: You can recognize tens of thousands of different words, and you can recognize them whether the words are printed in large type or small, *italics* or straight letters, UPPER CASE or lower. You can even recognize handwritten words, for which the variation from one to the next is huge.

THE VARIABILITY OF STIMULI WE RECOGNIZE

We recognize cats from the side or the front, whether we see them close up or far away.

In addition, your recognition of various objects, whether print or otherwise, is influenced in important ways by the *context* in which the objects are encountered. For example, consider Figure 3.8. The middle character is the same in both words, but the character looks more like an *H* in the left word and more like an *A* in the right. With this, you unhesitatingly read the left word as "THE" and not "TAE" and the right word as "CAT" and not "CHT."

This effect of context suggests that our discussion will need to consider two types of influences. Some influences come directly from the stimulus itself—that is, the features that are in view. These influences—coming from the stimulus—are sometimes called *stimulus driven* but more commonly are termed **bottom-up influences**. Other influences come from *you*, rather than the stimulus itself. These are again cases in which you go "beyond the information given," and, more specifically, they're cases in which you supplement the input with your broader knowledge (for example the knowledge that CAT is a common word, but CHT is not). These influences—relying on your knowledge—are sometimes called *knowledge driven* or *expectation driven,* but are more commonly called **top-down influences**.

How should we think about all this? What mechanism underlies both the top-down and bottom-up influences? In the next sections, we'll consider a classic proposal for what the mechanism might be. We'll then be able to build on this base, as we consider more recent modifications and elaborations of this proposal.

Features

Common sense suggests that many objects are recognized by virtue of their parts. You recognize an elephant because you see the trunk, the thick legs, the large body. You know a lollipop is a lollipop because you can see the circle shape on top of the straight stick. These notions, though, simply invite the next question: How do you recognize the parts themselves? How, for example, do you recognize the trunk, or the circle in the lollipop? The answer may be simple: Perhaps you recognize the parts by looking at *their* parts, their constituents—the arcs, for example, that make up the circle, or the (roughly) parallel lines that identify the elephant's legs.

To put this more generally, recognition might begin with the identification of **visual features** in the input pattern—the vertical lines, curves, diagonals, and so on. With these features appropriately catalogued, you could then start assembling the larger units: If you detect a horizontal together with a vertical, you know you're looking at a right angle; if you've detected four right angles, you know you're looking at a square.

This broad proposal lines up well with the neuroscience evidence we discussed in Chapter 2. There we saw that specialized cells in the visual system do seem to act as "feature detectors," providing exactly the right start for the ideas we're now considering. In addition, we've already noted that people can recognize many variations on the objects they encounter—cats in different positions, *A*'s in different fonts or different handwritings. An emphasis on features, though, might help with this point: The various *A*'s, for example, are different from each other in overall shape, but they do have certain things in common: two inwardly sloping lines and a horizontal crossbar. Focusing on features might allow us to concentrate on what's common to the various *A*'s, and so might allow us to recognize *A*'s despite their apparent diversity.

Various studies also make it clear that people are remarkably fast and efficient when searching for a target defined by a simple feature—for example, finding a vertical segment in a field of horizontals, or a green shape in a field of red shapes. People are much slower, in contrast, in searching for a target defined as a *combination* of features (see Figure 3.9). All of this is just what we would expect if feature analysis is an early step in your analysis of the visual world, and separate from the step in which you combine the features you've detected. (For more on this point, see Chapter 4.)

WORKBOOK
DEMONSTRATION 3.3

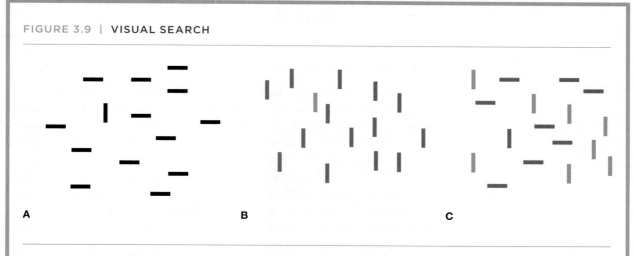

FIGURE 3.9 | **VISUAL SEARCH**

A   B   C

In (A), you can immediately spot the vertical, distinguished from the other shapes by just one feature. Likewise, in (B), you can immediately spot the lone green bar in the field of reds. In (C), it takes much longer to find the one red vertical, because now you need to search for a combination of features—not just for red or vertical, but for the one form that has both of these attributes.

Further support for these claims comes from studies of brain damage. Specifically, damage to the parietal cortex can lead to a disorder known as **integrative agnosia.** People with this disorder appear relatively normal in tasks requiring them simply to detect particular features in a display. These people are markedly impaired, in contrast, in tasks that require them to judge how the features are bound together to form complex objects (e.g., Behrmann, Peterson, Moscovitch, & Suzuki, 2006; Robertson, Treisman, Friedman-Hill, & Grabowecky, 1997).

Similar results have been obtained in studies in which *transcranial magnetic stimulation* (TMS) is used to disrupt portions of the brain in healthy individuals. (For more on TMS, see Chapter 2.) Ashbridge, Walsh, and Cowey (1997) found that disruption of the parietal lobe had no impact on performance when participants were searching a display for targets defined by a single feature (e.g., "Find the red shape"). However, the TMS markedly slowed performance when participants were searching for a target defined by a conjunction of features ("Find the shape that is red and round").

Word Recognition

Several lines of evidence, therefore, indicate that object recognition does begin with the detection of simple features. Then, once this detection is done, separate mechanisms are needed to put the features together, assembling them into complete objects. But how does this assembly proceed, so that we end up seeing not just the features but whole words, for example, or Chihuahuas, or fire hydrants? In tackling this question, it will be helpful to fill in some more facts that we can then use as a guide to our theory building.

Factors Influencing Recognition

In many studies, participants have been shown stimuli for just a brief duration—perhaps 20 or 30 ms (milliseconds). Older research did this by means of a **tachistoscope**, a device specifically designed to present stimuli for precisely controlled amounts of time. More modern research uses computers for this purpose, but the brief displays are still called "tachistoscopic presentations."

Each stimulus is followed by a post-stimulus **mask**—often just a random jumble of letters, such as "XJDKEL." The mask serves to interrupt any continued processing that participants might try to do for the stimulus just presented. This way, researchers can be certain that a stimulus presented for (say) 20 ms is visible for exactly 20 ms and no longer.

Can people recognize these briefly visible stimuli? The answer depends on many factors, including how *familiar* a stimulus is. If the stimulus is a word, for example, we can measure familiarity by literally counting how often that word appears in print, and these counts are an excellent predictor of tachistoscopic recognition. In one experiment, Jacoby and Dallas (1981) showed participants

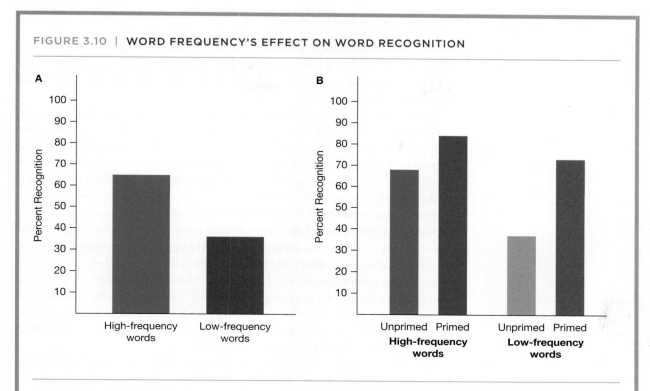

FIGURE 3.10 | WORD FREQUENCY'S EFFECT ON WORD RECOGNITION

In one study, recognition was much more likely for words appearing often in print, in comparison to words appearing only rarely—an effect of frequency. *Similarly, words that had been viewed recently were more often recognized, an effect of* recency *that, in this case, creates a benefit termed repetition priming. (After Jacoby & Dallas, 1981)*

words that were either very frequent (appearing at least 50 times in every million printed words) or infrequent (occurring only 1 to 5 times per million words of print). Participants viewed these words for 35 ms, followed by a mask; under these circumstances, they recognized twice as many of the frequent words (See Figure 3.10A.)

Another factor influencing recognition is recency of view. If participants view a word and then, a little later, view it again, they will recognize the word much more readily the second time around. The first exposure **primes** the participant for the second exposure; more specifically, this is a case of **repetition priming**.

As an example, participants in one study read a list of words aloud. The participants were then shown a series of words in a tachistoscope. Some of these words were from the earlier list and so had been primed; others were unprimed. For words that were high in frequency, 68% of the unprimed words were recognized, compared to 84% of the primed words. For words low in frequency, 37% of the unprimed words were recognized, compared to 73% of the primed words (see Figure 3.10B; Jacoby & Dallas, 1981).

The Word-Superiority Effect

Words that are frequently viewed are easier to perceive, as are words that have been viewed recently. It also turns out that words themselves are easier to perceive, as compared to isolated letters. This finding is referred to as the **word-superiority effect**.

This effect is usually demonstrated with a "two-alternative, forced-choice" procedure. Thus, in some trials, we might present a single letter—let's say *K*—followed by a poststimulus mask, and follow that with a question: "Which of these was in the display: an *E* or a *K*?" In other trials, we present a word—let's say "DARK"—followed by a mask, followed by a question: "Which of these was in the display: an *E* or a *K*?"

Notice that a participant has a 50-50 chance of guessing correctly in either of these situations, and so any contribution from guessing is the same for the letters as it is for the words. Note in addition that for the word stimulus, both of the letters we've asked about are plausible endings for the stimulus; either ending would create a common word ("DARE" or "DARK"). Therefore, a participant who saw only part of the display (perhaps "DAR") couldn't use his knowledge of the language to figure out what the display's final letter was. In order to choose between *E* and *K*, therefore, the participant really needs to have seen the relevant letter—and that, of course, is exactly what we want.

The results from this procedure are clear: Accuracy rates are higher in the word condition, and so, apparently, recognizing words is easier than recognizing isolated letters. To put this more precisely, participants are more accurate in identifying letters if those letters appear within a word, as opposed to letters appearing all by themselves (see Figure 3.11; Reicher, 1969; Rumelhart & Siple, 1974; Wheeler, 1970).

Degrees of Well-Formedness

The data are telling us, then, that it's easier to recognize an *E*, say, if the letter appears in context than it is if the letter appears on its own (and likewise for any other letter). But this benefit emerges only if the context is of the right sort. There's no context effect if we present a string like "HZYE" or "SBNE." An *E* presented within these strings will *not* show the word-superiority effect, that is, will not be recognized more readily than an *E* presented just on its own.

What about a context like "FIKE" or "LAFE"? These letter strings are not English words and are not familiar, but they nonetheless look like English strings and (related) are easy to pronounce. And strings like these do produce a context effect, and so letters in these contexts are easier to identify than letters alone (or letters in random strings).

The pattern is similar if we ask participants to report all of what they have seen, and not just to detect specific letters. Thus, a letter string like "JPSRW" is extremely difficult to recognize if presented briefly. With a stimulus like this and, say, a 30 ms exposure, participants may report that they only saw a flash, and no letters at all; at best, they may report a letter or two. But, with the same

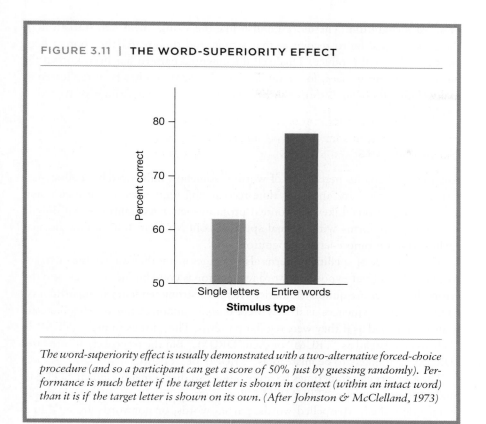

FIGURE 3.11 | THE WORD-SUPERIORITY EFFECT

The word-superiority effect is usually demonstrated with a two-alternative forced-choice procedure (and so a participant can get a score of 50% just by guessing randomly). Performance is much better if the target letter is shown in context (within an intact word) than it is if the target letter is shown on its own. (After Johnston & McClelland, 1973)

30 ms exposure, participants are reasonably likely to recognize strings like FIKE or LARE, although they do better still if the stimuli presented are actual, familiar words.

There are several ways to think about these findings. One approach emphasizes *pronounceability*, and the idea here is simple: Easily pronounceable strings (like FIKE or LAFE) do provide a context benefit. If the string is not readily pronounceable (e.g., HZYE), there's little or no context benefit. Likewise, pronounceable strings are generally easier to recognize, after a brief exposure, compared to unpronounceable strings.

A different and more precise approach emphasizes probabilities. We can, for example, work through a dictionary, counting how often the letter combination FI occurs, or the combination LA, or HZ. We can do the same for three-letter sequences (FIK, LAF, HZY, and so on). All of these counts will leave us with a tally that reveals which letter combinations are more probable in English spelling, and which are less. We can then use this tally to evaluate new strings—asking, for any string, whether its letter sequences are high-probability ones (occurring often) or low-probability (occurring rarely).

These statistical measures allow us to evaluate the "Englishness" of any letter string—i.e., the degree to which the letter sequence in the string conforms to the usual spelling patterns of English. Englishness, in turn, is a good predictor of word recognition: The more English-like the string (measured statistically), the easier it will be to recognize that string, and the greater the context benefit the string will produce. This well-documented pattern has been known for more than a century (see, for example, Cattell, 1885) and has been replicated in many studies (Gibson, Bishop, Schiff, & Smith, 1964; Miller, Bruner, & Postman, 1954).

Making Errors

Apparently, then, our perception of words is somehow influenced by spelling patterns, and so we have an easier time recognizing sequences that use common letter combinations. Likewise, context promotes letter recognition—but only if the context conforms with normal spelling; contexts that don't follow normal spelling don't promote letter recognition.

The influence of spelling patterns also emerges in another way: in the mistakes we make. With brief exposures, word recognition is good but not perfect, and the errors that occur are quite systematic: There is a strong tendency to misread less-common letter sequences as if they were more-common patterns; irregular patterns are misread as if they were regular patterns. Thus, for example, "TPUM" is likely to be misread as "TRUM" or even "DRUM." But the reverse errors are rare: "DRUM" is unlikely to be misread as "TRUM" or "TPUM."

These errors can sometimes be quite large—so that someone shown "TPUM" might instead perceive "TRUMPET." But, large or small, the errors show the pattern described: Misspelled words, partial words, or nonwords are read in a way that brings them into line with normal spelling. In effect, people perceive the input as being more regular than it actually is. Once again, therefore, our recognition seems to be guided by (or, in this case, misguided by) some knowledge of spelling patterns.

Feature Nets and Word Recognition

What lies behind this broad pattern of evidence? What are the processes inside of us that lead to the various findings we've described? Psychology's understanding of these points grows out of a theory published more than 50 years ago (Selfridge, 1959). Let's start with that theory, and then build on that base as we look at more modern work.

The Design of a Feature Net

Imagine that we want to design a system that will recognize the word "CLOCK" whenever it is in view. How might our "CLOCK" detector work? One option is to "wire" this detector to a C-detector, an L-detector, an O-detector, and so on. Then, whenever these letter detectors are activated, this would activate the word detector. But what activates the letter detectors? Perhaps the L-detector is "wired" to a horizontal-line detector, and also a vertical-line detector, and maybe

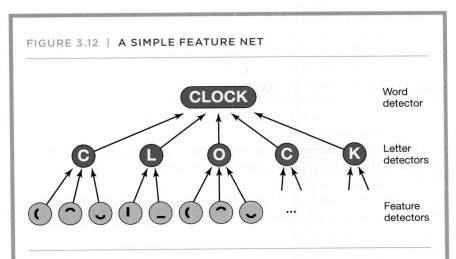

FIGURE 3.12 | A SIMPLE FEATURE NET

Word detector

Letter detectors

Feature detectors

An example of a feature net. Here the feature detectors respond to simple elements in the visual input. When the appropriate feature detectors are activated, they trigger a response in the letter detectors. When these are activated, in turn, they can trigger a response from a higher-level detector, such as a detector for an entire word.

also a corner detector, as shown in Figure 3.12. When all of these feature detectors are activated as a group, this activates the letter detector.

The idea, then, is that there is a network of detectors, organized in layers, with each subsequent layer concerned with more complex, larger-scale objects. The "bottom" layer is concerned with features, and that is why networks of this sort are often referred to as **feature nets**, and, using the term we introduced earlier, the flow of information would be *bottom-up*—from the lower levels toward the upper levels.

But what does it mean to "activate" a detector? At any point in time, each detector in the network has a particular **activation level**, which reflects the status of the detector at just that moment—roughly, how energized the detector is. When a detector receives some input, its activation level increases. A strong input will increase the activation level by a lot, and so will a series of weaker inputs. In either case, the activation level will eventually reach the detector's **response threshold**, and at that point the detector will *fire*—that is, send its signal to the other detectors to which it is connected.

These points parallel our description of neurons in Chapter 2, and that's no accident. If the feature net is to be a serious candidate for how humans recognize patterns, then it has to use the same sorts of building blocks that the brain does. However, let's be careful not to overstate this point: No one is suggesting that detectors are neurons, or even large groups of neurons. Instead, detectors likely involve complex assemblies of neural tissue. Nonetheless, it's plainly attractive that the hypothesized detectors, within the feature net, function in a way that's biologically sensible.

Within the net, some detectors will be easier to activate than others—that is, some detectors will require a strong input to make them fire, while others will fire even with a weak input. This difference is created in part by how activated each detector is to begin with. If the detector is moderately activated at the start, then only a little input is needed to raise the activation level to threshold, and so it will be easy to make this detector fire. If a detector is not at all activated at the start, then a strong input is needed to bring the detector to threshold, and so it will be more difficult to make this detector fire.

What determines a detector's starting activation level? As one factor, detectors that have fired recently will have a higher activation level (think of it as a "warm-up" effect). In addition, detectors that have fired frequently in the past will also have a higher activation level (think of it as an "exercise" effect). Thus, in simple terms, activation level is dependent on principles of *recency* and *frequency*.

We now can put these mechanisms to work. Why are frequent words in the language easier to recognize than rare words? Frequent words, by definition, appear often in the things you read. Therefore, the detectors needed for recognizing these words have been frequently used, and so they have relatively high levels of activation. Thus, even a weak signal (for example, a brief or dim presentation of the word) will bring these detectors to their response threshold and so will be enough to make these detectors fire. Hence, the word will be recognized even with a degraded input.

Repetition priming is explained in similar terms. Presenting a word once will cause the relevant detectors to fire. Once they have fired, activation levels will be temporarily lifted (because of recency of use). Therefore, only a weak signal will be needed to make the detectors fire again. As a result, the word will be more easily recognized the second time around.

The Feature Net and Well-Formedness

The net we've described so far cannot explain all of the data. Consider, for example, the effects of well-formedness—for instance, the fact that people are able to read letter strings like "PIRT" or "HICE" even when they're presented very briefly (or dimly, or in low contrast), but not strings like "ITPR" or "HCEI." This difference can't be explained in terms of letter detectors, since, as it turns out, the same letters are used in "PIRT" and "ITPR," yet one is easy to recognize and one is not. Likewise for "HICE" and "HCEI." These differences also can't be explained in terms of word detectors: None of these letter sequences is a word, and so word detectors would play no role in the recognition of these strings.

How, therefore, should we accommodate these results? One option is to add another layer to the net, a layer filled with detectors for *letter combinations*—pairs of letters, for example, or trios of letters. In Figure 3.13, we've added a layer of **bigram detectors**—detectors of letter pairs. These detectors, like all the rest, will be triggered by lower-level detectors and send their output to higher-level detectors. And just like any other detector, each bigram detector will start out with a certain activation level, influenced by the frequency with which the detector has fired in the past and by the recency with which it has fired.

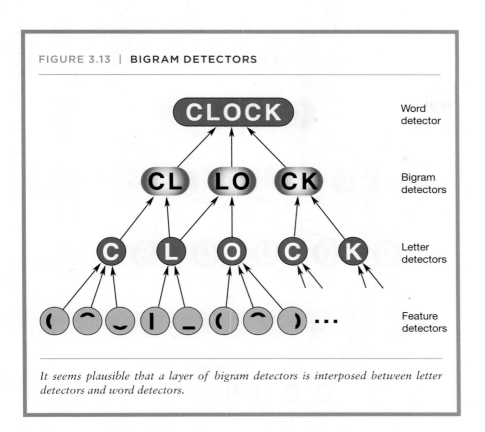

FIGURE 3.13 | BIGRAM DETECTORS

Word detector

Bigram detectors

Letter detectors

Feature detectors

It seems plausible that a layer of bigram detectors is interposed between letter detectors and word detectors.

This turns out to be all the theory we need. Why are English-like nonwords more easily recognized than strings not resembling English ("RSFK" or "IUBE")? Well-formed words involve familiar letter combinations. You have never seen the sequence "HICE" before, but you have seen the letter pair *HI* (in "HIT," "HIGH," or "HILL") and the pair *CE* ("FACE," "MICE," "JUICE"). The detectors for these letter groups, therefore, have high activation levels at the start, and so they don't need much additional input to reach their threshold. As a result, these detectors will fire with only weak input. That will make the corresponding letter combinations easy to recognize, facilitating the recognition of strings like "HICE." None of this is true for "RSFK." Because none of these letter combinations is familiar, this string will receive no benefits from priming. A strong input will therefore be needed to bring the relevant detectors to threshold, and so the string will be recognized only with difficulty. (For more on bigram detectors and how they work, see Grainger, Rey, & Dufau, 2008; Grainger & Whitney, 2004; Whitney, 2001; for some reservations, though, about the proposed bigram detectors, see Rayner & Pollatsek, 2011.)

Recovery From Confusion

Imagine that we present the word "CORN" for just 20 ms. With this brief presentation, the visual system has only a limited opportunity to analyze the input, so

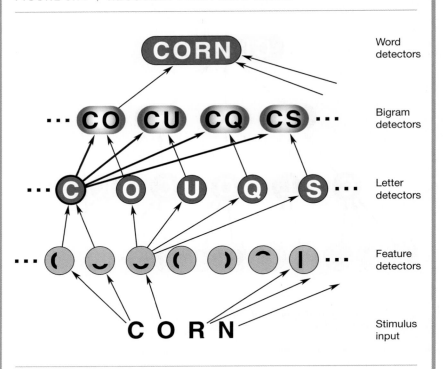

FIGURE 3.14 | RECOVERY FROM CONFUSION

If "CORN" is presented briefly, not all of its features will be detected. Imagine, for example, that only the bottom curve of the O is detected, and not the O's top or sides. This will (weakly) activate the O-detector, but it will also activate the detectors of various other letters having a bottom curve, including U, Q, and S. This will, in turn, send weak activation to the appropriate bigram detectors. The CO-detector, however, is well primed and so is likely to respond even though it is receiving only a weak input. The other bigram detectors (for CQ or CS) are less well primed and so will not respond to this weak input. Therefore, "CORN" will be correctly perceived, despite the confusion at the letter level caused by the weak signal.

it's possible that the visual system will miss some of the features that are present. For example, let's imagine that the second letter in this word—the O—is hard to see, so that, perhaps, only the bottom-curve is detected.

This partial information invites confusion: If all you know is "the second letter had a bottom curve," then perhaps this letter was an O, or perhaps it was a U, or a Q, or maybe an S. Figure 3.14 shows how this would play out in terms of the network: We've already said that you detected the bottom curve—and that means we're supposing the "bottom-curve detector" is activated. Activation of this detector, in turn, provides input to the O-detector, and also the detectors for U, Q, and S; that's guaranteed by the various connections that make up the network. Thus, activation in this *feature* detector causes activation in all of these *letter* detectors.

However, each of these letter detectors is wired so that it also receives input from other feature detectors. (And so usually the O-detector also gets input from detectors for left curves and right curves and top curves.) We've already said, though, that with this brief input these other features weren't detected this time around. As a result, the O-detector will only be weakly activated (because it's not getting its customary full input), and the same is true for the detectors for *U*, *Q*, and *S*.

Thus we so far have partial information at the feature level (again, because only one of the O's features was detected), leading to confusion at the letter level (specifically, too many letter detectors are firing, and all are firing weakly). What happens next? The information sent upward, from the letter level to the bigram level, reflects the confusion we've just described: The detector for the *CO* bigram is receiving a strong signal from the *C* detector (because the *C* was clearly visible) but only a weak signal from the *O* detector (because the *O* wasn't clearly visible). The *CU* detector is getting roughly the same input—a strong signal from the *C*-detector and a weak signal from the *U*-detector. Likewise for the *CQ* and *CS* detectors. Thus, to put this state-of-affairs crudely, the signal being sent from the letter-detectors is roughly, "maybe *CO* or maybe *CU* or maybe *CQ* or maybe *CS*."

This confusion is immediately sorted out at the bigram level: All four bigram detectors in this situation are receiving the same input—a strong signal from one of their letters and a weak signal from the other. However, the four detectors don't all respond in the same way. The *CO*-detector is well primed (because this is a frequent pattern), and so the activation this detector is receiving will probably be enough to fire this (primed) detector. The *CU*-detector is less primed (because this is a less frequent pattern); the *CQ*- and *CS*-detectors, if they even exist, are not primed at all. The input to these latter detectors is therefore unlikely to activate them—because, again, they're less-well primed, and so won't respond to this weak input.

What will the result of all this be? At the feature level, there was partial information (because only a subset of the input's features were detected). This produced confusion at the letter level (with too many detectors firing). But then, at the bigram level, it's only the *CO*-detector that fires, because, at this level, this is the detector that (because of priming) is most likely to respond to the weak input. In essence, then, the network has made a "choice"—that the input was *CO*- and not *CU*- or *CS*-. Thus, in a totally automatic fashion, the network recovers from its own confusion, and an error has been avoided.

Ambiguous Inputs

The logic just described also explains some other evidence. Look again at Figure 3.8 (p. 86). The second character shown is exactly the same as the fifth, but the left-hand string is perceived as "THE" (and the character is identified as an *H*), and the right-hand string is perceived as "CAT" (and the character as an *A*).

What's going on here? The ambiguous character in this display will trigger some of the features normally associated with an *A* and some normally associated with an *H*. This will cause the *A*-detector to fire, but only weakly (because only some of the *A*'s features are present), and likewise for the *H*-detector. At the letter level, therefore, there will be uncertainty about what the incoming character is.

The uncertainty is resolved at subsequent levels. Let's look, for example, at the network's response to the letter string on the left. The *T* is clearly in view, and so presumably the *T*-detector will fire strongly in response. The middle character is ambiguous, and so the *A*- and *H*-detectors will fire only weakly. As a result of this activity on the letter level, a moderate signal will be sent to both the *TH*- and the *TA*-detectors at the bigram level, and likewise to the *THE*- and *TAE*-detectors at the word level. But the *TH*-detector is enormously well primed; so is the *THE*-detector. If there were a *TAE*-detector, it would be barely primed, since this is a string rarely encountered. Thus, the *THE*- and *TAE*-detectors might be receiving similar input, but this input is sufficient only for the well-primed *THE*-detector, and so only it will respond. In this way, the net will recognize the ambiguous pattern as "THE," not "TAE." (And the same is true, with appropriate adjustment, for the ambiguous pattern on the right, perceived as "CAT," not "CHT.")

A similar explanation will handle the word-superiority effect (see, for example, Rumelhart & Siple, 1974). To take a simple case, imagine that we present the letter *A* in the context "AT." If the presentation is brief enough, participants may see very little of the *A*, perhaps just the horizontal crossbar. This would not be enough to distinguish among *A*, *F*, or *H*, and so all these letter detectors would fire weakly. If this were all the information the participants had, they'd be stuck. But let us imagine that the participants did perceive the second letter in the display, the *T*. It seems likely that the *AT* bigram is far better primed than the *FT* or *HT* bigrams. (That is because you often encounter words like "CAT" or "BOAT"; words like "SOFT" or "HEFT" are used less frequently.) Thus, the weak firing of the *A*-detector would be enough to fire the *AT* bigram detector, while the weak firing for the *F* and *H* might not trigger their bigram detectors. In this way, a "choice" would be made at the bigram level that the input was "AT" and not something else. Once this bigram has been detected, answering the question "Was there an *A* or an *F* in the display?" is easy. In this manner, the letter will be better detected in context than in isolation. This is not because context allows you to see more; instead, context allows you to make better use of what you see.

Recognition Errors

There is, however, a downside to all this. Imagine that we present the string "CQRN" to participants. If the presentation is brief enough, study participants will register only a subset of the string's features. Let's imagine, in line with an earlier example, that they register only the bottom bit of the string's second letter. This detection of the bottom curve will weakly activate the *Q*-detector, and

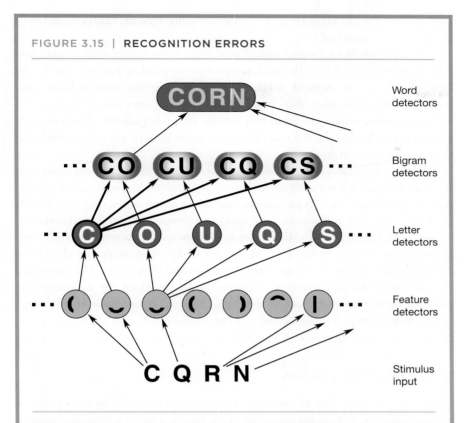

FIGURE 3.15 | RECOGNITION ERRORS

Word detectors

Bigram detectors

Letter detectors

Feature detectors

Stimulus input

If "CQRN" is presented briefly, not all of its features will be detected. Perhaps only the bottom curve of the Q is detected, and this will (weakly) activate various other letters having a bottom curve, including O, U, and S. However, this is the same situation that would result from a brief presentation of "CORN" (as shown in Figure 3.14); therefore, by the logic we have already discussed, this stimulus is likely to be misperceived as "CORN."

also the *U*-detector and the *O*-detector. The resulting pattern of network activation is shown in Figure 3.15.

Of course, the pattern of activation in this case is identical to the pattern in Figure 3.14: In both cases, perceivers have seen the features for the C, R and N and have only seen the second letter's bottom curve. And we've already walked through the network's response to this feature pattern: This configuration will lead to confusion at the letter level, and this confusion will get sorted out at the bigram level, with the (primed) *CO*-detector responding to this input, and other (less well primed) detectors *not* responding. Thus the stimulus will be identified as "CORN." In the situation we described in Figure 3.14, the stimulus actually was "CORN," and so the dynamic built into the net aids performance, allowing the network to recover from its initial confusion. In the case we're considering now (with "CQRN" as the stimulus), the exact same dynamic causes the network to misread the stimulus!

This example helps us understand how recognition errors come about, and why those errors tend to make the input look more regular than it really is. The basic idea is that the network is biased, inevitably favoring frequent letter combinations over infrequent ones. In effect, the network operates on the basis of "when in doubt, assume the input falls into the frequent pattern." The reason, of course, is simply that the detectors for the frequent pattern are well primed, and therefore easier to trigger.

This bias facilitates perception if the input is, in fact, a frequent word. But the bias will pull the network toward errors if the input has an unusual spelling pattern. Moreover, the bias guarantees that, when errors occur, they will reliably be of the same sort: turning irregular spelling into more frequent combinations.

Let's emphasize, though, that these errors are usually unproblematic. Low-frequency words are, as we've just discussed, likely to be misperceived, but (by definition) low-frequency words aren't encountered that often. The network's bias promotes the perception of frequent words, and these (by definition) are the words you encounter most of the time. Hence, the network's bias aids recognition in the more frequent cases and hurts recognition only in the rare cases. Necessarily, then, the network's bias helps perception more often than it hurts.

Distributed Knowledge

There is no question that the network's functioning is guided by knowledge of spelling patterns. This point is evident in the fact that letter strings are easier to recognize if they conform to normal spelling. The same point is shown by the fact that letter strings provide a context benefit only if they conform to normal spelling. Still more evidence comes from the fact that errors, when they occur, are shaped by normal spelling.

To explain these results, we've suggested that the network "knows" (for example) that *CO* is a common bigram in English, while *CF* is not, and likewise "knows" that *THE* is a common sequence but *TAE* is not. The network seems to rely on this "knowledge" in "choosing" its "interpretation" of unclear or ambiguous inputs. Similarly, the network seems to "expect" certain patterns and not others and is more efficient when the input lines up with those expectations.

Obviously, though, we've wrapped quotations around several of these words in order to emphasize that the sense in which the net "knows" facts about spelling, or the sense in which it "expects" things or makes "interpretations," is a bit peculiar. Knowledge about spelling patterns is not explicitly stored anywhere in the network. Nowhere within the net is there a sentence like "*CO* is a common bigram in English; *CF* is not." Instead, this memory (if we even want to call it that) is manifest only in the fact that the *CO*-detector happens to be more primed than the *CF*-detector. The *CO*-detector doesn't "know" anything about this advantage, nor does the *CF*-detector know anything about its disadvantage. Each simply does its job, and in the course of doing their jobs, occasions will arise that involve a "competition" between these detectors. (This sort of competition was illustrated in Figures 3.14 and 3.15.) When these competitions occur, they'll be "decided," in a straightforward way, by activation levels: The better-primed detector will be more likely to respond, and so that detector will be more likely to influence subsequent events. That's the entire mechanism through which these "knowledge effects" arise. That's how "expectations" or "inferences" emerge—as a direct consequence of the activation levels.

To put this into technical terms, the network's "knowledge" is not **locally represented** anywhere; it is not stored in a particular location or built into a specific process. Thus, we cannot look just at the level of priming in the CO-detector and conclude that this detector represents a frequent bigram, nor can we look at the *CF*-detector to conclude that it represents a rare bigram. Instead, we need to look at the *relationship* between their levels of priming, and we also need to look at how this relationship will lead to one detector being more influential than the other. The knowledge about bigram frequencies, in other words, is **distributed knowledge**—that is, it is represented in a fashion that's distributed across the network and detectable only if we consider how the entire network functions.

What is perhaps most remarkable about the feature net, then, lies in how much can be accomplished with a distributed representation, and thus with simple, mechanical elements correctly connected to one another. The net appears to make inferences and to know the rules of English spelling. But the actual mechanics of the net involve neither inferences nor knowledge (at least, not in any conventional sense). You and I can see how the inferences unfold by taking a bird's-eye view and considering how all the detectors work together as a system. But nothing in the net's functioning depends on the bird's-eye view. Instead, the activity of each detector is locally determined—influenced by just those detectors feeding into it. When all of these detectors work together, though, the result is a process that acts as if it knows the rules. But the rules themselves play no role in guiding the network's moment-by-moment activities.

Efficiency Versus Accuracy

One other point about the network also needs emphasis: The network does make mistakes, misreading some inputs and misinterpreting some patterns. As we've seen, though, these errors are produced by exactly the same mechanisms that are responsible for the network's main advantages—its ability to deal with ambiguous inputs, for example, or to recover from confusion. Perhaps, therefore, we should view the errors as the price you must pay in order to gain the benefits associated with the net: If you want a mechanism that's able to deal with unclear, or partial, inputs, you simply have to live with the fact that sometimes the mechanism will make mistakes.

This framing of things, however, invites a question: Do you really need to pay this price? After all, outside of the lab you're unlikely to encounter fast-paced tachistoscopic inputs. Instead, you see stimuli that are out in view for long periods of time, stimuli that you can inspect at your leisure. Why, therefore, don't you take the moment to scrutinize these inputs so that you can rely on fewer inferences and assumptions, and in that fashion gain a higher level of accuracy in recognizing the objects you encounter?

The answer to this question is straightforward. To maximize accuracy, you could, in principle, scrutinize every character on the page. That way, if a character were missing or misprinted, you would be sure to detect it. But the cost associated with this strategy would be insufferable: Reading would be unspeakably slow (in part because the speed with which you move your eyes is relatively slow—no more than four or five eye movements per second). In contrast, it's possible to make inferences about a page with remarkable speed, and this leads readers to adopt the obvious strategy: They read some of the letters and make inferences about the rest. And for the most part, those inferences are safe—thanks to the simple fact that our language (like most aspects of our world) contains some redundncies, so that one doesn't need every lettr to identify what a wrd is; oftn the missng letter is perfctly predctable from the contxt, virtually guaranteeing that inferences will be correct.

Thus, the efficient reader is not being careless, or hasty, or lazy. Given the redundancy of text, and given the slowness of letter-by-letter reading, the inferential strategy is the only strategy that makes sense.

WORKBOOK
DEMONSTRATION 3.4

Descendants of the Feature Net

As we mentioned early on, we've been focusing on the "classic" version of the feature net. This has allowed us to bring a number of important themes into view—including the trade-off between efficiency and accuracy and the notion of distributed knowledge built into a network's functioning.

Over the years, though, researchers have offered variations (and improvements) on this basic conceptualization, and, in the next sections, we'll consider three of these proposals. All three preserve the basic idea of a network of interconnected detectors, but all three extend this idea in important ways. We'll look first at a proposal that highlights the role of *inhibitory* connections among detectors. Then we'll turn to a proposal that applies the network idea to the recognition of complex three-dimensional objects. Finally, we'll consider a proposal that rests on the idea that your ability to recognize objects may depend on your viewing perspective when you encounter those objects.

The McClelland and Rumelhart Model

In the network proposal we've considered so far, activation of one detector serves to activate other detectors. Thus, activation of the horizontal and vertical feature detectors causes activation in the *L*-detector; activation in the letter detectors for *T* and *H* causes activation in the bigram detector for *TH*; and so on. Other models include this notion of spreading activation but also include the possibility of detectors inhibiting each other, so that activation of a detector can in fact serve to *decrease* the activation in other detectors.

One of the early (and highly influential) models of this sort was proposed by McClelland and Rumelhart (1981); a portion of their model is illustrated in Figure 3.16. This network, like the one we've been discussing, is better able to identify

FIGURE 3.16 | AN ALTERNATIVE CONCEPTION OF THE FEATURE NETWORK

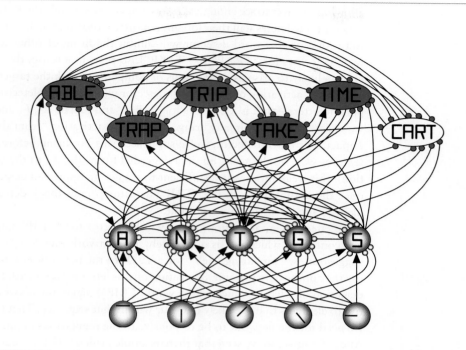

The McClelland and Rumelhart (1981) pattern-recognition model includes both excitatory connections (indicated by arrows) and inhibitory connections (indicated by connections with dots). Connections within a specific level are also possible—so that, for example, activation of the "TRIP" detector will inhibit the detectors for "TRAP," "TAKE," or "TIME."

well-formed strings than irregular strings; this net is also more efficient in identifying characters in context as opposed to characters in isolation. However, several attributes of this net make it possible to accomplish all this without bigram detectors.

In Figure 3.16, some of the connections are *excitatory*—so that activation of one detector causes activation in its neighbors. These **excitatory connections** are shown in the figure with arrows; for example, detection of a T serves to "excite" the "TRIP" detector. Other connections are *inhibitory*, and so (for example) detection of a *G* deactivates, or inhibits, the "TRIP" detector. These **inhibitory connections** are shown in the figure with dots. In addition, this model also allows for more complicated signaling than we've used so far. In our discussion, we have assumed that lower-level detectors trigger upper-level detectors, but not the reverse. The flow of information, it seemed, was a one-way street. In the McClelland and Rumelhart model, higher-level detectors (word detectors) can influence the lower-level detectors, and detectors at any level can also influence other detectors at the same level (e.g., letter detectors inhibit other letter detectors; word detectors inhibit other word detectors).

To see how this would work, let's say that the word "TRIP" is briefly shown, allowing a viewer to see enough features to identify, say, only the *R*, *I*, and *P*. Detectors for these letters will therefore fire, in turn activating the detector for "TRIP." Activation of this word detector will inhibit the firing of other word detectors (e.g., detectors for "TRAP" or "TAKE"), so that, in a sense, these other words are less likely to arise as distractions or competitors with the target word. At the same time, activation of the "TRIP" detector will excite the detectors for its component letters—that is, detectors for *T*, *R*, *I*, and *P*. The *R*-, *I*-, and *P*-detectors, we've assumed, were already firing, so this extra activation "from above" has little impact. But the *T*-detector, we've supposed, was not firing before. The relevant features were on the scene but in a degraded form (thanks to the brief presentation); this weak input was insufficient to trigger an unprimed detector. However, once the excitation from the "TRIP" detector primes the *T*-detector, it's more likely to fire, even with a weak input.

In effect, then, activation of the word detector for "TRIP" implies that this is a context in which a *T* is quite likely. The network therefore responds to this suggestion by "preparing itself" for a *T*. Once the network is suitably prepared (by the appropriate priming), detection of this letter is facilitated. In this way, the detection of a letter sequence (the word "TRIP") makes the network more sensitive to elements that are likely to occur within that sequence. That is exactly what we need for the network to be responsive to the regularities of spelling patterns. And, of course, we've seen that there is ample evidence that humans are sensitive to (and exploit) these regularities.

There are several reasons one might prefer this kind of net over the kind considered earlier. Perhaps the most conspicuous reason, though, is biological, because the sort of two-way communication being showcased here is ubiquitous in the nervous system: Neurons in the eyeballs send activation to the brain but also *receive* activation from the brain; neurons in the LGN send activation to the visual cortex but also receive activation from the cortex. These facts make it clear that visual processing is not a one-way process, with information flowing simply from the eyes toward the brain. Instead, signaling occurs in both an ascending (toward the brain) and a descending (away from the brain) direction, just as the McClelland and Rumelhart model claims.

Recognition by Components

The McClelland and Rumelhart model—like the feature net we started with—was designed initially as an account of how people recognize *printed language*. But, of course, we recognize many objects other than print, including the three-dimensional objects that fill our world—chairs and lamps and cars and trees. Can these objects also be recognized by a feature network? The answer turns out to be yes.

Consider, for example, a network theory known as the **recognition by components** (or RBC) **model** (Hummel & Biederman, 1992; Hummel & Stankiewicz,

FIGURE 3.17 | GEONS

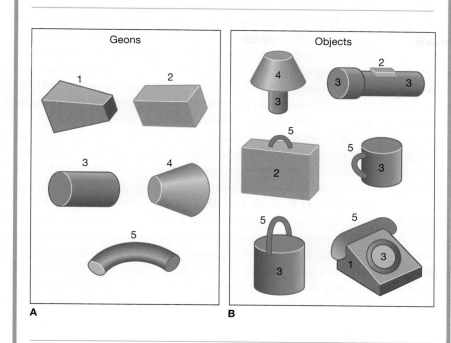

Panel A shows five different geons; Panel B shows how these geons can be assembled into objects. The numbers in Panel B identify the specific geons; for example, a bucket contains Geon 5 top-connected to Geon 3.

1998). This model includes several important innovations, one of which is the inclusion of an intermediate level of detectors, sensitive to **geons** (short for "geometric ions"). The idea is that geons might serve as the basic building blocks of all the objects we recognize; geons are, in essence, the alphabet from which all objects are constructed.

Geons are simple shapes, such as cylinders, cones, and blocks (see Figure 3.17A) And only a small set of these shapes is needed: According to Biederman (1987, 1990), we need (at most) three dozen different geons to describe every object in the world, just as 26 letters are all we need to spell all the words of English. These geons can be combined in various ways—in a top-of relation, or a side-connected relation, and so on—to create all the objects we perceive (see Figure 3.17B).

The RBC model, like the other networks we've been discussing, uses a hierarchy of detectors. The lowest-level detectors are feature detectors, which respond to edges, curves, vertices, and so on. These detectors in turn activate the geon detectors. Higher levels of detectors are then sensitive to combinations of geons. More precisely, geons are assembled into more complex arrangements called "geon assemblies," which explicitly represent the relations between geons (such as top-of or side-connected). These assemblies, finally, activate the *object model*, a representation of the complete, recognized object.

The presence of the geon and geon-assembly levels within this hierarchy buys us several advantages. For one, geons can be identified from virtually any angle of view, and so recognition based on geons is **viewpoint-independent**. Thus, no matter what your position is relative to a cat, you'll be able to identify its geons and thus identify the cat. Moreover, it seems that most objects can be recognized from just a few geons. As a consequence, geon-based models like RBC can recognize an object even if many of the object's geons are hidden from view.

In addition, several lines of evidence seem to confirm that geons do play a role in recognition. For example, recognition of simple objects is relatively easy if the geons are easy to discern; recognition is more difficult if the geons are hard to identify (Biederman, 1985). As an illustration, consider the objects shown in Figure 3.18. In Columns B and C, about two thirds of the contour has been deleted from each drawing. In Column B, this deletion has been carefully done so that the geons can still be identified; as you can see, these objects can be recognized without much difficulty. In Column C, however, the deletion has been done in a fashion that obscures geon identity; now object recognition is much harder. Thus, it does seem that the geons capture something crucial for identification of these objects. (For other evidence, see Behrmann et al., 2006.)

Recognition via Multiple Views

A number of researchers (Hayward & Williams, 2000; Tarr, 1995; Tarr & Bülthoff, 1998; Vuong & Tarr, 2004; Wallis & Bülthoff, 1999) have offered a different approach to object recognition. They propose that people have stored in memory a number of different views of each object they can recognize: an image of what a cat looks like when viewed head-on, a view of what it looks like from the left, and so on. According to this perspective, then, you'll recognize Felix (let's say) as a cat only if you can match your current view of Felix with one of these views in memory. However, the number of views in memory is limited—perhaps a half dozen or so—and so, in many cases, your current view won't line up with any of the available images. In that situation, you'll need to "rotate" the current view to bring it into alignment with one of the remembered views, and this mental rotation will cause a slight delay in the recognition.

The key, then, is that recognition sometimes requires mental rotation, and, as a result, will be slower from some viewpoints than from others. In other words, the speed of recognition will be **viewpoint-dependent**, and, in fact, this claim is confirmed by a growing body of data. To be sure, we can (as we've repeatedly noted) recognize objects from many different angles, and our recognition is generally fast. However, data indicate that recognition is faster from some angles than others, in a fashion consistent with this multiple-views proposal.

According to this perspective, how exactly does recognition proceed? One proposal resembles the network models we've been discussing (Riesenhuber &

FIGURE 3.18 | RECOGNIZING DEGRADED PICTURES

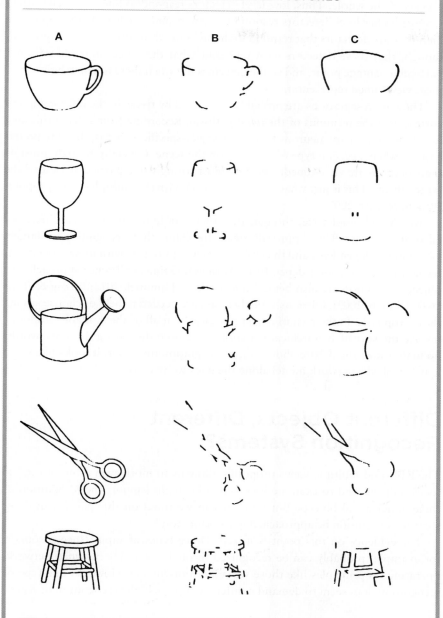

A   B   C

In Column B, you can still identify the objects' geons, and so the forms are easily recognized. In Column C, it is difficult to identify the geons and correspondingly difficult to identify the objects. This evidence adds strength to the claim that geon identification plays an important role in object recognition.

Poggio, 1999, 2002; Tarr, 1999). In this proposal, there is a hierarchy of detectors, with each successive layer within the network concerned with more complex aspects of the whole. Thus, low-level detectors respond to lines at certain orientations; higher-level detectors respond to corners and notches. At the top of the hierarchy are detectors that respond to the sight of whole objects. It is important, though, that these detectors each represent what the object looks like from a particular vantage point, and so the detectors fire when there is a match to one of these view-tuned representations.

These representations are probably supported by tissue in the inferotemporal cortex, near the terminus of the *what* pathway. Recording from cells in this area has shown that many neurons here seem object-specific—that is, they fire preferentially when a certain type of object is on the scene. Crucially, though, most of these neurons are view-tuned: They fire most strongly to a particular view of the target object. This is just what one might expect with the multiple-views proposal (Peissig & Tarr, 2007).

We should emphasize, though, that there continues to be debate between advocates of the RBC approach (with its claim that recognition is largely viewpoint-independent) and the multiple-views approach (with its argument that recognition is viewpoint-dependent). At the same time, still other approaches to object recognition are also being explored (e.g., Hummel, 2012; Peissig & Tarr, 2007; Ullman, 2007). Obviously, further data are needed to help us choose among these proposals. In the meantime, let's be clear that all of the available proposals involve the sort of hierarchical network we've been discussing. In other words, no matter how the debate about object recognition turns out, it looks like we're going to need a network model along the lines we've considered.

Different Objects, Different Recognition Systems?

The RBC and multiple-views proposals allow us to move away from our initial focus on print and to examine how networks might support the recognition of three-dimensional objects. But how far can we travel on this path? Can other sorts of recognition be approached in the same way?

The evidence on this point is mixed. Other types of input (speech sounds, for example) probably can be recognized through a suitably designed network, operating on principles like those we've been discussing. However, one type of recognition does seem to demand a different approach: the recognition of *faces*.

Faces Are Special

As we discussed in Chapter 2, damage to the visual system can produce a disorder known as *agnosia*—an inability to recognize certain stimuli. There are several subtypes of agnosia, one of which is **prosopagnosia**. People with this disorder lose their ability to recognize faces, even though their other visual abilities seem to be intact. This seems to imply the existence of a special neural

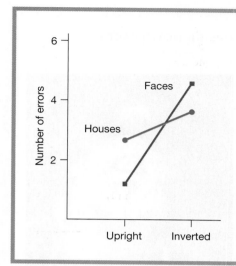

FIGURE 3.19 | FACES AND THE INVERSION EFFECT

People's memory for faces is quite good, when compared with memory for other pictures (in this case, pictures of houses). However, performance is very much disrupted when the pictures of faces are inverted. Performance with houses is also worse with inverted pictures, but the effect of inversion is far smaller. (After Yin, 1969)

structure involved almost exclusively in the recognition and discrimination of faces, and, of course, it's this structure that's damaged in people suffering from prosopagnosia (Behrman & Avidan, 2005; Burton, Young, Bruce, Johnston, & Ellis, 1991; Damasio, Tranel, & Damasio, 1990; De Renzi, Faglioni, Grossi, & Nichelli, 1991).

Face recognition is also specialized in another way—in its strong dependence on orientation. We've mentioned that there is debate about whether the recognition of houses, or teacups, or automobiles is viewpoint-dependent, but there can be no question about this for faces. In one study, four categories of stimuli were considered—right-side-up faces, upside-down faces, right-side-up pictures of common objects other than faces, and upside-down pictures of common objects. As can be seen in Figure 3.19, performance suffered for all of the upside-down stimuli. However, this effect was much larger for faces than for other kinds of stimuli (Yin, 1969).

The same point can be made informally. Figure 3.20 shows two upside-down photographs of former British prime minister Margaret Thatcher (from Thompson, 1980). You can probably detect that something is odd about them, but now try turning the book upside down so that the faces are right side up. As you can see, the difference between these faces is immense, and yet this fiendish contrast is largely lost when the faces are upside down. Once again, it seems that the perception of faces is strikingly different from other forms of perception, with face perception more strongly dependent on orientation. (Also see Rhodes, Brake, & Atkinson, 1993; Valentine, 1988.)

However, we need to adjust these claims a bit, because it's not just faces that are special in these ways. Consider first the evidence of prosopagnosia. In one case, a prosopagnosic bird-watcher has not only lost the ability to recognize faces, he has also lost the ability to distinguish the different types of warblers (Bornstein, 1963; Bornstein, Sroka, & Munitz, 1969). Another patient with prosopagnosia has lost

FIGURE 3.20 | **PERCEPTION OF UPSIDE-DOWN FACES**

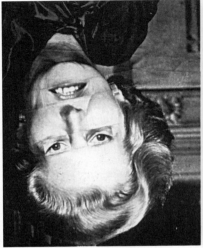

The left-hand picture looks somewhat odd, but the two pictures still look relatively similar to each other. Now try turning the book upside down (so that the faces are upright). In this position, the left-hand face (now on the right) looks ghoulish, and the two pictures look very different from each other. Perception of upside-down faces is apparently quite different from our perception of upright faces. (From Thompson, 1980)

the ability to tell cars apart; she is able to locate her car in a parking lot only by reading all the license plates until she finds her own (Damasio, Damasio, & Van Hoesen, 1982). Thus, prosopagnosia is not strictly a disorder of face recognition.

Likewise, in Chapter 2, we mentioned neuroimaging data showing that a particular brain site—the fusiform face area (FFA)—is specifically responsive to faces. It turns out, though, that tasks requiring subtle distinctions among birds, or among cars, also produce high levels of activation in this area (Gauthier, Skudlarski, Gore, & Anderson, 2000). Apparently, the neural tissue "specialized" for faces isn't used *only* for faces.

In the same way, other categories of stimuli, not just faces, can show the upside-down effect we have already described. For example, one study examined people who were highly experienced judges in dog shows, people who knew particular breeds extremely well. Diamond and Carey (1986) compared how well these judges recognized right-side-up and upside-down stimuli in each of two categories: faces and dogs in the familiar breed. Not surprisingly, performance was much worse with upside-down faces than with right-side-up faces, replicating the pattern of Figure 3.19. The critical result, though, is that performance suffered just as much with upside-down pictures of dogs. (For more on perceptual expertise, see Bukach, Gauthier & Tarr, 2006.)

It seems, then, that we do have a specialized recognition system, using its own brain tissue and especially sensitive to orientation. The key, though, is that this system doesn't operate only on faces. Instead, the system seems crucial whenever a task has two characteristics: The task has to involve recognizing specific individuals within a category, and the category has to be an extremely familiar one (although, for some complications, see McKone & Robbins, 2010; Richler, Cheug, & Gauthier, 2011; Richler, Wong & Gauthier, 2011; Wong, Palmeri, & Gauthier, 2009). The recognition of faces certainly meets these requirements, but other tasks do as well. Thus, this special system is used when expert birdwatchers are recognizing individual birds, when expert dog judges are recognizing individual dogs, and so on.

Holistic Recognition

So far, we've argued that recognition of faces (and some other targets) involves a system different from the network we've been focusing on. But what is this other system? How does it function? The networks we've been considering up until now all begin with an analysis of a pattern's *parts* (features, geons); the networks then assemble those parts into larger wholes. Face recognition, in contrast,

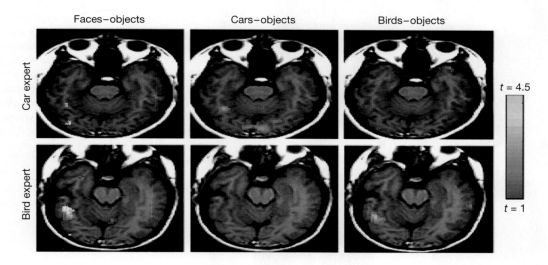

THE FUSIFORM FACE AREA AND NONFACE STIMULI

Pictures of faces, cars and birds were shown to a car "expert" and a bird "expert." fMRI data in the left column show activation (shown in red) in response to faces. The bird expert shows the expected pattern—with face stimuli leading to strong activation of the FFA; the car expert's FFA, it turns out, was slightly lower in his brain, and so, even though clearly activated, does not show in this scan. More important, when cars *were the stimuli the car expert (but not the bird expert) showed activation in the FFA. When* birds *were the stimuli, it was the bird expert who showed FFA activation. (From Gauthier, Skudlarski, Gore, & Anderson, 2000)*

doesn't depend on an inventory of a face's parts; instead, this recognition seems to depend on *holistic perception* of the face. In other words, the recognition depends on complex relationships created by the face's overall configuration—the spacing of the eyes relative to the length of the nose, the height of the forehead relative to the width of the face, and so forth.

Of course, a face's features still matter in this holistic process. The key, however, is that the features can't be considered one by one, apart from the context of the face. Instead, the features matter by virtue of the relationships and configurations they create. It's these relationships, and not the features on their own, that guide face recognition (cf. Rhodes, 2012; Wang, Li, Fang, Tian & Liu, 2012).

Some of the evidence for this holistic processing comes from the *composite effect* in face recognition. In an early demonstration of this effect, Young et al. (1987) combined the top half of one face with the bottom-half of another, and participants were asked to identify just the top half. This task is difficult if the two halves are properly aligned. In this setting, participants seem unable to focus only on the top half; instead, they see the top of the face as part of the whole (see Figure 3.21A). Thus, in the figure, it's difficult to see that the top half of the face is Harrison Ford's (shown in normal view in Figure 3.21C). This task is relatively

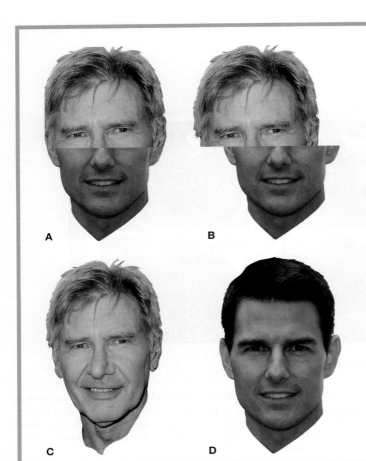

FIGURE 3.21 | **THE COMPOSITE EFFECT IN FACE RECOGNITION**

Participants were asked to identify the top half of composite faces like those in A and B. This task was much harder if the halves were properly aligned (as in A), easier if the halves weren't aligned (as in B). With the aligned faces, participants have a difficult time focusing on just the face's top (and so have a hard time recognizing Harrison Ford—shown in C). Instead, they view the face as a whole, and this context changes their perception of Ford's features, making it harder to recognize him. (The bottom of the composite face belongs to Tom Cruise, shown in D.)

easy, though, if the halves are misaligned (as in Figure 3.21B). Now, the stimulus itself breaks up the configuration, making it possible to view the top half on its own. (Also see Gauthier & Buach, 2007; McKone & Robbins, 2007; for related results, see Amishav & Kimchi, 2010.)

Further work is needed to specify exactly how the configurational system functions. In the meantime, it appears that the feature net approach we have discussed in this chapter is powerful and applicable to a wide variety of patterns, but it simply is not the whole story. Some patterns, including faces, seem to involve a different, more holistic, sort of pattern recognition. (For examples of other research on memory for faces, see Jones & Bartlett, 2009; Kanwisher, 2006; Michel, Rossion, Han, Chung, & Caldara, 2006; Rhodes, 2012.)

Top-Down Influences on Object Recognition

Feature nets can accomplish a great deal, and they are plainly crucial for the recognition of print, three-dimensional objects in our visual environment, and probably sounds as well. At the same time, feature nets are limited, because there are some targets—faces, and probably others—for which our recognition depends on configurations, rather than individual features.

It turns out, though, that there is another limit on the feature net, even if we're focusing on the targets for which the feature net *is* useful—print, common objects, and so on. Even in this domain, it turns out that the feature net must be supplemented with additional mechanisms. This requirement doesn't in any way undermine the importance of the feature net idea; the net is plainly needed as part of our theoretical account. The key word, however, is "part," because we need to place the feature net within a larger theoretical frame.

The Benefits of Larger Contexts

Earlier in the chapter, we saw that letter recognition is improved by context, so that the letter *V*, for example, is easier to recognize in the context "VASE," or even the nonsense context "VIMP," than it is if presented alone. These are examples of "top-down" effects—effects driven by your knowledge and expectations—and these particular top-down effects, based on spelling patterns, are easily accommodated by the network: Priming (from recency and frequency of use) guarantees that detectors that have often been used in the past will be easier to activate in the future. In this way, the network "learns" which patterns are common, and which are not, and is more receptive to inputs that follow the usual patterns.

Other top-down effects, however, require a different type of explanation. Consider, for example, the fact that words are easier to recognize if you see them as part of a sentence than they are if you see them in isolation. There are many formal demonstrations of this effect (e.g., Rueckl & Oden, 1986; Spellman, Holyoak, & Morrison, 2001; Tulving & Gold, 1963; Tulving, Mandler, & Baumal, 1964), but for our purposes, an informal example will be sufficient. Imagine that we tell research participants, "I am about to show you a word very briefly on a computer screen; the word is the name of something that you can eat." If we forced the participants to guess the word at this point, they would be unlikely to name the target word. (There are, after all, many things you can eat, and so the chances are slim of guessing just the right one.) But if we now briefly show the word "CELERY," we're likely to observe a large priming effect; that is, participants are more likely to recognize "CELERY" with this cue than they would have been without the cue.

Think about what this priming involves. First, the person needs to understand each of the words in the instruction. If she did not understand the word "eat" (if, for example, she mistakenly thought we had said, "something that you can beat"), we would not get the priming. Second, the person must understand the syntax of the instruction and thus the relations among the words in the instruction. Again, if she mistakenly thought we said "something that can eat you," we would expect a very different sort of priming. Third, the person has to know some facts about the world—namely, the kinds of things that can be eaten; without this knowledge, we would expect no priming.

Obviously, then, this instance of priming relies on a broad range of knowledge, and there is nothing special about this example. We could, after all, observe similar priming effects if we tell someone that the word about to be shown is the name of a historical figure, or that the word is related to the *Harry Potter* books. In each case, this instruction would facilitate perception, with the implication that in explaining these various priming effects we'll need to hook up our object-recognition system to a much broader library of information.

Notice, though, where all of this brings us: Examples like we have just considered tell us that we cannot view object recognition as a self-contained process. Instead, knowledge that is external to object recognition (e.g., knowledge about what is edible) is imported into and clearly influences the process. Put differently, the "CELERY" example (and others as well) does not depend just on the specific stimuli you've encountered recently or frequently. Instead, what is crucial for this sort of priming is what you know coming into the experiment, knowledge derived from a wide range of life experiences.

We have, therefore, reached an important juncture. We have tried in this chapter to examine object recognition in isolation from other cognitive processes, considering how a separate object-recognition module might function, with the module then handing its product (the object it had recognized) on to subsequent processes. We have made good progress in this attempt and have described how a significant piece of object recognition might proceed. But in the end we have run up against a problem—namely, top-down priming that draws on knowledge from outside of object recognition per se. This sort of priming plainly depends on what is in memory and on how that knowledge is accessed and used, and so we cannot tackle this sort of priming until we have said a great deal more about memory, knowledge, and thought. We therefore must leave object recognition for now in order to fill in some other pieces of the puzzle. We will have more to say about object recognition in later chapters, once we have some more theoretical machinery in place.

CHAPTER SUMMARY

- Visual perception is a highly active process in which the perceiver goes beyond the information given in organizing and interpreting the visual input. The process must specify a figure/ground organization for the input and how the figure is organized in depth. The interpretive process is guided by certain principles, including those catalogued by the Gestalt psychologists. Importantly, though, the interpretation seems to be guided simultaneously by the input's features and its overall configuration.

- We easily recognize a wide range of objects in a wide range of circumstances. Our recognition is heavily influenced by context, which can determine how or whether we recognize an object. To study these achievements, investigators have often focused on the recognition of printed language, using this case as a microcosm within which to study how object recognition in general might proceed.

- Many investigators have proposed that recognition begins with the identification of features in the (organized) input pattern. Crucial evidence for this claim comes from neuroscience studies showing that the detection of features is separate from the processes needed to assemble these features into more complex wholes.

- To study word recognition, investigators often use tachistoscopic presentations. In these studies, words that appear frequently in the language are easier to identify, and so are words that have been recently viewed—an effect known as repetition priming. The data also show a pattern known as the word-superiority effect; this refers to the fact that words are more readily perceived than isolated letters. In addition, well-formed nonwords are more readily perceived than letter strings that do not conform to the rules of normal spelling. Another reliable pattern is that recognition errors, when they occur, are quite systematic, with the input typically perceived as being more regular than it actually is. These findings together indicate that recognition is influenced by the regularities that exist in our environment (e.g., the regularities of spelling patterns).

- These results can be understood in terms of a network of detectors. Each detector collects input and fires when the input reaches a threshold level. A network of these detectors can accomplish a great deal; for example, it can interpret ambiguous inputs, recover from its own errors, and make inferences about barely viewed stimuli.

- The feature net seems to "know" the rules of spelling and "expects" the input to conform to these rules. However, this knowledge is distributed across the entire network and emerges only through the network's parallel processing. This setup leads to enormous efficiency in our commerce with the world because it allows us to recognize patterns and objects with relatively little input and under highly diverse circumstances. But these gains come at the cost of occasional error. This trade-off may be necessary, though, if we are to cope with the informational complexity of our world.

- A feature net can be implemented in different ways—with or without inhibitory connections, for example. With some adjustments (e.g., the addition of geon detectors), the net can also recognize three-dimensional objects. However, some stimuli—for example, faces—probably are not recognized through a feature net but instead require a different sort of recognition system, one that is sensitive to relationships and configurations within the stimulus input.

- The feature net also needs to be supplemented to accommodate top-down influences on object recognition. These influences can be detected in the benefits of larger contexts in facilitating recognition and in forms of priming that are plainly concept-driven rather than data-driven. These other forms of priming demand an interactive model, which merges bottom-up and top-down processes.

The Workbook Connection

See the *Cognition Workbook* for further exploration in recognizing objects:

- Demonstration 3.1: Adelson's Brightness Illusion
- Demonstration 3.2: A Size Illusion and a Motion Illusion
- Demonstration 3.3: Features and Feature Combinations
- Demonstration 3.4: Inferences in Reading
- Research Methods: Dealing With Confounds
- Cognitive Psychology and Education: Speed-Reading
- Cognitive Psychology and the Law: Cross-Race Identification

NEED HELP STUDYING?

 wwnorton.com/studyspace

Visit StudySpace to access free review material such as

- Chapter study plans
- Quizzes
- Flashcards, and more

Go to **wwnorton.com/zaps** for these online labs:

- Ames Room
- Visual Search
- Feature Net
- Word Frequency
- Word Superiority

CHAPTER FOUR

Paying Attention

Consider your circumstances right now. You're paying attention to this page, reading these words. However, there are thousands of other inputs available to you, things you could pay attention to if you chose. For example, you're paying attention to the meanings of these words, but you could choose instead to look at the shapes of the letters, rather than the words themselves. You could, if you chose, contemplate the color of the paper, or its texture. If you wanted to, you could look up from the page and look at any of the people or objects in the room with you. And these are just the *visual* inputs. There are also many sounds in the room. Perhaps there's music on, or perhaps you can hear someone at the next desk turning pages. Perhaps the room is silent, but even so, you could focus on the silence, much as a sentry listens carefully to detect intruders. For that matter, you could, if you wished, focus on *internal* events rather than external ones—and so, for example, you could start planning your weekend, or think about the term paper that's due next week.

This list could easily be extended, but by now the point should be clear: The stimulus you're attending to is only one of many that are available to you, and this fact invites two crucial observations. First, it seems clear that you could choose to pay attention to any of the things just mentioned, and if you did, you would be virtually oblivious to the

PREVIEW OF CHAPTER THEMES

- In this chapter, we argue that multiple mechanisms are involved in the seemingly simple act of paying attention. In other words, people must take many different steps to facilitate the processing of desired inputs; in the absence of these steps, their ability to pick up information from the world is dramatically reduced.

- Many of the steps we take in order to perceive have a "cost" attached to them: They require the commitment of mental resources. These resources are limited in availability, and this is part of the reason we cannot pay attention to two inputs at once: This would require more resources than we have.

- Divided attention (the attempt to do two things at once) can also be understood in terms of resources:

- We can perform two activities at the same time, provided that the activities do not require more resources than we have available.

- Some of the mental resources we use are specialized, and so they are required only for tasks of a certain sort. Other resources are more general, needed for a wide range of tasks. The resource demand of a task can, however, be diminished through practice.

- We emphasize that attention is best understood not as a process or mechanism, but as an *achievement*. Like most achievements, paying attention involves many different elements, all of which help us to be aware of the stimuli we're interested in and not be pulled off track by irrelevant distractors.

other things on the list. Indeed, until you read the previous paragraph, you probably were oblivious to the other stimuli we mentioned! How do you do this? How do you manage to avoid the distractors and focus your attention in just the manner you wish, selecting only one input of many? Second, there seems to be one thing you cannot do: You cannot pay attention to all of these things at once. If you start musing about your weekend, you're likely to lose track of what's on the page; if you start planning your paper, you won't finish the reading assignment. Of course, sometimes you *can* "multitask" and deal with two different inputs, or different chores, at once. You can, if you choose, hum a melody while reading these words; most people can walk and chew gum at the same time; and so on. But where are the limits? When can you do two (or more) things at the same time, and when can't you?

Selective Attention

William James is one of the historical giants of our field, and his writing, late in the 19th century, set out many of the key issues that psychology continues to pursue today. James is often quoted in the modern literature, and one of his most famous quotes provides our starting point in this chapter. Roughly 120 years ago, James wrote:

> *Everyone knows what attention is. It is the taking possession by the mind, in clear and vivid form, of one out of what seem several simultaneously possible objects or trains of thought. Focalization, concentration, of consciousness are of its essence. It implies withdrawal from some things in order to deal effectively with others, and is a condition which has a real opposite in the confused, dazed, scatterbrained state which in French is called distraction . . . (James, 1890, pp. 403–404).*

In this quote, James describes what attention *achieves,* but what processes or mechanisms produce these effects? What steps do you need to take in order to achieve this "focus," and why is it that the focus "implies withdrawal from some things in order to deal effectively with others"?

Dichotic Listening

Early studies of attention often used a setup called **dichotic listening**: Participants wore headphones, and heard one input in the left ear and a different input in the right ear. The participants were instructed to pay attention to one of these inputs—the **attended channel**—and told simply to ignore the message in the other ear (the **unattended channel**).

To make sure participants were paying attention, they were usually given a task called **shadowing**. The attended channel contained a recording of someone speaking, and, as participants listened to this speech, they were required to repeat it back, word for word, so that they were, in essence, simply echoing what they heard. Shadowing is initially challenging, but it becomes relatively easy after a minute of practice. (You might try it, shadowing a voice on the radio or TV.)

Participants' shadowing performance is generally close to perfect: they repeat almost 100% of the words they hear. At the same time, however, they hear remarkably little from the unattended channel. If we ask them, after a minute or so of shadowing, to report what the unattended message was about, they indicate that they have no idea at all (see Cherry, 1953, for an early study documenting this point). They can't even tell if the unattended channel contained a coherent message or just random words. In fact, in one study, participants shadowed coherent prose in the attended channel, while in the unattended channel they heard a text in Czech, read with English pronunciation. Thus, the individual sounds (the vowels, the consonants) resembled English, but the message itself was (for an English speaker) gibberish. After a minute of shadowing, only 4 of 30 participants detected the peculiar character of the unattended message (Treisman, 1964).

More-recent studies have documented a similar pattern with *visual* inputs. Participants in one study watched a TV screen that showed a team of players in white shirts passing a ball back and forth; the participants had to signal each time the ball changed hands. Interwoven with these players (and visible on the same

WORKBOOK
DEMONSTRATION 4.1

FIGURE 4.1 | THE INVISIBLE GORILLA

In this experiment, participants were instructed to keep track of the ballplayers in the white shirts. Intent on their task, they were oblivious to what the black-shirted players were doing. They also failed to see the person in the (black) gorilla suit strolling through the scene. (Figure provided by Daniel J. Simons)

TV screen) was another team, wearing black shirts, also passing a ball back and forth; participants were instructed to ignore these players. Participants easily did this selective task, but they were so intent on the white team that they didn't see other, rather salient, events that appeared on the screen, right in front of their eyes. For example, they entirely failed to notice when another player wearing a gorilla costume walked through the middle of the game, pausing briefly to thump his chest before exiting! (See Figure 4.1; Neisser & Becklen, 1975; Simons & Chabris, 1999). (For a similar result in which participants fail to perceive unattended faces, see Jenkins, Lavie, & Driver, 2005.)

However, people are not altogether oblivious to the unattended channel: In selective listening experiments, they easily and accurately report whether the unattended channel contained human speech, musical instruments, or silence. If the unattended channel contains human speech, they can report whether the speaker was male or female, had a high or low voice, or was speaking loudly or softly. (For reviews of this early work, see Broadbent, 1958; Kahneman, 1973.) Apparently, then, *physical attributes* of the unattended channel are heard, even though participants seem oblivious to the unattended channel's semantic content.

Some Unattended Inputs Are Detected

However, some results don't fit this pattern, and some bits of the unattended input do seem to "leak" through and get noticed. In one study, people were asked to shadow one passage while ignoring a second passage. Embedded within the unattended channel was a series of names, and roughly a third of the participants did hear their own name when it was spoken—even though (just like in other studies) they heard almost nothing else from the unattended input (Moray, 1959).

And it's not just names that can "catch" your attention. Mention of a movie you just saw, or mention of your favorite restaurant, will often be noticed in the unattended channel. More generally, words with some personal importance are often (but not always) noticed, even though the rest of the unattended channel is perceived only as an undifferentiated blur (Conway, Cowan, & Bunting, 2001; Wood & Cowan, 1995).

These results are often referred to under the banner of the **cocktail party effect.** There you are at a party, engaged in conversation. Many other conversations are taking place in the room, but somehow you're able to "tune them out." You are aware that other people in the room are talking, but you don't have a clue what they're saying. All you hear is the single conversation you're attending to, plus a buzz of background noise. But now imagine that someone a few steps away from you mentions the name of a close friend of yours. Your attention is immediately caught, and you find yourself listening to that other conversation and (momentarily) oblivious to the conversation you had been engaged in. This experience, easily observed outside the laboratory, is precisely parallel to the pattern of experimental data.

How can we put all of these results together? How can we explain both our general insensitivity to the unattended channel and also the cases in which the unattended channel "leaks through"?

Perceiving and the Limits on Cognitive Capacity

One option for explaining these results focuses on what you do with the *unattended* input. Specifically, the proposal is that you somehow block processing of the inputs you're not interested in, much as a sentry blocks the path of unwanted guests but stands back and does nothing when legitimate guests are in view, allowing them to pass through the gate unimpeded.

This sort of proposal was central for early theories of attention—so-called "bottleneck theories"—which suggested that you erect a **filter** that shields you from potential distractors. Desired information (the attended channel) is not filtered out and so goes on to receive further processing (Broadbent, 1958). More-recent evidence suggests, though, that this filtering is rather specific and is done on a distractor-by-distractor basis—as if the sentry lacked the broad ability to separate desirable guests in general from undesirable ones. Instead, the sentry seems to have the assignment of blocking specific, already-identified gate-crashers. Thus, you seem able to inhibit your response to *this* distractor and do the same for *that* distractor, but these efforts are of little value if some new, unexpected distractor comes along. In that case, you need to develop a new skill aimed specifically at blocking the new intruder (Fenske, Raymond, Kessler, Westoby, & Tipper, 2005; Jacoby, Lindsay, & Hessels, 2003; Tsushima, Sasaki, & Watanabe, 2006).

Apparently, then, the ability to ignore certain distractors—to shut them out—needs to be part of our theory. Other evidence, though, indicates that this is not the whole story. That's because not only do you block the processing of distractors, but you are also able to *promote* the processing of *desired* stimuli.

Inattentional Blindness

We saw in Chapter 3 that perception involves a lot of activity, as you organize and interpret the incoming stimulus information. It seems plausible that this activity requires some initiative and some resources from you—and the evidence suggests that it does.

In one experiment, participants were told that they would see large "+" shapes on a computer screen, presented for 200 milliseconds, followed by a pattern mask. (The "mask" is just a meaningless jumble on the screen, designed to interrupt any further processing.) If the horizontal bar of the "+" was longer than the vertical, the participants were supposed to press one button; if the vertical bar was longer, they had to press a different button. As a complication, participants weren't allowed to look directly at the "+." Instead, they fixated (pointed their eyes at) a mark in the center of the computer screen—a **fixation target**—and the "+" shapes were shown just off to one side (see Figure 4.2).

For the first three trials of the procedure, events proceeded just as the participants expected, and the task was relatively easy. On Trial 3, for example, participants made the correct response 78% of the time. On Trial 4, though, things were slightly different: While the target "+" was on the screen, the fixation target disappeared and was replaced by one of three shapes—a triangle, a rectangle, or a cross. Then the entire configuration (the "+" target and this new shape) was replaced by the mask.

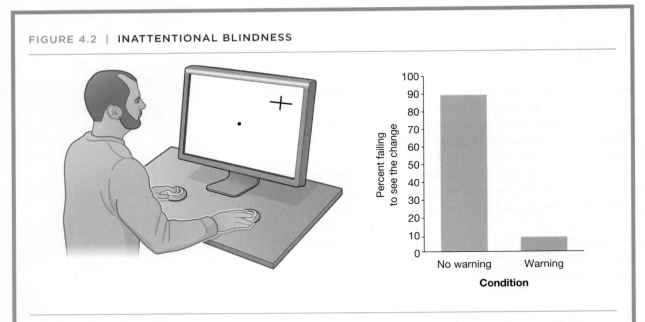

FIGURE 4.2 | **INATTENTIONAL BLINDNESS**

Participants were instructed to point their eyes at the dot, and to make judgments about the cross shown just off to the side. However, the dot itself briefly changed to another shape. If participants were not warned about this (and so were not paying attention to the dot), they routinely failed to detect this change—even though they had been pointing their eyes right at the dot the whole time! If participants were warned, though, and so alert for possible changes, then virtually all detected the change. (After Mack & Rock, 1998)

Immediately after the trial, participants were asked: Was there anything different on this trial? Was anything present, or anything changed, that wasn't there on previous trials? Remarkably, 89% of the participants reported that there was no change; they had apparently failed to see anything other than the (attended) "+." To probe the participants further, the researchers told them (correctly) that during the previous trial the fixation target had momentarily disappeared and had been replaced by a shape. The participants were then asked what that shape had been and were explicitly given the choices of a triangle, a rectangle, or a cross. The responses to this question were essentially random. Even when probed in this fashion, participants seemed not to have seen the shape that had been directly in front of their eyes (Mack & Rock, 1998; also see Mack, 2003).

What's going on here? Some researchers have proposed that the participants in this experiment did see the target shapes but, a moment later, couldn't *remember* what they'd just seen (e.g., Wolfe, 1999). However, Mack and Rock, the researchers who conducted the study, offer a stronger claim—namely, that the participants literally failed to see the shapes, even though they were staring straight at them. This failure to see, they argue, was caused by the fact that the participants were not expecting any shapes to appear and were not in any way prepared for these shapes. Mack and Rock dubbed this pattern **inattentional blindness** (Mack & Rock, 1998; also see Mack, 2003).

Which of these accounts is correct? Did participants fail to see the input? Or did they see it but, just a few milliseconds later, forget what they'd seen? For purposes of theory, this distinction is crucial, but for the moment let's emphasize

INATTENTIONAL BLINDNESS OUTSIDE OF THE LAB

Inattentional blindness is usually demonstrated in the laboratory, but has a number of real-world counterparts. Most people, for example, have experienced the peculiar situation in which they are unable to find the mayonnaise in the refrigerator (or the ketchup, or the salad dressing) even though they are staring right at the bottle! This is a situation in which the person is so absorbed in thoughts about other matters that he or she becomes blind to an otherwise salient stimulus.

what the two proposals have in common: By either account, our normal ability to see what's around us, and to make use of what we see, is dramatically diminished in the absence of attention.

There's more to be said about these issues, but, before we press on, let's note the important "real-world" implications of these findings. Chabris and Simons (2010) call attention to the reports of traffic accidents in which (for example) a driver says, "I never saw the bicyclist! He came out of nowhere! But then—suddenly—there he was, right in front of me." Or, as a much more mundane case, you go to the refrigerator to find the mayonnaise (or the ketchup, or the juice), and fail to find it, even though it is directly in front of you.

In these cases, we lament the neglectful driver, and your inability to find the mayonnaise may cause you to worry that you're losing your mind as well as your condiments. The response to all this, though, is to realize that these cases of failing-to-see are entirely normal. Perception requires more than "merely" having a stimulus in front of your eyes. Perception requires some work.

Conscious Perception, Unconscious Perception

Based on their work on inattentional blindness, Mack and Rock argue that there is no perception without attention. However, this claim needs an important refinement, and so, more precisely, Mack and Rock argue there is no *conscious* perception without attention (Mack & Rock, 1998, p. 14).

To see why this refinement is needed, consider the following experiment (Moore & Egeth, 1997; for other data pertinent to this claim, see Mack, 2003; Mack & Rock, 1998). Participants were shown a series of images on a computer screen; each image contained two horizontal lines surrounded by a pattern of black and white dots (see Figure 4.3A), and the participants' task was to decide which of the two lines was longer, the top one or the bottom. For the first three trials of this procedure, the background dots on the computer screen were arranged randomly. On Trial 4, however, and with no warning to participants, the pattern of dots shown was like the one in Figure 4.3B, creating a stimulus configuration that reproduces a standard geometric illusion, the Müller-Lyer illusion. Focusing their attention on the two horizontal lines, however, the participants didn't perceive this pattern. When they were asked immediately after the trial whether they had noticed any pattern in the dots, none reported seeing the pattern. They were then told directly that there had been a pattern and were asked to choose it (from among four options); 90% selected one of the incorrect patterns. Plainly, then, this experiment reproduces the finding of inattentional blindness.

Nonetheless, the participants were influenced by the dot pattern. In the standard Müller-Lyer display, the "fins" make the top horizontal line in Figure 4.3C appear longer than the bottom horizontal line, even though both lines are exactly the same length. The dot pattern in the Moore and Egeth displays did the same, and 95% of the participants reported that the top line in Figure 4.3B was longer than the bottom one, even though, in the display, both were the same length.

Notice, then, that the participants were completely unaware of the fins but were still influenced by them. No participant reported seeing the fins, but virtually

FIGURE 4.3 | UNCONSCIOUS PERCEPTION

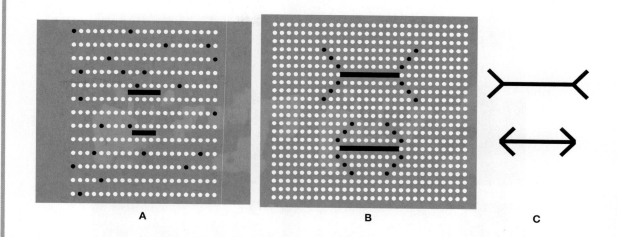

A   B   C

Participants were shown a series of images, each containing a pair of horizontal lines; their task was to decide which of the two lines was longer. For the first three trials, the background dots were arranged randomly (Panel A). For the fourth trial, the dots were arranged as shown in Panel B, roughly reproducing the configuration of the Müller-Lyer illusion; Panel C shows the standard form of this illusion. The participants in this study did not perceive the "fins" consciously, but they were nonetheless influenced by the fins—judging the top horizontal line in Panel B to be longer, fully in accord with the usual misperception of this illusion.

all responded in the length judgment in a fashion consistent with the fins. (For related data, see Russell & Driver, 2005.) The obvious conclusion, then, is that participants did perceive the fins in some way but did not consciously perceive them. We'll return to issues of conscious and unconscious perception in Chapter 13; for now, it seems attention may be needed for *conscious* perception, but perhaps you can unconsciously detect (and be influenced by) patterns in the world even in the absence of attention.

Change Blindness

The active nature of perception is also evident in studies of **change blindness**—observers' inability to detect changes in scenes they're looking at directly. In some experiments, participants are shown pairs of pictures separated by a brief blank interval (e.g., Rensink, O'Regan, & Clark, 1997). The pictures in each pair are identical except for some single aspect: an "extra" engine shown on the airplane in one picture and not in the other; a man not wearing a hat in one picture but wearing one in the other; and so on (see Figure 4.4). Participants know from the start that their task is to detect these changes, but even so, the task is difficult. If the change involves something central to the scene, observers may need as many

FIGURE 4.4 | CHANGE BLINDNESS

In some change-blindness demonstrations, participants see one picture, then a second, then the first again, then the second, and must spot the difference between the two pictures. Here we've displayed the pictures side by side, rather than putting them in alternation. Can you find the differences? For most people, it takes a surprising amount of time and effort to locate the differences—even though some of the differences are quite large. Apparently, therefore, having a stimulus directly in front of your eyes is no guarantee that you will perceive the stimulus!

as a dozen alternations between the pictures before they detect the change. If the change involves some peripheral aspect of the scene, then as many as 25 alternations may be required.

A related pattern emerges when participants watch videos. In one study, observers watched a movie of two women having a conversation. During the film, the camera first focused on one woman, then on the other, just as it would in an ordinary TV show or movie. The crucial element of this experiment, though, was that aspects of the scene changed every time the camera angle changed. For example, when the camera was pointing at Woman A, you could plainly see the red plates on the table between the women. When the camera was shifted to point at Woman B, just a fraction of a second later, the plates had miraculously turned white (see Figure 4.5). Most observers, however, noticed none of these changes. In one experiment, a film containing a total of nine changes was shown

FIGURE 4.5 | CHANGE BLINDNESS

In this video, every time there was a shift in camera angle, there was a change in the scene—so that the woman in the red sweater abruptly gained a scarf, the plates that had been red were suddenly white, and so on. When viewers watched the video, though, they noticed none of these changes!

to ten participants. Only one participant claimed to notice the changes, and when pressed, this participant merely said there was a difference in "the way people were sitting." When allowed to watch the film again and told explicitly to look out for changes, observers noticed (on average) only two of the nine changes (D. T. Levin & Simons, 1997; Shore & Klein, 2000; Simons, 2000).

Incredibly, the same pattern can be documented with live (i.e., not filmed) events. In a remarkable study, an investigator (let's call him "Leon") approached pedestrians on a college campus and asked for directions to a certain building. During the conversation, two men carrying a door approached and deliberately walked *between* Leon and the research participant. As a result, Leon was momentarily hidden (by the door) from the participant's view, and in that moment Leon traded places with one of the men carrying the door. A second later, therefore, Leon was able to walk away, unseen, while the new fellow (who had been carrying the door) stayed behind and continued the conversation with the participant.

Roughly half of the participants failed to notice this switch. They continued the conversation as though nothing had happened—despite the fact that Leon and his replacement were wearing different clothes, had easily distinguishable voices, and so on. When asked directly whether anything odd had happened in this event, many participants commented only that it was rude that the guys carrying the door had walked right through their conversation (Simons & Ambinder, 2005; Simons & Chabris, 2010). (For other studies of change blindness, see Most et al., 2001, and Rensink, 2002; for similar effects with auditory stimuli, see Gregg & Samuel, 2008; Vitevitch, 2003; for discussion of why some people notice these switches, while others do not, see Seegmiller, Watson, & Strayer, 2011.)

WORKBOOK
DEMONSTRATION 4.2

Early Versus Late Selection

In several paradigms, then, it's clear that people are oblivious to stimuli directly in front of their eyes—whether the stimuli are simple displays on a computer screen, photographs, movies, or real-life events. As we noted earlier, though, there are two ways we might think about these results: These studies may reveal genuine limits on *perception*, so that participants literally don't see these stimuli; or these studies may reveal limits on *memory*, so that people do see the stimuli but immediately forget what they've just seen.

Which proposal is correct? One approach to this question hinges on *when* the perceiver selects the desired input, and (correspondingly) when the perceiver ceases the processing of the unattended input. According to the **early selection** hypothesis, the attended input is identified and privileged from the start, so that the unattended input receives little (and maybe even zero?) analysis (and so is never perceived). According to the **late selection** hypothesis, however, all inputs receive relatively complete analysis, and the selection is done after all of this analysis is finished. Perhaps the selection is done just before the stimuli reach consciousness, and so we become aware only of the attended input. Or perhaps the selection is done later still—so that all inputs make it (briefly) into consciousness, but *then* the selection is done, so that only the attended input is remembered.

It turns out that each hypothesis captures part of the truth. On the one side, we've already considered a case in which people seem genuinely unaware of the distractors but are nevertheless influenced by them (pp. 124–125). This seems to be a case of *late selection*, with the selection done after the distractors were perceived, but before they made it to consciousness. On the other side, though, we can also find evidence for *early selection*, with distractor stimuli receiving little analysis and indeed falling out of the stream of processing at a very early stage. Relevant evidence comes, for example, from studies that record the electrical activity of the brain in the milliseconds after a stimulus has arrived. These studies confirm that the brain activity for attended inputs is distinguishable from that for unattended inputs just 80 ms or so after the stimulus presentation—a time interval in which early sensory processing is still under way (Hillyard, Vogel, & Luck, 1998). Apparently, in these cases, the attended input is privileged from the start.

Other data also provide evidence for early selection. For example, recordings from neurons in Area V4 of the visual cortex show that these neurons are more responsive to attended inputs than to unattended ones, almost as if attention made the light areas seem brighter and dim areas seem darker (Carrasco, Ling, & Read, 2004; Carrasco, Penpeci-Talgar, & Eckstein, 2000; McAdams & Reid, 2005; Reynolds, Pasternak, & Desimone, 2000). Other studies suggest that attention may modulate neural events even earlier in the stream of visual processing— perhaps as early as the lateral geniculate nucleus (O'Connor, Fukui, Pinsk, & Kastner, 2002; also see Yantis, 2008). These results argue powerfully that attention doesn't just change what we remember or what we're aware of. Attention can literally change what we perceive.

But what accounts for this mixed pattern? Why do the data sometimes indicate late selection, and sometimes early? The answer depends in part on the nature of the attended input. If this input is particularly complex, then the processing of this input will demand a lot of effort and a lot of cognitive resources. (We'll have more to say about these "resources" later in the chapter.) In this case, little effort will be left over for other stimuli, with the consequence that the other stimuli receive less processing, leading to a data pattern consistent with early selection. In contrast, if the attended input is relatively simple, processing will demand few resources, leaving more available for the unattended inputs. Here the unattended inputs will probably receive more analysis, and so we'll see the pattern of late selection (after Lavie, 2001, 2005, 2009; also Cohen, Alvarez & Nakayama, 2011; Macdonald & Lavie, 2008; Rensink, 2012; for some challenges to this claim, though, see Mack, 2003).

Selective Priming

Whether selection is early or late, though, it's clear that looking directly at an input isn't by itself enough to allow conscious perception. But, in that case, what else is needed? Likewise, we've noted that people seem to hear little from the unattended channel during dichotic listening but are reasonably likely to detect some inputs—such as their own name. How should we think about these facts? And, with this, we've also suggested that "resources" are needed for perceiving, but what are those resources? Let's tackle these questions.

In Chapter 3, we proposed that recognition requires a network of detectors, and we argued that these detectors fire most readily, and most quickly, if they're suitably primed. But what does that priming involve? In some cases, priming is produced by your visual experience—specifically, whether each detector has been used recently or frequently in the past. But as we suggested at the end of Chapter 3, priming can also come from another source: your expectations about what the stimulus will be.

The proposal, then, is that people can literally prepare themselves for perceiving by priming the suitable detectors. Let's hypothesize in addition that this priming isn't free. Instead, you need to spend some effort or allocate some resources in order to do the priming, and let's suppose that these resources are in limited supply.

These simple ideas help explain several findings we've already met. Why don't participants notice the shapes in the inattentional blindness studies? The answer lies in the fact that they don't expect any stimulus to appear, so they have no reason to prepare for any stimulus. As a result, the stimulus, when it's presented, falls on unprepared (thus, unprimed, unresponsive) detectors. The detectors therefore don't respond to the stimulus, and you end up not perceiving the stimulus.

What about selective listening? In this case, you're trying to listen to the attended channel and usually have no interest in the unattended input. Put differently, you *don't want to* hear the distractor, so devoting resources to the distractor would be, at best, a waste of these resources. Therefore, the detectors needed for the distractor receive no resources and thus are unprimed, literally making it more difficult to hear the distractor. But why, on this account, does attention sometimes "leak," so that we do hear some aspects of the unattended input? Think about what will happen if your name is uttered on the unattended channel. The detectors for this stimulus are already primed, but this is not because you are, at that moment, expecting to hear your name. Instead, the detectors for your name are primed simply because this is a stimulus you've often encountered in the past. Thanks to this prior exposure, the activation level of these detectors is already high; you don't need to prime them further. So these detectors will fire even if your attention is elsewhere.

Two Types of Priming

The idea before us, in short, is that perception requires primed detectors and that this priming can come from two different sources. Sometimes the priming is a simple matter of the stimuli you've encountered (recently or frequently) in the past. This type of priming takes no effort on your part, and requires no resources. This is the sort of priming that allows you to hear your name on the unattended channel. But a different sort of priming is also possible. This priming is under your control, and dependent on your expectations: Specifically, you can deliberately prime detectors for inputs you think are upcoming, so that you're ready for those inputs when they arrive. You don't do this priming for inputs you have no interest in, and you *can't* do this priming for inputs you can't anticipate. As a result, the detectors for these other inputs remain unprimed (and therefore unresponsive).

Can we document this pattern? In a classic series of studies, Posner and Snyder (1975) gave people a straightforward task: A pair of letters was shown on a computer screen, and participants had to decide, as swiftly as they could, whether the letters were the same or different. So someone might see "AA" and answer "same," or might see "AB" and answer "different."

Before each pair, participants saw a warning signal. In the neutral condition, the warning signal was a plus sign ("+"). This signal notified participants that the stimuli were about to arrive but provided no other information. In a different condition, the warning signal was itself a letter and actually matched the stimuli to come. So someone might see the warning signal "G" followed by the pair "GG." In this case, the warning signal actually served to prime the participants for the stimuli. In a third condition, though, the warning signal was misleading. The warning signal was again a letter, but it was a letter different from the stimuli to come. Participants might see "H" followed by the pair "GG." Let's call these three conditions *neutral*, *primed*, and *misled*.

In this simple task, accuracy rates are very high. But the *speed* of responding varies from condition to condition, and we can use these speeds as a way of exploring what's going on in the participants' minds. Specifically, in each condition, Posner and Snyder recorded how quickly people responded. By comparing these **response times** (or RTs) in the *primed* and *neutral* conditions, we can ask what benefit there is from the prime. Likewise, by comparing RTs in the *misled* and *neutral* conditions, we can ask what cost there is, if any, from being misled.

Before we turn to the results, though, we need one further complication: Posner and Snyder ran this procedure in two different versions (as shown in Table 4.1). In one version, the warning signal was an excellent predictor of the upcoming stimuli: For example, if the warning signal was an *A*, there was an 80% chance that the upcoming stimulus pair would contain *A*'s. In Posner and Snyder's terms, the warning signal provided a "high validity" prime. In a different version of the procedure, the warning signal was a poor predictor of the upcoming stimuli: If the warning signal was an *A*, there was only a 20% chance that the upcoming pair would contain *A*s. This is the "low validity" condition.

Let's consider the low-validity condition first, and let's focus on those rare occasions in which the prime did match the subsequent stimuli. That is, we're focusing on 20% of the trials and ignoring the other 80% for the moment. In this condition, the participant can't use the prime as a basis for predicting the stimuli because, after all, the prime is a poor indicator of things to come. Therefore, the prime should not lead to any specific expectations. Nonetheless, we do expect faster RTs in the *primed* condition than in the *neutral* condition: Why? Thanks to the prime, the relevant detectors have just fired, and so the detectors should still be warmed up. When the target stimuli arrive, therefore, the detectors should fire more readily, allowing a faster response. This is, in effect, a case of repetition priming, as described in Chapter 3.

TABLE 4.1 | **DESIGN OF POSNER AND SNYDER'S EXPERIMENT**

| | Type of Trial | TYPICAL SEQUENCE | | Provides Repetition Priming? | Provides Basis for Expectation? |
		Warning Signal	Test Stimuli		
Low-validity Condition	Neutral	+	AA	No	No
	Primed	G	GG	Yes	No
	Misled	H	GG	No	No
High-validity Condition	Neutral	+	AA	No	No
	Primed	G	GG	Yes	Prime leads to correct expectation
	Misled	H	GG	No	Prime leads to incorrect expectation

In the low-validity condition, misled *trials occurred four times as often as* primed *trials (80% versus 20%). Therefore, participants had reason not to trust the primes and, correspondingly, had no reason to generate an expectation based on the primes. In the high-validity condition, things were reversed: Now* primed *trials occurred four times as often as* misled *trials. Therefore, participants had good reason to trust the primes and good reason to generate an expectation based on the prime.*

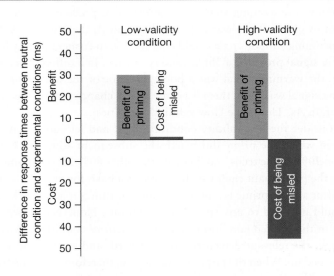

FIGURE 4.6 | THE EFFECTS OF PRIMING ON STIMULUS
PROCESSING

As one way of assessing the Posner and Snyder (1975) results, we can subtract the response times for the neutral condition from those for the primed condition; in this way, we measure the benefits of priming. Likewise, we can subtract the response times for the neutral condition from those for the misled condition; in this way, we measure the costs of being misled. In these terms, the low-validity condition shows a small benefit (from repetition priming) but zero cost from being misled. The high-validity condition, in contrast, shows a larger benefit, but also a substantial cost. The results shown here reflect trials with a 300 ms interval between the warning signal and the test stimuli; the results were somewhat different at other intervals.

The results bear this out. RTs were reliably faster (by roughly 30 ms) in the *primed* condition than in the *neutral* condition (see Figure 4.6, left side). Apparently, then, detectors can be primed by mere exposure to a stimulus. Or, to put it differently, priming is observed even in the absence of expectations. This priming, therefore, seems truly stimulus-based.

What about the *misled* condition? With a low-validity prime, misleading the participants had no effect: Performance in the *misled* condition was the same as performance in the *neutral* condition. Priming the "wrong" detector, it seems, takes nothing away from the other detectors—including the detectors actually needed for that trial. This fits with our discussion in Chapter 3: Each of the various detectors works independently of the others. Thus, priming one detector obviously influences the functioning of that specific detector but neither helps nor hinders the other detectors.

Let's look next at the high-validity primes. In this condition, people might see, for example, a "J" as the warning signal, and then the stimulus pair "J J." Presentation of the prime itself will fire the J-detectors, and this should, once again, "warm up" these detectors, just as the low-validity primes did. Thus, we expect a stimulus-driven benefit from the prime. However, the high-validity primes may also have another influence: High-validity primes are excellent predictors of the stimulus to come. Participants are told this at the outset, and they have lots of opportunity to see that it is true. High-validity primes will therefore produce a warm-up effect *and also* an expectation effect, whereas low-validity primes produce only the warm-up. We should therefore expect the high-validity primes to help participants more than low-validity primes—and that's exactly what the data show (Figure 4.6, right side). The combination of warm-up and expectations, in other words, leads to faster responses than warm-up alone. From the participants' point of view, it pays to know what the upcoming stimulus might be.

Explaining the Costs and Benefits

Thus, we do need to distinguish two types of primes. One type is stimulus-based—produced merely by presentation of the priming stimulus, with no role for expectations. The other type is expectation-based and is created only when the participant believes the prime allows a prediction of what's to come.

These types of primes can be distinguished in various ways. First, expectation-based priming takes longer to kick in than stimulus-based priming—presumably because you need a moment to form an expectation, and then a bit longer to activate the relevant detectors. Thus, in the data, stimulus-based priming can be observed immediately after the prime; priming based on expectations takes roughly a half-second to develop (Neely, 1977).

The two types of priming can also be distinguished in terms of their "cost." Stimulus-based priming appears to be "free," and so we can prime one detector without taking anything away from the other detectors. We see this in the low-validity condition, in the fact that the *misled* trials lead to responses just as fast as those in the *neutral* trials. Expectation-based priming, in contrast, does have a cost, and we see this in an aspect of Figure 4.6 that we've not yet mentioned: With high-validity primes, responses in the *misled* condition were slower than responses in the *neutral* condition. That is, misleading the participants actually hurt performance. As a concrete example, F-detection was slower if G was primed, compared to F-detection when the prime was simply the neutral warning signal ("+"). Put more broadly, it seems that priming the "wrong" detector takes something away from the other detectors, and so participants are worse off when they're misled than when they received no prime at all.

What produces this cost? As an analogy, think about being on a limited budget. Imagine that you have just $50 to spend on groceries. You can spend more on ice cream if you wish, but if you do, you'll have that much less to spend on other foods. Any increase in the ice cream allotment must be covered by a decrease somewhere else. This trade-off arises, though, only because of the limited budget. If you had unlimited funds, you could spend more on ice cream and still have enough money for everything else.

Expectation-based priming shows the same pattern. If the Q-detector is primed, this takes something away from the other detectors. Getting prepared for one target seems to make people less prepared for other targets. But we just said that this sort of pattern implies a limited "budget." If an unlimited supply of activation were available, you could prime the Q-detector and leave the other detectors just as they were. And that is the point: Expectation-based priming, by virtue of revealing costs when misled, reveals the presence of a **limited-capacity system**.

We can now put the pieces together. Ultimately, we need to explain the facts of selective attention, including the fact that while listening to one message you hear little content from other messages. To explain this, we've proposed that perceiving involves some work, and this work requires some limited mental resources. That is why you can't listen to two messages at the same time; doing so would demand more resources than you have. And now, finally, we're seeing evidence for those limited resources: The Posner and Snyder research (and many other results) reveals the workings of a limited-capacity system, just as our hypothesis demands.

Chronometric Studies and Spatial Attention

The Posner and Snyder study shows us that your expectations about an upcoming stimulus can influence the processing of that stimulus. But what exactly is the nature of these expectations? How precise, or how vague, are they?

As one way of entering this issue, imagine that participants in a study are told, "The next stimulus will be a T." In this case, they know exactly what to get ready for. But now imagine that participants are told, "The next stimulus will be a letter" or "The next stimulus will be on the left side of the screen." Will these cues allow people to prepare themselves?

These issues have been examined in studies of **spatial attention**—that is, the ability to focus on a particular position in space, and thus to be better prepared for any stimulus that appears in that position. In an early study, Posner, Snyder, and Davidson (1980) required their participants simply to detect letter presentations; the task was just to press a button as soon as a letter appeared. Participants kept their eyes pointed at a central fixation mark, and letters could appear either to the left or to the right of this mark.

For some trials, a neutral warning signal was presented, so that participants knew a trial was about to start but had no information about stimulus location. For other trials, an arrow was used as the warning signal. Sometimes the arrow pointed left, sometimes right; and the arrow was generally an accurate predictor of the location of the stimulus-to-come: If the arrow pointed right, the stimulus would be on the right side of the computer screen. (In the terms we used earlier, this is a high-validity cue.) On 20% of the trials, however, the arrow misled participants about location.

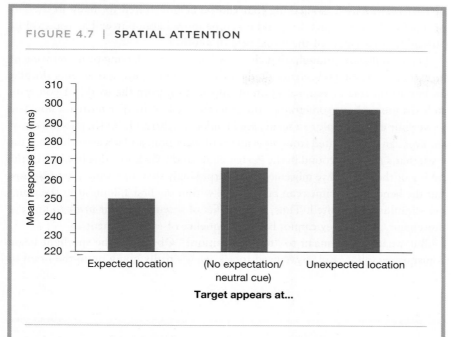

FIGURE 4.7 | SPATIAL ATTENTION

In the Posner et al. (1980) study, participants simply had to press a button as soon as they saw the target. If participants knew where the target would appear, they were slightly faster (although the procedure prevented them from moving their eyes to this target location). If, however, participants were misled about the target's position, their responses were slower than they were when the participants had no expectations at all.

The results show a familiar pattern (Posner et al., 1980): With high-validity priming, the data show a benefit from cues that correctly signal where the upcoming target will appear. The differences between conditions aren't large—a few hundredths of a second—but keep the task in mind: All participants had to do was detect the input. Even with the simplest of tasks, it pays to be prepared (see Figure 4.7).

What about the trials in which participants were misled? RTs in this condition were about 12% slower than those in the neutral condition. Once again, therefore, we're seeing evidence of a limited-capacity system: In order to devote more attention to (say) the left position, you have to devote *less* attention to the right. If the stimulus then shows up on the right, you're less prepared for it—hence the cost of being misled.

Attention as a Spotlight

Studies of spatial attention suggest to some psychologists that visual attention can profitably be compared to a spotlight beam that can "shine" anywhere in the visual field. The "beam" marks the region of space for which you are prepared, so inputs within the beam are processed more efficiently. The beam can be wide or narrowly focused, something that can be demonstrated formally in the lab, or informally (see Figure 4.8), and it can be moved about at will as you explore (attend to) one aspect of the visual field or another.

Let's emphasize, though, that the spotlight idea is referring to movements of *attention*, and not movements of the eyes. Of course, eye movements do play an important role in your selection of information from the world: If you want to learn more about something, you generally look at it. (For more on how you move your eyes to explore a scene, see Henderson, 2012.) Even so, movements of the eyes can be separated from movements of attention, and it's attention, not the eyes, that's moving around in the Posner et al. study. We know this because of the timing of the effects: Eye movements are surprisingly slow, requiring 180 to 200 ms. But the benefits of primes can be detected within the first 150 ms after the priming stimulus is presented. Thus, the benefits of attention occur *prior to* any eye movement, and so they cannot be a consequence of eye movements.

But what does it mean to "move attention?" Obviously, the spotlight beam is just a metaphor, and so we need to ask what's really going on in the brain to

WORKBOOK
DEMONSTRATION 4.3

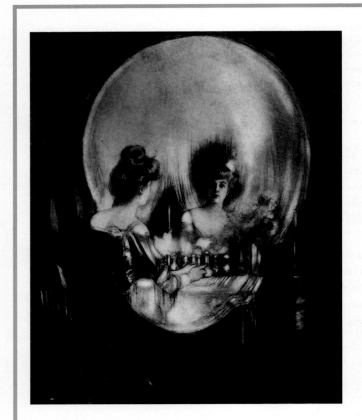

FIGURE 4.8 | **ADJUSTING THE "BEAM" OF ATTENTION**

Charles Allan Gilbert's painting All Is Vanity *can be perceived either as a woman at her dressing table or as a human skull. As you shift from one of these perceptions to the other, you need to adjust the spotlight beam of attention—to a narrow beam to see details (e.g., to see the woman) or to a wider beam to see the whole scene (e.g., to see the skull).*

produce these effects. Evidence suggests that the control of attention actually depends on a network of brain sites in the frontal cortex and parietal cortex (Posner & Rothbart, 2007; see Figure 4.9). Neural connections from these areas send activity to other brain sites (like the visual areas in the occipital cortex) that do the actual analysis of the incoming information. In this way, expectations (based on your goals and the information you've received so far) are supported by one group of brain areas, and are used to modulate activity in other areas directly responsible for handling the input (Corbetta & Shulman, 2002; Hampshire, Duncan, & Owen, 2007; Hon, Epstein, Owen, & Duncan, 2006; Hung, Driver, & Walsh, 2005; Miller & Cohen, 2001). Similarly, activity in the parietal cortex can modulate activity in regions crucial for memory, allowing you to pay attention to remembered events, rather than current inputs (e.g., Cabeza, Ciaramelli, Olson, & Moscovitch, 2008).

Thus there is no spotlight beam. Instead, neural mechanisms are in place that allow you to adjust your sensitivity to certain inputs. This is, of course, entirely in line with the proposal we're developing—namely, that a large part of "paying

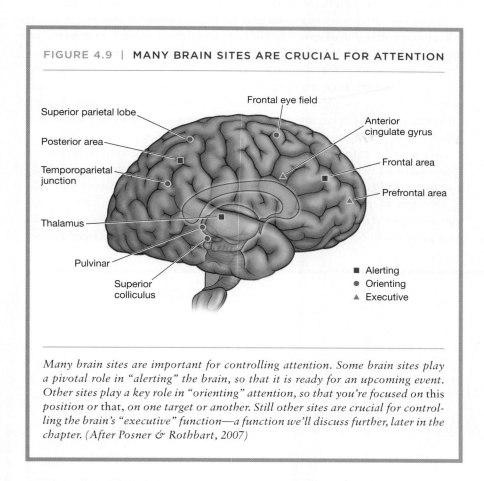

FIGURE 4.9 | MANY BRAIN SITES ARE CRUCIAL FOR ATTENTION

Many brain sites are important for controlling attention. Some brain sites play a pivotal role in "alerting" the brain, so that it is ready for an upcoming event. Other sites play a key role in "orienting" attention, so that you're focused on this position or that, on one target or another. Still other sites are crucial for controlling the brain's "executive" function—a function we'll discuss further, later in the chapter. (After Posner & Rothbart, 2007)

attention" involves priming: For stimuli you don't care about, you don't bother to prime yourself, and so those stimuli fall on unprepared (and unresponsive) detectors. For stimuli you do care about, you do your best to anticipate the input, then use these anticipations to prime the relevant processing channel. This increases your sensitivity to the desired input, which is of course just what you want.

Attending to Objects or Attending to Positions

Although just a metaphor, the spotlight beam is still a useful way to think about attention. (For a broad overview of spatial attention and the spotlight notion, see Cave, 2012; Rensink, 2012; Wright & Ward, 2008.) But the comparison to a spotlight raises a new question. Think about how an actual spotlight works. If, for example, a spotlight shines on a donut, then part of the beam will fall on the donut's hole and so illuminate the plate underneath the donut. Similarly, if the beam isn't aimed quite accurately, it may also illuminate the plate just to the left of the donut. The region illuminated by the beam, in other words, is defined purely in spatial terms: a circle of light at a particular position. That position may or may not line up with the boundaries of the object you're shining the beam on.

Is this how attention works—so that we pay attention to whatever it is that falls in a certain region of space? In this case, we might on some occasions end up paying attention to part of this object, part of that. An alternative is that we pay attention to *objects*, rather than to *positions in space*. To continue the example, the target of our attention might be the donut itself, rather than the donut's location. In that case, the plate just to the left and the bit of plate visible through the donut's hole might be close to our focus, but they aren't part of the attended object and so aren't attended.

Which is the correct view of attention? Do we pay attention to regions in space, whatever the objects (or parts of objects) are that fall in that region? Or do we pay attention to objects? It turns out that each view captures part of the truth.

One line of evidence comes from the study of people who have suffered forms of brain damage (typically in the parietal cortex) that produce extraordinary problems in paying attention. For example, patients with **unilateral neglect**

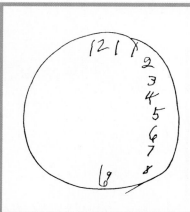

FIGURE 4.10 | **NEGLECT SYNDROME**

A patient with damage to the right parietal cortex was asked to draw a typical clock face. In his drawing, the patient seemed unaware of the left side, but he still recalled that all 12 numbers had to be displayed. The drawing shows how he resolved this dilemma.

syndrome seem to ignore all inputs coming from one side of the body. A patient with neglect syndrome will eat food from only one side of the plate, will wash only half of his or her face, and will fail to locate sought-for objects if they're on the neglected side (see Figure 4.10; Logie, 2012; Sieroff, Pollatsek, & Posner, 1988). This syndrome usually results from damage to the *right* parietal lobe, and so the neglect is for the *left* side of space. (Remember the brain's contralateral organization; see Chapter 2.) Thus, in the laboratory, neglect patients will read only the right half of words shown to them; that is, they will read "pigpen" as "pen," "parties" as "ties," and so on. If asked to cross out all the *E*s on a page, the patient will cross out the *E*s on only the right side of the page.

Taken at face value, these symptoms seem to support a space-based account of attention: The afflicted patient seems insensitive to all objects within a spatially defined region—namely, everything to the left of his current focus. If an object falls half within the region and half outside of it, then the spatially defined region is what matters, not the object's boundaries. This is clear, for example, in how these patients read words—responding only to the word's right half, apparently oblivious to the word's overall boundaries.

Other evidence, however, demands further theory. In one study, patients with neglect syndrome had to respond to targets that appeared within a barbell-shaped frame (see Figure 4.11). Not surprisingly, they were much more sensitive to the targets appearing within the red circle (on the right) and missed many of the targets appearing in the blue circle (on the left); this result simply confirms the patients' diagnosis. What's crucial, though, is what happened next: While the patients watched, the barbell frame was slowly spun around, so that the red circle, previously on the right, was now on the left, and the blue circle, previously on the left, was now on the right.

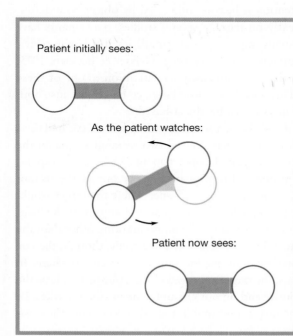

Patient initially sees:

As the patient watches:

Patient now sees:

FIGURE 4.11 | SPACE-BASED OR OBJECT-BASED ATTENTION?

Patients with unilateral neglect syndrome were much more sensitive to targets appearing within the red circle (on the right) and missed many of the targets appearing within the blue circle (on the left); this observation simply confirms their clinical diagnosis. Then, as the patients watched, the "barbell" frame rotated, so that now the red circle was on the left and the blue circle was on the right. After this rotation, participants were still more sensitive to targets in the red circle (now on the left), apparently focusing on this attended object even though it had moved into their "neglected" side.

What should we expect in this situation? If the patients consistently neglect a region of space, they should now be more sensitive to the (right-side) blue circle. A different possibility is more complicated: Perhaps these patients have a powerful bias to attend to the right side, and so initially they attend to the red circle. Once they have "locked in" to this circle, however, it's the object, and not the position in space, that defines their focus of attention. According to this view, if the barbell form rotates, they will continue attending to the red circle (this is, after all, the focus of their attention), even though it now appears on their "neglected" side. This prediction turns out to be correct: When the barbell rotates, the patients' focus of attention seems to rotate with it (Behrmann & Tipper, 1999).

To describe these patients, therefore, we need a two-part account. First, the symptoms of neglect syndrome plainly reveal a spatially defined bias: These patients neglect half of space. But, second, once attention is directed toward a target, it's the target itself that defines the focus of attention; if the target moves, the focus moves with it. In this way, the focus of attention is object-based, not space-based. (For more on these issues, and on some of the intriguing complications in neglect syndrome, see Chen & Cave, 2006; Logie & Della Salla, 2005; Richard, Lee, & Vecera, 2008.)

And it's not just people with brain damage who show this complex pattern: People with intact brains also show a mix of space-based and object-based attention. We've already seen evidence for the spatial base: The Posner et al. (1980) study and many results like it show that participants can focus on a particular region of space in preparation for a stimulus. In this situation, the stimulus has not yet appeared; there is no object to focus on. Therefore, the attention must be spatially defined.

In other cases, though, attention is heavily influenced by object boundaries. For example, we mentioned early on that, in several studies, participants have been shown displays with visually superimposed stimuli, as if a single television set were showing two channels at the same time (Neisser & Becklen, 1975; Simons & Chabris, 1999). Participants can easily pay attention to one of these stimuli and ignore the other. This selection cannot be space-based (because both stimuli are in the same place) and so must be object-based.

Similarly, Egly, Driver, and Rafal (1994; also Marino & Scholl, 2005) had their participants look at a computer screen that showed two rectangles, one on the left side of the screen and one on the right. The participants' task was to respond as soon as they saw a target at one end (top or bottom) of one of the rectangles. In the majority of trials, a cue signaled in advance where the target would appear—so that, let's say, the cue signaled the target would appear at the location marked 1 in Figure 4.12. (There was no "1," and no marking other than the briefly presented cue, in the actual experiment.) In some trials, though, the cue was misleading: It signaled one location but the target appeared elsewhere. In some of these (misleading) trials, the target appeared in the same rectangle as the cue, but at the rectangle's opposite end (in our example, the position marked 2); in other (misleading) trials, the target appeared in the other rectangle (the position marked 3).

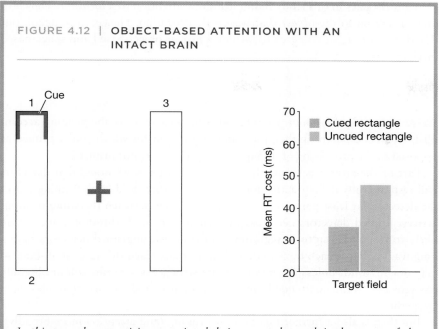

FIGURE 4.12 | OBJECT-BASED ATTENTION WITH AN
INTACT BRAIN

1

Cue

3

2

Mean RT cost (ms)

70
60
50
40
30
20

- Cued rectangle
- Uncued rectangle

Target field

In this procedure, participants pointed their eyes at the mark in the center of the screen; they then responded as rapidly as they could when the target arrived. However, they were slower if they'd been cued for one position (let's say: position 1) but the target—unexpectedly—appeared at the other end of the cued rectangle (position 2). But they were even slower if the target (unexpectedly) appeared in the uncued *rectangle. This condition produced a greater "cost." See the text for procedural details. (After Egly, Driver, & Rafal, 1994)*

Not surprisingly, participants were fastest when the cue accurately signaled where the target would be; this observation echoes other results we've already discussed. But what happened when the cue was misleading? Before describing the result, let's emphasize that the display was set up so that the *distance* between positions 1 and 2 was the same as the distance between positions 1 and 3. Therefore, if attention is governed by spatial position, then it won't matter if you expect position 1 but get position 2, or if you expect position 1 but get position 3. In either case, your "spotlight's focus" is off by the same amount.

Things will be different, though, if attention is governed by object boundaries, and not distance. If you expect position 1 and get position 2, you've been misled, but at least you're focusing on the proper rectangle. That's better than focusing on the wrong rectangle altogether!

The results favor the object-based account: Continuing our example, if the cue indicated that the target would appear at position 1 but instead it appeared at position 2, this bit of misdirection slowed the participants a bit—and so there was a "cost" (of about 35 ms) to being misled. But the cost was larger if the cue indicated a target would be at position 1, and instead it appeared at position 3. In this case, the misdirection slowed participants down by roughly 50 ms.

Thus the cues in this study didn't just draw attention to a *location*. They also drew attention to the *object* that was in that location. Hence, once again, our description of attention needs to include a mix of object-based and space-based mechanisms.

Feature Binding

We've now said a lot about priming, but what exactly does the priming accomplish? What's different in the processing of an input for which you're primed as opposed to the processing of an input for which you're not primed?

Part of the answer is straightforward: In Chapter 3, we noted that detectors will respond only if their activation rises to their threshold level. Priming moves the detectors at least part way to this level. Therefore, when the stimulus input arrives, primed detectors need less of a change to reach threshold, and so are likely to respond even to a weak input. In contrast, unprimed detectors have a long way to go to reach threshold, and so may not reach this level at all (and so may not respond) unless the input is quite strong. As a result, you are literally less sensitive to the unattended (unprimed) inputs—and so you often miss them altogether.

But there's also a further function for priming (and attention more broadly). In Chapter 2, we emphasized that different analyses of the input all go on in parallel. In other words, you figure out the color of the object in front of you at the same time that you figure out its shape and its position. A separate step is then needed to put these elements together, so that you perceive a single, unified object. In other words, you need to solve the *binding problem,* so that you don't just perceive orange + round + close by + moving, but instead see the basketball in its trajectory toward you.

Attention plays a key role in solving the binding problem. In Chapter 2 we mentioned that, if we overload attention (by giving participants some other task to perform while they're perceiving our displays), the participants often make *errors* in binding. Thus, we might show them a red triangle and blue circle, and yet the participants report seeing a blue triangle and a red circle. In other words, these distracted participants correctly catalogue the features that are in view, but, with attention diverted to another task, they fail to bundle the features the right way.

Further evidence comes from *visual search tasks*. We discussed these tasks in Chapter 3, when we mentioned that it's easy to search through a set of stimuli looking for a target defined by a single feature—finding a red object, for example, in a crowd of greens, or finding a round shape in a group of triangles. This was part of the evidence that *features* really do have priority in your perception.

The role of attention, however, comes into view when we consider the impact of *set size*. In visual search, set size refers to how many stimuli the participants have to search through in order to find the target. Thus, with a set size of four, the target appears within a cluster of four stimuli (target plus three irrelevant stimuli), and participants have to find the target within this group. With a set size of eight, the target appears within a cluster of eight stimuli. And so on.

When searching for a target defined by a single feature, set size has little effect. In this case, participants can search through six stimuli about as fast as they can search through two or three. Indeed, it seems wrong to use the word "search" in this setting; instead, the target seems to "pop out" from the display, with no effort (and little time) spent in hunting for it.

In contrast, set size has a large effect when searching for a target defined in terms of a *combination* of features. Imagine, for example, that you're looking at a computer screen, and some of the lines in view are red and some are green. Some of the lines in view are horizontal, and some are vertical. But there's just one line that's red *and* horizontal, and it's your job to find it. In this case, the time you'll need depends on set size, and, to put the matter simply, the larger the crowd to be searched through, the longer it takes.

To understand these results, imagine two hypothetical participants, both hunting for the combination red + horizontal. One (shown in Figure 4.13A) is trying to take in the whole display. He'll be able to quickly catalogue all the features that are in view (because he's looking at all the inputs simultaneously), but he'll also fail in his search for the red + horizontal combination: His catalogue of features tells him that both redness and horizontality are present, but the catalogue doesn't help him in figuring out if these features are linked or not. The observer in Figure 4.13B, in contrast, has focused his mental spotlight and so is carefully looking at just one stimulus at a time. This process is slower, because he'll have to examine the stimuli one by one, and therefore this observer will certainly be influenced by set size. But this focusing of attention gives the participant the information he needs: If, at any moment, he's only analyzing one item, he can be sure that the features he's detecting are all coming from that item. That tells him directly which features are linked to each other, and, for this task (and for many other purposes as well), that's the key. (For the "classic" statement of these ideas, see Treisman & Gelade, 1980; for a more modern take, see Rensink, 2012.)

Now let's put these pieces together. Expectation-based priming, by its very nature, is selective: You prime the detectors for just one location, or just one type of feature, and this creates a processing advantage for stimuli in that location, or stimuli with that feature. Returning to our earlier metaphor, priming shines the spotlight of attention on just one stimulus. That will often slow you down (because you won't pick up information from other stimuli, and so you'll need to turn to them later). But this selectivity gives you a substantial benefit: You've primed just one stimulus, and so you're receiving information from just one stimulus. Thus there's no risk of confusion about where the information is coming from, and so you can be sure that all the information you're picking up at a particular moment (the redness, and the orientation, and the size) is linked. In this way, the selectivity that's built into priming helps you in solving the binding problem.

FIGURE 4.13 | THE COSTS AND BENEFITS OF SELECTION

With attention aimed...

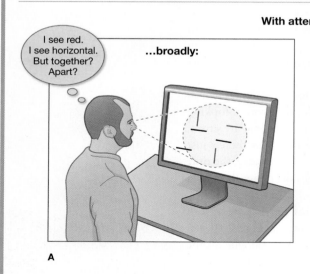

A

B

Focusing your attention involves a trade-off: If you focus your attention broadly, you can take in many inputs at once, and this is faster (because you don't have to search through the items one by one). But, since you're taking in multiple inputs simultaneously, you may not know which feature belongs with which. In contrast, if you focus your attention narrowly, you'll be slower in your search (because now you do have to search item by item), but, with information coming from just one input, you'll know how the features are combined.

Perceiving and the Limits on Cognitive Capacity: An Interim Summary

Our account is growing complex, so let's pause to take stock of where we are. At the broadest level, we've suggested that two different mechanisms are involved in selective attention. One mechanism serves to *inhibit*, or block out, the processing of *unwanted* inputs; this is, in effect, a mechanism for "ignoring" inputs in which you have no interest. A second mechanism *facilitates* the processing of *desired* inputs. This is a mechanism for "paying attention."

We've also seen, though, that the mechanism for paying attention has several parts: You're primed for some stimuli simply because you've encountered them often in the past. For other stimuli, if you know the target's identity in advance, you can prime the relevant detectors. If you know only *where* the target will appear, you can prime detectors for the appropriate region of space; then, once you locate the object in that region, and learn a bit about it, you can prime detectors appropriate for that object.

Moreover, there's some flexibility in *when* the selection takes place. In some circumstances, the perceiver makes an early selection of the desired input, so that the unattended input receives relatively little processing. In other circumstances, the unattended input receives a fuller analysis—even if that input never penetrates into the perceiver's conscious awareness.

And, finally, we've also seen that this selection accomplishes several things: Because of priming, you're more sensitive to the inputs you're interested in. Because you're *not* primed for irrelevant stimuli, you are *less* sensitive to them—and so less likely to be distracted. And because the priming is selective in this way, you end up receiving input from just one stimulus at a time. This diminishes the risk of confusion about where you're getting your information from, and so helps with the binding problem.

In light of all these points, it's best not to think of the term "attention" as referring to a particular process or a particular mechanism. Instead, we need to think of paying attention as an *achievement*, something that you are able to do. Like many other achievements (e.g., doing well in school, staying healthy, earning a good salary), paying attention involves many elements. The exact set of elements varies from occasion to occasion. Sometimes a strong distractor is on the scene, making it essential that you inhibit your response to that distractor. Sometimes no distractors are in view, so inhibition plays a smaller role. Sometimes you know in advance what the stimulus will be, so you can prime just the right detectors. Sometimes stimuli are less predictable, so your priming must be more diffuse. In all cases, multiple steps are needed to ensure that you end up aware of the stimuli you're interested in, and not pulled off track by irrelevant inputs.

Divided Attention

So far in this chapter, we've been emphasizing situations in which you want to focus on a single input. If other tasks and other stimuli are on the scene, they are mere distractors. Our concern, therefore, has been on how you manage to select just the desired information, while avoiding irrelevant distraction.

There are circumstances, however, in which you want to do multiple things at once, in which you want to divide your attention among various tasks or various inputs. In the last decade or so, people have referred to this as "multitasking." Psychologists, in contrast, use the term **divided attention**—the effort to "divide" your focus between multiple tasks or multiple inputs at the same time.

Sometimes, divided attention is easy. For example, almost anyone can walk and sing simultaneously; many people like to knit while they're holding a conversation or listening to a lecture. It's far harder, though, to do your calculus homework while listening to the lecture; and trying to get your reading done while watching TV is surely a bad bet. What lies behind this pattern? Why are some combinations difficult, while others are easy?

Our first step toward answering these questions is already in view. We've proposed that perceiving requires resources that are in short supply; the same is presumably true for other mental tasks—remembering, reasoning, problem

CAESAR THE MULTITASKER

Some writers lament the hectic pace at which we live our lives, and view this as a sad fact about the pressured reality of the modern world. But were things that different in earlier times? More than 2,000 years ago, Julius Caesar was praised for his ability to multitask. (That term is new, but the capacity is not.) According to the Roman historian Suetonius, Caesar could write, dictate letters, and read at the same time. Even on the most important subjects, he could dictate four letters at once, and, if he had nothing else to do, as many as seven letters at once.

solving. They, too, require resources, and without these resources, these processes cannot go forward. What are these resources? The answer includes a mix of things: certain mechanisms that do specific jobs, certain types of memory that hold onto information while you're working on it, energy supplies to keep the mental machinery going, and more. No matter what the resources are, though, a task will be possible only if you have the needed resources—just as a dressmaker can produce a dress only if he has the raw materials, the tools, the time needed, the energy to run the sewing machine, and so on.

All of this leads to a straightforward proposal: You can perform concurrent tasks only if you have the resources needed for both. If the two tasks, when combined, require more resources than you've got, divided attention will fail.

The Specificity of Resources

We need to be more specific, though, about how this competition for "mental resources" unfolds. Imagine two relatively similar tasks—say, reading a book and listening to a lecture. Both of these tasks involve thinking about, and using, language, and so it seems plausible that these tasks will have similar resource requirements. As a result, if you try to do these tasks at the same time, they're likely to *compete* for resources, since language-related resources in use for one of the tasks won't be available for the other task. On this basis, this sort of multitasking will be difficult.

Now think about two very different tasks, such as the example we mentioned earlier: *knitting* and listening to a lecture. These tasks are likely to have very different resource requirements, and, on that basis, won't interfere with each other: Even if all of your language-related resources are in use for the lecture, this won't matter for knitting, because it's not a language-based task.

In short, the prediction here is that divided attention will be easier if the simultaneous tasks are very different from each other, because, again, different tasks are likely to have distinct resource requirements. Thus, resources consumed by Task 1 won't be needed for Task 2, and so it doesn't matter for Task 2 that these resources are tied up in another endeavor. In settings like this, the tasks won't compete for resources, and so they won't interfere with each other.

Is this the pattern of the research data? In an early study by Allport, Antonis, and Reynolds (1972), participants heard a list of words presented through headphones into one ear, and their task was to shadow these words. At the same time, they were also presented with a second list. No immediate response was required to this second list, but later on, memory was tested for these items. In one condition, the second list (the memory items) consisted of words presented into the other ear, so the participants were hearing (and shadowing) a list of words in one ear while simultaneously hearing the memory list in the other. In a second condition, the memory items were presented visually. That is, while the participants were shadowing one list of words, they were also seeing, on a screen before them, a different list of words. Finally, in a third condition, the memory items consisted of pictures, also presented on a screen.

These three conditions have the same requirements—namely, shadowing one list while memorizing another. But the first condition (hear words + hear words) involves very similar tasks; the second condition (hear words + see words) involves less similar tasks; the third condition (hear words + see pictures), even less similar tasks. On the logic we've discussed, we should expect the most interference in the first condition, the least in the third. And that is what the data show (see Figure 4.14).

The Generality of Resources

Thus, task similarity matters for divided attention—but is not the whole story. If it were, then we'd observe less and less interference as we consider tasks further and further apart. Eventually, we'd find tasks that were so different from each other that we'd observe *no* interference between them. But that's not the pattern of the evidence.

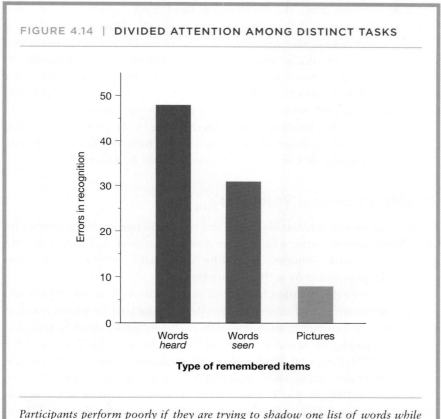

FIGURE 4.14 | DIVIDED ATTENTION AMONG DISTINCT TASKS

Participants perform poorly if they are trying to shadow one list of words while hearing *other words. They do somewhat better if shadowing while* seeing *other* words. *They do better still if shadowing while* seeing pictures. *In general, the greater the difference between two tasks, the easier it will be to combine the tasks. (After Allport, Antonis, & Reynolds, 1972)*

CELL-PHONE DANGERS FOR PEDESTRIANS

It's not just driving that's disrupted by cell-phone use. Pedestrians engaged in phone conversations tend to walk more slowly and more erratically, change directions more often, and are less likely to check traffic carefully before they cross a street. They're also less likely to notice things along their path: In one study, researchers observed pedestrians walking across a public square. If the pedestrian was walking with a friend (and so engaged in a "live" conversation), there was a 71% chance the pedestrian would notice the unicycling clown, just off the pedestrian's path. If the pedestrian was instead on the phone (and thus engaged in a telephonic conversation), the person had only a 25% chance of detecting the clown. (Hyman, Boss, Wise, McKenzie, & Caggiano, 2010)

Consider a situation that touches many of our lives: talking on a cell phone while driving. When you're on the phone, the main stimulus information comes into your ear, and your primary response is by talking. When you're driving, the main stimulation comes into your eyes, and your primary response involves control of your hands on the steering wheel and your feet on the pedals. For the phone conversation, you're relying on language skills. For driving, you need spatial skills. Overall, it looks like there's little overlap in the specific demands of these two tasks, and so little chance that the tasks will compete for resources.

It turns out, however, that driving and cell-phone use do interfere with each other; this is reflected, for example, in the fact that phone use has been implicated in many automobile accidents (Lamble, Kauranen, Laakso, & Summala, 1999). Even with a hands-free phone, drivers engaged in cell-phone conversations are more likely to be involved in accidents, more likely to overlook traffic signals, and slower to hit the brakes when they need to (see Figure 4.15; Kunar, Carter, Cohen, & Horowitz, 2008; Levy & Pashler, 2008; Strayer & Drews, 2007; Strayer, Drews, & Johnston, 2003; also see Spence & Read, 2003).

We should mention, though, that the data pattern is different if the driver is instead talking to a *passenger* in the car, rather than using the phone. Conversations with passengers seem to cause little interference with driving (Drews, Pasupathi, & Strayer, 2008), and the reason is simple: If the traffic becomes complicated, or the driver has to perform some tricky maneuver, the passenger can see this—either by looking out of the car's window or by detecting the driver's tension and focus. In these cases, passengers helpfully slow down their side of the conversation, which takes the load off of the driver, allowing the driver to focus on the road! (Hyman, Boss, Wise, McKenzie, & Caggiano, 2010; Nasar, Hecht & Wener, 2008.)

Identifying General Resources

Apparently, tasks as different as driving and talking compete with each other for some mental resource; otherwise, we have no explanation of the interference. But what is this resource—evidently needed for verbal tasks and spatial ones, tasks with visual inputs and tasks with auditory inputs?

The answer to this question has several parts, because there are actually several relevant resources, each contributing to the limits on how (or whether) we can divide attention between tasks. Some authors, for example, describe resources that serve (roughly) as an energy supply, drawn on by all tasks (Eysenck, 1982; Kahneman, 1973; Lavie et al. 2009). Other authors describe resources best thought of as "mental tools" rather than some sort of mental "energy supply" (Allport, 1989; Baddeley, 1986; Bourke & Duncan, 2005; Dehaene, Sergent & Changeux, 2003; Johnson-Laird, 1988; Just, Carpenter, & Hemphill, 1996; Norman & Shallice, 1986; Ruthruff et al., 2009; Vergaujwe, Barrouillet, & Camos, 2010; for some *reservations* about the resource idea, however, see Franconeri, 2011). One of these tools, for example, is a mental mechanism that seems to be required for *selecting* and *initiating* responses, including both physical responses and mental ones (such as the beginning of a memory search or the making of a decision; McCann &

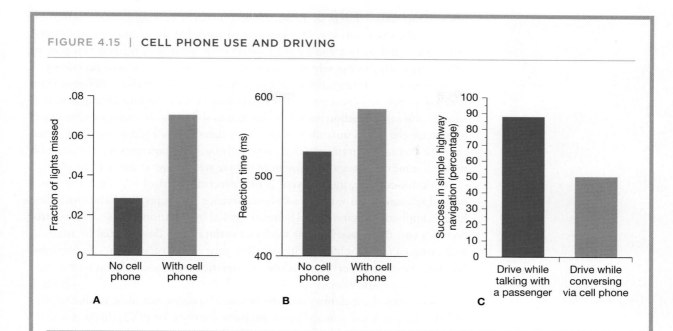

FIGURE 4.15 | CELL PHONE USE AND DRIVING

Many studies show that driving performance is impaired when the driver is on the phone (whether it's a hand-held or hands-free phone). (A) On the phone, drivers are more likely to miss a red light, and (B) certainly slower in responding to a red light. (After Strayer & Johnston, 2001) (C) Disruption is not observed, however, if the driver is conversing with a passenger, rather than on the phone. That's because the passenger is likely to adjust her conversation to accommodate changes in driving—such as not speaking while the driver is navigating an obstruction.

Johnston, 1992; Pashler, 1991, 1992, 1996; Pashler & Johnston, 1989; but also see Tombu & Jolicoeur, 2003). This **response selector** presumably plays a key role in coordinating the timing of your various activities and thus serves as a mental traffic cop, controlling which processes go forward at any moment in time.

Executive Control

A different mental resource is needed for many tasks: namely, the mind's "executive control." This is the mechanism that sets goals and priorities, chooses strategies, and, in general, directs the function of many cognitive processes (Baddeley, 1986, 1996; Brown, Reynolds & Braver, 2007; Duncan et al., 2008; Gilbert & Shallice, 2002; Kane, Conway, Hambrick & Engle, 2007; Miyake & Friedman, 2012; Vandierendonck, Liefooghe, & Verbruggen, 2010; we'll have more to say about executive control in Chapters 5 and 12).

Theorists disagree about the details of how the "executive" functions. As an illustration, though, let's look at one of the proposals. The idea here begins with the observation that much of your day-to-day functioning is guided by habit and prior associations (Engle & Kane, 2004; Unsworth & Engle, 2007). After all, many of the situations you find yourself in resemble those you've encountered in the past, and so you don't need to start from scratch in figuring out how to behave. Instead, you can rely on responses or strategies you've used previously.

In some cases, though, you want to behave in a fashion that's different from how you've behaved in the past—perhaps because your goals have changed, or perhaps because the situation itself has changed in some way. In such cases, you need to overrule the action or strategy supplied by memory. As a related problem, some circumstances contain triggers that powerfully evoke certain responses. If you wish to make some *other* response, you need to take steps to avoid the obvious trap.

With this context, the proposal is that executive control is a mental resource needed whenever you want to avoid interference from previous habit (including habits supplied by memory, and habits triggered by situational cues). This control provides two functions: First, it works to maintain the desired goal in mind, so that this goal (and not habit) will prevail in your choice of strategies and actions. Second, the control serves to *inhibit* automatic responses, helping ensure that these responses won't occur.

Evidence for these claims comes from several sources, including studies of people who have suffered damage to the prefrontal cortex (or PFC); this is (roughly) the brain area right behind your eyes. The PFC seems to play a crucial role in "goal maintenance"—the process of keeping your current goal in mind (Aron, 2008; Courtney, Petit, Maisog, Ungerleider, & Haxby, 1998; Huey, Krueger, & Grafman, 2006; Stuss & Knight, 2002). What happens, therefore, when someone has suffered damage to the PFC? Remarkably, people with this damage (including Phineas Gage, whom we met in Chapter 2, pp. 35–36) can often lead relatively normal lives; this is because, in their day-to-day behavior, they can usually rely on habit or routine, or can simply respond to prominent cues in their environment. With appropriate tests, though, we can reveal the disruption that results from frontal lobe damage. For example, in one commonly used task, patients with frontal lesions are asked to sort a deck of cards into two piles. At the start, the patients have to sort the cards according to color; later they need to switch strategies and sort according to the shapes shown on the cards. The patients have enormous difficulty making this shift and continue to sort by color, even though the experimenter tells them again and again that they're placing the cards onto the wrong piles (Goldman-Rakic, 1998). This is referred to as a **perseveration error,** a tendency to produce the same response over and over, even when it's plain that the task requires a change in the response.

These patients also show a pattern of **goal neglect**—failing to organize their behavior in a way that moves them toward their goals. For example, one patient was asked to copy Figure 4.16A; the patient produced the drawing shown in Figure 4.16B. The copy preserves features of the original, but close inspection reveals that the patient drew the copy with no particular plan in mind. The large rectangle that defines the shape was never drawn; the diagonal lines that organize the figure were drawn in a piecemeal fashion. Many details are correctly reproduced but were not drawn in any sort of order; instead, these details were added whenever they happened to catch the patient's attention (Kimberg, D'Esposito, & Farah, 1998).

Another patient, asked to copy the same figure, produced the drawing shown in Figure 4.16C. This patient started to draw the figure in a normal way, but then she got swept up in her own artistic impulses, adding stars and a smiley face (Kimberg et al., 1998). (For more on the complex topic of executive control, see Duncan et al., 2008; Gilbert & Shallice, 2002; Kane & Engle, 2003; Kimberg et al., 1998; Logie & Della Salla, 2005; Ranganath & Blumenfeld, 2005; Stuss & Levine, 2002.)

Divided Attention: An Interim Summary

Let's pause once again to take stock of where we are. Our consideration of *selective* attention drove us toward a several-part account, with one mechanism apparently serving to block out unwanted distractors and a number of other mechanisms serving to promote the processing of interesting stimuli. Now, in our discussion of *divided* attention, we again seem to require several elements in our theory. Interference between tasks is plainly increased if the tasks are similar to each other, presumably because similar tasks overlap in their processing requirements and so make competing demands on mental resources that are specialized for that sort of task.

But interference can also be demonstrated with tasks that are entirely different from each other—such as driving and talking on a cell phone. Thus, our account needs to include resources that are general enough in their use that they're drawn on by almost any task. We've noted that there are, in fact, likely to be several of these general resources: an energy supply needed for mental tasks; a response

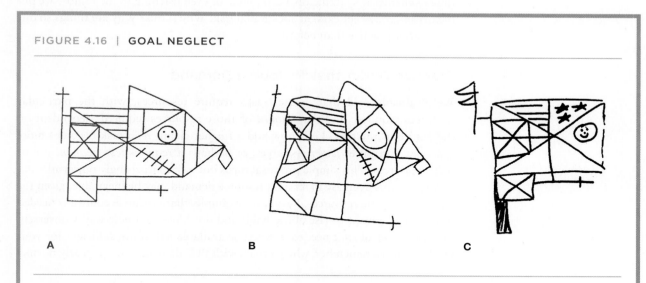

FIGURE 4.16 | GOAL NEGLECT

A   **B**   **C**

Patients who had suffered damage to the prefrontal cortex were asked to copy the drawing in A. One patient's attempt is shown in B; the drawing is reasonably accurate but seems to have been drawn with no overall plan (and so, for example, the large rectangle in the original, and the main diagonals, were created piecemeal, rather then being used to organize the drawing). Another patient's attempt is shown in C; this patient started to re-create the drawing, but then got swept up in her own artistic impulses.

selector needed whenever a task involves the launching of successive steps; executive control, needed whenever a task requires "rising above" prior habits and tendencies; and probably others as well. No matter what the resource, though, the key principle will be the same: Tasks will interfere with each other if their combined demand for a resource is greater than the amount available—that is, if the demand exceeds the supply.

Practice

We still need to add a complication to our account—namely, the effect of *practice*. To introduce the issue, let's return once again to the example of talking on a cell phone while driving. For a skilled driver, this task combination is easy if the driving is straightforward and the conversation is relatively simple. Indeed, it's plain that many drivers manage this pair of simultaneous tasks every day, without causing an endless string of horrible accidents. Things fall apart, though, the moment the conversation becomes complex or the driving becomes challenging; that's when these two tasks interfere with each other: Engaged in deep conversation, the driver misses a turn; while maneuvering through the intersection, the driver suddenly stops talking.[1]

Let's emphasize, though, that these points only apply to a skilled driver. For a *novice* driver, the task of driving is difficult all by itself, even on a straight road with no traffic. If, therefore, we ask the novice to do anything else at the same time—whether it's talking on a cell phone or even listening to the radio—we put the driver (and other cars) at substantial risk. Why is this? Why are things so different after practice than before?

Practice Diminishes Resource Demand

We've already said that mental tasks require resources, with the particular resources required, and the *amount* of those resources required, dependent on the nature of the task. Let's now add a further claim: As a task becomes more practiced it requires *fewer* resources, or perhaps it requires *less frequent* use of these resources. This simple proposal turns out to be surprisingly powerful.

In fact, this decrease in a task's resource demand may be inevitable, given the function of some resources. Recall, for example, that executive control is needed whenever you want to rise above habit and do things in a new way. Conversely, executive control *isn't* needed when your available habits are sufficient for your needs. (This is, remember, why patients with PFC damage can live nearly normal

---

1. As a practical note, let's emphasize that challenges like a sudden increase in the demands of driving, or a sudden shift in the conversation's complexity, can arise without warning. As a result, you never know when the conversation and driving will demand more resources than you've got (and so cause interference), and this is why most psychologists would recommend that you never talk on the cell phone while driving. If you follow that advice, then there's no risk that interference might unexpectedly arise.

lives—often our habits do serve us well.) But, of course, the option of relying on habits is only possible if you *have* habits, and, early in practice, when a task is brand new, you haven't formed any relevant habits yet, and so you have no habits to fall back on. As a result, executive control is needed all the time. Once you've done the task over and over, though, you can acquire a repertoire of suitable habits, and, as you rely on them more and more, the demand for executive control decreases.

Roughly the same logic applies to a different mental resource—the response selector. Early in practice, you need the selector to choose and then launch each step in your performance. After some practice, though, you know in advance what the steps will be, so you can approach the task with the entire sequence in mind and use the response selector just once: to launch the whole sequence. Thus, there's no need for a series of choices ("What do I do next?") and, with that, no need for a series of launches, one for each of the task's steps. Instead, you simply do a single memory lookup ("What was the sequence of steps I used last time?"), and the response selector is needed to launch this overall routine. Once that's done, you can run off the routine with no further need for the selector.

Based on this logic, it's sensible that, with practice, tasks make smaller demands on mental resources. These resources, it seems, are intimately tied up with the *control* of mental performance—making plans for what to do, launching each step, and so on. Once a routine is established, there's less need for this control and, with that, less need for the resources.

Of course, we've already argued that tasks will interfere with each other if their *combined resource demand* is greater than the amount of resources available. An obvious implication of this point is that it will be easier to combine two tasks if the resource demand of each task is low. We can now add the further idea that the resource demand will be lower after practice than before. Thus, it's no surprise that practice makes divided attention easier—allowing the skilled driver to continue chatting with her passenger as they cruise down the highway, even though this combination is hopelessly difficult for the novice driver.

Why Does Practice Improve Performance?

What about the other obvious effect of practice—namely, the fact that practice makes performance *better*? After all, there's no question that a pianist plays more beautifully after rehearsing a piece for a while, and that athletes play more skillfully after practice. Similar observations can be made for mental skills, such as solving problems, reading, or doing calculations. These, too, are more successful after practice than before. What produces this improvement?

The answer to this question has several parts, but one part hinges, once again, on the broad idea of resource availability. Let's start with the fact that most tasks that you do have multiple components, and you'll succeed in the tasks only if you can handle all the components. To continue our example of driving, a skilled driver needs to keep track of his steering *and* how fast he's going *and* how far he is from the car in front of him, and so on. If the driver neglects any of these elements, the result could be disastrous.

Cast in these terms, it appears that "divided attention" isn't just an issue for, say, people who want to knit while holding a conversation, or people who want to surf the web while listening to a lecture. Instead, divided attention can be an issue even for (what seems to be) a single task—because you need to divide your attention among the elements of the task. And that's where practice comes in. Early in practice, each part of a task requires resources, and that makes it impossible to think about all the tasks' parts at once. Thus, the new driver has to focus all his attention on steering, and, as a result, remains oblivious to the other elements of driving. With just a bit of practice, though, the resource demand of steering is diminished, allowing the novice to think about other parts of the overall task—such as controlling speed. Likewise, a novice tennis player getting ready to serve the ball must focus all her resources on how she tosses the ball upward. As a consequence, the player won't have any resources left over for other aspects of the serve—such as choosing where to aim. With practice, though, the tennis player can devote fewer resources to the chore of tossing the ball, freeing up resources so that she can start thinking about other dimensions of the game.

In a nutshell, then, practice decreases resource demand, and this makes divided attention easier. As a result, you can pay attention to, and coordinate, multiple aspects of your task, and this leads immediately to an improvement in your performance. Indeed, with more practice, the decrease in resource demand makes it possible for you to consider elements of the task that were, at the outset, entirely out of your reach. Thus, for an advanced tennis player, all of the game's elements are so well-practiced, and so easy, that she can start thinking about other, higher-order aspects of the game: What strategy does she want to develop as the game unfolds? Are there hints in her opponent's moves that signal *her* strategy? It's attention to these broader elements—made possible only because resources are no longer demanded by the lower-level steps—that allows the skilled tennis player (or driver, or chess player, or mathematician) to reach virtuoso levels of performance. (For more on expert performance, see Chapter 12, also Ericsson & Towne, 2012.)

Automaticity

We've now described why practice makes performance of a task *easier* and *better*. But practice also has another effect: It can make a task *difficult to control*.

In fact, this point flows naturally from claims we've already considered: We noted a moment ago that, with practice, you develop habits and routines, and so have less need for executive control. You also develop well-rehearsed sequences of steps, and so you only need the response selector once (to launch the sequence), rather than over and over (to launch each step). For both of these reasons, then, practice diminishes the *need* for moment-by-moment control of a task, and that's helpful. But, by the same logic, practice also undermines the *option* of moment-by-moment control of your performance, and sometimes that's not at all helpful! In other words, practice allows many mental processes to go forward untouched by control mechanisms; these processes are, as a result, uncontrollable.

To capture this idea, psychologists say that tasks that have been heavily practiced can achieve a state of **automaticity**. With this, many psychologists distinguish between **controlled tasks** and **automatic tasks**. Controlled tasks are typically novel (not yet practiced) or are tasks that continually vary in their demands (so that it's not possible for you to develop standardized "routines"). Automatic tasks, in contrast, are typically highly familiar and do not require great flexibility. With some practice, then, you can approach these tasks with a well-rehearsed procedure—a sequence of responses (often triggered by specific stimuli) that have gotten the job done in the past. Of course, this procedure is usually established through practice, but it can also be learned from some good advice or a skilled teacher (cf. Yamaguchi & Proctor, 2011). In any case, once the routine is acquired, the automatic task doesn't need to be supervised or controlled, and so it requires few resources.

There are many advantages associated with automaticity, because (as we've seen) it frees up resources for other chores, and we've discussed how this can improve performance. But automaticity has a downside: Since automatic tasks are not governed by the mind's control mechanisms, they are not controlled, and in some circumstances they can act as if they were "mental reflexes."

A striking example of this lack of control involves an effect known as **Stroop interference**. In the classic demonstration of this effect, study participants were shown a series of words and asked to name aloud the color of the ink used for each word. The trick, though, was that the words themselves were color names. So people might see the word "BLUE" printed in green ink and would have to say "green" out loud, and so on (see Figure 4.17; Stroop, 1935).

WORKBOOK
DEMONSTRATION 4.4

This task turns out to be extremely difficult. There is a strong tendency to read the printed words themselves rather than naming the ink color, and people make many mistakes in this task. Presumably, this reflects the fact that word recognition, especially for college-age adults, is enormously well practiced and, as a consequence, can proceed automatically. This is a condition, therefore, in which mental control should be minimal, and that is certainly consistent with the errors that we observe. (For discussion of the specific mechanisms that produce this interference, see Besner & Stolz, 1999a, 1999b; Durgin, 2000; Engle & Kane, 2004; Jacoby et al., 2003; Kane & Engle, 2003.)

Where Are the Limits?

We are nearing the end of our discussion of attention, and so it again may be useful to summarize where we are. Two simple ideas lie at the heart of our account: First, tasks require resources, and second, you cannot "spend" more resources than you have. These claims are central for almost everything we have said about selective and divided attention.

As we have seen, though, we need to complicate this account in two regards: First, there seem to be different types of resources, and second, the exact resource demand of a task depends on several factors. The nature of the task matters, of course, so that the resources required by a verbal task (e.g., reading) are different from those required by a spatial task (e.g., remembering a shape).

FIGURE 4.17 | STROOP INTERFERENCE

Column A	Column B
ZYP	RED
QLEKF	BLACK
SUWRG	YELLOW
XCIDB	BLUE
WOPR	RED
ZYP	GREEN
QLEKF	YELLOW
XCIDB	BLACK
SUWRG	BLUE
WOPR	BLACK

As rapidly as you can, name out loud the colors of the ink *in Column A. (And so you'll say, "black, green," and so on.) Now do the same for Column B—again, naming out loud the colors of the ink. You will probably find it much easier to do this for Column A, because in Column B you experience interference from the automatic habit of reading the words.*

The novelty of the task and amount of flexibility the task requires also matter. Connected to this, *practice* matters, with well-practiced tasks requiring fewer resources.

What, then, sets the limits on divided attention? When can you do two tasks at the same time, and when not? The answer varies, case by case. If two tasks make competing demands on task-specific resources, the result will be interference. If two tasks make competing demands on task-general resources (the response selector, or executive control), again the result will be interference. In addition, it will be especially difficult to combine tasks that involve similar stimuli— combining two tasks that both involve printed text, for example, or that both involve speech. This is because similar stimuli will demand similar resources, and also because these stimuli can sometimes "blur together," with a danger that you'll lose track of which elements belong in which input ("Was it the man who said 'yes,' or the woman?"; "Was the red dog in the top picture or the bottom?"). This sort of "crosstalk" (leakage of bits of one input into the other input) can itself compromise performance.

In short, it looks like we need a multipart theory of attention, with performance limited by different factors on different occasions. This draws us once more to a claim we made earlier in the chapter: Attention cannot be thought of as a skill, or a mechanism, or a capacity. Instead, attention is an *achievement*—an achievement of performing multiple activities simultaneously, or an achievement of successfully avoiding distraction when you wish to focus on a single task. And, as we have seen, this achievement rests on an intricate base, so that many skills, mechanisms, and capacities contribute to our ability to attend.

Finally, one last point. We have discussed various limits on human performance—that is, limits on how much you can do at any one time. How rigid are these limits? We have discussed the improvements in divided attention that are made possible by practice, but are there boundaries on what practice can accomplish? Can one perhaps gain new mental resources or, more plausibly, find new ways to accomplish a task in order to avoid the bottleneck created by some limited resource? At least some evidence indicates that the answer to these questions may be yes; if so, many of the claims made in this chapter must be understood as being claims about what is *usual*, and not claims about what is *possible* (Hirst, Spelke, Reaves, Caharack, & Neisser, 1980; Spelke, Hirst, & Neisser, 1976). With this, many traditions in the world—Buddhist meditation traditions, for example—claim it is possible to *train* attention so that one has better control over one's mental life; how do these claims fit into the framework we have developed in this chapter? These are issues in need of further exploration, and in truth, what is at stake here is a question about the boundaries on human potential, making these issues of deep interest for future researchers to pursue.

CHAPTER SUMMARY

- People are often oblivious to unattended inputs; they are unable to tell if an unattended auditory input was coherent prose or random words, and they often fail altogether to detect unattended visual inputs, even though such inputs are right in front of the viewer's eyes. However, some aspects of the unattended inputs are detected. For example, people can report on the pitch of the unattended sound and whether it contained human speech or some other sort of noise. Sometimes they can also detect stimuli that are especially meaningful; some people, for example, hear their own name if it is spoken on the unattended channel.

- These results suggest that perception may require the commitment of mental resources, with some of these resources helping to prime the detectors needed for perception. This proposal is supported by studies of inattentional blindness, studies showing that perception is markedly impaired if the perceiver commits no resources to the incoming stimulus information. The proposal is also supported by results showing that you perceive more efficiently when you can anticipate the upcoming stimulus (and so can prime the relevant detectors). In many cases, this anticipation is spatial—if, for example, you know that a stimulus is about to arrive at a particular location. This priming, however, seems to draw on a limited-capacity system, and so priming one stimulus or one position takes away resources that might be spent on priming some other stimulus.

- Your ability to pay attention to certain regions of space has encouraged many researchers to compare attention to a spotlight beam, with the idea that stimuli falling "within the beam" are processed more efficiently. However, this spotlight analogy is potentially misleading. In many circumstances, you do seem to devote attention to identifiable regions of space, no matter what falls within those regions. In other circumstances, though, attention seems to be object-based, not space-based, and so you pay attention to specific objects, not specific positions.

- Perceiving, it seems, requires the commitment of resources, and so do most other mental activities. This provides a ready account of divided attention: It is possible to perform two tasks simultaneously only if the two tasks do not in combination demand more resources than are available. Some of the relevant mental resources are task-general, and so are called on by a wide variety of mental activities. These include the response selector and executive control. Other mental resources are task-specific, required only for tasks of a certain type.

- Divided attention is clearly influenced by practice, and so it is often easier to divide attention between familiar tasks than between unfamiliar tasks. In the extreme, practice may produce automaticity, in which a task seems to require virtually no mental resources but is also difficult to control. One proposal is that automaticity results from the fact that decisions are no longer needed for a well-practiced routine; instead, one can simply run off the entire routine, doing on this occasion just what one did on prior occasions.

The Workbook Connection

See the *Cognition Workbook* for further exploration on paying attention:

- Demonstration 4.1: Shadowing
- Demonstration 4.2: Color-Changing Card Trick
- Demonstration 4.3: The Control of Eye Movements
- Demonstration 4.4: Automaticity and the Stroop Effect
- Research Methods: The Power of Random Assignment
- Cognitive Psychology and Education: ADHD
- Cognitive Psychology and the Law: What Do Eyewitnesses Pay Attention To?
- Cognitive Psychology and the Law: Guiding the Formulation of New Laws

NEED HELP STUDYING?

 wwnorton.com/studyspace

Visit StudySpace to access free review material such as
- Chapter study plans
- Quizzes
- Flashcards, and more

Go to **wwnorton.com/zaps** for these online labs:
- Attentional Blink
- Simon Effect
- Spatial Cueing
- Stroop Effect
- Dichotic Listening

Memory

As we move through our lives, we encounter new facts, gain new skills, and have new experiences. And we are often *changed* by all of this, and so, later on, we know things and can do things that we couldn't know or do before. How do these changes happen? How do we get new information into memory, and then how do we retrieve this information when we need it? And how much trust can we put in this process? Why is it, for example, that we sometimes fail to remember things (including important things)? And why is it that our memories are sometimes *wrong*—so that, in some cases, you remember an event one way, but your friend, who was present at the same event, remembers things differently?

We'll tackle all these issues in this section, and they will lead us to both theoretical claims and practical applications. We'll offer suggestions, for example, about how students should study their class materials, to maximize retention. We'll also discuss how police should question crime witnesses to maximize the quality of information the witnesses provide.

In our discussion, several themes will emerge again and again. One theme concerns the active nature of learning, and we'll discuss the fact that passive exposure to information, with no intellectual engagement, leads to poor memory. From this base, we'll consider why some forms of engagement with to-be-learned material lead to especially good memory but other forms do not.

The active nature of memory will also be central in our discussion of what it means to "remember." Here we'll see that in many cases what seems to be remembering is really after-the-fact reconstruction, and we'll need to consider how this reconstruction proceeds and what it implies for memory accuracy.

A second theme will be equally prominent: the role of memory connections. In Chapter 5 we'll see

that, at its essence, learning involves the creation of connections, and the more connections formed, the better the learning. In Chapter 6 we'll argue that these connections help because they can serve as "retrieval paths" later on—paths that, you hope, will lead you from your memory search's starting point to the information you're trying to recall. As we'll see, this notion has clear implications for when you will remember a previous event and when you won't.

Chapter 7 then explores a different ramification of the connections idea: Memory connections can actually be a source of memory errors. In learning, you create connections that knit together the new material with things you already know. These connections are helpful (because they serve as retrieval paths), but the more connections you create, the harder it will be to keep track of which remembered elements were contained within the episode itself and which are connected to that episode only because you connected them during the learning process. We'll ask what this means for memory accuracy overall, and we'll discuss what you can do to minimize error and to improve the completeness and accuracy of your memory.

CHAPTER FIVE

The Acquisition of Memories and the Working-Memory System

H ow does new information—whether it's a friend's phone number or a fact you hope to memorize for the Bio exam—become established in memory? Are there ways to learn that are particularly effective? And then, once information is in storage, how do you locate it and "reactivate" it later on? And why does search through memory sometimes fail—so that (for example) you're unable to recall a name while taking an exam (but then, to your chagrin, remember the name the moment you leave the exam room)?

In tackling these questions, there is an obvious way to organize our inquiry: Before there can be a memory, you need to gain, or "acquire" some new information. On this basis, **acquisition**—the process of gaining information and placing it into memory—should be our first topic. Then, once you've acquired this information, you need to hold it in memory until the information is needed. We refer to this as the **storage** phase. Finally, you *remember*. In other words, you somehow locate the

- We begin the chapter with a discussion of the broad architecture of memory. We then turn to a closer examination of one component of this architecture: working memory.

- We emphasize the active nature of working memory—activity that is especially evident when we discuss working memory's "central executive," a mental resource that serves to order, organize, and control our mental lives.

- The active nature of memory is also evident in the process of *rehearsal*: Rehearsal is effective only if the person engages the materials in some way; this

is reflected, for example, in the contrast between deep processing (which leads to excellent memory) and mere maintenance rehearsal (which produces virtually no memory benefit).

- Activity during learning appears to establish *memory connections*, which can serve as retrieval routes when it comes time to remember the target material. For complex material, the best way to establish these connections is to seek to understand the material; the better the understanding, the better the memory will be.

information in the vast warehouse that is memory and you bring it into active use; this is called **retrieval**.

This organization seems sensible; it fits, for example, with the way most "electronic memories" (e.g., computers) work. Information ("input") is provided to a computer (the acquisition phase). The information then resides in some dormant form, generally on the hard drive (the storage phase). Finally, the information can be brought back from this dormant form, often via a search process that hunts through the disk (the retrieval phase). And, of course, there's nothing special about a computer here; "low-tech" information storage works the same way. Think about a file drawer: Information is acquired (i.e., filed), rests in this or that folder, and then is retrieved.

Guided by this framework, we'll begin our inquiry by focusing on the acquisition of new memories, leaving discussion of storage and retrieval for later. As it turns out, though, we'll soon find reasons for challenging this overall approach to memory. In discussing acquisition, for example, we might wish to ask: What is good learning? What guarantees that material is firmly recorded in memory? As we will see, evidence indicates that what is good learning depends on how the memory is to be used later on, so that good preparation for one kind of use may be poor preparation for a different kind of use. Claims about acquisition, therefore, must be interwoven with claims about retrieval. These interconnections between acquisition and retrieval will be the central theme of Chapter 6.

In the same way, we cannot separate claims about memory acquisition from claims about memory storage. This is because how you learn (acquisition) depends heavily on what you already know (information in storage). This relationship needs to be explored and explained, and it will provide a recurrent theme in both this chapter and Chapter 7.

With these caveats in view, we'll nonetheless begin by describing the acquisition process. Our approach will be roughly historical. We'll start with a simple model, emphasizing data collected largely in the 1970s. We'll then use this as the framework for examining more recent research, adding refinements to the model as we proceed.

The Route Into Memory

For many years, theorizing in cognitive psychology was guided by a perspective known as **information processing**. Details aside, the notion was that complex mental events such as learning, remembering, and deciding actually involve a large number of discrete steps. These steps occur one by one, each with its own characteristics, and with each providing as its "output" the input to the next step in the sequence.

A lot of the theorizing within this approach focused on the process through which information was perceived and then moved into memory storage—that is, on the process of information acquisition. There was disagreement about the details but reasonable consensus on the bold outline of events. An early version of this model was described by Waugh and Norman (1965); later refinements were added by Atkinson and Shiffrin (1968). The consensus model came to be known as the **modal model**, and Figure 5.1 provides a (somewhat simplified) depiction of this model.

Updating the Modal Model

According to the modal model, information processing involves different kinds of memory. When information first arrives, it is stored briefly in *sensory memory*, which holds onto the input in "raw" sensory form—an *iconic memory* for visual inputs and an *echoic* memory for auditory inputs. A process of selection and interpretation then moves the information into *short-term memory*—the place you hold information while you're working on it. Some of the information is then transferred into *long-term memory*, a much larger and more permanent storage place.

This early conception of memory captured some important truths, but the conception needs to be updated in several ways. As one concern, the idea of "sensory memory" plays a much smaller role in modern theorizing, and so modern discussions of perception (like our discussion in Chapters 2 and 3) often make no mention of this memory. In addition, modern proposals use the term *working memory* rather than short-term memory, to emphasize the *function* of this memory: Ideas or thoughts in this memory are currently activated, currently

FIGURE 5.1 | AN INFORMATION-PROCESSING VIEW OF MEMORY

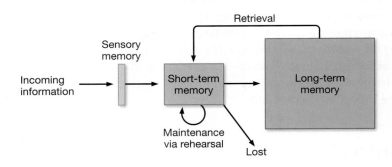

Diagrams like this one depict the flow of information hypothesized by the "modal model." The model captures many important truths, but must be updated in important ways. Current theorizing, for example, emphasizes that short-term memory (now called working memory*) is not a* place *serving as a "loading dock" outside of long-term memory. Instead, working memory is best understood as an* activity, *in ways described in the chapter.*

being thought about, and so they're the ideas you are currently *working on*. **Long-term memory (LTM)**, in contrast, is the vast repository that contains all of your knowledge and all of your beliefs—most of which you happen not to be thinking about (i.e., not working on) at this moment.

The modal model also needs updating in another way: Pictures like the one in Figure 5.1 suggest that working memory is a *storage place*, often described as the "loading dock" just outside of the long-term memory "warehouse." The idea, roughly, is that information has to "pass through" working memory on the way into longer-term storage. Likewise, the picture implies that memory retrieval involves the "movement" of information out of storage and back into working memory.

These ideas played an important role in the development of more modern views. In contemporary theorizing, though, researchers do not conceive of working memory as a "place" at all. Instead, working memory is (as we will see) simply the name we give to a *status*. Thus, when we say that ideas are "in working memory," this simply means that these ideas are currently activated and are currently being worked on by a specific set of operations.

We'll have much more to say about this modern perspective before we're through. It's important to emphasize, though, that the modern perspective also *preserves* some ideas central to the modal model: Specifically, modern theorizing continues to build on several of the modal model's claims about how working memory and long-term memory differ from each other, so let's start by counting through those differences.

First, working memory is limited in size; long-term memory is vast. Indeed, long-term memory *has to be* vast, because it contains all of your knowledge, including specific knowledge (e.g., how many siblings you have) and more general themes (you know that water is wet, that Dublin is in Ireland, that unicorns don't exist). Long-term memory also contains all your knowledge about events, including events early in your life as well as your more recent experiences.

Second, getting information *into* working memory is easy: If you think about some idea or some content, then you are, in effect, "working on" that idea or content, and so this information—*by definition*—is now in your working memory. In contrast, we'll see later in the chapter that getting information into long-term memory often involves some work.

Third, getting information *out of* working memory is also easy: Since (by definition) this memory holds the ideas you are thinking about right now, this information is already available to you. Finding information in long-term memory, on the other hand, can sometimes be effortful and slow, and in some settings it can fail altogether.

Fourth (and finally), the contents of working memory are quite fragile: Working memory, we emphasize, contains the ideas you're thinking about right now. If you shift your thoughts to a new topic, these new ideas will now occupy working memory, pushing out what was there a moment ago. Long-term memory, in contrast, is not linked to the current focus of your thoughts, and so is far less fragile: Information remains in storage whether or not you're thinking about it right now.

We can make all these claims more concrete by looking at some classic findings. These findings come from a task that's quite artificial (i.e., not the sort of memorizing you do every day!) but also quite informative.

Working Memory and Long-Term Memory: One Memory or Two?

In many studies, researchers have asked study participants to listen to a series of words, like "bicycle, artichoke, radio, chair, palace." In a typical experiment, the list contains 30 words and is presented at a rate of one word per second. Immediately after the last word is read, participants are asked to repeat back as many words as they can. They are free to report the words in any order they choose, which is why this is referred to as a **free recall** procedure.

People usually remember 12 to 15 words in such a test, in a consistent pattern: They are extremely likely to remember the first few words on the list, something known as the **primacy effect**, and they're also likely to remember the last few words on the list, a **recency effect**. The resulting pattern is a U-shaped curve describing the relation between position within the series—or **serial position**—and likelihood of recall (see Figure 5.2; Baddeley & Hitch, 1977; Deese & Kaufman, 1957; Glanzer & Cunitz, 1966; Murdock, 1962; Postman & Phillips, 1965).

What produces this pattern? We've already said that working memory contains the material someone is *working on* at just that moment. In other words, this memory contains whatever the person is currently thinking about, and, of course, during the list presentation, the participants are thinking about the words they're hearing. Therefore, it's these words that are in working memory. This

WORKBOOK
DEMONSTRATION 5.1

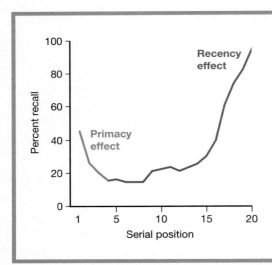

FIGURE 5.2 | PRIMACY AND RECENCY EFFECTS IN FREE RECALL

Research participants heard a list of 20 common words presented at a rate of 1 word per second. Immediately after hearing the list, participants were asked to write down as many of the words on the list as they could recall. The results show that position in the series strongly affected recall—participants had better recall for words at the beginning of the list (a pattern called the primacy effect) and for words at the end of the list (the recency effect).

memory, however, is limited in its size, capable of holding only five or six words. Consequently, as participants try to keep up with the list presentation, they will be placing the words *just heard* into working memory, and this will bump the previous words out of this memory. Thus, as participants proceed through the list, their working memories will, at each moment, contain only the half dozen words that arrived most recently. Any words earlier than these will have been pushed out by later arrivals.

Of course, the last few words on the list don't get bumped out of working memory, because no further input arrives to displace these words. Therefore, when the list presentation ends, those last few words stay in place. Moreover, our hypothesis is that materials in working memory are readily available—easily and quickly retrieved. When the time comes for recall, then, working memory's contents (the list's last few words) are accurately and completely recalled.

The key idea, then, is that the list's ending is still in working memory when the list ends (because nothing has arrived to push out these items), and working memory's contents are easy to retrieve. This is the source of the recency effect. The primacy effect, on the other hand, comes from a different source. We've suggested that it takes some work to get information into long-term memory (LTM), and it seems likely that this work requires some time and attention. Let's examine, then, how participants allocate their attention to the list items. As participants hear the list, they do their best to be good memorizers, and so, when they hear the first word, they typically repeat it over and over to themselves ("bicycle, bicycle, bicycle")—a process referred to as **memory rehearsal**. When the second word arrives, they rehearse it, too ("bicycle, artichoke, bicycle, artichoke"). Likewise for the third ("bicycle, artichoke, radio, bicycle, artichoke, radio"), and so on through the list. Note, though, that the first few items on the list are privileged: For a brief moment, "bicycle" is the only word participants have to worry about, and so it has 100% of their attention; no other word receives this privilege. When "artichoke" arrives, a moment later, participants divide their attention between the list's first two words, and so "artichoke" gets only 50% of the participants' attention—less than "bicycle" got, but still a large share of the participants' efforts. When "radio" arrives, it has to compete with "bicycle" and "artichoke" for the participants' time, and so it receives only 33% of their attention.

Words later in the list receive even less attention. Once six or seven words have been presented, the participants need to divide their attention among all of these words, which means that each one receives only a small fraction of the participants' focus. As a result, words later in the list are rehearsed fewer times than words early in the list—a fact we can confirm simply by asking participants to rehearse out loud (Rundus, 1971).

This view of things leads immediately to our explanation of the primacy effect—that is, the observed memory advantage for the early list items. These early words didn't have to share attention with other words (because the other words hadn't arrived yet!), and so more time and more rehearsal were devoted to these early words than to any others. This means that the early words have a greater chance of being transferred into LTM, and so a greater chance of being recalled after a delay. That's what shows up in our data as the primacy effect.

This account of the serial-position curve leads to many further predictions. First, note that we're claiming the recency portion of the curve is coming from working memory, while the other items on the list are being recalled from LTM. Therefore, any manipulation of working memory should affect recall of the recency items but should have little impact on the other items on the list. To see how this works, consider a modification of our procedure. In the standard setup, we allow participants to recite what they remember immediately after the list's end. In place of this, we can delay recall by asking participants to perform some other task prior to their report of the list items. For example, we can ask them, immediately after hearing the list, to count backward by threes, starting from 201. They do this for just 30 seconds, and then they try to recall the list.

We've hypothesized that at the end of the list working memory still contains the last few items heard from the list. But the chore of counting backward will itself require working memory (e.g., to keep track of where you are in the counting sequence). Therefore, this chore will *displace* working memory's current contents; that is, it will bump the last few list items out of working memory. As a result, these items won't benefit from the swift and easy retrieval that working memory allows, and, of course, that retrieval was the presumed source of the recency effect. On this basis, the simple chore of counting backward, even if only for a few seconds, will eliminate the recency effect. In contrast, the counting backward should have no impact on recall of the items earlier in the list: These items are (by hypothesis) being recalled from long-term memory, not working memory, and there's no reason to think the counting task will interfere with LTM. (That's because LTM, unlike working memory, is not dependent on current activity.)

Figure 5.3 shows that these predictions are correct: An activity interpolated between the list and recall essentially eliminates the recency effect, but it has no influence elsewhere in the list (Baddeley & Hitch, 1977; Glanzer & Cunitz, 1966; Postman & Phillips, 1965). In contrast, merely delaying the recall for a few

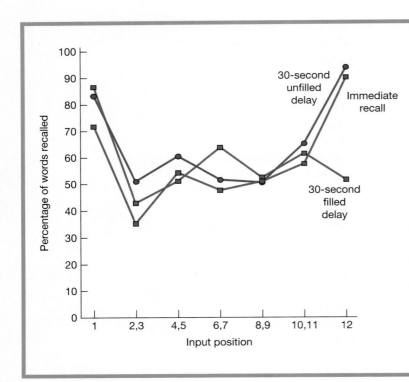

FIGURE 5.3 | THE IMPACT OF INTERPOLATED ACTIVITY ON THE RECENCY EFFECT

With immediate recall, or if recall is delayed by 30 seconds with no activity during this delay, a strong recency effect is detected. In contrast, if participants spend 30 seconds on some other activity between hearing the list and the subsequent memory test, the recency effect is eliminated. This interpolated activity has no impact on the pre-recency portion of the curve.

seconds after the list's end, with no interpolated activity, has no impact. In this case, participants can continue rehearsing the last few items during the delay and so can maintain them in working memory. With no new materials coming in, nothing pushes the recency items out of working memory, and so, even with a delay, a normal recency effect is observed.

This conception of what's going on in this procedure generates a different set of predictions for experiments that manipulate long-term memory rather than working memory. In this case, the manipulation should affect all performance *except* for recency (which, again, is dependent on working memory, not LTM). For example, what happens if we slow down the presentation of the list? Now participants will have more time to spend on all of the list items, increasing the likelihood of transfer into more permanent storage. This should improve recall for all items coming from LTM. Working memory, in contrast, is limited by its size, not by ease of entry or ease of access. Therefore, the slower list presentation should have no influence on working-memory performance. The results confirm these claims: Slowing the list presentation improves retention of all the pre-recency items but does not improve the recency effect (see Figure 5.4). Other variables that influence entry into long-term memory have similar effects. Using more familiar or more common words, for example, would be expected to ease entry into long-term memory and does improve pre-recency retention, but it has no effect on recency (Sumby, 1963).

Over and over, therefore, the recency and pre-recency portions of the curve are open to separate sets of influences and obey different principles. This strongly

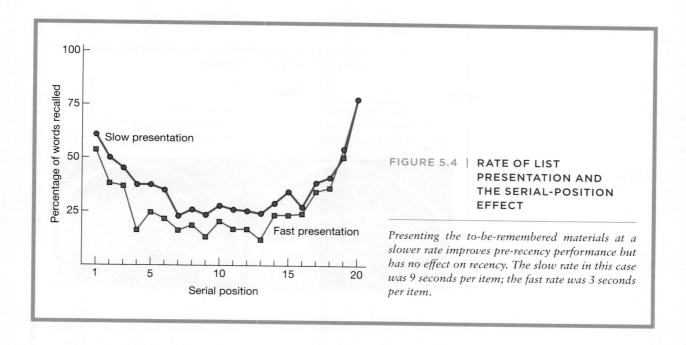

FIGURE 5.4 | RATE OF LIST PRESENTATION AND THE SERIAL-POSITION EFFECT

Presenting the to-be-remembered materials at a slower rate improves pre-recency performance but has no effect on recency. The slow rate in this case was 9 seconds per item; the fast rate was 3 seconds per item.

indicates that these portions of the curve are the products of different mechanisms, just as our theorizing proposes. In addition, fMRI scans suggest that memory for early items on a list depends on brain areas (in and around the hippocampus) that are associated with long-term memory; memory for later items on the list do not show this pattern (Talmi, Grady, Goshen-Gottstein, & Moscovitch, 2005; see Figure 5.5). This provides further (and powerful) confirmation for our memory model.

A Closer Look at Working Memory

We earlier counted through four fundamental differences between working memory and LTM—the *size* of these two stores, the *ease of entry*, the *ease of retrieval*, and the fact that working memory is dependent on current activity (and hence *fragile*) while LTM is not. These are all points proposed by the modal model, and preserved in current thinking. As we've said, though, our understanding of working memory has developed over the years. Let's pause, therefore, to examine the newer conception in a bit more detail.

The Function of Working Memory

Virtually all mental activities require the coordination of several pieces of information. Sometimes the relevant bits come into view one by one, and, if so, you need to hold onto the early-arrivers until the rest of the information is available, and only then weave all the bits together. Alternatively, sometimes the relevant bits

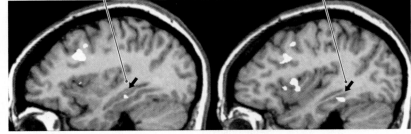

FIGURE 5.5 | BRAIN REGIONS SUPPORTING WORKING MEMORY AND LONG-TERM MEMORY

Retrieval from long-term memory specifically activates the hippocampus.

Retrieval from working memory specifically activates the perirhinal cortex.

We can confirm the distinction between working memory and long-term memory with fMRI scans. These scans suggest that memory for early items on a list depends on brain areas (in and around the hippocampus) that are associated with long-term memory; memory for later items on the list do not show this pattern (Talmi, Grady, Goshen-Gottstein, & Moscovitch, 2005).

are all in view at the same time—but you still need to hold onto them together, so that you can think about the relations and combinations. In either case, you'll end up with multiple ideas in your thoughts, all activated simultaneously, and thus several bits of information in the status we describe as "in working memory."

Framing things in this way makes it clear how important working memory is: You use working memory whenever you have multiple ideas in your mind, multiple elements that you're seeking to combine or compare. Let's now add that people differ in the "holding capacity" of their working memories: Some people are able to hold onto (and work with) more elements, and some with fewer. How exactly does this matter? To find out, we first need a means of *measuring* working memory's capacity, to find out if your memory capacity is above average, below, or somewhere in between. The procedure for obtaining this measurement, however, has changed over the years; looking at this change will help clarify what working memory *is*, and what working memory *is for*.

Digit Span

For many years, the holding capacity of working memory was measured with a **digit-span task**. In this task, people are read a series of digits (e.g., "8, 3, 4") and must immediately repeat them back. If they do so successfully, they're given a slightly longer list (e.g., "9, 2, 4, 0"). If they can repeat this one without error, they're given a still longer list ("3, 1, 2, 8, 5"), and so on. This procedure continues until the person starts to make errors—something that usually happens when the list contains more than seven or eight items. The number of digits the person can echo back without errors is referred to as that person's digit span.

Procedures such as this imply that working memory's capacity is typically around seven items or, more cautiously, at least five items and probably not more than nine items. These estimates are often summarized by the statement that this memory holds **"7 plus-or-minus 2"** items (Chi, 1976; Dempster, 1981; Miller, 1956; Watkins, 1977).

However, we immediately need a refinement of these measurements: If working memory can hold 7 plus-or-minus 2 items, what exactly is an "item"? Can we remember seven sentences as easily as seven words? Seven letters as easily as seven equations? In a classic paper, George Miller proposed that working memory holds 7 plus-or-minus 2 **chunks** (Miller, 1956). The term "chunk" is a deliberately unscientific-sounding term in order to remind us that a chunk does not hold a fixed quantity of information. Instead, Miller proposed, working memory holds 7 plus-or-minus 2 packages, and what those packages contain is largely up to the individual person.

The flexibility in how people "chunk" input can easily be seen in the span test. Imagine that we test someone's "letter span," rather than their "digit span," using the procedure we've already described. Thus, the person might hear "R, L" and have to repeat this sequence back, and then "F, J, S," and so on. Eventually, let's imagine that the person hears a much longer list, perhaps one starting "H, O, P, T, R, A, S, L, U . . ." If the person thinks of these as individual letters, she'll only remember 7 of them, more or less. But the same person might reorganize the list into "chunks," and, in particular, think of the letters as forming syllables ("HOP, TRA, SLU, . . ."). In this case, she'll still remember 7 plus-or-minus 2 items, but the items are the *syllables*, and, by remembering them, she'll be able to report back 15 letters or more.

WORKBOOK
DEMONSTRATION 5.2

The chunking process does have a cost attached, however, because often some effort is required to "repackage" the materials (i.e., assemble the letters into syllables or the syllables into words), and with some amount of attention spent in this way, less attention is available for rehearsing these items (Daneman & Carpenter, 1980; Hitch, Towse, & Hutton, 2001). Even so, chunking can have enormous effects, creating considerable flexibility in what working memory can hold. This is evident, for example, in a remarkable individual studied by Chase and Ericsson (1982; Ericsson, 2003). This fellow happens to be a fan of track events, and when he hears numbers, he thinks of them as finishing times for races. The sequence "3, 4, 9, 2," for example, becomes "3 minutes and 49.2 seconds, near world-record mile time." In this fashion, four digits become one chunk of information. This person can then retain 7 finishing times (7 chunks) in memory, and this can involve 20 or 30 digits! Better still, these chunks can be grouped into larger chunks, and these into even larger chunks. For example, finishing times for individual racers can be chunked together into heats within a track meet, so that, now, 4 or 5 finishing times (more than a dozen digits) become one chunk.

With strategies like this and with a considerable amount of practice, this person has increased his apparent memory span from the "normal" 7 digits to 79 digits!

However, let's be clear that what has changed through practice is merely this person's chunking strategy, not the capacity of working memory itself. This is evident in the fact that when tested with sequences of letters, rather than numbers, so that he can't use his chunking strategy, this individual's memory span is a (perfectly normal) 6 consonants. Thus, the 7-chunk limit is still in place for this man, even though (with numbers) he is able to make extraordinary use of these 7 slots.

Operation Span

Chunking provides one complication in our measurement of working memory's capacity. Another—and deeper—complication grows out of the very nature of working memory. We have mentioned that early theorizing about working memory was guided by the modal model, and this model, we said, implied that working memory is something like a box in which information is stored or a location in which information can be displayed. The traditional digit-span test fits well with this conception: If working memory is like a "box," then it's sensible to ask how much "space" there is in the box: How many slots, or spaces, are there in it? This is precisely what the digit span measures, on the notion that each digit (or each chunk) is placed in its own slot.

We've suggested, though, that the modern conception of working memory is more dynamic—so that working memory is best thought of as a *status* (something like "currently activated") rather than a *place* (see Figure 5.6). On this basis, perhaps we need to rethink how we measure this memory's capacity—seeking a measure that reflects working memory's active operation.

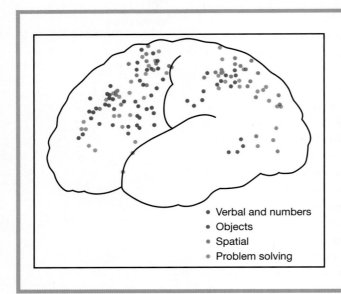

- Verbal and numbers
- Objects
- Spatial
- Problem solving

FIGURE 5.6 | **IS WORKING MEMORY A "PLACE"?**

Modern theorists argue that working memory is not a place at all, but is instead the name we give for a certain set of mental activities. Consistent with this modern view, there's no specific place within the brain that serves as working memory. Instead, working memory is associated with a wide range of brain sites, as shown here. (After Cabeza & Nyberg, 2000)

Modern researchers therefore measure this memory's capacity in terms of **operation span**, a procedure explicitly designed to measure working memory when it is "working." There are actually several ways to measure operation span, with the various types differing in what "operation" they use (Conway, Kane, Bunting, Hambrick, Wilhelm & Engle, 2005, but also see Cowan, 2010). One type, for example, is *reading span*, and, to measure this span, research participants might be asked to read aloud a series of sentences, like these:

Due to his gross inadequacies, his position as director was terminated abruptly.

It is possible, of course, that life did not arise on the Earth at all.

Immediately after reading the sentences, the participant is asked to recall the final words in the sentences—in this case, "abruptly" and "all." If the participant can do this with these two sentences, she's asked to do the same task with a group of three sentences, and then with four, and so on, until the limit on her performance is located. This limit defines the person's working-memory capacity, typically abbreviated WMC.

Think about what this task involves: storing some materials (the ending words) for later use in the recall test, while simultaneously working with other materials (the full sentences). This juggling of processes, as you move from one part of the task to the next, is exactly what working memory must do in its functioning in day-to-day life. Therefore, performance in this test is likely to reflect the efficiency with which working memory will operate in more natural settings.

Is the operation span a valid measure—that is, measuring what it's supposed to? Our hypothesis, of course, is that someone with a higher span has a larger working memory, and, if this is right, then someone with a higher span should have an advantage in tasks that make heavy use of this memory. Which tasks are these? They're tasks that require you to keep multiple ideas active at the same time, so that you can coordinate and integrate various bits of information. Thus, here's our prediction: People with a larger span (i.e., a greater WMC) should do better in tasks that require the coordination of different pieces of information.

Consistent with this claim, people with a greater WMC do have an advantage in many settings—in tests of reasoning, assessments of reading comprehension, standardized academic tests (including the verbal SAT), and more (e.g., Ackerman, Beier, & Boyle, 2002; Butler, Arrington & Weywadt, 2011; Daneman & Hannon, 2001; Engle & Kane, 2004; Gathercole & Pickering, 2000; Gray, Chabris, & Braver, 2003; Salthouse & Pink, 2008). For that matter, people with a larger WMC seem less likely to have their minds wander and so are more likely to keep their thoughts "on task," in comparison to people with a smaller WMC (Kane et al., 2007).

These results actually convey several messages: First, these correlations provide indications about when it's helpful to have a larger working memory, and this in turn helps us understand when and how working memory is used. Second, the link between WMC and measures of intellectual performance provides an intriguing

FIGURE 5.7 | DYNAMIC MEASURES OF WORKING MEMORY

$(7 \times 7) + 1 = 50$; dog
$(10/2) + 6 = 10$; gas
$(4 \times 2) + 1 = 9$; nose
$(3/1) + 1 = 5$; beat
$(5/5) + 1 = 2$; tree

Operation span can be measured in several different ways. In one procedure, participants must announce whether each of these "equations" is true or false, and then recall the words that were appended to each equation. If participants can do this with two equations, we ask them to do three; if they can do that, we ask them to try four. By finding out how far they can go, we measure their working-memory capacity.

hint about what we're measuring with tests (like the SAT) that seek to measure "intelligence." We'll return to this issue in Chapter 12, when we discuss the nature of intelligence. Third, it's important that these various correlations are obtained with the more active measure of working memory (operation span) but not with the more traditional (and more static) span measure. (We note, however, that there are several ways to measure operation span—see Figure 5.7.) This point confirms the advantage of the more dynamic measures and, more broadly, strengthens the idea that we're now thinking about working memory in the right way: not as a passive storage box but instead as a highly active information processor.

The Working-Memory System

Working memory's active nature is also evident in another way: in the actual structure of this memory. In Chapter 1, we introduced the idea that working memory is not a single entity but is instead a *system* built out of several components (Baddeley, 1986, 1992, 2012; Baddeley & Hitch, 1974). At the center of the system is a set of processes we discussed in Chapter 4: the executive control processes that govern the selection and sequence of our thoughts. In discussions of working memory, these processes have been playfully dubbed the *central executive*, as if there were a tiny agent somehow embedded in your mind, running your mental operations. Of course, there is no agent, and the central executive is merely a name we give to the set of mechanisms and processes that do run the show.

The central executive is needed for the "work" in working memory, and so if you have to plan a response or make a decision, these steps require the executive. But there are many settings in which you need less than this from working memory. Specifically, there are settings in which you need to keep ideas in mind, not because you're analyzing or integrating them, but because you're likely to need them *soon*. In this case, you don't need the executive. Instead, you can rely on the executive's "helpers," leaving the executive itself free to work on more difficult matters.

In Chapter 1, we discussed the fact that the executive has several helpers, including the *visuo-spatial buffer*, used for storing visual materials (such as mental images; see Chapter 10), and the *articulatory rehearsal loop*, used for storing verbal material. These helpers function in much the way a piece of scratch paper on your desk does: Imagine that a friend tells you a phone number, and you'll need to dial the number in a few minutes; odds are that you'll jot the number down on whatever piece of paper is nearby. That way, the number is "stored" so that you don't have to keep it in your thoughts, allowing you to turn your attention to other chores. Then, a few minutes later, when you're ready to dial the number, you can glance at the paper and see the digits, ready for use.

Working memory's helpers function in roughly the same way. For example, let's say that you wanted to multiply 23 times 12 in your head. To reach the answer, you'll probably proceed in three steps. First, you'll note that 20 times 12 is 240. Second, you'll note that 3 times 12 is 36. Then, finally, you'll add these numbers together to get the answer (276). The key, though, is what you did *between* the first and second steps: If you kept your attention focused on 240, you wouldn't have been able to think about the next step (the product of 3 x 12). But if you abandoned all thought of the 240, then at the end of the second step you would have lost the information you gained in the first step! You easily escape this dilemma, though, by shuffling the 240 off to one of working memory's helpers (probably, the rehearsal loop). That way, the 240 is stored in the loop, but the executive is free to do the next bit of multiplication. Then, for step 3, you can read the content of the loop (this is the equivalent of glancing at your piece of scrap paper), and finish the calculation.

The Central Executive

In Chapter 1, we described the functioning of working memory's rehearsal loop and discussed the (many) pieces of evidence that confirm this loop's existence. But what can we say about the main player within working memory—the central executive? Here, too, we can rely on earlier chapters, because (as we've already flagged) the central executive (a crucial concept for theorizing about working memory) is really the same thing as the *executive control processes* we described in Chapter 4 (where we introduced the executive as a key concept in our theorizing about attention).

In Chapter 4, we argued that executive control processes are needed to govern the sequence of your thoughts and actions; these processes allow you to set goals, to make plans for reaching those goals, and to select the steps needed for implementing those plans. Executive control processes also help you whenever you wish to rise above habit or routine, in order to "tune" your words or deeds to the current circumstances. However, these control processes can work on only one task at a time, and this is one of the important limits on people's ability to "multitask"—to divide their attention and do two things at once.

For purposes of the current chapter, though, let's emphasize that these same processes control the selection of ideas active at any moment in time. And, of course, these active ideas constitute the contents of working memory. It's inevitable, then, that we would link executive control with this type of memory.

With all these points in view, we're ready to move on. We've now updated the modal model (Figure 5.1) in important ways and, in particular, we've abandoned the notion of a relatively passive *short-term memory*, serving largely as storage container. We've shifted instead to a dynamic conception of *working memory*, with the proposal that this term is merely the name we give to an organized set of activities (especially the complex activities of the central executive). Thus, when we say an idea is "in" working memory, this does not suggest that a representation of the idea is in some specific place. Instead, if an idea is in working memory, this simply means that the idea is actively in your thoughts and is being worked on by the processes (including the executive) that define working memory. (For more on this modern view of working memory. see Jonides et al., 2008; Nee, Berman, Moore, & Jonides, 2008.)

But let's again emphasize that, in this modern conception, just as in the modal model, working memory is quite fragile: Each shift in attention brings new information into working memory, and newly arriving materials displace earlier items. Storage in this memory, therefore, is plainly temporary. Obviously, then, we also need some sort of enduring memory storage, so that we can remember things that happened an hour, or a day, or even years ago. Let's turn, therefore, to the functioning of long-term memory.

Entering Long-Term Storage: The Need for Engagement

We've already seen one important clue about how information becomes established in long-term storage: In discussing the primacy effect early in the chapter, we suggested that the more an item is rehearsed, the more likely it is that you'll remember that item later on. In order to pursue this point, though, we need to ask what exactly rehearsal is, and how it might work to promote memory.

Two Types of Rehearsal

The term "rehearsal" really means little beyond "thinking about." In other words, when a research participant rehearses an item on a memory list, she's simply thinking about that item—perhaps once, perhaps over and over; perhaps mechanically, or perhaps with close attention to what the item means. Clearly, therefore, there's considerable variety within the activities that count as rehearsal, and, in fact, psychologists find it useful to sort this variety into two broad types.

As one option, people can engage in **maintenance rehearsal**, in which they simply focus on the to-be-remembered items themselves, with little thought about what the items mean or how they are related to each other. This is a rote, mechanical process, recycling items in working memory simply by repeating them over and over. In contrast, **relational**, or **elaborative**, **rehearsal** involves thinking about what the to-be-remembered items mean and how they're related to each other and to other things you already know.

In general, relational rehearsal is vastly superior to maintenance rehearsal for establishing information in memory. Indeed, in many settings maintenance rehearsal provides no long-term benefits whatsoever. As an informal demonstration of this point, consider the following experience (although, for a more formal demonstration of this point, see Craik & Watkins, 1973). You're watching your favorite reality show on TV. The announcer says: "To vote for Contestant #4, dial 800-233-4830!" You reach into your pocket for your phone, but realize you left it in the other room. You recite the number to yourself while scurrying for your phone, but then, just before you dial, you see that you've got a text message. You pause, read the message, and then you're ready to dial, but . . . you realize at that moment that you don't have a clue what the number was.

What went wrong? You certainly heard the number, and you rehearsed it a couple of times while you were moving to fetch your phone. But, despite these rehearsals, the brief interruption (from reading the text) seems to have erased the number from your memory. But this isn't ultra-rapid forgetting. Instead, you never established the number in memory in the first place, because, in this setting, you relied only on maintenance rehearsal. This kept the number in your thoughts while you were moving across the room, but it did nothing to establish the number in long-term storage. And when you try to dial the number (again: after reading the text), it's long-term storage that you need.

The idea, then, is that if you think about something only in a mindless and mechanical fashion, the item will not be established in your memory. In the same way, long-lasting memories are not created simply by repeated exposures to the items to be remembered. If you encounter an item over and over but, on each encounter, barely think about it (or think about it in a mechanical fashion), then this, too, will not produce a long-term memory. As a demonstration, consider the ordinary penny. Adults in the United States have probably seen pennies tens of thousands of times. Adults in other countries have seen their own coins just as often. If sheer exposure is what counts for memory, people should remember perfectly what these coins look like.

But, of course, most people have little reason to pay attention to the penny. Pennies are a different color from the other coins, so they can be identified at a glance with no need for further scrutiny. If it's scrutiny that matters for memory, or, more broadly, *if we remember what we pay attention to and think about*, then memory for the coin should be quite poor.

The evidence on this point is clear: People's memory for the penny is remarkably bad. For example, most people know that Lincoln's head is on the "heads" side, but which way is he facing? Is it his right cheek that's visible, or his left? What other markings are shown on the coin? Most people do very badly with these questions; their answers to the "Which way is he facing?" question are close to random (see Figure 5.8; Nickerson & Adams, 1979); performance is similar for people in other countries remembering their own coins. (Also see Bekerian & Baddeley, 1980; and Rinck, 1999.)

WORKBOOK
DEMONSTRATION 5.3

FIGURE 5.8 | MEMORY FOR PENNIES

Despite having seen the U.S. penny thousands and thousands of times, people seem to have little recollection of its layout. Test yourself. Which of these versions is most accurate?

The Need for Active Encoding

It seems, then, that it takes some work to get information into long-term memory. Merely having an item in front of your eyes is not enough—even if the item is there over and over and over. Likewise, having an item in your thoughts doesn't, by itself, establish a memory. That's shown by the fact that maintenance rehearsal seems entirely ineffective at promoting memory.[1]

Further support for these claims comes from studies of brain activity during learning. In several procedures, researchers have used fMRI recording to keep track of the moment-by-moment brain activity in people who were studying a list of words (Brewer, Zhao, Desmond, Glover, & Gabrieli, 1998; Wagner, Koutstaal, & Schacter, 1999; Wagner et al., 1998). Later, the participants were able to remember some of the words they had learned, but not others, which allowed the investigators to return to their initial recordings and compare brain activity *during the learning process* for words that were later remembered and words that were later

---

1. We should acknowledge that maintenance rehearsal does have a lasting impact if memory is tested in just the right way, and we will return to this point in Chapter 6. (See, for example, Kelly, Burton, Kato, & Akamatsu, 2001; Wixted, 1991; for accurate *penny* memory, given just the right test, see Martin & Jones, 2006.) However, this does not change the fact that maintenance rehearsal is worthless for establishing the sorts of memories you need when simply trying to remember "Is this what I saw yesterday?" or "Is this what I heard ten minutes ago?"

FIGURE 5.9 | BRAIN ACTIVITY DURING LEARNING

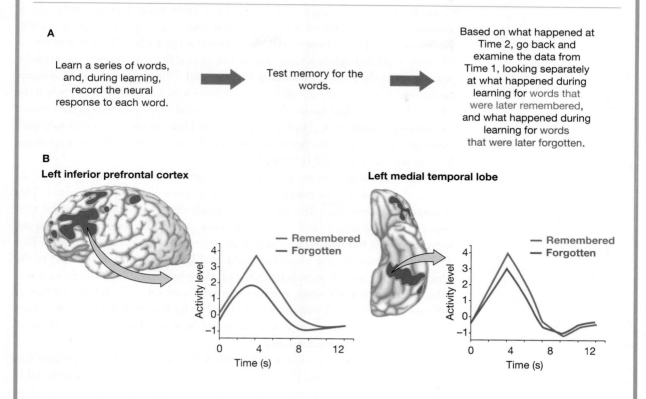

A

Learn a series of words, and, during learning, record the neural response to each word.

Test memory for the words.

Based on what happened at Time 2, go back and examine the data from Time 1, looking separately at what happened during learning for words that were later remembered, and what happened during learning for words that were later forgotten.

B

Left inferior prefrontal cortex

Left medial temporal lobe

(A) Participants in this study were given a succession of words to memorize, and their brain activity was recorded during this initial presentation. These brain scans were then divided into two types: those showing brain activity during the encoding of words that were remembered later on in a subsequent test, and those showing activity during encoding of words that were forgotten in the test. (B) As the figure shows, activity levels during encoding were higher for the later-remembered words than they were for the later-forgotten words. This confirms that whether a word is forgotten or not depends on participants' mental activity when they encountered the word in the first place.

forgotten. Figure 5.9 shows the results, with a clear difference, during the initial encoding, between these two types of words. Specifically, greater levels of brain activity (especially in the hippocampus and regions of the prefrontal cortex) were reliably associated with greater probabilities of retention later on.

These fMRI results are telling us, once again, that learning is not a passive process. Instead, activity is needed to lodge information into long-term memory, and, apparently, higher levels of this activity lead to better memory. But this demands some new questions: What is this activity? What does it accomplish? And if—as it seems—*maintenance* rehearsal is a poor way to memorize, what type of rehearsal is more effective?

Incidental Learning, Intentional Learning, and Depth of Processing

Consider a student taking a course in college. The student knows that her memory for the course materials will be tested later (e.g., in the course's exams). And presumably the student will take various steps to help herself remember: She may read through her notes again and again; she may discuss the material with friends; she may try outlining the material. Will these various techniques work—so that the student will have a complete and accurate memory when the exam takes place? And notice that the student is taking these steps in the context of wanting to memorize, hoping to memorize. How do these elements influence performance? Or, put another way, how does the *intention to memorize* influence how or how well material is learned?

In an early experiment, participants in one condition heard a list of 24 words; their task was to remember as many of these words as they could. This is **intentional learning**—learning that is deliberate, with an expectation that memory will be tested later on. Several other groups of participants heard the same 24 words but had no idea that their memories would be tested later. This allows us to examine the impact of **incidental learning**—that is, learning in the absence of any intention to learn. One of these incidental-learning groups was asked simply, for each word, whether the word contained the letter *e* or not. A different incidental-learning group was asked to look at each word and to report how many letters it contained. Another group was asked to consider each word and to rate how *pleasant* it seemed.

The results are shown in Figure 5.10A (Hyde & Jenkins, 1969). Performance was relatively poor for the "find the *e*" and "count the letters" groups but appreciably better for the "how pleasant?" group. What's especially striking, though, is that the "how pleasant?" group, with no intention to memorize, performed just as well as the intentional-learning group. The suggestion, then, is that the intention to learn doesn't add very much; memory can be just as good without this intention, provided that you approach the materials in the right way.

This broad pattern has been reproduced in countless other experiments (to name just a few: Bobrow & Bower, 1969; Craik & Lockhart, 1972; Hyde & Jenkins, 1973; Jacoby, 1978; Lockhart, Craik, & Jacoby, 1976; Parkin, 1984; Slamecka & Graf, 1978). As one example of this avalanche of findings, consider a study by Craik and Tulving (1975). In one of their experiments, participants were again led to do incidental learning (that is, the participants did not know their memories would be tested). For some of the words shown, the participants did **shallow processing**—that is, they engaged the material in a superficial fashion. Specifically, they had to say whether the word was printed in CAPITAL letters or not. (Other examples of shallow processing would be decisions about whether the words are printed in red or in green, high or low on the screen, and so on.) For other words, the participants had to do a moderate level of processing: They had to judge whether each word shown *rhymed* with a particular cue word. Then, finally, for other words, participants had to do **deep processing**. This is processing that requires some thought about what the words *mean*, and, specifically,

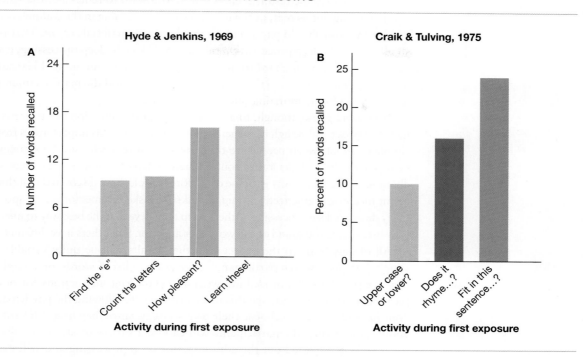

FIGURE 5.10 | THE IMPACT OF DEEPER PROCESSING

Hyde & Jenkins, 1969

A

Number of words recalled

Activity during first exposure

Find the "e"
Count the letters
How pleasant?
Learn these!

Craik & Tulving, 1975

B

Percent of words recalled

Activity during first exposure

Upper case or lower?
Does it rhyme...?
Fit in this sentence...?

The two sets of results here derive from studies described in the text, but are just part of an avalanche of data confirming the broad pattern: Shallow processing leads to poor memory. Deeper processing (paying attention to meaning) leads to much better memory. And what matters seems to be the level of engagement; the specific intention to learn (because someone knows their memory will be tested later on) contributes little.

Craik and Tulving asked whether each word shown would fit into a particular sentence.

The results are shown in Figure 5.10B. Plainly, there is a huge effect here of **level of processing**, with deeper processing (that is, more attention to meaning) leading to much better memory. In addition, Craik and Tulving (and many other researchers) have confirmed the Hyde and Jenkins finding that the intention to learn adds little. That is, memory performance is roughly the same in conditions in which participants do shallow processing *with* an intention to memorize, and conditions in which they do shallow processing *without* this intention. Likewise, the outcome is the same whether people do deep processing *with* the intention to memorize or *without*. In study after study, what matters is how people approach the material they're seeing or hearing. It's that approach, that manner of engagement, that determines whether memory will be excellent or poor later on. The intention to learn seems, by itself, not to matter.

WORKBOOK
DEMONSTRATION 5.4

The Intention to Learn

The message of these results seems clear: If you want to remember the sentences you're reading in this text, or the materials you're learning in the training sessions at your job, you should pay attention to what these materials *mean*. That is, you should try to do deep processing. And, in fact, if you do deep processing, it won't matter if you're trying hard to memorize the materials (intentional learning) or merely paying attention to the meaning because you find the material interesting, with no plan for memorizing (incidental learning).

We should pause, though, to acknowledge that the intention to memorize does have an impact—although it's generally an *indirect* one. This impact arises from the simple fact that, when people are trying to memorize, each uses the strategy that he or she thinks best. As it turns out, though, different people have different beliefs about what the "best" way is. Some of us, for example, have discovered that thinking about meaning is an effective strategy, and so, if asked to memorize, we spontaneously draw on deep processing. Others seem to believe that the best way to memorize is by listening to the sound of the word over and over. Still others have different ideas.

All of this leads to the expectation that results will be quite variable if we simply instruct research participants to memorize a list of words, or a paragraph, or a recipe. With this procedure, we're not providing instructions for how the participants should approach this task, and so we're allowing the participants to "self-instruct"—i.e., to choose their own strategy. Since they have different ideas about memorizing, the participants will choose a variety of strategies: Some of them will have figured out the advantages of deep processing and will use that strategy here, and they will therefore do well in our memory test. Others may not have discovered the advantages of deep processing and thus will use some other strategy—and hence perform more poorly. (For studies of people's spontaneous strategies, see Anderson & Bower, 1972; Brown, 1979.)

What, therefore, can we conclude about the role of intention in guiding the learning process? Intention does matter, because (among other considerations) someone who has no intention to learn may end up doing maintenance processing rather than elaborative processing, and this obviously will affect what is remembered. Likewise, someone who intends to learn will select the strategy she thinks best, and as we have seen, this choice of strategy will also affect the quality of memory. But these effects of intention are, as we said, indirect. The intention to learn leads people to approach the materials in a certain fashion, and it is the approach, not the intention, that matters for memory. If we can lead people to approach the materials in the same way without the intention, we get the same memory results.

The Role of Meaning and Memory Connections

The contrasts we've been considering are large: Maintenance rehearsal can leave you with no memory at all; elaborative rehearsal is vastly more productive. Likewise, the benefits of deeper processing are considerable: In many experiments, people are four or five times more likely to remember items that were processed deeply than to remember items processed in a shallow manner. But what lies behind these effects? Why is it, for example, that attention to meaning leads to such good recall? Let's start with a broad proposal; we'll then need to circle back and fill in the evidence for this proposal.

Connections Promote Retrieval

Perhaps surprisingly, the benefits of deep processing may not lie in the learning process itself. Instead, deep processing may influence subsequent events. More precisely, attention to meaning may help you by virtue of facilitating *retrieval* of the memory later on. To understand this point, consider what happens whenever a library acquires a new book. On its way into the collection, the new book must be catalogued and shelved appropriately. These steps happen when the book arrives, but the cataloguing doesn't literally influence the arrival of the book into the building. The moment the book is delivered, it's physically in the library, catalogued or not, and the book doesn't become "more firmly" or "more strongly" in the library because of the cataloguing.

But the cataloguing is crucial. If the book were merely tossed on a random shelf somewhere, with no entry in the catalogue, users might never be able to find it. Indeed, without a catalogue entry, users of the library might not even realize that the book was in the building. Notice, then, that cataloguing happens at the time of arrival, but the benefit of cataloguing isn't for the arrival itself. (If the librarians all went on strike, so that no books were being catalogued, books would continue to arrive, magazines would still be delivered, and so on. Again: The *arrival* doesn't depend on cataloguing.) Instead, the benefit of cataloguing is for events subsequent to the book's arrival: Cataloguing makes it possible (and maybe makes it *easy*) to find the book later on.

The same is true for the vast library that is your memory. The task of learning is not merely a matter of placing information into long-term storage. Learning also needs to establish some appropriate indexing; it must, in effect, pave a path to the newly acquired information, so that this information can be retrieved at some future point. Thus, one of the main chores of memory acquisition is to lay the groundwork for memory retrieval.

But what is it that facilitates memory retrieval? There are, in fact, several ways to search through memory, but a great deal depends on memory *connections*. Connections allow one memory to trigger another, and then that memory to trigger another, so that you are "led," connection by connection, to the sought-after information. In some cases, the connections link one of the items you're trying to remember to some of the other items; if so, finding the first will lead you to the others. In other settings, the connections might link some aspect of the context-of-learning to the target information, so that when you think again about the context ("I recognize this room—this is where I was last week"), you'll be led to other ideas ("Oh, yeah, I read that silly story in this room"). In all cases, though, this triggering will happen only if the relevant connections are in place—and *establishing those connections* is a large part of what happens during learning.

WHY DO MEMORY CONNECTIONS HELP?

When books arrive in a library, the librarians must catalog *them. This doesn't facilitate the "entry" of books into the library— the books are in the building whether they are catalogued or not. But cataloguing makes the books vastly easier to find later on. Memory connections may serve the same function: The connections don't "bring" material into memory, but they do make the material findable in long-term storage later.*

This line of reasoning has many implications, and we can use those implications as a basis for testing whether this proposal is correct. But, right at the start, it should be clear why, according to this account, deep processing (that is, attention to *meaning*) promotes memory. The key here is that attention to meaning involves thinking about relationships: "What words are related in meaning to the word I'm now considering? What words have *contrasting* meaning? What is the relationship between the start of this story and the way the story turned out?" Points like these are likely to be prominent when you're thinking about what some word (or sentence, or event) means, and these same points will help you to find (or, perhaps, to *create*) connections among your various ideas. It's these connections, we're proposing, that really matter for memory.

Elaborate Encoding

On the hypotheses just sketched, attention to meaning is an excellent way to improve memory: Paying attention to meaning forces you to think about relationships among ideas. Thinking about these relationships fosters (creates, strengthens) memory connections. And those memory connections will guide your search through memory later, when you're trying to locate the target materials.

Let's be clear, though, that, on this account, attention to meaning is not the only way to improve memory. Other strategies should also be helpful, provided that they help the memorizer to establish memory connections. As an example, consider another study by Craik and Tulving (1975). Participants were shown a word and then shown a sentence with one word left out. Their task was to decide whether the word fit into the sentence. For example, they might see the word "chicken," then the sentence "She cooked the _____." The appropriate response would be yes, since the word does fit in this sentence. After a series of these trials, there was a surprise memory test, with participants asked to remember all the words they had seen.

There was, however, an additional element in this experiment: Some of the sentences shown to participants were simple, while others were more elaborate. For example, a more complex sentence might be "The great bird swooped down and carried off the struggling _____." How did this matter? These more complicated sentences improved memory. More precisely, words were much more likely to be remembered if they appeared with these rich, elaborate sentences, than if they had appeared in the simpler sentences (see Figure 5.11).

To make their initial yes-or-no response to any of these sentences, the research participants obviously had to think about the meanings of the words they were reading. This is deep processing, and if deep processing were all that mattered for memory, then all of the words should be remembered equally. But that's not what the data show. Instead, deep and *elaborate* processing led to better recall than deep processing alone.

Why does elaborate processing help memory? The answer hinges on memory connections. Perhaps the "great bird swooped" sentence calls to mind a barnyard scene, with the hawk carrying a chicken away. Or perhaps it calls to mind thoughts about predator-prey relationships. One way or another, the richness of this sentence offers the potential for many connections as it calls other thoughts to mind, each of which can be connected, in your thinking, to the target sentence. These connections, in turn, provide potential **retrieval paths**—paths that can, in effect, guide your thoughts toward the content to be remembered. All of this seems less likely for the impoverished sentences, which will evoke fewer connections and so establish a narrower set of retrieval paths. Consequently, these sentences are less likely to be recalled later on.

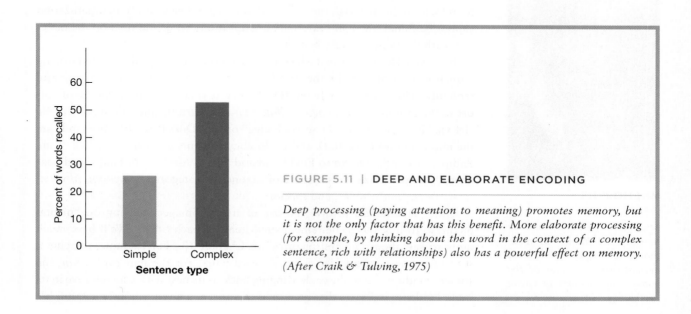

FIGURE 5.11 | DEEP AND ELABORATE ENCODING

Deep processing (paying attention to meaning) promotes memory, but it is not the only factor that has this benefit. More elaborate processing (for example, by thinking about the word in the context of a complex sentence, rich with relationships) also has a powerful effect on memory. (After Craik & Tulving, 1975)

Organizing and Memorizing

Sometimes, we've said, memory connections link the to-be-remembered material to other information already in memory. In other cases, the connections link one aspect of the to-be-remembered material to another aspect of the same material. Such a connection ensures that if any part of the material is recalled, then all will be recalled.

In all settings, though, the connections are important, and that leads us to ask how people go about discovering (or creating) these connections. More than 60 years ago, a German psychologist, George Katona, argued that the key lies in *organization* (Katona, 1940). Katona's argument, in fact, was that the processes of organization and memorization are inseparable: We memorize well when we discover the order within the material. Conversely, if we find (or impose) an organization on the material, we will easily remember it. These suggestions are fully compatible with the conception we're developing here, since what organization provides is, once again, memory connections.

Mnemonics

MNEMOSYNE

Strategies used to improve memory are known as mnemonic *strategies; the term derives from the name of the goddess of memory in Greek mythology—Mnemosyne.*

For thousands of years, people have longed for "better" memories; they have wished to learn more quickly and to remember more accurately. Motivated by these wishes, people in the ancient world devised a number of techniques to "improve" memory—techniques known as **mnemonic strategies**. People continue to invent new mnemonics, but many of the strategies still in use date back to ancient Greece (and, in fact, these techniques are named in honor of Mnemosyne, the goddess of memory in Greek mythology).

There are many types of mnemonics, but, in general, they all involve a straightforward principle—namely, that organization helps. If an organization can be found within the material, then this will lead to good memory. If an organization cannot be found, then an "external" organization can be imposed on the material, with the same memory benefit.

For example, one broad class of mnemonic, often used for memorizing sequences of words, links the *first letters* of the words into some meaningful structure. Thus, children rely on ROY G. BIV to memorize the sequence of colors in the rainbow (*red, orange, yellow . . .*) and learn the lines in music's treble clef via "Every Good Boy Deserves Fudge" or ". . . Does Fine" (the lines indicate the musical notes *E, G, B, D,* and *F*). Biology students use a sentence like "King Philip Crossed the Ocean to Find Gold and Silver" (or: ". . . to Find Good Spaghetti") to memorize the sequence of taxonomic categories: *kingdom, phylum, class, order, family, genus,* and *species.*

Other mnemonics involve the use of mental imagery, relying on "mental pictures" to link the to-be-remembered items to each other. (We'll have much more to say about "mental pictures" in Chapter 10.) For example, imagine a student trying to memorize a list of word pairs. For the pair *eagle-train*, the student might imagine the eagle winging back to its nest with a locomotive in its beak. Evidence indicates that images of this sort can be enormously helpful. It's

FIGURE 5.12 | MNEMONIC STRATEGIES

"You simply associate each number with a word, such as 'table' and 3,476,029."

To be effective, a mnemonic must provide some rich linkage among the items being memorized. Merely putting the items side-by-side is not enough.

important, though, that the images show the objects in some sort of relationship or interaction—again highlighting the role of *organization*. It doesn't help just to form a picture of an eagle and a train sitting side-by-side (Wollen, Weber & Lowry, 1972; for an example of the *wrong* sort of mnemonic use, *not* providing the linkage, see Figure 5.12).

A different type of mnemonic provides an external "skeleton" for the to-be-remembered materials, and here too mental imagery can be useful. Imagine, for example, that you want to remember a list of largely unrelated items, perhaps the entries on your shopping list or a list of questions you want to ask when you next see your adviser. For this purpose, you might rely on one of the so-called **peg-word systems**. These systems begin with a well-organized structure, such as this one:

One is a bun.

Two is a shoe.

Three is a tree.

Four is a door.

Five is a hive.

Six are sticks.

Seven is heaven.

Eight is a gate.

Nine is a line.

Ten is a hen.

This rhyme provides ten "peg words" ("bun," "shoe," "tree," and so on), and in memorizing something you can "hang" the materials to be remembered on these "pegs." Let's imagine, therefore, that you want to remember the list of topics you need to discuss with your adviser. If you want to discuss your unhappiness with your chemistry class, you might form an association between chemistry and the first peg, "bun." You might, for example, form a mental image of a hamburger bun floating in an Erlenmeyer flask. If you also want to discuss your after-graduation plans, you might form an association between some aspect of those plans and the next peg, "shoe." (Perhaps you might think about how you plan to pay your way after college by selling shoes.) If you continue in this fashion, when the time comes to meet with your adviser, all you have to do is think through that silly rhyme again. When you think of "one is a bun," it is highly likely that the image of the flask (and therefore of chemistry lab) will come to mind. When you think of "two is a shoe," you'll be reminded of your job plans. And so on.

Hundreds of variations on these techniques—the first-letter mnemonics, visualization strategies, peg-word systems—are available. Some of the variations are taught in self-help courses (you've probably seen the ads—"How to Improve Your Memory!"); some are presented by corporations as part of management training. All the variations, though, use the same basic scheme. To remember a list with no apparent organization, you impose an organization on it by using a skeleton or scaffold that is itself tightly organized. And, crucially, these systems all work: They help you remember individual items, and they also help you remember those items in a specific sequence. Figure 5.13 shows some of the data from one early study; many other studies confirm this pattern (e.g., Bower, 1970, 1972; Bower & Reitman, 1972; Christen & Bjork, 1976; Higbee, 1977; Roediger, 1980; Ross & Lawrence, 1968; Yates, 1966). All of this strengthens our central claim: Organizing improves recall. Mnemonics work because they impose an organization on the materials to be remembered, thus establishing connections between the material and some other easily remembered structure.

Mnemonics contribute to our theoretical understanding of memory, but of course they also have practical uses. Many students, for example, use mnemonics to help them in their studies. Indeed, for many topics, there are online databases containing thousands of useful mnemonics, helping medical students to memorize symptom lists, chemistry students to memorize the periodic table, neuroscientists to remember the brain's anatomy, and more.

Use of these mnemonics is sensible: We've already said that mnemonics can improve memory. But there's also a downside to mnemonics in educational settings: When you're using a mnemonic, you typically focus on just one aspect of the material you're trying to memorize—for example, just the first letter of the word to be remembered—and this focus usually means that you don't

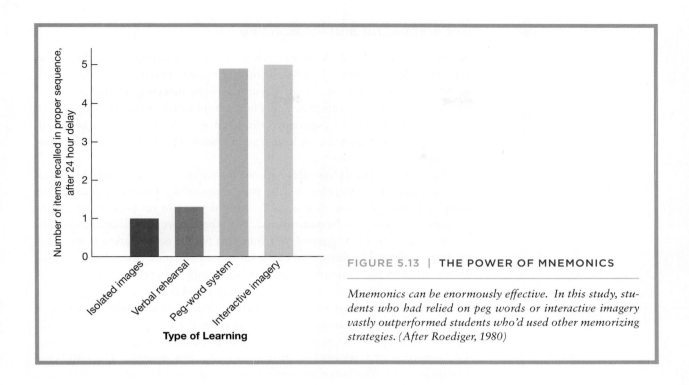

FIGURE 5.13 | **THE POWER OF MNEMONICS**

Mnemonics can be enormously effective. In this study, students who had relied on peg words or interactive imagery vastly outperformed students who'd used other memorizing strategies. (After Roediger, 1980)

pay much attention to *other* aspects of the material. As a result, you may cut short your effort toward understanding this material, and likewise your effort toward finding multiple connections between the material and other things you know.

To put this point differently, mnemonic use involves a trade-off: More attention focused on one or two memory connections means less attention spent on thinking about other connections, including other connections that might help you understand the material. This trade-off will be fine if you don't care very much about the meaning of the material. (Do you care why, in taxonomy, "order" is a subset of "class," rather than the other way around?) But this trade-off is troubling if you're trying to memorize material that is meaningful. In this case, you'd be better served by a memory strategy that leads you to seek out *multiple* connections between the material you're trying to learn and things you already know. Indeed, this effort toward multiple links will help you in two ways. First, it will foster your understanding of the material to be remembered, and so will lead to better, richer, deeper learning. Second, the multiple links will help you retrieve this information later on: We've already suggested that memory connections serve as retrieval paths, and the more paths there are, the easier it will be to find the target material later.

For these reasons, mnemonic use may be ill-advised in many situations. Nonetheless, the fact remains that mnemonics are immensely useful in some settings (what were those rainbow colors?), and this in turn confirms our initial point: Organization promotes memory.

Understanding and Memorizing

So far, we've said a lot about how people memorize rather impoverished stimulus materials—lists of randomly selected words, or colors that have to be learned in exactly the right sequence. In our day-to-day lives, however, we typically want to remember more meaningful, and more complicated, material. We want to remember the episodes we experience, the details of rich scenes we have observed, or the many-step arguments we have read in a book. Do the same memory principles apply to these cases?

The answer is clearly yes (although we'll have more to say about this broad issue in Chapter 7). In other words, your memory for events, or pictures, or complex bodies of knowledge is enormously dependent on your being able to organize the material to be remembered. With these more complicated materials, though, we've already suggested that your best bet for organization is not some arbitrary skeleton like those used in the various mnemonics. Instead, the optimal organization of these complex materials is generally dependent on understanding. That is, you remember best what you understand best.

There are many ways to show that this is true. For example, we can give people a sentence or paragraph to read and test their comprehension by asking questions about the material or by asking them to paraphrase the material. Sometime later, we can test their memory for this material. The results are straightforward: The better the participants' understanding of a sentence or a paragraph, the greater the likelihood that they will remember it later. The more accurately they could answer questions immediately after reading the material, the greater the chance that they will remember the material after a delay (e.g., Bransford, 1979).

A similar pattern can be demonstrated outside of the laboratory. For example, consider the material you are learning right now in the courses you are taking. Will you remember this material 5 years from now, or 10, or 20? The answer depends on how well you understand the material, and one measure of understanding is the grade you earn in a course: With full and rich understanding, you're likely to earn an A; with poor understanding, your grade is likely to be lower. This leads to an obvious prediction: If understanding is (as we've proposed) important for memory, we should expect that the higher someone's grade in a course, the more likely that person is to remember the course contents, even many years later. This is exactly what the data show, with A students remembering the material quite well, even years later, and C students remembering much less. Plainly, then, the better your understanding, the better (and longer-lasting) your memory will be (Conway, Cohen, & Stanhope, 1992).

The relationship between understanding and memory can also be demonstrated in another way: by *manipulating* whether people understand the material or not. For example, in an experiment by Bransford and Johnson (1972, p. 722), participants read this passage:

> *The procedure is actually quite simple. First you arrange items into different groups. Of course one pile may be sufficient depending on how much*

there is to do. If you have to go somewhere else due to lack of facilities that is the next step; otherwise you are pretty well set. It is important not to overdo things. That is, it is better to do too few things at once than too many. In the short run, this may not seem important but complications can easily arise. A mistake can be expensive as well. At first, the whole procedure will seem complicated. Soon, however, it will become just another facet of life. It is difficult to foresee any end to the necessity for this task in the immediate future, but then, one never can tell. After the procedure is completed one arranges the materials into different groups again. Then they can be put into their appropriate places. Eventually they will be used once more and the whole cycle will then have to be repeated. However, that is part of life.

You are probably puzzled by this passage; so are most research participants. The story is easy to understand, though, if we give it a title: "Doing the Laundry." In the experiment, some participants were given the title before reading the passage; others were not. Participants in the first group easily understood the passage and were able to remember it after a delay. The second group, reading the same words, were not confronting a meaningful passage and did poorly on the memory test. (For related data, see Bransford & Franks, 1971; Sulin & Dooling, 1974; for another example, see Figure 5.14.)

Similar effects can be documented with nonverbal materials. Consider the picture shown in Figure 5.15. At first it looks like a bunch of meaningless blotches; with some study, though, you may discover that a familiar object is depicted. Wiseman and Neisser (1974) tested people's memory for this picture. Consistent with what we have seen so far, their memory was good if they understood the picture, and bad otherwise. (Also see Bower, Karlin, & Dueck, 1975; Mandler & Ritchey, 1977; Rubin & Kontis, 1983.)

FIGURE 5.14 | **MEMORY FOR DIGITS**

$$1\ 4\ 9\ 1\ 6\ 2\ 5\ 3\ 6\ 4\ 9\ 6\ 4\ 8\ 1$$

Examine this series of digits for a moment, and then turn away from the page and try to recall all 15 in their proper sequence. The chances are good that you will fail in this task—perhaps remembering the first few and last few digits, but not the entire list. Things will go differently, though, if you discover the pattern within the list. Now you'll easily be able to remember the full sequence. What is the pattern? Try thinking of the series this way: 1, 4, 9, 16, 25, 36. . . . Here, as always, organizing and understanding aid memory.

FIGURE 5.15 | COMPREHENSION ALSO AIDS MEMORY FOR PICTURES

People who perceive this picture as a pattern of meaningless blotches are unlikely to remember the picture. People who perceive the "hidden" form do remember the picture. (After Wiseman & Neisser, 1974)

The Study of Memory Acquisition

This chapter has largely been about memory acquisition. How do we acquire new memories? How is new information, new knowledge, established in long-term memory? Or, in more pragmatic terms, what is the best, most effective, most efficient way to learn? We now have answers to these questions, but our discussion has also indicated that we need to place these questions into a broader context—looking not just at acquisition, but also at the substantial contribution from the memorizer, as well as the powerful interconnections among acquisition, retrieval, and storage.

The Contribution of the Memorizer

Over and over, we've seen that memory depends on *connections* among ideas, and these connections, in turn, are plainly fostered by steps toward organizing and understanding the materials to be remembered. Hand in hand with this, it appears that memories are not established by sheer contact with the items you're hoping to remember. If you are merely exposed to the items without giving them any thought, then subsequent recall of those items will be poor.

These points immediately draw our attention to the role played by the memorizer. If we wish to predict whether this or that event will be recalled, it isn't enough to know that someone was exposed to the event. Likewise, if we wish to predict memory performance, it isn't enough to describe the memory "equipment" possessed by each of us—for example, a working memory with various components, a long-term memory with a specific structure. Instead, if we wish to predict someone's recall performance, we need to pay attention to what the person was doing at the time of learning. Did she elect to do mere maintenance rehearsal, or did she engage the material in some other way? If the latter, how did she think about the material? Did she pay attention to the appearance of the words or to their meaning? If she thought about meaning, was she able to understand the material? Did she think about the material as involving separate bits, or did she find some unifying theme? These considerations are crucial for predicting the success of memory.

The contribution of the memorizer is also evident in another way. We've argued that learning depends on the person's making connections, but connections to what? If someone wants to connect the to-be-remembered material to other knowledge, to other memories, then the person needs to have that other knowledge; she needs to have other (potentially relevant) memories to "hook" the new material onto. Thus, what people contribute to learning also includes their own prior knowledge. If someone enters the learning situation with a great deal of knowledge that's relevant to the new information, then she arrives with a considerable advantage—a rich framework that the new materials can be woven into. If, in contrast, someone enters the learning situation with little relevant background, then there is no framework, nothing to connect to, and learning will be correspondingly more difficult. Thus, if we wish to predict the success of memorizing, we also need to consider what other knowledge the individual brings into the situation.

The Links Among Acquisition, Retrieval, and Storage

These points lead us to another theme of considerable importance. Our emphasis in this chapter has been on memory acquisition, but we've now seen several indications that claims about acquisition can't be separated from claims about memory storage and memory retrieval. For example, why is recall improved by organization and understanding? We have suggested that organization provides retrieval paths, making the memories "findable" later on when the time comes to remember the target information. Therefore, our claims about acquisition rest on assumptions about memory retrieval and the usefulness of memory connections within retrieval.

Likewise, we just noted that a person's ability to learn new material depends, in part, on having a framework of prior knowledge to which the new materials can be tied. In this way, claims about memory acquisition must be coordinated with claims about the nature of what is already in storage.

The same can be said about chunking, both in working memory and in long-term storage. In most cases, chunking depends on understanding, and understanding rests on things you already know. For example, the number series "1 4 9 1 6 . . ." (Figure 5.14) can be chunked as the squares of the digits only if you already know what the squares of the digits are. The passage about laundry is understood only by virtue of your prior knowledge about how clothing is washed. In both of these cases, therefore, chunking at the time of memory acquisition is dependent on knowledge you already have, and so again we see the interweaving of memory acquisition and knowledge already in storage.

We close this chapter, then, with a two-sided message. We have offered many claims about memory acquisition and about how memories are established. In particular, we've offered claims about the importance of memory connections, organization, and understanding. At the same time, though, these claims cannot stand by themselves. We've already seen that our account of acquisition needs to make references to the role of prior knowledge and the nature of memory retrieval. And, for the data themselves, we'll soon see that these interactions among acquisition, knowledge, and retrieval have important implications for learning, for forgetting, and for memory accuracy. We turn next to some of those implications.

 CHAPTER SUMMARY

- It is convenient to think of memorizing as having separate stages. First, one acquires new information (acquisition). Next, the information remains in storage until it is needed. Finally, the information is retrieved. However, this separation among the stages may be misleading. For example, in order to memorize new information, you form connections between this information and things you already know. In this fashion, the acquisition stage is inter-twined with the retrieval of information already in storage.

- Information that is currently being considered is held in working memory; information that is not currently active but is nonetheless in storage is in long-term memory. The distinction between these two forms of memory has traditionally been described in terms of the modal model and has been examined in many studies of the serial-position curve. The primacy portion of this curve reflects those items that have had extra opportunity to reach long-term memory; the recency portion of this curve reflects the accurate retrieval of items currently in working memory.

- Our conception of working memory has evolved in important ways in the last few decades. Crucially, psychologists no longer think of working memory as a "storage container," or even as a "place." Instead, working memory is a status—and so we say items are "in working memory" when they are being actively thought about, actively contemplated. This activity is governed by working memory's central executive. For mere storage, the executive often relies on a number of low-level assistants, including the articulatory rehearsal loop and the visuospatial buffer, which work as mental scratch pads. The activity inherent in this overall system is reflected in the flexible way material can be chunked in working memory; the activity is also reflected in current measures of working memory, via operation span.

- Maintenance rehearsal serves to keep information in working memory and requires little effort, but it has little impact on subsequent recall. To maximize your chances of recall, elaborative rehearsal is needed, in which you seek connections within the material to be remembered, or connections between the material to be remembered and things you already know.

- In many cases, elaborative processing takes the form of attention to meaning. This attention to meaning is called deep processing, in contrast to attention to sounds or visual form, which is considered shallow processing. Many studies have shown that deep processing leads to good memory performance later on, even if the deep processing was done with no intention of memorizing the target material. In fact, the intention to learn has no direct effect on performance; what matters instead is how someone engages or thinks about the material to be remembered.

- Deep processing has beneficial effects by creating effective retrieval paths that can be used later on. Retrieval paths depend on connections linking one memory to another; each connection provides a path potentially leading to a target memory. Mnemonic strategies build on this idea and focus on the creation of specific memory connections, often tying the to-be-remembered material to a frame (e.g., a strongly structured poem).

- Perhaps the best way to form memory connections is to understand the material to be remembered. In understanding, you form many connections within the material to be remembered, and also between this material and other knowledge. With all of these retrieval paths, it becomes easy to locate this material in memory. Consistent with these suggestions, studies have shown a close correspondence between the ability to understand some material and the ability to recall that material later on; this pattern has been demonstrated with stories, visual patterns, number series, and many other sorts of stimuli.

The Workbook Connection

See the *Cognition Workbook* for further exploration of the acquisition of memories and the working-memory system:

- Demonstration 5.1: Primacy and Recency Effects
- Demonstration 5.2: Chunking
- Demonstration 5.3: The Effects of Unattended Exposure

- Demonstration 5.4: Depth of Processing
- Research Methods: Replication
- Cognitive Psychology and Education: "How Should I Study?"
- Cognitive Psychology and the Law: The Video-Recorder View

NEED HELP STUDYING?

 wwnorton.com/studyspace

Visit StudySpace to access free review material such as
- Chapter study plans
- Quizzes
- Flashcards, and more

Go to **wwnorton.com/zaps** for these online labs:
- Iconic Memory
- Memory Span
- Operation Span
- Brown-Peterson Task
- Sternberg Search
- Serial Position Task

CHAPTER SIX

Interconnections Between Acquisition and Retrieval

P utting information into long-term memory helps you only if you can retrieve that information later on. Otherwise, it would be like putting money into a savings account without the option of ever making withdrawals, or like writing books that could never be read. It's equally clear that there are different ways to retrieve information from memory. You can try to *recall* the information ("What was the name of your tenth-grade homeroom teacher?") or to *recognize* it ("Was the name perhaps Miller?"). If you try to recall the information, a variety of cues may or may not be available (you might be told, as a hint, that the name began with an *M* or rhymed with "tiller").

In Chapter 5, we largely ignored these variations in retrieval. We talked as if material was well established in memory or was not, with no regard for how the material would be retrieved from memory. There's every reason to believe, however, that we cannot ignore these variations

- Learning does not simply place information in memory; instead, learning prepares you to retrieve the information in a particular way. As a result, learning that is good preparation for one sort of memory retrieval may be inadequate for other sorts of retrieval.

- In general, retrieval seems to be most likely if your mental perspective is the same during learning and during retrieval, just as we would expect if learning establishes retrieval paths that help you later only if you "travel" the same path in your effort toward locating the target material.

- Some experiences seem to produce unconscious memories, and an examination of these "implicit memory" effects will help us understand the broad set of ways in which memory influences you and will also help us see where the feeling of familiarity comes from.

- Finally, an examination of amnesia confirms a central theme of the chapter—namely, that we cannot speak of "good" or "bad" memory in general; instead, we need to evaluate memory by considering how, and for what purposes, the memory will be used.

in retrieval, and in this chapter we'll examine the interactions between how exactly a bit of information was learned and how it is retrieved later on.

As we'll see, this examination will lead us into several crucial issues. One will involve the conscious experience of *familiarity*, and we'll need to ask what causes this experience. This will in turn lead us into an intriguing set of cases in which people are influenced by memories that they aren't at all aware of—memories that are, in effect, unconscious. We'll also need to consider what "optimal" learning might be: If you want to maximize your chances of recalling what you learned in a college course, or if you want to remember as much as possible about some event in your life, how should you proceed? Our discussion will guide us toward some surprising answers to this question.

Learning as Preparation for Retrieval

Why should there be any relationship between the way you put information *into* memory and the way you take it *out*—i.e., between the particular way you learn and the particular form of memory retrieval? The answer begins with a point we made in Chapter 5: When you are learning, we argued, you're making connections between the newly acquired material and other representations already in your memory. These connections help you because they make the new knowledge "findable" later on. Specifically, the connections serve as *retrieval paths*: When you want to locate information in memory, you travel on those paths, moving from one memory to the next until you reach the target material.

These claims seem simple enough, but they have an important implication. To see this, bear in mind that retrieval paths—like any paths—have a starting point and an ending point: The path leads you from a certain Point A to a certain Point B. That's obviously useful if you want to move from A to B, but what if you're trying to reach B from somewhere else? What if you're trying to reach Point B, but at the moment you happen to be nowhere close to Point A? In that case, this path linking A and B may not help you.

As an analogy, imagine that you're trying to reach Chicago from the west. For this purpose, what you need is some highway coming in from the west. It won't be helpful that you've constructed a wonderful road coming into Chicago from the *south*. That road might be valuable in other circumstances, but it's not the path you need to get from where you are right now to where you're heading.

Do retrieval paths in memory work the same way? If so, we might find cases in which someone's learning is excellent preparation for one sort of retrieval, but useless for other types of retrieval—as if he's built a road coming in from one direction but now needs a road from another direction. Is this indeed the pattern of the data?

WORKBOOK
DEMONSTRATION 6.1

Context-Dependent Learning

Consider a broad class of studies on **context-dependent learning** (Eich, 1980; Overton, 1985). In one such study, Godden and Baddeley (1975) asked scuba divers to learn various materials. Some of the divers learned the material while sitting on dry land; others learned the material while 20 feet underwater, hearing the material via a special communication set. Within each group, half of the divers were then tested while above water, and half were tested below (see Figure 6.1).

Underwater, the world has a different look, feel, and sound, and this could easily influence what thoughts come to mind for the divers in this situation. Imagine, for example, that a diver is feeling a bit cold while underwater. This context will probably lead the diver to think "cold-related" thoughts, and so those thoughts will be in the diver's mind during the learning episode. This makes it likely that the diver will form some sort of memory connections between these thoughts and the materials he's trying to learn.

How will this learning context influence the data? If this diver is back underwater at the time of the memory test, it's plausible that he'll again feel cold, and this may once again lead him to "cold-related" thoughts. These thoughts, in turn, are now connected (we've proposed) to the target materials, and that gives us what we want: The cold triggers certain thoughts, and, thanks to the connections formed during learning, those thoughts can trigger the target memories.

Of course, all is not lost if the diver is tested for the same memory materials *on land*. In this case, the diver might have some other links, some other memory connections, that will lead to the target memories. Even so, the diver will be at a disadvantage: On land, the "cold-related" thoughts are not triggered, and so there will be no benefit from the connections that are now in place, linking those thoughts to the sought-after memories.

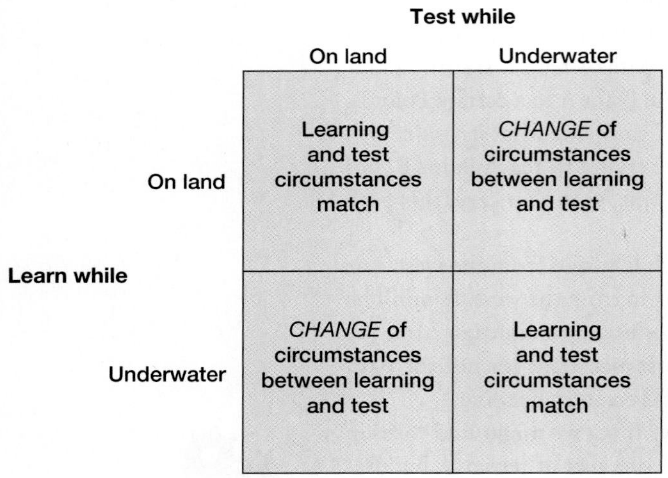

Test while

	On land	Underwater
On land	Learning and test circumstances match	*CHANGE* of circumstances between learning and test
Underwater	*CHANGE* of circumstances between learning and test	Learning and test circumstances match

Learn while

FIGURE 6.1 | THE DESIGN OF A CONTEXT-DEPENDENT LEARNING EXPERIMENT

Half of the participants (deep-sea divers) learned the test material while underwater; half learned while sitting on land. Then, within each group, half were tested while underwater; half were tested on land. We expect a retrieval advantage if the learning and test circumstances match. Hence, we expect better performance in the top left and bottom right cells.

By this logic, then, we should expect that divers who learn material while underwater will remember the material best if they're again underwater at the time of the test. This setting will allow them to use the connections they established earlier. In terms of our earlier analogy: They've built certain highways, and we've put them into a situation in which they can use what they've built. And, of course, the opposite is true for divers who learned while on land; they should do best if tested on land. And that is exactly what the data show (see Figure 6.2).

Similar results have been obtained in many other studies, including studies designed to mimic the life situation of a college student: In one experiment, the research participants read a two-page article on psychoimmunology, similar to the sorts of readings they might encounter in their college courses. Half the participants read the article in a quiet setting; half read it in noisy circumstances. When later given a short-answer test, those who read the article in quiet did best if tested in quiet—67% correct answers, compared to 54% correct if tested in a noisy environment. Those who read the article in a noisy environment did better if tested in a noisy environment—62% correct, compared to 46% (Grant et al., 1998; also see Balch, Bowman, & Mohler, 1992; Cann & Ross, 1989; Schab, 1990; Smith, 1985; Smith & Vela, 2001).

Smith, Glenberg, and Bjork (1978) report the same pattern if learning and testing take place in different *rooms*—with the rooms varying in their visual appearance, sounds, and even scent. The data showed that recall was best if done in the room in which the initial learning took place. In this study, though, there was an important twist: In one version of the procedure, the participants learned materials in one room and were tested in a different room. Just before testing, however, the participants were urged to think about the room in which they had learned— what it looked like and how it made them feel. When tested, these participants

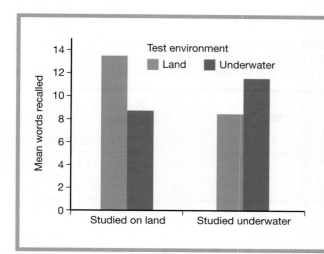

Mean words recalled

Test environment
■ Land ■ Underwater

Studied on land   Studied underwater

FIGURE 6.2 | CONTEXT-DEPENDENT LEARNING

Scuba divers learned materials either while on land, or while underwater. Then they were tested while on land, or underwater. Performance was best if the divers' circumstances at the time of test were matched to those in place during learning. (After Godden & Baddeley, 1975)

performed as well as those participants for whom there was no room change (Smith, 1979). What matters, therefore, is not the *physical* context but the *psychological* context—a result that's entirely consistent with our account of this effect.

Changes in Your Approach to the Memory Materials

In a number of settings, then, recall performance is best if your state at the time of testing matches your state at the time of learning. As a result, we can easily demonstrate a benefit of **context reinstatement**—that is, improved memory performance if we re-create the context that was in place during learning. Let's be clear, though, that the context has its effect only because it influences how you think about the materials to be remembered; it's these thoughts, and the perspective you had taken during learning and during the test, that matter for memory, not the physical environment per se.

Consistent with these ideas, we can get a similar result with no change at all in physical context—by manipulating someone's perspective directly. Fisher and Craik (1977) presented their research participants with a series of word pairs. The participants were instructed to learn the second word in each pair and to use the first word in the pair only "as an aid to remembering the target words." For half of the pairs, this other word was semantically associated with the target word; for example, if participants were shown "cat," they were also shown the context word "dog." This association should have encouraged them to think about the words' meanings. For the other pairs, the context word was one that rhymed with the target (e.g., if shown "cat," they were also shown the context word "hat"). This association should have encouraged participants to think about the target word's sound.

When the time came for a test, participants were given a hint—more properly called a **retrieval cue**—to help them recall each word. In some trials, the cue focused on meaning ("Was there a word on the list associated with 'dog'?"); in

| TABLE 6.1 | PERCENTAGE OF WORDS RECALLED AFTER PRIOR ASSOCIATION WITH EITHER MEANING OR SOUND |

Type of processing at time of learning	TYPE OF HINT		
	Meaning	Sound	Both combined
Meaning	44%	17%	30.5%
Sound	17%	26%	21.5%

SOURCE: AFTER FISHER & CRAIK (1977).

other trials, the cue concerned sound ("Was there a word on the list associated with 'hat'?"). Table 6.1 shows the results. Note, first, the column all the way to the right (averaging together trials with meaning hints and trials with sound hints). Consistent with the data in Chapter 5, thinking about meaning led to better memory, in this case with an advantage of 30.5% to 21.5%. Thus, people who thought about meaning at the time of learning remembered about 50% more than people who thought about sound. But now look at the table's other two columns. If participants thought about meaning at the time of learning, they did considerably better in the test if the cues provided by the experimenter concerned meaning. The same was true for sound: If they thought about sound at the time of learning, they did better with a cue concerning the word's sound.

In fact, the table shows two separate influences on memory working at the same time: an advantage for thinking about meaning (overall, performance is better in the top row) and an advantage for matched learning and test conditions (overall, performance is best in the main diagonal of the table). In the table's top left cell, these effects combine, and here performance is better (44%) than in any other condition. These two effects clash, though, in the column showing the results of the sound hint. The advantage from thinking about meaning favors the top cell in this column; the advantage from matched learning and test conditions favors the bottom cell. As it turns out, the match effect wins over the levels-of-processing effect: "Deep but unmatched" (17%) is inferior to "not so deep, but matched" (26%). Thus, the advantage for deep processing is simply overturned in this situation.

Encoding Specificity

The results we've been describing provide an important message about memory retrieval—and, in particular, help us understand why retrieval sometimes fails. But the results also illuminate another point: just what it is that's stored in memory. Let's go back to the scuba-diving experiment: The divers in this study didn't just remember the words they'd learned; apparently, they also remembered something about the context in which this learning took place. Otherwise, the data in Figure 6.2 (and related findings) make no sense: If the context had left no trace in memory, there'd be no way for a *return* to the context to influence the participants later.

The suggestion, then, is that what's preserved in memory is some record of the target material (that is, the information you're focusing on) *and also* some record of the connections you established during learning. To return to our analogy one more time: Your brain contains the target information *and* the highways you've now built, leading toward that information. These highways—the memory connections—can obviously influence your search for the target information; that's what we've been emphasizing so far. But the connections can do more: They can also change the *meaning* of what is remembered because, in many settings, "memory plus *this* set of connections" has a different meaning from "memory plus *that* set of connections." That change in meaning, in turn, can have profound consequences for how you remember the past.

In one experiment, participants read target words (e.g., "piano") in either of two contexts: "The man lifted the piano" or "The man tuned the piano." In each case, the sentence led the participants to think about the target word in a particular way, and it was this thought that was encoded into memory. Thus, what was placed in memory was not just the word "piano." Instead, what was recorded in memory was the idea of "piano as something heavy" or "piano as musical instrument."

This difference in memory content became clear when participants were later asked to recall the target words. If they had earlier seen the "lifted" sentence, they were quite likely to recall the target word if given the cue "something heavy." The hint "something with a nice sound" was much less effective. But if participants had seen the "tuned" sentence, the result reversed: Now the "nice sound" hint was effective, but the "heavy" hint was not (Barclay, Bransford, Franks, McCarrell, & Nitsch, 1974). In both cases, then, the cue was effective only if it was congruent with what was stored in memory.

Other experiments show a similar pattern, a pattern often dubbed **encoding specificity** (Tulving, 1983; also see Hunt & Ellis, 1974; Light & Carter-Sobell, 1970). This label reminds us that what you encode (i.e., place into memory) is indeed specific—not just the physical stimulus as it was encountered, but the stimulus together with its context. Then, if you're later presented with the stimulus in *some other context*, you ask yourself, "Does this match anything I learned previously?" and you *correctly* answer no. And we emphasize that this "no" response is indeed correct. It is as if you had learned the word "other" and were later asked whether you had been shown the word "the." In fact, "the" does appear as part of "other"—more precisely, the letters "t h e" do appear within the word "other." But it's the whole that people learn, not the parts. Therefore, if you've seen "other," it's entirely sensible to deny that you have seen "the" or, for that matter, "he" or "her," even though all these letter combinations are contained within "other."

Learning a list of words works in the same way. The word "piano" was contained in what the research participants learned, just as "the" is contained in "other." What was learned, however, was not just this word; instead, what was learned was the broader, integrated experience: the word as the perceiver

understood it. Therefore "piano-as-a-musical-instrument" *isn't* what participants learned if they saw the "lifted" sentence, and so they're correct in asserting that this item wasn't on the earlier list.

The Memory Network

In Chapter 5, we introduced the idea that memory acquisition—and, more broadly, *learning*—involves the creation (or strengthening) of memory connections. In this chapter, we've returned to the idea of memory connections, building on the notion that these connections serve as retrieval paths, guiding you toward the information you seek. But what are these connections? How do they work? And who (or what?) is traveling on these "paths"?

According to many theorists, memory is best thought of as a vast *network* of ideas. We'll postpone the question of how exactly these ideas are represented; we'll return to this issue in Chapters 8, 9, and 10. For now, though, let's think of these representations as **nodes** within the network, just like the knots in a fisherman's net. (In fact, the word "node" is derived from the Latin word for knot, *nodus.*) These nodes are then tied to each other via connections we'll call **associations,** or **associative links.** Some people find it helpful to think of the nodes as being akin to lightbulbs that can be turned on by incoming electricity and to imagine the associative links as wires that carry the electricity.

Spreading Activation

Theorists speak of a node becoming *activated* when it has received a strong enough input signal. Then, once a node has been activated, it can in turn activate other nodes: Energy will spread out from the just-activated node via its associations, and this will activate the nodes connected to the just-activated node.

To put all of this more precisely, nodes receive activation from their neighbors, and as more and more activation arrives at a particular node, the **activation level** for that node increases. Eventually, the activation level will reach the node's **response threshold**. Once this happens, we say that the node **fires**. This firing has several effects, including the fact that the node will now itself be a source of activation, sending energy to its neighbors and so activating them. In addition, firing of the node will summon attention to that node; this is what it means to "find" a node within the network.

Activation levels below the response threshold, so-called **subthreshold activation,** also have an important role to play: Activation is assumed to accumulate, so that two subthreshold inputs may add together, or **summate,** and bring the node to threshold. Likewise, if a node has been partially activated recently, it is in effect already "warmed up," so that even a weak input will be sufficient to bring the node to threshold.

These claims mesh well with points we raised in Chapter 2, when we considered how neurons communicate with each other. Neurons receive activation from other neurons; once a neuron reaches its threshold, it fires, sending activation to other neurons. All of this is precisely parallel to the suggestions we're describing here.

Our current discussion also parallels the claims we offered in Chapter 3, when we described how a network of detectors might function in object recognition. Thus, the network linking *memories* to each other will resemble the networks we've described, linking *detectors* to each other (e.g., Figures 3.14 and 3.16). Detectors, like memory nodes, receive their activation from other detectors; they can accumulate activation from different inputs, and once activated to threshold levels, they fire.

Returning to long-term storage, however, the key idea here is that activation travels from node to node via the associative links. As each node becomes activated and fires, it serves as a source for further activation, spreading onward through the network. This process, known as **spreading activation**, allows us to deal with a key question: How does one navigate through the maze of associations? If you start a search at one node, how do you decide where to go from there? Our initial proposal is that you do not "choose" at all. Instead, activation spreads out from its starting point in all directions simultaneously, flowing through whatever connections are in place.

Retrieval Cues

This sketch of the memory network leaves a great deal unspecified, but even so it allows us to explain some results we've already seen. For example, why do hints help you to remember? Why is it, for example, that you draw a blank if asked, "What's the capital of South Dakota?" but then remember if given the cue, "Is it perhaps a man's name?" Here's one likely explanation. Mention of South Dakota will activate nodes in memory that represent your knowledge about this state. Activation will then spread outward from these nodes, eventually reaching nodes that represent the capital city's name. It's possible, though, that there's only a weak connection between the SOUTH DAKOTA nodes and the nodes representing PIERRE. Perhaps you're not very familiar with South Dakota, or perhaps you haven't thought about this state's capital for some time. In either case, this weak connection will do a poor job of carrying the activation, with the result that only a trickle of activation will flow into the PIERRE nodes, and so these nodes won't reach threshold and won't be "found."

Things will go differently, though, if a hint is available. If you're told, "South Dakota's capital is also a man's name," this will activate the MAN'S NAME node, and so activation will spread out from this source at the same time that activation is spreading out from the SOUTH DAKOTA nodes. Therefore, the nodes for PIERRE will now receive activation from two sources simultaneously, and this will probably be enough to lift the nodes' activation to threshold levels. In this way, question-plus-hint accomplishes more than the question by itself (see Figure 6.3).

WORKBOOK
DEMONSTRATION 6.3

Context Reinstatement

Likewise, why is it that memory retrieval is more likely to succeed if your state during retrieval is the same as it was during learning? Why is it that, if you were underwater during learning, you'll have an easier time remembering what you learned if you're again underwater during the memory test?

We've already suggested that being underwater will bring certain thoughts to mind during your learning, and it seems likely that some of these thoughts will

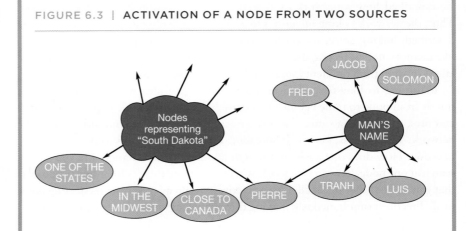

FIGURE 6.3 | ACTIVATION OF A NODE FROM TWO SOURCES

A participant is asked, "What is the capital of South Dakota?" This activates the SOUTH DAKOTA *nodes, and activation spreads from there to all of the associated nodes. However, it is possible that the connection between* SOUTH DAKOTA *and* PIERRE *is weak, so* PIERRE *may not receive enough activation to reach threshold. Things will go differently, though, if the participant is also given the hint "The capital is a man's name." Now the* PIERRE *node will receive activation from two sources: the* SOUTH DAKOTA *nodes and the man's name nodes. With this double input, it is more likely that the* PIERRE *node will reach threshold. This is why the hint ("man's name") makes the memory search easier.*

become associated with the materials being learned. With this base, the logic here is the same as it was in our discussion of hints. Imagine that you learn a list of words while underwater, including the words "home," "city," and "nose" (see Figure 6.4). If asked later, "What words were on the list?" activation will flow outward from the nodes representing your general thoughts about the list. Perhaps enough of this activation will reach the "HOME," "CITY," and "NOSE" nodes to activate them, but perhaps not. If, however, you're again underwater at the time of the test, then this will trigger certain thoughts, and we just suggested that the nodes representing these thoughts may be linked to the nodes representing the learned material. As a result, the "HOME," "CITY," and "NOSE" nodes will be receiving a double input: They will receive activation from the nodes representing thoughts about the list, and also from the nodes representing the underwater thoughts. This double input makes it more likely that they will be activated, leading to the memory advantage that we associate with context reinstatement.

Semantic Priming

The explanations we've just offered rest on a key assumption—namely, the *summation of subthreshold activation*. In other words, in explaining *memory cues*

FIGURE 6.4 | THE BASIS FOR CONTEXT REINSTATEMENT
EFFECTS

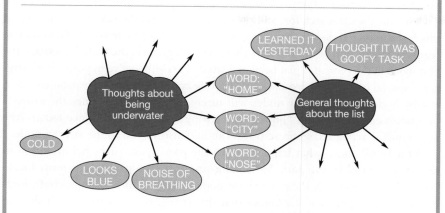

*Why is it helpful, when trying to recall something, to re-create the context? The
information you seek in memory is probably tied to the retrieval cue you're given
(e.g., "What was on the list?"), but it's possible that the information you seek
receives insufficient activation from this source. However, the information you seek
may also be tied in memory to thoughts that had been triggered by the learning
context (e.g., thoughts about being underwater). If you're back in that context at
the time of recall, the target nodes can receive a double input (i.e., activation from
two different sources), and this will help activate the target nodes.*

and *context reinstatement*, we've relied on the idea that the insufficient activation received from one source can add to the insufficient activation received from
another source. Either source of activation on its own would not be enough, but
the two can combine to activate the target nodes.

Can we document this summation more directly? In a **lexical-decision task**,
research participants are shown a series of letter sequences on a computer screen.
Some of the sequences spell words; other sequences aren't words (e.g., "blar"
or "plome"). The participants' task is to hit a "yes" button if the sequence
spells a word and a "no" button otherwise. Presumably, they perform this task
by "looking up" these letter strings in their "mental dictionary," and they base
their response on whether they find the string in the dictionary or not. We can
therefore use the participants' speed of response in this task as an index of how
quickly they can locate the word in their memories.

In a series of classic studies, Meyer and Schvaneveldt (1971; Meyer, Schvaneveldt, & Ruddy, 1974) presented participants with *pairs* of letter strings, and
participants had to respond "yes" if both strings were words and "no" otherwise.
Thus, participants would say "yes" in response to "chair, bread" but "no" in
response to "house, fime." In addition, if both strings were words, sometimes the
words were semantically related in an obvious way (e.g., "nurse, doctor") and

sometimes they were not ("lake, shoe"). Of central interest was how this relationship between the words would influence performance.

Consider a trial in which participants see a related pair, like "bread, butter." To choose a response, they first need to "look up" the word "bread" in memory. This means they'll search for, and presumably activate, the relevant node, and in this fashion they'll decide that, yes, this string is a legitimate word. Then they're ready for the second word. But note that, in this sequence, the node for BREAD (the first word in the pair) has just been activated. This will, we've hypothesized, trigger a spread of activation outward from this node, bringing activation to other, nearby nodes. These nearby nodes will surely include BUTTER, since the association between "bread" and "butter" is a strong one. Therefore, once BREAD (the first word) is activated, some activation should also spread to the BUTTER node.

Now think about what happens when the participant turns her attention to the second word in the pair. To select a response, the participant must locate "butter" in memory. If the participant finds this word (or, more precisely, finds the relevant node), then she knows that this string, too, is a word, and she can hit the "yes" button. But of course the process of activating the BUTTER node has already begun, thanks to the (subthreshold) activation this node just received from BREAD. This should accelerate the process of bringing this node to threshold (since it's already partway there!), and so it will require less time to activate. Hence, we expect quicker responses to "butter" in this context, compared to a context in which "butter" was preceded by some unrelated word.

Our prediction, therefore, is that trials with related words will produce **semantic priming.** The term "priming" is used to indicate that a specific prior event (in this case, the presentation of the first word in the pair) will produce a state of readiness (and hence faster responding) later on. There are various forms of priming (in Chapter 3, we discussed *repetition* priming). In the procedure we're considering here, the priming results from the fact that the two words in the pair are related in meaning—and hence this is *semantic* priming.

The results confirm these predictions—and thus semantic priming is observed. Participants' lexical-decision responses were faster by almost 100 ms if the stimulus words were related, so that the first word could prime the second in the fashion we just described (see Figure 6.5). This is exactly as we would expect on the model we are developing. (For other relevant studies, including some alternative conceptions of priming, see Hutchison, 2003; Lucas, 2000.)

Before pressing on, though, we should mention that this process of spreading activation—with one node activating nearby nodes—is not the whole story for memory search. As one complication, people surely have some degree of control over the *starting points* for their memory searches, relying on the processes of reasoning (Chapter 11) and the mechanisms of executive control (Chapters 4 and 5). In addition, evidence suggests that, once the spreading activation has begun, people have the option of "shutting down" some of this spread if they are convinced the wrong nodes are being activated (e.g., Anderson & Bell, 2001; Johnson & Anderson, 2004). Even so, spreading activation is a crucial mechanism—playing a central role in retrieval, and helping us understand why memory connections are so important and so helpful.

WORKBOOK DEMONSTRATION 6.4

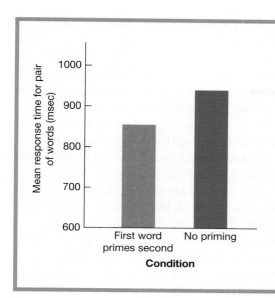

FIGURE 6.5 | SEMANTIC PRIMING

Participants were given a lexical-decision task involving pairs of words. In some pairs, the words were semantically related (and so the first word in the pair primed the second); in other pairs, the words were unrelated (and so there was no priming). Responses to the second word were reliably faster if the word had been primed—providing clear evidence of the importance of subthreshold activation. (After Meyer & Schaneveldt, 1971)

Different Forms of Memory Testing

Let's pause to take stock of where we are. In Chapter 5, we argued that learning involves the creation or strengthening of connections. This is why memory is promoted by understanding (because understanding consists, in large part, of seeing how new material is connected to other things you know). We also proposed that these connections later serve as *retrieval paths,* guiding your search through the vast warehouse that is memory. In this chapter, we've explored an important implication of this idea: that (like all paths) the paths through memory have both a starting point and an end point. Therefore, retrieval paths will be helpful only if you're at the appropriate starting point; this, we've proposed, is the basis for the advantage termed *context reinstatement.* And, finally, we've now started to lay out what these paths really are: connections that carry activation from one memory to another.

This theoretical base also helps us with another issue: the impact of different forms of memory *testing.* Both in the laboratory and in day-to-day life, we often want to **recall** information we encountered earlier. This means that we're presented a retrieval cue that broadly identifies the information that we seek, but then we need to come up with the information on our own: "What was the name of that great restaurant that your parents took us to?"; "Can you remember the words to that song?"; "Where were you last Saturday?"

In other circumstances, though, you draw information from your memory via **recognition**. This term refers to cases in which information is presented to you, and you must decide whether it's the sought-after information or not: "Is this the man who robbed you?"; "I'm sure I'll recognize the street when we get there"; "If you let me taste that wine, I'll tell you if it's the same one we had last time."

These two modes of retrieval—recall and recognition—turn out to be fundamentally different from each other. Recall, by its very nature, requires memory search because you have to come up with the sought-after item on your own; you need to locate that item within memory. As a result, recall depends heavily on the memory connections we've been emphasizing so far. Recognition, in contrast, turns out to be something of a "hybrid." To put this in concrete terms, imagine that you're taking a recognition test, and the fourth word on the test is "loon." You might say to yourself, "Yes, I remember seeing this word on the previous list, because I remember the image that came to mind when I saw this word." In this situation, you're making a recognition judgment (did you see this word before or not?), but you're actually basing your judgment on recall of the earlier episode. It's no surprise, then, that this sort of recognition follows the same rules as recall, and so is more likely if you formed the relevant connections during learning.

Sometimes, though, recognition works differently. Let's say that you're taking a recognition test, and the fifth word on the test is "butler." In response to this word, you might find yourself thinking this way, "I don't recall seeing this word on the list, but this word feels extraordinarily familiar, so I guess I must have seen it recently. Therefore, it must have been on the list." In this case you do not have what's called **source memory**; that is, you do not have any recollection of the *source* of your current knowledge. But you do have a strong sense of **familiarity**, and you're willing to make an inference about where that familiarity came from. In other words, you attribute the familiarity to the earlier encounter, and thanks to this **attribution**, you'll probably respond "yes" on the recognition test.

Familiarity and Source Memory

We need no new theory to talk about *source memory,* because this type of memory depends on the connections we've been discussing all along. Thus, in our example, you recall where you encountered the word "loon" because there's a connection in your memory between this word and an aspect of the prior episode ("I remember thinking about the image"). That remembered fact, in turn, is likely to be tied to other ideas in your memory, and these other ideas help to identify the context ("Oh yeah, it was in that room in the Psych Building . . ." or "it was late at night . . .").

But what about familiarity? What does this sort of remembering involve? As a start, let's be clear that familiarity is truly distinct from source memory. This is evident, for example, in the fact that the two types of memory are independent of each other, so that it's possible for an event to be familiar without any source memory, and also possible for you to have source memory without any familiarity. Indeed, this independence is reflected in the common experience in which you're watching a movie, realize that one of the actors is familiar, but (with considerable frustration, and despite a lot of effort) you're unable to recall where you've seen that actor before. Or you're walking down the street, see a familiar face, and immediately find yourself asking: "Where do I know that woman from? Does she work at the grocery store I shop in? Is she the driver of the bus I often take?" You're at a loss to answer these questions; all you know is that the face is familiar.

"FAMILIAR . . . BUT *WHERE DO I KNOW HIM FROM?!?*"

The photos here all show successful TV or film actors. The odds are good that, for some of them, you will immediately know their faces as familiar but will be uncertain why *they are familiar. You know you have seen these actors in some movie, but which one? (We provide the performers' names at the chapter's end.)*

In maddening cases like these, you cannot "place" the memory, you cannot identify the episode in which the face was last encountered. But you're certain the face is familiar, even though you don't know why—a clear example of familiarity without source memory.

The inverse case (source memory without familiarity) is less common but can also be demonstrated. For example, we considered an illustration of this pattern in Chapter 2 when we discussed Capgras syndrome. In this syndrome, the patient has detailed, complete, accurate memories of the past but no sense at all of familiarity, and so faces (of family members, of friends) seem hauntingly unfamiliar.

Source memory and familiarity are also distinguishable biologically. In a number of studies, participants have been asked, during a recognition test, to make a **"remember/know"** distinction—pressing one button (to indicate "remember") if they actually recall the episode of encountering a particular item, and pressing a different button ("know") if they don't recall the encounter but just have the broad feeling that the item must have been on the earlier list. In this latter case, participants are essentially saying, "This item seems very familiar, and so I *know* it was on the earlier list, even though I *don't remember* the experience of seeing it" (Gardiner, 1988; Hicks & Marsh, 1999; Jacoby, Jones, & Dolan, 1998).

We can use fMRI scans to monitor participants' brain activity while they are taking the memory tests, and these scans make it clear that "remember" and "know" judgments depend on different brain areas. The scans show heightened activity in the hippocampus when people indicate that they "remember" a particular test item, suggesting that this brain structure is crucial for source memory. In contrast, "know" responses are associated with activity in a different area—the anterior parahippocampus, with the implication that this brain site is crucial for familiarity (Aggleton & Brown, 2006; Diana, Yonelinas, & Ranganath, 2007; Dobbins, Foley, Wagner, & Schacter, 2002; Wagner, Shannon, Kahn, & Buckner, 2005; also see Rugg & Curran, 2007; Rugg & Yonelinas, 2003).

Familiarity and source memory can also be distinguished during *learning*. Specifically, if certain brain areas (e.g., the rhinal cortex) are especially active during learning, then the stimulus is likely to seem familiar later on (and so that stimulus is likely, later, to trigger a "know" response). The obvious suggestion is that this brain site plays a key role in establishing the familiarity (see Figure 6.6). In con-

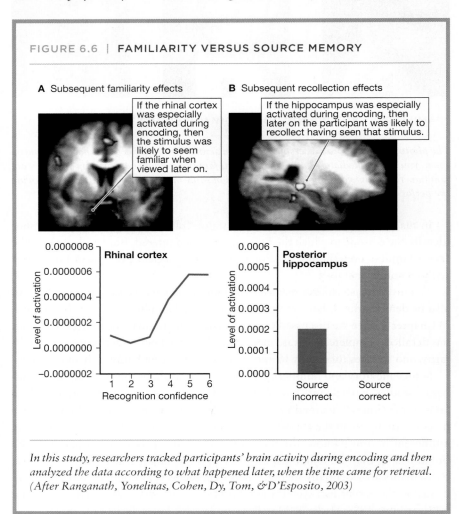

FIGURE 6.6 | **FAMILIARITY VERSUS SOURCE MEMORY**

A Subsequent familiarity effects

If the rhinal cortex was especially activated during encoding, then the stimulus was likely to seem familiar when viewed later on.

Rhinal cortex

Level of activation / Recognition confidence

B Subsequent recollection effects

If the hippocampus was especially activated during encoding, then later on the participant was likely to recollect having seen that stimulus.

Posterior hippocampus

Level of activation / Source incorrect / Source correct

In this study, researchers tracked participants' brain activity during encoding and then analyzed the data according to what happened later, when the time came for retrieval. (After Ranganath, Yonelinas, Cohen, Dy, Tom, & D'Esposito, 2003)

trast, if other brain areas (e.g., the hippocampal region) are particularly active during learning, there's a high probability that the person will offer a "remember" response to that stimulus when tested later on (e.g., Davachi & Dobbins, 2008; Davachi, Mitchell, & Wagner, 2003; Ranganath et al., 2003), implying that these brain sites are crucial for establishing source memory.

We still need to ask, though, what's going on in these various brain areas to create the relevant memories. Activity in the hippocampus is presumably helping to create the memory connections we've been discussing all along, and it is these connections, we've suggested, that promote source memory: The connections link a memory item to other thoughts that help identify the episode (the source) in which that item was encountered. This allows you to recall when and where you saw (or heard) that item. What about familiarity? What "record" does it leave in memory? The answer to this question turns out to be complicated and requires some discussion of a very different sort of "memory."

Implicit Memory

It's clear that some stimuli—a face that you see, a scent that reaches your nose— seem instantly and powerfully familiar to you. You're certain you've encountered the stimulus before; you know that it's somehow connected to your past. But what leads to this subjective sense of familiarity? As we'll see, our best path toward this issue begins with cases in which stimuli *are* familiar (i.e., they are part of your past) but *don't feel* familiar.

Memory Without Awareness

How can we find out if someone remembers a previous event? The obvious path is to ask her: "How did the job interview go?"; "Have you ever seen *Casablanca*?"; "Is this the book you told me about?" But as an alternative, we can expose some- one to an event, then later re-expose her to the same event, and assess whether her response on the second encounter is different from the first. Specifically, we can ask whether the first encounter somehow *primed* the person—got her ready—for the second exposure. If so, it would seem that the person must retain some record of the first encounter—she must have some sort of memory.

In a number of studies, participants have been asked to read through a list of words, with no indication that their memories would be tested later on. (They might be told, for example, that they're merely checking the list for spelling errors.) Then, sometime later, the participants are given a lexical-decision task: They are shown a series of letter strings and, for each, must indicate (by pressing one button or another) whether the string is a word or not. And, of course, some of the letter strings in the lexical-decision task are duplicates of the words seen in the first part of the experiment (that is, the words were on the list they checked for spelling), allowing us to ask whether this first exposure somehow primed the participants for the second encounter.

The result of such experiments is clear (e.g., Oliphant, 1983): Lexical decisions are appreciably quicker if the person has recently seen the test word; that is, lexical decision shows the pattern that (in Chapter 3) we called *repetition priming*. Remarkably, this priming is observed even when participants have no recollection for having encountered the stimulus words before. To demonstrate this, we can show participants a list of words and then test them in two different ways. One test assesses memory directly and uses a standard recognition procedure: "Which of these words were on the list I showed you earlier?" The other test is indirect and relies on lexical decision: "Which of these letter strings form real words?" In this setup, the two tests will often yield different results. At a sufficient delay, the direct memory test is likely to show that the participants have completely forgotten the words presented earlier; their recognition performance is essentially random. According to the lexical-decision results, however, they still remember the words—and so they show a robust priming effect. In this situation, then, participants seem to have no conscious memory of having seen the stimulus words, but they are nonetheless influenced by the earlier experience.

In other studies, participants have been asked to read a list of words aloud and have later been given a test in which words are presented very briefly on a computer screen; their task was simply to identify each word—to say what the word is (Jacoby, 1983; also Jacoby & Dallas, 1981; Winnick & Daniel, 1970). Unbeknownst to the participants, some of the words shown had also been presented during the procedure's initial phase, while other words were novel (i.e., had not been recently viewed). The question was whether this earlier exposure would influence performance.

Again, the result is clear (see Figure 6.7). In this task, performance was considerably improved if participants had recently viewed the test word, and again, this benefit did not depend on conscious recollection: Participants showed the repetition priming effect even for words that (when asked about directly) they could not recall seeing on the earlier list. So here, too, participants were influenced by a specific past experience that they seemed (consciously) not to remember at all—a pattern that some researchers refer to as "memory without awareness."

A different example draws on a task called **word-stem completion**. In this task, people are given three or four letters and must produce a word with this beginning. If, for example, they are given "CLA–," then "clam" or "clatter" would be an acceptable response, and the question of interest for us is which of these the person produces. It turns out (in line with the other results in this section) that people are more likely to offer a specific word if they've encountered it recently, and once again, this priming effect is observed even if participants, when tested directly, show no conscious memory of their recent encounter with that word (Graf, Mandler, & Haden, 1982).

Results like these lead psychologists to distinguish two types of memory. **Explicit memories** are those usually revealed by **direct memory testing**—testing that specifically urges you to remember the past. Recall is a direct memory test; so is a standard recognition test. **Implicit memories**, however, are typically revealed by **indirect memory testing** and are often manifested as priming effects. In this form of testing, your current behavior is demonstrably influenced by a prior event, but you may be quite unaware of this. Lexical decision, word-stem comple-

WORKBOOK
DEMONSTRATION 6.5

FIGURE 6.7 | EXPLICIT MEMORY IS DISTINCT FROM IMPLICIT MEMORY

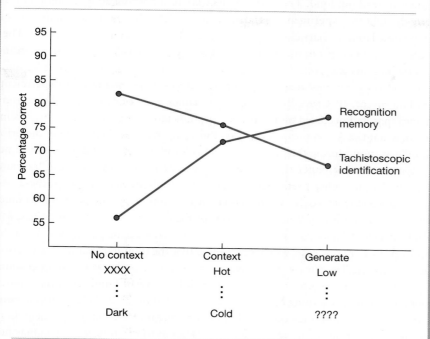

In this early study by Jacoby (1983), participants encountered words in one of three settings: In the No context setting, they saw a word and had to read it aloud. This condition did nothing to encourage any thoughts about the word's meaning, and correspondingly led to poor explicit memory (tested via a standard recognition test). But this condition forced participants to look at the word, and this led to good implicit memory (tested via tachistoscopic identification). The Generate condition produced the opposite result: In this condition, participants were given an antonym for the target word, and had to come up with the word on their own. This condition strongly encouraged thoughts about meaning, and led to good explicit memory, but involved no practice in looking at the word, and so led to poor implicit memory. The third condition, Context, produced intermediate results. Plainly, then, we see a factor (attention to meaning) that promotes explicit memory but not implicit, and a different factor (perceptual contact) that promotes implicit memory but not explicit.

tion, and many other tasks provide indirect means of assessing memory (Mulligan & Beskin, 2012).

What exactly is implicit memory? How is implicit memory different from explicit memory? We'll have more to say about these questions before we're done; first, though, we need to say more about how implicit memory *feels* from the rememberer's point of view. This will then lead us back into our discussion of familiarity and source memory.

False Fame

Jacoby, Kelley, Brown, and Jasechko (1989) presented participants with a list of names to read out loud. The participants were told nothing about a memory test; they thought the experiment was concerned with how they pronounced the names. Some time later, the participants were given the second step of the procedure. They were shown a new list of names and asked to rate each person on this list according to how famous each was. The list included some real, very famous people; some real but not-so-famous people; and some fictitious names (names the experimenters had invented). Crucially, the fictitious names were of two types: Some were names that had occurred on the prior ("pronunciation") list, and some were simply new names. A comparison between those two types will tell us how the prior familiarization (during the pronunciation task) influenced the judgments of fame.

For some participants, the "famous" list was presented right after the "pronunciation" list; for other participants, there was a 24-hour delay between these two steps. To see how this delay matters, imagine that you're a participant in the immediate-testing condition: When you see one of the fictitious-but-familiar names, you might decide, "This name sounds familiar, but that's because I just saw it on the previous list." In this case, you have a feeling that the (familiar) name is distinctive, but you also realize *why* it's distinctive, because you remember your earlier encounter with the name. In other words, you have both a sense of familiarity *and* a source memory, so there's nothing here to persuade you that the name belongs to someone famous, and you respond accordingly. But now imagine that you're a participant in the other condition, with the 24-hour delay. Thanks to this time span, you may not recall the earlier episode of seeing the name in the pronunciation task. Nonetheless, the broad sense of familiarity remains, and so in this setting you might say, "This name rings a bell, and I have no idea why. I guess this must be a famous person." And this is indeed the pattern of the data: When the two lists are presented one day apart, the participants are likely to rate the made-up names as being famous.

Apparently, the participants in this study noted (correctly) that some of the names did "ring a bell" and so did have a certain feeling of familiarity. The false judgments of fame, however, come from the way the participants *interpreted* this feeling and what conclusions they drew from it. To put it simply, participants in the 24-hour-delay condition forgot the real source of the familiarity (appearance on a recently viewed list) and instead filled in a bogus source ("Maybe I saw this person in a movie?"). And it's not hard to see why they made this particular misattribution. After all, the experiment was described to them as being about fame, and other names on the list were indeed those of famous people. From the participants' point of view, therefore, it's a reasonable inference under these circumstances that any name that "rings a bell" belongs to a famous person.

Let's be clear, though, that this misattribution is possible only because the feeling of familiarity produced by these names was relatively vague, and so open to interpretation. The suggestion, then, is that implicit memories may leave people with only a broad sense that a stimulus is somehow distinctive—that it "rings a bell" or "strikes a chord." What happens after this depends on how they interpret that feeling (see Figure 6.8).

FIGURE 6.8 | FAMILIARITY AND SPELLING

innoculate	vs.	inoculate?
embarrass	vs.	embarass?
argument	vs.	arguement?
harass	vs.	harrass?
cemetery	vs.	cemetary?
mispell	vs.	misspell?

In deciding how to spell a word, people often write out the word, then ask them-selves, "Does this look right?" This is a good strategy, but if you have regularly encountered the misspelled version of the word, these encounters can make that spelling "look right." As a result, regular encounters with the wrong *spelling can make that spelling look correct to you. This will be true even if you have no recollection of those encounters—another example of implicit memory's influence.*

Implicit Memory and the "Illusion of Truth"

How broad is this potential for *mis*interpreting an implicit memory? Participants in one study heard a series of statements and had to judge how interesting each statement was (Begg, Anas, & Farinacci, 1992). As an example, one sentence was, "The average person in Switzerland eats about 25 pounds of cheese each year." (This is false; the average is closer to 18 pounds.) Another was, "Henry Ford forgot to put a reverse gear in his first automobile." (This is true.) After hearing these sentences, the participants were presented with some more sentences, but now they had to judge the credibility of these sentences, rating them on a scale from *certainly true* to *certainly false*. Needless to say, some of the sentences in this "truth test" were repeats from the earlier presentation; the question of interest is how sentence credibility is influenced by sentence familiarity.

The result was a propagandist's dream: Sentences heard before were more likely to be accepted as true; that is, familiarity increased credibility (Begg, Armour, & Kerr, 1985; Brown & Halliday, 1990; Fiedler, Walther, Armbruster, Fay, & Naumann, 1996; Moons, Mackie, & Garcia-Marques, 2009; Unkelbach, 2007). To make things worse, this effect emerged even when the participants were explicitly warned in advance not to believe the sentences in the first list. In one procedure, participants were told that half of the statements had been made by men and half by women. The women's statements, they were told, were always true; the men's, always false. (Half the participants were told the reverse.) Then participants rated how interesting the sentences were, with each sentence attributed to either a man or a woman: "Frank Foster says that house mice can run an average of 4 miles per hour" or "Gail Logan says that crocodiles sleep with their eyes open." Later, participants were presented with more sentences and had to judge their truth, with these new sentences including the earlier assertions about mice, crocodiles, and so forth.

Let's focus on the sentences initially identified as being false—in our example, Frank's claim about mice. If someone explicitly remembers this sentence ("Oh yes—Frank said such and such"), then he should judge the assertion to be false ("After all, the experimenter said that the men's statements were all lies"). But what about someone without this explicit memory? Since the person doesn't remember whether the assertion came from a man or a woman, he can't use the source as a basis for judging the sentence's veracity. Nonetheless, the person might still have an implicit memory for the sentence left over from the earlier exposure ("Gee, that statement rings a bell"), and this might increase the credibility of the statement ("I'm sure I've heard that somewhere before; I guess it must be true"). This is exactly the pattern of the data: Statements plainly identified as false when they were first heard still created the so-called **illusion of truth**; that is, these statements were subsequently judged to be more credible than sentences never heard before.

The relevance of this result to the political arena, or to advertising, should be clear. A newspaper headline inquires, "Is Mayor Wilson a crook?" Or perhaps the headline declares, "Known criminal claims Wilson is a crook!" In either case, the assertion that Wilson is a crook has now become familiar. The Begg et al. data indicate that this familiarity will, by itself, increase the likelihood that you'll later believe in Wilson's dishonesty. This will be true even if the paper merely raised the question; it will be true even if the allegation came from a disreputable source. Malicious innuendo does in fact work nasty effects (Wegner, Wenzlaff, Kerker, & Beattie, 1981).

Attributing Implicit Memory to the Wrong Stimulus

In both the illusion-of-truth and the false-fame experiments, participants are misinterpreting a sense of familiarity: They know that a name or a sentence is familiar, but they don't realize that this is because it was on the previous list. Instead, they falsely conclude that the name is familiar because it belongs to someone famous or that the sentence is familiar because they read it in some authoritative source.

In other cases, the misinterpretation can go even further. In one experiment, participants were presented with bursts of noise and asked to judge how loud each noise was (Jacoby, Allan, Collins, & Larwill, 1988). Embedded within each burst of noise, though, was a sentence. Some of the sentences were new to participants, but—crucially—some of the sentences had been presented earlier.

In this study, memory appeared in an odd way. If a sentence was one of the previously presented ones, participants had an easier time hearing it against the backdrop of noise. This is just another case of repetition priming and so is consistent with results already described. But then the participants seemed to reason in this fashion: "Well, that sentence was easy to hear. I guess, therefore, the noise couldn't have been so loud." Likewise, for the unfamiliar sentences, they seemed to reason like this: "Gee, that noise must have been loud, since it really drowned out the sentence." As a result of these (completely unconscious) inferences, a noise that contained familiar sentences was (mis)perceived as being softer than it actually was. Noise containing novel sentences was (mis)perceived as being loud.

In this experiment, therefore, the participants seemed not to realize at all that the previously presented sentences were, in fact, familiar. All they realized is that it was easier to perceive the sentences in one condition than it was in the other, and they mistakenly attributed this difference to differing noise levels. In other words, the sentences were (objectively) familiar, but there was no subjective sense of familiarity. Indeed, the implicit memory didn't at all change how participants felt about the sentences. Instead, the memory showed its influence by changing how the participants felt about an entirely different stimulus—namely, the noise in which the sentences were embedded.

Attributing Implicit Memory to the Wrong Source

One last example will illustrate the range of cases in which you might be influenced by misplaced familiarity, and it is an example of some consequence. In a study by Brown, Deffenbacher, and Sturgill (1977), research participants witnessed a staged crime. Two or three days later, they were shown "mug shots" of individuals who supposedly had participated in the crime; but as it turns out, the people in these photos were different from the actual "criminals"—no mug shots were shown for the truly "guilty" individuals. Finally, after four or five more days, the participants were shown a lineup and asked to select the individuals seen in Step 1—namely, the original crime (see Figure 6.9).

The data in this study show a pattern known as **source confusion**. The participants correctly realized that one of the people in the lineup looked familiar, but they were confused about the source of the familiarity. They falsely believed they had seen the person's face in the original "crime," when, in truth, they'd seen that face only in a subsequent photograph. In fact, the likelihood of this error was quite high, with 29% of the participants (falsely) selecting from the lineup an individual they had seen only in the mug shots. (Also see Davis, Loftus, Vanous & Cucciare, 2008; for examples of similar errors that—sadly—interfere with a real-life criminal investigations, see Garrett, 2011.)

Theoretical Treatments of Implicit Memory

One message coming from all of these studies is that you're often better at remembering *that* something is familiar than you are at remembering *why* it is familiar. This is why it's possible to have a sense of familiarity without source memory ("I've seen her somewhere before, but I can't figure out where!"), and

FIGURE 6.9 | A PHOTO LINEUP

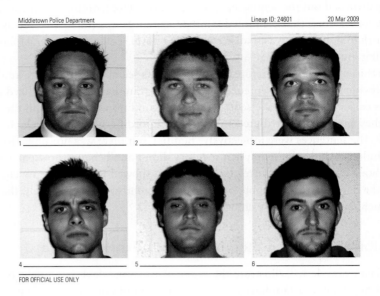

Middletown Police Department   Lineup ID: 24601   20 Mar 2009

1 _____   2 _____   3 _____

4 _____   5 _____   6 _____

FOR OFFICIAL USE ONLY

On TV, crime victims view a live lineup, but it's far more common in the United States for the victim (or witness) to see a "photo lineup" like this one. The victim (or witness) is told that the perpetrator may or may not be present and is asked to pick out the perpetrator if he's there. Unfortunately, victims sometimes pick the wrong person, and this error is more likely if the suspect is familiar to the victim for some reason other than the crime.

also why it's possible to be *correct* in judging familiarity but *mistaken* in judging source.

In addition, note that in many of these studies participants are being influenced by memories they are not aware of. In some cases, participants realize that a stimulus is somehow familiar, but they have no memory of the encounter that produced the familiarity. In other cases, people don't even have a sense of familiarity for the target stimulus; nonetheless, they're influenced by their previous encounter with the stimulus. We saw this latter pattern in the experiment involving noise judgments; other experiments show that participants often *prefer* a previously presented stimulus over a novel stimulus, even though they have no sense of familiarity with either stimulus. In such cases, people don't realize at all that their preference is being guided by memory (Murphy, 2001).

It does seem, then, that the phrase "memory without awareness" really is appropriate, and it does seem sensible to describe these memories as *implicit* memories. But what exactly are implicit memories? What is the content of these memories? It is to these questions that we now turn.

Implicit Memory: A Hypothesis

Our discussion so far—in this chapter, and in Chapters 3 and 4—has laid the foundation for a proposal about implicit memory. Let's build the argument, though, in steps: When a stimulus arrives in front of your eyes, it triggers certain detectors, and these trigger still other detectors, and these still others, until you recognize the object ("Oh, it's my stuffed bear, Blueberry"). We can think of this sequence as involving a "flow" of activation that moves from detector to detector, and we could, if we wished, keep track of this flow and in this way identify the "path" that the activation traveled through the network. Let's refer to this path as a **processing pathway**—the sequence of detectors, and the connections *between* detectors, that the activation flows through in recognizing a specific stimulus.

In the same way, we've proposed in this chapter that *remembering* often involves the activation of a node, and this node triggers other, nearby, nodes so that they become activated; they, in turn, trigger still other nodes, leading (eventually) to the information you seek in memory. So here, too, we can speak of a processing pathway—the sequence of nodes, and connections between nodes, that the activation flows through during memory retrieval.

We've also said the use of a processing pathway *strengthens* that pathway. This is because the baseline activation level of nodes or detectors increases if the nodes or detectors have been used frequently in the past, or if they've been used recently. Likewise, connections (between detectors or nodes) grow stronger with use. Thus, by thinking about the link between, say, Jacob and Iowa, you strengthen the connection between the corresponding nodes, and this will help you remember that Jacob lived in Iowa.

Now let's put the pieces together: Use of a processing pathway strengthens the pathway. As a result, the pathway will be a bit more efficient, a bit faster, the next time you use it. Theorists describe this fact by saying that use of a pathway increases the **processing fluency** of that pathway—that is, the speed and ease with which the pathway will carry activation.

In many cases, this is all the theory we need to explain implicit memory effects: Consider, for example, implicit memory's effect on lexical decision. In this procedure, you first are shown a list of words, including, let's say, the word "trifle." Then, later, we ask you to do the lexical-decision task and you're faster for words (like "trifle") that had been included in the earlier list. It's this increase in speed that provides our evidence for implicit memory. The explanation, though, is straightforward: When we show you "trifle" early in the experiment, you read the word, and this involves activation flowing through the appropriate processing pathway for this word. This "warms up" the pathway, and, as a result, the path's functioning will be more fluent the next time you use it. Then, in the lexical-decision task, you see a bunch of new words. If "trifle" is included in the test, it's handled by the processing pathway that you just warmed up. This increases your speed in recognizing this word—and that, of course, is the result we're trying to explain.

To explain other implicit-memory effects, though, we need a further assumption—namely, that people are sensitive to the *degree* of processing fluency. That is, just as people can easily tell whether they've lifted a heavy carton or a lightweight one, just as they can tell whether they've answered an easy question ("What's 2 + 2?") or a harder one ("What's 17 × 19?"), people also have a broad sense of when they have perceived easily and when they have perceived only by expending more effort. They likewise know when a sequence of thoughts was particularly fluent and when the sequence was labored. This fluency, however, is perceived in an odd way. When a stimulus is easy to perceive (for example), people do not experience something like, "That stimulus sure was easy to recognize!" Instead, they merely register a vague sense of specialness. They feel that the stimulus "rings a bell." No matter how it is described, though, this sense of specialness has a simple cause—namely, the detection of ease-in-processing, brought on by fluency, which in turn was created by practice.[1]

We need one more step in our hypothesis, but it's a step we have already introduced: When a stimulus feels special, people typically want to know why. Thus, the vague, hard-to-pinpoint feeling of specialness (again, produced by fluency) triggers an attribution process, as people seek to ask, "Why did that stimulus stand out?" In many circumstances, that question will be answered correctly, and so the specialness will be (accurately) interpreted as *familiarity* and attributed to the correct source. ("That picture seems distinctive, and I know why: It's the same picture I saw yesterday in the dentist's office.") In other situations, though, things may not go so smoothly, and so—as we have seen—people sometimes misinterpret their own processing fluency, falling prey to the errors and illusions we have been discussing.

The Nature of Familiarity

All of these points provide us—at last—with a proposal for what "familiarity" is, and the proposal is surprisingly complex. One might think that familiarity is a feeling produced more or less directly when you encounter a stimulus you have met before. The findings of the last few sections, though, point toward a different proposal—namely, that "familiarity" is more like a *conclusion that you draw* rather than a *feeling* triggered by a stimulus. Specifically, the evidence suggests that a stimulus will seem familiar whenever the following list of requirements is met: First, you have encountered the stimulus before. Second, because of that prior encounter (and the "practice" it afforded), you are now faster and more efficient in your processing of that stimulus; that's what we're calling "processing fluency." Third, you detect that fluency, and this leads you to register the stimulus as somehow distinctive or special. Fourth, you try to figure out *why* the stimulus seems special, and you reach a particular conclusion—namely, that the stimulus has this distinctive quality *because* it's a stimulus you have met before in some prior episode. And then, finally, you may

---

1. Actually, what people detect, and what makes a stimulus feel "special," may not be fluency per se. Instead, what they detect may be a *discrepancy* between how easy (or hard) it was to carry out some mental step and how easy (or hard) they expected it to be, in light of the context and their experience. (See, for example, Whittlesea, 2002.) A stimulus is registered as distinctive, or "rings a bell," when this discrepancy reaches too high a level. Having acknowledged this, however, we will, for simplicity's sake, ignore this complication in our discussion.

CHANGES IN APPEARANCE

The text emphasizes our sensitivity to increases in fluency, but we can also detect decreases. In viewing a picture of a well-known actor, for example, you might notice immediately that something is new in his appearance, but you might be clueless about what exactly the change involves. In this setting, the change in appearance disrupts your well-practiced steps of perceiving for an otherwise familiar face, and so the perception is less fluent than it has been in the past. This lack of fluency is what gives you the "something is new" feeling. But then the attribution step fails: You cannot identify what produced this feeling (and so you end up offering various lame hypotheses, like "Is that a new haircut?" when, in fact, it's the goatee that is new). This case therefore provides the mirror image of the cases we have been considering, in which familiarity leads to an increase in fluency, so that something "rings a bell" but you cannot say why.

draw a further conclusion about when and where you encountered the stimulus—in the experimenter's list of words, or yesterday in the newspaper, and so on.

Let's be clear, though, that none of these steps happens consciously; you're not aware of seeking an interpretation or trying to explain why a stimulus feels distinctive. All you experience consciously is the end product of all these steps: the sense that a stimulus feels familiar. Moreover, this conclusion about a stimulus isn't one you draw capriciously; instead, you arrive at this conclusion, and decide a stimulus is familiar, only when you have supporting information. Thus, imagine that you encounter a stimulus that "rings a bell." You're more likely to decide the stimulus is familiar if you also have an (explicit) source memory, so that you can recollect where and when you last encountered that stimulus ("I know this stimulus is familiar *because I can remember seeing it yesterday*"). You're also more likely to decide that a stimulus is familiar if the surrounding circumstances support it: If you are asked, for example, "Which of these words were on the list you saw earlier?" the question itself gives you a cue that some of the words were recently encountered, and so you're more likely to attribute fluency to that encounter.

The fact remains, though, that judgments of familiarity can go astray, which is why we need this complicated theory. We have considered several cases in

FIGURE 6.10 | THE CHAIN OF EVENTS LEADING TO THE SENSE OF "FAMILIARITY"

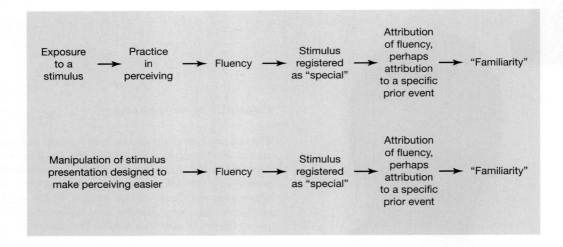

In the top line, practice in perceiving leads to fluency, and if the person attributes the fluency to some specific prior encounter, the stimulus will "feel familiar." The bottom line, however, indicates that fluency can be created in other ways: by presenting the stimulus more clearly or for a longer exposure. Once this fluency is detected, though, it can lead to steps identical to those in the top row. Hence, an "illusion of familiarity" can be created.

which a stimulus is objectively familiar (you've seen it recently) but does not *feel* familiar—just as our theory predicts. In these cases, you detect the fluency but attribute it to some other source ("The noise is soft" rather than "The sentence is familiar," or "That melody is lovely" rather than "The melody is familiar"). In other words, you go through all of the steps shown in the top of Figure 6.10 except for the last two: You do not attribute the fluency to a specific prior event, and so you do not experience a sense of familiarity.

We can also find the opposite sort of case—in which a stimulus is not familiar (i.e., you've not seen it recently) but feels familiar anyhow—and this, too, fits with the theory. This sort of *illusion of familiarity* can be produced, for example, if the processing of a completely novel stimulus is more fluent than you expected—perhaps because (without telling you) we've sharpened the focus of a computer display, or presented the stimulus for a few milliseconds longer than other stimuli you're inspecting (Jacoby & Whitehouse, 1989; Whittlesea, 2002; Whittlesea, Jacoby, & Girard, 1990). In cases like these, we have the situation shown in the bottom half of Figure 6.10, and as our theory predicts, these situations do produce an illusion: Your processing of the stimulus is unexpectedly fluent; you seek an attribution for this fluency, and you are fooled into thinking the stimulus is familiar—and so you say you've seen the stimulus before, when in fact you haven't. This illusion is a powerful confirmation that the sense of familiarity does rest on processes like the ones we've described. (For more on fluency, see Hertwig, Herzog, Schooler, & Reimer, 2008; Oppenheimer, 2008;

Tsai & Thomas, 2011. For a glimpse of what fluency amounts to in the nervous system, see Knowlton & Foerde, 2008.)

The Hierarchy of Memory Types

There's no question that we are often influenced by the past without being aware of that influence. We often respond differently to familiar stimuli than we do to novel stimuli, even if we have no subjective feeling of familiarity. Thus, our conscious recollection seriously underestimates what is in our memories, and researchers have only begun to document the ways in which unconscious memories influence what we do, think, and feel. (For examples, though, of some of the relevant research, see Coates, Butler, & Berry, 2006; Kahneman, 2011; Roediger & Marsh, 2005; or Thomson, Milliken & Smilek, 2010.)

In addition, the data are clearly telling us that there are two different kinds of memory: one typically conscious and deliberate, one typically unconscious and automatic. Moreover, evidence is piling up that these two broad categories must be further subdivided, as shown in Figure 6.11. Explicit memories can be subdivided into episodic memories (memory for specific events) and semantic memory (more general knowledge). Implicit memory is often divided into four subcategories, as shown in the figure. Our emphasis here has been on one of the subtypes—priming—largely because of its role in producing the feeling of familiarity. However, the other subtypes of implicit memory are also important

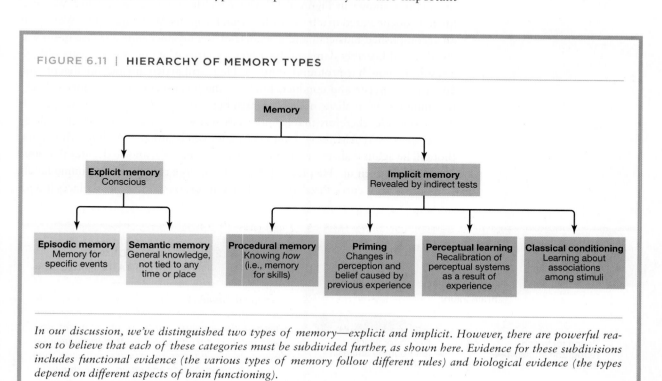

FIGURE 6.11 | HIERARCHY OF MEMORY TYPES

In our discussion, we've distinguished two types of memory—explicit and implicit. However, there are powerful reason to believe that each of these categories must be subdivided further, as shown here. Evidence for these subdivisions includes functional evidence (the various types of memory follow different rules) and biological evidence (the types depend on different aspects of brain functioning).

and can be distinguished from priming both in terms of their functioning (i.e., they follow somewhat different rules) and in terms of their biological underpinnings.

Some of the best evidence for all of these distinctions, though, comes from the clinic, not the laboratory. In other words, we can learn a great deal about these various types of memory by considering individuals who have suffered various forms of brain damage. Let's look at some of that evidence.

Amnesia

A variety of injuries or illnesses can lead to a loss of memory, or **amnesia**. Some forms of amnesia are *retrograde*, meaning that they disrupt memory for things learned *prior to* the event that initiated the amnesia (see Figure 6.12). **Retrograde amnesia** is often caused, for example, by blows to the head; the afflicted person is then unable to recall events that occurred just before the blow. Other forms of amnesia have the reverse effect, causing disruption of memory for experiences *after* the onset of amnesia; these are cases of **anterograde amnesia**. (We should note that many cases of amnesia involve both retrograde and anterograde memory loss.)

Disrupted Episodic Memory, but Spared Semantic Memory

Studies of amnesia can teach us many things. For example, do we need all the distinctions shown in Figure 6.11? Consider the tragic case of Clive Wearing, lovingly documented in a book by his wife, Deborah (Wearing, 2011). Wearing is an accomplished musician and a scholar of Renaissance music whose brain was invaded and horribly damaged by a Herpes virus when he was 47 years old. As a result, he now has profound amnesia. He is still articulate and intelligent, and able to play music and conduct. But Wearing has no episodic memories. Every few minutes, he realizes he can't remember anything from just a few seconds back, concludes therefore that he must have just woken up, and writes in his diary things like, "8:31 AM. Now I am really, completely awake." A short while later, though, he again realizes he can't recall the last seconds, and so decides that *now* he has just woken up. He picks up his diary to note this event, and immediately sees his previous entry. Puzzled by the entry, he crosses it out, and replaces it with

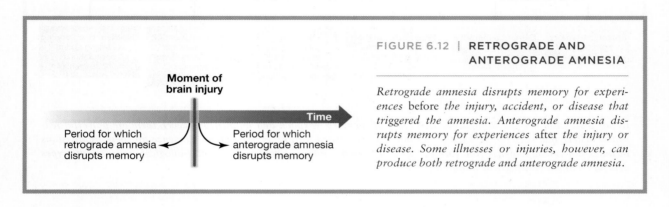

FIGURE 6.12 | RETROGRADE AND ANTEROGRADE AMNESIA

Retrograde amnesia disrupts memory for experiences before *the injury, accident, or disease that triggered the amnesia. Anterograde amnesia disrupts memory for experiences* after *the injury or disease. Some illnesses or injuries, however, can produce both retrograde and anterograde amnesia.*

Moment of brain injury

Time

Period for which retrograde amnesia disrupts memory

Period for which anterograde amnesia disrupts memory

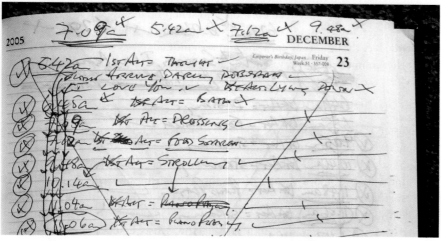

CLIVE WEARING

Clive Wearing (shown here with his wife) developed profound amnesia as a result of viral encephalitis, and now seems to have only a moment-to-moment consciousness. With no memory at all of what he was doing just moments ago, he is often convinced he just woke up, and repeatedly writes in his diary "Now perfectly awake (1st time)." On the diary page shown here, he has recorded his bath as his "1st act" because he has no memory of any prior activity. A few minutes later, though, he seems to realize again that he has no memory of any earlier events, and so he scribbles out the 6:45 entry and now records that dressing is his "1st act." The sequence repeats over and over, with Wearing never recalling what he did before his current activity, and so recording act after act as his "first."

"9:06 AM. Now I am perfectly, overwhelmingly awake." But then the process repeats, and so this entry gets scribbled out, and a new entry reads: "9:34 AM: Now I am superlatively, actually awake." (For other cases, also involving devastated episodic memory, see Rosenbaum et al., 2005; Schacter, 1996).

Wearing's episodic memory is massively disrupted, but his memory for generic information, and his deep love for his wife, seem to be entirely intact. Other patients show the reverse pattern—with disrupted semantic memory, but preserved episodic knowledge. One patient, for example suffered damage (from encephalitis) to the front portion of her temporal lobes. As a consequence, she has lost her memory of many common words, important historical events, famous people, and even the fundamental traits of animate and inanimate objects. "However, when asked about her wedding and honeymoon, her father's illness and death, or other specific past episodes, she readily produced detailed and accurate recollections" (Schacter, 1996, p. 152; also see Cabeza & Nyberg, 2000). (For more on amnesia, see Brown, 2002; Conway & Fthenaki, 1999; Kopelman & Kapur, 2001; Nadel & Moscovitch, 2001; Riccio, Millin, & Gisquet-Verrier, 2003.)

These cases (and other evidence as well) provide the *double dissociation* that demands a distinction between episodic and semantic memory. It is observations like these, therefore, that force us to a taxonomy like the one shown in Figure 6.11. (For evidence, though, that episodic and semantic memory are intertwined with each other in important ways, see McRae & Jones, 2012.)

Anterograde Amnesia

In Chapter 1, we mentioned the patient H.M. (For a review of H.M.'s case, see Milner, 1966, 1970; for more recent studies, see O'Kane, Kensinger, & Corkin, 2004; Skotko et al., 2004; Skotko, Rubin & Tupler, 2008.) H.M. suffered from profound epilepsy, and a variety of attempts at curing him had all failed. As a last resort, doctors sought (in 1953) to contain H.M.'s disorder by brain surgery, specifically by removing portions of the brain that seemed to be the source of the seizures. The surgery was, in a very narrow sense, a success, because it did improve the epilepsy. But more broadly the surgery was a disaster, because the cure for epilepsy came at an incredible cost: H.M. was now unable to learn anything new—a condition that lasted from the surgery (in 1953) until H.M.'s death in 2008, 55 years later.

H.M. could function normally in many regards and could, for example, hold a coherent, meaningful conversation. Within the conversation, he would even talk about prior events in his life, since he was able to recall many events that had taken place *prior to* the surgery. However, he couldn't recall anything that had taken place since the surgery. Episodes he had experienced, people he had met, books he had read—all seemed to leave no enduring record, as though nothing new could get into his long-term storage.

The severity of H.M.'s amnesia was evident in many ways, but the problem became instantly clear if a conversation with him was interrupted for some reason: If you spoke with him for a while, then (for example) left the room and came back 3 or

4 minutes later, he seemed to have totally forgotten that the earlier conversation ever took place; if the earlier conversation was your first meeting with H.M., he would, after the interruption, be quite certain he was now meeting you for the very first time.

H.M.'s case was unique, but a similar amnesia can be found in patients who have been longtime alcoholics. The problem is not the alcohol itself; the problem instead is that alcoholics tend to have inadequate diets, getting most of their nutrition from whatever they are drinking. It turns out, though, that most alcoholic beverages are missing several key nutrients, including vitamin B_1 (thiamine). As a result, longtime alcoholics are vulnerable to a number of problems caused by thiamine deficiency, including a disorder known as **Korsakoff's syndrome** (Rao, Larkin, & Derr, 1986; Ritchie, 1985).

Patients suffering from Korsakoff's syndrome seem in many ways similar to H.M. They typically have little problem in remembering events that took place before the onset of alcoholism. They can also maintain current topics in mind as long as there's no interruption. New information, though, if displaced from the mind, is seemingly lost forever. Korsakoff's patients who have been in the hospital for decades will casually mention that they arrived only a week ago; if asked the name of the current president or events in the news, they unhesitatingly give answers appropriate for two or three decades prior, whenever the disorder began (Marslen-Wilson & Teuber, 1975; Seltzer & Benson, 1974).

Anterograde Amnesia: What Kind of Memory Is Disrupted?

Other evidence complicates this portrait of anterograde amnesia, and returns us to issues of implicit and explicit memory. As it turns out, some of this evidence has been available for a long time: In 1911, a Swiss psychologist named Édouard Claparède (1911/1951) reported the following incident. He was introduced to a young woman suffering from Korsakoff's amnesia, and he reached out to shake her hand. However, Claparède had secretly positioned a pin in his own hand so that when they clasped hands the patient received a painful pinprick. (Respect for patient's rights would prevent any modern investigator from conducting this cruel experiment, but ethical standards were apparently different in 1911.) The next day, Claparède returned and reached out to shake hands with the patient. Not surprisingly, the patient gave no indication that she recognized Claparède or remembered anything about the prior encounter. (This simply confirms the diagnosis of amnesia.) Nevertheless, just before their hands touched, the patient abruptly withdrew her hand and refused to shake hands with Claparède. Claparède asked her why, and after some confusion the patient simply said vaguely that "sometimes pins are hidden in people's hands."

What's going on here? On the one side, this patient seemed to have no memory of the prior encounter with Claparède. She certainly did not mention the encounter in explaining her refusal to shake hands, and when questioned closely about the earlier encounter, she indicated no knowledge of it. On the other side, she plainly remembered something about the previous day's mishap; we see this clearly in her behavior.

A related pattern can be observed with other Korsakoff's patients. In one procedure, the researchers used a deck of cards like those used in popular trivia games. Each card contained a trivia question and some possible answers, offered in a multiple-choice format (Schacter, Tulving, & Wang, 1981). The experimenter showed each card to a Korsakoff's patient, and, if the patient didn't know the answer, he was told it. Then (unbeknownst to the patient) the card was replaced in the deck, guaranteeing that the same question would come up again in a few minutes. When the question did come up again, the patient was quite likely to get it right, and so apparently had learned the answer in the previous encounter and remembered the relevant information. Consistent with their diagnosis, though, the patients had no recollection of the learning: They were consistently unable to explain *why* their answers were correct. They did not say, "I know this bit of trivia because the same question came up just five minutes ago." Instead, they were likely to say things like, "I read about it somewhere" or "My sister once told me about it."

Many studies show similar results, with amnesic patients showing profound memory loss on some measures but performance within the normal range on other measures (Cohen & Squire, 1980; Graf & Schacter, 1985; Moscovitch, 1982; Schacter, 1996; Schacter & Tulving, 1982; Squire & McKee, 1993). Specifically, these patients seem completely incapable of recalling episodes or events, and so, in the terms we've been using, they seem to have no explicit memory. Even so, these patients do learn and do remember and thus seem to have intact implicit memories. Indeed, in many tests of implicit memory, amnesic patients seem indistinguishable from ordinary individuals.

Explicit Memory Without Implicit?

The results with amnesic patients add to the package of evidence we've been considering in this chapter. In particular, these patients provide powerful evidence that explicit memory is truly independent of implicit memory, with these patients plainly influenced (implicitly) by specific episodes in the past even though they have no conscious (explicit) recollection of those episodes.

Further data, also arguing for a separation between implicit and explicit memory, come from patients who have the reverse pattern of symptoms: implicit memory disrupted but explicit memory intact. One study involved a patient who had suffered brain damage to the hippocampus but not the amygdala and a second patient with the reverse problem—damage to the amygdala but not the hippocampus (Bechara et al., 1995). These patients were exposed to a series of trials in which a particular stimulus (a blue light) was reliably followed by a loud boat horn, while other stimuli (green, yellow, or red) were not followed by the horn. Later on, the patients were exposed to the blue light on its own and their bodily arousal was measured; would they show a fright reaction in response to this stimulus? In addition, the patients were asked directly, "Which color was followed by the horn?"

The patient with damage to the hippocampus did show a fear reaction to the blue light (assessed via the *skin conductance response*, a measure of bodily arousal), and so his data on this measure look just like results for control participants (i.e., people without brain damage; see Figure 6.13). However, when asked directly, this patient could not recall which of the lights had been associated with

FIGURE 6.13 | DAMAGE TO HIPPOCAMPUS AND AMYGDALA

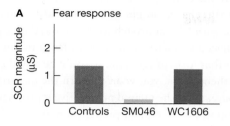

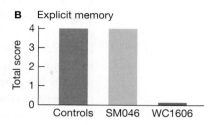

Panel A shows result for a test probing implicit memory; Panel B shows result for a test probing explicit memory. Patient SM046 had suffered damage to the amygdala, and shows little evidence of implicit memory (i.e., no fear response) but a normal level of explicit memory. Patient WC1606 had suffered damage to the hippocampus, and shows the opposite pattern: massively disrupted explicit memory, but a normal fear response. (After Bechara et al., 1995)

the boat horn. In contrast, the patient with damage to the amygdala showed the opposite pattern. She was able to report calmly that just one of the lights had been associated with the horn and that the light's color had been blue—demonstrating fully intact explicit memory. When presented with the blue light, however, she showed no fear response.

Optimal Learning

We're almost done with the chapter, but, before closing, let's put these amnesia findings into the broader context provided by the chapter's main themes. Throughout the chapter, we've argued that we cannot make claims about learning or memory acquisition without some reference to how the learning is going to be used later on. Thus, whether it's better to learn underwater or on land depends on where you will be tested. Whether it's better to learn while listening to jazz or while sitting in a quiet room depends on the music background of the memory test environment. Even whether it's best to attend to meaning depends to some extent on whether meaning will be prominent when the time comes for memory retrieval.

These ideas are echoed in the neuropsychology data. Specifically, it would be misleading to say that Korsakoff's amnesia disrupts someone's ability to learn or ruins their ability to create new memories. Instead, brain damage is likely to disrupt *some types* of learning but not others, and how this matters for the person depends on how the newly learned material will be accessed. Thus, someone who suffers hippocampal damage will likely appear normal on an indirect memory test but seem amnesic on a direct test, while someone who suffers amygdala damage will probably show the reverse pattern.

All of these points are enormously important for our theorizing about memory, but the same points have a practical implication. Right now, you are reading this material and presumably want to remember it later on. For that matter, you're also encountering new material in other settings (perhaps in other classes you are taking), and surely you want to remember that as well. How should you study all of this information if you want to maximize your chances of retaining it for later use?

At one level, the lesson of this chapter might be that the ideal form of learning would be one that is "in tune with" the approach to the material that you'll need later. If you're going to be tested explicitly, you want to learn the material in a fashion that prepares you for that form of retrieval. If you'll be tested underwater or while listening to music, then, again, you want to learn the material in a way that prepares you for that context and the mental perspective it produces. If you'll need source memory, then you want one type of preparation; if you'll need familiarity, you might want a different type of preparation.

The problem, though, is that during learning you often don't know how you'll be approaching the material later—whether your focus during retrieval will be on meaning or on sound, whether you'll need the information implicitly or explicitly, and so on. As a result, maybe the best strategy in learning would be to use *multiple perspectives*. To pick up our earlier analogy, imagine that you know that at some point in the future you'll want to reach Chicago, but you don't know yet whether you'll be approaching the city from the north, the south, or the west. In that case, your best bet might be to build multiple highways, so that you can reach your goal from any direction. Memory works the same way. If you initially think about a topic in different ways and in conjunction with many other ideas, then you'll establish many paths leading to the target material, and so you'll be able to access that material from many different perspectives. The real pragmatic message from this chapter, then, is that this multiperspective approach may, in fact, provide the optimal learning strategy.

 ## CHAPTER SUMMARY

- In general, the chances that someone will remember an earlier event are greatest if the physical and mental circumstances in place during memory retrieval match those in place during learning. This is reflected in the phenomenon of context-dependent learning, in which one is most likely to remember material learned while underwater if tested underwater, most likely to remember material learned while listening to music if again listening to music during the test, and so on.

- In the same vein, if you focused on the meaning of some material while learning it, then hints concerned with meaning will be especially helpful when the time comes to recall the material. If you focused on the sound of the material during learning, then hints concerned with sound will be most helpful at the time of recall.

- A similar pattern is reflected in the phenomenon of "encoding specificity." This term refers to the idea that you usually learn more than the specific material to be remembered itself; you also learn that material within its associated context.

- All these results arise from the fact that learning establishes connections among memories, and these connections serve as retrieval paths. Like any path, these lead from some starting point to some target. To use the path, therefore, you must return to the appropriate starting point. In the same way, if there is a connection between two memories, then activating the first memory is likely to call the second to mind. If the first memory is not activated, however, this connection, no matter how well established, will not help in locating the second memory, just as a large highway approaching Chicago from the south will not be helpful if you are trying to reach Chicago from the north.

- This emphasis on memory connections fits well with a conceptualization of memory as a vast "network," with individual nodes joined to each other via connections or associations. An individual node becomes activated when it receives enough of an input signal to raise its activation level to its response threshold. Once activated, the node sends activation out through its connections to all the nodes connected to it.

- Hints are effective because the target node can receive activation from two sources simultaneously—from nodes representing the main cue or question, and also from nodes representing the hint. The benefits of context reinstatement can be explained in a similar fashion.

- Activating one node does (as predicted) seem to prime nearby nodes through the process of spreading activation. This is evident (for example) in studies of semantic priming in lexical-decision tasks.

- Some learning strategies are effective as preparation for some sorts of memory tests but ineffective for other sorts of tests. Some strategies, for example, are effective at establishing source memory rather than familiarity; other strategies do the reverse. Source memory is essential for recall; recognition can often be achieved either through source memory or through familiarity.

- Different forms of learning also play a role in producing implicit and explicit memories. Implicit memories are those that influence you even when you have no awareness that you are being influenced by a specific previous event. In many cases, implicit-memory effects take the form of priming—for example, in word recognition or word-stem completion. But implicit memories can also influence you in other ways, producing a number of memory-based illusions.

- Implicit memory can be understood as the consequence of processing fluency, produced by experience in a particular task with a particular stimulus. The fluency is sometimes detected and registered as a sense of "specialness" attached to a stimulus. Often this specialness is then attributed to some cause, but this attribution can be inaccurate.

- Implicit memory is also important in understanding the pattern of symptoms in anterograde amnesia. Amnesic patients perform badly on tests requiring explicit memory and may not even recall events that happened just minutes earlier.

However, they often perform at near-normal levels on tests involving implicit memory. This disparity underscores the fact that we cannot speak in general about good and bad memories, good and poor learning. Instead, learning and memory must be matched to a particular task and a particular form of test; learning and memory that are excellent for some tasks may be poor for others.

The Workbook Connection

See the *Cognition Workbook* for further exploration of interconnections between acquisition and retrieval:

- Demonstration 6.1: Retrieval Paths and Connections
- Demonstration 6.2: Encoding Specificity
- Demonstration 6.3: Spreading Activation in Memory Search
- Demonstration 6.4: Semantic Priming
- Demonstration 6.5: Priming From Implicit Memory
- Research Methods: Chronometric Studies
- Research Methods: Double Dissociations
- Cognitive Psychology and Education: The Importance of Multiple Retrieval Paths
- Cognitive Psychology and Education: Familiarity Is Potentially Treacherous
- Cognitive Psychology and the Law: Unconscious Transference
- Cognitive Psychology and the Law: The Cognitive Interview

NEED HELP STUDYING?

 wwnorton.com/studyspace

Visit StudySpace to access free review material such as

- Chapter study plans
- Quizzes
- Flashcards, and more

Go to **wwnorton.com/zaps** for these online labs:

- Stereotypes
- Encoding Specificity
- Fan Effect
- Memory Bias
- Recalling Information
- Lexical Decision

The actors who appear on p. 213 are (top, from left) Elizabeth Banks, John Leguizamo, Jesse Williams; (bottom, from left) Padma Lakshmi, Joseph Gordon-Levitt, and Regina Hall.

CHAPTER SEVEN

Remembering Complex Events

In the last two chapters, we've said a great deal about how memory functions—how information enters storage in the first place, and then how the information is retrieved later. Most of the findings we've considered, though, come from studies that have used relatively simple materials: Research participants have been asked to memorize word lists or short sentences. We've probed memory for single pictures or brief bits of melody.

In your daily life, however, you encounter much more complex materials. You encounter (and then try to remember) complicated episodes involving many actions and, often, many players. And, crucially, these episodes are integrated into the fabric of your life: You come into these episodes already knowing things about the situation, and then, afterward, you're likely to encounter other information pertinent to the event you experienced initially.

How do these factors influence memory? In this chapter, we'll address this issue in two separate ways. First, we'll consider some of the *errors* that can arise when people try to remember episodes that are related to other things they know and have experienced. Second, we'll consider some of the factors that are directly pertinent to memory as it functions in day-to-day life. For example, we'll consider the impact of the *emotion* that is often part of an event, asking how it influences memory. We'll also consider the effect of *time*, asking how people remember events that happened years, or even decades, earlier.

- Outside the lab, you often try to remember materials that are related in some fashion to other things you know or have experienced. Over and over, we will see that this other knowledge, the knowledge you bring to a situation, helps you to remember by promoting retrieval, but it also hurts memory by promoting error.

- The memory errors produced by your prior knowledge tend to be quite systematic, and so you often end up recalling the past as more "normal," more in line with your expectations, than it actually was.

- Even if we acknowledge the memory errors, our overall assessment of memory can be quite positive.

This is because your memories are accurate most of the time, and the errors that do occur can be understood as the by-products of mechanisms that generally serve you well.

- Finally, we will consider three factors that play an important role in shaping memory outside of the laboratory: *involvement* with an event, *emotion*, and the *passage of time*. These factors require some additional principles as part of our overall theory, but they also confirm the power of more general principles—principles hinging (for example) on the role of memory connections.

Memory Errors, Memory Gaps

Where did you spend last summer? What country did you grow up in? Where were you five minutes ago? These are, of course, extremely easy questions. The sought-after information is in your memory, and you effortlessly retrieve the information the moment you need it. And the same is true for countless other bits of information; these, too, are at your fingertips, swiftly and easily recalled whenever you wish.

Simple observations like these testify to the breadth and efficiency of human memory, and if we want to understand memory, we need to understand how you locate these bits of information (and thousands of others just like them) so quickly and easily. But if we want to understand memory, we also need to account for some other observations: Sometimes, when you try to remember an episode, you simply draw a blank. On other occasions, you recall something, but with no conviction that you're correct: "I think her nickname was Dink, but I'm not sure." And sometimes, when you try to remember, things go wrong in a more serious way: You recall a past episode, but then it turns out that your memory is mistaken. Perhaps details of the event were different from the way you recall them. Or perhaps your memory is altogether wrong, misrepresenting large elements of the original episode. Worst of all, in some cases you can remember entire events that never happened at all!

In this chapter, we'll consider how, and how often, these errors arise. Let's start with some examples.

Memory Errors: Some Initial Examples

In 1992, an El Al cargo plane lost power in two of its engines just after taking off from Amsterdam's Schiphol Airport. The pilot attempted to return the plane to the airport but couldn't make it; a few minutes later, the plane crashed into an 11-story apartment building in the Bijlmermeer neighborhood of Amsterdam. The building collapsed and burst into flames; 43 people were killed, including the plane's entire crew.

Ten months later, researchers questioned 193 Dutch people about the crash, asking them in particular, "Did you see the television film of the moment the plane hit the apartment building?" More than half of the participants (107 of them) reported seeing the film, even though there was no such film. No camera had recorded the crash; no film (or any reenactment) was shown on television. The participants were remembering something that never took place (Crombag, Wagenaar, & van Koppen, 1996). (For similar data, with people remembering a nonexistent film of the car crash that killed Princess Diana and Dodi Fayed, see Ost, Vrij, Costall, & Bull, 2002; also Jelicic et al., 2006; but for a complication, see Smeets et al., 2006.)

In a follow-up study, the investigators surveyed another 93 people about the crash. These people were also asked whether they'd seen the (nonexistent) TV film, and then they were asked more detailed questions about exactly what they had seen in the film: Was the plane burning when it crashed, or did it catch fire a moment later? In the film, did you see the plane come down vertically with no forward speed, or did it hit the building while still moving horizontally at a considerable speed?

Two thirds of these participants remembered seeing the film, and most of them confidently provided details about what they had seen. When asked about the plane's speed, for example, only 23% prudently said that they couldn't remember. The others gave various responses, presumably based on their "memory" of the film; as it turns out, only 11% gave the correct answer.

This is not a case of one or two people making a mistake; instead, a large majority of the people questioned seemed to have a detailed recollection of the nonexistent film. In addition, let's emphasize that this plane crash was an emotional, important, and much-discussed event for these participants; the researchers were not asking them to recall a minor occurrence.

Perhaps these errors emerged simply because the research participants were trying to remember something that had taken place almost a year earlier. Is memory more accurate when the questions come after a shorter delay? In a study by Brewer and Treyens (1981), participants were asked to wait briefly in the experimenter's office prior to the procedure's start. After 35 seconds, participants were taken out of this office and told that there actually was no experimental procedure. Instead, the study was concerned with their memory for the room in which they'd just been sitting.

The participants' recollections of the office were plainly influenced by their prior knowledge—in this case, their knowledge about what an academic office typically contains. For example, participants surely knew in advance of the

FIGURE 7.1 | THE OFFICE USED IN THE
BREWER AND TREYENS STUDY

No books were in view in this office, but participants, biased by their expectations for what should be in a scholar's office, often remembered seeing books. (After Brewer & Treyens, 1981)

study that academic offices usually contain a desk and a chair; as it turns out, these pieces of furniture were present in this particular office. This agreement between prior knowledge and the specific experience led to accurate memory, and 29 of 30 participants correctly remembered that the office contained a desk and a chair. In other regards, however, this office was different from what the participants might have expected. Specifically, participants would expect an academic office to contain shelves filled with books, yet in this particular office no books were in view (see Figure 7.1). As it turns out, though, the participants' recall was often in line with their expectations and not with reality: Almost one third of them (9 of 30) remembered seeing books in the office when, in fact, there were none.

How could this be? How could so many Dutch participants be wrong in their recall of a significant emotional episode? How could intelligent, alert college students fail to remember what they'd seen in an office just moments earlier?

Memory Errors: A Hypothesis

Memory errors can happen in many ways, starting with errors that arise during the initial exposure to the episode to be remembered, and continuing through the moment of recall. In almost all cases, though, the errors involve the same simple mechanism. In Chapters 5 and 6, we emphasized the importance of memory connections, linking each bit of knowledge in your memory to other bits. Sometimes these connections tie together similar episodes, so that a trip to the beach ends up connected in memory to your recollections of other trips. Sometimes the connections tie an episode to certain ideas—ideas, perhaps, that were part of your understanding of the episode, or ideas that were triggered by some element within the episode.

With all of these connections in place, information ends up being stored in memory in a system that looks like a vast spider web, with each bit of information connected by many threads to other bits of information elsewhere in the web. This was the idea that, in Chapter 6, we described as a huge *network* of interconnected *nodes*. We need to be clear, though, that, within this network, there are no boundaries keeping memories of one episode separate from memories of other episodes. The episodes, in other words, aren't stored in separate "files," each distinct from the others. What is it, therefore, that holds together the various elements within each episode? It is simply the density of connections: There are many connections linking the various aspects of your "trip to the beach" to each other; there are fewer connections linking this event to other events.

As we have discussed, these connections play a crucial role in memory retrieval: Imagine, for example, that you're trying to recall the restaurant you ate at during your beach trip. You'll start by activating the nodes in memory that represent some aspect of the trip—perhaps your memory of the rainy weather. Activation will then flow outward from there, through the connections you've established, and this will energize the nodes representing other aspects of the trip. The flow of activation can then continue from there, eventually reaching the nodes you seek. In this way, we've said, the connections serve as *retrieval paths*, guiding your search through memory.

This perspective makes it clear that memory connections are a good thing; without them, you might never locate the information you're seeking. However, the connections can also create problems for you. As you add more and more links between the bits of *this* episode and the bits of *that* episode, you're gradually knitting these two episodes together. As a result, you may lose track of the "boundary" between episodes, and, more precisely, you're likely to lose track of which bits of information were contained within which event. Thus you become vulnerable to what we might think of as "transplant" errors, in which a bit of information encountered in one context is transplanted into another context.

In the same fashion, as your memory for an episode becomes more and more interwoven with other thoughts you've had about the episode, it becomes difficult to keep track of which elements are linked to the episode because they were, in truth, part of the episode itself, and which are linked because they were merely *associated with* the episode in your thoughts. This, too, can produce transplant errors—elements that were part of your thinking get misremembered as if they were actually part of the original experience.

Understanding Both Helps and Hurts Memory

It seems, then, that memory connections both help and hurt recollection. They *help* because the connections, serving as retrieval paths, allow you to locate information in memory. But the same connections *hurt* because they can make it difficult to see where the remembered episode stops and other, related knowledge begins. As a result, the connections encourage **intrusion errors**—errors in which other knowledge intrudes into the remembered event.

In fact, it's easy to show that factors that foster connections do both help and hurt memory. As one example, consider the role of *understanding* itself. In one study, half of the participants read the following passage (Owens, Bower, & Black, 1979):

> *Nancy arrived at the cocktail party. She looked around the room to see who was there. She went to talk with her professor. She felt she had to talk to him but was a little nervous about just what to say. A group of people started to play charades. Nancy went over and had some refreshments. The hors d'oeuvres were good but she wasn't interested in talking to the rest of the people at the party. After a while she decided she'd had enough and left the party.*

Other participants read the same passage, but with a prologue that set the stage:

> *Nancy woke up feeling sick again and she wondered if she really were pregnant. How would she tell the professor she had been seeing? And the money was another problem.*

All participants were then given a recall test in which they were asked to remember the sentences as exactly as they could. Table 7.1 shows the results; as can be seen, the participants who had read the prologue (the "theme condition") recalled much more of the original story. This is consistent with claims made in Chapter 5: The prologue provided a meaningful context for the remainder of the story, and this helped understanding. Understanding, in turn, promoted recall.

TABLE 7.1 | **NUMBER OF PROPOSITIONS REMEMBERED BY PARTICIPANTS**

STUDIED PROPOSITIONS (THOSE IN STORY)		INFERRED PROPOSITIONS (THOSE NOT IN STORY)	
Theme condition	Neutral condition	Theme condition	Neutral condition
29.2	20.2	15.2	3.7

In the theme condition, a brief prologue set the theme for the passage that was to be remembered.

SOURCE: AFTER OWENS ET AL., 1979.

At the same time, the story's prologue also led participants to include many things in their recall that were not mentioned in the original episode. In fact, participants who had seen the prologue made *four times* as many intrusion errors as did participants who had not seen the prologue. For example, they might recall, "The professor had gotten Nancy pregnant." This is not part of the story but is certainly implied, and so it will probably be part of the participants' understanding of the story. It's then this understanding (including the imported element) that is remembered.

The DRM Procedure

Similar effects, with memory connections both *helping* and *hurting* memory, can even be demonstrated with word lists, provided that the lists are arranged so that they make appropriate contact with prior knowledge. For example, in many experiments, participants have been presented with lists like this one: "bed, rest, awake, tired, dream, wake, snooze, blanket, doze, slumber, snore, nap, peace, yawn, drowsy." Immediately after hearing this list, participants are asked to recall as many of the words as they can.

As you may have noticed, all of the words in this list are associated with sleep, and the presence of this theme helps memory: The words that are on the list are relatively easy to remember. It turns out, though, that the word "sleep" is not itself included in the list. Nonetheless, research participants spontaneously make the connection between the list words and this associated word, and this almost invariably leads to a memory error: When the time comes for recall, participants are extremely likely to recall that they heard "sleep." In fact, they are just as likely to recall "sleep" as they are to recall the actual words on the list (see Figure 7.2)!

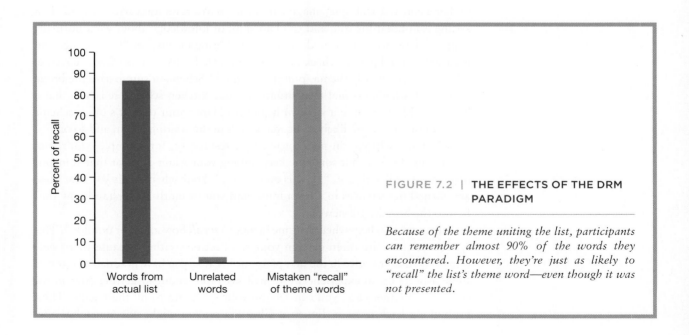

FIGURE 7.2 | **THE EFFECTS OF THE DRM PARADIGM**

Because of the theme uniting the list, participants can remember almost 90% of the words they encountered. However, they're just as likely to "recall" the list's theme word—even though it was not presented.

The same pattern emerges in recognition testing: If participants are shown test words and asked which of these appeared in the original list, they are just as likely to recognize "sleep" as being one of the list words as they are to recognize the actually presented list words. When asked how confident they are in their memories, participants are just as confident in their (false) recognition of "sleep" as they are in their (correct) recognition of genuine list words (Gallo, 2010; for earlier and classic papers in this arena, see Deese, 1957; Roediger & McDermott, 1995, 2000).

This paradigm is referred to as the **DRM procedure**, in honor of the investigators who developed it (Deese, Roediger, and McDermott). The procedure yields a large numbers of memory errors, even if participants are put on their guard before the procedure begins (i.e., told explicitly about the nature of the lists and the frequency with which these lists produce errors). Even with these warnings, participants still make the DRM errors (Gallo, Roberts, & Seamon, 1997; McDermott & Roediger, 1998). Apparently, the mechanisms leading to these memory errors are quite automatic, and not mechanisms that people can somehow inhibit.

Schematic Knowledge

The DRM procedure obviously relies on word lists for the to-be-remembered materials. We can document similar errors, though, with more complex materials—including the sorts of materials that you encounter in everyday life. This is because you enter most settings with some amount of background knowledge. This knowledge is usually helpful, because it guides you as you explore, think about, and interpret the situations you find yourself in. But this knowledge can also be a source of memory error.

For a concrete example, imagine that you go to a restaurant with a friend. This setting is familiar for you, and you have a lot of knowledge about what normally happens here. You'll be seated; someone will bring menus; you'll order, then eat; eventually, you'll pay the check and leave. Knowledge like this is often referred to with the Greek word **schema** (plural: *schemata*). Schemata summarize the broad pattern of what's normal in a situation: Your kitchen schema tells you that a kitchen is likely to have a stove in it, but no piano; your dentist's office schema tells you that there are likely to be magazines in the waiting room; and so on.

Schemata help you in many ways. In a restaurant, for example, you're not puzzled by the fact that someone keeps filling your water glass or that someone drops by the table to ask, "How is everything?" Your schema tells you that these are normal occurrences in a restaurant, and you instantly understand how they fit into the broader framework.

Schemata also help when the time comes to *recall* how an event unfolded. This is because there are often gaps in your recollection—either because there were things you didn't notice in the first place, or because you have gradually forgotten some aspects of an experience. (We will say more about forgetting later in the chapter.) In either case, you can rely on your schemata to fill these gaps. Thus, in thinking back to your dinner at Chez Pierre, you might not remember anything about the menus. Nonetheless, you can be reasonably sure that there were menus, and that they were given to you early on and taken away after you placed your order. On this basis, you're likely to include menus within your "recall" of the dinner, even if you have no memory for seeing the menus for this particular meal. In other words, you'll (unwittingly) supplement what you actually remember with a plausible reconstruction based on your schematic knowledge. And in most cases this after-the-fact reconstruction will be correct, since schemata do, after all, describe what happens most of the time.

Evidence for Schematic Knowledge

Clearly, then, schematic knowledge helps you—guiding your understanding and allowing you to reconstruct things you cannot remember. But schematic knowledge can also hurt you, promoting errors in perception and memory. Moreover, the *types* of errors produced by schemata are quite predictable: Bear in mind here that schemata summarize the broad pattern of your experience, and so your schemata tell you, in essence, what's typical or ordinary in a given situation. Any reliance on schematic knowledge, therefore, will be shaped by this information about what's "normal." Thus, if there are things you don't notice while viewing a situation or event, your schemata will lead you to fill these "gaps" with knowledge about what's normally in place in that setting. Likewise, if there are things you can't recall, your schemata will fill the gaps with knowledge about what's typical in that situation. As a result, a reliance on schemata will inevitably make the world seem more "normal" than it really is and will make the past seem more "regular" than it actually was.

Imagine, for example, that you visit a dentist's office, and this one happens not to have any magazines in the waiting room. It's possible that you won't notice this detail or that you'll forget about it after a while. What will happen, therefore, if you later try to recall this trip to the dentist? Odds are good that you'll rely on your schematic knowledge and "remember" that there were magazines (since, after all, there usually are some scattered around a waiting room). In this way, your recollection will make this dentist's office seem more typical, more ordinary, than it truly was.

This tendency toward "regularizing" the past is easily demonstrated in research. The classic demonstration, however, comes from studies published decades ago by Frederick Bartlett. Bartlett presented his British participants with a story taken from the folklore of Native Americans (the story is shown in Figure 7.3A; Bartlett, 1932). When tested later, the participants did reasonably well in recalling the gist of the story, but they made many errors in recalling the particulars (Figure 7.3B shows an example of participants' recall). The pattern of errors, though, was quite systematic: The details omitted tended to be ones that made little sense to Bartlett's participants. Likewise, aspects of the story that were unfamiliar were changed into aspects that were more familiar; steps of the story that seemed inexplicable were supplemented to make the story seem more logical.

Overall, then, the participants' memories seem to have "cleaned up" the story they had read—making it more coherent (from their perspective), more sensible,

FIGURE 7.3 | THE WAR OF THE GHOSTS

One night two young men from Egulac went down to the river to hunt seals, and while they were there it became foggy and calm. Then they heard war cries, and they thought; "Maybe this is a war party." They escaped to the shore and hid behind a log. Now canoes came up, and they heard the noise of paddles and saw one canoe coming up to them. There were five men in the canoe, and they said:

"What do you think? We wish to take you along. We are going up the river to make war on the people."

One of the young men said: "I have no arrows." "Arrows are in the canoe," they said. "I will not go along. I might be killed. My relatives do not know where I have gone. But you," he said, turning to the other, "may go with them."

So one of the young men went, but the other returned home. And the warriors went on up the river to a town on the other side of Kalama. The people came down to the water and they began to fight, and many were killed. But presently the young man heard one of the warriors say: "Quick, let us go home; that Indian has been hit." Now he thought, "Oh, they are ghosts." He did not feel sick, but they said he had been shot.

So the canoes went back to Egulac, and the young man went ashore to his house and made a fire. And he told everybody and said: "Behold I accompanied the ghosts, and we went to fight. Many of our fellows were killed, and many of those who attacked us were killed. They said I was hit, and I did not feel sick."

He told it all, and then he became quiet. When the sun rose, he fell down. Something black came out of his mouth. His face became contorted. The people jumped up and cried. He was dead. (Bartlett, 1932, p. 65)

A

EXAMPLE OF STORY RECALL

Indians were out fishing for seals in the Bay of Manpapan, when along came five other Indians in a war-canoe. They were going fighting. "Come with us," said the five to the two, "and fight." "I cannot come," was the answer of the one, "for I have an old mother at home who is dependent upon me." The other also said he could not come, because he had no arms. "That is no difficulty" the others replied, "for we have plenty in the canoe with us"; so he got into the canoe and went with them. In a fight soon afterwards this Indian received a mortal wound. Finding that his hour was come, he cried out that he was about to die. "Nonsense," said one of the others, "you will not die." But he did.

B

Bartlett presented his British participants with the story, shown in A, drawn from Native American folklore. When, later, the participants tried to remember the story, they did well in recalling the broad gist, but tended to alter the story so that it made more sense from their perspective. Specifically, they either left out or distorted elements that did not fit with their schema-based understanding. A typical recall is shown in B.

than it first seemed. This is exactly what we would expect if the memory errors derived from the participants' attempts to understand the story and, with that, their efforts toward fitting the story into a schematic frame. Elements that fit within the frame remained in their memories (or could be reconstructed later). Elements that did not fit dropped out of memory or were changed.

In the same spirit, consider the Brewer and Treyens study we mentioned at the start of this chapter—the study in which participants remembered seeing bookshelves full of books, even though there were none. This error was produced by schematic knowledge: During the event itself (i.e., while the participants were sitting in the office), schematic knowledge told the participants that academic offices usually contain many books, and this knowledge biased what the participants paid attention to. (If you're already certain that the shelves contain books, why should you spend time looking at the shelves? This would only confirm something you already know—cf. Vo & Henderson, 2009.) Then, when the time came to recall the office, participants used their schema to reconstruct what the office *must* contain—a desk, a chair, and of course lots of books. In this fashion, the memory for the actual office was eclipsed by generic knowledge about what a "normal" office contains.

Likewise, think back to our other early example—the misremembered plane crash. Here, too, the memory error distorted reality by making the past seem more regular, more typical, than it really was. After all, the Dutch survey respondents probably hear about most major news events via a television broadcast, and these broadcasts typically include vivid video footage. So here, too, the past as remembered seems to have been assimilated into the pattern of the ordinary. The event as it unfolded was unusual, but the event *as remembered* is quite typical of its kind—just as we would expect if understanding and remembering were guided by our knowledge of the way things generally unfold.

The Cost of Memory Errors

There's clearly a "good news, bad news" quality to our discussion so far. On the positive side of things, we've noted that memory connections serve as retrieval paths, allowing you to locate information in storage. The connections also enrich your understanding, because they highlight how each of your memories is related to other things you know. The links to schematic knowledge also allow you to supplement your (often incomplete) recollection with well-informed (and usually accurate) inference.

On the negative side, though, the same memory connections can undermine memory accuracy. We've now seen that the connections can lead you to remember things as more regular than they were, in some cases adding elements to a memory and in other cases "subtracting" elements, so that (in either case) the memory ends up making more sense (i.e., fitting better with your schemata). The connections can, in some circumstances, even lead you to recall whole episodes (e.g., seeing a plane crash on TV) that never happened.

These errors are troubling. As we've discussed in other contexts, you rely on memory in many aspects of our lives, and it's therefore unsettling that the memories you're relying on may be *wrong*—misrepresenting how the past unfolded. To make matters worse, the mistakes seem surprisingly frequent—with two thirds of the participants in one study remembering a nonexistent film, with one third of the participants in another study remembering books that weren't there at all, and so on. Perhaps worst of all, we can easily find circumstances in which these memory errors are deeply consequential. For example, memory errors in eyewitness testimony (e.g., in identifying the wrong person as the culprit or in misreporting how an event unfolded) can potentially send an innocent person to jail and allow a guilty person to go free.

How often do eyewitnesses make mistakes? A possible answer comes from American court cases in which DNA evidence, not available at the time of the trial, shows that the courts had convicted people who were, in truth, not guilty. There are now roughly 300 cases of these DNA exonerations—cases in which the courts have acknowledged their tragic error. The exonerees had (on average) spent more than a dozen years in jail for crimes they did not commit; many of them were on death row, awaiting execution.

These cases have been examined by psychologists, legal scholars, and journalists, and yield a clear message: Some of these men were convicted because of dishonest informants; some because analyses of forensic evidence had been botched. But by far the most common concern was eyewitness error. Indeed, according to most analyses, eyewitness errors account for three-quarters of these false convictions, more than all other causes combined (e.g., Garrett, 2011).

Cases like these make it plain that memory errors, including misidentifications, are profoundly important. What can we say, therefore, about the sources of these errors, and possible means of avoiding the errors? And can we identify specific problems within the legal system that might be producing the errors undeniably documented in the DNA exonerations?

Planting False Memories

One line of research has been modeled after the events that sometimes unfold when crime witnesses are questioned about what they have seen. In an early study, Loftus and Palmer (1974) showed participants a series of projected slides depict-

EXONERATION OF THE INNOCENT

Michael Anthony Green spent more than 27 years in prison for a rape he did not commit. He is one of the almost 300 people who were convicted in American courts but then proven innocent by DNA evidence. Mistaken eyewitness evidence accounts for more of these false convictions than all other causes combined.

ing an automobile collision. Sometime later, half the participants were asked, "How fast were the cars going when they hit each other?" Others were asked, "How fast were the cars going when they smashed into each other?" The difference between these questions ("hit" vs. "smashed") is slight, but it was enough to bias the participants' estimates of speed. Participants in the first group ("hit") estimated the speed to have been 34 miles per hour; participants in the second group ("smashed") estimated 41 miles per hour—20 percent higher (see Figure 7.4). But what is critical comes next: One week later, the participants were asked in a perfectly neutral way whether they had seen any broken glass in the slides. Participants who had initially been asked the "hit" question tended to remember (correctly) that no glass was visible; participants who had been asked the "smashed" question, though, often made this error. It seems, therefore, that the change of just one word within the initial question can have a large effect—in this case, more than doubling the likelihood of memory error.

In the "hit/smashed" study, the question implied to participants how they ought to think about the target event (with "smashed" suggesting a more violent collision). In other studies, participants have been asked questions that contain actual misinformation about an event. For example, they might be asked, "How fast was the car going when it raced by the barn?" when, in truth, no barn was in view. In still other studies, participants have been exposed to descriptions of the target event that allegedly were written by "other witnesses." They might be told, for example, "Here's how someone else recalled the crime; does this match what you recall?" Of course, the "other witness" descriptions contain some misinformation, allowing us to ask if our participants "pick up" these false leads (e.g., Paterson & Kemp, 2006; also Edelson, Sharon, Dolan, & Dudai, 2011). Finally, in other cases, participants have been asked questions about an event that required the participants themselves to *make up* the misinformation. For example, participants can be asked, "In the video, was the man bleeding from

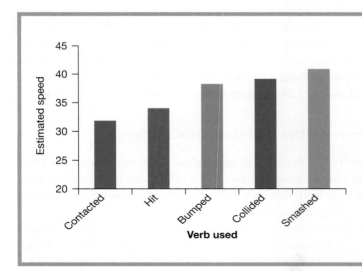

FIGURE 7.4 | **THE IMPACT OF LEADING QUESTIONS**

Witnesses asked how fast cars were going when they "hit" each other reported (on average) a speed of 34 miles per hour. Other witnesses, asked how fast the cars were going when they "smashed" into each other, gave estimates 20% higher. When all participants were later asked whether they'd seen broken glass in the scene, participants who'd been asked the "smashed" question were more likely to say "yes," although there was no broken glass. (After Loftus & Palmer, 1974)

his knee or from his elbow after the fall?" Even though it was clear in the video that the man wasn't bleeding at all, participants are still forced to choose one of these options (e.g., Chrobak & Zaragoza, 2008; Zaragoza, Payment, Ackil, Drivadahl, & Beck, 2001).

These procedures differ in important ways, but, even so, they are all variations on the same theme. In each case, the participant experiences an event and then is exposed to a misleading suggestion about how the event unfolded. Then some time is allowed to pass. At the end of this interval, the participant's memory is tested. And in each of these variations, the outcome is the same: A substantial number of participants—as many as one third of the participants in some studies—end up incorporating the false suggestion into their memory for the original event.

Of course, some attempts at manipulating memory are more successful, and some are less so. It's easier, for example, to plant *plausible* memories rather than implausible ones (although memories for implausible events can also be planted—see Hyman, 2000; Mazzoni, Loftus, & Kirsch, 2001; Pezdek, Blandon-Gitlin, & Gabbay, 2006; Scoboria, Mazzoni, Kirsch, & Jiminez, 2006; Thomas & Loftus, 2002). False memories are also more easily planted if the research participants don't just *hear* about the false event but, instead, are urged to *imagine* how the suggested event unfolded—an effect referred to as "imagination inflation." In one study, for example, participants were given a list of possible childhood events (going to the emergency room late at night; winning a stuffed animal at a carnival game; getting in trouble for calling 911). Participants were asked to "picture each event as clearly and completely" as they could, and this simple exercise was enough to increase participants' confidence that the event had really occurred (Garry, Manning & Loftus, 1996; also Mazzoni & Memon, 2003; Sharman & Barnier, 2008).

Even acknowledging these variations, though, let's emphasize the consistency of these findings: We can use subtle procedures (carefully worded questions) to plant false information in someone's memory, or we can use a more blatant procedure (demanding that the person make up the bogus facts). We can use printed stories as our to-be-remembered materials, or movies, or live events. In all cases, it is remarkably easy to alter someone's memory, with the result that the past as the person remembers it can differ from the past as it really was. (For more on research in this domain, see Chan, Thomas, & Bulevich, 2009; Frenda, Nichols & Loftus, 2011; Laney, 2012; Laney & Loftus, 2010; Seamon, Philbin, & Harrison, 2006.)

Are There Limits on the Misinformation Effect?

The pattern of results just described is referred to as the **misinformation effect** because the participants' memories are being influenced by misinformation they received after an episode was over. But what sorts of memory errors can be planted in this way? The answer, in brief, is: all sorts.

We've mentioned that researchers have led participants to remember broken glass when really there was none, and to remember barns when there were no buildings at all in view. Similar procedures have altered how *people* are remembered—

so that with just a few "suggestions" from the experimenter, people remember clean-shaven men as bearded, young people as old, and fat people as thin (e.g., Christiaansen, Sweeney, & Ochalek, 1983; Frenda et al., 2011).

We can celebrate the fact that these errors are relatively small, but, if so, we should simultaneously lament the fact that it's remarkably easy to produce these errors—with just one or two words ("hit" versus "smashed") enough to produce a "memory" for, say, broken glass that wasn't there at all. Indeed, think about what this means for police detectives, or medical investigators, or anyone else who needs to learn how some crucial event unfolded. Very small slips during an investigation can bias witnesses' memory—including memory for details that may be deeply consequential for the investigation.

What happens, though, if we ramp up our efforts toward planting false memories? Can we plant larger-scale errors? In one study, college students were told that the investigators were trying to learn how different people remember the same experience. The students were then given a list of events that they were told had been reported by their parents; the students were asked to recall these events as well as they could, so that the investigators could compare their recall with their parents' (Hyman, Husband, & Billings, 1995).

Some of the events on the list had, in fact, been reported by the participants' parents. Other events were bogus—made up by the experimenters. One of the bogus events was an overnight hospitalization for a high fever; in a different experiment, the bogus event was attending a wedding reception and accidentally spilling a bowlful of punch onto the bride's parents.

The college students were easily able to remember the genuine events (i.e., the events actually reported by their parents). In an initial interview, more than 80% of these events were recalled, but none of the students recalled the bogus events. However, repeated attempts at recall changed this pattern, and, by a third interview, 25% of the participants were able to remember the embarrassment of spilling the punch, and many were able to supply the details of this (entirely fictitious) episode. Other studies have yielded similar results, with participants led to recall details of particular birthday parties that, in truth, they never had (Hyman et al., 1995) or an incident of being lost in a shopping mall even though this event never took place, or a (fictitious) event in which they were the victim of a vicious animal attack (Loftus, 2003, 2004, 2005; also see Chrobak & Zaragoza, 2008; Geraerts et al., 2009; Laney et al., 2008; and many more).

Other researchers have taken a further step and have provided participants with "evidence" in support of the bogus memory. In one procedure, researchers obtained a real childhood snapshot of the participant (see Figure 7.5A for an example), and, with a few clicks of a computer mouse, created a fictitious picture like the one shown in Figure 7.5B. With this prompt, many participants were led to a vivid, detailed recollection of the hot-air balloon ride—even though it never occurred (Wade et al., 2002). Another study used an *unaltered* photo, showing the participants' second-grade class (see Figure 7.6). This was apparently enough to persuade participants that the experimenters really did have information about the participants' childhood. Thus, when the experimenters "reminded" the participants of an episode of their childhood misbehavior, the participants took

FIGURE 7.5 | THE BALLOON RIDE THAT NEVER WAS

In this study, participants were shown a faked photo (as in B) created from a real childhood snapshot (as in A). With this prompt, many participants were led to a vivid, detailed recollection of the balloon ride—even though it never occurred!

this reminder seriously. The result: Almost 80% of the participants were able to "recall" the episode, often in detail, even though it had never happened (Lindsay et al., 2004).

The same sort of result has been documented with children, and, in fact, evidence suggests that children are in many procedures more vulnerable than adults to this sort of memory "planting." In one study, children participated in an event with "Mr. Science," a man who showed them a number of fun demonstrations. Afterward, the parents (who were not at the event) were asked to discuss the event with their children—and were, in particular, urged to discuss several elements that (unbeknownst to the parents) actually had never occurred. Later on, the children were interviewed about their visit with Mr. Science, and many of them confidently remembered the (fictitious) elements they had discussed with their parents—including a time (that never happened) in which Mr. Science put something "yucky" in their mouths, or a time in which Mr. Science hurt the child's tummy (by pressing too hard when applying a sticker; Poole & Lindsay, 2001). Such results echo the misinformation results with adults, but they are also extremely important for their own sake, because (among other concerns) these results are relevant to children's testimony in the courtroom (Bruck & Ceci, 1999, 2009).

What, then, are the limits of false memory? It seems clear that your memory can sometimes be mistaken on small details (was there broken glass in view?), but memory can also fool you in larger ways: You can remember entire events

FIGURE 7.6 | PHOTOGRAPHS CAN ENCOURAGE MEMORY ERRORS

In one study, participants were "reminded" of a (fictitious) stunt they'd pulled while in the second grade. Participants were much more likely to "remember" the stunt (and so more likely to develop a false memory) if the experimenter showed them a copy of their actual second-grade class photo. Apparently, the photo convinced the participants that the experimenter really did know what had happened, and this made the experimenter's (false) suggestion much more persuasive.

that never took place. You can remember emotional episodes (like being lost in a shopping mall) that never happened. You can remember your own transgressions (spilling the punch bowl, misbehaving in the second grade), even when they never occurred.

These results fit well with our theorizing, and (more specifically) with our claims about how memory errors can arise. But these results also have pragmatic implications. As one example, participants changed their eating habits after a researcher persuaded them that, as children, they had become ill after eating egg salad (Geraerts et al., 2008). Or, as a deeply troubling example, studies of the justice system confirm that children sometimes accuse adults of abuse even when other evidence makes it clear the abuse never happened. Similarly, we know that—remarkably—people sometimes confess to (and apparently "remember") crimes that they did not commit (cf. Lassiter & Meissner, 2010; Leo, 2008; Kassin, Drizin, Grisso, Gudjonsson, Leo, & Redlich, 2010). It can be no surprise, therefore, that researchers continue to be deeply engaged in exploring how and when these false memories occur.

False memories can be quite consequential. In one study, participants were led to believe that, as children, they had gotten ill after eating egg salad. This "memory" then changed the participants' eating habits—over the next four months, they ended up eating less egg salad (Geraerts et al., 2008). Obviously, false memories can persist and have lasting behavioral effects.

Avoiding Memory Errors

Our discussion so far suggests that memory errors are far more common than most people expect. Even so, let's emphasize that, overall, our memories are generally accurate. In other words, evidence suggests that, in our daily lives, we can usually trust our memories, because, more often than not, our recollection is complete, detailed, long-lasting, and *correct*.

The fact remains, however, that the errors do occur, and can be both large and consequential (and so can, for example, lead a police investigation completely off track). Is there anything we can do, therefore, to avoid being misled by memory errors?

Memory Confidence

Perhaps we can find a way to *detect* memory errors when they've occurred, so that we can separate accurate memories from those likely to be false. How might we do this? Let's start with the fact that people sometimes announce that they're confident in their recall ("I distinctly remember her yellow jacket; I'm sure of it"), and sometimes they say the opposite ("Gee, I think she was wearing yellow, but I'm not certain"). And, it seems, people take these assessments quite seriously. In your own recall, you're more willing to take action based on confident memories than hesitant ones. The same is true when you're listening to others: In the courtroom, for example, juries place much more weight on a witness's evidence if the witness expresses confidence during the testimony; conversely, juries are often skeptical about testimony that is hesitant or hedged. Apparently, then, juries believe that *confident* recall is likely to be *accurate* recall (Brigham & Wolfskiel, 1983; Cutler, Penrod, & Dexter, 1990; Loftus, 1979; Wells, Lindsay, & Ferguson, 1979). And it's not just juries who hold this view: Judges believe the same, and they often instruct juries to put more faith in confident witnesses, less faith in hesitant ones. (Indeed, this notion of trusting *confident recall* is explicitly required by some judicial procedures—see, for example, *Neil v. Biggers*, 1972, a key ruling in U.S. courts that presumes that a confident witness is more likely to be accurate.)

This is an issue, however, on which common sense, juries, and the courts are all mistaken. Many studies have systematically compared people's confidence when they are reporting a correct memory with their confidence when they are reporting a false memory, and the pattern of evidence is clear: In many circumstances, there's little relationship between memory confidence and memory accuracy. Any attempt to categorize memories as correct or incorrect, based on someone's confidence, will therefore be riddled with errors. (For some of the evidence, see Busey, Tunnicliff, Loftus, & Loftus, 2000; Roediger & McDermott, 1995; Sporer, Penrod, Read, & Cutler, 1995; Wells & Quinlivan, 2009.)

WORKBOOK
DEMONSTRATION 7.2

How could this be? How could we be so poor in evaluating our own memories? One reason is that our confidence in a memory is often influenced by factors that have no impact on memory accuracy. When these factors are present, therefore, confidence will change (sometimes upward, sometimes downward) with no change in the accuracy level, and this will undermine any correspondence between confidence and accuracy.

For example, participants in one study witnessed a (simulated) crime and later were asked if they could identify the culprit from a group of pictures. Some of the participants were then given feedback ("Good, you identified the suspect"); others were not. This feedback could not possibly influence the *accuracy* of the identification, because the feedback arrived only after the identification was done. But the feedback did influence *confidence*, and witnesses who had received the feedback expressed a much higher level of confidence in their choice than did witnesses who received no feedback (see Figure 7.7; Douglas, Neuschatz, Imrich, & Wilkinson, 2009; Semmler & Brewer, 2006; Wells, Olson, & Charman, 2002, 2003). (For similar data *outside* of the lab, see Wright & Skagerberg,

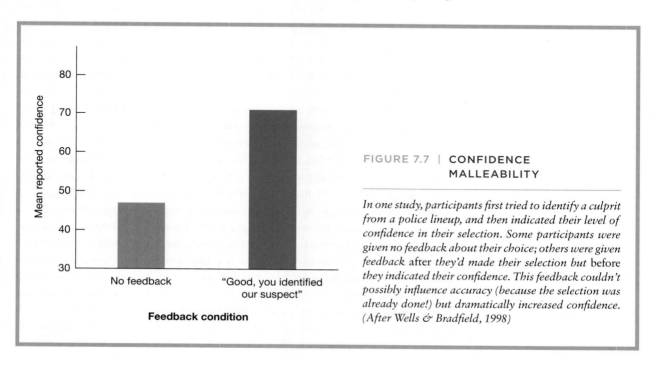

FIGURE 7.7 | CONFIDENCE MALLEABILITY

In one study, participants first tried to identify a culprit from a police lineup, and then indicated their level of confidence in their selection. Some participants were given no feedback about their choice; others were given feedback after they'd made their selection but before they indicated their confidence. This feedback couldn't possibly influence accuracy (because the selection was already done!) but dramatically increased confidence. (After Wells & Bradfield, 1998)

2007; for similar data with *children* as eyewitnesses, see Hafstad, Memon, & Logie, 2004.) Thus, with confidence inflated but accuracy unchanged, the linkage between confidence and accuracy was diminished. (For other factors contributing to the disconnection between accuracy and confidence, see Heathcote et al., 2009; Lampinen, Meier, Arnal, & Leding, 2005; Sampaio & Brower, 2009; Sharman, Manning, & Garry, 2005.)

The "Remember/Know" Distinction

Perhaps we can distinguish correct memories from false memories in some other way. Investigators have, for example, considered the emotion attached to a memory. We know that people often become quite emotional when recalling the events of their lives—and so they feel proud when thinking about some past triumph, and distressed when thinking about some past tragedy. Are they perhaps less emotional when remembering some memory fiction—an event that never occurred? If so, we could use the degree of emotion as a way of distinguishing accurate memories from false ones. This, too, turns out to be a dead end. False memories, memories of events that never actually happened, can be just as upsetting, just as emotional, as memories for real events (McNally et al., 2004).

Other investigators have examined the way a memory *feels*, relying on the "remember/know" distinction that we met in Chapter 6. This distinction rests on the fact that sometimes you can recall the episode in which you gained some information, and so you say things like: "I remember that there were books, because I recall thinking about how dusty they looked." Sometimes, though, you can't recall the episode, and so you say things like: "I know there were books, but, to tell you the truth, I don't remember anything about what they looked like." The first of these is a "remember" judgment; the second is a case of "know."

It turns out that a feeling of "remembering" is more likely with correct memories than with false memories (e.g., Conway, Collins, Gathercole, & Anderson, 1996; Lane & Zaragoza, 1995). Put differently, false memories often arrive with only a general sense of familiarity and no recollection of a particular episode. But there are numerous exceptions to this pattern—cases in which fully correct memories arrive in your thoughts with only a feeling of knowing, and false memories arrive with a detailed sense of remembering. As a result, the distinction between knowing and remembering, like the other efforts we have described, cannot serve as a reliable means of distinguishing correct memories from false ones (Frost, 2000; Holmes, Waters, & Rajaram, 1998; Roediger & McDermott, 1995).

Researchers continue to seek other means of distinguishing memory errors from accurate recall, but overall, the status of this research is easy to describe: A number of attributes are, statistically, somewhat more likely with accurate memories than with errors. We've just said this is true for a "remember" judgment. It's also true for response *speed*, with accurate memories (on average) recalled more rapidly than some errors (Dunning & Perretta, 2002, but also see Weber, Brewer, Wells, Semmler, & Keast, 2004). In some paradigms, there's even a statistical association between memory accuracy and confidence (Brewer & Wells, 2006). Crucially, though, in all cases the linkage at issue is quite weak. In the end, therefore, we have uncovered no indicator that can reliably guide us in deciding which memories to trust, and which not. For now, it seems that memory errors, when they occur, are usually undetectable.

Forgetting

We've been discussing the errors people sometimes make in recalling the past, but, of course, there's another way your memory can let you down: Sometimes you *forget*. You try to recall what was on the shopping list, or the name of an acquaintance, or what happened last week, and you simply draw a blank. Why does this happen? Are there things you can do to diminish forgetting?

The Causes of Forgetting

Why do you forget? Let's start with one of the more prominent examples of "forgetting"—which turns out not to be forgetting at all. Imagine meeting someone at a party, being told his name, and moments later realizing that you don't have a clue what his name is—even though you just heard it! This common (and embarrassing) experience is unlikely to be the result of ultra-rapid forgetting. Instead, the experience stems from a failure in acquisition. You were exposed to the name but barely paid attention to it and, as a result, never learned it in the first place.

What about "real" cases of forgetting—cases in which you once knew the information (and so plainly *had* learned it), but no longer do? For these cases, one of the best predictors of forgetting (not surprisingly) is the passage of time. Psychologists use the term *retention interval* to refer to the amount of time that elapses between the initial learning and the subsequent retrieval; as this interval grows, you're likely to forget more and more of the earlier event (see Figure 7.8). But why exactly does the passage of time matter?

One possible explanation is **decay**. With the passage of time, memories may fade or erode. Perhaps this is because the relevant brain cells die off. Or perhaps the connections among memories need to be constantly refreshed, and so, if they're not refreshed, the connections gradually weaken.

A different possibility is that new learning somehow interferes with older learning. This view is referred to as **interference theory**, and, according to this view, the passage of time is *correlated* with forgetting, but does not *cause* forgetting. Instead, the passage of time simply creates the opportunity for new learning, and it is the new learning that disrupts the older memories.

A third hypothesis blames **retrieval failure**. After all, the retrieval of information from memory is far from guaranteed, and we argued in Chapter 6 that retrieval is more likely if your perspective at the time of retrieval matches that in place at the time of learning. If we now assume that your perspective is likely to change as time goes by, we can make a prediction about forgetting: The greater the retention interval, the greater the likelihood that your perspective has changed, and therefore the greater the likelihood of retrieval failure.

Each of these hypotheses, therefore, is compatible with the fact that longer retention intervals lead to more forgetting. But which hypothesis is correct? It

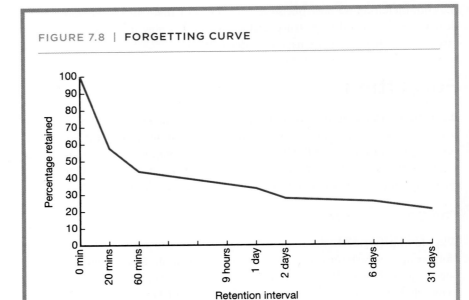

FIGURE 7.8 | **FORGETTING CURVE**

The figure shows retention after various intervals since learning. The data shown here are from classic work by Hermann Ebbinghaus, and so the pattern is often referred to as an "Ebbinghaus forgetting curve." The actual speed of forgetting (i.e., how "steep" the "drop-off" is) depends on how well learned the material was at the start. Across most situations, though, the pattern is the same—with the forgetting rapid at first, but then slower. Mathematically, this pattern is best described by an equation framed in terms of exponential decay.

turns out that they all are. There is, first of all, no doubt that retrieval failure does occur. In many circumstances, you're unable to remember some bit of information, but then, a while later, you do recall that information. Because the information was eventually retrieved, we know that it was not "erased" from memory through either decay or interference. Your initial failure to recall the information, then, must be counted as an example of retrieval failure.

Retrieval failure is usually complete—you can't recall anything about the target information. In some cases, though, retrieval failure is *partial*—you recall some aspects of the desired content, but not all. A maddening example of this sort comes from the common circumstance in which you're trying to think of a word, but can't come up with it. The word is, people say, on the "tip of your tongue," and, following this lead, psychologists refer to this as the TOT phenomenon. People experiencing this state can often recall the starting letter of the sought-after word, and approximately what it sounds like. Thus, a person might remember "it's something like *Sanskrit*" in trying to remember "scrimshaw," or "something like *secant*" in trying to remember "sextant" (Brown, 1991; Brown & McNeill, 1966; Harley & Brown, 1998; James & Burke, 2000; Schwartz & Metcalfe, 2011).

**WORKBOOK
DEMONSTRATION 7.3**

Retrieval failure, however, isn't the whole story of forgetting. In addition, memories do decay with the passage of time (e.g., Altmann & Gray, 2002; Wixted, 2004), and thus decay must also be part of our theorizing. Even so, we'll look at evidence later showing that memories can last an extremely long time; apparently, then, decay is not inevitable, and we'll have to address this point before we're done.

What about interference? In one early study, Baddeley and Hitch (1977) asked rugby players to recall the names of the other teams they had played against over the course of a season. Not all players made it to all games, because of illness, injuries, or schedule conflicts. These differences allow us to compare players for whom "two games back" means two weeks ago, to players for whom "two games back" means four weeks ago. Thus, we can look at the effects of retention interval (two weeks versus four) with the number of intervening games held constant. Likewise, we can compare players for whom the game a month ago was "three games back" to players for whom a month means "one game back." Now we have the retention interval held constant, and we can look at the effects of intervening events. In this setting, Baddeley and Hitch reported that the mere passage of time accounts for very little; what really matters is the number of intervening events (see Figure 7.9). This is just what we would expect if interference, and not decay, is the major contributor to forgetting.

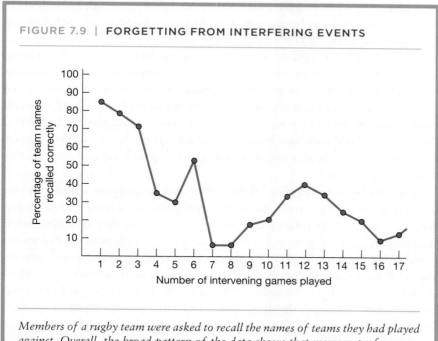

FIGURE 7.9 | **FORGETTING FROM INTERFERING EVENTS**

Members of a rugby team were asked to recall the names of teams they had played against. Overall, the broad pattern of the data shows that memory performance was powerfully influenced by the number of games that intervened between the game to be recalled and the attempt to remember. This pattern fits with an interference view of forgetting. (After Baddeley & Hitch, 1977)

But *why* does memory interference occur? Why can't the newly acquired information coexist with older memories? The answer has several parts, but a key element is linked to issues we've already discussed: In many cases, newly arriving information gets interwoven with older information, producing a risk of confusion about which bits are old (i.e., the event you're trying to remember) and which are new (i.e., information that you picked up after the event). This confusion is, of course, central for the misinformation effect, described earlier. In addition, in some cases, new information seems literally to replace old information—much as you no longer save the rough draft of one of your papers once the final draft is done. In this situation, the new information isn't woven into the older memory; instead, it erases it.

Undoing Forgetting

In some circumstances, forgetting can actually be helpful. If you experience some sad or painful event, for example, you're likely to hope that the memory for the event will eventually fade. In addition, forgetting can help you step away from specific details of your life experience, so that you can think about the experience in more general terms; this, in turn, can sometimes promote abstract thinking. We've also just suggested an analogy to replacing your "rough drafts" with newer, more polished versions. Continuing the analogy, the idea here is that forgetting sometimes allows you to replace old beliefs with (better-informed, more-thought-through) new beliefs, and that seems a positive step. (For more on the benefits of forgetting, see Storm, 2011.)

Even acknowledging these points, however, it's plain that people often want to *undo* forgetting, and to recover old memories. Is this possible? One option, often discussed, is *hypnosis*. The proposal in essence is that, under hypnosis, a person can "return" to an earlier event and remember virtually everything about the event, including aspects the person didn't even notice (much less think about) at the time. Similar claims have been made about certain drugs—sodium amytal, for example—with the idea that these, too, can help people remember things they otherwise never could.

Many studies have examined these claims, and the evidence is clear: Neither of these techniques improves memory. Hypnotized participants often do give detailed reports of the target event, but this isn't because they remember more; instead, they're just willing to *say* more in order to comply with the hypnotist's instructions. As a result, their "memories" are a mix of recollection, guesses, and inferences—and, of course, the hypnotized individual cannot tell you which of these are which (Lynn, Neuschatz, Fite, & Rhue, 2001; Mazzoni & Lynn, 2007; Spiegel, 1995). Likewise, the drugs sometimes given to improve memory work largely as sedatives, putting an individual in a less guarded, less cautious state of mind. This state allows people to report more about the past—not because they remember more, but simply because in this relaxed condition they're willing to say more.

A more exotic proposal is suggested by reports of people whose brains have been directly stimulated, usually as part of brain surgery. Patients are typically

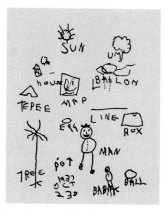

A Drawings done by hypnotized adult told that he was 6 years old

B Drawings done at age 6

HYPNOTIC AGE REGRESSION

In one study, participants were asked to draw a picture while mentally "regressed" to age 6. At first glance, their drawings (an example is shown in A) looked remarkably childlike. But when compared to the participants' own drawings made at that age (an example is shown in B), it's clear that the hypnotized adults' drawings were much more sophisticated. They represent an adult's conception of what a childish drawing is rather than being the real thing.

awake during this surgery, and the surgeon uses their responses to stimulation as a way of locating certain structures and regions within the brain. Sometimes, though, when the brain is prodded or poked, the patient suddenly remembers scenes from long ago, often in clear and remarkable detail (e.g., Penfield & Roberts, 1959). Could this be the way to defeat forgetting and to recover one's "lost past"? And if this procedure does undo forgetting, wouldn't that mean that forgetting does not involve decay or erasure (because the memories are still there, potentially recoverable in this way)? Wouldn't it mean, instead, that our memories are essentially permanent, with no information loss as the years go by?

The answer to all of these questions, however, is "no." In fact, only a small number of patients report recollections in response to this stimulation of the brain. The memories evoked in this fashion are extraordinary—clear and detailed, as though the patients were reliving the earlier experience. Unfortunately, though, we have no way of knowing whether these are really memories. The experiences might, for example, be hallucinations of some sort. Or they might be very vivid reconstructions. Because this evidence comes from an extreme circumstance, it has been difficult to track down the historical facts to confirm (or disconfirm) these patients' recollections. Until this is done, we have no evidence that they are remembering, much less remembering accurately. Hence, we have no basis for claiming that this technique promotes memory retrieval.

On the positive side, though, there are procedures that do improve memory and seem, therefore, to diminish forgetting. However, there's nothing exotic about these procedures. As we saw in Chapter 6, retrieval of memories from long-term storage is more likely if a suitable cue is provided. On this basis, researchers have explored various means of cueing memory; more specifically, they've developed a number of interview techniques—including the so-called *cognitive interview,* intended for use in police work—aimed at maximizing the quantity and accuracy of information obtained from eyewitnesses to crimes (Fisher & Schreiber, 2007). These techniques emphasize context reinstatement (i.e., re-creating the psychological state the person was in, during the event—see Chapter 6) and provide a diverse set of retrieval cues, on the idea that the more cues provided, the greater the chance of finding a successful cue. The well-documented success of these techniques reminds us, once again, that some forgetting is due to retrieval failure, and so can be undone.

In addition, rather than *undoing* forgetting, perhaps we can *avoid* forgetting: The passage of time has a much smaller impact on memory if you simply "revisit" the memory periodically. Each "visit" seems to refresh the memory, with the result that forgetting is much less likely. Researchers have examined this effect in several contexts, including one that is both theoretically interesting and pragmatically useful: Students often have to take exams, and this forces them to "revisit" the course materials. These revisits, we've just suggested, should slow forgetting, and, on this basis, exams can help students hang onto the material they've learned! Several studies have confirmed this optimistic suggestion—that is, have shown that the step of taking a college exam can promote long-term retention (e.g., Carpenter, Pashler, & Cepeda, 2009; Halamish & Bjork, 2011; Karpicke & Roediger, 2010; Karpicke & Blunt, 2011; McDaniel et al., 2007; Pahsler, Rohrer, Cepeda & Carpenter, 2007).

Memory: An Overall Assessment

Let's pause once again to recap some of our main themes. We've now seen that people sometimes recall with confidence events that never took place, and they sometimes forget information they'd hoped to remember. But we've also mentioned the positive side of things: how much people *can* recall, and the key fact that your memory is accurate far more often than not. Most of the time, it seems, you do recall the past as it truly was.

Perhaps most important, we've also suggested that memory's "failings" are simply the price you pay in order to gain crucial advantages. For example, we've argued that memory errors arise because the various episodes in your memory are densely interconnected with each other; it's these interconnections that allow elements to be transplanted from one remembered episode to another. But these connections are there for a purpose: They're the retrieval paths that make memory search possible. Thus, to avoid the errors, you would need to restrict the connections; but if you did that, you would lose the ability to locate your own memories within long-term storage!

The memory connections that lead to error also help you in other important ways. Our environment, after all, is in many ways predictable, and it's enormously useful for you to exploit that predictability. There's little point in scrutinizing a kitchen to make sure there's a stove in the room, because in the vast majority of cases there is. Why take the time, therefore, to confirm the obvious? Likewise, there's little point in taking special note that, yes, this restaurant does have menus and that, yes, people in the restaurant are eating and not having their cars repaired. These, too, are obvious points, and it would be a waste of effort to give them special notice.

On these grounds, reliance on schematic knowledge is a good thing: Schemata guide your attention to what's informative in a situation, rather than what's self-evident (e.g., Gordon, 2006), and they guide your inferences at the time of recall. If this use of schemata sometimes leads you astray, that is a small price to pay for the gain in efficiency that schemata allow. (For similar points, see Chapter 3.)

In the same fashion, we've also suggested that the blurring together of episodes may be a blessing, rather than a curse. Think, for example, about all the times in your life when you've been with a particular friend. These episodes are related to each other in an obvious way, and so they're likely to become interconnected in your memory. This will cause difficulties if you want to remember which episode is which, and whether you had a particular conversation in this episode or in that one. However, rather than lamenting this, perhaps we should *celebrate* what's going on here: Because of the "interference," all of the episodes will merge together in your memory, so that what resides in memory is one integrated package, containing in united form all of your knowledge about your friend. Thus,

SUPERIOR AUTOBIOGRAPHICAL MEMORY

What were you doing on, say, February 10, 1997? If asked about a randomly selected date, most people can recall little about that day. But a small number of people—including actress Marilu Henner (star of Taxi*)—seem to have hyper-thymesia, or "superior autobiographical recall." They're able to remember virtually every episode, every day, of their lives. They can, if asked, remember their activities on an afternoon a dozen years ago, and what they had for lunch that day, and what shoes they were wearing, and the weather, and more. When checked, these memories turn out to be uniformly accurate! This pattern has been documented only recently, and so far only a few dozen people have been identified who have this capacity. Researchers are just starting their inquiries on this fascinating topic!*

rather than complaining about memory confusion and "interference," we should rejoice over the memory *integration,* and "cross-referencing."

To put this point more broadly, many people have the idea that the function of memory is to supply encyclopedic knowledge about the past. Any slips in memory, therefore, or any gaps, are a problem. This perspective, though, is probably wrong. Instead, the function of memory is *to provide you with the information you need* in order to live your life, and, for this purpose, forgetting is often advantageous! (For more on the *benefits* produced by memory's apparent limitations, see Howe, 2011; Schacter, Guerin & St. Jacques, 2011; but for an intriguing challenge to these claims, see Parker, Cahill & McGaugh, 2006.)

In these ways, our overall assessment of memory can be rather upbeat. We have, to be sure, discussed a range of memory errors, but the errors are in most cases a side product of mechanisms that otherwise help you—to locate your memories within storage, to be efficient in your contact with the world, and to form general knowledge. Thus, even with the errors, even with forgetting, it seems that human memory functions in a fashion that serves us extraordinarily well.

Autobiographical Memory

We began this chapter by acknowledging that much of the evidence in Chapters 5 and 6 was concerned with memory for very simple stimuli—word lists, for example, or short sentences. In this chapter, we've considered memories for more complex materials, and this has drawn our attention to the ways in which your knowledge (whether knowledge of a general sort or knowledge about related episodes) can both improve memory and also interfere with it.

In making these points, we've considered memories in which the person was actually involved in the remembered episode, and not just an external witness (e.g., the false memory that you spilled that bowl of punch). We've also looked at studies that involved memories for emotional events (e.g., the plane crash we discussed at the chapter's start) and memory over the very long term (e.g., memories for childhood events "planted" in adult participants).

Do these three factors—involvement in the remembered event, emotion, and long delay—matter in any way, changing how or how well someone remembers? These factors are surely relevant to the sorts of remembering people do outside of the laboratory, and indeed, all three are central for **autobiographical memory**. This is the memory that each of us has containing the full recollection of our lives, and we've argued (e.g., in Chapters 1 and 6) that this sort of memory plays a central role in shaping how each of us thinks about ourselves and, thus, how we behave. (For more on the importance of autobiographical memory, see Baddeley, Aggleton, & Conway, 2002. For more on the distinction between these types of memory, including *biological* differences between autobiographical memory and "lab memory," see Cabeza & St. Jacques, 2007; Hodges & Graham, 2001; Kopelman & Kapur, 2001; Tulving, 1993, 2002.)

Let's look, therefore, at how the three factors we've mentioned, each seemingly central for autobiographical memory, influence what we remember.

Memory and the Self

Having some involvement in an event, rather than passively witnessing the event, turns out to have a large effect on memory. In part, this is because your involvement in an event often leads to the idea that the event is relevant to you and who you are, and, in general, information relevant to the self is better remembered than information that's not self-relevant (e.g., Symons & Johnson, 1997; also Westmacott & Moscovitch, 2003). This **self-reference effect** (the memory advantage for materials pertaining to the self) emerges in many forms, including an advantage in remembering things you have said as opposed to things others have said, better memory for adjectives that apply to you relative to adjectives that do not, better memory for names of places you have visited relative to names of places you've never been, and so on.

But here, too, we can find memory errors, in part because your "memory" for your own life is (just like other memories) a mix of genuine recall and some amount of schema-based reconstruction. Thus, you can "remember" how you spent last Tuesday by relying on your generic knowledge about how your Tuesdays generally unfold; you can "remember" that you were excited on New Year's Eve because you believe this is your usual pattern. These reconstructions are likely to be accurate in most cases, because your **self-schema**—just like any other schema—does reflect your usual or normal behavior. Even so, this schema-based construction is (as in all cases) open to error.

Consider, for example, the fact that most adults believe they've been reasonably consistent, reasonably stable, over their lifetimes. They believe, in other words, that they've always been pretty much the same as they are now. This notion of consistency, in other words, is part of their self-schema. When the time comes to remember the past, therefore, people will rely to some extent on this belief, and so reconstruct their own history in a biased fashion—one that maximizes the (apparent) stability of their lives. Thus, people recall their past attitudes, the past status of their romantic relationships, and their health in a fashion that emphasizes consistency and thereby makes the past look more like the present than it really was (M. Conway & Ross, 1984; Holmberg & Homes, 1994; for related results, see Levine, 1997; Marcus, 1986; McFarland & Buehler, 2012; Ochsner & Schacter, 2000; Ross & Wilson, 2003).

It's also true that most of us would prefer to have a positive view of ourselves, including a positive view of how we've acted in the past. This, too, can shape memory. As one illustration, Bahrick, Hall, and Berger (1996) asked college students to recall their high school grades as accurately as they could, and the data showed a clear pattern of self-service: When students forgot a good grade, their (self-serving) reconstruction led them to the (correct) belief that the grade must have been a good one; consistent with this, 89% of the A's were correctly remembered. But when students forgot a poor grade, reconstruction led them to the (false) belief that the grade must have been okay; as a result, only 29% of the D's were correctly recalled. Overall, then, students consistently recalled their grades as being better than they actually were. (For other mechanisms through which current motivations can color autobiographical recall, see Conway & Holmes,

2004; Conway & Pleydell-Pearce, 2000; Forgas & East, 2003; Kunda, 1990; Mather, Shafir, & Johnson, 2000.)

Memory and Emotion

Another factor important for autobiographical memory is *emotion*. You don't get emotional when memorizing a researcher's list of words or a story that you read in the lab. But many of your experiences in life *do* cause emotion; how does this influence memory?

In general, emotion helps you to remember. At a biological level, emotional arousal seems to promote the process of memory **consolidation**—the process through which memories are biologically "cemented in place." Consolidation takes place "behind the scenes"—that is, without you thinking about it—during the hours following an event (Hardt, 2010; Wang & Morris, 2010). If the consolidation is interrupted for some reason (for example, because of fatigue, or injury, or even extreme stress), no memory is established and so recall later will be impossible. (That's because there's no information in memory for you to retrieve; you can't read text off a blank page!) But, on the positive side, some circumstances—including the biological aspects of emotionality—enhance consolidation. Specifically, emotional events trigger a response in the amygdala, and the amygdala in turn increases activity in the hippocampus. The hippocampus is, as we've seen, crucial for getting memories established (see Chapter 6; for reviews of emotion's biological effects on memory, see Buchanan, 2007; Dudai, 2004; Hamann, 2001; Hoschedidt, Dongaonkar, Payne & Nadel, 2010; Joels, Fernandez & Roosendaal, 2011; Kensinger, 2007; LaBar, 2007; LaBar & Cabeza, 2006; Öhman, 2002; Phelps, 2004).

Emotion also shapes memory through other mechanisms. An emotional event is likely to be important to you, virtually guaranteeing that you'll pay close atten-

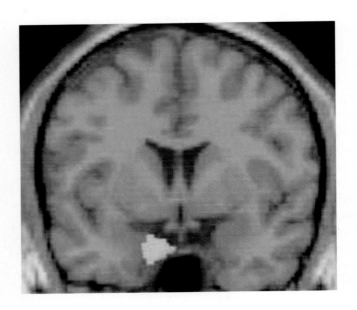

AMYGDALA ACTIVATION IN EMOTIONAL MEMORY

Higher levels of activity in the left amygdala (shown here in yellow) are associated with successful retrieval of emotional pictures. Increased amygdala activation during encoding is also associated with better memory.

tion as the event unfolds, and we've seen (e.g., in Chapter 5) that attention and thoughtful processing help memory. Moreover, you tend to mull over emotional events in the minutes (or hours) following the event, and this is tantamount to memory rehearsal. For all of these reasons, it's unsurprising that emotional events are well remembered (Reisberg & Heuer, 2004).

In addition, many authors have argued that emotion changes what you pay attention to within an event, and this changes the pattern of what is and is not remembered from an emotional episode. One proposal is that emotion leads to a "narrowing" of attention, so that in an emotional event all of your attention will be focused on just a few aspects of the scene (Easterbrook, 1959). This narrowing helps guarantee that these attended aspects are firmly placed into memory, but it also implies that the rest of the event, excluded from this narrowed focus, won't be remembered later (e.g., Gable & Harmon-Jones, 2008; Reisberg & Heuer, 2004; Steblay, 1992). A related proposal suggests that emotional events tend to set *goals*: If you're afraid, your goal is to escape; if you're angry, your goal is to deal with the person who's made you angry; if you're happy, your goal may be to relax and enjoy! In each case, you're more likely to pay attention to aspects of the scene directly relevant to your goal, and this, too, will color how you remember the emotional event (Fredrickson, 2000; Levine & Edelstein, 2009).

Flashbulb Memories

Some people believe that one group of emotional memories is in a category all its own. These are the so-called **flashbulb memories**—memories of extraordinary clarity, typically for highly emotional events, retained despite the passage of many years. When Brown and Kulik (1977) introduced the term "flashbulbs," they pointed as a paradigm case to the memories people have of first hearing the news of President John F. Kennedy's assassination. Their participants, interviewed more than a decade after that event, remembered it "as though it were yesterday," recalling details of where they were at the time, what they were doing, and whom they were with. Many participants were able to recall the clothing worn by people around them, the exact words uttered, and the like. Notice that these memories are not just vivid and long-lasting, they are also quite *personal:* The memories focus on the specific experience of the person who holds the memory—what they were doing at the time, who brought them the news, and so on. These memories tend to contain much less information about the main event that triggered the flashbulb, and so people usually can't recall who else was wounded in the attack, or whether Kennedy died immediately, or only later in the hospital. (Texas Governor Connally was seriously wounded; Kennedy was alive—but with no chance of survival—when he reached the hospital and was declared dead while still in the emergency room.)

Many other events have also produced flashbulb memories. People who were at least 10 or 12 years old in 1997 have vivid memories of hearing the news about Princess Diana's death that year. Most Americans can clearly recall where they were when they first heard about the attack on the World Trade Center in 2001. Many young people vividly remember what they were doing in 2009 when they first heard that Michael Jackson had died (see Pillemer, 1984; Rubin & Kozin, 1984; also see Weaver, 1993; Winograd & Neisser, 1993).

What is going on in all of these cases? More than a century ago, William James proposed a biological (albeit metaphorical) explanation, suggesting that "an impression may be so exciting emotionally as almost to leave a scar upon the cerebral tissues" (James, 1890, p. 670). Informally, people sometimes speak about these events being "burned" into their brains. Is this the right way to think about flashbulb memories?

In evaluating these notions, let's start with a key question: Flashbulb memories certainly seem extraordinarily vivid, but are these memories *correct?* In fact, research indicates that some flashbulb memories contain large-scale errors. For example, Neisser and Harsch (1992) interviewed college students one day after the 1986 explosion of the space shuttle *Challenger*, asking questions designed to probe the usual content of flashbulb memories: How had the students first heard about the explosion? Who brought them the news? What they were doing at the time? Neisser and Harsch then reinterviewed these students three years later, asking the same questions about the explosion. The results show remarkably little agreement between the immediate and delayed reports, even with regard to major facts such as who delivered the news or where the person was when the news arrived (see Figure 7.10). It appears, then, that the three-year reports are mostly false, although it should be said that the students were highly confident

FLASHBULB MEMORIES

People often have especially clear and long-lasting memories for events like their first hearing about Princess Diana's death, or the attack on the World Trade Center in September 2001, or the news of Michael Jackson's death in 2009. These memories—called flashbulb memories—are vivid and compelling, but they are not always accurate.

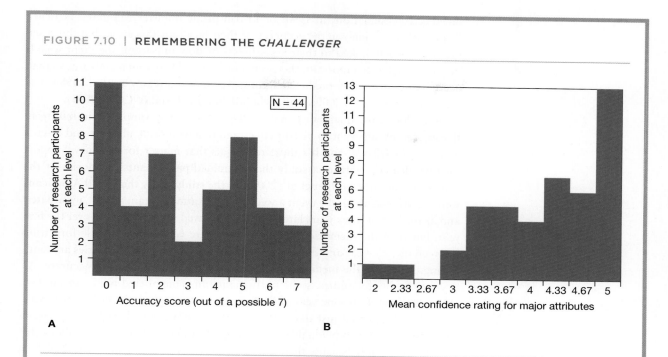

FIGURE 7.10 | REMEMBERING THE *CHALLENGER*

A

B

Three years after the tragic explosion of the space shuttle Challenger, *research participants had very poor memories for the event—but high confidence in their (false) recollections. Panel A shows how many of the 44 participants obtained each of the possible accuracy scores (and so 11 participants had a score of zero, four had a score of 1, and so on). Panel B shows a parallel breakdown for* confidence *ratings (and so one participant had a confidence level, averaged across questions, of 2.0; two had an average confidence level of 3.0, and so on). While 25% of the participants got a zero score on the memory test, and half of them a score of 2 or lower, confidence ratings were generally at the high end of the scale. (After Neisser & Harsch, 1992)*

about the accuracy of these reports. (For similar data, see Rubin & Talarico, 2007; Talarico & Rubin, 2003; Wagenaar & Groeneweg, 1990.)

Other data, though, tell a different story, suggesting that some flashbulb memories are accurate. Why should this be? Why are some flashbulb events remembered well, while others are not? One key factor may be the consequentiality of the flashbulb event. If the event matters directly for the participant's life, it is more likely to be remembered accurately. If the event is inconsequential for that person, memory accuracy will be poor. This point is well illustrated in a study that examined people's memory for the 1989 San Francisco earthquake. For individuals who lived in Georgia, thousands of miles from the earthquake's epicenter, memory accuracy was quite low, and so errors were as common for this event as they'd been in students' recollection of the space shuttle explosion. In contrast, for people who lived in Santa Clara, near the earthquake's epicenter, the quake was remembered accurately and in detail (Neisser, Winograd, & Weldon, 1991; Palmer, Schreiber, & Fox, 1991). Similarly, another study examined people's memories for the unexpected resignation (in 1990) of British prime minister Margaret Thatcher. People differed widely in the accuracy of their recall for this event, but this accuracy was closely linked to their assessments of how important the event was: If they regarded it as important, they were much more likely to remember it, so that, again, consequentiality predicted accurate recollection (Conway et al., 1994; also see Luminet & Curci, 2009; Tinti, Schmidt, Sotgiu, Testa, & Curci, 2009).

Why does consequentiality matter? The answer may simply lie in *rehearsal*: If you perceive an event to be consequential, then you think about it and discuss it with your friends, and it's these rehearsals that matter for memory. Support for this idea comes from a study that examined participants' memories of the September 11 attack (Hirst et al., 2009). In the study, more than 3000 Americans were questioned about the event a week after the attack, again almost a year later, and again almost three years later. The data showed some forgetting over the first year, but then the memories stabilized and there was relatively little forgetting between the one-year and three-year tests. Clearly, then, these memories are long-lasting. However, the memories were neither complete nor totally accurate. As in other flashbulb studies, some participants misremembered the event (and so reported things in the one-year or three-year test that were flatly inconsistent with what they'd reported just days after the event). Crucially, though, these errors were less likely for individuals who'd engaged in many conversations about the event—presumably because these conversations served as memory rehearsal.

Overall, though, let's not lose track of the fact that some flashbulb memories are marvelously accurate; others are filled with error. Therefore, the "burned into the brain" proposal is surely mistaken. In addition, it's important that, from the point of view of the person who has a flashbulb memory, there's no detectable difference between an accurate flashbulb and an inaccurate one: Either will be recalled with great detail; either will be recalled with enormous confidence. In each case, the memory can be intensely emotional. Apparently, then, memory errors can occur even in the midst of our strongest, most vivid recollection.

Traumatic Memories

Flashbulb memories tend to be highly emotional: People often feel deeply angry (or profoundly sad) when they recall the September 11 attack; many people still get upset when they think about Michael Jackson's death. But, unfortunately, we can easily find cases of far stronger emotion evoked by someone's experience. This leads us to ask: How are *traumatic* events remembered? If someone has witnessed wartime atrocities, can we count on the accuracy of their testimony in a war crimes trial? If someone suffers through the horrors of a sexual assault, will the painful memory eventually fade? Or will the memory remain as a horrific remnant of the brutal experience?

Evidence suggests that most traumatic events are well remembered for many years; indeed, victims of some atrocities often seem plagued by a cruel enhancement of memory, leaving them with extra-vivid and long-lived recollections of the terrible event (e.g., Alexander et al., 2005; Goodman et al., 2003; Peace & Porter, 2004; Porter & Peace, 2007; Thompsen & Berntsen, 2009). In fact, people who have experienced trauma sometimes complain about having "too much" memory and wish they remembered *less*.

This enhanced memory is best understood in terms of a mechanism we've already mentioned: consolidation. This process is promoted by the conditions that accompany bodily arousal, including the extreme arousal typically present in a traumatic event (Buchanan & Adolphs, 2004; Hamann, 2001). But this does not mean that traumatic events are always well remembered. There are, in fact, cases in which people who have suffered through extreme events have little or no recall of their experience (e.g., Arrigo & Pezdek, 1997). In addition, we can sometimes document substantial errors in someone's recall of a traumatic event (Paz-Alonso & Goodman, 2008). We need to ask, therefore, why some traumatic events—in contrast to the broader pattern—are completely forgotten.

In some cases, the forgetting of a traumatic event can be understood simply in terms of the person's *age*. In general, people have difficulty recalling events (traumatic or otherwise) from the first years of life, and so a failure to recall very early trauma may just be part of this broader pattern. In other cases, traumatic events are accompanied by sleep deprivation, head injuries, or substance abuse, each of which can disrupt memory, making it unsurprising that these traumas aren't recalled (McNally, 2003). In still other cases, the extreme stress associated with the event can disrupt the consolidation processes and so no memory is ever established (Hasselmo, 1999; Joels et al., 2011; McGaugh, 2000; Payne, Nadel, Britton, & Jacobs, 2004).

Finally, one last hypothesis is highly controversial: Several authors have argued that highly painful memories will be repressed—pushed out of awareness as a step toward self-protection. These memories, it is claimed, will not be consciously available but will still exist in a person's long-term storage and, in suitable circumstances, may be "recovered"—that is, made conscious once again. (See, for example, Freyd, 1996, 1998; Terr, 1991, 1994.)

Consistent with this broad claim, we know that memories can, in fact, be "lost" for some time and then recovered (e.g., Geraerts et al., 2007). The mechanism behind this pattern, however, remains uncertain, and, in truth, most memory researchers are skeptical about the repression idea (e.g., Kihlstrom, 2006). As one consideration, painful events—including events that seem likely candidates for repression—are typically well remembered, and this is, of course, not at all what we would expect if repression is in place as a self-protective mechanism. In addition, when painful events are forgotten, the rate of forgetting seems similar to the rate at which ordinary events are forgotten—again not what we'd expect if painful memories are especially likely to be banished through repression. Third, at least some of the "recovered memories" may, in fact, have been remembered all along, and so provide no evidence of repression. In these cases, the memories had appeared to be "lost" because the person refused to discuss the memories for many years (presumably because the remembered events were quite painful); the "recovery" of these memories simply reflects the fact that the person is at last willing to discuss these memories out loud. Such a recovery may be extremely consequential—emotionally and perhaps legally—but it does not tell us anything about how memory works.

Moreover, the pattern of memories lost and then found, when it does occur, may just reveal the effects of ordinary retrieval failure. This certainly is a mechanism that can hide memories from view for long periods of time, only to have the memories reemerge once a suitable retrieval cue is available. In this case, too, the recovery is of enormous importance for the person finally remembering the long-lost episodes; but again, this merely confirms the role of an already-documented memory mechanism; there is no need here for any theorizing about repression.

Finally, and most troubling, we need to acknowledge the possibility that at least some of these "recovered memories" may, in fact, be false memories. After all, we know that false memories occur and that they are more likely when one is recovering the distant past than when one is trying to remember recent events. It is also relevant that many recovered memories emerge only with the assistance of a therapist who is genuinely convinced that the client's psychological problems stem from long-forgotten episodes of childhood abuse. Even if the therapists scrupulously avoid leading questions, bias might still lead them to shape their clients' memory in other ways—by giving signs of interest or concern if the clients hit on the "right" line of exploration, by spending more time on topics related to the alleged memories, and so forth. In these ways, the climate within a therapeutic session could guide the clients toward finding exactly the "memories" the therapist expects to find.

These are, of course, difficult issues, especially when we bear in mind that recovered memories often involve horrible episodes, such as episodes of sexual abuse; if these memories are accurate, they are evidence for repugnant crimes. But here, as in all cases, the veracity of recollection cannot be taken for granted. This caveat is important in evaluating any memory, and it is far more so for anyone wrestling with this sort of traumatic recollection. (For discussion of this difficult issue, see, among others, Geraerts et al., 2009; Ghetti et al., 2006; Giesbrecht et al., 2008; Kihlstrom & Schacter, 2000; Loftus & Guyer, 2002; Read, 1999.)

Long, Long-Term Remembering

We've now touched on two of the key elements for autobiographical memory: the relationship to the self, and the influence of emotion (including extreme emotion). One other element is also important: In the laboratory, a researcher might ask you to recall a word list you read just minutes ago, or perhaps a film you saw a week ago. Away from the lab, however, people routinely try to remember events from years—and perhaps decades—back. We've already mentioned that these longer *retention intervals* are, in general, associated with a greater amount of forgetting. But, impressively, memories from long ago can sometimes turn out to be wonderfully accurate.

We've discussed the fact that flashbulb memories can be long-lasting, but memory across very long intervals can also be observed with more mundane materials. For example, Bahrick, Bahrick, and Wittlinger (1975) tracked down the graduates of a particular high school—people who had graduated in the previous year, and the year before, and the year before that, and, ultimately, people who had graduated 50 years before. All of these alumni were shown photographs from their own year's high school yearbook. For each photo, they were given a group of names and had to choose the name of the person shown in the picture. The data for this "name matching" task show remarkably little forgetting; performance was approximately 90% correct if tested 3 months after graduation, the same after 7 years, and the same after 14 years. In some versions of the test, performance was still excellent after 34 years (see Figure 7.11).

Recall performance in this study was slightly worse than recognition but was still impressive. When asked (in a "picture cueing" task) to come up with the names on their own, rather than choosing the correct name from a list, the participants were able to name 70% of the faces when tested 3 months after graduation, and 60% after 9 months. Remarkably, they were still able to name 60% of their classmates after 7 years.

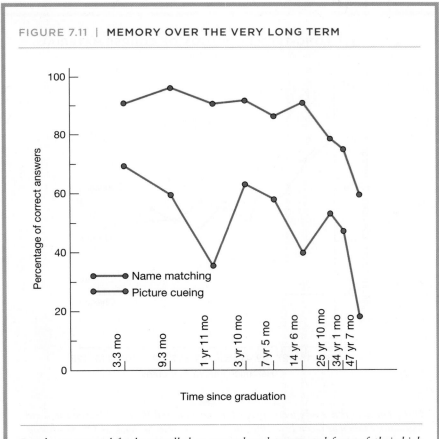

FIGURE 7.11 | **MEMORY OVER THE VERY LONG TERM**

People were tested for how well they remembered names and faces of their high school classmates; memory was remarkably long-lasting. (See the text for a description of the tasks.) The data do show a drop-off after 47 years, but it is unclear whether this reflects an erosion of memory or a more general drop-off in performance caused by the normal process of aging. (After Bahrick et al., 1975)

As a different example, what about the material you're learning right now? You are presumably reading this textbook as part of a course on cognitive psychology. Five years from now, will you still remember things you learned in this course? How about a decade from now? Conway, Cohen, and Stanhope (1991) explored these questions, testing students' retention of a cognitive psychology course taken years earlier. The results broadly echo the pattern we've already seen: Some forgetting of names and specific concepts was observed during the first 3 years after the course. After the third year, however, performance stabilized, so that students tested after 10 years still remembered a fair amount and, indeed, remembered just as much as students tested after 3 years (see Figure 7.12). Memory for more general facts and memory for research methods showed even less forgetting.

Some loss of memories is observed in these studies, but what is remarkable is how much people do remember, and for how long. In study after study, there

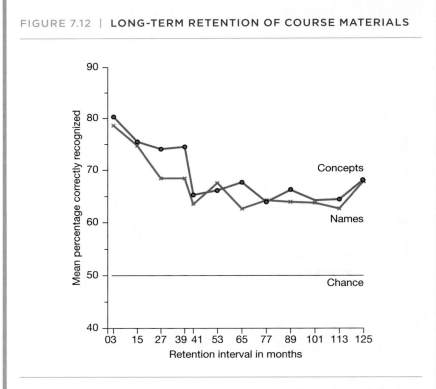

FIGURE 7.12 | **LONG-TERM RETENTION OF COURSE MATERIALS**

Participants in this study were quizzed about material they had learned in a college course taken as recently as three months ago, or as far back as 125 months ago (more than a decade!). The data showed some forgetting, but then performance leveled off, and so memory seemed remarkably stable from three years onward. Note that, in a recognition task, memory is probed with "familiar-or-not" questions, and so someone with no memory, responding at random, would get 50% right just by chance. (After Conway, Cohen, & Stanhope, 1991)

is an initial period of forgetting, generally for the first 3 or 4 years. After that, performance remains impressively consistent, despite the passage of several decades. How can we reconcile this with our earlier assertion that the retention interval is crucial for memory? In a previous section, we argued that memory gets worse and worse as times goes by. Here, in contrast, we're seeing little effect of the retention interval. How should we put these pieces together?

The solution to this puzzle is easy: The retention interval *is* crucial for memory, and it is, in general, more difficult to remember things from long ago, compared to memory for more recent events. However, *how much* the interval matters— that is, how quickly memories "fade"—depends on how well established the memories were in the first place. Thus, the high school students in the Bahrick et al. study had seen their classmates day after day, for (perhaps) several years. Hence they knew their classmates' names very, very well—and this is why the passage of time has only a slight impact on their memories for the names. Likewise, students in the Conway et al. study had, apparently, learned their psychology quite well—and so retained what they'd learned for a very long time. Indeed, we first met this study in Chapter 5, when we mentioned that students' *grades* in the course were good predictors of how much the students would still remember many years after the course was done. Here, too, the better the original learning, the slower the forgetting.

Indeed, Bahrick (1984) suggests that some memories can achieve a state of **permastore** (short for "permanent storage"), a state in which these memories are essentially immune to the passage of time. As we've just seen, memories are more likely to reach this status if the material is extremely well learned in the first place (Bahrick, 1984; Bahrick & Hall, 1991; Conway, Cohen, & Stanhope, 1991, 1992). It also helps if you revisit the material once in a while; as we noted earlier, this too slows forgetting.

We can maintain our claim, therefore, that the passage of time is the enemy of memory: Longer retention intervals produce lower levels of recall. However, there are also steps you can take—making sure the material is very well learned, and then taking the moments to revisit the material periodically—that can diminish (although probably not eliminate) the impact of the passing years.

How General Are the Principles of Memory?

There is certainly more to be said about autobiographical memory. For example, there are clear patterns for how much each individual remembers from specific portions of his or her lifetime: People tend to remember very little from the early years of childhood (before age 3 or so), both because a toddler's brain is immature and because the young child lacks the skills needed for encoding memories that will be retrievable later on (Bauer, 2007; Hayne, 2004; Howe, Courage, & Rooksby, 2009; Morrison & Conway, 2010). In contrast, some periods of life seem to be especially *well remembered*. For example, older adults tend to have especially clear memories of their adolescence and early adulthood, a pattern known as the *reminiscence bump* (see Figure 7.13; Conway & Haque, 1999; Dickson, Pillemer & Bruehl, 2011; Rathbone, Moulin & Conway, 2008). Thus,

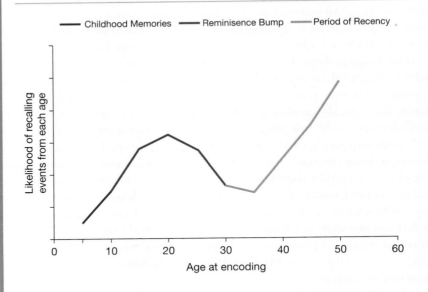

FIGURE 7.13 | THE LIFE SPAN RETRIEVAL CURVE

— Childhood Memories   — Reminisence Bump   — Period of Recency

Likelihood of recalling events from each age

Age at encoding

This graph represents the likelihood of someone being able to recall events experienced at various ages during the life span. (The data here are hypothetical, but the pattern is remarkably consistent from one individual to the next.) The life span retrieval curve contains four different parts. From birth to age 5 is a period of so-called childhood amnesia; from age 5 to 10 is a period of childhood memories; from 10 to 30 years old is the reminiscence bump; and last is a period from the end of the reminiscence bump to present time. The reminiscence bump has been observed on the life span retrieval curve in multiple studies.

WORKBOOK
DEMONSTRATION 7.4

for many Americans, the last years of high school, and the years they spend in college, are likely to be the most memorable period of their lives.

But, with an eye on the broader themes of this chapter, where does our brief survey of autobiographical memory leave us? In many ways this form of memory is similar to other sorts of remembering. Autobiographical memories can last for years and years, but so can memories that do not refer directly to your own life. Autobiographical remembering is far more likely if the person occasionally revisits the target memories; these rehearsals dramatically reduce forgetting. But the same is true in nonautobiographical remembering.

Autobiographical memory is also open to error, just as other forms of remembering are. We saw this in cases of flashbulb memories that turn out to be false. We've also seen that misinformation and leading questions can plant false autobiographical memories—about birthday parties that never happened and trips to the hospital that never took place (also see Brown & Marsh, 2008). Misinformation can even reshape memories for traumatic events, just as it can alter memories for trivial episodes in the laboratory (Paz-Alonso & Goodman, 2008).

These facts strengthen a claim that has been implicit in much of our discussion over the last three chapters: Certain principles seem to apply to memory in general, independent of what is being remembered. All memories depend on connections. The connections promote retrieval. The connections also facilitate interference because they allow one memory to blur into another. The connections can fade with the passage of time, producing memory gaps, and the gaps are likely to be filled via reconstruction based on generic knowledge. All of these things seem to be true whether we're talking about relatively recent memories or memories from long ago, emotional memories or memories of calm events, memories for complex episodes or memories for simple word lists.

But this does not mean that all principles of memory apply to all types of remembering. As we saw in Chapter 6, for example, the rules that govern implicit memory may be different from those that govern explicit memory. And, as we've now seen, some of the factors that play a large role in shaping autobiographical remembering (e.g., the role of emotion) may be irrelevant to other sorts of memory.

In the end, therefore, our overall theory of memory is going to need more than one level of description. We will need some principles that apply to only certain types of memory (e.g., principles specifically aimed at emotional remembering). But we'll also need broader principles, reflecting the fact that some themes apply to memory of all sorts (e.g., the importance of memory connections). As we have seen over the last three chapters, these more general principles have moved us forward considerably in our understanding of memory in many different domains and have allowed us to illuminate many aspects of learning, of memory retrieval, and of the sources of memory error.

CHAPTER SUMMARY

- Your memory is usually accurate, but errors do occur and can be quite large. In general, these errors are produced by the connections that link your memories to each other and link memories for specific episodes to other, more general knowledge. These connections help you because they serve as retrieval paths. But the connections can also "knit" separate memories together, making it difficult to keep track of which elements belong in which memory.

- Some memory errors are produced by your understanding of an episode. The understanding promotes memory for the episode's gist but also encourages memory errors. A similar pattern emerges in the DRM procedure, in which a word related to other words on a list is (incorrectly) recalled as being part of the list. Closely related effects arise from schematic knowledge. This knowledge helps you understand an episode, but at the same time, a reliance on schematic knowledge can lead you to remember an episode as being more "regular," more "normal," than it actually was.

- Memory errors can also arise through the misinformation effect, in which people are exposed to some (false) suggestion about a previous event. Such suggestions can easily change the details of how an event is remembered and can, in some cases, plant memories for entire episodes that never occurred at all.

- People seem genuinely unable to tell apart their accurate and inaccurate memories. This is because false memories can be recalled with just as much detail, emotion, and confidence as a historically accurate memory. Nor can we reliably detect false memories by relying on the contrast between whether people say they "remember" the past or whether they say they merely "know" what happened in the past. The absence of a connection between memory accuracy and memory confidence contrasts with the common-sense belief that you should rely on someone's degree of certainty in assessing their memory. The problem in this common-sense notion lies in the fact that confidence is influenced by factors (such as feedback) that have no impact on accuracy, and this influence undermines the linkage between accuracy and confidence.

- While memory errors are easily documented, cases of accurate remembering can also be observed, and they are probably more numerous than cases involving memory error. Memory errors are more likely, though, in recalling distant events rather than recent ones. One reason for this is decay of the relevant memories; another reason is retrieval failure. Retrieval failure can be either complete or partial; the tip-of-your-tongue pattern provides a clear example of partial retrieval failure. Perhaps the most important source of forgetting, though, is interference.

- People have sought various means of undoing forgetting, including hypnosis and various drugs. These procedures, however, seem ineffective. Forgetting can be diminished, though, through procedures that provide a rich variety of retrieval cues, and it can be avoided through occasional revisits to the target material.

- Although memory errors are troubling, they may simply be the price you pay in order to obtain other advantages. For example, many errors result from the dense network of connections that link your various memories. These connections sometimes make it difficult to recall which elements occurred in which setting, but the same connections serve as retrieval paths, and without the connections you might have great difficulty in locating your memories in long-term storage. Even forgetting may have a positive side, by virtue of trimming details from memory in a fashion that may foster abstract thinking.

- Autobiographical memory is influenced by the same principles as any other form of memory, but it is also shaped by its own set of factors. For example, episodes connected to the self are, in general, better remembered—a pattern known as the self-reference effect.

- Autobiographical memories are also often emotional, and this has multiple effects on memory. Emotion seems to promote memory consolidation, but it may also produce a pattern of memory narrowing. Some emotional events give rise to very clear, long-lasting memories called flashbulb memories. Despite their subjective clarity, these memories, like memories of any other sort, can contain errors and, in some cases, can be entirely inaccurate. At the extreme of emotion, trauma has mixed effects on memory. Some traumatic events are not remembered, but most traumatic events seem to be remembered for a long time and in great detail.

- Some events can be recalled even after many years have passed. In some cases, this is because the knowledge was learned so well that it reached a state of permastore. In other cases, occasional rehearsals preserve a memory for a very long time.

The Workbook Connection

See the *Cognition Workbook* for further exploration on remembering complex events:

- Demonstration 7.1: Associations and Memory Error
- Demonstration 7.2: Memory Accuracy and Confidence
- Demonstration 7.3: The Tip-of-the-Tongue Effect
- Demonstration 7.4: Childhood Amnesia
- Research Methods: External Validity
- Cognitive Psychology and Education: Overconfidence
- Cognitive Psychology and Education: Remembering for the Long Term
- Cognitive Psychology and the Law: Jurors' Memory

NEED HELP STUDYING?

 wwnorton.com/studyspace

Visit StudySpace to access free review material such as

- Chapter study plans
- Quizzes
- Flashcards, and more

Go to **wwnorton.com/zaps** for these online labs:

- Feature Net
- Lexical Decision
- Sentence Verification
- Word Frequency
- Word Superiority

Knowledge

I n Parts 2 and 3, we saw case after case in which your interactions with the world are guided by knowledge: In perceiving, you make inferences guided by knowledge about the world's regular patterns. In attending, you anticipate inputs guided by your knowledge about what's likely to occur. In learning, you connect new information to things you already know. And so on. But what is knowledge? How is knowledge represented in your mind? How do you locate knowledge in memory when you need it?

We've already taken some steps toward answering these questions—by arguing in previous chapters that knowledge is represented in the mind by means of a network of interconnected nodes. In this section, though, we'll flesh out this proposal in important ways: In Chapter 8, we'll describe the basic building blocks of your knowledge—your individual concepts—and consider several hypotheses about how concepts are represented in the mind. We'll see that each hypothesis captures a part of the truth, and so we'll be driven toward a several-part theory combining the various views. We'll also see that your knowledge about individual concepts depends on linkages to many other related concepts. Thus, you cannot know what a "dog" is without also understanding what an "animal" is, what a "living thing" is, and so on. As a result, connections among ideas will be crucial for us here, just as they were in previous chapters.

Chapters 9 and 10 look at two special types of knowledge: your knowledge about language, and your knowledge about visual images. In Chapter 9, we'll see that your knowledge of language is highly creative in the sense that you can produce new words and new sentences that no one has ever used before. But at the same time, the creativity is constrained, and so there are some words, and some sequences of words, that are considered unacceptable by virtually any speaker. In order to understand this pattern of "constrained creativity," we'll consider the possibility that language knowledge involves abstract rules that are, in some fashion, known and honored by every user of the language.

In Chapter 10, we'll discuss the fact that mental images seem to involve representations that are qualitatively distinct from those involved in other forms of knowledge, but we'll also consider some of the ways in which memory for visual appearances is governed by the same principles as other forms of knowledge.

CHAPTER EIGHT

Concepts and Generic Knowledge

No adult takes any pride in knowing what a dog is, or a bird, or a house, or a tree. These concepts are so ordinary, so common, that there seems to be nothing special about knowing—and being able to think about—these simple ideas. However, ordinary concepts like these are, in an important way, the building blocks out of which all your knowledge is created, and as we've seen in previous chapters, you depend on your knowledge in many aspects of your day-to-day functioning. Thus, you know what to pay attention to in a restaurant because you understand the basic concept of "restaurant." You're able to understand a simple story about a child checking her piggy bank because you understand the concepts of "money," "shopping," and so on.

The idea, then, is that you need concepts in order to have knowledge, and you need knowledge in order to function. In this way, your understanding of ideas like "dog" and "house" might seem commonplace, but it is an ingredient without which cognition cannot proceed.

But what exactly does it mean to understand simple concepts like these? How is this knowledge represented in the mind? In this chapter, we'll tackle these questions, and as we'll see, describing these concepts is appreciably more difficult than you might guess.

We'll begin with the obvious hypothesis: that understanding a concept is analogous to knowing a dictionary definition, and so, if someone

- Basic concepts—like "chair" and "dog"—are the building blocks of all your knowledge. However, attempts at *defining* these concepts usually fail because we easily find exceptions to virtually any definition that might be proposed.

- This leads to a suggestion that knowledge of these concepts is cast in terms of *probabilities*, so that a creature that has wings and feathers, and that flies and lays eggs, is *probably* a bird.

- Many results are consistent with this probabilistic idea and show that the more a test case resembles the "prototype" for a category, the more likely people are to judge the case as being in that category.

- Other results, however, indicate that conceptual knowledge includes other beliefs—beliefs that link a concept to other concepts and also specify why the concept is as it is.

- We are driven, therefore, to a multipart theory of concepts. Your conceptual knowledge must include a prototype for each category and also a set of remembered exemplars. But you also seem to have a broad set of beliefs about each concept—beliefs that provide a "theory" for why the concept takes the form it does, and you use this theory in a wide range of judgments about the concept.

knows what a *house* is, or a *taxi*, they can offer us something like a definition for these terms, and likewise for all the other concepts in each person's knowledge base. As we will see, though, this hypothesis quickly runs into problems, and so we'll need to turn to a richer—and more complicated—proposal.

Definitions: What Is a "Dog"?

You know perfectly well what a dog is. If someone sends you to the pet shop to buy a dog, you're sure to succeed. If someone tells you that a particular disease is common among dogs, you know that your pet terrier is at risk and so is the Doberman who lives down the block. Clearly, your store of knowledge about dogs will support these not-very-exciting achievements. But what is that knowledge?

One possibility is that you know something akin to a dictionary definition. That is, what you know is of this form: "A dog is a creature that (a) is mammalian, (b) has four legs, (c) barks, (d) wags its tail." You could then use this definition in straightforward ways: When asked whether a candidate creature is a dog, you could use the definition as a checklist, scrutinizing the candidate for the various defining features. When told that "a dog is an animal," you would know that you hadn't learned anything new, because this information is already contained, presumably, within the definition. If you were asked what dogs, cats, and horses have in common, you could scan your definition of each one looking for common elements.

This proposal is surely correct in some cases, and so, for example, you certainly know definitions for concepts like *triangle* or *even number*. But what about more commonplace concepts? The concern here was brought to light by the 20th-century philosopher Ludwig Wittgenstein, who argued (e.g., Wittgenstein, 1953) that the simple terms we all use every day actually don't have definitions. For example, consider the word "game." You know this word, and can use it sensibly, but what is a game? As an approach to this question, we could ask, for example, about the game of hide-and-seek. What makes hide-and-seek a "game"? Hide-and-seek (a) is an activity most often practiced by children, (b) is engaged in for fun, (c) has certain rules, (d) involves multiple people, (e) is in some ways competitive, and (f) is played during periods of leisure. All these are plausible attributes of games, and so we seem well on our way to defining "game." But are these attributes really part of the *definition* of "game"? What about the Olympic Games? The competitors in these games are not children, and runners in marathon races don't look like they're having a great deal of fun. Likewise, what about card games played by one person? These are played alone, without competition. For that matter, what about the case of professional golfers?

It seems that for each clause of the definition, we can easily find an exception: an activity that we call a game but that doesn't have the relevant characteristic. And the same is true for almost any concept. We might define "shoe" as an item of apparel made out of leather, designed to be worn on the foot. But what about wooden shoes? What about a shoe designed by a master shoemaker and intended only for display and never for use? What about a shoe filled with cement, which therefore cannot be worn? Similarly, we might define "dog" in a way that includes four-leggedness, but what about a dog that has lost a limb in some accident? We might specify "communicates by barking" as part of the definition of dog, but what about the Egyptian basenji, which has no bark? Examples like these make it clear that even simple terms, terms denoting concepts we use easily and often, resist being defined. In each case, we can come up with what seems to be a plausible definition, but then it's easy to find exceptions to it.

Family Resemblance

Plainly, then, we can't say things like, "A dog is a creature that has fur and four legs and barks." That's because, as we've seen, it's easy to find exceptions to this rule (a hairless Chihuahua? a three-legged dog? the barkless basenji?). But surely we *can* say, "Dogs *usually* are creatures that have fur, four legs, and bark, and a creature without these features is *unlikely to be* a dog." This probabilistic phrasing preserves what's good about definitions—the fact that they do name sensible, relevant features, shared by most members of the category. But this phrasing also allows a degree of uncertainty, some number of exceptions to the rule.

In a similar spirit, Wittgenstein proposed that members of a category have a **family resemblance** to each other. To understand this term, think about the

THE HUNT FOR DEFINITIONS

It is remarkably difficult to define even very familiar terms. For example, what is a "dog"? Most people include "has fur" in the definition, but what about the hairless Chihuahua? Many people include "communicates by barking" in the definition, but what about the Basenji (one of which is shown here)—a breed of dog that does not bark?

WORKBOOK
DEMONSTRATION 8.1

TYPICALITY IN FAMILIES

In the Smith family, many (but not all) of the brothers have dark hair, so dark hair is typical for the family (i.e., is found in many family members) but does not define the family (i.e., is not found in all family members). Likewise, wearing glasses is typical for the family but not a defining feature, and so is having a mustache and a big nose. Many concepts have the same character—with many features shared among the instances of the concept, but no features shared by all of the instances.

resemblance pattern in an actual family—your own, perhaps. There are probably no "defining features" for your family—features that every family member has. Nonetheless, there are features that are *common* in the family, and so, if we consider family members two or even three at a time, we can usually find some shared attributes. Thus, you, your brother, and your mother might all have the family's beautiful blonde hair and the same wide lips; as a result, you three look alike to some extent. Your sister, on the other hand, doesn't have these features; she's a narrow-lipped brunette. Nonetheless, she's still recognizable as a member of the family, because she (like you and your father) has the family's typical eye shape and the family's distinctive chin. Thus, there are common features, but the *identity* of those common features depends on what "subgroup" of the family you're considering—hair color shared for *these* family members; eye shape shared by *those* family members; and so on.

One way to think about this pattern is by imagining the "ideal" for each family—someone who has *all* of the family's features. (In our example, this would be someone who is blonde and has wide lips, and also has just the right eye and chin shapes.) In many families, this person may not exist, and there may be no one who has all of the family's features, so no one who looks like the "perfect Jones" (or the "perfect Martinez" or the "perfect Goldberg"). Nonetheless, each member of the family has at least some features in common with this ideal, and therefore some features in common with other family members. This is why the family members resemble each other, and it's how we manage to recognize these individuals as being within the family.

Wittgenstein proposed that ordinary categories like "dog" or "game" or "furniture" work in the same way. There may be no features that are shared by all dogs or all games, just as there are no features shared by everyone in your family. Even so, we can identify "characteristic features" for each category—features that many (and perhaps most) category members have. And the more of these features an object has, the more likely you are to believe it is in the category. Family resemblance is a matter of degree, not all-or-none.

There are several ways we might translate all of this into a psychological theory, but the most influential translation was proposed by Eleanor Rosch in the mid-1970s (Rosch, 1973, 1978; Rosch & Mervis, 1975; Rosch, Mervis, Gray, Johnson, & Boyes-Braem, 1976), and it's to her model that we now turn.

Prototypes and Typicality Effects

One way to think about definitions is that they set the "boundaries" for a category. If a test case has certain attributes, then it's "inside" the boundaries. If a test case doesn't have the defining attributes, then it's outside the category. **Prototype theory**, in contrast, begins with a different tactic: Perhaps the best way to identify a category, to characterize a concept, is to specify the "center" of the category, rather than the boundaries. Just as we spoke earlier about the "ideal" family member, perhaps the concept of "dog" (for example) is represented in the mind by some depiction of the "ideal" dog, and all judgments about dogs are made with reference to this ideal; likewise for "bird" or "house" or any other concept in your repertoire—in each case, the concept is represented by the appropriate prototype.

But what is a prototype? In some cases, a prototype literally represents the ideal for the category, and so, for example, the prototype diet soft drink might have zero calories but still taste great (although see Kim & Murphy, 2011). More commonly, a prototype will be an average of the various category members you've encountered. Thus, the prototype dog will be the average color of the dogs you've seen, the average size of the dogs you've seen, and so forth.

Notice, then, that different people may have different prototypes. If a prototype reflects the ideal for a category, people may disagree about what that ideal would involve. If a prototype reflects the average of the cases you've encountered, then an American's prototype for "house" might have one form, while for someone living in Japan the prototype "house" might be rather different. We'll therefore need some flexibility in how we characterize prototypes. Nonetheless, in all cases the prototype will serve as the anchor, the benchmark, for our conceptual knowledge. When you reason about a concept or use your conceptual knowledge, your reasoning is done with reference to the prototype.

Prototypes and Graded Membership

To see how prototypes are used, let's start with the simple task of categorization: deciding whether something is a dog or not. To make this decision, you compare the creature currently before your eyes with the prototype in your

CATEGORIES HAVE PROTOTYPES

As the text describes, people seem to have a prototype in their minds for a category like "dog." For many people, the German Shepherd shown here is close to that prototype, and the other dogs depicted are more distant from the prototype.

memory. If there's no similarity between them, the creature standing before you is probably not in the category; if there's considerable similarity, you draw the opposite conclusion.

This sounds plausible enough, but note an important implication: Membership in a category depends on resemblance to the prototype, and resemblance is a matter of degree. (After all, some dogs are likely to resemble the prototype rather closely, while others will have less in common with this ideal.) As a result, membership in the category is not a simple "yes or no" decision; instead, it's a matter of "more" or "less." In technical terms, we'd say that categories, on this view, have a **graded membership**, such that objects closer to the prototype are "better" members of the category than objects farther from the prototype. Or, to put this concretely, some dogs are "doggier" than others, some books "bookier" than others, and so on for all the other categories you can think of.

Testing the Prototype Notion

In a **sentence verification task**, research participants are presented with a succession of sentences; their job is to indicate (by pressing the appropriate button) whether each sentence is true or false. In most experiments, what we are interested in is *how quickly* participants can do this task, and it turns out that their speed of response varies from item to item within a category. For example, response times are longer for sentences like "A penguin is a bird" than for "A robin is a bird"; longer for "An Afghan hound is a dog" than for "A German shepherd is a dog" (Smith, Rips, & Shoben, 1974).

Why should this be? According to a prototype perspective, participants make these judgments by comparing the thing mentioned (e.g., penguin) to their prototype for that category (i.e., their bird prototype). When there is much similarity between the test case and the prototype, participants can make their decisions quickly; judgments about items more distant from the prototype take more time. And, given the results, it seems that penguins and Afghans are more distant from their respective prototypes than are robins and German shepherds.

Other results can also be understood in these terms. For example, in a **production task** we ask people to name as many birds or dogs as they can (Mervis, Catlin, & Rosch, 1976). According to a prototype view, they will do this task by first locating their bird or dog prototype in memory and then asking themselves what resembles this prototype. In essence, they'll start with the center of the category (the prototype) and work their way outward from there. Thus, birds close to the prototype should be mentioned first; birds farther from the prototype, later on.

Notice, then, that the first birds to be mentioned in the production task should be the birds that yielded fast response times in the verification task; that's because what matters in both tasks is proximity to the prototype. Likewise, the birds mentioned later in production should have yielded slower response times in verification. This is exactly what happens.

In fact, this sets the pattern of evidence for prototype theory: Over and over, in category after category, members of a category that are "privileged" on one task (e.g., yield the fastest response times) turn out also to be privileged on other tasks (e.g., are most likely to be mentioned). That is, various tasks *converge* in the sense that each task yields the same answer—that is, indicates the same category members as special.

As a further illustration of this converging pattern, consider the data from **rating tasks.** In these tasks, participants are given instructions like these (Rosch, 1975; also Malt & Smith, 1984): "We all know that some birds are 'birdier' than others, some dogs are 'doggier' than others, and so on. I'm going to present you with a list of birds or of dogs, and I want you to rate each one on the basis of how 'birdy' or 'doggy' it is." People are easily able to render these judgments, and quite consistently they rate items as being very "birdy" or "doggy" when these instances are close to the prototype (as determined in the other tasks). They rate items as being less "birdy" or "doggy" when these are farther from the prototype.

This suggests that, once again, people perform this task by comparing the test item to the prototype (see Table 8.1).

We get a related result if we simply ask people to *think* about categories (e.g., Rosch, 1977a). In one study, participants were asked to generate simple sentences about a category. If the category was "birds," for example, a participant might say, "I saw two birds in a tree" or "I like to feed birds in the park." Next, the experimenters rewrote these sentences, substituting for the category name either the name of a prototypical member of the category (e.g., robin) or a not-so-prototypical member (e.g., penguin). In our example, we would get "I like to feed robins in the park" and "I like to feed penguins in the park." Finally, these new, edited sentences were shown to a different group of participants; they were asked to rate how silly or implausible the sentences seemed.

TABLE 8.1 | PARTICIPANTS' TYPICALITY RATINGS FOR THE CATEGORY "FRUIT" AND THE CATEGORY "BIRD"

Fruit	Rating	Bird	Rating
Apple	6.25	Robin	6.89
Peach	5.81	Bluebird	6.42
Pear	5.25	Seagull	6.26
Grape	5.13	Swallow	6.16
Strawberry	5.00	Falcon	5.74
Lemon	4.86	Mockingbird	5.47
Blueberry	4.56	Starling	5.16
Watermelon	4.06	Owl	5.00
Raisin	3.75	Vulture	4.84
Fig	3.38	Sandpiper	4.47
Coconut	3.06	Chicken	3.95
Pomegranate	2.50	Flamingo	3.37
Avocado	2.38	Albatross	3.32
Pumpkin	2.31	Penguin	2.63
Olive	2.25	Bat	1.53

Ratings were made on a 7-point scale, with 7 corresponding to the highest typicality. Note also that the least "birdy" of the birds isn't (technically speaking) a bird at all!

SOURCE: AFTER MALT & SMITH (1984).

The hypothesis here is that when people think about a category they are in fact thinking about the prototype for that category. Therefore, in making up their sentences, participants will come up with statements appropriate for the prototype. It follows from this that the meaning of the sentence will be pretty much unchanged if we substitute a prototypical category member for the category name, since that will be close to what the participant had in mind in the first place. Substituting a nonprototypical member, in contrast, may yield a peculiar, even ridiculous proposition. This is fully in line with the data. When the new group of participants rated these sentences, they rated as quite ordinary the sentences into which we placed a prototypical case ("I saw two robins in a tree") and rejected as silly the sentences into which we placed a nonprototypical case ("I saw two penguins in a tree").

Basic-Level Categories

It seems, then, that certain category members are indeed "privileged," just as the prototype theory proposes. It turns out, in addition, that certain *types of category* are also privileged—in their structure and how they are used. Thus, imagine that we show you a picture like the one in Figure 8.1 and simply ask, "What is this?" You're likely to say "a chair" and unlikely to offer a more specific response ("upholstered armchair") or a more general one ("an item of furniture"). Likewise, we might ask, "How do people get to work?" In responding, you're unlikely

FIGURE 8.1 | **BASIC VERSUS SUPERORDINATE LABELING**

What is this? The odds are good that you would answer by saying it is a "chair," using the basic-level description, rather than using the superordinate label ("It's a piece of furniture") or a more specific description ("It's an upholstered armchair"), even though these other descriptions would certainly be correct.

to say, "Some people drive Fords; some drive Toyotas." Instead, your answer is likely to use more general terms, such as "cars," "trains," and "buses."

In keeping with these observations, Rosch and others have argued that there is a "natural" level of categorization, neither too specific nor too general, that you tend to use in your conversations and your reasoning. The special status of this **basic-level categorization** can be demonstrated in many ways. Basic-level categories are usually represented in our language via a single word, while more specific categories are identified only via a phrase. Thus, "chair" is a basic-level category, and so is "apple." The more specific ("subordinate") categories of "lawn chair" or "kitchen chair" are not basic level; neither is "Granny Smith apple" nor "Golden Delicious apple." In addition, if asked to describe an object, you're likely to use the basic-level term. If asked to explain what members of a category have in common with one another, you have an easy time with basic-level categories ("What do all chairs have in common?") but some difficulty with more-encompassing ("superordinate") categories ("What does all furniture have in common?"). And so on.

WORKBOOK
DEMONSTRATION 8.3

It seems, then, that basic-level categorization is important for a variety of purposes (also see Pansky & Koriat, 2004). Indeed, in studies of children who are learning how to talk, basic-level terms are often acquired earlier than either the more specific subcategories or the more general, more encompassing categories. Thus, basic-level categories do seem to reflect a natural way to categorize the objects in our world (Rosch et al., 1976; for more on these points, see Corter & Gluck, 1992; Rogers & Patterson, 2007).

Exemplars

Let's return, though, to our main agenda. As we've seen, a broad spectrum of tasks reflects the "graded membership" of mental categories: Some members of the categories are "better" than others, and the better members are recognized more readily, mentioned more often, judged more typical, and so on. (For yet another way you're influenced by typicality, see Figure 8.2.) Likewise, in diagnosing diseases, physicians often seem to function as if asking themselves, "How much does this case resemble a typical case of disease X? How closely does it resemble a typical case of disease Y?" The greater the resemblance to this or that diagnostic prototype, the more likely the diagnosis will be of that disease. (See, for example, Klayman & Brown, 1993; Kulatunga-Moruzi, Brooks, & Norman, 2011.)

All of this fits well with the notion that conceptual knowledge is represented via a prototype and that we categorize by making comparisons to that prototype. It turns out, though, that prototype theory isn't the only way you can think about these data.

Analogies From Remembered Exemplars

Imagine that we place a wooden object in front of you and ask, "Is this a chair?" According to the prototype view, you'll answer this question by calling up your

FIGURE 8.2 | TYPICALITY AND ATTRACTIVENESS

Typicality influences many judgments about category members, including attractiveness. Which of these pictures shows the most attractive-looking fish? Which shows the least attractive looking? In several studies, participants' ratings of attractiveness have been closely related to (other participants') ratings of typicality—so that people seem to find more-typical category members to be more attractive (e.g., Halberstadt & Rhodes, 2003). Plainly, the influence of typicality is rather broad.

chair prototype from memory and then comparing the candidate to that prototype. If the resemblance is great, you'll announce, "Yes, this is a chair."

But you might make this decision in a different way. You might notice that this object is very similar to an object in your Uncle Jerry's living room, and you know that the object in Uncle Jerry's living room is a chair. After all, you've seen Uncle Jerry sitting in the thing, reading his newspaper. If Jerry's possession is a chair, and if the new object resembles Jerry's, then it's a safe bet that the new object is a chair too.

The idea here is that in some cases categorization can draw on knowledge about specific category members rather than on more general information about the overall category. In our example, the categorization is supported by memories of a specific chair—Jerry's, rather than remembered knowledge about chairs in general. This is referred to as exemplar-based reasoning, with an exemplar being defined as a specific remembered instance—in essence, an example.

The exemplar-based approach is in many ways similar to the prototype view. According to each of these proposals, you categorize objects by comparing them to a mentally represented "standard." The difference between the views lies in what that standard is: For prototype theory, the standard is the prototype—an average representing the entire category; for exemplar theory, the standard is provided by whatever example of the category comes to mind (and, of course, different examples may come to mind on different occasions). In either case, though, the process is then the same. You assess the similarity between a candidate object and this standard. If the resemblance is great, you judge the candidate as being within the relevant category; if the resemblance is minimal, you seek some alternative categorization.

Explaining Typicality Data With an Exemplar Model

Consider a task in which we show people a series of pictures and ask them to decide whether each picture shows a fruit or not. We already know that they'll respond more quickly for typical fruits (apple, orange, banana) than for less typical fruits (kiwi, olive, cranberry), and we've seen how this result is handled by a prototype account. It turns out, however, that an exemplar-based account can also explain this result, and so this result favors neither the prototype nor the exemplar theory; instead, it's fully compatible with both.

How would an exemplar-based account handle this result? Let's imagine that you're trying to decide whether a picture shows a fruit or not. To make your decision, you'll try to think of a fruit exemplar (again: a memory for a particular fruit) that resembles the object in the picture. If you find a memory that's a good match to this object, then you know the object in the picture is indeed a fruit. No match? Then it's not a fruit.

How this sequence will play out, however, depends on the picture. If the picture shows, say, an apple, then your memory search will be extremely fast: Apples are common in your experience (often seen, often eaten, often mentioned), and so you've had many opportunities to establish apple memories. Moreover, these memories will be well primed, thanks to your frequent encounters with apples. As a result, you'll easily find a memory that matches the picture, and so you will swiftly respond that, yes, the picture does show a fruit. But if the picture shows, say, a fig or a starfruit, then your memory search will be more difficult: You probably don't have many memories that will match these pictures, and these memories aren't well primed. Hence you'll need more time to locate one of these memories, and your response will be slow.

A similar argument will handle the other tasks showing the graded-membership pattern—for example, the production task. Let's say that you're asked to name as many fruits as you can. You'll quickly name apples and oranges because these fruits are represented many times in your memory, thanks to the many encounters

WHICH ARE THE TYPICAL FRUITS?

If asked to name fruits, you're more likely to name typical fruits (like apples or oranges) than atypical fruits (figs, starfruit). According to a prototype account, this result emerges because you start your memory search with the prototype and "work outwards" from there. According to an exemplar account, the result emerges because you have many memories of apples and oranges, and these are well-primed; it's no surprise, therefore, that these are the fruit memories that come easily to mind for you.

you've had with them. These memories are also well primed, making them easy to retrieve. Fig and starfruit memories, however, will have neither of these advantages, and so they'll come to mind less easily. In this way, your production will favor the typical fruits—not because of prototyping, but because of the pattern of what's available in memory.

A Combination of Exemplars and Prototypes

It seems, then, that exemplar-based views can easily explain typicality effects, and so the data we've reviewed so far favor neither theory over the other; both are compatible with the evidence. Which theory, therefore, is correct? The answer, actually, is that *both* are correct, and you rely on both prototypes *and* exemplars in your thinking about categories.

What purpose is served by this double mode of representation? Prototypes provide an economical representation of what's typical for a category, and there are circumstances in which this quick summary is quite useful. But exemplars, for their part, provide information that's lost from the prototype. For example, people routinely "tune" their concepts to match the circumstances, and so they think about birds differently when thinking about Chinese birds than when thinking about American birds; they think about gifts differently when thinking about gifts for a student rather than gifts for a faculty member (Barsalou, 1988; Barsalou & Sewell, 1985). In fact, people can adjust their categories in fairly precise ways: not just "gift," but "gift for a 4-year-old" or "gift for a 4-year-old who recently broke her wrist" or "gift for a 4-year-old who likes sports but recently broke her wrist."

This pliability in concepts is easy to understand if people are relying on exemplars; after all, different settings, or different perspectives, would trigger different memories and thus bring different exemplars to mind. If someone is then relying on these exemplars in his reasoning, it makes sense that his reasoning will vary as he moves from one circumstance to the next, or as he shifts his perspective.

It's useful, then, that conceptual knowledge includes *both* prototypes *and* exemplars, because each carries its own advantages (also see Figure 8.3). And, in fact, the mix of exemplar and prototype knowledge may vary from person to person and from concept to concept. One person, for example, might have extensive knowledge about individual horses, and so she has many exemplars in memory; the same person might have only general information (a prototype, perhaps) about snowmobiles. Some other person might show the reverse pattern. And for all people, the pattern of knowledge might depend on the size of the category and on how confusable the category memories are with each other (with exemplars used when the individuals are more distinct).

The pattern of knowledge can also *change* for a particular person: When you're first learning about *palm trees*, say, you might only have seen a couple

FIGURE 8.3 | **DISTINCTIONS WITHIN CATEGORIES**

The chapter suggests that you have knowledge of both exemplars and prototypes. As a further complication, though, you also have special knowledge about distinctive individuals within a category. Thus, you know that Kermit has many frogly properties (he's green, he eats flies, he hops), but also has unusual properties that make him a rather unusual frog (since, after all, he can talk, he can sing, and he's in love with a pig).

of these trees, so you'll rely on this exemplar knowledge for all your thinking about this category. With more experience, though, you might start to lose track of which individual is which, so you'll rely more and more on prototype knowledge. Then, with even more experience, you might again become aware of individuals within the category—and so, at that point, you have an even mix of prototype and exemplar knowledge. (For discussion of these points, including how the mix of exemplars and prototypes will be shaped by various factors, see Brooks, Norman, & Allen, 1991; Homa, Dunbar, & Nohre, 1991; Minda & Smith, 2001; Rips, Smith, & Medin, 2012; Rouder & Ratcliff, 2006; Smith, 2002; Vanpaemel & Storms, 2008.)

Overall, though, it cannot be surprising that you have the option of *combining* prototype and exemplar models, because, as we've said, the two types of model are similar in crucial ways. In either case, an object before your eyes triggers some information in memory (either a specific instance, according to exemplar theory, or the prototype, according to prototype theory). In either case, you assess the resemblance between this conceptual knowledge, supplied by memory, and the novel object now before you: "Does this object resemble my sister's couch?" If so, the object is a couch. "Does the object resemble my prototype for an ashtray?" If so, it's probably an ashtray.

Thus exemplar and prototype models rely on the same processes—a triggering of a memory, then a judgment of resemblance, and finally a conclusion based on this resemblance. Given these similarities, it seems sensible that we might merge the models, with each of us on any particular occasion relying on whichever sort of information (exemplar or prototype) comes to mind more readily.

The Difficulties With Categorizing via Resemblance

We are moving, it seems, toward a relatively clear-cut set of claims. For most concepts, definitions are not available. For many purposes, though, you don't need a definition and can rely instead on a mix of prototypes and exemplars. In addition, there's no question that *typicality* plays a huge role in people's thinking, with more-typical category members being "privileged" in many regards. And typicality is exactly what we would expect if category knowledge does, in fact, hinge on prototypes and exemplars.

All of this seems straightforward enough. However, there are some results that do not fit into this picture, so the time has come to broaden our conception of concepts.

The Differences Between Typicality and Categorization

In the view we've been developing, judgments of *typicality* and judgments of *category membership* both derive from the same source: resemblance to an exemplar or to a prototype. If the resemblance is great, then a test case will be judged to be typical, and will also be judged to be a category member. If the resemblance is small, the test case will be judged atypical and probably not a category member. Thus, typicality and category membership should go hand in hand.

It turns out, though, that typicality and category membership sometimes *don't* go hand in hand. Armstrong, Gleitman, and Gleitman (1983), for example, gave their participants this peculiar instruction: "We all know that some numbers are even-er than others. What I want you to do is to rate each of the numbers on this list for how good an example it is for the category 'even number.'" Participants were then given a list of numbers (4, 16, 32, and so on) and had to rate "how even" each number was. The participants thought this was a strange task but were nonetheless able to render these judgments and, interestingly, were just as consistent with each other using these stimuli as they were with categories like "dog" or "bird" or "fruit" (see Table 8.2).

Of course, participants responded differently (and correctly!) if asked directly which numbers on the list were even and which were odd. Therefore, the participants could judge category membership as easily as they could judge typicality, but, importantly, these judgments were entirely independent of each other: Participants believed that 4 is a more typical even number than 7534, but also knew this has nothing to do with the fact that both are unmistakably in the category *even number.* Clearly, therefore, there's some basis for judging category membership that's separate from the assessment of typicality, and we have no explanation for that point in our theory so far.

TABLE 8.2 | PARTICIPANTS' TYPICALITY RATINGS FOR WELL-DEFINED CATEGORIES

EVEN NUMBER		ODD NUMBER	
Stimulus	Typicality rating	Stimulus	Typicality rating
4	5.9	3	5.4
8	5.5	7	5.1
10	5.3	23	4.6
18	4.4	57	4.4
34	3.6	501	3.5
106	3.1	447	3.3

Participants rated each item on how "good an example" it was for its category. Ratings were on a 0 to 7 scale, with 7 meaning the item is a "very good example." Participants rated some even numbers as being "better examples" of even numbers than others, although mathematically this is absurd: Either a number is even (divisible by 2 without a remainder), or it is not. The same remarks apply to the category of odd numbers. Either a number is odd or it is not, but even so, participants rate some odd numbers as being odder than others.

SOURCE: AFTER ARMSTRONG ET AL. (1983).

Perhaps there's something peculiar, though, about *mathematical concepts* like "even number." Maybe, then, we shouldn't be too concerned about a result obtained with this concept. However, this suggestion is quickly rebutted, because many other concepts show a similar distinction between category membership and typicality. Thus, robins strike us as being closer to the typical bird than penguins do; even so, most of us are certain that both robins and penguins are birds. Likewise, Moby Dick was definitely not a typical whale, but he certainly was a whale; Abraham Lincoln was not a typical American, but he was an American. These informal observations, like the even-number result, drive a wedge between typicality and category membership. (For confirmation of these points in a formal study, see McCloskey & Glucksberg, 1978.)

These (and other) results tell us that category judgments can be made on some basis *other than* typicality. But what is this other basis? As an approach to this question, let's think through an example. Consider a lemon. Paint the lemon with red and white stripes. Is it still a lemon? Most people believe that it is. Now inject the lemon with sugar water, so it has a sweet taste. Then run over the lemon with a truck, so that it's flat as a pancake. What have we got at this point? Do we have a striped, artificially sweet, flattened lemon? Or do we have a non-lemon? Most people still accept this poor, abused fruit as a lemon, but let's consider what this judgment entails. We've taken steps to make this object more and more distant from the prototype and also very different from any specific lemon you've ever encountered (and thus very different from any remembered exemplars). But this

CATEGORIZATION OUTSIDE OF TYPICALITY

Moby Dick was not a typical whale, but he unmistakably was a whale, even so. Clearly, then, typicality can, in some settings, be separated from category membership.

seems not to shake your faith that the object remains a lemon. To be sure, we have a not-easily-recognized lemon, an exceptional lemon, but it's still a lemon. Apparently, something can be a lemon with virtually no resemblance to other lemons. (For discussion of a similar case, with category members being transformed by exposure to toxic waste, see Rips, 1989.)

Related points emerge in research with children. In one early study, preschool children were asked what makes something a "coffeepot," a "raccoon," and so on (Keil, 1986). As a way of probing their beliefs, the children were asked whether it would be possible to turn a toaster into a coffeepot. Children often acknowledged that this would be possible. We would have to widen the holes in the top of the toaster and fix things so that the water wouldn't leak out of the bottom. We'd also need to design a place to put the coffee grounds. But the children saw no obstacles to these manipulations and were quite certain that, with these adjustments in place, one would have created a bona fide coffeepot.

Things were different, though, when the children were asked a parallel question—namely, whether one could, with suitable adjustments, turn a skunk into a raccoon. The children understood that we could dye the skunk's fur, teach it to climb trees, and, in general, teach it to behave in a raccoon-like fashion. Even with these provisions, the children steadfastly denied that we would have created a raccoon. A skunk that looks, sounds, and acts just like a raccoon might be a very peculiar skunk, but it is a skunk nonetheless. (For related data, see Gelman & Wellman, 1991; Keil, Smith, Simons, & Levin, 1998; Walker, 1993. For other evidence suggesting that people reason differently about *naturally occurring items* like raccoons and *manufactured items* like coffeepots, see Caramazza & Shelton, 1998; Estes, 2003; German & Barrett, 2005; Levin, Takarae, Miner, & Keil, 2001; also see pp. 308–311.)

What lies behind all of these judgments? If people are asked why the abused lemon still counts as a lemon, they're likely to mention the fact that it grew on a lemon tree, is genetically a lemon, and so on. It's these "deep" features that matter, and not the lemon's current properties. And so, too, for raccoons: In the child's view, being a raccoon is not merely a function of having the relevant features; instead, in the eyes of the child, the key to being a raccoon involves (among other things) having a raccoon mommy and a raccoon daddy. Thus, a raccoon, just like a lemon, is defined in ways that refer to deep properties and not to mere appearances.

We need to be clear, however, that these claims about an object's "deeper" properties depend, in turn, on a web of other beliefs, beliefs that are, in each case, "tuned" to the particular category being considered. Continuing with our example, you are, we've suggested, more likely to think that a creature is a raccoon if you're told that it has raccoons as parents. But this is true only because you have some ideas about how a creature comes to be a raccoon—ideas that are linked to your broader understanding of biological categories and inheritance. This understanding tells you that parentage is relevant here, even though it's *not* relevant in other cases. Thus, for a contrasting example, consider the steps you'd go through in deciding whether someone really is a doctor. In this case, you're unlikely to worry about whether she has a doctor mommy and a doctor daddy, because your other beliefs tell you that, for this category, parentage doesn't matter.

A SPANIEL, NOT A WOLF, IN SHEEP'S CLOTHING?

Both of these creatures resemble the prototype for sheep, and both resemble many sheep exemplars you've seen (or perhaps read about). But are they really sheep?

As a different example, think about the category of *counterfeit money*. A counterfeit bill, if it's skillfully produced, will bear a near-perfect resemblance to the prototype for legitimate money, but, despite this resemblance, you understand that a counterfeit bill is not in the category of legitimate money. So here, too, your categorization doesn't depend on resemblance to the prototype. Instead, your categorization depends on a web of other beliefs, including beliefs about circumstances of printing: A $20 bill is legitimate, you believe, only if it was printed with the approval of, and under the supervision of, the relevant government agencies. And once again, these beliefs arise only because you have a broader understanding of what money is and how government regulations apply to monetary systems. In other words, you consider circumstances of printing only because your understanding tells you that the circumstances are relevant here, and you won't consider circumstances of printing in a wide range of other cases. If asked, for example, whether a copy of the Lord's Prayer is "counterfeit" or not, your beliefs tell you that the Lord's Prayer is the Lord's Prayer no matter where (or by whom) it was printed. Instead, what's crucial for the prayer's "authenticity" is simply whether the words are the correct words.

Across these and other cases, therefore, your judgments are guided by your sense of what's essential for a category and what's not. And what counts as "essential" depends on your *understanding* of that category—and so you consider parentage in some cases but not others; circumstances of printing in some cases but not others. And, finally, this "understanding," guiding your judgment, seems to depend on a web of other beliefs—about biological inheritance, monetary systems, and so on.

All of this, however, simply leads to the next question: What are these "other beliefs" that seem to be guiding your thinking? And how does typicality (which, without question, does have a powerful influence) fit into this enlarged picture? We'll turn to these issues in a moment; first, though, we need to consider another perspective on the issues in play here.

The Complexity of Similarity

The prototype and exemplar views both depend, at their base, on judgments of *resemblance*—resemblance to the prototype or to some remembered instance. Cases like the mutilated lemon and the counterfeit bill, however, suggest that resemblance may not be the key here. The mutilated lemon doesn't resemble the lemon prototype, but it's still a lemon. A counterfeit bill *does* resemble the prototype for real money, but it still isn't legal. These observations suggest that we cannot base category membership on resemblance alone.

There is, however, a way we might try to "rescue" resemblance: An abused lemon doesn't resemble the lemon prototype *perceptually*, but you might say that it resembles the lemon prototype *in the ways that matter*. For example, the abused lemon has a DNA pattern that resembles the DNA pattern of the prototype. Likewise, the abused lemon has seeds inside it that, if planted, would grow into lemon trees; this, too, is a property of the prototype, and so another basis for claiming resemblance. If only we could focus on these essential properties, therefore, and ignore the superficial attributes, we could maintain the claim that category membership depends on properties shared with the prototype or shared with exemplars. In this way, we could preserve the claim that category membership depends on resemblance.

The problem, though, lies in explaining what we mean by resembling the prototype "in the ways that matter." How do you decide which properties of the prototype are really important, and should be given a lot of weight when judging resemblance, and which properties you can ignore as irrelevant? This seems once again to demand that your judgments be guided by some further knowledge—including beliefs about what it is that really matters for each category. And this brings us right back to where we were: In order to use your category knowledge, you've got to have other beliefs about what is essential for the category and what's not.

It may help to make this point more broadly, by considering what judgments of "resemblance" actually involve. You might think that two objects will be seen to resemble each other if they share properties: Both objects are big, for example, or both are green, or slow-moving, or whatever. And presumably, the more properties shared, the greater the resemblance. But it turns out that resemblance is more complicated than this. To see the point, consider plums and lawn mowers; how much do these two things resemble each other? Actually, these two have many properties in common (Murphy & Medin, 1985): Both weigh less than a ton, both are found on Earth, both have a detectable odor, both are used by people, both can be dropped, both cost less than a thousand dollars, both are bigger than a grain of sand, both are unlikely birthday presents for your infant daughter,

both contain carbon molecules. And on and on and on. (For discussion, see Goldstone & Son, 2012; Goodman, 1972; Markman & Gentner, 2001; Medin, Goldstone, & Gentner, 1993.) Of course, you ignore most of these shared features in judging these two entities, and, as a result, you regard plums and lawn mowers as rather different from each other. But that brings us back to a familiar question: How do you decide which features to ignore when assessing similarity and which features to consider? How do you decide, in comparing a plum and a lawn mower, which of their features are essential and which can be set aside?

We have already suggested an answer to these questions: A decision about which features are important depends on your beliefs about the concept in question. Thus, in judging the resemblance between plums and lawn mowers, you were unimpressed that they share the feature "cost less than a thousand dollars." This is because you believe cost is irrelevant for these categories. (Imagine a lawn mower covered with diamonds; it would still be a lawn mower, wouldn't it?) But, of course, guided by your beliefs, you do consider cost for other categories. (Consider a necklace selling for $1; you're unlikely to categorize this necklace as a "luxury item.") Likewise, you don't perceive plums to be similar to lawn mowers even though both weigh less than a ton, because you know this attribute, too, is irrelevant for these categories. But you do consider weight in thinking about other categories. (Does a sumo wrestler resemble a hippopotamus? In this case, you might be swayed by weight.) Thus it seems clear that the importance of an attribute—cost, or weight, or whatever—varies from category to category, and it varies, in particular, according to your beliefs about what matters for that category.

Concepts as Theories

Let's pause to take stock. Early in the chapter, we saw many results indicating that typicality plays an important role when you're categorizing the objects you encounter; typicality also guides you when you are reasoning about concepts. Our theorizing about concepts, therefore, needs to explain how these typicality effects emerge, and the best way to do this, we suggested, is by including prototypes and exemplars in our theories.

At the same time, our theorizing about concepts needs more than prototypes and exemplars. This was evident in our discussion of counterfeit money and mutilated lemons. More broadly, though, it seems that, whenever you *use* a prototype or exemplar, you're relying on a judgment of resemblance, and resemblance, we've now seen, depends on other knowledge: knowledge about which attributes to pay attention to in judging resemblance, and which to regard as trivial.

It seems plain, then, that we're moving toward a multipart theory of concepts. On the one side, there are prototypes and exemplars, often shaping how you reason in tasks requiring conceptual knowledge. On the other side, there are other beliefs and other knowledge, guiding and supplementing your use of prototypes. But how should we characterize these other beliefs? And within this broader context, exactly what role is played by prototypes and exemplars?

Categorization Heuristics

In your day-to-day thinking about the world, it seems plausible that you'd want to rely on strategies that are as accurate as possible, strategies that would rarely lead you astray. There is a danger, though, that such strategies might be slow and take a lot of effort. If so, you might be better off with a **heuristic** strategy, one that gives up the guarantee of accuracy in order to gain some efficiency. After all, which would you prefer: to be right *all* of the time but needing 18 hours for every judgment you make, or to be right *most* of the time but able to make your judgments in a matter of moments?

We've met this trade-off between efficiency and accuracy in other contexts (e.g., in Chapters 3 and 5), and in fact it's a widespread feature of our mental lives, one that will come up again in later chapters. But in any case, the proposal to be offered here should be obvious: Categorization via resemblance is a heuristic strategy, a relatively efficient (even if imperfect) way to think about categories. What makes this strategy efficient? In most cases, resemblance to a prototype or exemplar is judged on the basis of superficial features, and this is precisely what you want for a categorization heuristic: Superficial traits can be judged swiftly, allowing comparisons that are quick and easy.

Like any other heuristic, however, the use of typicality will occasionally lead to error: If you rely on the bird prototype to categorize flying creatures, you may misidentify a bat. That is the price you pay for heuristic use. But let's keep in mind that prototypes, by their very nature, represent the most common features of a category, and so prototypes will be representative of most category members. Thus, categorization via prototypes will usually be accurate: Most members of the category do resemble the prototype, even if some members do not. And the same points apply to a reliance on exemplars: As we have seen, the exemplars coming to mind will usually be examples of typical category members and so, more often than not, will resemble the new category members you encounter.

This view of things, therefore, preserves a central insight of both the prototype and the exemplar views: We cannot equate typicality with membership in a category. But even so, membership and typicality are clearly related to each other: Creatures closely resembling the prototype bird are not guaranteed to be birds, but they are highly likely to be birds. This is what allows you to use typicality as a fast and efficient basis for judging category membership.

Explanatory Theories

We've repeatedly said, though, that there's more to category knowledge than prototypes and exemplars. What is the "more"?

In the several cases we've considered, your understanding of a concept seems to involve a network of interwoven beliefs linking the target concept to other concepts. To understand what counterfeit is, you need to know what money is, and probably what a government is, and what crime is. To understand what a raccoon is, you need to understand what parents are, and with that, you need to know some facts about life cycles, heredity, and the like.

Perhaps, therefore, we need to broaden our overall approach. We've been trying throughout this chapter to characterize concepts one by one, as though each concept could be characterized independently of other concepts. We talked about the prototype for bird, for example, without any thought about how this prototype is related to the animal prototype or the egg prototype. Perhaps, though, we need a more holistic approach, one in which we place more emphasis on the interrelationships among concepts. This would allow us to include in our accounts the wide network of beliefs in which concepts seem to be embedded.

To see how this might play out, let's once again consider the concept "raccoon." Your knowledge about this concept probably includes a raccoon prototype and some exemplars, but it also includes your belief that raccoons are biological creatures (and therefore the offspring of adult raccoons), and also your belief that raccoons are wild animals (and therefore usually not pets, usually living in the woods). These various beliefs may not be sophisticated, and they may sometimes be inaccurate, but nonetheless they provide you with a broad cause-and-effect understanding of why raccoons are as they are. (Various authors have suggested different proposals for how we should conceptualize this web of beliefs. See, among others, Bang, Medin & Atran, 2007; Keil, 1989, 2003; Lakoff, 1987; Markman & Gentner, 2001; Murphy, 2003; Rips et al., 2012.)

Guided by these considerations, many authors have suggested that each of us has something that we can think of as a "theory" about raccoons—what they are, how they act, and why they are as they are—and likewise a "theory" about most of the other concepts we hold. The theories are less precise, less elaborate, than a scientist's theory, but they serve the same function: They provide a crucial knowledge base that you rely on in most of your thinking about an object, event, or category; and they allow you to understand any new facts you might encounter about the relevant object or category.

The Function of Explanatory Theories

Implicit "theories" about concepts influence you in many ways. We've already suggested that these "theories" influence how you *categorize* things—that is, your decisions about whether a test case is or is not in a particular category. This was crucial, for example, in our discussion of the abused lemon, the transformed raccoon, and the counterfeit bill. In each case, you relied on your background knowledge in deciding which features were crucial for the categorization and which were not; then, with the features "selected" in this fashion, the new case before your eyes could be categorized appropriately.

As a different example, imagine that you saw someone at a party jump fully clothed into a pool. Odds are good that you would decide this person belongs in the category "drunk," but why is this? Jumping into a pool in this way is surely not part of the *definition* of being drunk, and it's also unlikely to be part of the *prototype* (Medin & Ortony, 1989). But each of us also has certain beliefs about how drunks behave; we have, in essence, a "theory" of drunkenness. This theory allows us to think through what being drunk will cause someone to do and not to do, and on this basis we would decide that, yes, someone who jumped into the pool fully clothed probably was inebriated.

You also draw on a "theory" when thinking about new possibilities for a category. For example, could an airplane fly if it were made out of wood? What if it were ceramic? How about one made of whipped cream? You immediately reject this last option, because you know that a plane's function depends on its aero-

A WOODEN AIRPLANE?

Could an airplane be made out of wood? Made from ceramic? Made from whipped cream? You immediately reject the last possibility, because your implicit "theory" about airplanes tells you that planes can fly only because of their wings' shape, and whipped cream wouldn't maintain this shape. Planes can, however, be made of wood—and this one (the famous Spruce Goose) was!

dynamic properties, and those, in turn, depend on the plane's shape. Whipped cream wouldn't hold its shape, and so isn't a candidate for airplane construction. This is an easy conclusion to draw—but only because your concept "airplane" contains some ideas about why airplanes are as they are.

Your "theories" also affect how quickly you can learn new concepts. Imagine that you're given a group of objects and must decide whether each belongs in Category A or Category B. Category A, you are told, includes all the objects that are metal, have a regular surface, are of medium size, and are easy to grasp. Category B, on the other hand, includes objects that are not made of metal, have irregular surfaces, and are small and hard to grasp. This sorting task would be difficult—unless we give you another piece of information: namely, that Category A includes objects that could serve as substitutes for a hammer. With this clue, you immediately draw on your other knowledge about hammers, and in this way you can see *why* the features are as they are. This allows much more rapid learning of the new category. Indeed, when research participants are given this "theme," they learn the category more rapidly and more accurately (Medin, 1989; Wattenmaker, Dewey, Murphy, & Medin, 1986; for related findings, see Heit & Bott, 2000; Kaplan & Murphy, 2000; Rehder & Ross, 2001).

It's helpful, therefore, to understand how a concept's features hang together, but, again, let's be clear that this understanding rests on a broader set of cause-and-effect beliefs. You understand why "metal" and "easy to grasp" go together for the category "hammer substitutes" because you understand what a hammer is and how it's used. Thus, your "theory" about hammers is what gives this category its coherence, and the coherence, in turn, makes the category easier to learn.

Inferences Based on Theories

Here's another way theories guide your everyday concept use. If you meet my pet, Boaz, and decide that he's a dog, then you instantly know a great deal about Boaz—the sorts of things he's likely to do (bark, beg for treats, chase cats) and the sorts of things he's unlikely to do (climb trees, play chess, hibernate all winter). Likewise, if you learn some new fact about Boaz, you'll be able to make broad use of that knowledge—applying it to other creatures of his kind. If, for example, you learn that Boaz has sesamoid bones, you'll probably conclude that all dogs have sesamoid bones—and that perhaps other animals do too.

These examples remind us of one of the reasons that categorization is so important: Categorization allows you to apply your general knowledge (e.g., knowledge about dogs) to new cases you encounter (e.g., Boaz). Conversely, categorization allows you to draw broad conclusions from your experience (so that things you learn about Boaz can be applied to other dogs you meet). All of this is possible, though, only because you realize that Boaz *is a dog*; without this simple realization, you wouldn't be able to use your knowledge in this way. But how exactly does this use-of-knowledge proceed?

Early research indicated that inferences about categories were guided by typicality. In one study, participants who were told a new fact about robins were willing to infer that the new fact would also be true for ducks. If they were told a new fact

WHY IS CATEGORIZATION SO IMPORTANT?

If you decide that Boaz is a dog, then you instantly know a great deal about him (e.g., that he's likely to bark and chase cats, unlikely to climb trees or play chess). In this way, categorization allows you to apply your general knowledge to new cases. And if you learn something new about Boaz (e.g., that he's at risk for a particular virus), you're likely to assume the same is true for other dogs. Thus categorization also allows you to draw broad conclusions from specific experiences.

about ducks, however, they would not extrapolate to robins (Rips, 1975). Apparently, people were willing to make inferences from the typical case to the whole category, but not from an atypical case to the category. (For discussion of *why* people are more willing to draw conclusions from typical cases, see Murphy & Ross, 2005.)

However, your inferences are also guided by your beliefs about cause and effect, and so, once again, we meet a case of concept use being guided by the background knowledge that accompanies each concept. For example, if told that gazelle's blood contains a certain enzyme, people are willing to conclude that lion's blood contains the same enzyme. However, if told that lion's blood contains the enzyme, people are less willing to conclude that gazelle's blood does too. The obvious explanation is that, in the first case, people find it easy to imagine the property being transmitted from gazelles to lions via the food chain. Likewise, if told that grass contains a certain chemical, people are willing to believe that cows have the same chemical inside them. This makes perfect sense if people are thinking of the inference in terms of cause and effect, relying on their beliefs about how these concepts are related to each other (Medin, Coley, Storms, & Hayes, 2003; also see Heit, 2000; Heit & Feeney, 2005; Rehder & Hastie, 2004).

Different Profiles for Different Concepts

This proposal about theories and background knowledge has another important implication: People may think about different concepts in different ways. For example, most people believe that *natural kinds* (groups of objects that exist naturally in the world, like bushes or alligators or stones or mountains) are as they are because of forces of nature, forces that are consistent across the years. As a result, the properties of these objects are relatively predictable: There are, in effect, certain properties that a bush must have in order to survive as a bush; certain properties that a stone must have because of its chemical composition. Things are different, though, for *artifacts*, objects made by human beings. If we wished to make a table with 15 legs rather than 4, or one made out of gold, we could do this. The design of tables, after all, is up to us; and the same is true for most artifacts.

This leads to the proposal that people will reason differently about natural kinds and artifacts—because they have different beliefs about why categories of either sort are as they are. We have already seen one result consistent with this idea: the finding that children would agree that toasters could be turned into coffeepots but not that skunks could be turned into raccoons. Plainly, the children had different ideas about artifacts (like toasters) than they had about animate objects (like skunks). Other results confirm this pattern: In general, people tend to assume more homogeneity when reasoning about biological kinds (like raccoons or skunks) than when reasoning about artifacts (Atran, 1990; Coley, Medin, & Atran, 1997; Rehder & Hastie, 2001).

Related, consider the ways in which you think about categories of *people*. You probably believe that some of these categories exist naturally, while others derive from a diverse set of environmental or cultural factors. How do these beliefs shape your thinking? Consider the concepts "woman" and "stamp collector." People tend to assume that the category "woman" has relatively sharp boundaries (you either are a woman or you're not), that membership in the category is involuntary and immutable, and that many of the category's observable features reflect deep, unchanging attributes (such as a genetic pattern or facts about anatomy) that make women what they are. (As it turns out, each of these assumptions is—at best—debatable, but that's not crucial here; what's relevant is that, for better or worse, most people do make these assumptions.) People make very different assumptions for "stamp collector"—the category has fuzzy boundaries, membership can be temporary, and so on (Prentice & Miller, 2007). In both cases, the rationale is straightforward: People draw on their cause-and-effect beliefs (which may not be accurate!) about how someone gets to be a woman or how someone gets to be a stamp collector, and they reason about each of these categories in a fashion guided by those beliefs.

These variations—whether from one concept to another (*woman* vs. *stamp collector*) or from one class of concepts to another (*artifact* vs. *natural kind*)—can also be detected in neuroscience evidence. For example, fMRI scans tell us that, in healthy, intact brains, different sites are activated when people are thinking about living things than when they are thinking about nonliving things (e.g., Chao et al., 2002). Likewise, people who have suffered brain damage sometimes lose the ability to name certain objects, or to answer simple questions about these objects ("Does a whale have legs?"). Often the problem is specific to certain categories, so some patients lose the ability to name living things but not nonliving things; other patients show the reverse pattern (Mahon & Caramazza, 2009).

Indeed, sometimes the symptoms caused by brain damage are even more specific, with some patients losing the ability to answer questions about fruits and vegetables, but still able to answer questions about other objects, living or not living (see Figure 8.4). These data certainly suggest that separate brain systems are responsible for different types of conceptual knowledge—and so damage to a particular brain area disrupts one type of knowledge but not others.

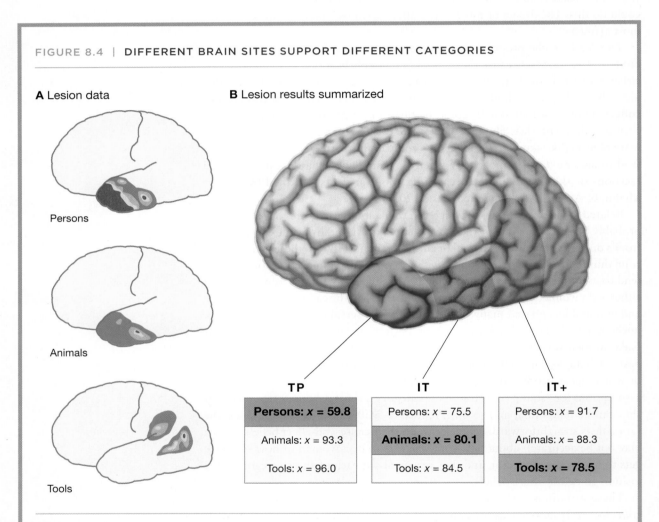

FIGURE 8.4 | DIFFERENT BRAIN SITES SUPPORT DIFFERENT CATEGORIES

A Lesion data

Persons

Animals

Tools

B Lesion results summarized

TP

| Persons: $x = 59.8$ |
| Animals: $x = 93.3$ |
| Tools: $x = 96.0$ |

IT

| Persons: $x = 75.5$ |
| Animals: $x = 80.1$ |
| Tools: $x = 84.5$ |

IT+

| Persons: $x = 91.7$ |
| Animals: $x = 88.3$ |
| Tools: $x = 78.5$ |

Brain damage often causes anomia—*an inability to name common objects. But the specific loss depends on where exactly the brain damage was. Panel A summarizes lesion data for patients who had difficulty naming persons (top), animals (middle) or tools (bottom). The colors indicate the percentage of patients with damage at each site: red, most patients; purple, few. Panel B offers a different summary of the data: Patients with damage in the brain's temporal pole (TP, shown in blue) had difficulty naming persons (only 59.8% correct) but were easily able to name animals and tools. Patients with damage in the inferotemporal region (IT, shown in red) had difficulty naming persons and animals, but did somewhat better naming tools. Finally, patients with damage in the lateral occipital region (IT+) had difficulty naming tools, but did reasonably well naming animals and persons. (After Damasio, Grabowski, Tranel, Hichwa, & Damasio, 1996)*

In addition, brain scans also reveal activation in *sensory* and *motor* areas when people are thinking about various concepts (Mahon & Caramazza, 2009; McRae, 2012)—with a strong suggestion that abstract conceptual knowledge is intertwined with knowledge about what particular objects look like (or sound like or feel like) and also with knowledge about how one might interact with the object. (For related data, see Binder & Desai, 2011.) These findings fit well with another theme we have been developing—namely, that conceptual knowledge has many elements (and so cannot be reduced, say, to just a representation of a prototype, or a definition).

Clearly, then, our theorizing is going to need some complexities: We need to distinguish between categories that represent natural kinds and categories of artifacts. We need to include, in a category's representation, "sensory knowledge" and "muscular" knowledge. We may need to adjust our claims according to the particular concept being considered—with concepts differing in their permanence, the fuzziness of their boundaries, and perhaps other ways as well. Across all of this diversity, though, one theme emerges again and again: How you think about your concepts, how you use your concepts, and, indeed, what your concepts *are*, is shaped heavily by a broad web of beliefs and background knowledge.

The Knowledge Network

Over and over, then, we're seeing a role for background knowledge, and this raises a new question for us: How is this knowledge represented in memory? In the remainder of this chapter, we'll tackle this broad question, and, as we'll see, the answer draws us back to some issues raised in earlier chapters.

Traveling Through the Network to Retrieve Knowledge

In Chapters 5, 6, and 7, we explored the notion that information in long-term memory is represented by means of a network, with associative links connecting the nodes to each other. Let's now carry this proposal one step further: The associative links don't just tie together the various bits of knowledge; they also help *represent* the knowledge. You know, for example, "George Washington was an American president." As a first approximation, this simple idea can be represented as an associative link between a node representing WASHINGTON and a node representing AMERICAN PRESIDENT. In other words, the link itself is a constituent of the knowledge.

The overarching idea, however, is that knowledge is stored via the memory network, and so, whenever you draw on your knowledge, you're retrieving information from the network. This retrieval presumably uses the processes we described in earlier chapters—with activation spreading from one node to the next—and this leads us to a prediction: Activation spreads quickly through the network, but, even so, this spread does take time, and the further the activation must travel, the more time needed. Therefore, you'll need less time to retrieve knowledge involving closely related ideas, more time to retrieve knowledge about more distant ideas.

Collins and Quillian (1969) explored this issue many years ago, using the *sentence verification task* described earlier in this chapter. Their participants were shown sentences, such as "A robin is a bird" or " "Cats have claws" or "Cats have hearts." Mixed together with these obviously true sentences were a variety of false sentences (e.g., "A cat is a bird"). In response to each sentence, participants had to hit a "true" or "false" button as quickly as they could.

Participants presumably perform this task by "traveling" through the network, seeking a connection between nodes. Thus, when the participant finds the connection from, say, the ROBIN node to the BIRD node, this confirms that there is, in fact, an associative path linking these nodes, and this tells the participant that the sentence about these two concepts is true. This travel should require little time if the two nodes are directly linked by an association, as ROBIN and BIRD probably are (see Figure 8.5). In this case, we'd expect participants to answer "true" rather quickly. The travel will require more time, however, if the two nodes are connected only indirectly (e.g., ROBIN and ANIMAL), and so we'd expect slower responses to sentences that require a "two-step" connection than to sentences that require a single connection.

In addition, Collins and Quillian argued that there is no point in storing in memory the fact that cats have hearts *and* the fact that dogs have hearts *and* the fact that squirrels have hearts. Instead, they proposed, it would be more efficient just to store the fact that these various creatures are animals, and then the separate fact that animals have hearts. Hence, the property "has a heart" would be associated with the ANIMAL node rather than the nodes for each individual animal, and the same is true for all the other properties of animals, as shown in

---

FIGURE 8.5 | HYPOTHETICAL MEMORY STRUCTURE FOR KNOWLEDGE ABOUT ANIMALS

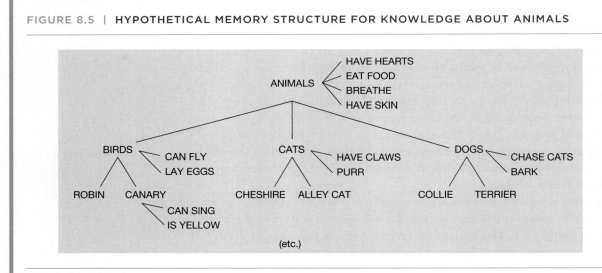

Collins and Quillian proposed that the memory system avoids redundant storage of connections between CATS and HAVE HEARTS, and between DOGS and HAVE HEARTS, and so on for all the other animals. Instead, HAVE HEARTS is stored as a property of all animals. To confirm that cats have hearts, therefore, you must traverse two links: from CATS to ANIMALS, and from ANIMALS to HAVE HEARTS. (After Collins & Quillian, 1969).

the figure. According to this logic, we should expect relatively slow responses to sentences like "Cats have hearts," since, to choose a response, a participant must locate the linkage from CAT to ANIMAL and then a second linkage from ANIMAL to HEART. We would expect a quicker response to "Cats have claws," because here there would be a direct connection between CAT and the node representing this property: All cats have claws, but other animals do not, and so this information could not be entered at the higher level.

As Figure 8.6 shows, these predictions are all borne out. Responses to sentences like "A canary is a canary" take approximately 1 second (1,000 ms). This is presumably the time it takes just to read the sentence and to move your finger on the response button. Sentences like "A canary can sing" require an additional step of traversing one link in memory and yield slower responses. Sentences like "A canary can fly" require the traversing of two links, from CANARY to BIRD and then from BIRD to CAN FLY, so they are correspondingly slower.

We should note, though, that subsequent data have clouded this picture somewhat. For example, we saw earlier in the chapter that verifications are faster if a sentence involves creatures close to the prototype—and so responses are faster to, say, "A canary is a bird" than "An ostrich is a bird". This difference isn't reflected in Figure 8.6, nor is it explained by the layout in Figure 8.5. Clearly, then, the Collins and Quillian view is incomplete.

In addition, the principle of "nonredundancy" proposed by Collins and Quillian doesn't always hold. For example, the property of "having feathers" should, on their view, be associated with the BIRD node rather than (redundantly) with the ROBIN node, the PIGEON node, and so forth. This fits with the fact that responses are relatively slow to sentences like "Sparrows have feathers." However,

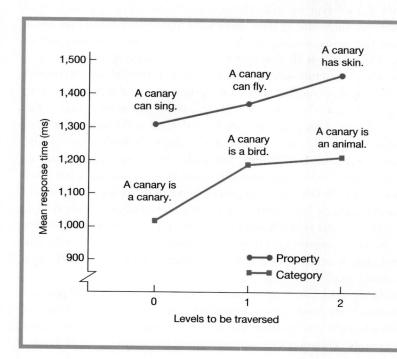

FIGURE 8.6 | TIME NEEDED TO CONFIRM VARIOUS SEMANTIC FACTS

In a sentence verification task, participants' responses were fastest when the test required them to traverse zero links in memory ("A canary is a canary"), slower when the necessary ideas were separated by one link, and slower still if the ideas were separated by two links. Responses were also slower if participants had to take the additional step of traversing the link from a category label ("bird") to the node representing a property of the category ("can fly"). (After Collins & Quillian, 1969).

it turns out that participants respond rather quickly to a sentence like "Peacocks have feathers." This is because in observing peacocks, you often think about their prominent tail feathers (Conrad, 1972). Thus, even though it is informationally redundant, a strong association between PEACOCK and FEATHERS is likely to be established.

Even noting these complications, the fact remains that we can often predict the speed of knowledge access by counting the number of nodes participants must traverse in answering a question. This observation powerfully confirms the claim that associative links play a pivotal role in knowledge representation.

Propositional Networks

To represent the full fabric of your knowledge, however, we'll need more than simple associations. After all, we need somehow to represent the contrast between "Sam has a dog" and "Sam is a dog." If all we had is an association between SAM and DOG, we wouldn't be able to tell these two ideas apart. Early theorizing sought to deal with this problem by introducing different types of associative links, with some representing equivalence (or partial equivalence) relations and others representing possessive relations. These links were termed *isa* links, as in "Sam *isa* dog," and *hasa* links, as in "A bird *hasa* head" or "Sam *hasa* dog" (Norman, Rumelhart, & Group, 1975).

This proposal moves us forward—but it is still inadequate, for the simple reason that you're able to remember, and think about, a wide range of relationships, not just equivalence and possession. You can, for example, consider the relationship "is the opposite of" or the relationship "is analogous to," and a thousand others as well. If each type of relationship is represented by a specific type of associative link, we might end up with a thousand types of links, and that would complicate our theorizing considerably. In addition, we'd then need some sort of "link reader," and it's not at all clear how this "reader" could operate.

Researchers have therefore sought other mechanisms through which network models might represent complex ideas. One proposal was developed by John Anderson (1976, 1980, 1993; Anderson & Bower, 1973), and at the center of this conception is the idea of **propositions**, which are defined as the smallest units of knowledge that can be either true or false. For example, "Children love candy" is a proposition, but "Children" is not; "Susan likes blue cars" is a proposition, but "blue cars" is not. Propositions are easily represented as sentences, but this is merely a convenience. In fact, the same proposition can be represented in a variety of different sentences: For example, "Children love candy," "Candy is loved by children," and "Kinder lieben Bonbons" all express the same proposition. For that matter, the same proposition can also be represented in various nonlinguistic forms, including a structure of nodes and linkages, and that is exactly what Anderson's model does.

In Anderson's model, propositions are represented as shown in Figure 8.7. The ellipses identify the propositions themselves (and so each ellipse identifies a new proposition). Associations connect an ellipse to the ideas that are the proposition's constituents. These associations are labeled, but only in general terms—

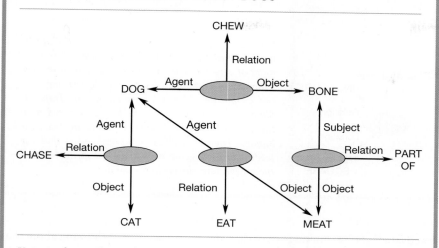

FIGURE 8.7 | NETWORK REPRESENTATION OF SOME OF YOUR KNOWLEDGE ABOUT DOGS

Your understanding of dogs—what dogs are, what they are likely to do—is represented by an interconnected network of propositions, with each proposition indicated by an ellipse. Labels on the arrows indicate each node's role within the proposition. (After Anderson, 1980)

terms that specify the constituent's role within that proposition. This allows us to distinguish, say, the proposition "Dogs chase cats" (shown in the figure) from the proposition "Cats chase dogs" (not shown).

The model can also distinguish between timeless truths such as "Jacob feeds the pigeons" and more specific statements such as "Last spring, Jacob fed the pigeons in Trafalgar Square." The model does this by incorporating time and location nodes as part of propositions, and in this fashion it can mark when and where the proposition was true. This additional information allows the network to represent facts about specific episodes (see Figure 8.8).

Anderson's model shares many claims with the network theorizing we discussed in earlier chapters: Nodes are connected by associative links. Some of these links are stronger than others. The strength of a link depends on how frequently and recently it has been used. Once a node is activated, the process of spreading activation causes nearby nodes to become activated as well. The model is distinctive, however, in its attempt to represent knowledge in terms of propositions, and the promise of this approach has attracted the support of many researchers.

Distributed Processing

There are also other ways that knowledge might be represented within a network. Specifically, in a model like Anderson's, individual ideas are represented with **local representations**: Each node represents one idea, so that when that node

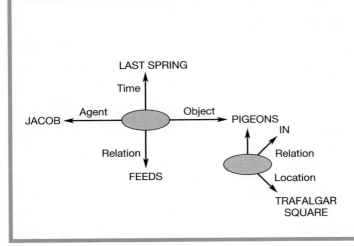

FIGURE 8.8 | REPRESENTING EPISODES WITHIN A PROPOSITIONAL NETWORK

In order to represent episodes, the propositional network includes time and location nodes. This fragment of a network represents two propositions: the proposition that Jacob fed pigeons last spring, and the proposition that the pigeons are in Trafalgar Square. Note that no time node is associated with the proposition about pigeons being in Trafalgar Square. Therefore, what is represented is that the feeding of the pigeons took place last spring but that the pigeons are always in the square.

is activated, you're thinking about that idea, and when you're thinking about that idea, that node is activated. In contrast, **connectionist networks** rely on **distributed representations**, so that any particular idea is represented only by a pattern of activation across the network. To take a simple case, the concept "birthday" might be represented by a pattern in which nodes B, F, H, N, P, and R are firing, whereas the concept "computer" might be represented by a pattern in which nodes C, G, H, M, O and S are firing. Note that node H is part of both of these patterns and probably part of the pattern for many other concepts as well. Therefore, we can't attach any meaning or interpretation to this node by itself; we can only learn what is being represented by looking at many other nodes simultaneously to find out what pattern of activation exists across the entire network. (For more on local and distributed representations, see Chapter 3.)

This reliance on distributed representation has important consequences for how a connectionist network functions. Imagine being asked what sort of computer you use. For you to respond, the idea "computer" needs to trigger the idea "MacBook" (or "Dell" or whatever it is you have). In a distributed network, this means that the many nodes representing "computer" have to manage collectively to activate the many nodes representing "MacBook." To continue our simple illustration, node C has to trigger node L at the same time that node G triggers node A, and so on, leading ultimately to the activation of the L-A-F-J-T-R combination that, let's say, represents "MacBook." In short, a network using distributed *representations* must use *processes* that are similarly distributed, so that one widespread activation pattern can have broad enough effects to evoke a different (but equally widespread) pattern. In addition, the steps bringing this about must all occur simultaneously—in parallel—with each other, so that one entire representation can smoothly trigger the next. This is why connectionist models are said to involve **parallel distributed processing** (PDP).

Many argue that models of this sort make biological sense. We know that the brain relies on parallel processing, with ongoing activity in many regions simultaneously. We also know that the brain uses a "divide and conquer" strategy, with complex tasks broken down into small components, and with separate brain areas working on each component. In addition, PDP models are remarkably powerful: According to many researchers, computers relying on this sort of processing have learned the rules of English grammar, have learned how to read, and have even learned how to play strategic games like backgammon. Related, PDP models have an excellent capacity for detecting *patterns* in the input they receive, despite a range of variations in how the pattern is implemented. Thus, the models can recognize a variety of different sentences as all having the same structure, and a variety of game positions as all inviting the same next move. As a result, these models are impressively able to generalize what they have "learned" to new, never-seen-before, variations on the pattern.

Learning as the Setting of Connection Weights

How do PDP models manage to detect patterns? How do these models "learn"? Recall that, in any associative network, knowledge can be represented by the associations themselves. To return to our earlier example, the knowledge that "George Washington was president" is represented via a link between the nodes representing GEORGE WASHINGTON and those representing PRESIDENT. When we first introduced this example, we phrased it in terms of local representations, with individual nodes having specific referents. The idea, however, is the same in a distributed system. What it means to know this fact about Washington is to have a pattern of connections among the many nodes that together represent "Washington" and the many nodes that together represent "president." Once these connections are in place, activation of either of these patterns will lead to the activation of the other.

Notice, then, that knowledge refers to a *potential* rather than to a *state*. If you know that Washington was a president, then the connections are in place so that if the "Washington" pattern of activations occurs, this will lead to the "president" pattern of activations. And, of course, this state of readiness will remain even if you happen not to be thinking about Washington right now. In this way, "knowing" something, in network terms, corresponds to how the activation will flow *if* there is activation on the scene. This is different from "thinking about" something, which corresponds to which nodes are active at a particular moment, with no comment about where that activation will spread next.

In this view, "learning" must involve some sort of adjustments of the connections among nodes, so that after learning, activation will flow in a fashion that can represent the newly gained knowledge. Technically, we would say that learning involves the adjustment of **connection weights**—the strength of the individual connections among nodes. Moreover, in this type of modeling, learning requires the adjustment of *many* connection weights: We need to adjust the connections, for example, so that the thousands of nodes representing "Washington" manage, together, to activate the thousands of nodes representing "president." Thus, learning, just like everything else in the connectionist scheme, must be a distributed process involving thousands of changes across the network.

This learning is made possible by a number of powerful computing schemes, called "learning algorithms," that adjust connection weights through mechanisms governed entirely by "local" considerations—that is, activity in the immediate vicinity of each connection. One type of algorithm, for example, is governed by whether neighboring nodes are activated at the same time. If they are, the connection between them is strengthened; but if they are activated at different times, the connection is weakened. This gives the network a means of learning what-goes-with-what in experience—learning, for example, that "Q" is usually followed by "U," that the taste of apples is usually accompanied by the sight of an apple, and so on. (The biological version of this learning is called Hebbian learning, in honor of an important neuroscientist, Donald Hebb. The learning is sometimes described with the rule that "cells that fire together wire together.")

Another type of learning relies on feedback: In this algorithm, nodes that led to an inappropriate response receive an **error signal** from some external source, and this causes a *decrease* in the node's connections to the other nodes that led it to the error. (It's as if the node were saying to its inputs, "You misled me, and so I will listen to you less carefully in the future.") In addition, the node receiving the feedback is able to transmit the error signal to the nodes that misled it, allowing them to make their own adjustments. (Again, it's as if the initial node is saying, "You misled me, so I'll listen to you less in the future, but, in addition, notice that you had it wrong; therefore, you should put less faith in the nodes that misled *you*.") In this fashion, the error signal is transmitted backward through the network—starting with the nodes that immediately triggered the incorrect response, but with each node then passing the error signal back to the nodes that had caused it to fire. This process, called **back propagation**, allows the entire network to make use of the feedback even though each node is only being influenced by the nodes in its immediate vicinity.

Concepts: Putting the Pieces Together

We have now covered a lot of ground—discussing both individual concepts and also how these concepts might be woven together, via the network, to form larger patterns of knowledge. We've also talked a bit about how the network itself might be set up—with knowledge perhaps represented by propositions, or perhaps via a connectionist network. But, in the end, where does all of this leave us?

You might think that there's nothing glorious or complicated about knowing what a dog is, or a lemon, or a fish. Your use of these concepts is effortless and ubiquitous, and so is your use of thousands of other concepts. No one over the age of 4 takes special pride in knowing what an odd number is, nor do people find it challenging to make the elementary sorts of judgments we've considered throughout this chapter.

As we've seen, though, human conceptual knowledge is impressively complex. At the very least, this knowledge contains several parts. People probably have a prototype for most of their concepts, as well as a set of remembered exemplars, and use them for a range of fast and easy judgments about the relevant category. People also seem to have a set of beliefs about each concept they hold, and (among other points) these beliefs reflect the person's understanding of cause-and-effect relationships in the world—and so why it is that drunks act as they do, or how it could be that enzymes found in gazelles might be transmitted to lions. These beliefs, in turn, are woven into the broader network that manages to store all the information in your memory, and that network influences how you categorize items and also how you reason about the objects in your world.

Apparently, then, even our simplest concepts require a multifaceted representation in our minds, and at least part of this representation (the "theory") seems reasonably sophisticated. It is all this richness, presumably, that makes human conceptual knowledge extremely powerful and flexible—and so easy to use in a remarkable range of circumstances.

CHAPTER SUMMARY

- People cannot provide definitions for most of the concepts they use; this suggests that knowing a concept and being able to use it competently do not require knowing a definition. However, when trying to define a term, people mention properties that are indeed closely associated with the concept. One proposal, therefore, is that your knowledge specifies what is typical for each concept, rather than naming properties that are truly definitive for the concept. Concepts based on typicality will have a family resemblance structure, with different category members sharing features but with no features being shared by the entire group.

- Concepts may be represented in the mind via prototypes, with each prototype representing what is most typical for that category. This implies that categories will have graded membership, and many results are consistent with this prediction. The results converge in identifying some category members as "better" members of the category. This is reflected in sentence verification tasks, production tasks, explicit judgments of typicality, and so on.

- In addition, basic-level categories seem to be the categories we learn earliest and use most often. Basic-level categories (like "chair") are more homogeneous than their superordinate categories ("furniture") and much broader than their subordinate categories ("armchair"), and they are also usually represented by a single word.

- Typicality results can be also be explained with a model that relies on specific category exemplars, and with category judgments made by the drawing of analogies to these remembered exemplars. The exemplar model can explain your ability to view categories from a new perspective. Even so, prototypes provide an efficient summary of what is typical for the category. Perhaps it is not surprising, therefore, that your conceptual knowledge includes exemplars and prototypes.

- Sometimes categorization does not depend at all on whether the test case resembles a prototype or a category exemplar. This is evident with some abstract categories ("even number") and some weird cases (a mutilated lemon), but it is also evident with more mundane categories ("raccoon"). In these examples, categorization seems to depend on knowledge about a category's essential properties.

- Knowledge about essential properties is not just a supplement to categorization via resemblance. Instead, knowledge about essential properties may be a *prerequisite* for judgments of resemblance. With this knowledge, you are able to assess resemblance with regard to just those properties that truly matter for the category and not be misled by irrelevant or accidental properties.

- The properties that are essential for a category vary from one category to the next. The identification of these properties seems to depend on beliefs held about the category, including causal beliefs that specify why the category features are as they are. These beliefs are implicit theories, and they describe the category not in isolation but in relation to various other concepts.

- Prototypes and exemplars may serve as categorization heuristics, allowing efficient and usually accurate judgments about category membership. These heuristics may not be adequate, though, for some of the ways you use your category knowledge; for these, your implicit theories about the concept play a pivotal role.

- Researchers have proposed that your knowledge is stored within the same memory network that we have discussed in earlier chapters. Searching through this network seems to resemble travel in the sense that greater travel distances (more connections to be traversed) require more time.

- Early proposals tried to represent knowledge with a small number of types of associative links, including *isa* and *hasa* links. However, to store all of knowledge, the network may need more than simple associations. One proposal is that the network stores propositions, with different nodes each playing the appropriate role within the proposition.

- A different proposal is that knowledge is contained in memory via distributed representations. These representations require distributed processes, including the processes that adjust connection weights to allow the creation of new knowledge.

The Workbook Connection

See the *Cognition Workbook* for further exploration of concepts and generic knowledge:

- Demonstration 8.1: The Search for Definitions
- Demonstration 8.2: Assessing Typicality

- Demonstration 8.3: Basic-Level Categories
- Research Methods: Converging Operations
- Cognitive Psychology and Education: Learning New Concepts
- Cognitive Psychology and the Law: Defining Legal Concepts

NEED HELP STUDYING?

 wwnorton.com/studyspace

Visit StudySpace to access free review material such as
- Chapter study plans
- Quizzes
- Flashcards, and more

Go to **wwnorton.com/zaps** for these online labs:
- Sentence Verification

CHAPTER NINE

Language

Virtually every human knows and uses a language; some of us know and use several languages. Indeed, to find a human who *cannot* use language, we need to seek out people in extraordinary circumstances—people who have suffered serious brain damage or people who have grown up completely isolated from other humans. In sharp contrast, no other species has a language comparable to ours in complexity or communicative power. In a real sense, then, knowing a language is a key part of being human—a near-universal achievement in our species, yet unknown in its full-blown form in any other species.

Language seems no less central if we consider how it is used and what it makes possible. We use language to convey our ideas to each other, and our wishes, and our needs. Without language, our social interactions would be grossly impoverished, and cooperative endeavors would be a thousand times more difficult. Without language, the transmission of information and the acquisition of knowledge would be enormously impaired. (How much have you learned by listening to others or by reading?) Without language, there would be no science and no culture. Language is thus at the heart of, and essential for, a huge range of human activities and achievements. What is this tool, therefore, that is universal for our species, unique to our species, and crucial for so much of what our species does?

We'll start by considering the elements of language—its sounds, its words, its syntax; this will help us understand what it is people need to

- Language can be understood as having a hierarchical structure—with phonemes put together to form morphemes, morphemes put together to form words, and words put together to form sentences.

- At each level, you can endlessly combine and recombine units, but the combinations seem to be governed by rules of various sorts. The rules provide our explanation of why some combinations of elements are rare and others seem prohibited outright. Within the boundaries created by these rules, language is *generative*, so that any user of the language can create new forms (new sound combinations, new words, new phrases).

- A different set of principles describes how, moment by moment, people interpret the sentences they hear or read; in this process, people are guided by many factors, including syntax, semantics, and contextual information.

- In interpreting sentences, people seem to use a "compile as you go" strategy, trying to figure out the role of each word the moment it arrives. This approach is often efficient, but it can lead to error.

- Our extraordinary skill in using language is made possible in part by the fact that large portions of the brain are specialized for language use, making it clear that we are, in a literal sense, a "linguistic species."

- Finally, language surely influences our thoughts, but in an indirect fashion: Language is one of many ways to draw our attention to this or that aspect of the environment. This shapes our experience, which in turn shapes our cognition.

know in order to be competent users of English, or Spanish, or whatever language they speak. We'll then shift our focus to some of the processes people use in order to "decode" the sentences they encounter. We will turn next to the biological roots of language, and then, finally, to the ways that our language skills might shape the way that we think.

The Organization of Language

Language, at its heart, involves a special type of translation. I might, for example, want to tell you about a funny scene I saw earlier, and so I need to translate my ideas about the scene into sounds that I can utter. You, in turn, detect those sounds and need to convert them into some sort of comprehension. How does this translation—from ideas to sounds, and then back to ideas—take place?

The answer lies in the fact that language use relies on consistent and well-defined patterns—patterns in how individual words are used, patterns in how words are put together into phrases. I follow those patterns when I express my ideas, and the same patterns guide you when you're figuring out what I just said. In essence, then, we're both using the same "codebook," and so (most of the time) you can understand my messages, and I yours.

But what's in this "codebook"? What are the patterns of English (or whatever language you speak) that—apparently—we all know and use? As a first step toward tackling these issues, let's note that language has a structure, as depicted in Figure 9.1. At the highest level of the structure (not shown in the figure) are the ideas intended by the speaker, or the ideas that the listener derives from the input. These ideas are typically expressed in **sentences**—coherent sequences of words that express the intended meaning of a speaker. Sentences, in turn, are composed of phrases, which are in turn composed of words. Words are composed of **morphemes**, the smallest language units that carry meaning. Some morphemes, like "umpire" or "talk," are units that can stand alone, and they typically refer to particular objects or ideas or actions. Other morphemes get "bound" onto these "free" morphemes and add information crucial for interpretation. Examples of bound morphemes in Figure 9.1 are the past-tense morpheme "ed" and the plural morpheme "s."

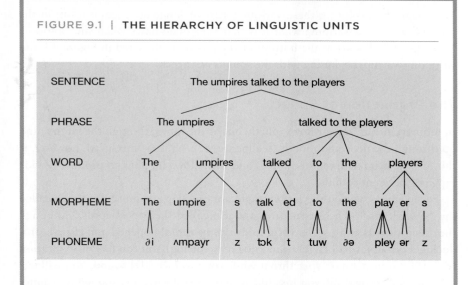

FIGURE 9.1 | THE HIERARCHY OF LINGUISTIC UNITS

It is useful to think of language as having a hierarchical structure. At the top of the hierarchy, there are sentences. These are composed of phrases, which are themselves composed of words. The words are composed of morphemes, and, when the morphemes are pronounced, the units of sound are called phonemes. In describing phonemes, the symbols correspond to the actual sounds produced, independent of how these sounds are expressed in ordinary writing.

In spoken language, morphemes are conveyed by sounds called **phonemes**, defined as the smallest unit of sound that can serve to distinguish words in language. Some phonemes are easily represented by letters of the alphabet, but others are not, and that is why the symbols look strange in the bottom row of Figure 9.1; the symbols correspond to the actual sounds produced, independent of how those sounds are expressed in our (or any other) alphabet.

Within each of these levels, language is also organized in another way. In each level, people can combine and recombine the units to produce novel utterances—assembling the phonemes into brand-new morphemes or assembling words into brand-new phrases. Crucially, though, not all combinations are possible—so that a new breakfast cereal (for example) might be called "Klof" but would probably seem strange to English speakers if it were called "Tlof." Likewise, someone might utter the novel sentence, "I admired the lurking octopi" but almost certainly would not say, "Octupi admired the I lurking." What lies behind these points? Why are some sequences acceptable—even if strange—while others seem awkward or even unacceptable? We will need to explore these points before we are done.

Phonology

Let's begin by exploring these various forms of language organization; in the process, we'll be describing what it is that someone knows when she "knows a language." We'll start at the bottom of the hierarchy depicted in Figure 9.1 and work our way up, beginning with the *sounds* of speech.

The Production of Speech

In ordinary breathing, air flows quietly out of the lungs, through the larynx, and up through the nose and mouth (see Figure 9.2). Noise is produced, however, if this airflow is interrupted or altered, and this allows humans to produce a wide range of different sounds.

For example, within the larynx there are two flaps of muscular tissue called the "vocal folds." (These structures are also called the "vocal cords," although they're not cords at all.) The vocal folds can be rapidly opened and closed, producing a buzzing sort of vibration known as **voicing**. You can feel this vibration by putting your palm on your throat while you produce a [z] sound. You will feel no vibration, though, if you hiss like a snake, producing a sustained [s] sound. (Try it!) The [z] sound is voiced; the [s] is not.

You can also produce sound by narrowing the air passageway within the mouth itself. For example, hiss like a snake again and pay attention to your tongue's position. To produce this sound, you placed your tongue's tip near the roof of your mouth, just behind your teeth; the [s] sound is the sound of the air rushing through the narrow gap you created.

If the gap is elsewhere, a different sound results. For example, to produce the [sh] sound (as in "shoot" or "shine"), the tongue is positioned so that it creates a

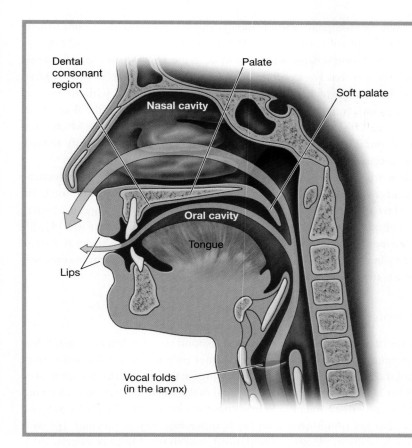

Dental
consonant
region

Palate

Soft palate

Nasal cavity

Oral cavity

Tongue

Lips

Vocal folds
(in the larynx)

FIGURE 9.2 | THE HUMAN VOCAL TRACT

Speech is produced by air flow from the lungs that passes through the larynx and from there through the oral and nasal cavities. Different vowels are created by movements of the lips and tongue, which change the size and shape of the vocal cavity. Consonants are produced by various articulatory movements that temporarily obstruct the air flow through the vocal tract.

narrow gap a bit further back in the mouth; air rushing through this gap causes the desired sound. Alternatively, the narrow gap can be more toward the front. Pronounce an [f] sound; in this case, the sound is produced by air rushing between your bottom lip and your top teeth.

These various aspects of speech production provide a basis for *categorizing* speech sounds. We can distinguish sounds, first, according to how the airflow is restricted; this is referred to as **manner of production**. Thus, air is allowed to move through the nose for some speech sounds but not others. Similarly, for some speech sounds, the flow of air is fully stopped for a moment (e.g., [p], [b], and [t]). For other sounds, the air passage is restricted, but air continues to flow (e.g., [f], [z], and [r]).

Second, we can distinguish between sounds that are voiced—produced with the vocal folds vibrating—and those that are not. The sounds of [v], [z], and [n] (to name a few) are voiced; [f], [s], [t], and [k] are unvoiced. (You can confirm this by running the hand-on-throat test while producing each of these sounds.) Finally, sounds can be categorized according to where the airflow is restricted; this is referred to as **place of articulation**. Thus, you close your lips to produce "bilabial" sounds like [p] and [b]; you place your top teeth close to your bottom lip to produce "labiodental" sounds like [f] and [v]; and you place your tongue just behind your upper teeth to produce "alveolar" sounds like [t] and [d].

This categorization scheme allows us to describe any speech sound in terms of a few simple features. For example, what are the features of a [p] sound? First, we specify the manner of production: This sound is produced with air moving through the mouth (not the nose) and with a full interruption to the flow of air. Second, voicing: The [p] sound happens to be unvoiced. Third, place of articulation: the [p] sound is bilabial. These features are all we need to identify the [p], and if any of these features changes, so does the sound's identity.

Put differently, these few features in varying combinations allow us to describe all the sounds our language needs. In English, these features are combined and recombined to produce 40 or so different phonemes. Other languages use as few as a dozen phonemes; still others, many more. (For example, there are 141 different phonemes in the language of Khoisan, spoken by the Bushmen of Africa; Halle, 1990.) In all cases, though, the phonemes are created by simple combinations of the features just described.

WORKBOOK
DEMONSTRATION 9.1

The Complexity of Speech Perception

The features of speech production also correspond to what listeners hear when they're listening to speech. Phonemes that differ only in one production feature sound similar to each other; phonemes that differ in multiple features sound more distinct. This is reflected in the errors people make when they try to understand speech in a noisy environment: Their misperceptions are usually off by just one feature, so that [p] is confused with [b] (a difference only in voicing), [p] with [t] (a difference only in place of articulation), and so on (Miller & Nicely, 1955; Wang & Bilger, 1973).

This makes it seem like the perception of speech may be a straightforward matter: A small number of features is sufficient to characterize any particular speech sound. All the perceiver needs to do, therefore, is detect these features, and, with this done, the speech sounds are identified.

It turns out, though, speech perception is more complicated than this. As one small concern, speech is *fast*. Normal speaking rate is around 180 words per minute—about 15 phonemes per second—but people can follow speech that's as fast as 250 words per minute. A deeper concern is evident in Figure 9.3, which shows the moment-by-moment sound amplitudes produced by a speaker uttering a brief greeting. It's these amplitudes, in the form of air-pressure changes, that reach the ear, and so, in an important sense, the figure shows the pattern of input with which "real" speech perception begins.

WORKBOOK
DEMONSTRATION 9.2

Notice that within this stream of speech there are no markers to indicate where one phoneme ends and the next begins. Likewise, there are, for the most part, no gaps to indicate the boundaries between successive syllables or successive words. Therefore, as a first step prior to phoneme identification, you need to "slice" this stream into the appropriate segments—a step known as **speech segmentation**.

For many people, this pattern comes as a surprise. Most of us are convinced that there are pauses between words in the speech that we hear, and it's these

FIGURE 9.3 | THE ACTUAL PATTERN OF SPEECH

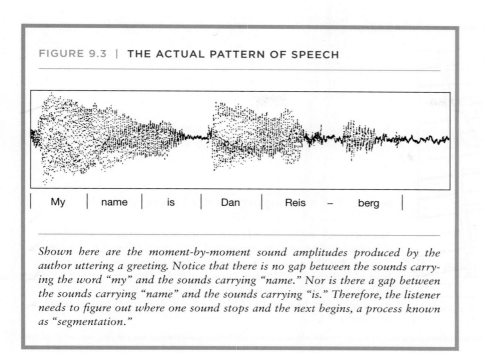

| My | name | is | Dan | Reis | – | berg | |

Shown here are the moment-by-moment sound amplitudes produced by the author uttering a greeting. Notice that there is no gap between the sounds carrying the word "my" and the sounds carrying "name." Nor is there a gap between the sounds carrying "name" and the sounds carrying "is." Therefore, the listener needs to figure out where one sound stops and the next begins, a process known as "segmentation."

pauses, we assume, that mark the word boundaries. This perception, however, turns out to be an illusion, and we are "hearing" pauses that, in truth, aren't there. This is evident when we "hear" the pauses in the "wrong places" and thus segment the speech stream in a way the speaker didn't intend (see Figure 9.4). The illusion is also revealed when we physically measure the speech stream (as we did in order to create Figure 9.3) or when we listen to speech we can't understand—for example, speech in a foreign language. In the latter circumstance, we lack the skill needed to segment the stream, so we are unable to "supply" the word boundaries. As a consequence, we hear what is really there: a continuous, uninterrupted flow of sound. That is why speech in a foreign language often sounds so fast.

Speech perception is further complicated by a phenomenon known as **coarticulation** (Liberman, 1970; also Daniloff & Hammarberg, 1973). This term refers to the fact that, in producing speech, you don't utter one phoneme at a time. Instead, the phonemes "overlap," and so, while you're producing the [s] sound in "soup" (for example), your mouth is getting ready to say the vowel. While uttering the vowel, you're already starting to move your tongue, lips, and teeth into position for producing the [p].

This overlap allows speech production to be faster and considerably more fluent. But the overlap also has consequences for the sounds produced, and so the [s] you produce while getting ready for one upcoming vowel is actually different from the [s] you produce while getting ready for a different vowel. As a result, we can't point to a specific acoustical pattern and say, "This is the pattern of an [s] sound." Instead, the acoustical pattern is different in different contexts. Speech perception therefore has to "read past" these context differences in order to identify the phonemes produced.

WORKBOOK
DEMONSTRATION 9.3

"Boy, he must think we're pretty stupid to fall for that again."

FIGURE 9.4 | AMBIGUITY IN SEGMENTATION

Virtually every child has heard the story of Chicken Little. No one believed this poor chicken when he announced "The sky is falling." It turns out, though, that the acoustic signal—the actual sounds produced—would have been the same if Chicken Little had said, "This guy is falling." The difference between these utterances ("The sky . . ." vs. "This guy...") is not in the input. Instead, the difference lies in how the listener segments the sounds.

Aids to Speech Perception

The need for segmentation in a continuous speech stream, the variations caused by coarticulation, and also the variations from speaker to speaker, make speech perception surprisingly complex. Nonetheless, you manage to perceive speech accurately and easily; how do you do it?

WORKBOOK DEMONSTRATION 9.4

Part of the answer lies in the fact that the speech you encounter, day by day, is surprisingly limited in its range. Each of us knows tens of thousands of words, but most of these words are rarely used. In fact, it has been estimated that the 50 most commonly used words in English make up more than half of the words you actually hear (Miller, 1951).

In addition, the perception of speech shares a crucial attribute with all other types of perception: You don't rely only on the stimuli you receive; instead, you *supplement* this input with a wealth of other knowledge—including knowledge about what the words are in our language. Thus, on one proposal, the moment you hear the first phoneme in a word, you activate all the words in your vocabulary that have this starting sound; the moment you hear the *second* phoneme, you narrow this "cohort" of words so that you're thinking only about words that start with this pair of phonemes. Continuing in this way, speech perception ends up as not just a matter of receiving and identifying sounds. Instead, it is a process in which you actively seek a match between the sounds arriving at your ears and the words actually in your vocabulary (Marslen-Wilson, 1987, 1990; Massaro, 1994).

(For more on how vocabulary can guide speech perception, see McClelland, Mirman & Holt, 2006.)

In other cases, speech perception is guided by knowledge of a broader sort, knowledge that relies on the context in which a word appears. This is evident, for example, in the **phonemic restoration effect**. To demonstrate this effect, researchers start by modifying tape-recorded sounds. For example, the [s] sound in the middle of the word "legislatures" might be removed and replaced by a brief burst of noise. This now-degraded stimulus is then presented to participants, embedded in a sentence such as

> The state governors met with their respective legi*latures convening in the capital city.

When asked what they had just heard, participants reported hearing the complete word, "legislatures," accompanied by a burst of noise. Apparently, they used the context to figure out what the word must have been, and then, in essence, they supplied the missing sound on their own (Repp, 1992; Samuel, 1987, 1991).

More, the participants don't just *infer* what the missing sound was; they literally seem to *"hear"* the sound. We can show this by simply asking participants to specify when, within the sentence, the noise burst occurred—simultaneous with the first syllable in "legislature"? the second? Remarkably, the participants cannot tell—with the clear implication that participants cannot tell which sounds within this word were truly part of the stimulus presentation and which were missing (but "supplied" by the participants themselves).

How much do context effects like these actually help us? Pollack and Pickett (1964) tape-recorded a number of naturally occurring conversations. From these recordings, they spliced out individual words and presented them, now in isolation, to their research participants. With no context to guide them, participants were able to identify only half of the words. If restored to their original context, though, the same stimuli were easy to identify. Apparently, the benefits of context are considerable.

Categorical Perception

Speech perception also benefits from a pattern called **categorical perception.** This term refers to the fact that you're much better at hearing the differences *between* categories of sounds than you are at hearing the variations *within* a category of sounds. Said differently, you're very sensitive to the differences between, say, a [g] sound and a [k], or the differences between a [d] and a [t]. But you're surprisingly insensitive to differences within each of these categories, so you have a hard time distinguishing, say, one [p] sound from another, somewhat different [p] sound. And, of course, this pattern is precisely what you want, because it allows you to hear the differences that matter without hearing (and being distracted by) inconsequential variations within the category.

Demonstrations of categorical perception generally rely on a series of stimuli, created by computer. The first stimulus in the series might, for example, be a [ba] sound. Another stimulus might be a [ba] that's been distorted a tiny bit, to make it a little bit closer to a [pa] sound. A third stimulus might be a [ba] that's been distorted a bit more, so that it's a notch closer to a [pa], and so on. In this fashion we create a series of stimuli, each slightly different from the one before, ranging from a clear [ba] sound at one extreme, through a series of "compromise" sounds, until we reach at the other extreme a clear [pa] sound.

How do people perceive these various sounds? Figure 9.5A shows the pattern we might expect. After all, our stimuli are gradually shading from a clear [ba] to a clear [pa]. Therefore, as we move through the series, we might expect people to be less and less likely to identify each stimulus as a [ba], and correspondingly more and more likely to identify each as a [pa]. In the terms we used in Chapter 8, this would be a "graded-membership" pattern: Test cases close to the [ba] prototype should be reliably identified as [ba]. As we move away from this prototype, cases should be harder and harder to categorize.

However, the actual data, shown in Figure 9.5B, don't fit with this prediction. Even though the stimuli are gradually changing from one extreme to another, participants "hear" an abrupt shift, so that roughly half the stimuli are reliably categorized as [ba], and half are reliably categorized as [pa]. Moreover, participants seem indifferent to the differences *within* each category. Across the first dozen stimuli, the syllables are becoming less and less [ba]-like, but this is certainly not reflected in how the listeners identify the sounds. Likewise, across the last dozen stimuli, the syllables are becoming more and more [pa]-like, but again, this is not reflected in the data. What listeners seem to hear is either a [pa], or a [ba] with no fine gradations inside of either category (Liberman, Harris, Hoffman, & Griffith, 1957; for reviews, see Handel, 1989; Yeni-Komshian, 1993).

CATEGORICAL PERCEPTION IN OTHER SPECIES

The pattern of categorical perception is not limited to language, or to humans. A similar pattern, for example, with much greater sensitivity to between-category *differences than to* within-category *variations has been documented in the hearing of the chinchilla.*

FIGURE 9.5 | CATEGORICAL PERCEPTION

HYPOTHETICAL IDENTIFICATION DATA

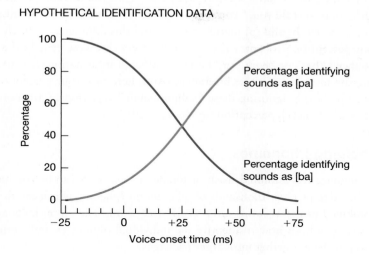

A

ACTUAL IDENTIFICATION DATA

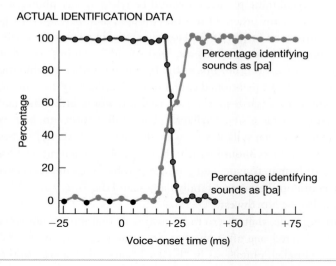

B

With computer speech, we can produce a variety of compromises between a [pa] and a [ba] sound, differing only in when the voicing begins (i.e., the voice-onset time, or VOT). Panel A shows a plausible prediction about how these sounds will be perceived: As the sound becomes less and less like an ordinary [ba], people should be less and less likely to perceive it as a [ba]. The bottom panel, however, shows the actual data: Research participants seem indifferent to small variations in the [ba] sound, and they categorize a sound with a 10 ms or 15 ms VOT in exactly the same way that they categorize a sound with a 0 VOT. The categorizations also show an abrupt categorical boundary between [pa] and [ba], although there is no corresponding abrupt change in the stimuli themselves. (After Lisker & Abramson, 1970)

It seems, then, that your perceptual apparatus is "tuned" to provide you just the information you need: After all, you want to respond differently if told to "bat the ball" or "pat the ball." You'll give different answers if asked, "What's your favorite bark?" or "What's your favorite park?" And you certainly want to know whether someone told you, "You're the best" or "You're the pest." Plainly, the difference between [b] and [p] matters to you, and this difference is clearly marked in your perception. In contrast, you usually don't care how exactly the speaker pronounced "bat" or "bark" or "best"—that's not information that matters for getting the meaning of these utterances. And, here too, your perception serves you well by largely ignoring these "subphonemic" variations. (For more on the broad issue of speech perception, see Mattys, 2012.)

Combining Phonemes

Each language has a limited stock of phonemes, but they can be combined and recombined to produce thousands of different morphemes, which can themselves be combined to create word after word after word. Therefore, language users need to know both how to identify the individual phonemes and—crucially—how to put them together into larger packages.

The step of combining phonemes would be trivial if any phoneme could be put side by side with any other. It turns out, though, that there are rules governing these combinations, and users of the language reliably respect these rules. Thus, in English, certain sounds (such as the final sound in "going" or "flying") can occur at the end of a word but not at the beginning. Other combinations seem prohibited outright. We mentioned earlier, for example, that the sequence "tlof" seems anomalous to English-speakers; indeed, no words in English contain the "tl" combination within a single syllable. (The combination can, however, occur at the boundary between syllables — as in "motley" or "sweetly.") These limits, however, are simply facts about English; they are not at all a limit on what human ears can hear or human tongues can produce. (Note, for example, *Nguyen* is one of the most common Vietnamese family names, and the *Tlingit* are an indigenous people of the Pacific Northwest.)

There are also rules that govern the adjustments that must occur when certain phonemes are uttered one after another. For example, consider the "s" ending that marks the English plural—as in "books," "cats," or "tapes." In these cases, the plural is pronounced as an [s]. In other contexts, though, the plural ending is pronounced differently. Say these words out loud: "bags," "duds," "pills." If you listen carefully, you will realize that these words actually end with a [z] sound, not an [s]. The choice between these—a [z] pronunciation or an [s]—depends on how the base noun ends. If it ends with a voiced sound, the [z] ending is used to make the plural. If the base noun ends with an unvoiced sound, the plural is created with an [s]. (For more on phonological rules, see Chomsky & Halle, 1968; Halle, 1990.)

A speaker's obedience to these principles can be demonstrated even with novel, made-up cases. For example, I have one wug, and now I acquire another. Now, I have two . . . what? Without hesitation, people pronounce "wugs" using the [z] ending—in accord with the standard pattern. Indeed, even young children

FIGURE 9.6 | KNOWING A WORD

(1)	She can place the books on the table.
(2)	* She can place on the table.
(3)	* She can sleep the books on the table.
(4)	She can sleep on the table.

Part of what it means to "know a word" is knowing how to use a word. For example, a word like "place" demands an object, so that Sentence 1 (with an object) sounds fine, but Sentence 2 is anomalous. Other words have other demands. "Sleep," for example, does not take an object, and so Sentence 3 is anomalous, but Sentence 4 is fine.

pronounce "wugs" with a [z], and so, it seems, they too have internalized—and obey—the relevant principles (Berko, 1958).

Morphemes and Words

The average American high school graduate knows about 45,000 different words (Miller, 1991). For college graduates, the estimate is higher: 75,000–100,000 words (Oldfield, 1963). For each word, the speaker typically has several bits of information. First, the speaker knows the word's *sound*—that is, the sequence of phonemes that make up the word. Second, in a literate culture, the speaker generally knows the word's *orthography*—that is, the sequence of letters that spell the word. Third, the speaker also knows how to use the word within various phrases, governed by the rules of syntax (see Figure 9.6). Finally—and obviously—the speaker needs to know the *meaning* of a word; he must have a *semantic representation* for the word to go with the *phonological* representation, essentially connecting the meaning to the sound. But what is this "meaning"?

Word Meaning

Most words are used to name objects or events in the world around us. The word "page," for example, refers to the sort of thing you're looking at right now; the word "reading" refers to the activity you are now engaged in; and so on. What a word refers to is called the word's **referent**. With this context, one might propose that the meaning of a word or phrase is linked to the word's (or phrase's) referent: If you know the referent of "bird," you know what the word "bird" means; if you know the referent of "football player," you know what the phrase means; and so on.

There is certainly an element of truth here, and so, if someone were clueless about what the word "page" referred to, we would suspect she did not know what the word meant. Even so, there are key differences between a word's reference and its meaning. Note, for example, that some phrases have no referent because they refer to things that don't exist ("unicorn"? "X-ray vision"? "perfect world"?), but even so the phrases seem meaningful. In addition, sometimes a word's reference is temporary or a matter of coincidence. Thus, the referent of "president of the United States" changes at regular intervals, but the meaning of the phrase seems more stable than that. For these (and other) reasons, word meanings must involve more than reference.

What is the "more"? Theorizing about this issue runs parallel to the points we encountered when we discussed *concepts* in Chapter 8. After all, many words do express single concepts, and more generally, you can understand a word's meaning only if you understand the relevant concepts. For present purposes, therefore, let us just say that a large part of "knowing a word" is knowing the relevant concept; we can then rely on the previous chapter for a discussion of what it means to know a concept. This may seem an inelegant proposal, but it is a proposal demanded by the complexities we encountered in Chapter 8. Conceptual knowledge turns out to be complicated—even for simple concepts like "bird" and "dog" and car." The same complications apply to *semantic* knowledge. (For some contrasts, though, between concepts and words, see Rips et al., 2012.)

Building New Words

We mentioned estimates of vocabulary size for typical Americans (e.g., 45,000 words for high school graduates), but these estimates are rough at best, because the size of someone's vocabulary is quite fluid. Why is this? One reason is that new words are created all the time. This happens, for instance, whenever a new style of music or clothing demands a correspondingly new vocabulary. The world of computers offers other examples: Someone who wants to know something will often *google* it; *spam* has now become a verb (and not just a type of canned meat), and most of us are no longer fooled by the *phishing* we see in occasional (and malicious) *email*. The terms *software* and *hardware* have been around for a while, but *spyware* and *malware* are new.

These new words don't arrive in the language as isolated entries, however, because language users immediately know how to create variations on each word by adding the appropriate morphemes. Imagine, for example, that you have just heard the word "hack" for the first time. You know instantly that someone who does this activity is a "hacker" and that the activity itself is called "hacking," and you understand someone who says, "I've been hacked." In these ways, the added morphemes allow you to use these words in new ways—indeed, the morphemes allow you to create entirely new words. For example, the word "wave" has long been in our language, but with a few added morphemes the term "unmicrowavable" is of recent vintage (Pinker, 1994).

Once again, therefore, let's highlight the **generativity** of language—that is, the capacity to create an endless series of new combinations, all built from the same set of fundamental units. Thus, someone who "knows English" (or, for that matter, someone who knows *any* language) has not just memorized the vocabulary of the language and some set of phrases. Instead, someone who "knows English" knows how to create new forms within the language: He knows how to combine morphemes to create new words; he knows how to "adjust" phonemes when they're put together into novel combinations; and so on. This knowledge isn't conscious—and so most English speakers could not (for example) articulate the principles governing the sequence of morphemes within a word, or why they pronounce "wugs" with a [z] sound rather than an [s]. Nonetheless, speakers honor these principles with remarkable consistency in their day-by-day use of the language and in their day-to-day *creation* of novel words.

WORKBOOK
DEMONSTRATION 9.5

Syntax

The generativity of language is even more salient when we consider the upper levels in the hierarchy shown in Figure 9.1—the levels of *phrases* and *sentences*. After all, you can combine production features to create a few dozen phonemes, and you can combine these to produce thousands of morphemes and words. But think about what you can do with those words: If you have 40,000 words in your vocabulary, or 60,000, or 80,000, how many sentences can you build from those words? How many sentences are you able to understand or to produce?

Sentences can range in length from the very brief ("Go!" or "I do") to the absurdly long. Most sentences, though, contain 20 words or fewer. With this length limit, it has been estimated that there are 100,000,000,000,000,000,000 possible sentences in English (Pinker, 1994). For comparison, if you could read off sentences at the insane rate of 1,000 per second, you'd still need over 30,000 *centuries* to read through this list!

Once again, though, there are limits on which combinations (i.e., which sequences of words) are acceptable and which not. Thus, in English you could say, "The boy hit the ball" but not "The boy hit ball the." Likewise, you could say, "The bird squashed the car" but not "The bird the car," or "The bird squashed the," or just "Squashed the car." Virtually any speaker of the language would agree these sequences have something wrong in them, suggesting that speakers somehow respect the rules of **syntax**—rules governing the sequence of words in a phrase or sentence.

One might think that the rules of syntax depend on *meaning*, so that meaningful sequences are accepted as "sentences" while meaning*less* sequences are rejected as nonsentences. This suggestion, though, is plainly wrong. As one concern, many nonsentences do seem meaningful ("Me Tarzan"). In addition, consider these two sentences:

'Twas brillig, and the slithy toves did gyre and gimble in the wabe.

Colorless green ideas sleep furiously.

(The first of these is from Lewis Carroll's famous poem "Jabberwocky"; the second was penned by the important linguist Noam Chomsky.) These sentences are, of course, without meaning: Colorless things aren't green; ideas don't sleep; toves

aren't slithy. Nonetheless, speakers of English, after a moment's reflection, regard these sequences as grammatically acceptable in a way that "Furiously sleep ideas green colorless" is not. It seems, therefore, that we need principles of syntax that are separate from considerations of semantics or sensibility.

Phrase Structure

But what is syntax? The answer is complicated, but one part seems to involve **phrase structure rules.** These are stipulations that list the elements that must appear in a phrase, as well as (for some languages) the sequence of those elements. The rules also specify the overall organization of the sentence.

One phrase structure rule, for example, stipulates that a sentence (S) must consist of a **noun phrase** (**NP**) and a **verb phrase** (**VP**). A different rule stipulates that noun phrases (at least in English) can include a "determiner," some number of adjectives, and then the noun itself. Verb phrases can take several different forms but often consist of a verb followed by a noun phrase.

One way to depict these rules is with a **tree structure** like the one shown in Figure 9.7. You can read the structure from top to bottom, and, as you move from one level to the next, you can see that each element has been "expanded" in a fashion that's strictly governed by the phrase structure rules.

Prescriptive Rules, Descriptive Rules

Before pressing on, though, we should be clear about what sorts of rules we're discussing here. Let's begin with the fact that most of us were taught, at some stage of our education, how to talk and write "properly." We were taught

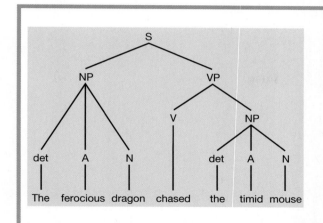

FIGURE 9.7 | A PHRASE STRUCTURE TREE

The diagram shows that the overall sentence itself (S) consists of a noun phrase (NP) plus a verb phrase (VP). The noun phrase is composed of a determiner (det) followed by an adjective (A) and a noun (N). The verb phrase is composed of a verb (V) followed by a noun phrase (NP).

never to say "ain't." Many of us were scolded for writing in the passive voice, or starting a sentence with "And." Injunctions like these are the result of **prescriptive rules**—rules describing how language is "supposed to be." Language that doesn't follow these rules, it's claimed, is "improper," or maybe just "wrong."

We should be skeptical, however, about these prescriptive rules. After all, languages change with the passage of time, and what's "proper" in one period is often different from what seems right at other times. A generation back, for example, many people insisted it was wrong to end a sentence with a preposition; modern speakers think this prohibition is silly. Likewise, consider the split infinitive. Prominent writers of the 18th and 19th centuries (Ben Franklin, William Wordsworth, Henry James) commonly split their infinitives; grammarians of the early 20th century, in contrast, energetically condemned this construction. Now, in the 21st century, most English speakers seem entirely indifferent to whether their infinitives are split or not (and may not even know what a "split infinitive" *is*).

This pattern of change makes it difficult to justify prescriptive rules. Many people, for example, insist that split infinitives are "improper," and must be avoided. This suggestion, however, seems to rest on the idea that the English spoken in, say, 1926 was "good, proper, correct English," and that the English spoken a few decades before or after this "Golden Age" is somehow inferior. It's hard to think of any justification for this assessment. The selection of prescriptive rules, therefore, may simply reflect the preferences of a particular group—and, in most settings, the group that defines these rules will of course be the group with the most prestige or social cachet (Labov, 2007). Thus, people will often strive to follow these rules with the simple aim of joining these elite groups.

Phrase structure rules, in contrast, are not at all prescriptive; they are instead **descriptive rules**—that is, rules characterizing the language as it is ordinarily used by fluent speakers and listeners. There are, after all, strong regularities in the

THE (SOMETIMES) PECULIAR NATURE OF PRESCRIPTIVE RULES

According to an often-repeated story, an editor had rearranged one of Winston Churchill's sentences to avoid ending it in a preposition, and the Prime Minister, proud of his style, scribbled this note in reply: "This is the sort of English up with which I will not put." We note, though, that there's some debate about the historical roots of this story!

way English is used, and the rules we are discussing describe these patterns. No value judgment is offered (nor should one be) about whether these patterns constitute "proper" or "good" English. These patterns simply describe how English is structured—or perhaps we should say, *what English is.*

The Function of Phrase Structure

Let's be clear that no one is claiming English speakers are consciously aware of their language's phrase structure rules, or that speakers of other languages are aware of their language's rules. Nonetheless, in some fashion, we have all internalized these rules; this is evident in the fact that many aspects of language use are reliably in line with the rules.

For example, people reject some sequences of words as "ungrammatical" and accept others as fine, independent of whether the sequences are meaningful. And, quite consistently, people accept sequences that follow the rules, and balk at sequences that do not.

In addition, people have clear intuitions about how the words in a sentence should be grouped. As an illustration, consider the simple sentence, "The boy loves his dog." The sentence seems to break naturally into two parts: The first two words, "the boy," identify what the sentence is about; the remaining three words ("loves his dog") then supply some information about the boy. These latter words, in turn, also break easily into two parts: the verb, "loves," and then two more words ("his dog") identifying what is loved. These groups are, of course, precisely what we would expect based on the phrase structure rules. The first grouping ("The boy" and "loves his dog") respects the boundary between the sentence's NP and its VP. The next group ("loves" and "his dog") respects the main components of the VP.

The groupings provided by the phrase-structure therefore organize a sentence, and this shapes our intuitions about a sentence's parts. The organization can also influence memory: In one study, the investigator asked listeners to memorize strings of nonsense words they heard spoken. Some of the strings had no structure at all ("Yig wur vum rix hom im jag miv"). Other strings included function morphemes that allowed the participants to discern a phrase structure ("The yigs wur vumly rixing hom im jagest miv"). One might think strings of the second type would be harder to memorize, because they're longer. But the opposite is true: Once organized into a phrase structure, these sequences were much easier to recall (Epstein, 1961; also see Figure 9.8)

Most important, though, phrase structure rules help us *understand* the sentences we hear or read, because syntax in general specifies the relationships among the words in each sentence. For example, the NP + VP sequence typically divides a sentence into the "doer" (the NP) and some information about that doer (the VP). Likewise, the V + NP sequence usually indicates the action described by the sentence, and then the recipient of that action. In this way, the phrase structure of a sentence provides an initial "road map" useful in understanding the sentence. Thus (to take a simple case), it's syntax that tells us who's doing what when we hear, "The boy chased the girl." Without syntax (if, for example, our sentences were merely lists of words, such as "boy, girl, chased"), we'd have no way to know who was the chaser and who was chaste.

This role of phrase structure, in guiding understanding, can be confirmed in a fashion that's informative and often funny: Sometimes, two different phrase structures can lead to the same sequence of words, and if you encounter those words you may not know which phrase structure was intended. How will this affect you?

The large tomato	The
made	large tomato made
a satisfying splat	a satisfying
when	splat when it
it hit	hit the
the floor.	floor.

FIGURE 9.8 | **PHRASE STRUCTURE ORGANIZATION AIDS THE READER**

The panel on the left shows a sentence written so that the breaks between lines correspond to breaks between phrases; this makes reading easier because the sentence has, in effect, been visually "pre-organized." In the panel on the right, the sentence has been rewritten so that the visual breaks don't correspond to the boundaries between phrases. Reading is now slower and more difficult.

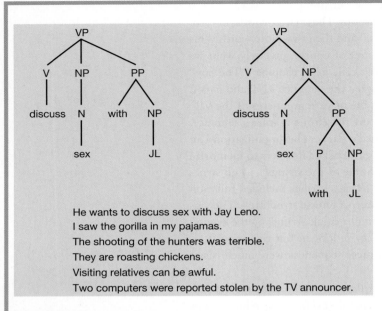

He wants to discuss sex with Jay Leno.
I saw the gorilla in my pajamas.
The shooting of the hunters was terrible.
They are roasting chickens.
Visiting relatives can be awful.
Two computers were reported stolen by the TV announcer.

FIGURE 9.9 | PHRASE STRUCTURE AMBIGUITY

Often the words of a sentence are compatible with more than one phrase structure; in such cases, the sentence will be ambiguous. Thus, you can understand the first sentence here either as describing a discussion with Leno or as describing sex with Leno; both analyses of the verb phrase are shown. Can you find both interpretations for the remaining sentences?

WORKBOOK
DEMONSTRATION 9.6

If, as we've suggested, phrase structures guide interpretation, then, with multiple phrase-structures available, there should be more than one way to interpret the sentence. This turns out to be correct—often with comical consequences (see Figure 9.9).

Linguistic Universals

Let's pause to take stock. We have climbed up the linguistic hierarchy—from basic features (like voicing or place of articulation) to phonemes, then to morphemes, words, and finally full sentences. At each step, we've seen how linguistic elements can be combined to create larger and more sophisticated units. In the process, we have seen how a small number of elements can be used to create a vast number of combinations.

We've suggested, though, that the combinations at each level seem to be rule-governed. The rules determine which units can be combined, and in what order. The rules also specify a *structure* within the larger units. And, remarkably, the rules are quite similar as we move from one language to the next.

Of course, languages differ. In English, adjectives are usually placed before the noun ("the blue house"); in Spanish, the adjective comes after the noun ("la casa azul"). Even so, there are a number of regularities across languages, even when we consider languages as diverse as, say, English, Japanese, and Turkish, or Walbiri and Kivunjo. Indeed, some experts have argued that these regularities constitute **linguistic universals**—that is, principles applicable to every human language (Chomsky, 1965, 1975, 1986; also see Comrie, 1981; Cook, 1988; Greenberg, Ferguson, & Moravcsik, 1978; Hawkins, 1988; for some reservations about the idea of linguistic universals, see Penn & Povinelli, 2012).

The proposed universals are of various sorts. Some identify the inventory of linguistic constituents, and so all languages, for example, include both nouns and

NOAH'S ARC

Sometimes linguistic ambiguity involves the interpretation of a phrase's organization. And sometimes the ambiguity involves the interpretation of a single word. Sometimes the ambiguity is evident in spoken *language but not in* written *language.*

verbs; all languages include pronouns. Some universals, in contrast, are framed in terms of probabilities. Thus, in all the world's languages, some sequences of words are common, while other sequences are quite rare. As an example, it's possible in English to put a sentence's object before the sentence's subject ("A bear he shot"), but this isn't the normal pattern for English—the normal pattern, instead, is subject-verb-object. And it's not only English that shows this pattern. The subject of a sentence tends to precede the object in roughly 98% of the world's languages. The sequence of subject before verb is preferred in roughly 80% of the world's languages (Crystal, 1987).

Other universals concern linguistic features that seem to come and go together. For example, if a language's preferred word order is subject-object-verb, the language is likely to form its questions by adding some words at the end of the question. If, in contrast, a language's preferred sequence is subject-verb-object (as in English), the language will place its question words at the beginning of the question (as in, "Where did he . . . ?" or "When did they . . . ?").

The existence of these linguistic universals opens an intriguing possibility. Consider the fact that every human child learns how to speak, and, indeed, the learning process is quite rapid—with sophisticated language use in place by the time the child is 4 years old. Moreover, what is learned seems quite complex—with rules governing the combinations of phonemes and different rules governing the combinations of morphemes and the structure of phrases. How is all this complexity mastered so quickly?

Some researchers suggest that language learning occurs so rapidly because each child begins the process with an enormous head start: a biological heritage that somehow stipulates the broad outline of human language. In other words, the child *begins* language learning already knowing the universal rules; the task for the child, therefore, is to figure out exactly how the rules are realized within the language community in which she is raised. The child needs to learn, for example, whether she lives in a community that prefers the subject-verb-object sequence or the subject-object-verb order. Having learned that, the child can then set the "switches" properly on the "language machinery" that she was born with and, in that way, be well on her way to speaking in the fashion that's appropriate for her language community— whether it's a community of Portuguese speakers, or Urdu, or Mandarin.

There is ongoing debate about these issues (e.g., Bates et al. 2001). Even so, the claims just offered strike many researchers as plausible. Let's be clear, though, that this plausibility rests on the observation that the rules we have discussed do seem, with the appropriate adjustments of parameters, universal. (For more on these points, see Bloom, 1994; Lidz, Waxman, & Freedman, 2003.)

Sentence Parsing

As we have discussed, a sentence's phrase structure conveys crucial information about who did what to whom, and so, once you know the phrase structure, you're well on your way to understanding the sentence. But how do you figure out the phrase structure in the first place? This would be an easy question if sentences were uniform in their structure: "The boy hit the ball. The girl chased the cat. The elephant trampled the geraniums." But, of course, sentences are more variable than this, which makes the identification of a sentence's phrase structure appreciably more difficult.

How, therefore, do you **parse** a sentence—that is, figure out each word's syntactic role? One possibility is that you wait until the sentence's end and only then go to work on figuring out the structure. With this strategy, your comprehension might be slowed a little (because of the wait for the sentence's termination), but you'd avoid errors, because your interpretation could be guided by full information about the sentence's content.

We've already seen that people don't use this wait-for-all-the-information strategy in perceiving *words* (pp. 330–331). Instead, they begin the identification process as soon as they hear the word's very first phoneme. Evidence suggests the same pattern occurs when people are interpreting *sentences*. Specifically, people seek to parse sentences as they hear them, trying to figure out the role of each word the moment it arrives (e.g., Marcus, 2001; Savova et al., 2007; Tanenhaus & Trueswell, 2006). This approach is more efficient (since there's no waiting), but it can lead to error in ways that we will describe in a moment. This turns out, therefore, to be one more case in which humans favor a strategy that is quick but occasionally misleading, in comparison to a strategy that is less efficient but more accurate.

Garden Paths

Even relatively simple sentences can be ambiguous if you're open-minded (or perverse) enough:

> Mary had a little lamb. (But I was quite hungry, so I had the lamb and also a bowl of soup.)

Time flies like an arrow. (But fruit flies, in contrast, like a banana.)

Temporary ambiguity is also common inside a sentence. More precisely, the early part of a sentence is often open to multiple interpretations, but then the later part of the sentence clears things up. For instance, consider this example:

The old man the ships.

In this sentence, most people read the initial three words as a noun phrase: "the old man." However, this interpretation leaves the sentence with no verb, and so a different interpretation is needed, with the subject of the sentence being "the old" and with "man" as the verb. (Who mans the ships? It is the old, not the young. The old man the ships.) Likewise:

The secretary applauded for his efforts was soon promoted.

Here one tends to read "applauded" as the sentence's main verb, but it isn't. Instead, this sentence is just a shorthand way of answering the question, "Which secretary was soon promoted?" (Answer: "The one who was applauded for his efforts.")

These examples are referred to as **garden-path sentences**: You are initially led to one interpretation (you are, as they say, "led down the garden path"), but this interpretation then turns out to be wrong. Hence, you need to reject your first construal and seek an alternative. Here are two more examples:

Fat people eat accumulates.

Because he ran the second mile went quickly.

Garden-path sentences highlight the risk attached to the strategy of interpreting a sentence as it arrives: The information you need in order to understand these sentences arrives only late in the sequence, and so, to avoid an interpretive dead end, you'd be well advised to remain neutral about the sentence's meaning until you've gathered enough information. That way, you'd know that "the old man" couldn't be the sentence's subject, that "applauded" couldn't be the sentence's main verb, and so on. But this is plainly not what you do. Instead, you commit yourself fairly early to one interpretation and then try to "fit" subsequent words, as they arrive, into that interpretation. This strategy is often effective, but it does lead to the "double-take" reaction when late-arriving information forces you to abandon your interpretive efforts so far (Grodner & Gibson, 2005).

Syntax as a Guide to Parsing

What is it that leads you down the garden path? More specifically, why do you initially choose one interpretation of a sentence, one parsing, rather than another? Many cues are relevant, and this tells us that many types of information influence parsing. For one, parsing is guided by an assumption of so-called **minimal attachment**. Roughly, this means that the listener or reader proceeds through a sentence seeking the simplest phrase structure that will accommodate the words heard so far. To see how this plays out, consider the earlier sentence, "The secretary applauded for his efforts was soon promoted." As you read "The secretary applauded," you had the option of interpreting this as a noun phrase plus the beginning of a separate clause modifying "secretary." This is, of course, the correct construal and is demanded by the way the sentence ends. However, the principle of minimal attachment led you to ignore this possibility, at least initially, and to proceed instead with a simpler interpretation—of a noun phrase + verb, with no idea of a separate embedded clause.

The tendency to misread the "secretary" sentence is also encouraged by other factors. People tend to assume that they'll be hearing (or reading) *active* sentences rather than *passive*, so they generally interpret a sentence's initial noun phrase as the "doer" of the action and not the recipient. As it happens, most of the sentences we encounter are active, not passive, so this assumption is usually correct (Svartik, 1966). However, this assumption works against us whenever we do encounter a passive sentence, and that's why active sentences are usually easier to understand than passive sentences (Hornby, 1974; Slobin, 1966). And, of course, this assumption adds to your difficulties with the "secretary" sentence: The embedded clause in this sentence is in the passive voice (the secretary was applauded by someone else); your tendency to assume active voice, therefore, works against the correct interpretation of this sentence.

Not surprisingly, parsing is also influenced by the function words that appear in a sentence and by the various morphemes that signal syntactic role (Bever, 1970). Thus, for example, people easily grasp the structure of "He gliply rivitched the flidget." That's because the "-ly" morpheme indicates that "glip" is an adverb; the "-ed" identifies "rivitch" as a verb; and "the" signals that "flidget" is a noun— all excellent cues to the sentence structure. This factor, too, is relevant to the "secretary" sentence, which included none of the helpful function words. Notice that we didn't say, "The secretary who was applauded . . . ." If we had, the chance of misunderstanding would have been much reduced.

With all these factors stacked against you, it's no wonder you were (temporarily) confused about "the secretary." Indeed, with all these factors in place, garden-path sentences can sometimes be enormously difficult to comprehend. For example, spend a moment puzzling over this (fully grammatical) sequence:

The horse raced past the barn fell.

(If you get stuck with this sentence, try adding the word "that" after "horse.")

Background Knowledge as a Guide to Parsing

Parsing is also guided by background knowledge. In general, people parse sentences in a way that makes sense to them, and so (for example) readers are unlikely to misread the headline *Drunk Gets Six Months in Violin Case* (Gibson, 2006; Pinker, 1994; Sedivy, Tanenhaus, Chambers, & Carlson, 1999). And this point, too, matters for the "secretary" sentence: Your background knowledge tells you that women secretaries are more common than men, and this likely added to your confusion in this case about who was applauding and who was applauded.

How can we document these knowledge effects? Several studies have tracked how people move their eyes while reading, and these movements reveal the confusion readers go through in reading a garden-path sentence. Specifically, the moment readers realize they've misinterpreted the sentence so far, they backtrack and reread the sentence's start, and, with appropriate instruments, we can easily detect these backwards eye movements (MacDonald, Pearlmutter & Seidenberg, 1994; Trueswell, Tanenhaus & Garnsey, 1994).

Using this technique, investigators have examined the effects of *plausibility* on readers' expectations for the words they're seeing. For example, participants might be shown a sentence beginning "The detectives examined . . . " The participants sensibly assume that "examined" is the sentence's main verb and are therefore puzzled when the sentence continues "by the reporter . . ." (see Figure 9.10). We detect this puzzlement in their eye movements: They pause and look back at "examined," realizing that their initial interpretation was wrong. Then, after this recalculation, they press onward.

Things go differently if the sentence begins "The evidence examined . . . " Here, readers can draw on the fact that "evidence" can't examine anything, and so "examined" can't be the sentence's main verb. Hence they're quite unsurprised when the sentence continues "by the reporter . . . ": Their understanding of the

---

FIGURE 9.10 | INTERPRETING COMPLEX SENTENCES

A The detectives examined by the reporter revealed the truth about the robbery.

B The evidence examined by the reporter revealed the truth about the robbery.

Readers are momentarily confused when they reach the "by the reporter" phrase in Sentence A. That is because they had interpreted "examined" as the sentence's main verb. Readers aren't confused by Sentence B, because their background knowledge told them that "examined" couldn't be the main verb (because evidence is not capable of examining anything).

world had already told them that the first three words were the start of a passive sentence, not an active one.

As a related point, people are also sensitive to statistical properties in the language and so, if a word has several meanings, they assume its most frequent meaning whenever they encounter the word. They therefore tend to assume that "train" means the thing on tracks rather than the activity one engages in to teach tricks to a dog. Likewise, they tend to assume that "tree" refers to a type of plant rather than an action (as in "The hounds want to tree the raccoon"). Similarly, they tend to assume that adjectives will be followed by nouns. This isn't an obligatory pattern, but it is certainly a frequent one, so the assumption seems safe.

Once again, we can see these factors in action in some of the garden-path sentences: The assumption that adjectives will be followed by nouns primes us to read the phrase "fat people" as an adjective-noun pair, and this gets us in trouble when we encounter "Fat people eat accumulates." Likewise, our reliance on frequent meanings is part of our problem in understanding sentences like "The old man ships" or "The new train quickly, but the old train more slowly."

The Extralinguistic Context

Let's be clear that you use all the strategies we've listed—minimal attachment, an assumption of active sentences, a reliance on function words *and* on background knowledge—in your parsing of every sentence you encounter. The role of these strategies is more obvious when the strategies mislead you, as they do with garden-path sentences, but that doesn't change the fact that these strategies are used for *all* sentences, and generally lead you to the correct parsing.

And, it turns out, our catalog of strategies isn't done, because you also make use of another factor: the *context* in which you encounter sentences, including the *conversational context*. Thus, the garden-path problem is much less likely to occur in the following setting:

Jack: Which horse fell?
Kate: The horse raced past the barn fell.

Just as important is the **extralinguistic context**—the physical and social setting in which you encounter sentences. To see how this factor matters, consider the following sentence:

Put the apple on the towel into the box.

At its start, this sentence seems to be an instruction to put an apple onto a towel; this interpretation must be abandoned, though, when the words "into the box" arrive. Now you realize that the box is the apple's destination; "on the towel" is simply a specification of which apple is to be moved. (Which apple should be put into the box? The one that is on the towel.) In short, this is another garden-path sentence—initially inviting one analysis, but eventually demanding another.

This confusion is avoided, however, if the sentence is uttered in the appropriate setting. Imagine that two apples are in view, as shown in Figure 9.11. In this context, a listener hearing the sentence's start ("Put the apple . . .") would immediately see the possibility for confusion (which apple is being referred to?) and so would expect the speaker to specify which apple is to be moved. When the phrase "on the towel" is uttered, the listener immediately understands it (correctly) as the needed specification. Hence, there is no confusion and no garden path (Eberhard, Spivey-Knowlton, Sedivy, & Tanenhaus, 1995; Tanenhaus & Spivey-Knowlton, 1996).

The Use of Language: What Is Left Unsaid

What does it mean to "know a language"—to "know English," for example? As we've discussed, each language user seems somehow to know (and obey) a rich set of rules—with these rules determining which sound combinations and which sequences of words seem acceptable, and which do not. In addition, we've now seen that language users rely on a further set of principles whenever they perceive and understand linguistic inputs. Some of these principles are rooted in syntax (e.g., minimal attachment); others depend on semantics (e.g., knowing that detectives can "examine" but evidence can't); others seem statistical in nature (e.g., knowing which usages are more common); and still others seem pragmatic (e.g., considerations of the extralinguistic context). These factors then seem to interact in an intricate fashion, so that your understanding of the sentences you hear (or see in print) is guided by all of these principles at the same time.

These points, however, still *understate* the complexity of language use and, with that, the complexity of the knowledge someone must have in order to "know a language." For illustration, note that we have said nothing about another source

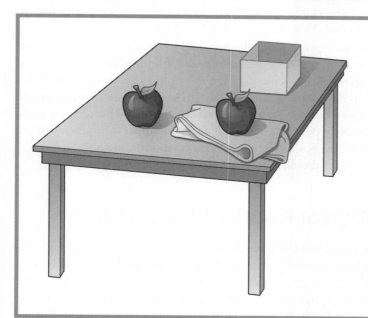

FIGURE 9.11 | **THE EXTRALINGUISTIC CONTEXT**

"Put the apple on the towel into the box." Without the setting shown here, this sentence causes momentary confusion: The listener will initially think she is supposed to put the apple onto the towel and is then confused by the sentence's last three words. If the sentence is presented together with this picture, however, there's no confusion. Now the listener immediately sees the potential for confusion (which apple is being discussed?), counts on the speaker to provide clarification for this point, and immediately understands "on the towel" as specification, not a destination.

of information useful in parsing: the rise and fall of speech intonation and the pattern of pauses. These rhythm and pitch cues, together called **prosody**, play an important role in speech perception. Prosody can reveal the mood of a speaker; it can also direct the listener's attention by, in effect, specifying the focus or theme of a sentence (Jackendoff, 1972). Prosody can also render unambiguous a sentence that would otherwise be entirely confusing (Beach, 1991). (Thus, garden-path sentences and ambiguous sentences are much more effective in print, where prosody provides no information.)

Likewise, we have not even touched on several other puzzles: How is language produced? How does one turn ideas, intentions, and queries into actual sentences? How does one turn the sentences into sequences of sounds? These are important issues, but we have held them to the side here.

Finally, what happens after one has parsed and understood an individual sentence? How is the sentence integrated with earlier sentences or subsequent sentences? Here, too, more theory is needed to explain the inferences you routinely make in ordinary conversation. If you are asked, for example, "Do you know the time?" you understand this as a request that you report the time—despite the fact that the question, understood literally, is a yes/no question about the extent of your temporal knowledge. In the same vein, consider this bit of conversation (Pinker, 1994):

> Woman: I'm leaving you.
>
> Man: Who is he?

We easily provide the soap-opera script that lies behind this exchange, but we do so by drawing on a rich fabric of additional knowledge, including knowledge of **pragmatics** (i.e., of how language is ordinarily used) and, in this case, also knowledge about the vicissitudes of romance. (For discussion, see Ervin-Tripp, 1993; Graesser, Millis, & Zwaan, 1997; Hilton, 1995; Kumon-Nakamura, Glucksberg, & Brown, 1995; Noveck & Reboul, 2008; Noveck & Sperber, 2005.)

These other topics—prosody, production, and pragmatics—are central concerns within the study of language, but for the sake of brevity we have not tackled them here. Even so, we mention these themes to emphasize a key message of this chapter: Each of us uses language all the time—to learn, to gossip, to instruct, to persuade, to express affection. We use this tool as easily as we breathe; we spend more effort in choosing our clothes in the morning than we do in choosing the words we will utter. But these observations must not hide the fact that language is a remarkably complicated tool, and we are all exquisitely skilled in its use.

The Biological Roots of Language

How is all of this possible? How is it that ordinary human beings—indeed, ordinary two-and-a-half-year-olds—manage the extraordinary task of mastering and fluently using language? According to many authors, the answer lies in the fact that humans are equipped with sophisticated neural machinery specialized for learning, and then using, language. Let's take a quick look at this machinery.

Aphasias

As we've seen in other chapters, brain damage can cause a variety of effects, depending on where and how widespread the damage is. For a number of brain sites, though, damage causes disruption of language—a disruption (which we first mentioned in Chapter 2) known as **aphasia**. Aphasias take many forms and are often quite specialized, with the particular symptoms largely dependent on the locus of the brain damage. As a rough summary of the data, however, investigators find it useful to distinguish two broad classes of aphasia. Damage to the left frontal lobe of the brain, and especially a region known as **Broca's area** (see Figure 9.12), usually produces a pattern of symptoms known as **nonfluent aphasia**. In extreme cases, a patient with this disorder is unable to utter or write a word. In less severe cases, only a part of the patient's vocabulary is lost, but the patient's speech becomes labored and fragmented, and articulating each word requires special effort. The resulting speech can sound something like, "Here . . . head . . . operation . . . here . . . speech . . . none . . . talking . . . what . . . illness" (Luria, 1966, p. 406).

Different symptoms are associated with damage to a brain site known as **Wernicke's area** (see Figure 9.12) and usually involve a pattern known as **fluent aphasia**. In these cases patients do produce speech, but even though they talk freely they actually say very little. The sentences they produce are composed largely of little filler words that provide scant information. One patient, for example, uttered, "I was over the other one, and then after they had been in the department, I was in this one" (Geschwind, 1970, p. 904).

Let's be clear, though, that this broad distinction—between fluent and nonfluent aphasia—captures the data only in the broadest sense. One reason lies in the fact that—as we've seen—language use involves the coordination of many different steps, many different processes. These include processes needed to "look up" word meanings in your "mental dictionary," processes needed to figure out the

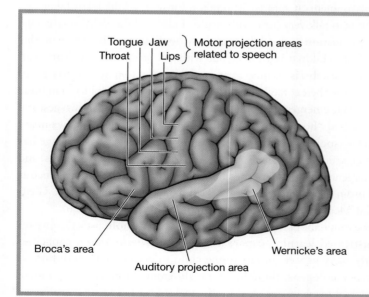

Tongue Jaw } Motor projection areas
Throat Lips } related to speech

Broca's area

Auditory projection area

Wernicke's area

FIGURE 9.12 | BRAIN AREAS CRUCIAL FOR THE PERCEPTION AND PRODUCTION OF LANGUAGE

Multiple brain regions are involved in the use of language. For most individuals, most of these regions are in the left cerebral hemisphere (as shown here). Broca's area is heavily involved in language production; Wernicke's area plays a crucial role in language comprehension.

structural relationships within a sentence, processes needed to integrate information about a sentence's structure with the meanings of the words within the sentence, and so on. Each of these processes relies on its own set of brain pathways, so damage to those pathways disrupts the process. As a result, the language loss observed in aphasia can sometimes be quite specific, with impairment just to a particular processing step (Cabeza & Nyberg, 2000; Demonet, Wise, & Frackowiak, 1993; Martin, 2003). Related, it's becoming clear that brain sites other than Broca's area and Wernicke's area play a role in language processing, and it will likely be some years before we've catalogued the full set of brain areas crucial for language (e.g., Dronkers et al., 2004; Poeppel & Hickok, 2004).

As a further complication, let's also note that brain lesions—produced by injury or by stroke—are often large enough to disrupt *multiple* brain areas, and so can produce a mixture of symptoms. Because of this point, aphasias are often difficult to classify precisely, and it's sometimes hard to see a correspondence between a patient's symptoms and the site of the patient's brain damage.

Even with these complexities, the point here is that humans do have a considerable amount of neural tissue that is specialized for language. Damage to this tissue can disrupt language understanding, language production, or both. And in all cases, the data make it clear that our skill in using language rests in part on the fact that we have a lot of neural apparatus devoted to precisely this task.

The Biology of Language Learning

The biological roots of language also show up in another way—in the way that language is learned. As we've mentioned, this learning is remarkably fast: By the age of 3 or 4, almost every child is able to converse at a reasonable level—and so able to convey her wishes and desires and, for that matter, to communicate sophisticated beliefs. Importantly, this learning proceeds at a normal pace in an astonishingly wide range of environments. Children who talk a lot with adults learn language, and so do children who talk very little with adults. Indeed, children learn language even if their communication with adults is entirely nonlinguistic! Evidence on this last point comes from children born deaf but with no opportunity to learn sign language. (In some cases, this is because their caretakers don't know how to sign; in other cases, it's because their caretakers choose not to teach signing.) Even in these extreme cases, language emerges: Children in this situation *invent* their own gestural language (usually called "home sign"), and the language they invent shows many parallels to ordinary (spoken) language. For example, their invented language has many of the formal structures routinely seen in the world's existing languages, and the pattern of emergence for these invented languages follows the same sequence as that observed in ordinary language learning (Feldman, Goldin-Meadow, & Gleitman, 1978; Goldin-Meadow, 2003; Senghas, Román & Mavillapalli, 2006).

How should we think about this? According to many psychologists, the answer lies in the sophisticated learning capacities that all humans share, capacities that contribute to many aspects of the young child's development, and not just language. Other psychologists, though, offer a different claim: that the human brain contains several mechanisms specifically evolved for language learning, so that, in effect, language learning is "wired into" our brains from the start.

What might these specialized mechanisms be? Earlier in the chapter, we suggested that children may be born with brain structures that somehow define the broad structure of human language. In this view, the learning process is one in which the child simply has to figure out how the universal structure is realized within his language community—what the parameters are for that particular language, what the vocabulary items are, and so on. This is why language learning is so fast and why the learning can proceed with truly minimal input; it is also why the various languages of the world all end up having the same basic structure.

Support for these claims comes from many sources, including observations of **specific language impairment** (SLI). Children with this disorder have normal intelligence and no problems with the muscle movements needed to produce language. Nonetheless, they are slow to learn language and, throughout their lives, have difficulty in understanding and producing many sentences. They are also impaired on tasks designed specifically to test their linguistic knowledge. They have difficulty, for example, completing passages like this one: "I like to blife. Today I blife. Tomorrow I will blife. Yesterday I did the same thing. Yesterday I _____." Most 4-year-olds know that the answer is, "Yesterday I blifed." But adults with SLI cannot do this task—apparently having failed to learn this simple rule of language (Bishop & Norbury, 2008; Lai, Fisher, Hurst, Vargha-Khadem, & Monaco, 2001; van der Lely, 2005).

Claims about SLI remain controversial, but many authors point to this disorder as evidence for brain mechanisms that are somehow specialized for language learning. Disruption to these mechanisms throws language off-track but, remarkably, seems to leave other aspects of the brain's functioning undisturbed.

The Processes of Language Learning

Even with these biological contributions, there's no question that learning does play a crucial role in the acquisition of language. After all, children who grow up in Paris learn to speak French; children growing up in China learn Chinese. In this rather obvious way, language learning depends on the child's picking up information from her environment.

But what learning mechanisms are involved here? One might think that language learning depends heavily on imitation (so that children in Paris imitate the French speakers around them, and so on), but, in truth, the data offer several challenges for an account hinging on imitation. For example, consider how English-speaking children learn to form the past tense. Initially, they proceed in a word-by-word fashion, so they memorize that the past tense of "play" is "played," the past tense of "climb" is "climbed," and so on. By age 3 or so, however, children seem to realize that they don't have to memorize each word's past tense as a separate vocabulary item. Instead, they realize they can produce the past tense by manipulating morphemes—that is, by adding the "-ed" ending onto a word. Once children make this discovery, they're able to apply this principle to many new verbs, including verbs they've never encountered before. Thus, Berko (1958) showed children a picture and told them, "Here is a man who likes to rick. Yesterday he did the same thing. Yesterday he _____." Prompted in this way, 3-year-olds unhesitatingly supply the past tense: "ricked."

However, children seem to get carried away with this pattern, and their speech at this age contains many **overregularization errors**: They say things like, "Yesterday we goed" or "Yesterday I runned." The same thing happens with other morphemes, and so children of this age also overgeneralize their use of the plural ending—they say things like "I have two foots" or "I lost three tooths" (Marcus et al., 1992). They also generalize on contractions, and, having heard "she isn't" and "you aren't," they say things like "I amn't." These errors are interesting for many reasons, but notice that they rule out any direct contribution from imitation, for the simple reason that adults almost never produce these overregularizations. The children, therefore, are producing forms they've "invented" for themselves, and not a form they're imitating from others.

In the same way, we might think that language learning is a matter of explicit instruction, with adults somehow "teaching" their children to speak. But this too turns out to be mistaken. Studies of child-adult interaction make it plain that adults rarely correct their children's grammar, nor do they reward children for speaking "correctly." Instead, adults usually react to the *messages* that children convey in their language—and so (for example) they respond positively to the message, "Love 'oo, Mommy," more concerned with the content than with the syntax. And in those rare occasions in which adults *do* correct children's grammar ("You shouldn't say 'holded,' Susie. Say, 'held'"), children seem largely oblivious to the correction (Bellugi, 1971).

What, then, *do* the learning mechanisms involve? Once again, the answer has many parts, but a key element rests on the fact that children are exquisitely sensitive to patterns and regularities in what they hear, as though each child were an astute statistician, keeping track of the frequency-of-occurrence of this form or that. In one study, 8-month-old infants heard a 2-minute tape recording that sounded something like "bidakupadotigolabubidaku." These syllables were spoken in a monotonous tone, with no difference in stress from one syllable to the next and no pauses in between any of the syllables. But there was a pattern. The experimenters had decided in advance to designate the sequence "bidaku" as a word. Therefore, they arranged the sequences so that if the infant heard "bida," then "ku" was sure to follow. For other syllables, there was no such pattern. For instance, "daku" (the end of the nonsense word "bidaku") would sometimes be followed by "go," sometimes by "pa," and so on. Astonishingly, the babies detected these patterns and their frequencies. In a subsequent test, the babies showed no evidence of surprise if they heard the string "bidakubidakubidaku." From the babies' point of view, these were simply repetitions of a word they already knew. However, the babies did show surprise if they were presented with the string "dakupadakupadakupa." This was not a "word" they had heard before, although of course they had heard each of its syllables many times. Thus, the babies had learned the vocabulary of this made-up language. They had detected the statistical pattern of which syllables followed which, despite their rather brief, entirely passive exposure to these sounds and despite the absence of any supporting cues such as pauses or shifts in intonation (Aslin,

Saffran, & Newport, 1998; Marcus, Vijayan, Rao, & Vishton, 1999; Saffran, 2003; Xu & Garcia, 2008).

In addition, language learning relies on a theme that has been in view throughout this chapter: Language has many elements (syntax, semantics, phonology, prosody, etc.), and these elements interact in ordinary language use (and so we rely on a sentence's syntactic form to figure out its meaning; we rely on semantic cues in deciphering the syntax). In the same fashion, language learning also relies on all these elements in an interacting fashion. Thus, children rely on prosody (again: the rise and fall of pitch, the pattern of timing) as clues to syntax, and adults speaking to children helpfully exaggerate these prosodic signals, easing the children's interpretive burden. Children also rely on their vocabulary, listening for words they already know as clues helping them to process more complex strings. Likewise, children rely on their knowledge of semantic relationships as a basis for figuring out syntax—a process known as **semantic bootstrapping** (Pinker, 1987). In this way, the very complexity of language is both a burden for the child (because there's so much to learn in "learning a language"!) and an aid (because the child can use each of the elements as sources of information in trying to figure out the other elements).

Language and Thought

One last topic will bring our consideration of language to a close. There is no question that language can—and often does—shape your thoughts. To take a trivial example, if you hear someone say, "I saw a dog," this input will lead you to different ideas than if you'd heard the speaker say, "I saw a cat." In this simple way, the language that you use (and, in this case, the language that you hear) can of course shape the flow of your ideas—that is, can shape what you think.

Other influences of language are, however, less obvious. For instance, verbal descriptions often provide a convenient label for a complex experience, and the labels, in turn, provide an economical way of coding, or chunking, that experience—with important consequences for memory (see Chapter 5). Thus, it is vastly easier to remember the label "tree" than it is to remember the corresponding image, easier to remember the label "trips to the zoo" than it is to remember all the details associated with those trips. In this fashion, labeling— made possible by language—has a powerful effect on memory.

Likewise, language can influence how you reason and how you make decisions. One illustration of this is in so-called "framing effects" (see Chapter 11). Thus, for just one case, a patient is more likely to choose a medical treatment if told that the treatment has a 50% chance of success than if told it has a 50% chance of failure—again, a powerful effect of language.

Linguistic Relativity

All of this invites a further question: If language shapes thought, then do people who speak different languages end up *thinking differently*? Some of the early

MYTHS ABOUT LANGUAGE AND THOUGHT

Many people believe that the native peoples of the far north (including the Inuit) have an enormous number of terms for the various forms of snow, and are correspondingly skilled in discriminating types of snow. It turns out, though, that the initial claim (the number of terms for snow) is wrong; the Inuit have roughly the same number of snow terms as do people living further south. In addition, if the Inuit people are more skilled in discriminating snow types, is this because of the language that they speak? Or is it because their day to day lives demand that they stay alert to the differences among snow types? (After Raberson, Davies, & Davidoff, 2000)

evidence on this question was offered by the anthropologist Benjamin Whorf, a strong proponent of the view that the specific language you speak does force you into certain modes of thought—a claim usually known as **linguistic relativity** (Whorf, 1956). The "results" Whorf offered, however, were quite weak. He tried to show, for example, that Hopi speakers think about time differently than English speakers do, but his evidence came largely from the ways that Hopi expressed themselves when talking about various events. This evidence is without value: Perhaps the Hopi think in the same ways that English speakers do, but they express these thoughts differently because their language differs from English. In this case, the evidence indicates only that the way you express your thoughts is influenced by your language—a conclusion that is both unsurprising and not very interesting.

More recent researchers have therefore tried to find more rigorous tests of Whorf's proposal. One line of work has examined how you perceive the colors in your world, building on the fact that some languages have many terms for colors (red, orange, mauve, puce, salmon, fawn, ocher, etc.) and others have few (see Figure 9.13). Do these differences among languages affect perception? Recent findings suggest, in fact, that people who speak languages with a richer color vocabulary may perceive colors differently—making finer and more sharply defined distinctions (Özgen, 2004; Roberson, Davies, & Davidoff, 2000).

FIGURE 9.13 | COLORS IN DIFFERENT LANGUAGES

A English naming

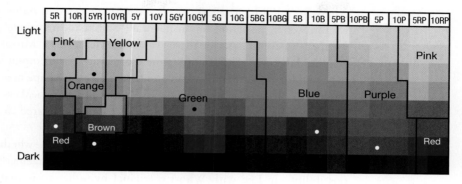

B Berinmo naming

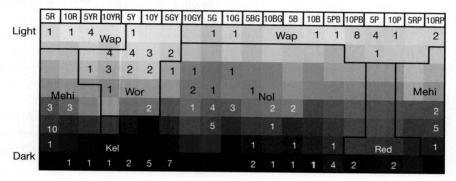

The Berinmo people, living in Papua New Guinea, have only five words for describing colors, and so, for example, use a single word ("nol") to describe colors that English speakers call "green" and colors we call "blue." (The letters and numbers in these panels refer to a system often used for classifying colors.) These differences, from one language to the next, have an impact on how people perceive and remember colors. This effect is best understood, however, in terms of attention: Language can draw our attention to some aspect of the world and in this way can shape our experience and thus our cognition. (After Roberson, Davies, & Davidoff, 2000)

Language Effects Beyond Color

Languages also differ in how they describe spatial arrangement—with some languages, for example, emphasizing absolute directions (akin to north or east, which are defined in a fashion independent of which way you're currently facing), while other languages emphasize relative directions (akin to left or right, which *do* depend on which way you're facing). Several studies have suggested that these language differences lead to corresponding differences in how people remember, and perhaps how they perceive, spatial position (Majid, Bowerman, Kita, Haun, & Levinson, 2004; Pederson et al., 1998).

Similarly, languages differ in expressions of time and number, and these differences, again, seem in some studies to be reflected in how people *think about* time and number (e.g., Boroditsky, 2011). Languages also differ in how they describe events. In English, we tend to use active sentences that name the agent of the action, even if the action was accidental ("Sam made a mistake"). It sounds awkward or evasive to describe these events in other terms ("Mistakes were made"). In other languages, including Japanese or Spanish, it's common *not* to mention the agent for an accidental event, and this in turn can shape memory: After viewing videos of accidental events, Japanese and Spanish speakers are less likely to remember the person who triggered the accident, compared to English speakers (Boroditsky, 2011).

But how should we think about all of these results—whether we're focused on color perception, or the perception of spatial arrangement or events? One possibility—in line with Whorf's original hypothesis—is that language has a direct impact on cognition, so that the categories recognized by your language become the categories used in your thought. In this view, language has a unique effect on cognition (because no other factor can shape cognition in this way). And, because language's influence is unique, it is also irreversible: Once your language has led you to think in certain ways, you will forever think in those ways. Thus, from this perspective, there are literally some ideas that a Japanese speaker (for example) can contemplate but that an English speaker cannot, and vice versa, and likewise, say, for a Hopi or French speaker.

A different possibility is more modest—and also much more plausible: Language influences cognition by shaping what you pay attention to. This effect is important, and sometimes powerful, but let's bear in mind that many other factors also shape attention. These other factors, therefore, can, in some settings, erase any impact that language might have on cognition.

To see how these points play out, let's look at a concrete case: When English speakers describe an event, our language requires us to name (and thus to pay attention to) the actor who caused the event; when a Spanish speaker describes the same event, her language doesn't have this requirement, and so doesn't force her to think about the actor. Thus, the structure of each language shapes what people are likely to pay attention to, and this will often have consequences for thinking and for memory.

But, of course, we could, if we wished, simply give the Spanish speaker an instruction: "Pay attention to the actor." Or we could make sure that the actor is wearing a brightly colored coat, using a perceptual cue to guide attention. These simple steps can (and often do) offset the bias created by language. For this reason, the effect of language on cognition is often *not* observed, and is surely not a permanent effect, forever defining (and perhaps limiting) how someone thinks.

What about the effect of language on color perception? If you're a speaker of Berinmo (a language spoken in New Guinea), your language makes no distinction between "green" and "blue," so your language never leads you to think about these as separate categories. If you're an English speaker, your language does make this distinction, and this can draw your attention to what all green objects have in common, and what all blue objects have in common. If your attention is drawn to this point again and again, you'll gain familiarity with the distinction and eventually become better at making the distinction. Once more, then, language does matter—but it matters because of language's impact on attention.

Similar logic applies to language's other effects—including its impact on the perception of spatial direction, or its influence on how people think about time. In these cases, too, the terms used in your language guide your attention, and this shapes your experience and thus shapes what you end up thinking. But, as in the other cases we've described, further factors also influence your attention and can therefore eliminate language's effects.

Let's be clear, though, that different cues will guide attention in different settings. As a result, sometimes language effects will be observed, and sometimes these effects will be offset by other factors. This is, in fact, the pattern of the evidence, with some studies showing an influence of language, and some studies finding no effect. Thus, for example, some studies have observed differences in how English and Chinese speakers think about time (e.g., Boroditsky, 2001), but these differences have not appeared at all in several other studies (e.g., Chen, 2007; January & Kako, 2007).

In addition, this emphasis on attention suggests that, within an experiment, we'll often be able to undo the effects of language by using some other means to redirect someone's attention. This, too, is correct: For example, English speakers and speakers of Mandarin Chinese seem initially to think about spatial relations differently—because their languages do bias them toward different interpretive habits. But the difference between English and Chinese speakers can be eradicated by a brief conversation, leading them to consider other ways one might think about space (Li & Gleitman, 2002; also Li, Abarbanell, Gleitman, & Papafragou, 2011).

Where, then, does this leave us? Having a language at all certainly influences cognition, and so our human language-guided thoughts are different from the thoughts of our nonlinguistic primate relatives (gorillas, chimps, etc.). In addition, speaking a *specific* language (English or Tzeltal, Mandarin or French) does influence your thoughts—but in ways that are not at all mysterious. Of course, someone can say, "Look at the bird" and thus guide your attention to the bird. In the same fashion, a specific language, by virtue of having a verbal label for a category, can call your attention to this category and in this way shape your experience, and thus your cognition. But language's effects are neither inevitable nor permanent. A half-century ago, Whorf argued that language plays a unique role in shaping thought and has a lifelong impact in determining quite literally what we can or cannot think, what ideas we can or cannot entertain. There is no persuasive evidence in favor of this stronger claim. (For more on these issues, see Gleitman & Papafragou, 2012; Hanako & Smith, 2005; Hermer-Vazquez, Spelke, & Katsnelson, 1999; Kay & Regier, 2007; Özgen & Davies, 2002; Papafragou, Li, Choi & Han, 2007; Stapel & Semin, 2007.)

Bilingualism

There's one more—and intriguing—way that language is said to influence cognition. It comes from cases in which someone knows more than one language.

Children who are raised in bilingual homes learn both languages as quickly and as well as monolingual children learn their single language (Kovelman, Shalinksy, Berens, & Petitto, 2008). Bilingual children do tend to have smaller vocabularies, compared to monolingual children, but this contrast is evident only at an early age, and bilingual children soon catch up on this dimension (Bialystok, Craik, Green & Gollan, 2009).

These findings surprise many people, on the expectation that bilingual children would become confused—blurring together their languages, and getting mixed up about which words and which rules belong in each language. But, remarkably, this confusion seems not to occur. In fact, children who are raised bilingually seem to develop skills that specifically help them avoid this sort of confusion. More broadly, they develop an impressive ability to switch between tasks—turning off *these* habits in *that* setting, and turning off *those* habits in *this* setting. This ability obviously supports their language learning—so that they don't use their French-interpretive habits when hearing English, or vice versa—but the ability may also help them in other settings (Bialystok et al., 2009; Hernández, Costa, & Humphreys, 2012; Hilchey & Klein, 2011; Zelazo, 2006). In Chapter 4, we introduced the idea of executive control, and the suggestion here is that being raised bilingually may encourage *better* executive control. As a result, bilinguals of all ages are often better at avoiding distraction, switching between competing tasks, or holding information in mind while working on some other task.

These are intriguing findings with important implications—for politics, for education, and for parenting. These findings are also quite *encouraging*, since roughly a fifth of the population in the United States speaks a language at home that is different from the English they use in other settings (Shin & Kominski, 2010). These points to the side, though, modern research on bilingualism provides one more argument that—in a positive and perhaps surprising way—language use can indeed shape cognition.

CHAPTER SUMMARY

- All speech is built up from a few dozen phonemes, although the selection of phonemes varies from language to language. Phonemes in turn are built up from a small number of production features, including voicing, place of articulation, and manner of production. Phonemes can be combined to form more complex sounds, but combinations are constrained by a number of rules.

- Speech perception is more than a matter of detecting the relevant features in the input sound stream. The perceiver needs to deal with speaker-to-speaker variation in how sounds are produced; she also needs to segment the stream of speech and cope with coarticulation. The process of speech perception is helped enormously by context, but we also have the impressive skill of categorical perception, which makes us keenly sensitive to differences between categories of speech sounds but insensitive to distinctions within each category.

- People know many thousands of words, and for each one they know the sound of the word, its syntactic role, and its semantic representation. Our understanding of words is also generative, allowing us to create limitless numbers of new words. Some new words are wholly made up (e.g., "geek"), but more often new words are created by combining familiar morphemes.

- The rules of syntax govern whether a sequence of words is grammatical. One set of rules governs phrase structure, and the word groups identified by these rules do correspond to natural groupings of words. Phrase structure rules also guide interpretation. Like all the rules discussed in this chapter, though, phrase structure rules are descriptive, not prescriptive.

- To understand a sentence, a listener or reader needs to parse the sentence, determining each word's syntactic role. Evidence suggests that people parse a sentence as they see or hear each word, and this sometimes leads them into parsing errors that must be repaired later; this is revealed by garden-path sentences. Parsing is guided by syntax, semantics, and the extralinguistic context.

- The biological roots of language are revealed in many ways. The study of aphasia makes it clear that some areas of the brain are specialized for learning and using language. The rapid learning of language also speaks to the biological basis for language; this rapid learning is certainly helped by the existence of linguistic universals—structural properties shared by all languages.

- Processes of imitation and direct instruction play relatively small parts in language learning. This is evident in the fact that children produce many forms (often, overregularization errors) that no adult produces; these forms are obviously not the result of imitation. Children also receive little direct instruction about language; adults tend to respond to the content of what children are saying, rather than its form. Language learning is, however, strongly influenced by children's remarkable sensitivity to statistical patterns in the language they hear. Children can also use their understanding of one aspect of language (e.g., phonology or vocabulary) to help them learn about other aspects (e.g., syntax).

- There has been considerable discussion about the ways in which thought might be shaped by the language one speaks. Language certainly guides and influences your thoughts, and the way a thought is formulated into words can have an effect on how you think about the thought's content. In addition, language can call your attention to a category or to a distinction, and this makes it likely that you will have experience in thinking about the category or distinction. This experience, in turn, can promote fluency in these thoughts. However, these effects are not unique to language (because other factors can also draw your attention to the category), nor are they irreversible. Hence, there is no evidence that language can shape what you *can* think.

- Research on bilingualism shows that children raised in bilingual homes learn both languages as quickly and as well as monolingual children learning their single language. In fact, bilingual children seem to develop an impressive ability to switch between languages, and this ability may also help them in other settings that demand executive control of mental processes.

The Workbook Connection

See the *Cognition Workbook* for further exploration of language:

- Demonstration 9.1: Phonemes and Subphonemes
- Demonstration 9.2: The *Speed* of Speech
- Demonstration 9.3: Coarticulation
- Demonstration 9.4: The Most Common Words
- Demonstration 9.5: Patterns in Language
- Demonstration 9.6: Ambiguity
- Research Methods: Metalinguistic Judgments
- Cognitive Psychology and Education: Writing
- Cognitive Psychology and the Law: Jury Instructions
- Cognitive Psychology and the Law: Remembering Conversation

NEED HELP STUDYING?

 wwnorton.com/studyspace

Visit StudySpace to access free review material such as

- Chapter study plans
- Quizzes
- Flashcards, and more

CHAPTER TEN

Visual Knowledge

People have knowledge of many different types. They know what a fish is (for example), but they also know what fish smells like when it's cooking and what a fish looks like. They know what a guitar is, but they also know what one sounds like. Likewise, people describe their *thoughts* in a variety of ways: Sometimes, they claim, their thoughts seem to be formulated in words. Sometimes, their thoughts seem more abstract—a sequence of ideas that lacks any concrete form. But sometimes, people claim, their thoughts involve a sequence of *pictures*, or *sounds*, or other sensory impressions.

What can we say about this variety? How are specific sights or sounds or smells represented in the mind? How should we think about the proposal that people sometimes "think in pictures"? In this chapter, we'll explore these questions, asking broadly about nonverbal knowledge but focusing largely on *visual* knowledge and *visual* thoughts. Our focus on visual knowledge reflects the fact that far more is known about this modality than about any other (e.g., auditory knowledge, or olfactory knowledge, or knowledge for tastes). As we proceed, though, you

- Mental images are, in important ways, picture-like, representing in a direct fashion the spatial layout of the represented scene. It's not surprising, therefore, that there is considerable overlap between imagery and perception—in how each functions and also in their neural bases.

- People can also use spatial imagery, which is not visual and which may instead be represented in the mind in terms of movements, or perhaps in some more abstract format.

- Although they are picture-like, images (visual or spatial) are plainly not pictures; instead, images (like percepts) seem to be organized and already interpreted in a fashion that pictures are not.

- Even though images in working memory provide a distinctive form of representation, information about appearances in long-term memory may not be distinctive. In fact, long-term memory for sensory information seems to obey all the principles we described, in earlier chapters, for verbal or symbolic memories.

should keep an eye on how the questions we're asking might be applied to other forms of nonverbal knowledge.

We'll will begin by examining how people describe their own mental images, but we will quickly run into the limitations of this "self-report" evidence. We'll turn, therefore, to more objective means of assessing imagery. Then, later in the chapter, we will consider your broader knowedge about visual appearance—how you remember the shapes, sizes, and colors of things you have seen at some point in the past, asking how this "sensory" information might be represented in long-term memory.

Visual Imagery

How many windows are there in your house or your apartment? Who has bushier eyebrows—Justin Bieber or Simon Cowell? For most people, questions like these seem to elicit "mental pictures." You know what Bieber and Cowell look like, and you call a "picture" of each before your "mind's eye" in order to make the comparison. Likewise, you call to mind a "map" of your apartment and count the windows by inspecting this map. Many people even trace the map in the air when they're counting the windows, moving their finger around to "follow" the imagined map's contours.

Various practical problems also seem to evoke images. There you are in the store, trying on a new sweater. Will the sweater look good with your blue pants? To decide, you'll probably try to visualize the blue of the pants, using your "mind's eye" to ask how they'll look with the sweater. Similarly, if a friend asks you, "Was David in class yesterday?" you might try to recall by visualizing what the room looked like during the class; is David "visible" in your image?

These examples illustrate the common, everyday use of visual images—as a basis for making decisions, as an aid to remembering. But surely there is no tiny eye somewhere deep in your brain; thus, the phrase "mind's eye" cannot be taken literally. Likewise, mental "pictures" cannot be actual pictures; with no eye deep inside the brain, who or what would inspect such pictures? In light of these puzzles, what *are* images?

Introspections About Images

Mental images have been described and discussed for thousands of years. However, it's only within the last century or so that psychologists have begun to gather systematic data about imagery. Among the earliest researchers was Francis Galton, who asked various people simply to describe their images and to rate them for vividness (Galton, 1883). In other words, Galton asked his research participants to *introspect* or "look within" (a method that we first met in Chapter 1) and to report on their own mental contents. The **self-report data** he obtained fit well with common sense: The participants reported that they could "inspect" their images much as they would inspect a picture. Their descriptions also made it clear that they were "viewing" their images from a certain position and a certain distance—just as they'd look at an actual scene from a specific viewing perspective. They also reported that they could "read off" from the image details of color and texture. All of this implies a mode of representation that is, in many ways, picture-like, and that is of course quite consistent with our informal manner of describing mental images as "pictures in the head," to be inspected with the "mind's eye."

There was also another side of these early data: Galton's participants differed widely from each other in their self-reports. Many described images of photographic clarity, rich in detail, almost as if they were actually *seeing* the imaged scene rather than visualizing it. Other participants, in contrast, reported very sketchy images or no images at all. They were able to think about the scenes or objects Galton named for them, but they insisted that in no sense were they "seeing" these scenes. Their reports rarely included mention of color or size or viewing perspective; indeed, their reports were devoid of *any* visual qualities.

These observations are in themselves interesting: Do people really differ in the nature of their imagery—so that some people are "visualizers" and some people are not? Are some people *incapable* of forming visual images? If so, what consequences does this variety have? Are there tasks that the visualizers can do that the "nonvisualizers" cannot (or vice versa)? If so, this could provide crucial information about how visual imagery is used and what it is good for.

Before we can answer these questions, though, we need to address a methodological concern raised by Galton's data, and it's a concern about self-report that we first met in Chapter 1: Perhaps all of Galton's participants had the *same* imagery skill, but some were cautious in how they chose to describe their imagery, while others were more extravagant. Thus, some chose to keep their descriptions brief and undetailed, while others took pleasure in providing elaborate and flowery descriptions. In this way, Galton's data might reveal differences in how people *talk about* their imagery rather than differences in imagery per se.

What seems required, therefore, is a more objective means of assessing imagery—one that does not rely on the subjectivity inherent in self-reports. With this more objective approach, we could assess the differences, from one individual to the next, suggested by Galton's data. Indeed, with this more objective approach, we could hope to find out exactly what images are.

Chronometric Studies of Imagery

Imagery researchers have, in the last 50 years, been keenly sensitive to these concerns about self-report, and this is why imagery experiments usually don't ask participants to *describe* their images. Instead, to gain more objective data, these experiments ask people to *do something* with their images—usually, to make a judgment based on the image. We can then examine how fast people are in these judgments, and with appropriate comparisons we can use these measurements as a basis for testing hypotheses about imagery. In other words, the data are generally chronometric ("time measuring") and give us a much more accurate portrait of imagery than could ever be obtained with self-report.

For example, chronometric studies allow us to ask what sorts of information are prominent in a mental image and what sorts are not, and we can then use these evaluations as a basis for asking how "picture-like" mental images really are. To see the logic, think about how actual, out-in-the-world pictures are different from verbal descriptions. Concretely, consider what would happen if you were asked to *write a paragraph* describing a cat. It seems likely that you'd mention the distinctive features of cats—their whiskers, their claws, and so on. Your paragraph probably wouldn't include the fact that cats have heads, since this is too obvious to be worth mentioning. But now consider, in contrast, what would happen if we asked you to *draw a sketch* of a cat. In this format, the cat's head would be prominent, for the simple reason that the head is relatively large and up front. The claws and whiskers might be less salient, because these features are small and so would not take up much space in the drawing.

The point here is that the pattern of what information is included, as well as what information is prominent, depends on the mode of presentation. For a *description*, the features that are prominent will be those that are distinctive and strongly associated with the object being described. For a *depiction*, distinctiveness and association won't matter; instead, size and position will determine what's prominent and what's not.

Against this backdrop, let's now ask what information is available in a visual image. Is it the pictorially prominent features, which would imply a depictive mode of representation, or the verbally prominent ones, implying a descriptive mode? Self-reports about imagery surely indicate a picture-like representation; is this confirmed by the data?

In an early study by Kosslyn (1976), research participants were asked to form a series of mental images and to answer yes/no questions about each. For example, they were asked to form a mental image of a cat and asked, "Does the cat have a head? Does the cat have claws?" Participants responded to these questions quickly, but—strikingly—responses to the head question were quicker than those to the claws question. This difference suggests that information quickly available in the image follows the rules for pictures, not paragraphs. In contrast, a different group of participants was asked merely to think about cats (with no mention of imagery). These participants, when asked the same questions, gave quicker responses to claws than to head—the reverse pattern of the first group. Thus, it seems that people have the option of thinking about cats via imagery and also the option of thinking about cats without imagery; as the mode of representation changes, so does the pattern of information availability.

In a different experiment, participants were asked to memorize the fictional map shown in Figure 10.1 and, in particular, to memorize the locations of the various landmarks: the well, the straw hut, and so on (Kosslyn, Ball, & Reiser, 1978). The experimenters made sure participants had the map memorized by asking them to draw a replica of the map from memory; once they could do this,

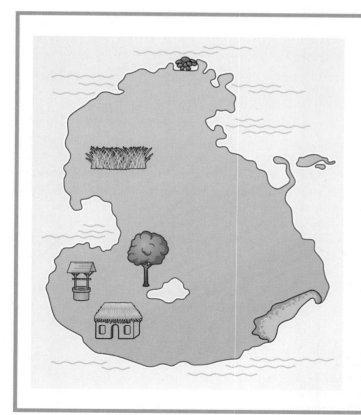

FIGURE 10.1 | FICTIONAL ISLAND USED IN IMAGE-SCANNING EXPERIMENTS

Participants in the study first memorized this map, including the various landmarks (the hut, the well, the patch of grass, and so on). They then formed a mental image of this map for the scanning procedure. (After Kosslyn, 1983)

the main experiment began. Participants were asked to form an image of the island and to point their "mind's eye" at a specific landmark—let's say, the well. Another landmark was then mentioned, perhaps the straw hut, and participants were asked to imagine a black speck moving in a straight line from the first landmark to the second. When the speck "reached" the target, participants pressed a button, stopping a clock. This provided a measure of how long the participants needed to "scan" from the well to the hut. The same was done for the well and the tree, and the hut and the patch of grass, so that the researchers ended up with scanning times for each of the various pairs of landmarks.

Figure 10.2 shows the results. The data from this **image-scanning procedure** clearly suggest that participants scan across their images at a constant rate, so that doubling the scanning "distance" doubles the time required for the scan, and tripling the distance triples the time required.

Similar results are obtained if participants are given a task that requires them to "zoom in" on their images (e.g., a task that requires them to inspect the image for some small detail) or a task that requires them to "zoom out" (e.g., a task that requires a more global judgment). In these studies, response times are directly proportional to the amount of zoom required, suggesting once again that travel in the imaged world resembles travel in the actual world, at least with regard to timing. As

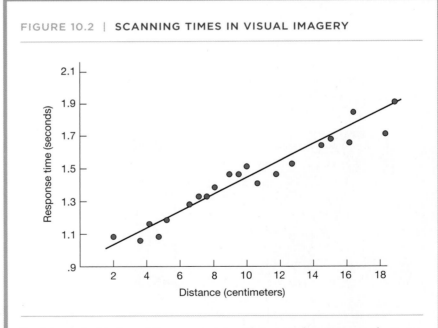

FIGURE 10.2 | **SCANNING TIMES IN VISUAL IMAGERY**

Participants had to "scan" from one point on their mental image to another point; they pressed a button to indicate when their "mind's eye" had arrived at its destination. Response times were closely related to the "distance" participants had to scan across on the image, implying that mental images are similar to actual pictures in how they represent positions and distance. (After Kosslyn, 1983)

ZOOMING IN ON MENTAL PICTURES

Just as it takes time to "scan across" a mental image, it also takes time to "zoom in" on one. Thus participants respond slowly if they are instructed to imagine a mouse standing with an elephant, and then asked: Does the mouse have whiskers? To answer this question, participants need a bit of time (which we can measure) to zoom in on the mouse, to bring the whiskers "into view."

a concrete example, participants in one study were asked to imagine a mouse standing next to an elephant and were then asked to confirm, by inspecting their image, that the mouse had whiskers. Participants were relatively slow in responding, presumably because they first needed time to zoom in on the image in order to "see" the whiskers. Response times were faster if the participants were initially asked to imagine the mouse standing next to a paper clip. For this image, participants start with a "close-up" view, so no zooming was needed to "see" the whiskers.

Whether you're scanning across a mental image, therefore, or zooming in on one, there's a clear relationship between "travel time" and "travel distance"—and, specifically, "traveling" a greater "distance" requires more time. This is the same relationship we would observe if we asked our participants to move their eyes across an actual map (rather than an image of one) or literally to zoom in on a real picture: In these cases, too, traveling a greater distance would require more time. All of this points toward the similarity between mental images and actual out-in-the-world pictures.

More precisely, though, these mental imagery data are telling us a great deal about the *nature* of mental images: According to these results, images represent a scene in a fashion that preserves all of the distance relationships within that scene: Points close to each other in the scene are somehow "close" to each other in the image; points that are farther apart in the scene are somehow "farther apart" in the image. Thus, in a very real sense, the image preserves the spatial layout of the represented scene. With this, the image will necessarily represent information about all the shapes and sizes within the scene, and it will also preserve a diverse set of spatial relationships (relationships such as one point being *between* two other points, or *aligned* with other points, and so on). It's in this fashion that images directly represent the *geometry* of the scene, and it's in this way that images *depict* the scene rather than describing it, and so are much more similar to pictures or maps than they are to descriptions.

Mental Rotation

Other results make a similar point with regard to the *transformation* of mental images. In a series of experiments by Shepard, Cooper, and Metzler, participants were asked to decide whether displays like the one in Figure 10.3A showed two different shapes or just one shape viewed from two different perspectives (Cooper & Shepard, 1973; Shepard & Metzler, 1971; Shepard & Cooper, 1982). In other words, is it possible to "rotate" the form shown on the left in Figure 10.3A so that it will end up looking just like the form on the right? What about the two shapes shown in Figure 10.3B or the two in 10.3C?

To perform this **mental rotation** task, participants seem first to imagine one of the forms rotating into alignment with the other. Then, once the forms are oriented in the same way, participants can make their judgment. This step of imagined rotation takes some time; in fact, the amount of time it takes depends on how

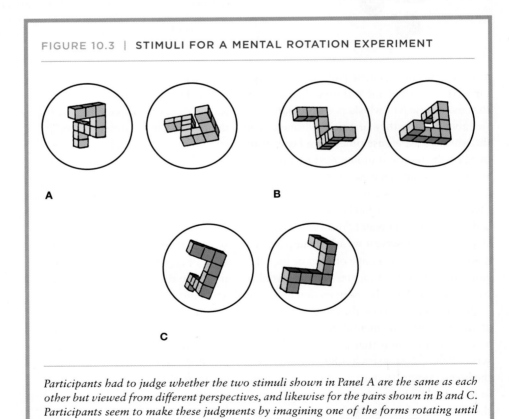

FIGURE 10.3 | **STIMULI FOR A MENTAL ROTATION EXPERIMENT**

A

B

C

Participants had to judge whether the two stimuli shown in Panel A are the same as each other but viewed from different perspectives, and likewise for the pairs shown in B and C. Participants seem to make these judgments by imagining one of the forms rotating until its position matches that of the other form. (After Shepard & Metzler, 1971)

much rotation is needed. Figure 10.4 shows the data pattern, with response times clearly being influenced by how far apart the two forms were in their initial orientations. Thus, once again, imagined "movement" resembles actual movement: The farther you have to imagine a form rotating, the longer the evaluation takes.

This task can also be used to answer some further questions about imagery. For example, notice that if you were to cut out the left-hand drawing in Figure 10.3A and spin it around while leaving it flat on the table, you could align it with the drawing on the right. The relevant rotation, therefore, is a rotation that leaves the pictures within the two-dimensional plane in which they are drawn. In contrast, the two forms shown in Figure 10.3B are identical except for a rotation in depth. No matter how you spin the *picture* on the left, it will not line up with the picture on the right. You can align these forms, but to do so you need to spin them around a vertical axis, in essence lifting them off the page.

People have no trouble with mental rotation in depth. They make very few errors (with accuracy levels around 95%), and the data resemble those obtained with picture-plane rotation (compare Figures 10.4A and 10.4B). Apparently, participants can represent three-dimensional forms in their

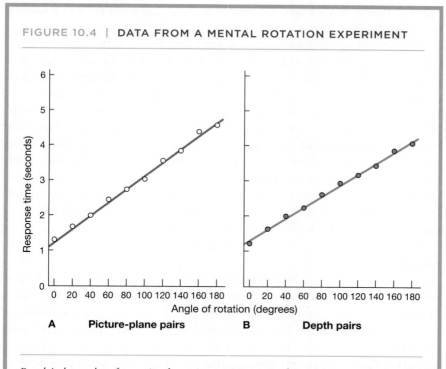

FIGURE 10.4 | DATA FROM A MENTAL ROTATION EXPERIMENT

A   **Picture-plane pairs**   **B**   **Depth pairs**

Panel A shows data from stimulus pairs requiring mental rotation in two dimensions, so that the imaged forms stay within the imagined picture plane. Panel B shows data from pairs requiring an imagined rotation in depth. The data are similar, indicating that participants can imagine three-dimensional rotations as easily, and as swiftly, as they can imagine two-dimensional rotations. In both cases, the greater the degree of rotation required, the longer the response times. (After Shepard & Metzler, 1971)

images, and they can imagine these forms moving in depth. In some circumstances, therefore, visual images are not mental pictures; they are more like mental sculptures.

Avoiding Concerns About Demand Character

In both mental rotation and mental scanning, the farther the imagined "travel," the longer it takes. We've interpreted these results as revealing the way in which images represent spatial layout—with points that are more distant in the represented scene somehow farther apart in the image. But there's another way one might try to interpret the data. Participants in these studies obviously know that movement through the world takes time and that moving a longer distance takes more time. Perhaps, therefore, the participants simply control the timing of their responses in order to re-create this "normal" pattern.

This proposal can be fleshed out in a variety of ways, but, to phrase things strongly, perhaps participants in these studies are not imagining rotations or scanning across an image at all. Instead, they might be thinking, "The experimenter just asked me to scan a long way, and I'd like to make it look like I'm obeying. I know that a long scan takes a long time, and so let me wait a moment before hitting the response button."

Why should participants act in this way? One reason is that participants in experiments usually want to be helpful, so they do all they can to give the experimenter "good" data. As a result, they are very sensitive to the **demand character** of the experiment—that is, cues that might signal how they are "supposed to" behave in that situation (Intons-Peterson, 1983, 1999; Intons-Peterson & White, 1981). A different possibility is that this sort of "simulation" is, in fact, what imagery is really all about. Perhaps whenever someone tries to "imagine" something, he draws on his knowledge about how an event in the world would actually unfold, and then he does his best to simulate this event. In this case, a longer scan or a greater rotation requires more time, not because there really is some "travel" involved, but because people know that these manipulations should take more time and do their best to simulate the process (Pylyshyn, 1981).

As it turns out, though, we can set aside these concerns, allowing us to maintain the claims we've already sketched—namely, that the scanning and rotation data are as they are, not through simulation, but indeed *because of how images represent spatial layout*. Several lines of evidence support this claim, including (crucially) data we will turn to, later in the chapter, examining the neural bases for imagery. But, in addition, we can tackle the concern about demand character directly. In several studies, the experimenters have asked participants to make judgments about spatial layout but have taken care never to mention to participants that imagery was relevant to the task (e.g., Finke & Pinker, 1982). This should diminish the demand character of the procedure and so avoid any suggestion to participants that they should simulate some sort of "mental travel." Even without imagery instructions, though, the participants in these procedures spontaneously form images and scan across them, and their responses show the standard pattern: longer response times observed with lon-

There is, of course, no "box" trapping this mime. Instead, the mime is simulating what would happen if he were trapped in a box. In the same fashion, researchers have asked whether study participants, guided by an experiment's demand character, are simply simulating (re-creating?) how they'd act if they were looking at a picture.

ger scans. Apparently, this result really does emerge whenever participants are using visual imagery—whether the result is encouraged by the experimenters' instructions or not.

Interactions Between Imagery and Perception

It seems, therefore, that there really are parallels between visual images and actual visual stimuli, and this leads to a question: If images are so much like pictures, then are the processes used to inspect images similar to those used to inspect stimuli? To put it more broadly, what is the relation between imaging and perceiving?

In a study by Segal and Fusella (1970, 1971), participants were asked to detect very faint signals—either dim visual stimuli or soft tones. On each trial, the task was merely to indicate whether a signal had been presented or not. Participants did this in one of two conditions: either while forming a visual image before their "mind's eye" or while forming an auditory image before their "mind's ear." Thus, we have a 2 × 2 design: two types of signals to be detected, and two types of imagery.

Let's hypothesize that there's some overlap between imaging and perceiving—that is, there are some mental processes that are used by both activities. Therefore, if these processes are occupied with imaging, they're not available for perceiving, and vice versa; we should thus expect competition if participants try to do both activities at once. That is exactly what Segal and Fusella observed: Their results indicate that forming a visual image interferes with seeing and that forming an auditory image interferes with hearing (see Figure 10.5; also see Farah & Smith, 1983).

Percentage of Detections

	Visual signal	Auditory signal
While visualizing	61%	67%
While maintaining an auditory image	63%	61%

Percentage of False Alarms

	Visual signal	Auditory signal
While visualizing	7.8%	3.7%
While maintaining an auditory image	3.6%	6.7%

Participants were less successful in detecting a weak visual signal if they were simultaneously maintaining a visual image than if they were maintaining an auditory image. (The effect is small but highly reliable.) The reverse is true with weak auditory signals: Participants were less successful in this detection if maintaining an auditory image than if visualizing. In addition, visual images often led to "false alarms" for participants trying to detect visual signals; auditory images led to false alarms for auditory signals. (After Segal & Fusella, 1970)

Notice, though, that the Segal and Fusella participants were trying to visualize one thing while perceiving something altogether different. What happens if participants are contemplating a mental image *related to* the stimulus they're trying to perceive? Can visualizing a possible input "pave the way" for perception? Farah (1985) had participants visualize a form (either an *H* or a *T*). A moment later, either an *H* or a *T* was actually presented, but at a very low contrast, making the letter difficult to perceive. With this setup, perception was facilitated if participants had just been visualizing the target form, and the effect was quite specific: Visualizing an *H* made it easier to perceive an *H*; visualizing a *T* made it easier to perceive a *T*. This result provides further confirmation of the claim that visualizing and perceiving draw on similar mechanisms, so that one of these activities can serve to prime the other. (For further discussions, see Heil, Rösler, & Hennighausen, 1993; also see McDermott & Roediger, 1994.)

Similar conclusions can be drawn from biological evidence. As we discussed in Chapter 2, we know a great deal about the specific brain structures required for vision, and it turns out that many of the same structures are crucial for imagery. This can be documented in several ways, including procedures that rely on the neuroimaging techniques (like PET or fMRI) that map the moment-by-moment activity in the brain (see Figure 2.8 on p. 47). These techniques confirm that vision relies heavily on tissue located in the occipital cortex (and so these brain areas are highly activated whenever you are examining a visual stimulus). It turns out that activity levels are also high in these areas when participants are visualizing a stimulus before their "mind's eye" (Behrmann, 2000; Isha & Sagi, 1995; Kosslyn, 1994; Miyashita, 1995; Thompson & Kosslyn, 2000).

The biological parallels between imagery and perception can be documented even at a fine grain: Specifically, we know that different areas of the occipital cortex are involved in different aspects of visual perception, and so, for example, Areas V1 and V2 in the cortex are involved in the earliest stages of visual perception, responding to the specific low-level features of the input. It's striking, therefore, that these same brain areas are particularly active whenever participants are maintaining highly detailed images, and that the amount of brain tissue showing activation increases as participants imagine larger and larger objects (Behrmann, 2000; Kosslyn & Thompson, 2003). In a similar fashion, Area MT/MST in the brain is highly sensitive to motion in ordinary visual perception, and it turns out that the same brain area is particularly activated when participants are asked to *imagine* movement patterns (Goebel, Khorram-Sefat, Muckli, Hacker, & Singer, 1998). Likewise, brain areas that are especially active during the perception of faces are also highly activated when people are imagining faces (O'Craven & Kanwisher, 2000).

Further evidence comes from *transcranial magnetic stimulation* (TMS), a technique that we first described in Chapter 2. As its name implies, TMS creates a series of strong magnetic pulses at a specific location on the scalp; this causes a (temporary!) disruption in the brain region directly underneath this scalp area (Helmuth, 2001). In this fashion, it's possible to disrupt Area V1 temporarily in an otherwise normal brain; Area V1, recall, is the brain area where axons from the visual system first reach the occipital cortex (see Chapter 2). Not surprisingly, using TMS in this way causes problems in vision, but it also causes parallel problems in visual imagery, providing a powerful argument that Area V1 is crucial both for the processing of visual information and for the creation and maintenance of visual images (Kosslyn et al., 1999).

Still more evidence comes from studies of brain damage, and here, too, we find parallels between visual perception and visual imagery. For example, in some patients brain damage has disrupted the ability to perceive color; in most cases these patients also lose the ability to imagine scenes in color. Likewise, patients who, because of brain damage, have lost the ability to perceive fine detail seem also to lose the ability to visualize fine detail; and so on (Farah, Soso, & Dasheiff, 1992; Kosslyn, 1994; let's note, though, that we'll need to add some complications to this point later in the chapter).

Brain damage also causes parallels in how people *pay attention* to visual inputs and to visual images. In one case, a patient had suffered a stroke and, as a result, had developed the "neglect syndrome" we described in Chapter 4: If this patient was shown a picture, he seemed to see only the right side of it; if asked to read a word, he read only the right half. The same pattern of neglect was evident in the patient's imagery: In one test, the patient was urged to visualize a familiar plaza in his city and to list the buildings "in view" in the image. If the patient imagined himself standing at the northern edge of the plaza, he listed all the buildings on the plaza's western side (i.e., on his right), but none on the east-

NEGLECT SYNDROME IN VISUAL IMAGERY

Because of brain damage, a patient had developed the pattern (first discussed in Chapter 4) of unilateral neglect—*and so he paid attention only to the right half of the visual world. He showed the same pattern in his visual images: When asked to imagine himself standing at the southern edge of the Piazza Del Duomo, and to describe all he could "see" in his image, he only listed buildings on the Piazza's eastern side. When he imagined himself standing at the northern edge of the Piazza, he only listed buildings on the western side. In both cases, he neglected the left half of the (visualized) Piazza.*

ern. If the patient imagined himself standing on the southern edge of the plaza, he listed all the sights on the plaza's eastern side, but none on the western. In both cases, he neglected the left half of the imaged scene, just as he did with perceived scenes (Bisiach & Luzzatti, 1978; Bisiach, Luzzatti, & Perani, 1979).

Sensory Effects in Imagery

Clearly, then, the neural "machinery" needed for imagery overlaps with that needed for perception. If the machinery is occupied with one of these functions, it's not available for the other. If the machinery is disrupted (permanently, by a stroke, or temporarily, by TMS), then both activities are compromised. If we scrutinize activation patterns, we find that to a large extent the same brain structures are involved in visualizing and in vision. All of this indicates an intimate relationship between imagery and perception.

Because of these shared neural mechanisms, we might expect imagery and perception to *function* in similar ways, and research indicates that they do. The research, in other words, indicates a **functional equivalence** between many aspects of visual imagery and aspects of visual perception. For example, consider **visual acuity**—the ability to see fine detail. In vision, acuity is much greater at the center of the visual field than in the visual periphery. Can we find a comparable pattern in imagery? Is it easier to discern detail at the image's center than at its periphery?

In measurements of "two-point acuity," observers are shown two dots. If the dots are far enough apart, the observer can easily see that they're separate. When the dots are very close together, though, the observer has trouble seeing the gap between them, and so the dots seem to fuse together. We can assess acuity, therefore, by measuring how far apart the dots have to be before the observer can see that they're separate; this tells us how well the observer can perceive fine detail.

In vision, two-point acuity is greatest when people are looking directly at the dots; under these circumstances, even minuscule gaps can be detected. However, if we position the dots 10° away from someone's line of vision, acuity is far worse. What about imagery? In one study, participants were first shown two dots of the appropriate size. The dots were then removed, but participants were asked to imagine that the dots were still present. The participants then moved their eyes away from the (imagined) dots' position, and as they looked farther and farther away, they had to judge whether they could still "see" that the dots were separate. In this way, "two-point acuity" was measured with imaginary stimuli (Finke & Kosslyn, 1980).

The data show a remarkable correspondence between participants' performance with actually perceived dots and their performance with imagined dots. In both cases, acuity fell off abruptly if the dots were not in the center of vision; indeed, the pattern of falloff was virtually the same in perception and in imagery. Moreover, in vision, acuity falls off more rapidly if participants look above or below the two dots, rather than to the left or right. This pattern was also observed in the imagery condition. Thus, qualitatively and quantitatively, the imagery data match the perceptual data.

Spatial Images and Visual Images

We are building an impressive case, then, for a close relationship between imagery and perception. Indeed, the evidence so far implies that we can truly speak of imagery as being *visual* imagery, drawing on the same mechanisms and having the same traits as actual vision. Other results, however, add some complications.

A number of studies have examined imagery in people blind since birth (Carpenter & Eisenberg, 1978; Giudice, Betty & Loomis, 2011; Kerr, 1983; Marmor & Zabeck, 1976; also see Jonides, Kahn, & Rozin, 1975; Paivio & Okovita, 1971; Zimler & Keenan, 1983). Obviously, the procedures need to be adapted in important ways—so that (for example) the stimuli to be imaged are presented initially as sculptures to be explored with the hands, rather than as pictures to be examined visually. Once this is done, however, experimental procedures parallel to those we have described can be carried out with the blind—procedures examining how the blind scan across an image, for example, or how they imagine a form in rotation. And the data show what is by now a familiar pattern: In tests involving mental rotation or image scanning, blind individuals yield data quite similar to those obtained with sighted research participants, with response times being proportionate to the "distance" traveled, and so on.

It seems unlikely that people blind since birth are using a sense of what things "look like" to perform these tasks. Presumably, therefore, they have some other means of thinking about spatial layout and spatial relations. This "spatial imagery" might be represented in the mind in terms of a series of imagined movements, so that it is body imagery or motion imagery rather than visual imagery. Alternatively, perhaps spatial imagery is not tied to any sensory modality but is instead part of our broader cognition about spatial arrangements and layout.

One way or another, though, it looks like we need to distinguish between *visual* and *spatial* imagery. Visual imagery represents an arrangement or a shape in terms of how things *look*. Spatial imagery, we've just suggested, might represent arrangement or shapes in terms of *movements*, or *body feelings*, or perhaps in some more abstract format. Blind individuals presumably use spatial imagery to carry out the tasks we have been discussing in this chapter; it seems plausible that sighted people can use either visual or spatial imagery to carry out these tasks. (For a related distinction among several types of imagery, see Kosslyn & Thompson, 1999, 2003; for other data emphasizing the importance of the visual/spatial distinction, see Hegarty, 2004; Hegarty & Stull, 2012; Klauer & Zhao, 2004.)

This distinction between visual and spatial imagery is confirmed by neuroscience evidence. For example, fMRI data tell us that the brain areas activated for visual tasks are different from those activated by spatial tasks (Thompson, Slotnick, Burrage, & Kosslyn, 2009). Likewise, we've already noted the cases in which brain damage seems to produce similar patterns of disruption in seeing and imaging. Thus, patients who (because of brain damage) have lost their color vision also seem to lose the ability to imagine scenes in color; patients who have lost their ability to perceive motion also lose the ability to imagine movement. However, there are exceptions to this pattern—that is, cases in which brain damage causes problems in imagery but not perception, or vice versa. For example, Goldenberg, Müllbacher, and Nowak (1995) describe a patient whose bilateral occipital lobe lesions have produced blindness, but despite this profound deficit, the patient does well on many (but not all) imagery tasks. Similarly, investigators have documented a number of patients who do well on imagery tasks despite visual agnosia. Other patients show the pattern of neglect syndrome in their vision but not in their imagery (and other patients show the reverse—neglect in imagery but not in vision). And so on. (For discussion of these patients, see, for example, Bartolomeo et al., 1998; Behrmann, 2000; Logie & Della Sala, 2005; Servos & Goodale, 1995.)

This might seem like a contradictory data pattern—with brain damage sometimes causing similar problems in imagery and in perception, and sometimes not. However, there is no contradiction here. *Visual* imagery relies on brain areas also needed for vision, and so damage to these areas disrupts both imagery and vision. *Spatial* imagery, in contrast, relies on different brain areas, and so damage to visual areas won't interfere with this form of imagery, and damage to brain sites needed for this imagery won't interfere with vision.

Similar claims emerge if we zoom in for a closer look at the imagery tasks that brain-damaged individuals can or cannot do. A patient known as L.H., for example, suffered brain damage in an automobile accident and, as a result, now has enormous difficulty in tasks requiring judgments about visual appearance—for example, judgments about *color* (Farah, Hammond, Levine, & Calvanio, 1988). In contrast, L.H. performs well on tasks like image scanning or mental rotation. More generally, he shows little disruption on tasks requiring spatial manipulations or memory for spatial positions. To make sense of L.H.'s profile, therefore, it seems once again crucial to distinguish between visual tasks and spatial ones and, correspondingly, between visual imagery and spatial imagery.

Individual Differences

Multiple lines of evidence, therefore, suggest there are at least two types of imagery—one visual and one spatial—and, presumably, most people have the capacity for both types: They can "visualize" and they can "spatialize." But this invites a new question: When do people use one type of imagery, and when do they use the other?

To some extent, the answer depends on the task. For example, to think about *colors*, you need to imagine exactly what something *looks like*; it won't be enough just to think about shapes or spatial positions. In this case, therefore, you'll need visual imagery, not spatial. But in many other cases, either form of imagery will get the job done. (You can, for example, think about what a speck would *look like* as it zoomed across an imagined scene, or you can think about what it would *feel like* to move your finger across the scene.) In these cases, the choice between visual and spatial imagery will depend on other factors, including your preferences and the exact instructions you receive.

The choice between these forms of imagery will also be influenced by each individual's ability levels: Some people may be poor visualizers but good "spatializers," and they would surely rely on spatial imagery, not visual, in most tasks. And, of course, for other people, this pattern would be reversed.

How should we think about these differences from one person to the next? Recall Galton's data, mentioned early on in this chapter. If we take those data at face value, they imply that people differ markedly in their conscious experience of imaging. People with vivid imagery report that their images are truly picture-like—in color, quite detailed, and with all of the depicted objects viewed from a particular distance and a particular viewing angle. People without vivid imagery, in contrast, will say none of these things. Their images, they report, are not at all picture-like, and it's meaningless to ask them whether an image is in color or in black and white; their image simply isn't the sort of thing that could be in color or in black and white. Likewise, it's meaningless to ask whether their image is viewed from a particular perspective; their image is abstract in a way that makes this question inapplicable. In no sense, then, do these "non-imagers" feel like they're "seeing" with the "mind's eye." From their perspective, these figures of speech are (at best) loosely metaphorical. This stands in clear contrast to the reports offered by vivid imagers; for them, mental seeing really does seem like actual seeing.

Roughly 10% of the population will, in this fashion, "declare themselves entirely deficient in the power of seeing mental pictures" (Galton, 1883, p. 110). As William James (1890) put it, they "have no visual images at all worthy of the name" (p. 57).

But what should we make of this? Is it truly the case that members of our species differ in whether or not they're capable of experiencing visual images?

To explore this issue, a number of studies have compared "vivid imagers" and "non-imagers" on tasks that depend on mental imagery, with the obvious prediction that people with vivid imagery will do better in these tasks and those with sparse imagery will do worse. The results, however, have often been otherwise, with many studies finding no difference between vivid imagers and sparse imagers in how they do mental rotation, how quickly or accurately they scan across their images, and so on (e.g., Ernest, 1977; Katz, 1983; Marks, 1983; Richardson, 1980).

Notice, though, that when people describe their images as "vivid," they are rather specifically reporting how much their image experience is *like seeing*, and so the self-report, it seems, provides an assessment of *visual* imagery. In contrast, tasks like mental rotation or scanning can be performed with either spatial imagery or visual imagery. Perhaps it's unsurprising, therefore, that there's no relationship between this self-report and the performance of these tasks: The self-report is reflecting a capacity (visual imagery) that isn't at all necessary for the tasks.

On this basis, though, there should be a relationship between image vividness and how well people perform on tasks that really do require visual imagery. Consider, for example, the two-point acuity experiment already described. This experiment, at its heart, requires someone to imagine exactly what the two dots *would look like* if they were viewed from a certain angle. Therefore, it seems plausible that this task would be performed more accurately by people with clear visual imagery—and it is. People who describe their imagery as "vivid" yield data in this experiment in close correspondence to the perceptual data; people with less-vivid imagery do not show this correspondence (Finke & Kosslyn, 1980). Many other findings can be understood in similar terms (Cui, Jeter, Yang, Montague, & Eagleman, 2006; Kozhevnikov, Kosslyn, & Shephard, 2005; McKelvie, 1995; Pearson, Rademaker & Tong, 2011).

All of this suggests that imagery self-reports do reveal genuine differences from one person to the next in the quality of their imagery experience. Again, these differences are differences in *visual* imagery, and so relevant to performance only if the task requires visual imagery. But, in any case, this point invites many questions: How do these differences in experience influence people outside of the laboratory, away from experimenters' tasks? What can people "with imagery" do that people "without imagery" cannot? There is, as just one illustration, some suggestion that these differences among people may determine their career choices: Visual imagers are likely to succeed in the arts; people with spatial imagery may be better suited to careers in science or engineering (Kozhevnikov et al., 2005). These are tantalizing suggestions, and they are obviously a target for further research.

Eidetic Imagery

For people with vivid imagery, it is surprising to hear that other individuals (including the author of this book!) seem to lack this capacity. But the differences among people are just as striking if we consider variation in the other direction: people who have "super-skills" in imagery.

FIGURE 10.6 | EIDETIC IMAGERY

Eidetic imagery is vastly more detailed than ordinary imagery. In one study (Haber, 1969), a 10-year-old was shown a picture like this one for 30 seconds. After the picture was taken away, the boy was unexpectedly asked detail questions: How many stripes were there on the cat's back? How many leaves on the front flower? The child was able to give completely accurate answers, as though his memory had perfectly preserved the picture's content.

There is a lot of folklore associated with the idea of "photographic memory," but this term needs to be defined carefully: Some people have fabulously detailed, wonderfully long-lasting memories, but without any "photographic" quality in their memory. These people often use careful rehearsal, or complex, well-practiced mnemonics, to remember the value of pi to a hundred decimal places, or the names of a hundred people they've just met—but these memories are not in any way "visual," and imagery is not necessary for these memorization strategies.

Other people, in contrast, do seem to have exquisitely detailed imagery that can indeed be described as "photographic," and researchers refer to this type of imagery as **eidetic imagery**, and people with this skill are called *eidetikers*. This form of imagery is sometimes found in people who have been diagnosed as autistic: These individuals can glance at a complex scene, and then draw incredibly detailed reproductions of the scene, as though they really had taken a "photograph" of the scene when first viewing it. Likewise, Stromeyer (1982) described a woman who could recall poetry written in a language she did not understand, even years after she'd seen the poem; she was also able to recall complicated random dot patterns after viewing them only briefly. Similarly, Haber (1969; also Haber & Haber, 1988) showed a picture like Figure 10.6 to a 10-year-old eidetiker for just 30 seconds. After the picture was taken away, the boy was unexpectedly asked detail questions: How many stripes were there on the cat's back? How many leaves on the front flower? The child was able to give completely accurate answers, as though his memory had perfectly preserved the picture's content.

However, we know remarkably little about this form of imagery. We do know that this capacity is rare. We know that some people who claim to have this

Hamlet: *My father—methinks I see my father—*
Horatio: *Where, my lord?*
Hamlet: *In my mind's eye, Horatio.*

(Hamlet, *Act 1, scene 2.*)

William Shakespeare is often credited with being the originator of the phrase "the mind's eye."

capacity do not: They often *do* have fabulous memories, but they rely on mnemonics, not some special form of imagery. But, beyond these obvious points, this remains a truly intriguing phenomenon in need of further research.

Images Are Not Pictures

Let's return, though, to more "normal" (at least, more ordinary) forms of imagery. At many points in this chapter, we've referred to mental images (especially *visual* images) as "mental pictures." That comparison is hardly new; the phrase "the mind's eye" was coined by Shakespeare four centuries ago and is embedded in the way most of us talk about our imagery. And, as we've seen, the comparison is in several ways appropriate: Visual images do depict a scene in a fashion that seems quite pictorial. In other ways, though, this comparison may be misleading.

We've already seen that mental images can represent three-dimensional figures and so may be more like mental sculptures than mental pictures. We've also distinguished visual images and spatial images, and so *some* images are like pictures to be explored with the mind's eye, and other images are not. But, on top of these points, there is a further complication. To introduce this issue, let's review some points we first raised in Chapter 3, and with that, an example we first met in that chapter. Figure 10.7 shows the figure known as the Necker cube (see also Figure 3.1 on page 78). The drawing of this cube—the stimulus itself—is ambiguous: It can be understood as a depiction of a cube viewed from above, or it can be understood as a depiction a cube viewed from below. The picture itself, in other words, doesn't specify in any way which of these two cubes it shows, and so, in this sense, the picture is neutral with regard to interpretation—and fully compatible with either interpretation.

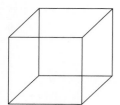

FIGURE 10.7 | THE NECKER CUBE

The cube can be perceived as if viewed from above or as if viewed from below.

Unlike the picture, though, our *perception* of the cube is not neutral, is not indeterminate with regard to depth. Instead, at any moment in time we perceive the cube as having one arrangement in depth or another. Our perception, in other words, "goes beyond the information given" by specifying a configuration in depth, a specification that in this case supplements an ambiguous drawing in order to create an unambiguous perception.

As we discussed in Chapter 3, the configuration in depth is just one of the ways that perception goes beyond the information given in a stimulus. Our perception of a stimulus also specifies a figure/ground organization, the form's orientation (e.g., identifying the form's "top"), and so on. These specifications serve to organize the form and have an enormous impact on the subjective appearance of the form, and with that, what the form is seen to resemble and what the form will evoke in memory.

We need to be clear, then, that our **percepts** (i.e., our mental representations of the stimuli we're perceiving) are in some ways similar to pictures, but in other ways different. Like pictures, percepts are *depictions*, representing key aspects of the three-dimensional layout of the world. Percepts, in other words, are not descriptions of a stimulus; instead, percepts, just like pictures, show directly what a stimulus looks like. At the same time, percepts are in some ways different from pictures: They are organized and unambiguous in a fashion that pictures are not.

What about visual images? Are they just like pictures—neutral with regard to organization, and so open to different interpretations? Or are they organized in the way percepts seem to be, and so, in a sense, already interpreted? One line of evidence comes from studies of ambiguous figures. In one experiment, participants were first shown a series of practice stimuli to make sure that they understood what it meant to reinterpret an ambiguous figure (Chambers & Reisberg, 1985). They were then shown a drawing of one more ambiguous figure (such as the Necker cube in Figure 10.7 or the duck/rabbit in Figure 10.8); then, after this figure had been removed from view, they were asked to form a mental image of it. Once the image was formed, they were asked if they could reinterpret this image, just as they had reinterpreted the practice figures.

The results are easily summarized. Across several experiments, not one of the participants succeeded in reinterpreting his or her images: They reliably failed to find the duck in a "rabbit image" or the rabbit in a "duck image." Is it possible that they didn't understand their task, or perhaps didn't remember the figure? To rule out these possibilities, participants were given a blank piece of paper immediately after their failure at reinterpreting their images and were asked to draw the figure based on their image. Now, looking at their own drawings, all of the participants were able to reinterpret the configuration in the appropriate way.

FIGURE 10.8 | **THE DUCK/RABBIT**

If people are visualizing this ambiguous figure, they have great difficulty reinterpreting it. That is, people imaging the "duck" have great difficulty in discovering the "rabbit"; people imaging the "rabbit" have great difficulty in discovering the "duck." Of course, once someone knows that both interpretations are possible, he can hop from one to the other. What seems enormously difficult, though, is discovering the alternative interpretation of the imaged figure in the first place.

Thus, we have 100% failure in reinterpreting these forms with images, and 100% success a moment later with drawings.

Apparently, therefore, what participants "see" in their image (even if it's a *visual* image, not a spatial one) is not a "picture"—neutral with regard to interpretation, and so open to new interpretations. Instead, images are inherently organized, just as percepts are. As such, images are entirely unambiguous and strongly resistant to reinterpretation. (For more on these issues, see Peterson, Kihlstrom, Rose, & Glisky, 1992; Thompson, Kosslyn, Hoffman, & Kooij, 2008; for a discussion on how image-based discovery is used in a real-world setting, see Verstijnen, Hennessey, van Leeuwen, Hamel, & Goldschmidt, 1998; Verstijnen, van Leeuwen, Goldschmidt, Hamel, & Hennessey, 1998).

WORKBOOK
DEMONSTRATION 10.1

Images and Pictures: An Interim Summary

Images, both visual and spatial, provide a distinctive means of representing the world, and so *visualizing* a robot (for example) is quite different from thinking about the word "robot," or merely contemplating the idea "robot." As one key difference, images are, without question, like pictures in the fact that images show exactly what

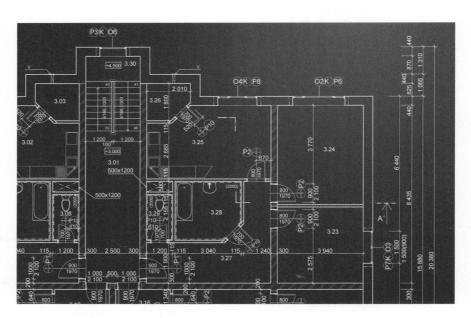

CHANGING A FRAME OF REFERENCE

In many professions—architecture, for example—designers visualize *the early stages of their ideas without needing to sketch the designs on paper. Research suggests, though, that there may be limits on this image-based process and that some discoveries are much more likely if the designers put their ideas down on paper and then inspect the drawings. This is because the drawing, on its own, has no interpretive "reference frame," making it much easier for the designer to impose a new reference frame.*

a form looks like. Visualizing a robot, therefore, will highlight the robot's appearance in your thoughts and make it much more likely that you'll be reminded of other forms having a similar appearance. Thinking about the robot without an image might not highlight appearance and so will probably call different ideas to mind.

Creating an image will also make some attributes of a form more prominent and others less so (the cat's head, for example, rather than its whiskers—see pp. 366–7). This, too, can influence what further ideas the image calls to mind, and so, again, putting your thoughts into imagery can literally shape the flow and sequence of your ideas.

At the same time, we've highlighted ways in which images are *not* picture-like: Images, it seems, are inherently organized in a fashion that pictures are not, and this organization can itself influence the sequence of your thoughts—with your understanding of the image (your understanding of where its "top" and "front" are, your understanding of its figure/ground organization, and so on) guiding which discoveries will, and which will not, easily flow from an image.

Where does all this leave us? Images have a great deal in common with pictures, but they are also different from pictures in important ways. Thus, the common phrase "mental pictures" is misleading, although, unmistakably, mental images are certainly picture-*like*. And, above all, we need to keep track of both sides of this story—the resemblances between images and pictures, and also the differences—if we are to understand how imagery functions in shaping our thoughts.

Long-Term Visual Memory

So far, our discussion has focused on "active" images—images currently being contemplated, images presumably held in working memory. What about visual information in long-term memory? For example, if you wish to form an image of an elephant, you need to draw on your knowledge of what an elephant looks like. What is this knowledge, and how is it represented in long-term storage? Likewise, if you recognize a picture as familiar, this is probably because you've detected a "match" between it and some memory of an earlier-viewed picture. What is the nature of this memory?

Image Information in Long-Term Memory

In earlier chapters, we suggested that your concept of "birthday" (for example) is represented by some number of nodes in long-term memory. Perhaps we can adapt this proposal to account for long-term storage of visual information (and likewise information for the other sensory modalities).

One possibility is that nodes in long-term memory represent entire, relatively complete pictures. Thus, to form a mental image of an elephant, you would activate the ELEPHANT PICTURE nodes; to scrutinize an image of your father's face, you would activate the FATHER'S FACE nodes; and so on.

However, evidence speaks against this idea (e.g., Kosslyn, 1980, 1983). Instead, images seem to be stored in memory in a piecemeal fashion. To form an image,

This picture shows "three rows of dots." The same picture also shows "four columns of dots." There is, in short, no difference between a picture of rows and a picture of columns. There is a difference, however, between a mental image of "three rows of dots" and a mental image of "four columns of dots." The latter image, for example, takes longer to generate and is more difficult to maintain, presumably because it contains a larger number of units—four columns, rather than three rows.

therefore, you first have to activate the nodes specifying the "image frame," which depicts the form's global shape. Then elaborations can be added to this frame, if you wish, to create a full and detailed image.

Many research results support this claim. First, images containing *more parts* take longer to create, just as we would expect if images are formed on a piece-by-piece basis (see Figure 10.9). Second, images containing *more detail* also take longer to create, in accord with our hypothesis. Third, we know that imagers have some degree of control over how complete and detailed their images will be, so that (depending on the task, the imagers' preferences, etc.) images can be quite sketchy or quite elaborate (Reisberg, 1996). This variation is easily explained if imagers first create an image frame and only then add as much detail as they want.

But how does the imager know *how to* construct the image—what its form should be and what it should include? The relevant information is drawn from **image files** in long-term memory. Each file contains the information needed in order to create a mental image—information about how to create the image frame, and then information about how to elaborate the frame in this way or that, if desired. How is this information represented within the image file? One proposal is that the image files contain something like a set of instructions, or even a "recipe," for creating an image. By analogy, someone could instruct you in how to create a picture by uttering the appropriate sentences: "In the top left, place a circle. Underneath it, draw a line, angling down . . ." Such instructions would allow you to create a picture, but notice that there is nothing pictorial about the instructions themselves; the instructions are sentences, not pictures. In the same way, the instructions within an image file allow you to create a representation that, as we have repeatedly seen, is picture-like in important ways. In long-term memory, however, this information may not be at all picture-like.

Verbal Coding of Visual Materials

The proposal before us, therefore, is that visual information is represented in long-term memory in a fashion that isn't itself "visual." Instead, visual information may be represented in long-term memory via propositions, and these provide a "recipe" to be used, when needed, for creating an image.

In some cases, though, visual information is represented in long-term storage in an even simpler format—namely, a verbal label. This point is relevant to issues we met in Chapter 9, concerning the interplay between language and thought. Specifically, evidence tells us that individuals with large color vocabularies have better color memories, probably because they're remembering the verbal label for the color rather than the color itself, and it's easier to remember a word than it is to recall a tint.

A related point was made in a classic study by Carmichael, Hogan, and Walters (1932). Their research participants were shown pictures like those in the center column of Figure 10.10. Half of the participants were shown the top form and told, "This is a picture of eyeglasses." The other half were told, "This is a picture of a barbell." Later, the participants were asked to reproduce these pictures, as

FIGURE 10.10 | THE INFLUENCE OF VERBAL LABELS ON
VISUAL MEMORY

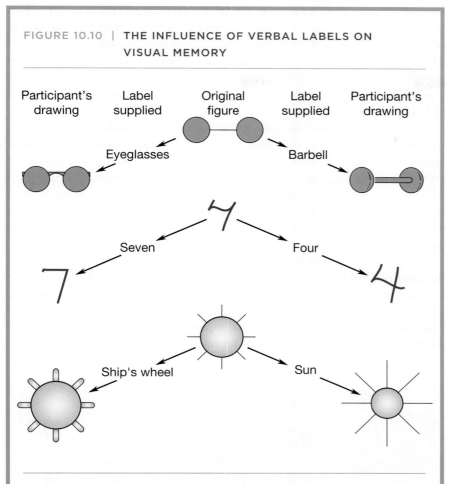

Participants were shown the figures in the middle column. If the top figure was presented with the label "eyeglasses," participants were later likely to reproduce the figure as shown on the left. If the figure was presented with the label "barbell," they were likely to reproduce it as shown on the right. (And so on for the other figures.) One interpretation of these data is that participants were remembering the verbal label and not the drawing itself, and then, at the time of the test, they reconstructed what the drawing must have been based on the remembered label. (After Carmichael, Hogan, & Walters, 1932)

carefully as they could, and those who had understood the picture as eyeglasses produced drawings that resembled eyeglasses; those who understood the picture as weights distorted their drawings appropriately. This is again what one would expect if the participants had memorized the description rather than the picture itself, and were re-creating the picture on the basis of this description.

It seems, then, that in some cases visual information may be stored in memory, not via imagery but as a description of the previously viewed object. A similar message emerges from tasks that require participants to reason about spatial position. In one study, participants were asked, "Which is farther north: Seattle or Montreal? Which is farther west: Reno, Nevada; or San Diego, California?" Many participants responded that Montreal is farther north and that San Diego is farther west, but both of these responses are wrong. Montreal, for example, is at roughly the same latitude as Portland, Oregon, a city almost 200 miles south of Seattle (Stevens & Coupe, 1978).

These errors arise because participants seem to be reasoning this way: "Montreal is in Canada; Seattle is in the United States. Canada is north of the United States. Therefore, Montreal must be farther north than Seattle." This kind of reasoning is sensible, since it will often bring you to the correct answer. (That's because most parts of Canada are, in fact, farther north than most parts of the United States.) Even so, this reasoning will sometimes lead to error, and it does so in this case. (The logic is obviously the same for the Reno/San Diego question.)

Of course, what is of interest here is not the participants' knowledge about the longitude and latitude of these particular cities. What is important is that the sort of reasoning revealed in these studies hinges on propositional knowledge, and not on any sort of mental images or maps. Apparently, at least some of our spatial knowledge relies on a symbolic/propositional code. (For more on reasoning about geography, see Friedman & Brown, 2000a, 2000b.)

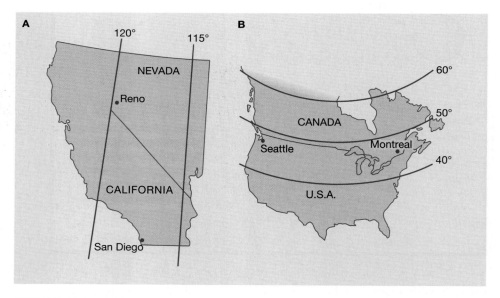

CONCEPTUAL MENTAL MAPS

Research participants tend to judge San Diego to be west of Reno and Montreal to be north of Seattle. But these judgments are in error. (A) A map of California and Nevada with lines of longitude, which show that, in fact, San Diego is east of Reno. (B) A map of the United States and southern Canada with lines of latitude, which show that Seattle is slightly north of Montreal.

Imagery Helps Memory

No matter how images are stored in long-term memory, however, it's clear that images influence memory in important ways and, in general, imagery improves memory. For example, materials that evoke imagery are considerably easier to remember than materials that do not evoke imagery. This can be demonstrated in many ways, including the following two-step procedure. First, participants are presented with a list of nouns and asked to rate each noun, on a scale from 1 to 7, for how readily it evokes an image (Paivio, 1969; Paivio, Yuille, & Madigan, 1968). Examples of words receiving high ratings are "church," with an average rating of 6.63, and "elephant," rated at 6.83. Words receiving lower ratings include "context" (2.13) and "virtue" (3.33).

As a second step, we ask whether these imagery ratings, generated by one group of participants, can be used to predict memory performance with a new group of participants. The new participants are asked to memorize lists of words, using the words for which we have imagery ratings. The data reliably indicate that participants learn high-imagery words more readily than low-imagery words (Paivio, 1969; Paivio, Smythe, & Yuille, 1968).

In the same fashion, memory can be enormously aided by the use of imagery mnemonics. In one study, some participants were asked to learn pairs of words by rehearsing each pair silently. Other participants were instructed to make up a sentence for each pair of words, linking the words in some sensible way. Finally, other participants were told to form a mental image for each pair of words, with the image combining the words in some interaction. The results showed poorest recall performance by the rehearsal group, and intermediate performance by the group that generated the sentences. Both of these groups, though, did appreciably worse than the imagery group (Bower & Winzenz, 1970; for discussion of other mnemonic techniques, see Chapter 5).

WORKBOOK
DEMONSTRATION 10.2

If forming images helps memory, does it matter what sort of image you create? Quite reliably, memory is best if the images you form show the objects to be remembered *interacting* in some way, and not just side by side (Wollen, Weber, & Lowry, 1972). This is not surprising: As we saw in Chapter 5, memory is improved in general if you can find ways to organize the material; interacting images provide one means of achieving this organization.

In addition, it's sometimes suggested that imagery mnemonics are most effective if the mental "picture" is in some fashion *bizarre*, rather than just showing some ordinary interaction. Evidence for this point, is mixed, however, with some studies showing an effect of bizarreness and some studies showing the opposite. The explanation for this mixed pattern probably lies in the *sequence* of stimuli employed in these studies. If participants see only a succession of bizarre images, one after another, they cease thinking of the images as bizarre, and so bizarreness has no impact on the data. If, instead, the bizarre images are mixed together with more-common images, the bizarreness is noticed and contemplated, leading to a memory improvement. (For reviews, see Einstein, McDaniel, & Lackey, 1989; McDaniel & Einstein, 1986, 1990.)

Dual Coding

There's no question, then, that imagery improves memory. But why is this? What memory aid does imagery provide?

One proposal is that imageable materials, such as high-imagery words, will be doubly represented in memory: The word itself will be remembered, and so will the corresponding picture. This pattern is referred to as **dual coding**, and its advantage should be obvious: When the time comes to retrieve these memories, either record—the verbal or the image—will provide the information you seek. This gives you a double chance of locating the information you need, thereby easing the process of memory search.

Of course, framing things in this way builds on the idea that you have (at least) two types of information in long-term storage: memories that represent the content of symbolic (and perhaps verbal) materials, and memories that represent imagery-based materials. Paivio (1971), the source of the dual-coding proposal, argues that these two types of memory differ from each other in important ways—including the information that they contain, and also the ways they are accessed. Access to symbolic memories, he suggests, is easiest if the cue provided is a word, as in, "Do you know the word 'squirrel'?" Access to an image-based memory, in contrast, is easiest if one begins with a picture: "Do you recognize this pictured creature?" Moreover, Paivio argues, some types of information—for example, semantic associations—are more easily stored via symbolic memories. Other types of information, such as information about size or shape, are more readily accessed from the remembered images. (Also see Paivio & Csapo, 1969; Yuille, 1983.)

Memory for Pictures

Paivio (1971) also proposed that there are two separate memory systems: one containing the symbolic memories, the other containing images. However, many psychologists are skeptical about this claim, arguing instead that there's just one long-term memory, holding both of these types of information (and perhaps other types as well). Within this single memory, each type of content does have its own traits, its own pattern of functioning. But, even with these differences, the two types of information are contained in a unified memory—much as a single library building, with one indexing system and one set of rules, can hold both books and photographs, sound recordings as well as videos. (For discussion of this point, see Heil, Rösler, & Hennighausen, 1994.)

On this basis, we would expect the two types of memory to have many traits in common, thanks to the fact that both reside within a single memory system. This expectation turns out to be correct, and so many of the claims we made in Chapters 5, 6, and 7 apply with equal force to visual memories and verbal memories. Recall of both memory types, for example, is dependent on memory connections; priming effects can be observed with both types of memory; encoding specificity is observed in both domains; and so on.

Likewise, visual memory (like memory in general) is heavily influenced by schema-based, generic knowledge—knowledge about how events unfold in general. Chapter 7 described how these knowledge effects influence memory for sentences and stories, but similar effects can easily be demonstrated with pictures. In an early study, Friedman (1979) showed participants pictures of scenes such as a typical kitchen or a typical barnyard. In addition, the pictures also contained some unexpected objects. The kitchen picture, for example, included some items rarely found in a kitchen, such as a fireplace. Participants were later given a recognition test in which they had to discriminate between pictures they'd actually seen and altered versions of these pictures in which something had been changed.

Participants' memories were plainly influenced by their broader knowledge of what "should be" included in a kitchen picture. Thus, in some of the test pictures, one of the ordinary, expected, objects in the scene had been changed—and so, for example, participants might be shown a test picture in which a different kind of stove appeared in place of the original stove, or one in which the toaster on the counter was replaced by a radio. Participants rarely noticed these changes, and thus tended (incorrectly) to respond that this new picture was in fact "old"—i.e., had been seen before. This is sensible on schema grounds: Both the original and altered pictures were fully consistent with the kitchen schema, so both would be compatible with a schema-based memory.

However, participants almost always noticed changes to the unexpected objects in the scene. If the originally viewed kitchen had a fireplace and the test picture did not, participants consistently detected this alteration. Again, this is predictable on schema grounds: The fireplace did not fit with the kitchen schema and so was likely to be specifically noted in memory. In fact, Friedman recorded participants' eye movements during the original presentations of the pictures. Her data showed that participants tended to look twice as long at the unexpected objects as they did at the expected ones; clearly, these objects did catch the participants' attention. (For more on schema guidance of eye movements, see Henderson & Hollingworth, 2003; Vo & Henderson, 2009.)

A different line of evidence also shows schema effects in picture memory. Recall our claim that, in understanding a story, people place the story within a schematic frame. As we saw in Chapter 7, this can often lead to intrusion errors, as people import their own expectations and understanding into the story, and thus end up remembering the story as including more than it actually did.

A similar pattern can be demonstrated with picture memory, in a phenomenon known as **boundary extension** (Intraub & Bodamer, 1993; Intraub & Dickinson, 2008; Intraub, Gottesman, & Bills, 1998; Intraub, Hoffman, Wetherhold, & Stoehs, 2006). That is, people remember a picture as including more than it actually did, in effect extending the boundaries of the remembered depiction. For example, participants shown the top panel in Figure 10.11 were later asked to sketch what they had seen. Two of the participants' drawings are shown at the bottom of

Figure 10.11, and the boundary extension is clear: Participants remember the scene as less of a close-up view than it actually was, and correspondingly, they remember the scene as containing more of the backdrop than it did. This effect is observed whether participants initially see a few pictures or many, whether they are tested immediately or after a delay, and even when they are explicitly warned about boundary extension and urged to avoid this effect.

Intraub has argued that this boundary extension arises from the way in which people perceive these pictures in the first place: People understand a picture, she claims, by means of a perceptual schema. This schema places the picture in a larger context, informing the perceiver about the real-world scene only partially revealed by the picture. Intraub suggests that this leads people to a series of expectations about what they might see if they could somehow look beyond the picture's edges, and these expectations become part of the experience of viewing

FIGURE 10.11 | BOUNDARY EXTENSION IN PICTURE MEMORY

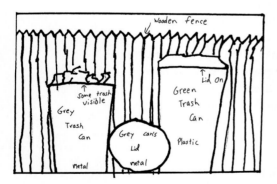

Participants were initially shown the photograph at the top of this figure. The two panels below show the scene as drawn from memory by two different participants. The participants clearly recalled the scene as a wide-angle shot, revealing more of the background than it actually did. (After Intraub & Richardson, 1989)

the picture. It's then the *experience* that is remembered—and so your memory includes both the picture itself, and also your understanding of what you'd see if you explored further—leading to the boundary extension that reliably emerges in the data.

Overall, then, it looks like picture memory follows the same rules and is influenced by the same factors, as memory for verbal materials. Schema effects, we've just seen, can be found in both domains. Similarly, participants show primacy and recency effects when they learn a series of pictures (Tabachnick & Brotsky, 1976), just as they do when they learn a series of words (Chapter 5). Spread of activation can be demonstrated with nonverbal materials (Kroll & Potter, 1984), just as it can be with verbal materials (Chapter 8). In short, there's considerable commonality between picture memory and memory of other sorts, confirming our suggestion of a single memory system, a system that holds diverse contents but with a uniform set of operating principles.

The Diversity of Knowledge

Notice, then, where the data are leading us: When you're thinking about an image—and thus holding the image in working memory—there's no question that you're considering a distinctive form of mental representation. Images in working memory contain different information than other representations do; they make different information prominent; they require a set of operations (like scanning, or rotation, or zooming) that are irrelevant to other sorts of memory contents. Hence our theorizing about active images has to be different from our theorizing about other forms of representation.

The situation is different, however, when we turn to long-term memory and consider your long-term retention for what a circus clown looks like or your recollection of what an earlier-viewed picture contained. The *content* of these memories is different from, say, your memory for stories. But even so, the image-based memories seem to be stored in the same memory system as every other memory—and so are influenced by exactly the same principles. In support of this claim, we can find many commonalities in the ways people remember diverse types of knowledge. We've mentioned some of these commonalities already, but, in addition, let's add that memory for faces benefits from rehearsal (Sporer, 1988), just as memory for stories does. Similarly, a separation between *familiarity* and *source memory* (see Chapter 6) can be demonstrated for remembered music or remembered faces (Brigham & Cairns, 1988; Brown, Deffenbacher, & Sturgill, 1977), just as it can be for remembered words. And so on.

It would appear, therefore, that there really is just one long-term memory, with a set of rules consistently applicable to all its diverse contents. However, we should attach one caution to this claim. In this chapter, we've focused on visual memories, and one might well ask whether similar conclusions would emerge with other categories of knowledge. For example, do memories for tastes or smells benefit from rehearsal, show schema effects, and the like? Do memories for emotions or for pain benefit from deep processing? Do they show the effects we

WORKBOOK
DEMONSTRATION 10.3

called (in Chapter 6) "implicit memory" effects? Relatively little research speaks to these issues.

It's on this basis, then, that the claims about the singularity of long-term memory should remain tentative, and that is one of the reasons that, throughout this chapter, our agenda has been both substantive and methodological. We've obviously surveyed what is known about visual imagery and visual memory, but, at the same time, we've tried to illustrate the questions that you might ask, and the methods you might use, in exploring other types of knowledge—asking whether the content is distinctive in working memory, and what evidence we'd need in order to propose a separate system within long-term memory. We've seen how things stand on these issues with regard to visual materials. However, the field awaits additional data before these issues can be resolved for other modalities.

CHAPTER SUMMARY

- People differ enormously in how they describe their imagery experience, particularly the vividness of that experience. However, concerns about how we should interpret these self-reports have led investigators to seek more objective means of studying mental imagery.

- Chronometric studies indicate that the pattern of what information is more available and what is less available in an image closely matches the pattern of what is available in an actual picture. Likewise, the times needed to scan across an image, to zoom in on an image to examine detail, or to imagine the form rotating all correspond closely to the times needed for these operations with actual pictures. These results emerge even when the experimenter makes no mention of imagery, ruling out an account of these data in terms of the demand character of the experiments.

- In many settings, visual imagery seems to involve mechanisms that overlap with those used for visual perception. This is reflected in the fact that imaging one thing can make it difficult to perceive something else, or that imaging the appropriate target can prime a subsequent perception. Visual images also show sensory effects similar to those observed in vision. Further evidence comes from neuroimaging and studies of brain damage; this evidence confirms the considerable overlap between the biological basis for imagery and that for perception.

- Not all imagery, however, is visual, so that we need to distinguish between *visual* and *spatial* imagery. This proposal is confirmed by studies of individuals with brain damage, some of whom seem to lose the capacity for visual imagery but retain their capacity for spatial imagery. This proposal may also help us understand the pattern of individual differences in imagery ability, with some individuals being particularly skilled in visual imagery, and some in spatial.

- Just as some individuals seem to have little or no visual imagery, other individuals—called eidetikers—seem to have fabulously detailed, photographic imagery. There is no question that this astonishingly vivid imagery exists in some people, but the mechanisms behind it remain unknown.

- Even when imagery is visual, mental images are picture-*like*, and not actually pictures. Unlike pictures, mental images seem to be accompanied by a perceptual reference frame that guides the interpretation of the image and also influences what can be discovered about the image.

- To create a mental image, you draw on information stored in an image file in long-term memory. These image files can be thought of as "recipes" for the construction of a mental image, usually by first constructing a frame and then by elaborating the frame as needed. In addition, at least some information about visual appearance or spatial arrangement is stored in long-term memory in terms of verbal labels or conceptual frameworks. For example, information about the locations of cities may be stored in terms of propositions ("Montreal is in Canada; Canada is north of the United States") rather than being stored in some sort of mental map.

- Imagery helps people to remember, and so word lists are more readily recalled if the words are easily imaged; similarly, instructions to form images help people to memorize. These benefits may be the result of dual coding: storing information in both a verbal format and a format that encodes appearances; this approach doubles the chances of recalling the material later on.

- When you're trying to remember combinations of ideas, it is best to imagine the objects to be remembered interacting in some way. There has been some dispute over whether bizarre images are more easily remembered than ordinary images, and evidence suggests that bizarre images will have an advantage only if the other images to be remembered are not bizarre.

- Memory for pictures can be accurate, but it follows most of the same rules as any other form of memory; for example, it is influenced by schematic knowledge.

- It is unclear what other categories of memory there may be. In each case, other kinds of memory are likely to have some properties that are distinctive and also many properties that are shared with memories of other sorts.

The Workbook Connection

See the *Cognition Workbook* for further exploration of visual knowledge:

- Demonstration 10.1: Imaged Synthesis
- Demonstration 10.2: Mnemonic Strategies
- Demonstration 10.3: Auditory Imagery

- Research Methods: Expectations, Motivation, and Demand
- Cognitive Psychology and Education: Using Imagery
- Cognitive Psychology and the Law: Lineups

NEED HELP STUDYING?

 wwnorton.com/studyspace

Visit StudySpace to access free review material such as
- Chapter study plans
- Quizzes
- Flashcards, and more

Go to **wwnorton.com/zaps** for these online labs:
- Mental Scanning
- Mental Rotation 2-D
- Mental Rotation 3-D

Thinking

M any people believe that the capacity for complex *thought* is what makes us human. And there's no question that we rely on this capacity all the time. We draw conclusions—about whether a friend is trustworthy; whether Volvos are especially safe; whether drinking red wine leads to headaches the next morning. We make choices—to go to this college or that; to buy an iPhone or a Droid; to get married or not. We solve problems—whether it's figuring out a way to repair a bicycle or finding a means to restore a damaged friendship.

But how do we achieve these things? How do we think? And how *well* do we think? In this section, we'll see that human thinking is often flawed, and we'll encounter examples of bad judgment, improper reasoning, and highly inefficient problem solving.

What produces this poor performance? The answer is not laziness or stupidity; instead, the answer reflects a theme that has already arisen in our discussion: In a wide range of settings, humans rely on mental shortcuts—strategies that are efficient but risk error. These shortcuts played an important part in Chapter 3, when we discussed object recognition; in Chapter 7, when we discussed memory errors; and in Chapter 8, when we discussed categorization. Similar shortcuts will emerge in this section, and as we'll see, they play a central (and sometimes destructive) role in guiding human thought.

However, let's not overemphasize these shortcomings in human thinking, because it's also clear that, in many circumstances, people rise above the shortcuts and think carefully and well! This will, at the least, drive us toward a multilayered conception of thinking, because we'll need to describe both the shortcuts that people use and also the more careful strategies that people often turn to. In addition, we'll need to tackle the obvious questions of *why and when* people rely on one sort of thinking or the other. What are the circumstances, or what are the reasons, that lead to efficient-but-risky thinking, and what are the triggers for slower-but-better thinking?

It's also important that people seem to differ in their thinking: Some people are wonderfully logical, others seem capricious. Some people are creative problem solvers, others are stymied by even simple problems. Some people seem fabulously intelligent, others seem less so. In this section, we'll tackle these differences as well.

Finally, one other set of issues will arise in this section: How much of thought is conscious? Are there benefits associated with conscious thought, as opposed to unconscious thought? We will tackle these questions in Chapter 13, but we'll do this largely by pulling together points we've made in earlier chapters; in this way, Chapter 13 will provide something of a review for the text at the same time that it tackles a series of enormously important theoretical questions.

CHAPTER ELEVEN

Judgment and Reasoning

The activity of "thinking" takes many forms. For a start, people often draw conclusions from their experiences—conclusions about a friend's personality, or where in town to get the best pizza, or whether the weather is generally decent in Chicago. Can we count on these conclusions? How exactly—and how well—do people learn from experience?

Then, once people have drawn a conclusion, they often take another step—trying to think through the implications of their new belief. What does this process look like?

Then, finally, people make countless decisions every day. Many of the decisions are trivial. (Soup or salad? Wear the blue shirt or the red? Coke or Pepsi?) But other decisions can change their lives—when, for example, they decide where to go school, whether to marry, and more. What mental processes govern these decisions?

In this chapter, we'll tackle these issues, asking how these various processes unfold, and also how *well*—that is, how good a job people do of drawing conclusions, or reasoning things through. We'll also consider what steps we can take to make people better, more critical, more astute thinkers.

- In a wide range of circumstances, people use cognitive shortcuts, or "heuristics," to make judgments. These heuristics tend to be relatively efficient and often lead to sensible conclusions. However, heuristic use can lead to error.

- People use these heuristics even when they're trying to be careful in their judgment, and even when they're highly motivated to be accurate. The heuristics are used both by experts and by ordinary people, and so expert judgments, too, are vulnerable to error.

- However, heuristic use is far from inevitable, and in some circumstances people rely on more sophisticated forms of reasoning—and so they judge covariation accurately, are sensitive to base rates, are alert to the problems of drawing a conclusion from a small sample of evidence, and so on.

- We will consider when people use their more sophisticated ("System 2") reasoning and when they rely on heuristics ("System 1"). Evidence suggests that System 2 comes into play only if the circumstances are right and only if the case being judged contains the appropriate triggers for this form of reasoning.

- The quality of people's thinking is also uneven when we turn to the broad domain of deduction.

- For example, people often show a pattern of "confirmation bias" and so are more sensitive to, and more accepting of, evidence that supports their beliefs than they are of evidence that challenges their beliefs.

- Errors in logical reasoning are also easy to document, and these errors follow patterns suggesting that people are guided by principles other than those of logic. In fact, people's reasoning is heavily influenced by the *content* of what they're reasoning about, although the exact reasons for this remain uncertain.

- People seem not to base their decisions on utility calculations; this is evident in the fact that many factors (including the decision's frame) have a strong impact on decisions, even though these factors do not change utilities in any way. Instead, people seem to make decisions that they feel they can explain and justify, and so are influenced by factors that make one choice or another seem more compelling.

- Another factor influencing decision making is emotion, but here the complication is that people are often inept in predicting their future emotions and so work hard to avoid regret that they wouldn't have felt anyhow, and spend money for things that provide only short-term pleasure.

Judgment

Experience is an extraordinary teacher, and so we all put considerable faith in the judgments a physician makes, based on her years of experience, or the advice we hear from a car mechanic, based on the many cars he's worked on.

But there are surely limits on what we can learn from experience. After all, sometimes the information provided by the world is ambiguous or incomplete.

And sometimes our *memories* for our experience are selective, or even distorted. We need to ask, therefore, how deeply these considerations cut into our ability to make judgments and to draw conclusions based on what we have seen, heard, or read.

Attribute Substitution

Imagine that you're choosing courses for next year, and, as part of that decision, you're trying to determine just how difficult your school's Organic Chemistry course really is. To figure this out, you might ask yourself, "How well have my friends done in this course? How many have gotten good grades, and how many have done poorly?" These are sensible questions to ask, and notice that they're questions about *frequencies*—assessments of how often various events have happened in the past. In this fashion, *frequency estimates* are often crucial for our judgments.

It's likely, however, that you've not kept an ongoing tally of your friends' grades. Even if you have, you may not be able, right now, to recall a dozen friends who've taken this course and the grade for each friend. Therefore, you'll have trouble estimating the relevant frequencies. What can you do instead? You're likely to rely on **attribute substitution,** a strategy of using easily available information that (you hope) is a plausible substitute for the information you seek. Specifically, in this situation you're likely to do a quick scan through memory, looking for relevant cases. If you can easily think of four friends who got good grades in Organic Chemistry, you'll probably conclude that this is a frequent occurrence and thus decide that the course isn't all that challenging. In contrast, if you can think of few friends with good grades, or if the relevant memories come to mind only slowly, you'll draw the opposite conclusion: This must be a rare occurrence.

With this strategy, you're basing your judgment on *availability*—that is, *how easily* and *how quickly* you can come up with relevant examples. That is why Tversky and Kahneman (1973) refer to this strategy as the **availability heuristic.** Let's be clear, though, that this heuristic is, at its heart, a case of attribute substitution. You need to judge frequency (how common something is in the world), but you don't have direct or easy access to information about frequency. So you rely on a plausible substitute: availability in memory, using this logic: "Examples leap to mind? Must be a common, often experienced event. A struggle to come up with examples? Must be a rare event."

Here's a different case: Imagine that you're applying for a job. You hope that the employer will carefully examine your credentials and make a thoughtful judgment about whether you'd be a good hire. It's likely, though, that the employer will rely on a faster, easier strategy—one that involves a different sort of attribute substitution. Specifically, the employer may barely glance at your résumé and instead ask himself how much you resemble other people he's hired who have worked out well. Do you have the same mannerisms, the same look as Joan, say, an employee that he's very happy with? If so, you're likely to get the job. In this case, the employer wants to judge a *probability* (namely: the probability that you'd

TABLE 11.1 | DIFFERENT TYPES OF ATTRIBUTE SUBSTITUTION

You want to judge . . .	Instead you rely on . . .	This usually works because . . .	But this strategy can lead to error because . . .
Frequency of occurrence in the world	Availability in memory: How easily can you think of cases?	Events that are frequent in the world are likely to be more available in memory	Many factors *other than* frequency in the world can influence availability from memory!
Probability of an event being in a category or having certain properties	Resemblance between that event and other events that are in the category	Many categories are homogeneous enough so that the category members do resemble each other	Many categories are not homogeneous!

work out well if hired) and instead relies on *resemblance*. This particular substitution is referred to as the **representativeness heuristic**. Let's look at these two heuristics—availability and representativeness—in more detail. (See Table 11.1 for a summary comparison of these two heuristics; for a broad discussion of heuristics, see Griffin, Gonzalez, Koehler & Gilovich, 2012).

The Availability Heuristic

Heuristics (which we first met in Chapter 8) are efficient strategies that usually lead you to the right answers. The key word, however, is "usually." Heuristics allow errors, but that's simply the price you pay in order to gain the efficiency.

The availability and representativeness heuristics both fit this profile. In each case, the attribute being used (availability or resemblance) is easy to assess, and that is the source of the efficiency. And in each case, the attribute being relied on is correlated with the target dimension, so that it can usually serve as a proxy for the target. Events or objects that are frequent are, in fact, likely to be easily available in memory, and so generally you can rely on availability as an index for frequency. And many categories are homogeneous enough so that members of the category do resemble each other; that's why you can often rely on resemblance as a way of judging probability of category membership.

Nonetheless, these strategies can lead to error. To take a simple case, ask yourself, "Are there more words in the dictionary beginning with the letter *R* ('rose,' 'rock,' 'rabbit') or more words with an *R* in the third position ('tarp,' 'bare,' 'throw')?" Most people assert that there are more words beginning with *R* (Tversky & Kahneman, 1973, 1974), but the reverse is true—by a margin of at least two to one.

Why do people get this wrong? The answer lies in availability. If you search your memory for words starting with *R*, many will come to mind. (Try it: How many *R*-words can you name in 10 seconds?) But if you search your memory for words with an *R* in the third position, fewer will emerge. (Again, try this for 10 seconds.) This difference, favoring the words beginning with *R*, arises because your memory is organized roughly like a dictionary, with the words sharing a starting sound all grouped together. As a consequence, it's easy to search memory using "starting letter" as your cue; a search based on "*R* in third position" is more difficult. Thus, the organization of memory creates a bias in what's easily available, and this bias in availability leads to an error in frequency judgment.

The Wide Range of Availability Effects

The *R*-word example is not very interesting on its own—how often do you need to make judgments about spelling patterns? But the example is, as they say, the tip of a large iceberg, because people rely on availability in a wide range of other cases, including cases in which they're making judgments of some importance.

For example, people regularly overestimate the frequency of events that are, in actuality, quite rare (Attneave, 1953; Lichtenstein, Slovic, Fischhoff, Layman, & Combs, 1978). This probably plays a part in people's willingness to buy lottery tickets; they overestimate the likelihood of winning! Likewise, physicians often overestimate the likelihood of a rare disease and, in the process, fail to pursue other, more appropriate, diagnoses (e.g., Elstein et al., 1986; Obrecht, Chapman, & Gelman, 2009).

What causes this pattern? There's little reason to spend time thinking about familiar events ("Oh look—that airplane has wings!"), but you're likely to notice and think about rare events, especially rare *emotional* events ("Oh God—that airplane crashed!"). As a result, rare events are likely to be well recorded in memory, and this will, in turn, make these events easily available to you. As a consequence, if you rely on the availability heuristic, you'll overestimate the frequency of these distinctive events and, correspondingly, overestimate the likelihood of similar events happening in the future.

Here's a rather different example: Participants in one study were asked to think about episodes in their lives in which they'd acted in an assertive fashion (Schwarz et al., 1991; also see Raghubir & Menon, 2005). Half of the participants were asked to recall six of these episodes; half were asked to recall 12 episodes. Then all the participants were asked some general questions, including how assertive overall they thought they were.

Participants in this study had an easy time coming up with six episodes, and so, using the availability heuristic, they concluded, "Those cases came quickly to mind; therefore, there must be a large number of these episodes; therefore, I must be an assertive person." In contrast, participants asked for 12 episodes had some difficulty generating this longer list, and so they concluded, "If these cases are so difficult to recall, I guess the episodes can't be typical for how I act."

Consistent with these suggestions, participants who recalled fewer episodes judged themselves to be more assertive. Notice, ironically, that the participants who recalled *more* episodes actually had more evidence in their view for their own assertiveness. But it's not the quantity of evidence that matters. Instead, what matters is the ease of coming up with the episodes. Participants who were asked for a dozen episodes had a hard time with the task *because they'd been asked to do something difficult*—namely, to come up with a lot of cases! But the participants seemed not to realize this. They reacted only to the fact that the examples were difficult to generate and, using the availability heuristic, concluded that being assertive was relatively infrequent in their past.

As a different sort of example, imagine that you've been asked to vote on how much money the government should spend on various research projects, all aimed at saving lives. It seems sensible that you'd choose to spend your resources on the more frequent causes of death, rather than investigating rare problems. On this basis, how will you vote? Should we spend more on preventing death from motor vehicle accidents or death from stomach cancer? Which is more common? Should we spend more on preventing homicides or diabetes? People reliably assert that motor vehicle accidents and homicide are the more frequent, although the opposite is true in both pairs—by a substantial margin (Combs & Slovic, 1979; Slovic, Fischhoff, & Lichtenstein, 1982).

What produces this error? In estimating the likelihood of these events, people are heavily influenced by the pattern of media coverage. Homicide makes the front page, while diabetes does not, and this is reflected in participants' estimates of frequency—estimates that are, in this case, far from the truth.

The Representativeness Heuristic

Similar points can be made about the representativeness heuristic, the strategy of relying on *resemblance* when what you're really after is a judgment of *probability*, including the probability that a particular case belongs in a specific category. Just like availability, this strategy is efficient and often leads to the correct conclusion. But here, too, the strategy can lead you astray.

How does the representativeness heuristic work? Let's start with the fact that many of the categories you encounter are relatively homogeneous: The category *birds,* for example, is homogeneous with regard to the traits of *having wings, having feathers*, and so on. Virtually every member of the category has these traits, and so, in these regards, each member of the category resembles all the others. Likewise, the category *motels* is homogeneous with regard to traits like *has beds in each room, has a Bible in each room*, and *has an office*, and so, again, in these regards each member of the category (each motel) resembles all the others.

The representativeness heuristic capitalizes on this homogeneity: We expect each individual to resemble the other individuals in the category (and thus we expect each individual to be *representative* of the category overall). As a result, we can use resemblance as a basis for judging the likelihood of category membership. Thus, if a creature resembles other birds you've seen, you conclude that the creature probably is a bird. We first met this approach in Chapter 8, when we were discussing simple categories like *bird* or *chair* or *fruit*. But the same approach can be used more broadly—and this is the heart of the representativeness strategy. Thus, if a job candidate resembles successful hires you've made, you conclude the person will probably be a successful hire; if someone you meet at a party resembles engineers you've known, you assume the person is likely to be an engineer.

Of course, since many categories *are* homogeneous, reasoning in this fashion will often lead you to sensible judgments. Even so, the use of this heuristic can lead to error. Imagine, for example, tossing a coin over and over and let's say that the coin has landed heads up six times in a row. Many people believe that, on the next toss, the coin is more likely to come up tails. But this conclusion, often called the *gambler's fallacy*, is wrong. The "logic" leading to this fallacy seems to be that if the coin is fair, then a series of tosses should contain equal numbers of heads and tails. If no tails have appeared for a while, then some are "overdue" to bring about this balance.

Let's be clear, though, that the coin has no "memory," so it has no way of knowing (or being influenced by) how long it's been since the last tails. Therefore, the likelihood of a tail on any particular toss must be independent of what has happened on previous tosses; there's no way that the previous tosses could influence the next one. Hence, the probability of a tail on toss number 7 is .50, just as it was on the first toss, and on every toss.

What produces the gambler's fallacy? The explanation lies in the assumption of category homogeneity. We all know that, in the long run, a fair coin will produce equal numbers of heads and tails. Thus, the category of "all tosses" has this property. Our assumption of homogeneity, though, leads us to expect that any "representative" of the category will also have this property—that is, any sequence of tosses will also show the 50-50 split. But this isn't true: Some sequences of tosses are 75% heads, some are 5% heads. It is only when we combine these sequences that the 50-50 split emerges.

WORKBOOK
DEMONSTRATIONS 11.1
AND 11.2

Reasoning From a Single Case to the Entire Population

In the gambler's fallacy, people seem to believe that each subset of a category should have the same properties as the category overall; this is, we've said, a consequence of people assuming that categories are homogeneous. But the assumption of homogeneity can also lead to the opposite error—an expectation that the entire category will have the same properties as the individual category members. Thus, concretely, people will be far too willing to extrapolate from a few instances to the entire set (see Figure 11.1).

Hamill, Wilson, and Nisbett (1980) showed their participants a videotaped interview in which a prison guard discussed his job. In one condition, the guard was compassionate and kind; in another condition, the guard expressed contempt for the prison inmates and scoffed at the idea of rehabilitation. Before seeing either video, though, some participants were told that this guard was typical of those at the prison; other participants were told that he was quite *atypical*, chosen for the interview precisely because of his extreme views.

Participants were later questioned about their own views of the criminal justice system, and they were plainly influenced by the interview they'd just seen: Those who had seen the humane guard indicated that they believed prison guards in general were decent people; those who had seen the inhumane guard reported

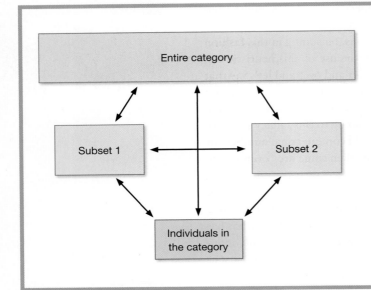

Entire category

Subset 1

Subset 2

Individuals in
the category

FIGURE 11.1 | IMPLICATIONS OF
ASSUMING CATEGORY
HOMOGENEITY

If a category is truly homogeneous, then we know what the category's subsets will be like, based on information about the overall category, and we know what the category will be like, based on the subsets. Likewise, if the category is truly homogeneous, then we know what the individual category members will be like, based on information about the category, and vice versa. Unfortunately, though, people are far too quick to assume that categories are homogeneous, and so they make all these inferences even when they shouldn't!

more negative views of guards. What's remarkable, though, is that participants seemed to ignore the information about whether the interviewed guard was typical or not. Those explicitly told the guard was atypical were influenced by the interview just as much as those told that the guard was typical.

In this study, participants drew a conclusion about an entire category ("prison guards") based on a single case—and did so even when explicitly warned *against* this extrapolation. Similarly, imagine that you're shopping for a new car. You've read various consumer magazines and decided, based on their test data, that you'll buy a Smacko brand car. You report this to a friend, who is aghast. "Smacko? You must be crazy. Why, I know a man who bought a Smacko, and the transmission fell out two weeks after he got it. Then the alternator went. Then the brakes. How could you possibly buy a Smacko?"

In this instance, your friend is offering a "man who" argument (a term proposed by Nisbett & Ross, 1980); what should you make of this argument? The consumer magazines tested many cars and reported that, say, 2% of all Smackos break down. In your friend's "data," 100% of the Smackos (one out of one) broke down. Should this "sample of one" outweigh the much larger sample tested by the magazine? Your friend presumably believes he's offering a persuasive argument, but, if so, your friend must be assuming that the category will resemble the instance; only in that case would reasoning from a single instance be appropriate.

If you listen to conversations around you, you'll regularly hear "man who" (or "woman who") arguments. "What do you mean cigarette smoking causes cancer?! I have an aunt who smoked for 50 years, and she runs in marathons!" Often these arguments seem persuasive. But they have force only by virtue of the representativeness heuristic—and thus your willingness to extrapolate from a tiny sample.

Detecting Covariation

It cannot be surprising that people often rely on mental shortcuts. It's unsettling, though, that people use these shortcuts even when making consequential judgments, or when making judgments about familiar domains. And to make things worse, the errors caused by the heuristics can, in turn, trigger other sorts of errors, including errors in judgments about **covariation**. This term has a technical meaning, but for our purposes we can define it this way: X and Y "covary" if X tends to be on the scene whenever Y is, and if X tends to be absent whenever Y is absent. For example, exercise and stamina covary: People who do the first tend to have a lot of the second. Owning audio CDs and going to concerts also covary, although less strongly than exercise and stamina. (Some people own many CDs but rarely go to concerts.) Thus, covariation can be strong or weak, and can also be negative or positive. Exercise and stamina, for example, covary positively (as exercise increases, so does stamina). Exercise and body fat covary negatively (as exercise increases, body fat decreases).

Covariation is important for many reasons—including the fact that it's what you need to consider when checking on a belief about cause and effect. Does education lead to a higher-paying job? If so, then degree of education and salary should covary. Likewise, do you feel better on days in which you eat a good breakfast? If so, then the presence or absence of breakfast in the morning should covary with how you feel as the day wears on. Similarly for other cause-effect questions: Are you more likely to fall in love with someone tall? Do vertical stripes make you look thinner? Does your car start more easily if you pump the gas? These are all questions about covariation, and they are the sorts of questions people frequently ask. So how well do people do in judging covariation?

Illusions of Covariation

In the Rorschach test, people are shown inkblots and asked to describe them. Psychologists then examine the descriptions, looking both for patterns and for specific types of responses. Responses that mention humans in motion, for example, are said to indicate imagination and a rich inner life; responses that describe the white spaces around the inkblot are taken as indications of rebelliousness.

Is this valid? Do specific responses really covary with certain personality traits? And how astutely do people detect this covariation? To attack these questions, Chapman and Chapman (1971) created (fictitious) transcripts of people's responses to the inkblots; they also made up fictitious descriptions of the people who'd supposedly offered these responses: One transcript was attributed to a man who "believes other people are plotting against him"; another was attributed to a man who "has sexual feelings toward other men."

The Chapmans *randomly paired* the transcripts and the personality descriptions, and these pairs were shown to a group of undergraduates, students who had no experience with the Rorschach test and did not know the theory behind the test. These students were asked to examine the pairs and to determine what

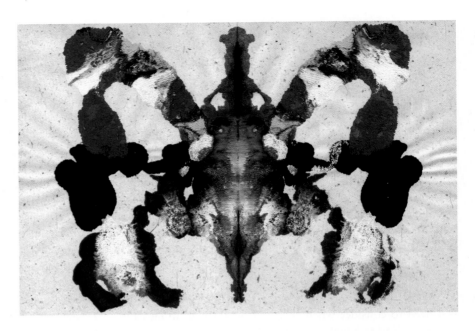

RORSCHACH IMAGES

The Rorschach inkblots are often used as part of a clinical assessment, probing for a variety of traits and potential disorders.

responses covaried with what traits. In particular, the students were asked which responses covaried with homosexuality.

Before pressing on, we need to emphasize that the Chapmans' research was done years ago, at a time when many psychiatrists viewed homosexuality as a "disorder." In the years since their work, however, psychiatrists and psychologists have abandoned this utterly indefensible view, and thus we discuss the Chapmans' research as a classic study of covariation, and not because it tells us anything about homosexuality.

Returning to the study itself, the students did see a pattern in these data. Certain responses, they claimed, were more commonly offered by gay respondents than by straights, so these responses (in the participants' view) were good indicators of sexual orientation. For example, they reported that homosexual respondents were particularly likely to perceive buttocks in the inkblots. Therefore, mention of buttocks was an indication, they claimed, that the respondent was gay.

The pattern "perceived" by these students, though, was unmistakably an illusion—the students were seeing something that was not there! After all, the Rorschach data they'd reviewed were—as we already mentioned—assembled *randomly,* so there was no covariation here. What's especially striking, though, is that the covariation "detected" by these students was identical to that reported by trained clinicians. The clinicians had extensive experience in using the Rorschach test, and, based on this professional experience, they too were convinced that use of the "buttocks" response covaried with sexual orientation, with homosexuals more likely to offer this response.

It turns out, though, that the pattern observed by the clinicians *is also illusory*. Researchers have examined the actual Rorschach responses from homosexuals and heterosexuals and asked statistically whether "buttocks" responses are more likely from one group than the other. The data are clear: The two groups do not differ at all in the likelihood of this response, so the clinicians are seeing a "pattern" that really isn't there. With all of their training, then, and with years of experience, the clinicians are caught by the same illusion as the lab participants. (For related evidence, see Arkes & Harkness, 1983; Schustack & Sternberg, 1981; Shaklee & Mims, 1982; Smedslund, 1963.)

What Causes Illusions in Covariation?

Illusions about covariation are easy to document. For example, many people are convinced there's a relationship between a person's handwriting and personality, yet no serious study has documented this covariation (King & Koehler, 2000). Likewise, many people believe they can predict the weather by paying attention to their arthritis pain ("My knee always acts up when a storm is coming"). This, too, turns out to be groundless and is another case in which people perceive covariation when in truth there is none (Redelmeier & Tversky, 1996).

What causes illusions like these? One proposal focuses on the evidence that people consider in judging covariation, because, in making these judgments, people seem to consider only a *subset* of the evidence, and it's a subset that's skewed by their prior expectations (Baron, 1988; Evans, 1989; Gilovich, 1991; Jennings, Amabile, & Ross, 1982). This virtually guarantees mistaken judgments, since even if the judgment process were 100% fair, a biased input would lead to a biased output.

Specifically, when judging covariation, your selection of evidence is likely to be guided by **confirmation bias**, a tendency to be more responsive to evidence that *confirms* your beliefs, rather than to evidence that might *challenge* your beliefs (Nisbett & Ross, 1980; Tweney, Doherty, & Mynatt, 1981). We'll have more to say about confirmation bias later, but for now, note how confirmation bias could distort the assessment of covariation. Let's say, for example, that you have the belief that big dogs tend to be vicious. With this belief, you're more likely to notice big dogs that are, in fact, vicious and little dogs that are friendly. As a result, a biased sample of dogs is available to you, in the dogs you perceive and the dogs you remember. Therefore, if you're asked to estimate covariation between dog size and temperament, you'll probably overestimate the covariation. This isn't because you're ignoring the facts, nor is it because you're incompetent in thinking about covariation. The problem instead lies in your "data"; and if the data are biased, so will be your judgment.

Base Rates

Assessment of covariation can also be pulled off track by another problem: neglect of **base-rate information**—information about how frequently something occurs in general. To make this concrete, imagine that we're testing a new drug, in hopes that it will cure hepatitis. Here we're trying to find out if *taking the drug* covaries with a better medical outcome, and let's say that our study tells us that 70% of the patients taking the drug do recover from the illness. This result is on its own uninterpretable, because we need the base rate: We need to know in general how often people recover from hepatitis. If it turns out (for example) that the overall recovery rate is 70%, then our new drug is having no effect whatsoever.

Similarly, do good-luck charms help? Let's say that you wear your lucky socks whenever your favorite team plays, and the team has won 85% of its games. Here, too, we need to ask about base rates: How many games has your team won over the last few years? Perhaps the team has won 90% overall. In that case, your socks are actually a jinx (also see Table 11.2).

Despite the importance of base rates, people often ignore them. In a classic study, Kahneman and Tversky (1973) asked participants this question: If someone is chosen at random from a group of 70 lawyers and 30 engineers, what is his profession likely to be? Participants understood perfectly well that, in this setting, the probability of the person being a lawyer is .70. Here people *are* using base-rate information sensibly.

Other participants were given a similar task, but instead of base rates, they were given brief descriptions of certain individuals, and asked, based on these descriptions, whether each individual was more likely to be a lawyer or an engineer. Some of the descriptions had been crafted (based on common stereotypes) to suggest that the person was a lawyer; some suggested engineer; some were relatively neutral.

TABLE 11.2 | **THE IMPORTANCE OF BASE RATES: AN EXAMPLE**

DO LEECHES CURE FEVER?		
	Fever cured	Fever not cured
Patients treated with leeches	195	105
Patients not treated with leeches	130	70

Years ago, physicians believed that attaching leeches to the body would cure fever. Here we've provided some fictitious data to illustrate why many people believed this claim—and also why the claim is false. Notice that in these data, 195 people treated with leeches were cured. If we focus on just these cases, we might decide leeches are effective. ("I know a man who . . .") In addition, among people treated this way, two thirds (roughly 200 out of 300) were cured. If we focused on this fact, we might again be impressed with leeches' efficacy. We draw the opposite (and correct) conclusion, though, when we consider the base rate: The overall cure rate, in these data, is also 2/3, and so your chances of cure are the same with leeches or without. Can you think of modern examples of bogus cures that show the same data pattern?

Not surprisingly, participants' judgments were guided by these thumbnail sketches. Thus, it appears that participants are responsive to base rates if this is the only information they have, and they use information about the individual if this is all they have. But now let's ask: What happens if we provide *both* sorts of information—the base rates *and* information about the specific person?

Participants in a third group were given the thumbnail descriptions and also told that these individuals had been selected at random from a group of 70 lawyers and 30 engineers. We've just seen that participants understand the value of either type of information, when it's presented on its own. When given *both* types of information, therefore, we should expect the participants to combine these inputs as well as they can. Thus, if both the base rate and the diagnostic information favor the lawyer response, participants should offer this response with confidence. If the base rate indicates one response and the diagnostic information the other response, participants should temper their estimates accordingly.

However, this is not what participants do. When provided with both types of information, participants rely only on the descriptive information about the individual. Indeed, they respond the same way if the base rates are as already described (70 lawyers, 30 engineers) or if the base rates are reversed (30 lawyers, 70 engineers). This reversal has no impact on participants' judgments, confirming that they are indeed ignoring the base rates.

What produces this neglect of base rates? The answer, in part, is attribute substitution: When asked whether a particular person—Tom, let's say—is a lawyer or an engineer, people seem to turn this question about category membership into a question about resemblance. (In other words, they rely on the representativeness heuristic!) Thus, to ask whether Tom *is* a lawyer, they ask themselves how much Tom *resembles* (their idea of) a lawyer. This substitution is (as we've discussed) often helpful, but note that this strategy provides no role for base rates—and this guarantees that people will routinely ignore base rates. Consistent with this claim, base-rate neglect is indeed widespread and can be observed both in laboratory tasks and in many real-world judgments (Dawes, 1988; Griffin et al., 2012; Klayman & Brown, 1993).

WORKBOOK
DEMONSTRATION 11.3

Dual-Process Models

We seem to be painting a grim portrait of human judgment. There are several sources of error, and even experts make the errors—experienced therapists evaluating Rorschach responses (and falling prey to illusory covariation), skilled financial managers making claims about investments (e.g., Hilton, 2003; Kahneman, 2011) and even physicians diagnosing cancer (but ignoring base rates; Eddy, 1982). These errors occur even when people are doing their best to be careful. Indeed, in some studies participants have been offered cash bonuses if they perform accurately. These bonuses do increase accuracy, but, even so, a substantial number of errors remain (Arkes, 1991; Gilovich, 1991; Hertwig & Ortmann, 2003).

Cheat death.

The antioxidant power of
pomegranate juice.

FTC Complaint Charges Deceptive Advertising by POM Wonderful

Agency Proceedings Will Determine Whether Health Claims for Pomegranate Products Are False and Not Supported by Scientific Evidence

As part of its ongoing efforts to uncover over-hyped health claims in food advertising, the Federal Trade Commission has issued an administrative complaint charging the makers of POM Wonderful 100% Pomegranate Juice and POMx supplements with making false and unsubstantiated claims that their products will prevent or treat heart disease, prostate cancer, and erectile dysfunction.

MIRACLE CURES?

People are remarkably ready to believe in a variety of "miracle cures," and advertisers are certainly ready to take advantage of these beliefs. One seller of pomegranate juice, for example, made extraordinary claims about the health benefit of their product . . . until the Federal Trade Commission stepped in. Because of the FTC ruling, POM is no longer allowed to make these (unsubstantiated) claims about their product's benefits.

Could it be, then, that human judgment is fundamentally flawed? If so, this might explain why people are so ready to believe in telepathy, astrology, and a variety of bogus cures (Gilovich, 1991; King & Koehler, 2000). Indeed, perhaps these points help us understand why warfare, racism, neglect of poverty, and environmental destruction are so widespread; perhaps these ills are the inevitable outcome of people's inability to understand facts and to draw decent conclusions.

More-Sophisticated Judgment Strategies

Before we make these claims, however, let's acknowledge—and celebrate—another side to our story: Sometimes, human judgment rises above the heuristics we've described so far. Thus, people often rely on availability in judging frequency, but sometimes they seek other (more accurate) bases for making their judgments (Oppenheimer, 2004; Schwarz, 1998; Winkielman & Schwarz, 2001). Likewise, a reliance on representativeness is easy to document, but sometimes people do better: In using representativeness, for example, people are willing to draw conclusions from a tiny sample of evidence. (This is why "man who" stories are often persuasive.) In other settings, though, people refuse conclusions if the data sample is too small. As an illustration, consider the following dialogue:

> Bart: I've got a great system for choosing lottery numbers! I chose a number yesterday, and I won!

> Lisa: Come on—that doesn't mean your system's great; maybe you just got lucky.

In this setting, Lisa's response seems right; we all know that lucky accidents do happen, and Bart's boast does sound unjustified. For contrast, however, consider this bit of dialogue:

Marge: I've got a great system for choosing lottery numbers! I've tried it 11 times, and I won every time!

Homer: Come on—that doesn't mean your system's great; maybe you just got lucky each time.

Here, Homer's response sounds odd, and Marge's boast does seem sensible. Yes, lucky accidents do happen, but they don't keep happening over and over. If something happens over and over, it's probably not an accident.

These are easy points to grasp, and it's precisely this ease of understanding that's important here, because it reveals a comprehension of some crucial facts about sample size. Specifically, you understand these bits of dialogue only because you already know that it's dangerous to draw conclusions from a small sample of evidence. This is why you side with Lisa, not Bart. Likewise, you side with Marge because you understand that it's legitimate to draw conclusions from a larger sample; you know that a pattern in a larger set is less likely to be the result of an accident.

System 1, System 2

Here's a blunt summary of where we are: Sometimes people make judgment mistakes, and sometimes they don't. Sometimes people rely on heuristics—and so they're fooled by extraneous factors that influence availability; they draw conclusions from "man who" stories; they ignore base rates—and sometimes they don't. How can we make sense of this mixed pattern?

The obvious suggestion is that people must have two ways of thinking. One type of thinking is fast and easy; the heuristics we've described fall into this category. And sometimes people turn to a different type of thinking that is slower, more effortful, and more accurate. This is why people don't always make heuristic-based errors.

Researchers have offered many proposals that build on this simple idea; in all cases, what is being proposed is called a **dual-process** model (Evans, 2003, 2006, 2012a; Ferreira, Garcia-Marques, Sherman & Sherman, 2006; Kahneman, 2011; Pretz, 2008; Shafir & LeBoeuf, 2002; for thoughtful reviews, though, including some concerns about dual-process models, see De Neys, Vartanian, & Goel, 2008; Evans, 2008; Griffin et al. 2012; Keysers et al., 2008; Kruglanski & Orehek, 2007; Osman, 2004). The various dual-process models differ in their specifics and use different terminology. We'll rely, though, on the rather neutral terms suggested by Stanovich and West (2000), and so we'll use **System 1** as the label for the fast, easy sort of thinking and **System 2** as the label for the slower, more effortful thinking (but also see Stanovich, 2012).

When do people use System 1, and when do they use System 2? One hypothesis is that people *choose* when to rely on each system, and, presumably, they shift to the less efficient, more accurate System 2 when making a judgment that really matters. As we've seen, however, people rely on System 1's heuristics even when incentives are offered for accuracy, even when making important professional judgments, even when making medical diagnoses that may, in some cases, literally be matters of life and death. Surely people would choose to use System 2 in these cases if they could, and yet they still rely on System 1 and fall into error. On these grounds, it's difficult to argue that using System 2 is a matter of deliberate choice.

Instead, evidence suggests that System 2 comes into play only if triggered by certain cues and only if the circumstances are right. We've already suggested, for example, that System 2 judgments are slower than System 1's, and on this basis, it's not surprising that heuristic-based judgments (and so heuristic-based *errors*) are more likely when judgments are made under time pressure (Finucane, Alhakami, Slovic, & Johnson, 2000). We've also said that System 2 judgments require *effort*, so this form of thinking is more likely if the person can focus attention on the judgment being made (De Neys, 2006; Ferreira et al., 2006; Gilbert, 1989; for some complexity, though, see Chun & Kruglanski, 2006).

The Importance of Data Format

Factors like time pressure and focus, however, cannot be our whole story, because even alert, focused people sometimes make judgment errors, and, often, people who are rushed or distracted still get things right! We therefore need to ask what other factors govern the use of System 1 or System 2.

Evidence suggests that several features of the judgment being made are crucial, so that certain judgments seem more likely to "trigger" System 2's operation. For example, we've discussed the widespread neglect of base-rate information. Presumably, this is a result of System 1 thinking, with people relying on heuristics in judging covariation and, in the process, not taking base rates into account. However, the error is avoided, and sensitivity to base rates is markedly increased, if the base rates are presented the right way.

In many experiments, people have been presented with base rates cast in terms of probabilities or proportions: "There is a .01 chance that people like Mary will have this disease"; "Only 5% of the people in this group are lawyers." But the same information can be conveyed in terms of *frequencies*, and it turns out that people are more likely to use the base rates if they're conveyed in this "frequency format." Thus, people are more alert to a base rate phrased as "12 out of every 1,000 cases" than they are to the same information cast as a percentage ("1.2%") or a probability (.012) (Gigerenzer & Hoffrage, 1995; also Brase, 2008; Cosmides & Tooby, 1996).

There is debate about *why* frequency information is advantageous (Evans, Handley, Perham, Over, & Thompson, 2000; Fiedler, Brinkmann, Betsch, & Wild, 2000; Girotto & Gonzalez, 2001; Lewis & Keren, 1999; Mellers, Hertwig, & Kahneman, 2001), but there's no question that participants' performance in dealing with judgment problems is improved if the data are cast in terms of frequencies. This obviously helps us to understand why judgment about evidence is sometimes so poor and sometimes accurate. It depends on how the problem is presented, with some presentations more "user-friendly" than others.

WORKBOOK
DEMONSTRATION 11.4

Codable Data

The use of System 2 is also more likely if the role of *chance* is more conspicuous in a problem. If this role is salient, people are more likely to realize that the "evidence" they're considering may just be a fluke, or an accident, and not an indication of a reliable pattern. With this, people are more likely to pay attention to the *quantity* of evidence, on the (sensible) idea that a larger set of observations is less vulnerable to chance fluctuations.

In one study, participants were asked about someone who assessed a restaurant based on just one meal (Nisbett, Krantz, Jepson, & Kunda, 1983). The participants were more alert to considerations of sample size if the diner chose his entrée by blindly dropping a pencil onto the menu (presumably because participants realized that a different sample, and perhaps different views of the restaurant, might have emerged if the pencil had fallen on a different selection). In another study, participants were asked about a high school student who chose what college to go to based on her campus visit; they, too, were more alert to issues of sampling if told that the student chose which classes to sit in on entirely at random (e.g., Baratgin & Noveck, 2000; Gigerenzer, 1991; Gigerenzer, Hell, and Blank, 1988; Nisbett et al., 1983; Tversky & Kahneman, 1982).

Likewise, people are more accurate in their judgments, and less prone to heuristic use, when confronting evidence that is easily understood in statistical terms (Holland, Holyoak, Nisbett, & Thagard, 1986; Kunda & Nisbett, 1986). The suggestion here is that people do have some understanding of basic statistical concepts (such as the importance of sample size); that was our point in the earlier dialogues between Bart and Lisa, Marge and Homer. Often, though, people don't realize these concepts are *applicable* to a judgment they're trying to make. Thus, they might not realize that the evidence they're contemplating can be understood as a *sample of data* drawn from a larger set of potential observations. If they do have this insight, however, their judgment is improved.

For example, it's clear that an athlete's performance in a game's first quarter is just a sample of evidence and may or may not reflect his performance in other samples (other quarters or other games). It's also clear how to measure performance (points or other sports statistics). For these reasons, the evidence is already "packaged" in a way that leads people to think in statistically sophisticated terms, and this explains why people are better at judging covariation, and more likely to be sensitive to the size of the sample of evidence, when thinking about sports (Jepson, Krantz, & Nisbett, 1983).

In contrast, other evidence is less easily coded in these terms. If an employer interviews a job candidate, the employer may not realize that the 10 minutes of interview can be thought of as just a "sample" of evidence, and that other impressions might come from other samples (e.g., reinterviewing the person on a different day or seeing the person in another setting). It's also not clear how to quantify the employer's impressions during the interview—how to measure how responsible the candidate seemed, or how motivated. In the eyes of most people, evidence like this doesn't lend itself to statistical treatment, and, in fact, this sort of evidence tends not to evoke System 2 thinking. Instead, the employer is likely to rely on simple heuristics in thinking about the job candidate—and to make less justifiable decisions in the process.

Background Knowledge and Skills

It's clear, then, that the use of System 2 thinking depends on factors in the situation (e.g., the presence of time pressure) and also factors in the evidence considered (whether the evidence is presented in terms of frequencies, rather than probabilities; whether the evidence is "codable" or not). The use of System 2 thinking also depends on the knowledge and skills each person possesses. Thus, for just one example, people know that samples of a mineral all tend to resemble each other, but that humans vary enormously in their body shapes. As a result, people are willing to draw conclusions from a single sample of a mineral, but hesitate to draw conclusions about a tribe based on what a single tribe member looks like (see Figure 11.2; Nisbett et al., 1983).

Likewise, people are more sensitive to base rates if their background knowledge leads them to see a meaningful linkage between the base rate and the dimension being judged. In one study, participants were asked to predict whether a particular student would pass an upcoming exam (Ajzen, 1977; also Tversky & Kahneman, 1982). The participants were told some facts about this student, but they were also told the base rate—namely, that in the last few years, only 30% of the students who'd taken this exam passed it. In this situation, participants perceived the base rate as meaningful: The low pass rate meant that the exam was quite difficult. Interpreted in this way, participants made sensible use of the base rate and did not show the pattern of base-rate neglect observed in other studies (also see Krynski & Tenenbaum, 2007; Oppenheimer, 2004; Winkielman & Schwarz, 2001).

In addition—and quite optimistically—you're more likely to use System 2 if you've been *educated* in the right way. Fong, Krantz, and Nisbett (1986) provided research participants with just a half-hour of training, focusing on the importance of sample size. The participants were reminded that accidents do happen but that accidents don't keep happening over and over. Therefore, a small sample of data might be the result of some accident, but a large sample probably isn't. Consequently, large samples are more reliable, more trustworthy, than small samples.

This brief training was remarkably effective: Once trained, the participants were more likely to apply considerations of sample size to novel cases. Moreover, their application of this knowledge tended to be reasonable and appropriate.

Similarly, Fong et al. conducted a telephone survey of "opinions about sports," calling students who were taking an undergraduate course in statistics. Half of the students were contacted during the first week of the semester; half were contacted during the last week. There was no indication to the students that the telephone interview was connected to their course; as far as they knew, they had been selected entirely at random.

In the phone interview, one of the questions involved a comparison between how well a baseball player did in his first year and how well he did in the remainder of

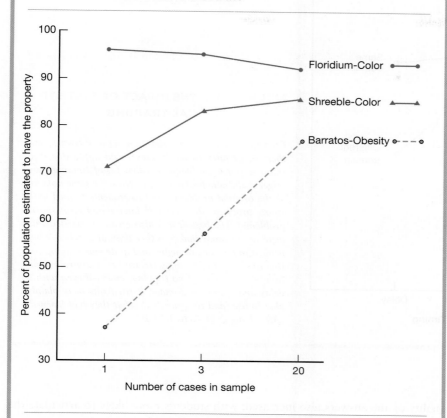

FIGURE 11.2 | THE IMPACT OF SAMPLE SIZE DEPENDS ON THE JUDGMENT DOMAIN

Participants were told that they were visitors to an island, and told they had viewed one native—from the Barratos tribe—and had observed he was obese. They were then asked how likely they thought it was that all Barratos were obese. Other participants were asked whether they would draw a conclusion after seeing three Barratos, or twenty? Participants were also asked whether they would draw conclusions after observing one Shreeble (a type of bird on the island) or three, or twenty. Participants were likewise asked whether they would draw conclusions after observing samples of a new mineral, Floridium. The data show that participants' willingness to draw conclusions depended heavily on the category— presumably because participants were guided by the background knowledge that samples of minerals tend to resemble each other; individual birds, however, can differ from each other, and certainly tribal members can differ from each other. Hence, with the more diverse groups, participants insisted on gaining more evidence before drawing any conclusions. (After Nisbett, Krantz, Jepson, & Kunda, 1983.)

his career. This is, in effect, a question about sample size (with the first-year being just a sample of the player's overall performance). Did the students realize that sample size was relevant here? For those contacted early in the term, only 16% gave answers that showed any consideration of sample size. For those contacted later, the number of answers influenced by sample size more than doubled (to 37%). The

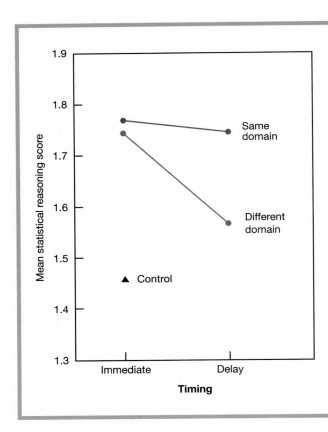

FIGURE 11.3 | THE IMPACT OF STATISTICAL TRAINING

Participants were given brief training in statistics, and then tested later to see if they could apply this new training to new problems. The benefits of training were larger if the new problems came from the same domain as the original problems (and so students trained with sports problems did better if later tested with sports problems). The benefit was also greater if participants were tested immediately, rather than at a delay. What is most important, though—and quite encouraging—is that the benefit of training (relative to a control condition, which involved no training) emerged even with a delay and a shift in domain. Participants were plainly able to use (and to generalize) what they had learned! (After Fong & Nisbett, 1991.)

quality of the answers also increased, with students more likely to articulate the relevant principles correctly at the end of the semester than at the beginning.

It seems, then, that students' reasoning about evidence can be improved, and the improvement applies to problems in new domains and in new contexts. (Also see Figure 11.3; Fong & Nisbett, 1991.) Training in statistics, it appears, can have widespread benefits. (For more on education effects, see Ferreira et al., 2006; Gigerenzer, Gaissmaier, Kurz-Milcke, Schwartz, & Woloshin, 2008; Lehman & Nisbett, 1990; Schunn & Anderson, 1999.)

Thinking About Evidence: Some Conclusions

How, then, should we think about the results described so far? As we have seen, it's easy to document judgment errors in bright, motivated undergraduates or in highly trained professionals. But there's also ample evidence of more-sophisticated judgment—cases in which people are sensitive to sample size and sample bias, cases in which people judge covariation accurately and do consider base rates.

It's this pattern that demands a dual-process model, distinguishing between System 1 thinking and System 2 thinking. People surely don't want to use System 2 all the time; that would be too slow, too effortful. But they probably do want to use System 2 when the stakes are high and a judgment really matters. It's troubling, then, that System 2's use is not a matter of choice, and so, even when people are motivated to use System 2 (because the judgment is an important one), they often use System 1 nonetheless. System 2 seems to enter the scene only when circumstances allow it and only when this system is appropriately triggered.

However, it's encouraging that we can identify steps that *promote* System 2's use. We can, for example, change features of the environment (e.g., recasting numbers as frequencies rather than proportions), so that we seek what one paper calls "environments that make us smart" (Todd & Gigerenzer, 2007). It's also important that *training* can improve judgment and make judgment errors less likely. Thus, with training, you're more likely to realize that an interview can be thought of as a small sample of data and perhaps should be trusted less than other sources of information based on a larger sample of evidence. Likewise, you can think of an athlete's rookie year in these terms, or a dancer's audition. Once the situation is coded in this fashion, the application of statistical rules is more straightforward and more likely.

We close this section, then, on an optimistic note. Errors in judgment are ubiquitous and consequential. But these errors are not the result of deep flaws in people's capacity for making judgments. Instead, the errors arise largely because the situation does not trigger our (System 2) abilities for making sensible, defensible judgments. And, crucially, education can improve this state of affairs, allowing people to use better judgment in a range of settings. Education doesn't eliminate judgment errors, nor does it guarantee the triumph of System 2 thinking. But education of the right sort substantially decreases the danger of someone making the errors we've catalogued so far.

Confirmation and Disconfirmation

So far in this chapter, we've been looking at judgments that fall within the domain of **induction**—the process through which you make forecasts about *new* cases, based on the cases you've observed so far. Thus, you've observed one prison guard, and you're making a forecast about what others will be like. You've observed a baseball player's performance in one season, and you're predicting how he'll do in other seasons.

Just as important, though, is **deduction**—cases in which you start with claims or assertions that you count as "given" and ask what follows from these premises. For example, perhaps you're already convinced that red wine gives you headaches, or that relationships based on physical attraction rarely last. You might want to ask: What follows from this? What implications do these claims have for your other beliefs or actions?

Deduction has many functions for you, including the fact that it helps keep your beliefs in touch with reality. After all, if deduction leads you to a prediction based on your beliefs, and the prediction then turns out to be *wrong*, this indicates that something is off track in your beliefs—and that claims you thought to be solidly established aren't so solid after all.

"MY PARENTS DIED. THEIR PARENTS DIED. THEIR PARENTS DIED...
IT RUNS IN THE FAMILY."

DRAWING CONCLUSIONS FROM EVIDENCE

We rely on induction in many settings. Sometimes we misread the pattern. Sometimes we detect the pattern, but draw the wrong conclusions.

Does human reasoning respect this principle? If you encounter evidence confirming your beliefs, does this strengthen your convictions? If evidence challenging your beliefs should come your way, do you adjust? And what if you realize from the start that you're uncertain about a belief? What evidence do you seek to check on the belief?

Confirmation Bias

It seems sensible that, in evaluating any belief, you'd want to take a balanced approach—considering evidence that *supports* the belief and weighing it against evidence that might *challenge* the belief. And, in fact, scientists and philosophers often highlight the role of the latter evidence (evidence that challenges you); this evidence, they claim, can be more informative than evidence that seems to support you (e.g., Popper, 1934).

There's a substantial gap, however, between these suggestions about what people *should* do in evaluating their beliefs, and what they actually do. Specifically, people routinely display a pattern we've already mentioned, the pattern known as *confirmation bias*: a greater sensitivity to confirming evidence, and a tendency to neglect disconfirming evidence. Let's be clear, however, that this is an "umbrella" term, because confirmation bias can take many different forms (see Figure 11.4). What all the forms have in common, though, is the capacity to protect your beliefs from challenge (see, among others, Bilalić, McLeod & Gobet, 2010; Evans, 1982; Gilovich, 1991; Kassin, Bogart, & Kerner, 2012; Schulz-Hardt, Frey, Lüthgens, & Moscovici, 2000; Stangor & McMillan, 1992).

FIGURE 11.4 | CONFIRMATION BIAS

Confirmation bias takes many forms:

- First, when people are assessing a belief or a hypothesis, they're more likely to seek evidence that might confirm the belief than evidence that might disconfirm it.

- Second, when disconfirming evidence is made available to them, people often fail to use it in adjusting their beliefs.

- Third, when people encounter confirming evidence, they take it at face value; when they encounter disconfirming evidence, they reinterpret the evidence to diminish its impact.

- Fourth, people often show better memory for confirming evidence than for disconfirming evidence, and, if they do recall the latter, they remember it in a distorted form that robs the evidence of its force.

- Finally, people often fail to consider alternative hypotheses that might explain the available data just as well as their current hypothesis does.

Confirmation bias is a blanket term that refers to many specific effects; we've listed some of those effects here. Confirmation bias is often a good thing; it helps you to maintain stability in your understanding of the world, and often leads you to overrule evidence that should, in fact, be overruled. (If, for example, someone told you they saw a unicorn yesterday, would you believe them?) But confirmation bias can also create many problems.

In a classic demonstration of confirmation bias, Wason (1966, 1968) presented research participants with a series of numbers, such as "2, 4, 6." The participants were told that this trio of numbers conformed to a specific rule, and their task was to figure out what the rule was. Participants were allowed to propose their own trios of numbers ("Does '8, 10, 12' follow the rule?"), and in each case the experimenter responded appropriately ("Yes, it does follow the rule" or "No, it doesn't"). Then, once participants were satisfied they'd discovered the rule, they announced their "discovery."

The rule was, in fact, quite simple: The three numbers had to be in ascending order. Thus, "1, 3, 5" follows the rule, but "6, 4, 2" does not, and neither does "10, 10, 10." Despite this simplicity, participants had difficulty discovering the rule, often requiring many minutes. This was largely due to the type of information they requested as they sought to evaluate their hypotheses: To an overwhelming extent, they sought to confirm the rules they had proposed; requests for disconfirmation were relatively rare. And, we should note, those few participants who *did* seek out disconfirmation for their hypotheses were more likely to discover the rule! It seems, then, that confirmation bias was strongly present in this experiment, and interfered with performance. (For related data, see Mahoney & DeMonbreun, 1978; Mitroff, 1981; Mynatt, Doherty, & Tweney, 1977, 1978.)

Reinterpreting Disconfirming Evidence

It's also the case that, when people encounter confirmation, they're likely to take it at face value. When they encounter disconfirming evidence, however, they're often skeptical about it and scrutinize this new evidence with care, seeking flaws or ambiguities.

Ironically, this mental activity sometimes makes people more likely to remember disconfirming evidence than they are to remember confirming evidence. However, they remember the disconfirming evidence in a way that robs this evidence of its force, leaving their beliefs unchallenged.

As an illustration, one study examined gamblers who bet on professional football games (Gilovich, 1983; also Gilovich & Douglas, 1986). These people all believed they had good strategies for picking winning teams, and their faith in these strategies was undiminished by a series of losses. Why is this? It's because the gamblers didn't remember their losses as "losses." Instead, they remembered them as flukes or oddball coincidences: "I was right. New York was going to win if it hadn't been for that crazy injury to their running back"; "I was correct in picking St. Louis. They would have won except for that goofy bounce the ball took after the kickoff." In this way, winning bets were remembered as wins, but losing bets were remembered as "near wins" (Gilovich, 1991). No wonder, then, that the gamblers maintained their views despite the (seemingly) contrary evidence provided by their own empty wallets.

Belief Perseverance

Even when disconfirming evidence is undeniable, people sometimes don't use it, leading to a phenomenon called **belief perseverance**. Participants in one study were asked to read a series of suicide notes; their task was to figure out which notes were authentic, collected by the police, and which were fake, written by other students as an exercise. As participants offered their judgments, they were provided with feedback about how well they were doing—that is, how accurate they were in detecting the authentic notes. The trick, though, was that the feedback was predetermined and had nothing to do with participants' actual judgments. By prearrangement, some participants were told that they were performing at a level well above average in this task; other participants were told the opposite—that they were much below average (Ross, Lepper, & Hubbard, 1975; also Ross & Anderson, 1982).

Later on, participants were debriefed. They were told that the feedback they had received was utterly bogus and had nothing to do with their performance. Indeed, they were shown the experimenter's instruction sheet, which had assigned them in advance to the *success* or *failure* group. They were then asked a variety of additional questions, including questions for which they had to assess their own "social sensitivity." Specifically, they were asked to rate their actual ability, as they perceived it, in tasks like the suicide-note task.

Let's emphasize that participants were making these judgments about themselves after they'd been told explicitly that the feedback they'd received was randomly determined and had no credibility whatsoever. Nonetheless, participants were influenced by the feedback: Those who had received the "above average" feedback continued to think of their social sensitivity as being above average, and likewise their ability to judge suicide notes. Those who had received the "below average" feedback showed the opposite pattern. The participants, in other words, persevered in their beliefs even when the basis for the belief had been completely discredited.

What's going on here? Imagine yourself in the place of one of the participants, and let's say that we've told you that you're particularly bad at the suicide-note task. As you digest this new "information" about yourself, you'll probably ask yourself, "Could this be true? Am I less sensitive than I think I am?" To check on this possibility, you might search through your memory, looking for evidence that will help you evaluate this suggestion.

What sort of evidence will you seek? This is where confirmation bias comes into play. Because of this bias, chances are good that you'll check on the researcher's information by seeking other facts or other episodes in your memory that might confirm your lack of social perception. As a result, you'll soon have two sources of evidence for your social insensitivity: the (bogus) feedback provided by the researcher, and the supporting information you came up with yourself, thanks to your (selective) memory search. Thus, even if the researcher discredits the information he provided, you still have the information you provided, and on this basis you might maintain your belief. (For discussion, see Nisbett & Ross, 1980; also Johnson & Seifert, 1994.)

Of course, in this experiment, participants could be led either to an enhanced estimate of their own social sensitivity or to a diminished estimate, depending on which false information they were given in the first place. Presumably, this is because the range of episodes in participants' memories is rather wide: In some previous episodes they've been sensitive, and in some they haven't been. Therefore, if they search through their memories seeking to confirm the hypothesis that they've been sensitive in the past, they will find confirming evidence. If they search through memory seeking to confirm the opposite hypothesis, this too will be possible. In short, they can confirm either hypothesis via a suitably selective memory search. This highlights the dangers built into a selective search of the evidence and, more broadly, the danger associated with confirmation bias.

Logic

In displaying confirmation bias, people sometimes seem to be reasoning this way: "If my gambling strategy is good, then I'll win my next bet. But I lose the bet. Therefore, my strategy is good!" This is patently illogical and suggests that, in some cases, people fail to grasp even the simplest principles of logic. How widespread a pattern is this? To find out, researchers have asked how people perform when we explicitly invite them to think things through in a logical manner.

Reasoning About Syllogisms

A number of theorists have proposed that thought generally does follow the rules of logic (Boole, 1854; Henle, 1962, 1978; Mill, 1874; Piaget, 1952). If people make reasoning errors, therefore, it's not because of flaws in their thinking. Instead, the

All M are B.
All D are M.
    Therefore, all D are B.

All X are Y.
Some A are X.
    Therefore, some A are Y.

Some A are not B.
All A are G.
    Therefore, some G are not B.

FIGURE 11.5 | EXAMPLES OF CATEGORI-
CAL SYLLOGISMS

All of the syllogisms shown here are valid; that is, if the two premises are true, then the conclusion must be true.

errors must come from other sources—carelessness, perhaps, or a misinterpretation of the problem.

It turns out, however, that errors in logical reasoning are ubiquitous. If people are careless or misread problems, they do so with great frequency. This is evident, for example, in studies using **categorical syllogisms**—a type of logical argument that begins with two assertions (the problem's **premises**) each containing a statement about a category, as shown in Figure 11.5. The syllogism can then be completed with a conclusion that may or may not follow from these premises. The cases shown in the figure are all **valid syllogisms**—that is, the conclusion *does* follow from the premises stated. In contrast, here is an example of an **invalid syllogism**:

All P are M.
All S are M.
Therefore, all S are P.

To see that this is invalid, try translating it into concrete terms, such as "All plumbers are mortal" and "All sadists are mortal." Both of these are surely true, but it doesn't follow from this that "All sadists are plumbers."

Research participants who are asked to reason about syllogisms do remarkably poorly—a fact that has been clear in the research for many years. Chapman and Chapman (1959), for example, gave their participants a number of syllogisms, including the one just discussed, with premises of "All P are M," and "All S are M." The vast majority of participants, 81%, endorsed the invalid conclusion "All S are P." Another 10% endorsed other invalid conclusions; only 9% got this problem right. Other studies, with other problems, yield similar data—with error rates regularly as high as 70% to 90%. (Gilhooly, 1988, provides a review; also see Khlemani & Johnson-Laird, 2012.) Participants' performance is somewhat better when the syllogisms are spelled out in concrete terms, but here, too, performance remains relatively low (for the classic data, see Wilkins, 1928).

HOW LOGICAL ARE WE?

Errors in logic are extraordinarily common—in adults and in children, and even when we are contemplating very simple logical arguments.

Sources of Logical Errors

Errors in logical reasoning are not just common, they're also quite *systematic* and thus don't look at all like the product of mere carelessness. For example, people often show a pattern dubbed **belief bias**: If a syllogism's conclusion happens to be something people believe to be true anyhow, they're likely to judge the conclusion as following logically from the premises. Conversely, if the conclusion happens to be something they believe to be false, they're likely to reject the conclusion as invalid (Evans, 2012b; Handley et al., 2011; Klauer, Musch, & Naumer, 2000).

This strategy at first appears reasonable: Why wouldn't you endorse conclusions you believe to be true, based on the totality of your knowledge, and reject claims you believe to be false (Evans & Feeney, 2004)? Let's be clear, though, that there's a problem here: When people show the belief-bias pattern, they're failing to distinguish between good arguments (those that are truly persuasive) and bad ones. As a result, they'll endorse an illogical argument if it happens to lead to conclusions they like, and they'll reject a logical argument if it leads to conclusions they have doubts about.

Other logical errors seem to be the result of a low-level "matching strategy"— a strategy of endorsing conclusions if the words "match" those in the premise. Thus, if a participant sees "All A are B" and then "All D are B," the participant is likely to accept a conclusion like "All A are D," because this conclusion "matches" the wording and structure of the premises. Likewise, a participant who sees premises like "Some A are not X" and "Some B are not X" is likely to accept a conclusion like "Some A are not B"—again, because of the "match" in wording and structure (Gilhooly, Logie, Wetherick, & Wynn, 1993; Johnson-Laird, 1983; Wetherick, 1989; an earlier version of this idea, dubbed the "atmosphere effect," was proposed by Woodworth & Sells, 1935). But, of course, this "matching strategy" is illogical and will lead to errors like the one in the "plumbers and sadists" example.

The Four-Card Task

Similar conclusions derive from research on a different aspect of logic: reasoning about **conditional statements**. These are statements of the familiar "If X, then Y" format, with the first statement providing a *condition* under which the second statement is guaranteed to be true.

Overall, reasoning about conditionals is quite poor, with error rates again as high as 80% or 90% (Evans, 1982; Evans, Newstead, & Byrne, 1993; Rips, 1990; Wason & Johnson-Laird, 1972; see Figure 11.6). And here, too, belief bias plays a role: People will endorse a conclusion if they happen to believe it to be true, even

---

FIGURE 11.6 | **ERRORS IN LOGIC**

Affirming the consequent
(1) If A is true, then B is true.
     B is true.
     Therefore, A is true.

Denying the antecedent
(2) If A is true, then B is true.
     A is not true.
     Therefore, B is not true.

Many people accept these arguments as valid, but they are not. To see this, consider some concrete cases:

(3) If the object in my hand is a frog, then the object is green.
     The object in my hand is green.
     Therefore, it is a frog.
(4) If the object in my hand is a frog, then the object is green.
     The object in my hand is not a frog.
     Therefore, it is not green.

People commonly make the errors called "affirming the consequent" and "denying the antecedent." However, a moment's reflection, guided by a concrete case, makes it clear that reasoning in these patterns is, in fact, incorrect.

if the conclusion doesn't follow from the stated premises. Conversely, people will reject a conclusion if they happen to believe it to be false, even if the conclusion is logically demanded by the premises.

Often psychologists study conditional reasoning directly: "If Q is true then R is true. R is not true. What follows from this?" More commonly, though, researchers have turned to the **selection task** (sometimes called the **four-card task**). In this task, participants are shown four playing cards, as in Figure 11.7 (after Wason, 1966, 1968). The participants are told that each card has a number on one side and a letter on the other. Their task is to evaluate this rule: "If a card has a vowel on one side, it must have an even number on the other side." Which cards must be turned over to put this rule to the test?

In Wason's research, 33% of the participants turned over the "A" card to check for an even number. Another 46% turned over both the "A" and the "6." The correct answer, however, was obtained by only 4% of the participants—turning over the "A" and the "7." Plainly, then, performance is atrocious in this problem, with 96% of the participants giving wrong answers. (See the caption for Figure 11.7 for an explanation of *why* this is the right answer!)

FIGURE 11.7 | THE FOUR-CARD TASK

Which cards would you turn over to test this rule: "If a card has a vowel on one side, it must have an even number on the other side"? If we turn over the "A" card and find an even number, that's consistent with the rule. But if we turn it over and find an odd number, that's inconsistent. Therefore, by turning over the "A," we'll discover if this card is consistent with the rule or not. In other words, there's something to be learned by turning over this card. What about the "J"? The rule makes no claims about what is on the flip side of a consonant card, so no matter what we find on the other side, it will not challenge the rule. Therefore, there's nothing to be learned by turning over this card; we already know (without flipping the card over) that it's consistent with the rule. By similar reasoning, we'll learn nothing by turning over the "6"; no matter what we find, it satisfies the rule. Finally, if we turn over the "7" and a consonant is on the other side, this fits with the rule. If there's a vowel on the other side, this doesn't fit. Therefore, we do want to turn over this card, because there is a chance that we might find something informative.

Performance is much better, though, with some variations of the four-card task. For example, Griggs and Cox (1982) asked their participants to test rules like this one: "If a person is drinking beer, then the person must be at least 21 years old." As in the other studies, the participants were shown four cards and asked which cards they would need to turn over to test the rule (see Figure 11.8). In this version, participants did quite well: 73% (correctly) selected the card labeled "Drinking a beer" and also the card labeled "16 years of age." They did not select "Drinking a Coke" or "22 years of age." Griggs and Cox also tested their participants with the "standard" version of the test (if vowel, then even number), and none of their participants got this problem right.

It would seem, then, that how you think—and how *well* you think—depend on what you're thinking about. The problems posed in Figures 11.7 and 11.8 have the same logical structure, but they yield very different performances. What produces this difference? Researchers have offered a variety of answers to this question, but, so far, the data don't allow us to choose which account is preferable. (For a hypothesis cast in terms of evolution, see Cosmides, 1989; Cummins, 2004; Cummins & Allen, 1998; Gigerenzer & Hug, 1992. For a hypothesis cast in terms of day-to-day learning, see Cheng & Holyoak, 1985; Cheng, Holyoak, Nisbett, & Oliver, 1986; Nisbett, 1993, also see Figure 11.9. For still other options, see Almor & Sloman, 2000; Girotto, 2004; Oaksford & Chater, 1995; Polk & Newell, 1995; Sperber, Cara, & Girotto, 1995.)

Even with this unsettled issue, though, it's important to note the parallels between these points and our earlier discussion of how people make judgments about the evidence they encounter. In both domains (inductive judgments

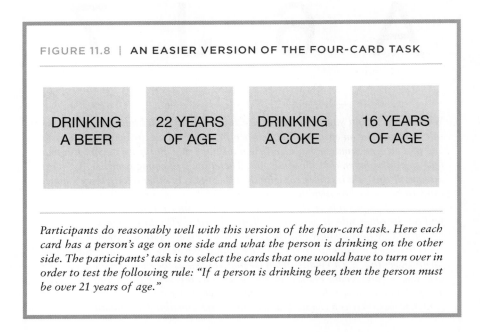

FIGURE 11.8 | AN EASIER VERSION OF THE FOUR-CARD TASK

| DRINKING A BEER | 22 YEARS OF AGE | DRINKING A COKE | 16 YEARS OF AGE |

Participants do reasonably well with this version of the four-card task. Here each card has a person's age on one side and what the person is drinking on the other side. The participants' task is to select the cards that one would have to turn over in order to test the following rule: "If a person is drinking beer, then the person must be over 21 years of age."

FIGURE 11.9 | THE ROLE OF A RATIONALE IN THE
FOUR-CARD PROBLEM

ENTERING	TRANSIT	CHOLERA	OTHER

Participants were asked which cards they would need to turn over to find out if the following rule is true: "If the form says 'ENTERING' on one side, then the other side includes cholera among the list of diseases." Some participants were simply given this problem, and their performance was quite poor. Other participants, though, were provided with a rationale for the rule: They were told that a country was undergoing an outbreak of cholera. Passengers who landed at the country's airport and intended to enter the country therefore needed to be inoculated. On the other hand, passengers who were merely passing through (and not leaving the airport) did not need an inoculation. This rationale helped tie the case to ordinary pragmatic reasoning, and, with this pragmatic framework, participants' reasoning was quite good.

and deductive reasoning), it's remarkably easy to document errors in people's thinking. But in both domains, we can also document higher-quality, more-sophisticated thinking. This more-sophisticated thinking seems to play a role, however, only in the "right" circumstances. When we were discussing judgment, we listed several factors that can trigger System 2 thinking. In our discussion of logic, we've now seen that a problem's *content* can sometimes trigger more accurate reasoning. Thus, the quality of thinking is certainly uneven— but, with the right triggers (and, it turns out, proper education), it can be improved.

WORKBOOK
DEMONSTRATION 11.5

Decision Making

We turn now to a final type of thinking: the thinking that underlies *choices*. Choices, big and small, fill your life, whether you're choosing what courses to take next semester, which candidate to support in an election, or whether to stay with your current partner. How do you make any of these decisions?

Utility Theory

Each of us has our own values—things we like, things we prize, or conversely, things we hope to avoid. Likewise, each of us has a series of goals—things we hope to accomplish or things we hope to see. The obvious suggestion, then, is that we use these values and goals in making decisions. In choosing courses for next semester, for example, you'll choose classes that are interesting (something you value) and also those that help fill the requirements for your major (one of your goals). In choosing a medical treatment, you hope to avoid pain, and you also hope to retain your physical capacities as long as possible.

To put this a bit more formally, each decision will have certain costs attached to it (i.e., consequences that will carry you farther from your goals) and also benefits (consequences moving you toward your goals and providing you with things you value). In deciding, you weigh the costs against the benefits and seek a path that will minimize the former and maximize the latter. When you have several options, you choose the one that provides the best balance of benefits and costs.

Often, though, the costs and benefits you're considering are highly disparate. For example, should you go to Miami for your vacation this year, or Tucson? The weather is better in Tucson, but the flight to Miami is less expensive. To make your choice, therefore, you'll need to weigh the pleasure made possible by good weather against the $90 you might save in airfare, and of course there's no direct way to compare these—no objective procedure for asking how much your pleasure is worth. Your only option, then, is to compare these factors *subjectively*, asking, in effect, how important each factor is to you. This is often expressed as the **subjective utility** of each factor, meaning, simply, the value of that factor for you. Thus, to choose your vacation destination, you'll need to assess the subjective utility of each option (and so, for Tucson, you'll need to calculate the utility of a pleasant vacation *minus* the "disutility" of spending more on airfare). With that done, you can compare your options, obviously choosing the option with the greatest utility.

In most decisions, however, there's a further complication: a degree of uncertainty. The weather isn't always great in Tucson, and often Miami's weather is fine. How should you factor these points into your decision? Likewise, imagine a medical patient, trying to decide whether to take a new medication. Five percent of the people who use this drug, he learns, suffer serious side-effects; should he take the chance that he'll be in this unfortunate group?

One way to think about these uncertainties follows a model formalized by von Neumann and Morgenstern (1947). Within their model, you calculate the **expected value** of each option using this simple equation:

EXPECTED VALUE
= (PROBABILITY OF A PARTICULAR OUTCOME) × (UTILITY OF THE OUTCOME)

Thus, imagine that I offer to sell you a lottery ticket. The ticket costs $5 but gives you a one-in-a-hundred chance of winning $200. In this case, the expected value of the ticket is (.01 × $200), or $2. At a cost of $5, I'm selling the ticket for more than it's worth.

Or, as a more ambitious case, let's say that you're choosing courses for next year. Course 1 looks interesting, but has a heavy workload. To evaluate this course, therefore, you first need to estimate the subjective utility of taking an interesting course and then the disutility of being burdened by a heavy workload. Next, you have to factor in the uncertainties. Perhaps there's a 70% chance that the course will be interesting but a 90% chance that it will have a heavy workload. In this case, the overall utility for this course will be (.70 × the utility of an interesting course) minus (.90 × the disutility of a heavy workload). You could then make similar calculations for the other courses available to you and choose the one with the greatest expected value.

All of this points the way toward a theory of choice, and it's a theory endorsed by many economists: The claim is that in making choices you seek to maximize utility. You do this by consistently selecting the option with the greatest expected utility, calculated as described. (For discussion, see von Neumann & Morgenstern, 1947; also see Baron, 1988; Speekenbrink & Shanks, 2012.)

Framing of Outcomes

It's remarkably easy, however, to find cases in which decision making is not guided by the principle of utility maximization. Part of the reason is that we are all powerfully influenced by factors having nothing to do with utilities.

Consider the problem posed in Figure 11.10. In this choice, a huge majority of people—72%—choose Program A, selecting the sure bet rather than the gamble (Tversky & Kahneman, 1987; also Willemsen, Böckenholt & Johnson, 2011). But

---

FIGURE 11.10 | THE ASIAN DISEASE PROBLEM: POSITIVE FRAME

Imagine that the United States is preparing for the outbreak of an unusual Asian disease, which is expected to kill 600 people. Two alternative programs to combat the disease have been proposed. Assume that the exact scientific estimates of the consequences of the programs are as follows:

If Program A is adopted, 200 people will be saved.

If Program B is adopted, there is a one-third probability that 600 people will be saved, and a two-thirds probability that no people will be saved.

Which program would you prefer? There is clearly no right answer to this question; one could defend selecting the "risky" choice (Program B) or the less-rewarding but less-risky choice (Program A). The clear majority of people, however, lean toward Program A, with 72% choosing it over Program B. Note that this problem is "positively" framed in terms of lives "saved."

Imagine that the United States is preparing for the outbreak of an unusual Asian disease, which is expected to kill 600 people. Two alternative programs to combat the disease have been proposed. Assume that the exact scientific estimates of the consequences of the programs are as follows:

If Program A is adopted, 400 people will die.

If Program B is adopted, there is a one-third probability that nobody will die, and a two-thirds probability that 600 people will die.

Which program would you prefer? This problem is identical in content to the one shown in Figure 11.10: 400 dead out of 600 people is the same as 200 saved out of 600. Nonetheless, people react to the problem shown here rather differently than they do to the one in Figure 11.10. In the "lives saved" version, 72% choose Program A. In the "will die" version, 78% choose Program B. Thus, by changing the phrasing we reverse the pattern of people's preferences.

now consider the problem in Figure 11.11. Here, an enormous majority—78%—choose Program B, and so this time people prefer the gamble, rather than the sure bet. The puzzle, of course, lies in the fact that the two problems are objectively identical: 200 people saved out of 600 is the same as 400 dead out of 600. Nonetheless, this change in how the problem is phrased—that is, the **frame** of the decision—has an enormous impact, turning a 3-to-1 preference in one direction into a 4-to-1 preference in the opposite direction.

Let's emphasize that there's nothing wrong with participants' individual choices. In either Figure 11.10 or Figure 11.11, there's no "right answer," and you can persuasively defend either the decision to avoid risk (by selecting Program A) or the decision to gamble (by choosing Program B). The problem lies in the contradiction created by choosing Program A in one context and Program B in the other context. Indeed, if a single participant is given both frames on slightly different occasions, the participant is quite likely to contradict himself. For that matter, if you wanted to manipulate someone's evaluation of these programs (if, for example, you wanted to manipulate voters or shoppers), then framing effects provide an effective way to do this.

Related effects are easy to demonstrate. Consider, for example, the two problems shown in Figure 11.12. When participants are given the first problem, almost three quarters of them (72%) choose Option A—the sure gain of $100. Participants contemplating the second problem generally choose Option B, with 64% going for this choice (Tversky & Kahneman, 1987). Note, though, that the problems are once again identical. Both pose the question of whether you'd rather end

FIGURE 11.12 | FRAMING EFFECTS IN MONETARY CHOICES

Problem 1

Assume yourself richer by $300 than you are today. You have to choose between:

A. a sure gain of $100

B. 50% chance to gain $200 and 50% chance to gain nothing

Problem 2

Assume yourself richer by $500 than you are today. You have to choose between:

A. a sure loss of $100

B. 50% chance to lose nothing and 50% chance to lose $200

These two problems are identical. In both cases, the first option leaves you with $400, while the second option leaves you with an even chance between $300 and $500. Despite this identity, people prefer the first option in Problem 1 (72% select this option) and the second option in Problem 2 (64% select this option). Once again, by changing the frames we reverse the pattern of preferences.

up with a certain $400 or with an even chance between $300 and $500. Despite this equivalence, participants treat these problems very differently, preferring the sure thing in one case and the gamble in the other.

In fact, there's a reliable pattern in these data: If the frame casts a choice in terms of *losses*, decision makers tend to be **risk seeking**; that is, they prefer to gamble, presumably because they hope to avoid or reduce the loss. (This pattern is especially strong when people contemplate *large* losses—see Harinck, Van Dijk, Van Beest, & Mersmann, 2007; also see LeBoeuf & Shafir, 2012.) Thus, when the Asian disease problem (for example) is cast in terms of lives lost, people choose Program B, apparently attracted by the (slim) possibility that, with this program, they may avoid the loss. Likewise, Problem 2 in Figure 11.12 casts the options in terms of financial losses, and this, too, triggers risk-seeking: Here people reliably choose the 50-50 gamble over the sure loss.

In contrast, if the frame casts the choice in terms of gains, decision makers tend to be **risk averse**: they refuse to gamble, choosing instead to hold tight to what they already have. Thus, Figure 11.10 casts the Asian disease problem in terms of gains (the number of people saved), and this leads people to prefer the risk-free choice (Program A) over the gamble offered by Program B. (And likewise for Problem 1 in Figure 11.12.)

Again, let's emphasize that there's nothing wrong with either of these strategies by itself: If someone prefers to be risk-seeking, this is fine; if someone prefers to be risk averse, this is okay too. The problem arises, though, when people

WORKBOOK
DEMONSTRATION 11.6

FIGURE 11.13 | THE INFLUENCE OF HOW A QUESTION IS FORMED

Imagine that you serve on the jury of an only-child sole-custody case following a relatively messy divorce. The facts of the case are complicated by ambiguous economic, social, and emotional considerations, and you decide to base your decision entirely on the following few observations. To which parent would you award sole custody of the child?

Parent A   average income
average health
average working hours
reasonable rapport with the child
relatively stable social life

Parent B   above-average income
very close relationship with the child
extremely active social life
lots of work-related travel
minor health problems

When asked the question shown here, 64% of the research participants decided to award custody to Parent B. Other participants, however, were asked a different question: "To which parent would you deny sole custody?" Asked this question, 55% of the participants chose to deny custody to Parent B (and so, by default, to award custody to Parent A). Thus, with the "award" question, a majority votes for granting custody to Parent B; with the "deny" question, a majority votes for granting custody to Parent A.

flip-flop between these strategies, depending on how the problem is framed. The flip-flopping, in brief, leaves people wide open to manipulation, inconsistency, and self-contradiction.

Framing of Questions and Evidence

So far, we've considered changes in the way your *options* are framed. Related effects emerge with changes in how a *question* is framed. For example, imagine that you're on a jury in a messy divorce case; the parents are battling over who will get custody of their only child. The two parents have the attributes listed in Figure 11.13. To which parent will you award sole custody of the child?

Research participants asked this question tend to favor Parent B by a 64% to 36% margin. After all, this parent does have a close relationship with the child and has a good income. Note, though, that we asked to which parent you would *award* custody. Things are different if we ask participants to which parent they would *deny* custody. In this case, 55% of the participants choose to deny custody to Parent B (and so, by default, end up awarding custody to Parent A). Thus, the decision is simply reversed: With the "award" question, the majority of participants awards custody to Parent B. With the "deny" question, the majority denies custody to Parent B—and so gives custody to Parent A. (Also see Downs & Shafir, 1999; Shafir, 1993.)

People are also influenced by how *evidence* is framed. Thus, they rate a basketball player more highly if the player has made 75% of his free throws, compared to their ratings of a player who has missed 25% of his free throws. They're more likely to endorse a medical treatment with a "50% success rate" than they are to endorse one with a "50% failure rate." And so on (Levin & Gaeth, 1988; Levin, Schnittjer, & Thee, 1988; also Dunning & Parpal, 1989).

None of this makes sense from the perspective of utility theory, since these differences in framing should, on most accounts, have no impact on the expected utilities of the options. Yet these differences in framing can dramatically change people's choices. (For further, related evidence, see Lichtenstein & Slovic, 2006; Mellers, Chang, Birnbaum, & Ordóñez, 1992; Schneider, 1992; Schwarz, 1999.)

WORKBOOK DEMONSTRATIONS 11.7 AND 11.8

Maximizing Utility Versus Seeing Reasons

How should we think about all of this? One possibility is that people are trying to use (something like) utility calculations when making decisions, but they aren't very good at it. As a result, they're pulled off track by various distractions, including how the decision is framed.

A different possibility, though, is more radical: Perhaps we're not guided by utilities at all. Instead, suppose our goal is simply to make decisions that we feel good about, decisions that we think are reasonable and justified. This view of decision making is called **reason-based choice**. To see how the account plays out, let's go back to the divorce/custody case just described. Half of the participants in this study were asked to which parent they would *award* custody. These participants therefore asked themselves: "What would justify giving custody to one parent or another?" and this drew their attention to each parent's positive traits. As a result, they were swayed by Parent B's above-average income and close relationship with the child. The other participants were asked which parent they would *deny* custody to, and this led them to ask: "What would justify this denial?" This drew attention to the parents' negative attributes—and thus Parent B's heavy travel schedule and health problems.

In both cases, then, the participants relied on *justification* in making their decision. As it turns out, though, the shift in framing caused a change in the factors relevant to that justification, and this is why the shift in framing reversed the pattern of decisions!

For a different example, consider a study by Shafir, Simonson, and Tversky (1993). Half their participants were asked to consider Scenario A in Figure 11.14. In this scenario, 66% of the participants said that they would buy the Sony; only 34% said that they'd prefer to wait until they had checked out other models.

FIGURE 11.14 | THE INFLUENCE OF OTHER ALTERNATIVES ON DECISION MAKING

Scenario A

Suppose you are considering buying a compact disc player and have not yet decided which model to buy. You pass a store that is having a 1-day clearance sale. It offers a popular Sony player for just $99, well below the list price. Do you

    a. buy the Sony player?
    b. wait until you learn more about the various models?

Scenario B

Suppose you are considering buying a compact disc player and have not yet decided which model to buy. You pass a store that is having a 1-day clearance sale. It offers a popular Sony player for just $99 and a top-of-the-line Aiwa player for just $169, both well below the list price. Do you

    a. buy the Sony player?
    b. buy the Aiwa player?
    c. wait until you learn more about the various models?

When people were given the choice shown in Scenario A, 66% chose to buy the Sony player, and only 34% chose to continue shopping. In Scenario B, however, 46% of the participants chose to continue shopping, and only 27% chose to buy the Sony. Thus, in the first context people thought that the Sony was a better choice than continued shopping, but in the second choice they thought that continued shopping was a better choice than buying the Sony.

Other participants, though, were presented with Scenario B, which also offered another player, popular at the time of the study. In this situation, 27% chose the Aiwa, 27% chose the Sony, and a much larger number—46%—chose to wait until they'd learned about other models. How should we think about this? From a utility perspective, the results from Scenario A tell us that the perceived value of the Sony is greater than the perceived value of continued shopping; that's why (by a margin of two to one) participants chose to buy. But the choices in Scenario B show the reverse preference—with continued shopping preferable to either the Sony or the Aiwa (again, by almost two to one). It seems, then, that participants are again flip-flopping: The purchase of the Sony is preferable to continued shopping in one case; continued shopping is preferable to purchasing the Sony in the other.

If we calculate utilities, therefore, people are being foolish. This switch makes sense, however, if we assume that people are looking for *reasons* for their decisions. When only the Sony is available, there are compelling arguments for buying

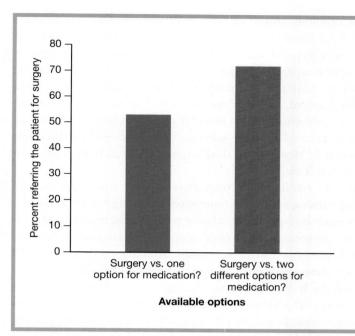

FIGURE 11.15 | THE COST OF TOO MANY OPTIONS

Practicing physicians were given a description of a patient, and asked to choose a treatment. For one group of physicians, the choices offered were surgery and a specific medication. For a second group, the choices included surgery, the same medication, and a different medication. The results were virtually identical to the Aiwa/Sony results. When doctors were choosing between one drug and surgery, many thought the drug was worth a try, and only 53% referred the patient for surgery. When the doctors had three choices, though, they found it difficult to justify choosing either drug over the other, and so most—72%—opted for surgery instead. This is, of course, the same pattern we have already seen: When the doctors couldn't justify one drug option over the other, they chose neither. (After Redelmeier & Shafir, 1995)

it. (It's a popular model, it's available at a good price, and it's available at that price for just one day.) But when both the Sony and the Aiwa are available, it's harder to find persuasive arguments for buying one rather than the other. (Both, after all, are available at a good price for just one day. The Sony is cheaper, which is attractive, but the Aiwa is top of the line.) With no good argument in view for preferring one of these models, people buy neither. (For similar data, see Figure 11.15; also see Schwartz, Chapman, & Brewer, 2004.)

WORKBOOK DEMONSTRATIONS 11.9 AND 11.10

Emotion

There's still another factor that needs to be included in our theorizing: For many people, the idea of *utility maximization* makes it sound like your decisions are governed by calm and dispassionate calculations. To be sure, the assessment of utilities is a subjective matter, but, once the utilities are "measured," the rest of the decision depends largely on arithmetic. Likewise, an emphasis on *reasons* seems to suggest that decision making is a cold, intellectual exercise. But, despite these implications, it's clear that your decisions are powerfully influenced by *emotion*. (See, among others, Kahneman, 2003; Loewenstein, Weber, Hsee, & Welch, 2001; Medin, Schwartz, Blok, & Birnbaum, 1999; Slovic, Finucane, Peters, & MacGregor, 2002; Weber & Johnson, 2009.)

For example, decision making is often influenced by the emotion of *regret*. People are strongly motivated to avoid regret and this guides their decision making: Whenever possible, they select options that will minimize the chances for regret later on. (For more on regret, see Connolly & Zeelenberg, 2002; Gilovich & Medvec, 1995; Gilovich, Medvec, & Kahneman, 1998; Mellers, Schwartz, & Ritov, 1999.)

Likewise, many decisions involve an element of risk. (Should you try out a new, experimental drug? Should we rely more on nuclear power? Should you sign up for the new professor's course, even though you don't know much about her?) In these cases, people seem to assess the risk in emotional terms. Specifically, they ask themselves (for example) how much dread they experience when thinking about a nuclear accident, and they use that dread as an indicator of risk (Fischhoff, Slovic, & Lichtenstein, 1978; Slovic et al., 2002). Notice, by the way, that this is another instance of attribute substitution (pp. 401–402): Rather than asking a hard question—"How risky is this?"—people instead rely on an easier substitute: "How does this make me feel?"

Here's another way emotion influences decisions. We know that certain memories can cause a strong bodily reaction: In remembering a scary movie, for example, you once again become tense and your palms might begin to sweat. In remembering a romantic encounter, you once again become aroused. In the same fashion, *anticipated* events can also produce bodily arousal, and Damasio (1994) suggests that you use these sensations—**somatic markers**, as he calls them—as a guide to decision making. In making a choice, he argues, you literally rely on your "gut feelings" to assess your various options, and this pulls you toward options associated with positive feelings and away from ones that trigger negative feelings.

Damasio argues, in addition, that a particular region of the brain—the orbitofrontal cortex (at the base of the frontal lobe, just above the eyes)—is crucial in your use of these somatic markers, because it is this brain region that allows you to interpret your emotions. Evidence comes from patients who have suffered damage to the orbitofrontal cortex. In one study, participants were required to choose cards from one stack or another; each card, when turned over, showed the amount of money the participant had won or lost on that trial. The cards in one stack often showed large payoffs, but sometimes they showed huge penalties, and thus, overall, it was better to choose cards from the other stack (which had smaller payoffs but much smaller penalties).

Participants *without* orbitofrontal damage figured out this pattern as they worked their way through the task, so they ended up making most of their choices from the less risky stack (and thus earned more overall). Participants *with* orbitofrontal damage, in contrast, continued (unwisely) to favor the risky deck. Because of their brain damage, they were unable to use the somatic markers normally associated with risk—so they failed to heed the "gut feeling" that could have warned them against a dangerous choice (Damasio, 1994; Naqvi, Shiv, & Bechara, 2006; also see Bechara, Damasio, Tranel, & Damasio, 2005; Coricelli, Dolan, & Sirigu, 2007; Dunn et al., 2010; Maia & McClelland, 2005).

Predicting Emotions

Emotion's role in decision making draws our attention to one more complication—and, unfortunately, one more obstacle to good decision making. When emotion shapes decisions, this influence is generally based on a *prediction about the future*: Thus, when people assess the risk associated with nuclear power, they seem to be asking themselves how they would react if, someday, there were a

off the mark .com   by Mark Parisi

THE ROLE OF REGRET

In making decisions, people are powerfully motivated to avoid decisions they might regret later. It turns out, though, that when decisions work out badly, people generally experience far less regret over their choice than they'd anticipated.

nuclear accident. Likewise, if you're trying to avoid regret, you're again looking toward a (possible) future: "If I buy the Sony and I don't like it, I'll feel regret about my own decision, and I'd like to avoid that regret."

These observations demand that we ask: Are people accurate in making these predictions about their own feelings? As it turns out, research suggests that **affective forecasting**—the ability to predict your own emotions—is surprisingly poor. For example, people tend to overestimate how much they'll later regret their errors (Gilbert, Morewedge, Risen, & Wilson, 2004). As a result, people probably give more weight to "regret avoidance" than they should, since they're working to avoid something that, in the end, really won't be that bad.

In the same way, imagine that you're choosing between two apartments that you might rent for next year. One is cheaper and larger but faces a noisy street. Will you just grow used to the noise, so that it ceases to bother you? If so, then you should take the apartment. Or will the noise grow more and more obnoxious to you as the weeks pass? If so, you should pay the extra money for the other apartment. Here, too, your decision depends on a prediction about the future—in this case, a prediction about how your likes and dislikes will change as time goes by.

Several studies suggest that people are rather inept at making these predictions; in particular, people tend to underestimate how swiftly they'll get used to changes in fortune, and likewise underestimate how easily they'll find excuses and rationalizations for their own mistakes (Hsee & Hastie, 2005; Kahneman & Snell, 1992; Loewenstein & Schkade, 1999; Sevdalis & Harvey, 2007; Wilson, Wheatley, Meyers, Gilbert, & Axsom, 2000). Thus, to name a few examples, researchers have shown that people generally overpredict their own reactions to events that are as diverse (and as powerful) as "breaking up with a romantic partner, losing an election, receiving a gift, learning they have a serious illness, failure to secure a

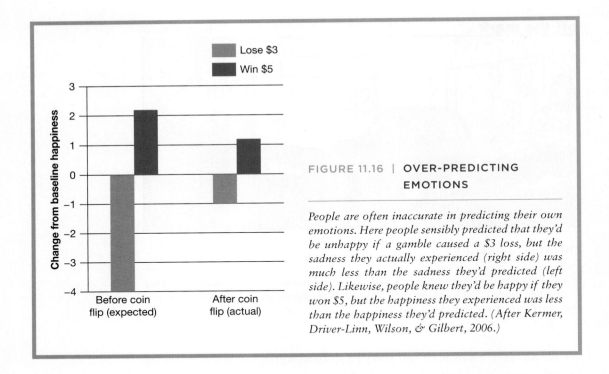

FIGURE 11.16 | OVER-PREDICTING EMOTIONS

People are often inaccurate in predicting their own emotions. Here people sensibly predicted that they'd be unhappy if a gamble caused a $3 loss, but the sadness they actually experienced (right side) was much less than the sadness they'd predicted (left side). Likewise, people knew they'd be happy if they won $5, but the happiness they experienced was less than the happiness they'd predicted. (After Kermer, Driver-Linn, Wilson, & Gilbert, 2006.)

promotion, scoring well on an exam," and so on (Gilbert & Ebert, 2002, p. 503; Kermer, Driver-Linn, Wilson, & Gilbert, 2006; see also Figure 11.16).

In these various cases, people seem to be convinced that things that bother them now will continue to bother them in the future, and that things that please them now will continue to bring pleasure in the future. In both directions, people underestimate their own ability to adapt and, as a result, work to avoid things that they'd soon get used to anyhow and spend money for things that provide only short-term pleasure.

Research on Happiness

Earlier in this chapter, we saw that people often make errors in judgment and reasoning. It now appears that people also lack skill in decision making, relying on strategies that leave them open to manipulation and self-contradiction. And, of course, errors in affective forecasting guarantee that people will often take steps to avoid regrets that, in reality, they wouldn't have felt, and pay for expensive toys that they'll lose interest in before long.

Some investigators draw strong conclusions from these findings. Perhaps people really are incompetent in making decisions. Perhaps people really don't know what will make them happy and what won't and so might be better served by having someone else make their choices for them! (See, for example, Gilbert, 2006; Hsee, Hastie, & Chen, 2008; but for different views, see Kahneman, 2011; Keys & Schwartz, 2007; Weber & Johnson, 2009.)

These are, of course, strong (and fascinating) claims, and have been the subject of considerable debate. One author, for example, simply asserts that people are "predictably irrational" in their decision making, and we're stuck with that (Ariely, 2009). Another author suggests that people truly don't know what's best for them, so they're unable to move efficiently toward happiness; the best they can do is "stumble on happiness" (Gilbert, 2006). Yet another author notes that we all like to have choices but argues that having too many choices actually makes us less happy—a pattern he calls the "paradox of choice" (Schwartz, 2003).

Plainly, these are issues that demand scrutiny, with implications for how each of us lives our life, and also, perhaps, implications that might guide government policies or business practices, helping people to become happy (Layrd, 2010; Thaler & Sunstein, 2009). Indeed, the broad study of "subjective well-being"— what it is, what promotes it—has become an active and exciting area of research. In this way, the study of *how* people make decisions has led to important questions—and perhaps some helpful answers—regarding how they *should* make decisions. In the meantime, the research certainly highlights some traps to avoid, and also suggests that each of us should be a bit more careful in making the choices that shape our lives.

CHAPTER SUMMARY

- Induction often relies on attribute substitution, so that (for example) people estimate frequency by relying on availability. Thus they judge an observation to be frequent if they can easily think of many examples of that observation. The more available an observation is, the greater the frequency is judged to be.

- Judgments based on the availability heuristic are often accurate, but they do risk error. This is because many factors influence availability, including the pattern of what is easily retrievable from memory, bias in what you notice in your experiences, and bias in what the media report.

- People also use the representativeness heuristic, relying on the assumption that categories are relatively homogeneous, so that any case drawn from the category will be representative of the entire group. Because of this assumption, people expect a relatively small sample of evidence to have all the properties that are associated with the entire category; one example of this is the gambler's fallacy. Similarly, people seem insensitive to the importance of sample size, so they believe that a small sample of observations is just as informative as a large sample. In the extreme, people are willing to draw conclusions from just a single observation, as in "man who" arguments.

- People are also likely to make errors in judging covariation. In particular, their beliefs and expectations sometimes lead them to perceive illusory covariations. These errors have been demonstrated not just in novices working with unfamiliar materials but also in experts dealing with the sorts of highly familiar materials they encounter in their professional work. The errors are probably attributable to the fact that confirmation bias causes people to notice and remember a biased sample of the evidence, which leads to bad covariation judgments.

- People also seem insensitive to base rates, and again, this can be demonstrated both in novices evaluating unfamiliar materials and in experts making judgments in their professional domains.

- Use of heuristics is widespread, and so are the corresponding errors. However, we can also find cases in which people rely on more-sophisticated judgment strategies, and thus are alert to sample size and sample bias, and do consider base rates. This has led many theorists to propose dual-process models of thinking. One process (often called System 1) relies on fast, effortless shortcuts; another process (System 2) is slower and more effortful, but is less likely to lead to error.

- System 1 thinking is more likely when people are pressed for time or distracted. However, System 1 thinking can be observed even in the absence of time pressure or distraction, and even when the matter being judged is both familiar and highly consequential.

- System 2 thinking seems more likely when the data are described in terms of frequencies rather than probabilities and also when the data are easily coded in statistical terms (as a *sample* of data, with *chance* playing a role in shaping the sample). System 2 thinking is also more likely if people bring to a situation background knowledge that helps them to code the data and to understand the cause-and-effect role of sample bias or base rates. Training in statistics also makes System 2 thinking more likely, leading us to the optimistic view that judging is a *skill* that can be improved through suitable education.

- Reasoning often shows a pattern of confirmation bias: People tend to seek evidence that might confirm their beliefs rather than evidence that might challenge their beliefs. When evidence challenging a belief is in view, it tends to be underused or reinterpreted. One manifestation of confirmation bias is belief perseverance, a pattern in which people continue to believe a claim even after the basis for the claim has been thoroughly discredited. This is probably because people engage in a biased memory search, seeking to confirm the claim. The evidence provided by this search then remains even when the original basis for the claim is removed.

- People's performance with logic problems such as categorical syllogisms or problems involving conditional statements is often quite poor. The errors are not the product of carelessness, but often derive from belief bias, or a primitive matching strategy.

- How well people reason depend on what they are reasoning about. This is evident in the four-card task, in which some versions of the task yield reasonably good performance, even though other versions yield enormous numbers of errors.

- According to utility theory, people make decisions by calculating the expected utility of each of their options. Evidence suggests, however, that decisions are often influenced by factors that have nothing to do with utilities—for example, how the question is framed or how the possible outcomes are described. If the outcomes are described as potential gains, decision makers tend to be risk averse; if they are described as potential losses, decision makers tend to be risk seeking.

- Some investigators have proposed that your goal in making decisions is not to maximize utility but, instead, to make decisions that you think are reasonable or justified. When you cannot justify a decision, you sometimes decide *not* to decide.

- Decisions are also clearly influenced by emotion. This influence is evident in decision makers' efforts toward avoiding regret; it is also evident in decision makers' reliance on their own bodily sensations as a cue for evaluating their various options. Decision makers are surprisingly inept, however, at predicting their own future reactions. This is true both for predictions of regret and for predictions of future enjoyment or future annoyance.

The Workbook Connection

See the *Cognition Workbook* for further exploration of judgment:

- Demonstration 11.1: Sample Size
- Demonstration 11.2: Relying on the Representativeness Heuristic
- Demonstration 11.3: Applying Base Rates
- Demonstration 11.4: Frequencies Versus Percentages
- Demonstration 11.5: The Effect of Content on Reasoning
- Demonstration 11.6: Wealth Versus Changes in Wealth
- Demonstration 11.7: Probabilities Versus Decision Weights
- Demonstration 11.8: Framing Questions
- Demonstration 11.9: Mental Accounting
- Demonstration 11.10: Seeking Reasons
- Research Methods: Systematic Data Collection
- Research Methods: The Community of Scientists
- Cognitive Psychology and Education: Making People Smarter
- Cognitive Psychology and Education: The Doctrine of Formal Disciplines
- Cognitive Psychology and the Law: Juries' Judgment
- Cognitive Psychology and the Law: Pretrial Publicity
- Cognitive Psychology and the Law: Confirmation Bias in Police Investigation

NEED HELP STUDYING?

 wwnorton.com/studyspace

Visit StudySpace to access free review material such as
- Chapter study plans
- Quizzes
- Flashcards, and more

Go to **wwnorton.com/zaps** for these online labs:
- Syllogisms
- Wason Selection Task
- 2-4-6 Task
- Misconceptions
- Decision Making

CHAPTER TWELVE

Problem Solving and Intelligence

I n many ways, humans are remarkably alike. We all have two arms, one nose. We all have roughly the same biochemistry, and, to a large extent, we all have roughly the same brains, with the structures inside your skull virtually identical to the ones in mine. Perhaps it's no surprise, then, that throughout this book we've been able to discuss truths that apply to all of us—the ways in which we all pay attention, the ways in which we all learn and remember.

But people also differ—in their personalities, their values, and their cognition. We've occasionally mentioned these differences, but the time has come to focus on these differences more directly. In this chapter, we'll start with people's ability to solve problems, and we'll look at how people differ in this domain. Then we'll turn to the often-controversial topic of intelligence. We all know people who seem amazingly smart, and people who we regard as lamentably slow. But what do these differences amount to? What is "intelligence"? Can it be measured? Can it be improved? We'll address all these questions before we're done.

- Often people solve problems by using general heuristics that help them narrow their search for the problem's solution. One of these heuristics is means-end analysis, which leads people to divide problems into a series of simpler subproblems. In other cases, people solve problems by drawing analogies based on problems they've solved in the past. As helpful as they are, however, analogies are often underused.

- Training can improve someone's skill in problem solving. The training can draw someone's attention to a problem's deep structure, which promotes analogy use. Training can also help someone see how a problem can be divided into subproblems. Experts consistently attend to a problem's deep structure and are quite sensitive to a problem's parts. Experts also benefit from their highly cross-referenced knowledge in their domain of expertise.

- Problem solving is often stymied by how people approach the problem in the first place, and that leads to a question of how people find new and creative approaches to problems.

- When closely examined, creative approaches seem to be the result of the same processes that are evident in "ordinary" problem solving—processes hinging on analogies, heuristics, and the like. Hence, the creative *product* is often extraordinary, but the creative *process* may not be.

- Measures of intelligence turn out (to many people's surprise) to be reliable and, on many assessments, valid. Moreover, the data suggest that we can truly speak of "intelligence in general," intelligence that applies to a wide range of tasks. This general intelligence may be a result of mental speed and may be a result of better executive control, with some people better able to control their own thoughts.

- We can easily demonstrate that genetic and environmental factors both matter for intelligence, but, crucially, these factors interact in producing someone's level of intelligence.

- Men and women do not differ on overall intelligence, but there are some tasks in which (on average) men do better, and some tasks in which (on average) women do better. American Whites and American Blacks do differ in the average scores for each group; at least part of the explanation is the inferior nutrition and inferior education provided for many American Blacks. For both the race differences and the sex differences, however, social stereotypes play a large role in how individuals are trained and encouraged, and in the expectations individuals hold for their own performance.

General Problem-Solving Methods

People solve problems all the time. Some problems are pragmatic ("I want to reach the store, but Tom borrowed my car. How should I get there?"). Others are social ("I really want Amy to notice me; how should I arrange it?"). Others are academic ("I'm trying to prove this theorem. How can I do it, starting from these axioms?"). Across this diversity, though, in each case the person has a goal and is trying to figure out how to reach that goal—and so is engaged in the process we call **problem solving**. How do people solve problems?

Problem Solving as Search

Researchers often compare problem solving to a process of *search*, as though you were navigating through a maze, seeking a path toward your goal (cf. Newell & Simon, 1972, also Bassok & Novick, 2012; Mayer, 2012). You begin with an **initial state** (the knowledge and resources you have at the outset) and, to move toward the goal, you have a set of **operators**—actions that can change your state. There are also **path constraints** (such as limited time or money, or ethical limits) that rule out some solutions.

To make this concrete, consider the Hobbits and Orcs problem in Figure 12.1. For this problem, the operators are the moves you can make (transporting creatures back and forth). The path constraints are the requirement that no Hobbits be eaten and the limited size of the boat. Together, all these elements leave you with a set of options shown graphically in Figure 12.2. More precisely, the figure shows the moves available early in the solution and depicts the options as a tree, with each step leading to more branches. All the branches together form the **problem space**—that is, the set of all states that can be reached in solving this problem.

Framing things in this way suggests that one strategy in solving this problem would be to trace through the entire problem space, exploring each branch in turn. This would be akin to exploring every possible corridor in a maze, and this approach would guarantee that you'd eventually find the solution. For most problems, however, this "brute force" approach would be hopeless. Consider, for

---

FIGURE 12.1 | **THE HOBBITS AND ORCS PROBLEM**

Five Orcs and five Hobbits are on the east bank of the Muddy River. They need to cross to the west bank and have located a boat. In each crossing, at least one creature must be in the boat, but no more than three creatures will fit in the boat.

And, of course, if the Orcs ever outnumber the Hobbits on either side of the river, they will eat the Hobbits! Therefore, in designing the crossing we must make certain that the Hobbits are never outnumbered, either on the east bank of the river or on the west.

How can the creatures get across without any Hobbits being eaten?

This problem has been used in many studies of problem-solving strategies. Can you solve it?

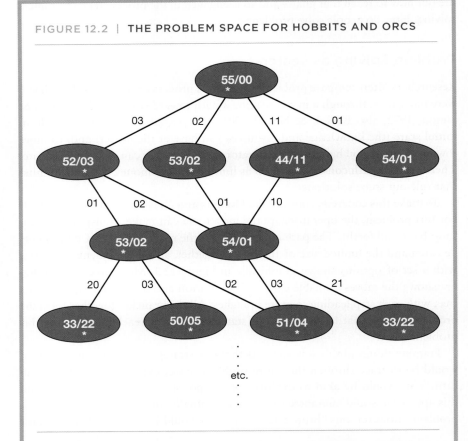

Each circle shows a possible problem state. The state 54/01, for example, indicates that five Hobbits and four Orcs are on the east bank; there are no Hobbits, but one Orc, on the west bank. The star shows the position of the boat. The numbers alongside each line indicate the number of creatures in the boat during each river crossing. The move 02, for example, transports no Hobbits, but two Orcs. The problem states shown here are all the legal states. (Other states, and other moves, would result in some of the Hobbits being eaten.) Thus, there are four "legal" moves one can make, starting from the initial state. From these, there are four possible moves one can make, but these lead to just two problem states (53/02 and 54/01). From these two states, there are four new states that can be reached, and so on. We have here illustrated the first three moves that can be made in solving this problem; the shortest path to the problem's solution involves 11 moves.

example, the game of chess: In chess, which move is best at any point in the game depends in part on what your opponent will be able to do in response to the move, and then what you'll do next. To make sure you're choosing the best move, therefore, you need to think through a few cycles of play, so that you can select as your current move the one that leads to the best sequence.

Let's imagine, therefore, that you decide to look ahead just three cycles of play—three of your moves, and three of your opponent's. Some quick calculation, however, tell us that, for three cycles of chess play, there are roughly 700 million possibilities for how the game could go; and this number immediately rules out the option of considering every possibility. If you could evaluate 10 sequences per second, you'd still need more than two years, on a 24/7 schedule, to evaluate the full set of options, each time you wanted to select a move! And, of course, there's nothing special here about chess, because most real-life problems offer so many options that you couldn't possibly explore every one.

Thus, you somehow need to narrow your search through a problem space, but of course this involves an element of risk: If you don't consider every option, there's a chance you'll miss the *best* option. However, you have no choice about this, since the alternative—the strategy of considering each possibility—would be absurd.

What you need, therefore, is a problem-solving heuristic. Heuristics are, we've said, strategies that are efficient, but at the cost of occasional errors. In the domain of problem solving, a heuristic is a strategy that narrows your search through the problem space—but (you hope) in a fashion that still leads to the problem's solution.

General Problem-Solving Heuristics

What problem-solving heuristics do people use? One common approach involves the **hill-climbing strategy**. To understand this term, imagine that you're hiking through the woods and trying to figure out which trail leads to the mountaintop. You obviously need to climb uphill to reach the top, so whenever you come to a fork in the trail, you select the path that's going uphill. The problem-solving strategy works the same way: At each point, you simply choose the option that moves you in the direction of your goal.

This strategy is often helpful but is surely of limited use: This is because many problems require that you briefly move *away* from your goal; only then, from this new position, can the problem be solved. For instance, if you want Mingus to notice you more, it might help if you go away for a while; that way, he'll be more likely to notice you when you come back. This ploy would never be discovered, though, if you relied on the hill-climbing strategy.

Even so, people often rely on this heuristic. As a result, they have difficulties whenever a problem requires them to "move backward in order to go forward." Often, at these points, people drop their current plan and seek some other solution to the problem: "This must be the wrong strategy; I'm going the wrong way." (See, for example, Jeffries, Polson, Razran, & Atwood, 1977; Thomas, 1974.)

Fortunately, though, people also have other heuristics available to them. For example, people often rely on **means-end analysis**. To use this strategy, you compare your current state to the goal state, and ask, "What means do I have to make these more alike?" Figure 12.3 offers a commonsense example of how this strategy plays out.

FIGURE 12.3 | EXAMPLE OF MEANS-END ANALYSIS

I want to take my son to nursery school. What's the difference between what I have and what I want? One of distance. What changes distance? My automobile. My automobile won't work. What is needed to make it work? A new battery. What has new batteries? An auto repair shop. I want the repair shop to put in a new battery; but the shop doesn't know I need one. What is the difficulty? One of communication. What allows communication? A telephone.... (from Newell & Simon, 1972, p.416)

People use a variety of heuristics to solve problems, but one common strategy is means-end analysis. To use this strategy, you compare your current status to your desired status, and ask: "What means do I have to make these more alike?" Among its other benefits, this strategy helps you to break a problem into small subproblems.

Notice that a means-end analysis leads you to break a problem into smaller **subproblems,** each with its own goal. By solving the subproblems one by one, you address the larger problem. In fact, some have suggested that this identification of subproblems is itself a powerful problem-solving heuristic: By breaking a problem into smaller pieces, you make the initial problem easier to solve.

Pictures and Diagrams

People also have other options in their mental toolkit. For example, it's often helpful to translate a problem into concrete terms, relying on a mental image or a picture. Indeed, the histories of science, art, and engineering are filled with instances in which great discoveries emerged in this way (Hegarty & Stull, 2012; Miller, 1986; Reed, 1993; Shepard, 1988).

As a simple illustration, consider the problem described in Figure 12.4. Most people try an algebraic solution to this problem (width of each volume, multiplied by the number of volumes, divided by the worm's eating rate) and end up with the wrong answer. People generally get this problem right, though, if they start by visualizing the arrangement. Now they can discern the actual positions of the worm's starting point and end point, and this usually takes them to the correct answer (see Figure 12.5).

For this problem, it doesn't matter whether you rely on an actual picture or a "mental picture"—that is, an image (J. R. Anderson, 1993; R. Anderson & Helstrup, 1993; Reed, 1993). But sometimes, mental images are preferable: For example, it's easy to imagine moving patterns; it's harder to depict motion with

FIGURE 12.4 | THE BOOKWORM PROBLEM

Solomon is proud of his 26-volume encyclopedia, placed neatly, with the volumes in alphabetical order, on his bookshelf. Solomon doesn't realize, though, that there's a bookworm sitting on the front cover of the A volume. The bookworm begins chewing his way through the pages on the shortest possible path toward the back cover of the Z volume.

Each volume is 3 inches thick (including pages and covers), so that the entire set of volumes requires 78 inches of bookshelf. The bookworm chews through the pages and covers at a steady rate of ¾ of an inch per month. How long will it take before the bookworm reaches the back cover of the Z volume?

People who try an algebraic solution to this problem often end up with the wrong answer.

a diagram. Thus, if a problem solution depends on motion, the problem may be more easily solved with imagery than with a picture.

Sometimes, though, the advantage goes the other way. Elaborate or detailed forms are difficult to image clearly, so, if a problem depends on such forms, problem solving via image will be difficult. Likewise, there seem to be limits on what can be discovered from a mental image, but you can escape these limits by drawing a picture based on the image. The picture allows you a "start fresh" in interpreting the form, and this can lead to new perspectives or new ideas. The advantage of "externalizing" the image can easily be demonstrated in the laboratory (Reisberg, 2000); it can also be demonstrated in real-world settings—for example, with architects who gain by sketching out their designs rather than by trying to work out the design entirely "in their heads" (Verstijnen, Hennessey, van Leeuwen, Hamel, & Goldschmidt, 1998).

Drawing on Experience

Where does all of this leave us with regard to the questions with which we began—and, in particular, the ways in which people differ from each other in their mental abilities? There's actually little difference from one person to the next in the use of strategies like hill-climbing or means-end analysis—most people can and do use these strategies. People do differ, of course, in their drawing ability and in their imagery prowess (see Chapter 10), but these points are relevant only for some problems. Where, then, do the broader differences in problem-solving skill arise?

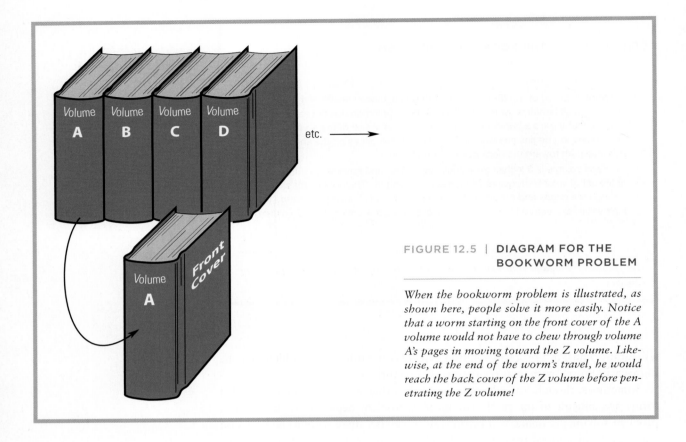

FIGURE 12.5 | DIAGRAM FOR THE BOOKWORM PROBLEM

When the bookworm problem is illustrated, as shown here, people solve it more easily. Notice that a worm starting on the front cover of the A volume would not have to chew through volume A's pages in moving toward the Z volume. Likewise, at the end of the worm's travel, he would reach the back cover of the Z volume before penetrating the Z volume!

Problem Solving via Analogy

Often a problem reminds you of other problems you've solved in the past, and so you can rely on your experience in tackling the current challenge. In other words, you solve the current problem by means of an analogy with other, already-solved, problems.

Analogies have certainly been helpful in the history of science—with scientists furthering their understanding of the heart by comparing it to a pump, and extending their knowledge of gases by comparing molecules to billiard balls. Analogies are also useful in the classroom—with the atom described to students as (roughly) resembling the solar system, or with memory compared to a library (Donnelly & McDaniel, 1993; for more on the powerful effects of analogy use, see Gentner & Smith, 2012; Holyoak, 2012).

WORKBOOK DEMONSTRATION 12.1

What about ordinary problem solving? The tumor problem (see Figure 12.6A) is difficult, but people generally solve it if they're able to use an analogy: Gick and Holyoak (1980) first had their participants read about a related situation (see Figure 12.6B), then presented them with the tumor problem. When participants were encouraged to use this hint, 75% were able to solve the tumor problem. Without the hint, only 10% solved the problem.

However, despite the clear benefit of using analogies, people routinely fail to use them. Gick and Holyoak had another group of participants read the "general

FIGURE 12.6 | THE TUMOR PROBLEM

A Suppose you are a doctor faced with a patient who has a malignant tumor in his stomach. To operate on the patient is impossible, but unless the tumor is destroyed the patient will die. A kind of ray, at a sufficiently high intensity, can destroy the tumor. Unfortunately, at this intensity the healthy tissue that the rays pass through on the way to the tumor will also be destroyed. At lower intensities the rays are harmless to healthy tissue but will not affect the tumor. How can the rays be used to destroy the tumor without injuring the healthy tissue?

B A dictator ruled a country from a strong fortress, and a rebel general, hoping to liberate the country, vowed to capture the fortress. The general knew that an attack by his entire army would capture the fortress, but he also knew that the dictator had planted mines on each of the many roads leading to the fortress. The mines were set so that small groups of soldiers could pass over them safely, since the dictator needed to move his own troops to and from the fortress. However, any large force would detonate the mines, blowing them up and also destroying the neighboring villages.

The general knew, therefore, that he couldn't just march his army up one of the roads to the fortress. Instead, he devised a simple plan. He divided his army into small groups and dispatched each group to the head of a different road. When all were ready, he gave the signal and each group marched up a different road to the fortress, with all the groups arriving at the fortress at the same time. In this way, the general captured the fortress and overthrew the dictator.

The tumor problem, designed by Duncker (1945), has been studied extensively. Can you solve it? One solution is to aim multiple low-intensity rays at the tumor, each from a different angle. The rays will meet at the site of the tumor and so, at just that location, will sum to full strength. People are much more likely to solve this problem if encouraged to use the hint provided by the problem shown in B.

and fortress" story, but no further hints were given. In particular, these participants were not told that this story was relevant to the tumor problem. Only 30% solved the tumor problem (see Figure 12.7) (also see Hayes & Simon, 1977; Ross, 1984, 1987, 1989; Weisberg, DiCamillo, & Phillips, 1978).

Apparently, then, people benefit from analogies if suitably instructed, but spontaneous, uninstructed use of analogies is surprisingly rare. One reason lies in how people search through memory when seeking an analogy: In solving a problem about tumors, people seem to ask themselves, "What else do I know about tumors?" This search will help them remember other situations in which they thought about tumors, but of course it won't lead them to the "general and fortress" problem (e.g., Bassok, 1996; Cummins, 1992; Hahn et al., 2010; Wharton, Holyoak, Downing, & Lange, 1994). This (potential) analogue will therefore lie dormant in memory and provide no help.

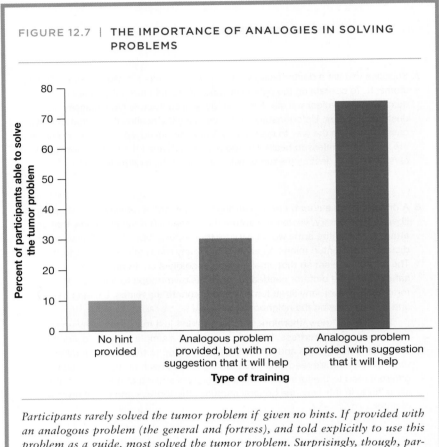

FIGURE 12.7 | THE IMPORTANCE OF ANALOGIES IN SOLVING PROBLEMS

Participants rarely solved the tumor problem if given no hints. If provided with an analogous problem (the general and fortress), and told explicitly to use this problem as a guide, most solved the tumor problem. Surprisingly, though, participants often failed to make use of the analogy unless they were specifically encouraged to. (After Gick & Holyoak, 1980.)

Thus, to locate helpful analogies in memory, people often need to get beyond the superficial features of the problem, and think instead about the principles governing the problem—focusing on what's sometimes called the problem's "deep structure," rather than its "surface structure." Related, people can use analogies only if they figure out how to map the prior case onto the problem now being solved—only if they realize, for example, that converging groups of soldiers correspond to converging rays, and that a fortress-to-be-captured corresponds to a tumor-to-be-destroyed. This mapping process can be difficult (Holyoak, 2012), and failures to figure out the mapping are another reason that people regularly fail to find and use analogies.

Strategies to Make Analogy Use More Likely

Perhaps, then, people who are better problem solvers are those who make better use of analogies. Presumably, this is because the better problem solvers pay attention to a problem's dynamic, rather than its superficial traits, and this helps them both to find analogies and to master the mapping.

Consistent with these claims, it turns out that we can *improve* problem solving by encouraging people to pay attention to problems' underlying dynamic. For example, Cummins (1992) instructed participants in one group to analyze a series of algebra problems one by one. Participants in a second group were asked to *compare* the problems to each other, describing what the problems had in common. This latter instruction forced participants to think about the problems' underlying structure, and, guided by this perspective, these participants were more likely, later on, to use the training problems as a basis for analogies.

Likewise, Needham and Begg (1991) presented participants with a series of training problems. Some participants were told that they'd need to recall these problems later and were encouraged to work at memorizing them. Other participants were encouraged to work at *understanding* each solution, so that they'd be able to explain it later to another person. When the time came for the test problems, participants in the second group were more likely to transfer what they'd learned earlier. As a result, those who had taken the "understand" approach were able to solve 90% of the test problems; participants who had taken the "memorize" approach solved only 69%. (For related data, see Catrambone, Craig, & Nersessian, 2006; Kurtz & Loewenstein, 2007; Lane & Schooler, 2004; Pedrone, Hummel & Holyoak, 2001.)

Expert Problem Solvers

How far can we go with these points? Can we use these simple ideas to explain the difference between ordinary problem solvers and genuine experts? To some extent, we can.

We've claimed, for example, that it's helpful to think about problems in terms of their deep structure, and this is, it seems, the way experts think about problems. In one study, participants were asked to categorize simple physics problems (Chi, Feltovich, & Glaser, 1981). Novices tended to place together all the problems involving inclined planes, all the problems involving springs, and so on, in each case focusing on the surface form of the problem, independent of what physical principles were needed to solve the problem. In contrast, experts (Ph.D. students in physics) ignored these details of the problems and, instead, sorted according to the physical principles relevant to the problem's solution. (For more on expertise, see Ericsson & Towne, 2012.)

We've also claimed that attention to a problem's structure promotes analogy use, so if experts are more attentive to this structure, they should be more likely to use analogies—and they are (e.g., Bassok & Novick, 2012). Novick and Holyoak (1991) found that participants with greater math expertise (measured via quantitative SAT scores) were more likely to use analogies when working on math problems. There was no relationship, though, between analogy use and verbal SAT scores; what mattered, therefore, was specifically expertise in the relevant domain.

Experts' reliance on analogies is also evident in real-world settings. Christensen and Schunn (2007) recorded work meetings of a group of expert engineers. The engineers were trying to create new products for use in the medical world, and, as they discussed their options, analogy use was frequent—with an analogy offered in the discussion every 5 minutes!

Chunking and Subgoals

Experts have another advantage: We mentioned earlier that it's often helpful to break a problem into subproblems, so that the problem can be solved part by part rather than all at once. This, too, is a technique often used by experts.

Classic evidence on this point comes from studies of chess experts (De Groot, 1965, 1966; also see Chase & Simon, 1973). The data show that these experts are particularly skilled in *organizing* a chess game—in seeing the structure of the game, understanding its parts, and perceiving how the parts are related to each other. This is revealed, for example, in how chess masters remember board positions. In one procedure, chess masters were able to remember the positions of 20 pieces after viewing the board for just 5 seconds; novices remembered many fewer (see Figure 12.8). In addition, there was a strong pattern to the experts' recollection: In recalling the layout of the board, the experts would place four or five pieces in their proper positions, then pause, then recall another group, then pause, and so on. In each case, the group of pieces was one that made "tactical sense"—for example, the pieces involved in a "forked" attack, a chain of mutually defending pieces, and the like.

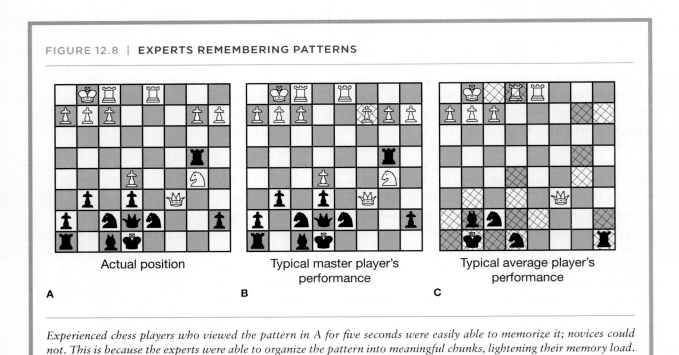

FIGURE 12.8 | EXPERTS REMEMBERING PATTERNS

Actual position

A

Typical master player's performance

B

Typical average player's performance

C

Experienced chess players who viewed the pattern in A for five seconds were easily able to memorize it; novices could not. This is because the experts were able to organize the pattern into meaningful chunks, lightening their memory load. Cross-hatched squares indicate memory errors.

It seems, then, that the masters had memorized the board in terms of higher-order units, defined by their strategic function within the game. Consistent with this suggestion, the masters showed no memory advantage if asked to memorize random configurations of chess pieces. Here there were no sensible groupings, and so the masters were unable to organize (and thus memorize) the board. (For similar data with other forms of expertise, see Egan & Schwartz, 1979; Tuffiash, Roring, & Ericsson, 2007.)

This perception of higher-order units helps organize the expert's thinking. By focusing on the units and how they're related to each other, the expert keeps track of broad strategies without getting bogged down in the details. Likewise, these units set subgoals for the expert: Having perceived a group of pieces as a coordinated attack, the expert sets the subgoal of preparing for the attack. Having perceived another group of pieces as the early development of a pin, the expert creates the subgoal of avoiding the pin. Thus, the higher-order units lend structure to the expert's thinking and guide the expert in choosing the next move.

Can nonexperts be trained to use subgoals in this way? Participants in one study were shown a new mathematical procedure. For some participants, key steps of the procedure were labeled in a fashion that highlighted the function of those steps; for other participants, no labels were provided (Catrambone, 1998). The idea here is that the labels can help participants to divide the procedure into meaningful parts, and, in fact, participants given the labels were better able to use this new procedure in solving novel problems.

Let's be clear, though, that experts also have other advantages, including the simple fact that they know much more about their domains of expertise than novices do. Experts in many cases have also received feedback or explicit instruction, improving their performance (Campitelli & Gobet, 2011; Ericsson, 2005, Ericsson & Towne, 2012; Ericsson & Ward, 2007). Experts also organize their knowledge more effectively than novices. In particular, studies indicate that experts' knowledge is heavily cross-referenced, so that each bit of information has associations to many other bits (e.g., Bédard & Chi, 1992; Heller & Reif, 1984). As a result, experts have better access to what they know.

In short, there is a stack of differences separating novices from experts. None of these differences, though, is exotic or mysterious. Instead, the differences all hinge on the processes we've already discussed—with an emphasis on analogies, subproblems, memory search, and the benefits of sheer practice. All this provides an indication both that our theorizing is sensible and that we can use this theorizing to describe how people (in particular, novices and experts) differ from each other.

Defining the Problem

Novices, we've said, often define problems in terms of superficial features; experts, in contrast, define a problem in their area of expertise in terms of the problem's underlying dynamic. As a result, the experts are more likely to break the problem into meaningful parts, more likely to realize what other problems are analogous to the current problem, and so are more likely to benefit from analogies.

All of this clearly implies that there are better and worse ways to define a problem—ways that will lead to a solution, and ways that will obstruct it. But what does it mean to "define" a problem? And what determines how people define the problems they encounter?

Ill-Defined and Well-Defined Problems

For many problems, the initial state, goal, and operators are clearly stated at the start: Get all the hobbits to the other side of the river, using the boat. Solve the math problem, using the axioms stated. Many of the problems people encounter, though, are rather different. For example, we all hope for peace in the world, but what exactly will this goal look like? There will be no fighting, of course, but what other traits will the goal have? Will the nations currently on the map still be in place? How will disputes be settled? It's also unclear what steps should be tried in an effort toward reaching this goal. Would diplomatic adjustments work? Or would economic measures be more effective?

Problems like this one are said to be **ill-defined**, with no clear statement at the outset of how the goal should be characterized or what operations might be used to reach that goal. Other examples of ill-defined problems include "having a good time while on vacation," "saving money for college," or "choosing a good paper topic" (Halpern, 1984; Kahney, 1986; Schraw, Dunkle, & Bendixen, 1995; Simon, 1973).

When confronting ill-defined problems, your best bet is often to create subgoals, because many ill-defined problems have reasonably well-defined parts, and, by solving each of these, you can move toward solving the overall problem. A different strategy is to add some structure to the problem, by adding extra constraints or extra assumptions. In this way, you gradually render the problem well-defined instead of ill-defined—perhaps with a narrower set of options in how you might approach the problem, but with a clearly specified goal state and, eventually, with a manageable set of operators to try.

Functional Fixedness

Even for well-defined problems, however, there's often more than one way to understand the problem. This point is evident in the contrast between superficial and deeper-level descriptions of a problem, but other examples are easy to find.

Consider the problem in Figure 12.9. To solve it, you need to cease thinking of the box as a container, and instead think of it as a potential platform. Thus, solving the problem depends heavily on how the box is represented, and we can show this by *encouraging* one representation or another. In one study, participants were given the equipment shown in Figure 12.9A: some matches, a box of tacks, and a candle. This configuration (implicitly) underscored the box's conventional function. As a result, this configuration increased **functional fixedness**—the tendency to be rigid in how you think about an object's function. With fixedness in place, the problem was rarely solved (Duncker, 1945; Fleck & Weisberg, 2004).

Other participants were given the same tools, but configured differently. They were given some matches, a pile of tacks, the box (now empty), and a candle. In

FIGURE 12.9 | THE CANDLE PROBLEM

You are given the objects shown: a candle, a book of matches, and a box of tacks. Your task is to find a way to attach the candle to the wall of the room, at eye level, so that it will burn properly and illuminate the room.

Initial state:

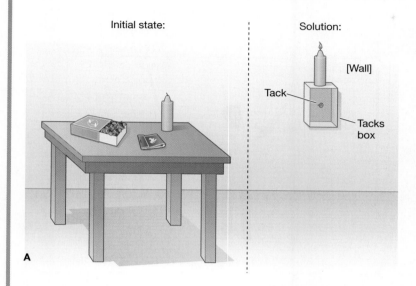

A

Solution:

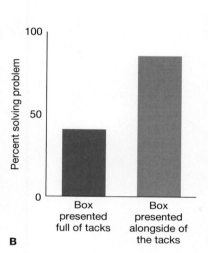

[Wall]

Tack

Tacks box

B

What makes this problem so difficult is the tendency to think of the box of tacks as a box—that is, as a container. The problem is readily solved, though, once you think of the box as a potential platform.

this setting, the participants were less likely to think of the box as a container for the tacks, and so less likely to think of the box *as a container*. As a result, they were more likely to solve the problem (Duncker, 1945). (Also see German & Barrett, 2005 for a demonstration of fixedness in a group of hunter-horticulturalists living in the Amazon jungle!; for a similar problem, see Figure 12.10; for more on *escaping* the limits imposed by fixedness, see McCaffrey, 2012.)

Einstellung

A related obstacle to problem solving arises when people start work on a problem and, because of their early steps, get locked into a particular line of thinking. In this case, too, people can end up the victims of their own assumptions, rigidly following a path that no longer serves them well.

Some investigators describe this rigidity as a **problem-solving set**—the collection of beliefs and assumptions a person makes about a problem. Other investigators use the term **Einstellung**, the German word for "attitude," to

FIGURE 12.10 | THE TWO-STRING PROBLEM

You enter a room in which two strings are hanging from the ceiling and a pair of pliers is lying on a table. Your task is to tie the two strings together. Unfortunately, though, the strings are positioned far enough apart so that you can't grab one string and hold on to it while reaching for the other. How can you tie them together?

The two-string problem is difficult—because of functional fixedness. The trick here is not to think of the pliers in terms of their usual function—squeezing or pulling. Instead, the trick is simply to think of the pliers as a weight. The solution to the puzzle is to tie the pliers to one string, and push the pliers away from the other string. While this pendulum is in motion, go and grab the second string, and then, when the pendulum swings back toward you, grab it and you're all set.

describe the problem solvers' perspective (their beliefs, habits, preferred strategies, and so on).

A classic demonstration of Einstellung uses the water jar problem. In this problem, you're given three jars: Jar A, which holds 18 ounces; Jar B, which holds 43 ounces; and Jar C, which holds 10 ounces. You have access to an unlimited supply of water. You also have a large, uncalibrated bucket. Your task is to pour exactly 5 ounces of water into the bucket. How would you do it?

Most participants find the solution (shown in Figure 12.11) after a little thought. Then, once they've solved this problem, we give them a new one. Jar A now holds 9 ounces, Jar B holds 42, and Jar C holds 6. The goal is to end up with 21 ounces. Once they've solved this, they get another problem: Jar A holds 21; B holds 127; C holds 3; the goal is 100 ounces.

The problems in this series can all be solved in the same way: You start by filling the largest jar (B). Then you pour from Jar B into Jar A and Jar C, filling

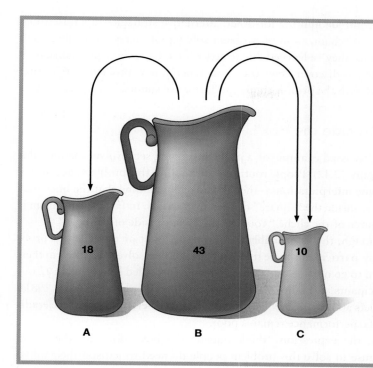

FIGURE 12.11 | THE WATER JAR
PROBLEM

You're given these three jars, an unlimited supply of water, and an uncalibrated bucket. You want to pour exactly 5 ounces of water into the bucket; how can you do it? The solution is shown here. Once participants have solved a couple of problems, though, each of which can be solved the same way, they seem to grow blind to other solution paths.

them both. Next, you dump Jar C's contents and fill it again, still from Jar B. This sequence leaves the desired amount in Jar B.

After solving several problems with this design, participants are given one more problem: Jar A holds 18 ounces; Jar B holds 48 ounces; Jar C holds 4 ounces. The goal is 22 ounces. Participants generally solve this problem the same way they've solved the previous problems, failing to see that a more direct route to the goal is possible—by filling A, filling C, and combining them (18 + 4). Their prior success in using the same procedure over and over renders them blind to the more efficient alternative.

More troubling, consider what happens if participants are given the training problems just described, all solved via the same path, and then given this problem: Jar A holds 28 ounces; Jar B holds 76; Jar C holds 3. The goal is 25 ounces. The participants attack this problem by using their tried-and-true method: B, minus A, minus C twice. But this time the method fails (yielding 42 ounces, instead of the desired 25). When participants realize this, they're often stymied; their well-practiced routine won't work here, and they fail to see the simpler path that would work (28 minus 3 equals 25). Remarkably, 64% of the participants in one study failed to solve this problem, thanks to their history of using a now-inapplicable strategy (Luchins, 1942; Luchins & Luchins, 1950, 1959).

Let's be clear that, in a way, participants are doing something sensible here: Once you discover a strategy that "gets the job done," you might as well use that strategy. Correspondingly, once you discover a strategy that works, there's little reason to continue hunting for other, alternative strategies. It's unsettling, though, that this mechanization of problem solving interferes with subsequent performance: Once they've learned one strategy for solving these problems, people seem less able to discover new strategies. When a new problem arrives that cannot be solved with the prior formula, performance suffers.

Thinking "Outside the Box"

Another often-discussed example of a problem-solving set involves the nine-dot problem (see Figure 12.12). People routinely fail to solve this problem, because—according to some interpretations—they (mistakenly) assume that the lines they draw need to stay inside the "square" defined by the dots. In fact, this problem is probably the source of the cliché "You need to think outside of the box."

Ironically, though, this is probably the wrong account of the nine-dot problem. In one study, participants were told explicitly that to solve this problem their lines would need to go outside the square. This hint provided little benefit: 12 out of the 15 participants still failed to find the solution (Weisberg & Alba, 1981). Apparently, beliefs about "the box" are not the obstacle here; even when we eradicate these beliefs, performance remains poor.

Nonetheless, the expression "think outside the box" does get the broad idea right, because to solve this problem people do need to jettison their initial approach. Specifically, most people assume that the lines they draw must begin and end on dots. People also have the idea that they'll need to maximize the number of dots "canceled" with each move; as a result, they seek solutions in which each line cancels a full row or column of dots. It turns out, though, that these assumptions

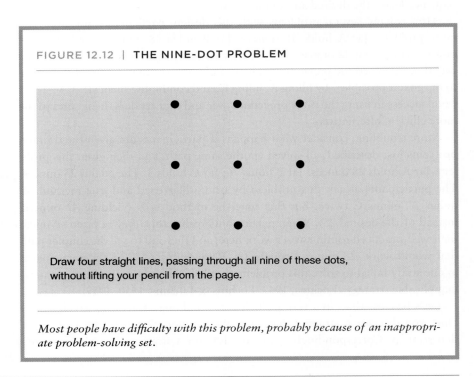

FIGURE 12.12 | THE NINE-DOT PROBLEM

Draw four straight lines, passing through all nine of these dots, without lifting your pencil from the page.

Most people have difficulty with this problem, probably because of an inappropriate problem-solving set.

"Actually, I got some pretty good ideas when I was in the box."

THINKING OUTSIDE THE BOX

The expression "thinking outside the box" captures an important truth: Often our problem solving is limited by unnecessary or misleading assumptions, and it's helpful to break free of those assumptions. However, the likely source of this expression (the nine-dot problem) involves far more than just thinking outside the box (i.e., the square formed by the dots).

are wrong, and so, guided by these mistaken beliefs, people find this problem quite hard (Kershaw & Ohlsson, 2004; MacGregor, Ormerod, & Chronicle, 2001).

Once again, therefore, people seem to be victims of their own problem-solving set; to find the problem's solution, they need to change that set. This phrasing of things, however, makes it sound like a set is a bad thing, blocking the discovery of a solution, so it's important once more to remind ourselves that sets also provide enormous benefits. This is because (as we mentioned early on) most problems offer a huge number of options as you seek the solution—an enormous number of moves you might try or approaches you might consider. A problem-solving set helps you, therefore, by narrowing your options, which in turn eases the search for a solution. Thus, in solving the nine-dot problem, you didn't waste any time wondering whether you should try drawing the lines while holding the pencil between your toes, or whether the problem was hard because you were sitting down while you worked on it and you should have been standing up. Likewise, you didn't consider the option of waiting for Martians to visit, so that they could whisper the solution in your ear. These are all foolish ideas, so you brushed past them. But what identifies them as foolish? It is your problem-solving set, which tells you, among other things, which options are plausible, which are physically possible, and the like.

In short, there are costs and benefits to a problem-solving set. A set can blind you to important options, and so it can be an obstacle. But a set also blinds you to a wide range of futile strategies, and this is a good thing: It allows you to focus, much more productively, on options that are likely to work out. Indeed, without a set, you might be so distracted by silly notions that even the simplest problem would become insoluble.

Creativity

Problem-solving sets are helpful, we've just argued, but there's no question that your efforts toward a problem's solution are often *hindered* by your set, and this observation points us toward one more way in which people differ: Some people are remarkably flexible in their approaches to life's problems; they seem easily able to "think outside the box." Other people, in contrast, seem far-too-ready to rely on routine, so they're more vulnerable to the obstacles we've just described.

How should we think about these differences? Why is it that some people reliably produce novel and unexpected solutions, while other people offer only mundane and familiar solutions? This is, in effect, a question of why some people are *creative*, and others are not—a question that forces us to ask: What is creativity?

Case Studies of Creativity

One way to approach this question is by examining individuals who've been enormously creative—artists like Picasso and Bach, or scientists like Charles Darwin and Marie Curie. By studying these giants, perhaps we can draw hints about the nature of creativity when it arises, on a much smaller scale, in day-to-day life—when, for example, you find a creative way to begin a term paper, or a creative way to repair a damaged friendship. As some researchers put it, we may be able to learn about "little-c creativity" (the every day sort) by studying "Big-C Creativity" (the sort shown by people we count as scientific or artistic geniuses—cf. Simonton & Damian, 2012).

Research suggests in fact that highly creative people like Bach or Curie tend to have certain things in common, and perhaps we can think of these shared elements as "prerequisites" for creativity (e.g., Hennessey & Amabile, 2010). These individuals, first of all, generally have great knowledge and skills in their domain. (This point can't be surprising: If you don't know a lot of chemistry, you can't be a creative chemist. If you're not a skilled storyteller, you can't be a great novelist.) Second, to be creative, it seems that you need certain personality traits: a willingness to take risks, a willingness to ignore criticism, an ability to tolerate ambiguous findings or situations, and an inclination not to "follow the crowd." Third, highly creative people tend to be motivated by the pleasure of their work rather than by the promise of external rewards. With this, highly creative people tend to work extremely hard on their endeavors and to produce a lot of their product, whether these products are poems, paintings, or scientific papers. Fourth, these highly creative people have generally been "in the right place at the right time"—that is, in environments that allowed them freedom, provided them with the appropriate supports, and offered them problems "ripe" for solution with the resources available.

Notice, then, that creativity involves factors outside of the person, as well as the person's own capacities and skills. The external environment, for example, is the source of the relevant knowledge and often defines the problem itself; this is why many authors have suggested that we need a systematic "sociocultural approach" to creativity—one that considers the social, cultural, and historical context, as well as the processes unfolding inside the creative individual's mind (e.g., Sawyer, 2006). Even so, we still need to ask: What does go on in a creative mind? If a person has all the prerequisites just listed, what happens next to produce the creative step forward?

In truth, there is wide disagreement on these issues. A recent review, for example, celebrates a diversity of approaches to creativity but describes the theoretical options as "plentiful but murky" (Hennessey & Amabile, 2010, p. 576; also Mumford & Antes, 2007). It will be instructive, though, to examine a proposal offered many years ago by Wallas (1926). As we'll see, Wallas's notion fits well with some commonsense ideas about creativity, and this is one of the reasons his framework continues to guide modern research. Nonetheless, we'll soon see that the evidence forces us to question several of Wallas's central claims.

The Moment of Illumination

According to Wallas, creative thought proceeds through four stages. In the first stage, **preparation**, the problem solver gathers information about the problem. This stage is characterized by periods of effortful, often frustrating work on the problem, but with little progress. In the second stage, **incubation**, the problem solver sets the problem aside and seems not to be working on it. Wallas argued, though, that the problem solver continues to work on the problem during this stage, albeit unconsciously. Thus, the problem's solution is continuing to develop, unseen, just as the baby bird develops, unseen, inside the egg. This period of incubation leads to the third stage, **illumination**, in which some key insight or new idea emerges, paving the way for the fourth stage, **verification**, in which the person confirms that the new idea really does lead to a problem solution and works out the details.

Was Wallas right? Historical evidence suggests that many creative discoveries don't include the steps he described or, if they do, include these steps in a complex, back-and-forth sequence (Weisberg, 1986). Likewise, the moment of great illumination celebrated in Wallas's proposal may be more myth than reality: When we examine creative discoveries (Watson and Crick's discovery of the double helix, Calder's invention of the mobile as a form of sculpture, etc.), we find that these ideas developed through a succession of "mini-insights," each moving the process forward in some way, rather than springing forth, full-blown, from some remarkable "Aha!" moment (Sawyer, 2006).

For that matter, what exactly does the "Aha!" experience—the moment in which people feel they've made a great leap forward—involve? Wallas proposed that this moment indicates the arrival of a key insight that leads to the solution, but is this right? Metcalfe (1986; Metcalfe & Weibe, 1987) gave her participants a series of "insight problems" like those shown in Figure 12.13A. As participants

FIGURE 12.13 | INSIGHT PROBLEMS

A

Problem 1

A stranger approached a museum curator and offered him an ancient bronze coin. The coin had an authentic appearance and was marked with the date 544 B.C. The curator had happily made acquisitions from suspicious sources before, but this time he promptly called the police and had the stranger arrested. Why?

Problem 2

A landscape gardener is given instructions to plant four special trees so that each one is exactly the same distance from each of the others. How should the trees be arranged?

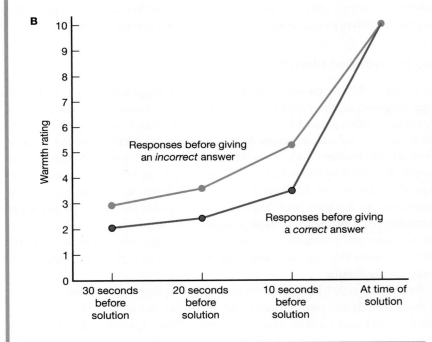

As participants worked on these problems, they were asked to judge their progress by using an assessment of "warmth" ("I'm getting warmer . . . , I'm getting warmer . . . , I'm getting hot!"). For the first problem, you must realize that no one in the year 544 BC knew that it was 544 BC; that is, no one could have known that Christ would be born exactly 544 years later. For the second problem, the gardener needs to plant one of the trees at the top of a tall mound and then plant the other trees around the base of the mound, with the three together forming an equilateral triangle and with the four forming a triangle-based pyramid (i.e., a tetrahedron). (After Metcalfe, 1986.)

worked on each problem, they rated their progress by using a judgment of "warmth" ("I'm getting warmer . . . , I'm getting warmer . . ."), and these ratings did capture the "moment of insight": Initially, the participants didn't have a clue how to proceed and gave warmth ratings of 1 or 2; then, rather abruptly, they saw how to solve the problem, and at that instant their warmth ratings shot up to the top of the scale.

To understand this pattern, though, we need to look separately at those participants who subsequently announced the correct solution to the problem and those who announced an *incorrect* solution. Remarkably, the pattern is the same for these two groups (see Figure 12.13B). Thus, some participants abruptly announced that they were getting "hot" and, moments later, solved the problem. Other participants made the same announcement and, moments later, slammed into a dead end.

It seems, then, that when you say, "Aha!" it means only that you've discovered a new approach, one that you've not yet considered. This is by itself important, because often a new approach is just what you need. But there's nothing magical about the "moment of illumination." This moment doesn't signal the fact that you have at last discovered a path leading to the solution. Instead, it means only that you've discovered something new to try, with no guarantee that this "something new" will be helpful. (For more on these issues, see Bassok & Novick, 2012; Chronicle, MacGregor, & Ormerod, 2004; Fleck, 2012; Jones, 2003; Knoblich, Ohlsson, & Raney, 2001; Topolinski & Reber, 2010; Smith & Ward, 2012; van Steenburgh, Fleck, Beeman & Kounios, 2012; for discussion of the neural mechanisms underlying insight, see Fleck, Beeman & Kounios, 2012; Qiu et al., 2008.)

Incubation

What about Wallas's second stage, the stage of incubation? In this stage, problem solvers seem to set the problem aside, but they (allegedly) continue to work on it unconsciously and, as a result, make considerable progress.

Many people find this an appealing idea, since most of us have had an experience along these lines: You're working on a problem but getting nowhere. After a while, you give up and turn your thoughts to other matters. Sometime later, though, you're thinking about something altogether different when the solution suddenly pops into your thoughts.

Many examples of this pattern have been recorded, with a number of authors pointing out that great scientific discoveries have often been made in this manner (e.g., Kohler, 1969). However, more-systematic data tell us that the incubation effect is (at best) unreliable: Some studies do show that time away from a problem helps in finding the problem's solution, but many studies find no effect (see Christensen & Schunn, 2005; Dodds, Ward, & Smith, 2007; Segal, 2004; Sio & Ormerod, 2009).

More important, it's not clear, when an interruption *does* help, *why* it helps, and the answer probably involves a mix of factors. For one, in Chapter 8 we described the process of *spreading activation*, through which one memory can activate related memories. It is possible that when consciously working on a

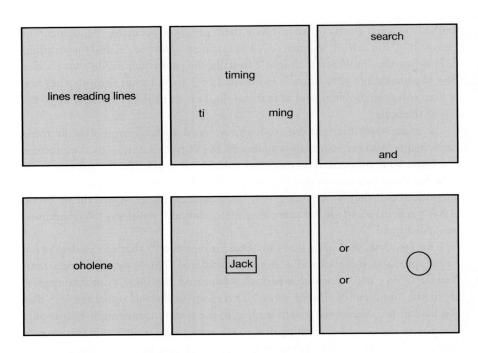

AN INCUBATION BENEFIT FROM SIMPLE FORGETTING

Each panel refers to a familiar word or phrase. Clues were given for each problem, but for many of the problems the clues were designed to be misleading. Control participants had a minute to work on each puzzle; other participants worked on each puzzle for 30 seconds, then were interrupted, and later returned to the puzzle for an additional 30 seconds. This interruption did improve performance, so that problem solution was more likely for the "incubation" group. Crucially, though, Smith and Blankenship (1991) also tested participants' memory for the misleading clues, and the researchers found that the incubation participants were less likely to remember the clues. Smith and Blankenship argued that this forgetting is what created the "incubation" advantage: After the interruption, participants were no longer misled by the bad clues, and their performance improved accordingly. The solutions to these puzzles are given at the end of the chapter.

problem, people try to direct this flow of activation—and may end up directing it in unproductive ways. When someone is not actively thinking about a problem, in contrast, the activation can flow wherever the memory connections take it, and this may lead to new ideas being activated (cf. Ash & Wiley, 2006; Bowden, Jung-Beeman, Fleck, & Kounios, 2005; Smith & Ward, 2012). This process provides no guarantee that *helpful* or *productive* ideas will come to mind, only that *more* (and perhaps unanticipated) ideas will be activated. In this way, incubation is like illumination—a source of new possibilities which may or may not pay off.

In addition, time away from a problem may be helpful for other, more prosaic, reasons. For example, the interruption may allow you to gather new information—perhaps because, during the time away from the problem, you stumble across some clue in the environment or in your own memory (Moss, Kotovsky, & Cagan, 2011). In other cases, your early efforts with a problem may have been tiring or frustrating, and the interruption may provide an opportunity for this frustration or fatigue to dissipate. Likewise, your early efforts with a problem may have been dominated by a particular approach, a particular set. If you put the problem aside for a while, it's possible you'll forget about these earlier tactics, freeing you to explore other, more productive avenues (Smith & Blankenship, 1989, 1991; Storm, Angello & Bjork, 2011; Vul & Pashler, 2007).

WORKBOOK DEMONSTRATIONS 12.2 AND 12.3

The Nature of Creativity

We all stand in awe of creative geniuses like da Vinci, Einstein, and Beethoven. So remarkable are their accomplishments, so different from what you and I produce, that it's natural to assume that their thought processes are no less distinctive. You and I, equipped with heuristics, analogies, and subgoals, have troubles enough with Hobbits and Orcs. It seems unlikely, therefore, that the same intellectual tools could have led to the creativity obvious in great works of art, great innovations of science, and great inventions. On this basis, the suggestion must be that great creativity arises from some other source—some different form of thinking, some other approach to problem solving.

When we examine Darwin's notebooks, though, or Picasso's early sketches, we discover that they relied on analogies and hints and heuristics, and a lot of hard work, just as the rest of us do (Gruber, 1981; Sawyer, 2006; Weisberg, 1986). Likewise, when we examine processes like illumination and incubation, we realize that these processes are less mysterious than they first seem. As we've seen, the "Aha!" feeling of illumination reflects only the fact that a person has discovered new things to try, new approaches to explore, in working on a problem. These new approaches bring no guarantee of success, and often people shout "Aha!" only to discover that their new insight leads them no closer to their goal.

Similarly, even when an "incubation" effect is observed, the process is not a magical one. Instead, incubation can be explained in terms of the ordinary mechanism of spreading activation, as well as the dissipation of fatigue, opportunity for discovering new clues, and the like.

Of course, highly creative people may have certain advantages. There's some suggestion, for example, that they're especially skilled in "divergent thinking"— the ability to spot novel connections among ideas, connections that others had missed (Guilford, 1967, 1979; Carson, Peterson, & Higgins, 2005; Vartanian, Martindale, & Matthews, 2009; see Figure 12.14; for a related notion, see Figure 12.15; also see Gupta, Jang, Mednick, & Huber, 2012). Even so, they seem to use the same search processes as anyone else when hunting through memory (or the world), looking for these novel connections. Thus, the point remains that there's no evidence that Darwin, Picasso, or Georgia O'Keefe possessed some special "creativity mechanism." Instead, they seem to be relying on the same processes, and the same strategies, as ordinary problem solvers.

What then, can we say about how Newton or Michelangelo achieved what they did? The creative *products* from these giants were extraordinary, but the possibility before us is that their creative *processes* were the same ones you and I use in tackling day-to-day problems. These creative titans may have had an edge in the depth of their knowledge, the intensity of their motivation, or their skill

FIGURE 12.14 | CREATIVITY AS DIVERGENT THINKING

Tests of divergent thinking require you to think of new uses for simple objects or new ways to think about familiar ideas. How many different uses can you think of for a brick?

As a paperweight.
As the shadow-caster in a sundial (if positioned appropriately).
As a means of writing messages on a sidewalk.
As a stepladder (if you want to grab something just slightly out of reach).
As a nutcracker.
As a pendulum useful for solving the two-string problem.

Choose five names, at random, from the telephone directory. In how many different ways could these names be classified?

According to the number of syllables.
According to whether there is an even or odd number of vowels.
According to whether their third letter is in the last third of the alphabet.
According to whether they rhyme with things that are edible.

Guilford (1967, 1979) argued that creativity lies in the ability to take an idea in a new, unprecedented direction. Among its other items, his test of creativity asks people to think of new uses for a familiar object. Some possible responses are listed here.

with spreading activation—but these are only differences of degree, and certainly not differences in the type of thinking they used (cf. DeHaan, 2011; Goldenberg, Mazursky, & Solomon, 1999; Klahr & Simon, 2001; Simonton, 2003, 2009a; Simonton & Damian, 2012; Weisberg, 2006).

These extraordinary individuals probably were distinctive, though, in one crucial way. Many of us are smart; many of us are willing to take risks and to ignore criticism; many of us live in a cultural setting that might support a new discovery. What may distinguish creative geniuses, though, is that they are the special few people who happen to have *all* of the ingredients together—the right intellectual tools, the right personality characteristics, living in the right context, plenty of motivation, and so on. Many people have some of these ingredients, but very few have them all, and it is the convergence of these elements that may, perhaps, be the recipe for achieving monumental creativity.

Intelligence

We turn now to another way in which people differ—in their *intelligence*. Everyone acknowledges that these differences exist, and we celebrate those people whom we count as wonderfully smart and express concerns about (and try

FIGURE 12.15 | CREATIVITY AS THE ABILITY TO FIND NEW CONNECTIONS

For each trio of words, think of a fourth word that is related to each of the first three. For example, for the trio "snow, down, out," the answer would be "fall" ("snowfall"; "downfall"; "fallout").

1. off   top   tail

2. ache   sweet   burn

3. dark   shot   sun

4. arm   coal   peach

5. tug   gravy   show

Mednick (1962; Mednick & Mednick, 1967) argued that creativity is the ability to find new connections among ideas. This ability is measured in the Remote Associates Test, for which some sample items are shown here. The solutions are (1) "spin" ("spin-off," "topspin," "tailspin"); (2) "heart," (3) "glasses," (4) "pit," and (5) "boat."

WORKBOOK
DEMONSTRATION 12.4

to help) those we consider intellectually dull. But, when we try to define these differences, or measure them, we rapidly descend into controversy. Part of the controversy derives from widespread cynicism about the tests used to measure intelligence—whether the standard intelligence tests, or the (closely related) tests of "academic aptitude." The cynicism takes several forms but is certainly fueled by the fact that students can often bump their scores upward by taking a "test prep" course, suggesting perhaps that a student's scores depend on how test savvy she is, rather than her true level of ability.

In addition, we all know people who perform well in academic settings but seem to lack common sense. Conversely, there are people whose performance in academic settings is mediocre but who have remarkable artistic ability, or great practical intelligence, or wonderful "people skills." These points suggest that standard measures may lead us to overlook and undervalue other important abilities.

There's also a large worry about *bias* built into standard forms of intellectual testing. Undeniably, this testing has an ugly history and was for many years used to "justify" horrific forms of discrimination (Gould, 1981; Kamin, 1974). More recently, there's been heated (and, in the eyes of many people, racist) debate focused on the comparison between the test scores of African Americans and those of White Americans. It turns out that the average score for African Americans is, in many data sets, lower than the average for Whites, but what does this mean? Is this apparent difference telling us something about the intellectual functioning of Whites and Blacks? Or does the difference merely reflect some form of discrimination built into the test? Amidst all this controversy, what's the reality? Do intelligence tests measure what they're designed to measure? Are there crucial skills *not* tapped by these tests? Are the tests biased? And, perhaps most basic, what *is* intelligence?

Defining and Measuring Intelligence

More than a dozen years ago, a group of 52 experts offered their definition of intelligence: "the ability to reason, plan, solve problems, think abstractly, comprehend complex ideas, learn quickly and learn from experience," an ability that must be distinguished from "book learning . . . or test-taking smarts." The experts also noted that this is an ability crucial for "'catching on,' 'making sense' of things, or 'figuring out' what to do" (Gottfredson, 1997a, p. 13).

This many-part definition, however, played no role in the early efforts toward measuring intelligence. These efforts took place a century ago in France, when the French minister of public instruction appointed a committee with the specific task of identifying children who were performing badly in school and who would benefit from remedial education. In this project, Alfred Binet (1857–1911) and his colleagues began simply with the notion that intelligence is a capacity that matters for many aspects of cognitive functioning. They therefore created a test that included a range of tasks: copying a drawing, repeating a string of digits, understanding a story, arithmetic reasoning, and so on. They knew that someone might do well on one or two of these tasks just by luck or because of some specific experience, but they were convinced that only a truly intelligent person would do well on all the tasks. Therefore, intelligence could be measured, they thought, by a composite score, with the diversity of the tasks ensuring that the test wasn't measuring some specialized talent but was instead a measure of ability in general.

In its original form, the test score was computed as a ratio between a child's "mental age" (the level of development reflected in the test performance) and chronological age. (The ratio was then multiplied by 100 to get the final score.) This ratio—or *quotient*—was the source of the test's name: The test evaluated the child's "intelligence quotient," or IQ.

Modern forms of the test no longer calculate this ratio, but, even so, they're still called IQ tests. One commonly used test is the Wechsler Intelligence Scale for Children (WISC; Wechsler, 2003). Adult intelligence is often evaluated with the Wechsler Adult Intelligence Scale (WAIS) and, like Binet's original test, these modern tests rely on numerous subtests. In the WAIS, for example, there are tests to assess general knowledge, vocabulary, and comprehension; a perceptual-reasoning scale includes visual puzzles like the one shown in Figure 12.16A. Separate subtests assess working memory and speed of intellectual processing. (Other commonly used tests include the fifth edition of the Stanford Binet test [Roid, 2003], and the Kaufman Assessment Battery for Children, or KABC [Kaufman & Kaufman, 2004].)

FIGURE 12.16 | INTELLIGENCE TEST ITEMS

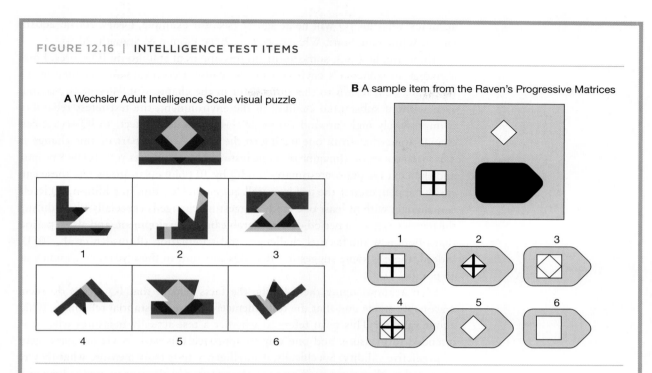

A Wechsler Adult Intelligence Scale visual puzzle

B A sample item from the Raven's Progressive Matrices

Panel A shows a sample item from the Wechsler Adult Intelligence Scale; the task is to assemble some of the parts to form the pattern shown. Panel B shows an easy item from the Raven's Progressive Matrices; the task is to pick the figure that completes the pattern. The test items get harder and harder as the test progresses!

Other intelligence tests have different formats. For example, the Raven's Progressive Matrices Test (Figure 12.16B) hinges entirely on someone's ability to analyze figures and detect patterns. This test presents the test taker with a series of grids (these are the "matrices"), and she must select an option that sensibly completes the pattern in each grid. This test is designed to minimize any influence from verbal skills or background knowledge.

WORKBOOK
DEMONSTRATION 12.5

Reliability and Validity

Whenever we design a test—to assess intelligence, personality, mental health, or anything else—we need to check on whether the test is *reliable* and *valid*. **Reliability** refers to how consistent the measure is and is often evaluated by assessing **test-retest reliability**. This assessment boils down to a simple question: If we give the test, wait a while, and then give it again, do we get essentially the same outcome?

Intelligence tests actually have high test-retest reliability—even if the two test occasions are widely separated. There is, for example, a high correlation between measurements of someone's IQ at, say, age 6 and measurements of IQ when she's 18. Likewise, if we know someone's IQ at age 11, we can predict with reasonable accuracy what his IQ will be at age 27 (see, for example, Deary, 2001a, 2001b; Deary, Whiteman, Starr, Whalley, & Fox, 2004; Plomin & Spinath, 2004).

There are, however, some limits on this apparent stability in IQ scores. First, a change in someone's environment can cause a corresponding change in his IQ score; we'll return to this point later in the chapter (pp. 484–487). Second, even without substantial changes in the environment, the test-retest reliability is impressively high (around .70 or .80)—but it's not perfect, so IQ scores can change somewhat from one testing to the next. At least part of this change is measurement error. (Imagine that one testing underestimates your IQ by 8 points, and the next testing overestimates the IQ by 10 points; variations like these can easily happen, even if the test is overall quite reliable.) But, in addition, IQ levels can change, with at least one study suggesting change is especially likely during the teenage years—a period of considerable brain development, and also a period that offers new intellectual challenges and stimulation (Ramsden et al., 2011). Indeed, there is some suggestion that IQs can shift in these years by as much as 15 points.

Even acknowledging these limits, the facts remain that IQ scores do seem reasonably stable and that the tests themselves have substantial reliability. What about **validity**? This term refers to whether a test actually measures what it is intended to measure, and one way to approach this issue is via an assessment of **predictive validity**: Specifically, if intelligence tests truly measure what they're supposed to, then someone's score on the test should allow us to predict how well that person will do in settings that require intelligence. And here, too, the results are promising. For example, there's roughly a +.50 correlation between someone's IQ and subsequent measures of academic performance (e.g., grade-point average; Arneson, Sackett, & Beatty, 2011; Deary, 2012; Kuncel, Hezlett, & Ones, 2004; Strenze, 2007). This is far from a perfect correlation, and that's important, because it tells us that we'll easily locate exceptions to the pattern: lower-IQ students who do well in school, and higher-IQ students who do poorly. IQ does not define someone's destiny! Still, this correlation is strong enough to indicate that IQ scores do allow us to make predictions about academic success—as they should, if the scores are valid.

IQ scores are also good predictors of performance outside the academic world, and, indeed, are strong predictors of success in the workplace (Sackett et al., 2008; Schmidt & Hunter, 1998, 2004). Sensibly, though, IQ matters more for some jobs than others. Jobs of low complexity require relatively little intelligence, so, not surprisingly, the correlation between IQ and job performance is small (although still positive) for such jobs—for example, a correlation of .20 between IQ and performance on an assembly line. As jobs become more complex, intelligence matters more, so the correlation between IQ and performance gets stronger (Gottfredson, 1997b). Thus we find correlations between .50 and .60 when we look at IQ scores and people's success as accountants or shop managers.

Other results also confirm the validity of IQ scores. For example, people with higher IQ scores tend, overall, to earn more money during their lifetime, end up with higher-prestige careers, and even live longer. Likewise, higher-IQ individuals are less likely to die in automobile accidents (see Table 12.1) and less likely

TABLE 12.1 | THE RELATION BETWEEN IQ AND HIGHWAY DEATHS

IQ	DEATH RATE PER 100,000 DRIVERS
115	51.3
100–115	51.5
85–99	92.2
80–84	146.7

to have difficulty following a doctor's instructions (Deary, Weiss & Batty, 2010; Gottfredson, 2004; Kuncel et al., 2004; Lubinski, 2004.)

Let's emphasize, however, that—like the correlation between IQ and grades—these correlations between IQ and life outcomes are all appreciably lower than +1.00. Again, this reminds us that there are often exceptions to the pattern we're describing—and so there are obviously low-IQ people who end up in high-prestige jobs, and some high-IQ people who end up with lousy jobs, low salaries, and a short life expectancy. These exceptions remind us that (of course) intelligence is just one of the factors influencing life outcomes, and so, inevitably, the correlation between IQ and life success isn't perfect. As we said before, IQ is not destiny, and there are other routes to success that do not require a high IQ score. Nonetheless, there is a statistical linkage between IQ scores and important life outcomes—suggesting, first, that IQ tests do have predictive validity, and, more broadly, that these tests do measure something interesting and consequential.

General Versus Specialized Intelligence

It certainly seems, then, that IQ tests are measuring something that helps people to lead healthier, wealthier, and more productive lives. But can we be more precise about what this "something" is? This question is often framed in terms of two broad options. On one side, Binet and his collaborators assumed that the test measured a singular ability that can apply to virtually any content. In other words, they supposed that someone's score on an IQ test revealed their *general* intelligence, a capacity that would provide an advantage on any mental task (see Kaufman, 2012).

On the other side, however, many authors argue that there's no such thing as being intelligent in a general way. Instead, each person has a collection of more specific talents—you might be "math smart" but not so strong with language, or "highly verbal" but perform poorly with tasks requiring visualization. From this perspective, if we represent your capacities with a single number—an IQ score—this is only a crude summary of what you can do, because it averages together the things you're good at and the things you're not.

Which proposal is correct? One way to find out relies on the fact that, as we've said, many intelligence tests include numerous subtests, allowing us to compare a person's score on each subtest with his or her scores on other subtests. When we make these comparisons, we find an impressive level of consistency: People who do well on one portion of the test tend to do well across the board; people who do poorly on one subtest tend to do poorly on other subtests as well. Of course, each person does have his or her own profile of strengths and weaknesses, but the variations within this profile tend to be small, so that we can meaningfully speak of how well the person performs in general.

This pattern suggests that the various parts of the intelligence test overlap somehow in what they're measuring. To evaluate this overlap, psychologists rely on a statistical technique known as **factor analysis**. As its name implies, this procedure looks for common factors—"ingredients" that are shared by several scores. And, in fact, this form of analysis confirms that there's a common element shared by all the components of the IQ test; indeed, this single common element seems to account for roughly half of the overall data pattern (Arnau & Thompson, 2000; Deary, 2012; Johnson, Carothers & Deary, 2008; Watkins et al., 2006). Some of the subtests (e.g., someone's comprehension of a simple story) depend heavily on this general factor; others (e.g., someone's ability to recall a string of digits) depend less on the factor. Nonetheless, this general factor matters across the board, and that's why all the subtests end up correlated with each other.

Years ago, Charles Spearman gave a name to this common element. He called it **general intelligence**, usually abbreviated with the letter *g*. Spearman (1927) proposed that *g* is called on for virtually any intellectual task, and so individuals with a lot of *g* have an advantage in every intellectual endeavor; if *g* is in short supply, the individual will do poorly on a wide range of tasks.

A Hierarchical Model of Intelligence

The data are clear, however, that *g* is not the whole story, because people also have more specialized skills. One of these skills, for example, involves aptitude for verbal and linguistic tasks, so performance on (say) a reading-comprehension test depends on how much *g* a person has *and also* on the strength of these verbal skills. A second specialized ability involves quantitative or numerical aptitude, so performance on an arithmetic test depends on how much *g* a person has and also the strength of these skills.

Putting these pieces together, we can think of intellectual performance as having a hierarchical structure as shown in Figure 12.17. Researchers disagree about the details of this hierarchy; but by most accounts, *g* is at the top of the hierarchy and contributes to virtually all tasks. At the next level down are the abilities we just described—language and quantitative—and several more, including spatial skill, a specialized ability for fast-paced mental tasks, and a specialized ability to learn new materials. Then at the next level are even more specific capacities—at least 80 have been identified—each useful for a narrow and specialized set of tasks (Carroll, 1993; Flanagan, McGrew & Ortiz, 2000; Johnson, Nijenhuis, & Bouchard, 2007; McGrew, 2009; Snow, 1994, 1996).

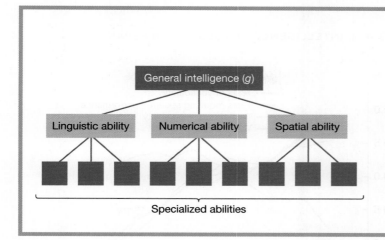

FIGURE 12.17 | A HIERARCHICAL MODEL OF INTELLIGENCE

Most modern researchers regard intelligence as having a hierarchical structure. General intelligence (g) is an ability called on to some extent by virtually all mental tasks. At the next level, broad linguistic or numerical ability is called on by a wide range of tasks of a certain type. At the next level down, more than 80 specific abilities have been identified, each applicable to a specialized type of task.

This hierarchical conception leads to a prediction that, if we choose tasks from two different categories—say, a verbal task and a task requiring arithmetic—we should find a correlation in performance. This is because, no matter how different these tasks seem, they do have something in common: They both draw on g. If we choose tasks from the *same* category, though—say, two verbal tasks, or two quantitative tasks—we should find a *higher* correlation because these tasks have two things in common: They both draw on g, and both draw on the more specialized capacity needed for just that category. The data confirm both of these predictions—moderately strong correlations among all of the IQ test's subtests, and even stronger correlations among subtests in the same category.

It seems, then, that both of the broad hypotheses we introduced earlier are correct: There is some sort of general capacity, useful for all mental endeavors, but there are also various forms of more-specialized intelligence. Each person has some amount of the general capacity and draws on it in all tasks; this is why there's an overall consistency in each person's performance. At the same time, the consistency isn't perfect, because each task also requires more specialized abilities. Each of us has our own profile of strengths and weaknesses for these skills, and thus things we do relatively well, and things we do less well.

Fluid and Crystallized Intelligence

We need one more complication in our theorizing, though, because, alongside of verbal, quantitative, and spatial skills, there are two more forms of intelligence that, on many proposals, should be included in the second level of the hierarchy shown in Figure 12.17: *fluid intelligence* and *crystallized intelligence* (Carroll, 2005; Horn, 1985; Horn & Blankson, 2005).

Fluid intelligence refers to the ability to deal with new and unusual problems. It's the form of intelligence you need when you have no well-practiced routines you can bring to bear on a problem. **Crystallized intelligence**, on the other hand, refers to your acquired knowledge, including your verbal knowledge and your broad repertoire of skills—skills useful for dealing with problems similar to those already encountered.

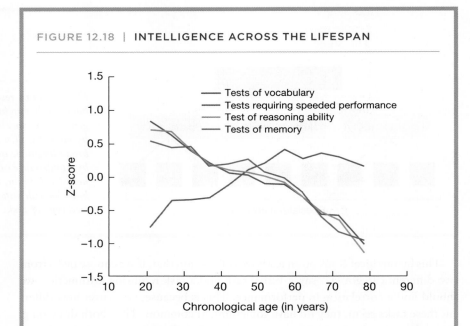

FIGURE 12.18 | INTELLIGENCE ACROSS THE LIFESPAN

Tests that involve crystallized intelligence (like tests of vocabulary) often show a genuine improvement in test scores across the lifespan, declining only when—at age 70 or so—the person's overall condition starts to deteriorate. In contrast, tests that involve fluid intelligence (like tests requiring speeded performance) peak at age 20 or so, and decline thereafter. The "Z-scores" used here are a common statistical measure used for comparing tests with disparate scoring schemes.

Fluid and crystallized intelligence differ in many ways. Crystallized intelligence usually increases with age, but fluid intelligence reaches its peak in early adulthood and then, for most of us, declines steadily across the lifespan (see Figure 12.18; Horn, 1985; Horn & Noll, 1994; Salthouse, 2004, 2012). Similarly, many factors—including alcohol consumption, fatigue, and depression—cause more impairment in tasks requiring fluid intelligence than in those dependent on crystallized intelligence (Duncan, 1994; Hunt, 1995). Thus, someone who is tired will probably perform adequately on tests involving familiar routines and familiar facts. That same individual, however, may be markedly impaired if the test requires quick thinking or a novel approach—earmarks of fluid intelligence.

The Building Blocks of Intelligence

It's clear, then, that intelligence has many components. However, one component—*g*—is crucial, for the simple reason that this aspect of intelligence is relevant to virtually all mental activities. But what exactly is *g*? What, inside a person, gives him or her more *g*, or less?

One proposal is simple: Mental processes are quick but do take some time, and perhaps the people we consider intelligent are those who are especially fast in these processes. This speed would allow them to perform intellectual tasks more quickly; it also would give them time for more steps in comparison with those of us who aren't so quick (Coyle, Pillow, Snyder & Kochunov, 2011; Deary, 2012; Eysenck, 1986; Nettelbeck, 2003; Sheppard, 2008; Vernon, 1987). (For discussions of the possible biological basis for this speed, see Miller, 1994; Rae, Digney, McEwan, & Bates, 2003.)

Support for this idea comes from measures of **inspection time**—the time someone needs to decide which of two lines is longer, or which of two tones is higher. Measures of inspection time correlate around –.50 with intelligence scores (Bates & Shieles, 2003; Danthiir, Roberts, Schulze, & Wilhelm, 2005; Deary & Derr, 2005; Ravenzwaaij, Brown & Wagenmakers, 2011); the correlation is negative because lower response times go with higher scores on intelligence tests.

A different proposal about g centers on the notion of *working-memory capacity* (WMC). We first met this notion in Chapter 5, and there we saw that WMC is a measure of *executive control*—and so a measure of how well people can monitor and direct their own thought processes. We mentioned in the earlier chapter that people with a larger WMC do better on many intellectual tasks, including, we can now add, tests specifically designed to measure g; this linkage is especially strong for *fluid* intelligence (Burgess et al., 2011; Fukuda, Vogel, Mayr, & Awh, 2011). Perhaps, therefore, the people we call intelligent are those who literally have better control of their own thoughts, so they can coordinate their priorities in an appropriate way, avoid distraction, override errant impulses, and in general proceed in a deliberate manner when making judgments or solving problems.

As a related proposal, some theorists emphasize the *task model* you need to construct in order to perform mental tasks. This "model" is a mental representation that reflects your understanding of the task's goals, rules, and requirements, and, once constructed, it provides an "agenda" for work on the task, defining the sequence of steps that must be taken. Tasks differ in the complexity of the model they require, with more complicated models needed if the task involves multiple goals or demands a change in goals as certain cues come into view. Evidence suggests that the ability to handle this complexity is strongly linked to measures of g—so that higher-g individuals are able to maintain more complex task models, allowing them to outperform lower-g people whenever such models are required (Duncan et al., 2008).

Both of these notions—one emphasizing executive control, and one emphasizing task models—are compatible with the **parieto-frontal integration theory** (P-FIT) of intelligence suggested by Jung & Haier (2007). This theory grows out of neuroimaging studies that compare the brains of individuals at differing levels of intelligence; based on these comparisons, the theory identifies a network of brain sites that seem crucial for intellectual performance. Some of the sites are in the parietal lobe and heavily involved in the control of attention. Other sites are in the frontal lobe and essential for working memory. Still other important sites are crucial for language processing (see Figure 12.19). The P-FIT conception

FIGURE 12.19 | THE P-FIT MODEL

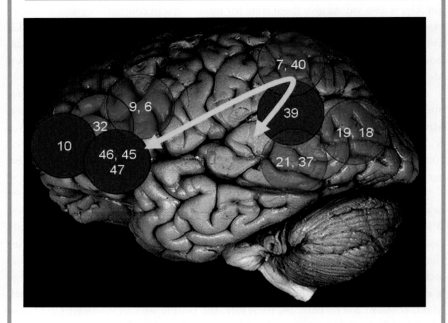

The P-FIT model identifies many brain sites as crucial for intelligence. The dark circles indicate brain areas that are especially relevant in the left *hemisphere; the light circles indicate brain areas that are relevant in* both *hemispheres. The yellow arrow indicates especially important connections. Finally, the numbers refer to a numbering scheme (so-called Brodmann Areas) commonly used for labeling brain regions. (After Jung & Haier, 2007.)*

emphasizes, though, that what really matters for intelligence is the *integration* of information from all of these sites, and thus the coordinated functioning of many cognitive components. (For more on this theory, see Colom et al., 2009; Gläscher et al., 2010; Schmithorst, 2009.)

Other Contributions to Intellectual Functioning

The capacity we call *g* is also shaped by attributes you might not think of as "intellectual" capacities. These include motivation, attitude toward intellectual challenges, and willingness to persevere when a problem becomes frustratingly difficult (e.g., Hannon & McNaughton-Cassill, 2011). Indeed, these factors will be crucial for us later in the chapter, when we turn to differences among various groups in their performance on intelligence tests.

Plainly, therefore, being intelligent—even if we focus just on *g*—requires a large set of attributes. If we choose, in light of these points, to represent someone's intelligence with a single number—an IQ score, or an assessment of their *g*—this seems both useful and misleading. The score is *useful* because it does summarize someone's performance, and (as we have seen) allows us to predict how the person will perform in a range of settings. At the same time, this single number blurs diverse constituents together. As a result, if we wish to understand intelligence—and more important, if we want to find ways to *improve* someone's intelligence—we need to look past this single measurement and examine the many components contributing to that score.

Intelligence Beyond the IQ Test

Our theory of intelligence is growing complicated—with many elements in the hierarchy, and with several ingredients contributing to g at the top of the hierarchy. Even so, we need some further complications, because there are aspects of intelligence not included in this portrait—aspects that are separate from the capacities we measure with conventional intelligence tests.

For example, you probably know people who are "street-smart" or "savvy," but not "school-smart." These people may lack the analytic skill required in the classroom, but they're astute in dealing with the practical world. In fact, Robert Sternberg has celebrated the importance of **practical intelligence**, the kind of intelligence needed for skilled reasoning in day-to-day settings (Sternberg, 1985; also see Henry, Sternberg, & Grigorenko, 2005; Sternberg, Kaufman, & Grigorenko, 2008; Wagner, 2000).

A different sort of complexity has been highlighted by Keith Stanovich, who argues that there are central aspects of cognition not tapped by the standard intelligence tests. As part of his evidence, Stanovich reminds us that we all know people who are very smart according to their test scores but who nonetheless ignore facts, are overconfident in their judgment, are insensitive to inconsistencies in their views, and more. As a result, they are especially prone to the reasoning errors we described in the last chapter—including belief perseverance and confirmation bias. In light of such cases (and a great deal of other evidence), Stanovich (2009) argues that we need separate measures of *intelligence* and *rationality*, with the latter term defined (in Stanovich's view) roughly as the capacity for critically assessing information as it is gathered in the natural environment.

Still other authors highlight the importance of **emotional intelligence**—the ability to understand your own emotions and others', and also the ability to control your emotions when appropriate (Mayer et al., 2008; Salovey & Mayer, 1990; also Brackett et al., 2006). Tests have been constructed to measure this form of intelligence, and people who score well on these tests are judged to create a more positive atmosphere in the workplace, and are judged to have more leadership potential (Lopes, Salovey, Côté, & Beers, 2005; Grewal & Salovey, 2005). Likewise, college students who score well on these tests are rated by friends as more caring and more supportive; they're also less likely to experience conflict with peers (Brackett & Mayer, 2003; Mayer, Roberts, & Barsade, 2008).

Thus, our list of intellectual capacities probably does need to include other talents. Indeed, in his theory of **multiple intelligences**, Howard Gardner (1983, 2006) argues for *eight* types of intelligence: Three of these are included in standard IQ tests: linguistic intelligence, logical-mathematical intelligence, and spatial intelligence. But Gardner also argues that we should acknowledge musical intelligence,

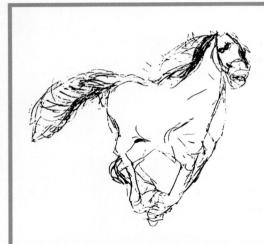

FIGURE 12.20 | AN "AUTISTIC SAVANT"

Nadia is an often-mentioned example of a child who, on the one side, appears to be severely retarded, but, at the same time, has remarkable drawing skill. This horse was drawn when Nadia was four years old. She preferred to draw in fine point pen, and showed little interest in the use of color. The pattern of her artistic production was also odd: Rather than beginning with an outline, Nadia would begin with details (such as a hoof, or the horse's mane) and only later connect these features.

bodily-kinesthetic intelligence (the ability to learn and create complex patterns of movement), interpersonal intelligence (the ability to understand other people), intrapersonal intelligence (the ability to understand ourselves), and naturalistic intelligence (the ability to understand patterns in nature).

Some of Gardner's evidence comes from the study of people with so-called **savant syndrome.** These individuals have a single extraordinary talent, even though they're otherwise disabled to a profound degree. Some display unusual artistic talent (see Figure 12.20). Others are "calendar calculators," able to answer immediately when asked questions like "What day of the week was March 17 in the year 1682?" Still others have remarkable musical skills and can effortlessly memorize lengthy and complex musical works (Hill, 1978; Miller, 1999).

Gardner's claims have been controversial (see, for example, Cowan & Carney, 2006; Deary, 2012; Thioux et al., 2006; Visser, Ashton, & Vernon, 2006; White 2008). Some of the disagreement concerns his data, but a deeper issue centers on Gardner's basic conceptualization: There is, of course, no question that some individuals—savants or otherwise—have remarkable talents, but is it appropriate to think of these talents as forms of intelligence? Or might we be better served by a distinction between *intelligence* and *talent*? It does seem peculiar to use the same term, *intelligence,* to describe both the capacity that Albert Einstein displayed in developing his theories and the capacity that Eli Manning displays on the football field. Similarly, we might celebrate the vocal talent of Adele or Katy Perry; but is theirs the same type of talent—and therefore sensibly described by the same term, *intelligence*—that a skilled debater relies on in rapidly thinking through the implications of an argument?

Gardner has certainly drawn our attention to abilities that are often ignored and undervalued, and it's clear that our culture does far too little to celebrate the talents displayed by an artist at her canvas, a skilled dancer in the ballet, or an empathetic clergyman in a hospital room. It's debatable whether these other abilities should be counted as forms of intelligence, but they're surely talents to be highly esteemed and, as much as possible, nurtured and developed.

The Roots of Intelligence

Plainly, people differ from one another in their intelligence and their talents, and, as we have seen, these differences *matter*. But what causes the differences? Why does one person end up with a high level of intelligence, while other people end up with a lower level? Answers to these questions are often framed in terms of two alternatives—the notion that what matters is genetics and heredity, or the notion that what matters is environment (and so learning and experience). The options, in other words, are boiled down to the dichotomy of "nature versus nurture."

As we'll see, this framing of the issue is misleading in important ways. Before we get to that point, though, let's establish the basics, by asking, first, whether genetic factors matter at all, and then doing the same for environmental factors.

Genetics and Individual IQ

One of the key methods for assessing genetic influences begins by asking whether people who resemble each other genetically also resemble each other in terms of the target trait. Often, the best evidence on this point comes from a comparison between the two types of twins. **Identical**, or **monozygotic (MZ)**, **twins** originate from a single fertilized egg. Early in development, that egg splits into two exact replicas, which develop into two genetically identical individuals. In contrast, **fraternal**, or **dizygotic (DZ)**, **twins** arise from two different eggs, each fertilized by a different sperm cell. As a result, fraternal twins share only half of their genetic material, just as ordinary (nontwin) siblings do (see Figure 12.21).

Identical twins, therefore, resemble each other genetically more than fraternal twins do. It turns out that identical twins also resemble each other in their IQs more than fraternal twins do—just as we'd expect if genetic factors play an important role in shaping IQ. In one early data set, for example, the correlation for identical twins was .86; the correlation for fraternal twins was notably lower, around .60 (Bouchard & McGue, 1981). More recent data confirm this pattern (see Figure 12.22), strongly suggesting a genetic component in the determination of IQ, with greater genetic similarity (in identical twins) leading to greater IQ similarity.

Further evidence comes from identical twins who were separated soon after birth, adopted by different families, and reared in different households. The data show a correlation for these twins of about .75 (Bouchard, Lykken, McGue, Segal, & Tellegen, 1990; McGue, Bouchard, Iacono, & Lykken, 1993; Plomin & Spinath, 2004). It seems, then, that identical genetic profiles lead to highly similar IQs even when the individuals grow up in different environments. (For other data, confirming the influence of genetic factors, see Plomin, Fulker, Corley, & DeFries, 1997; Plomin & Spinath, 2004; for some possible limits on these data,

FIGURE 12.21 | MONOZYGOTIC AND DIZYGOTIC TWINS

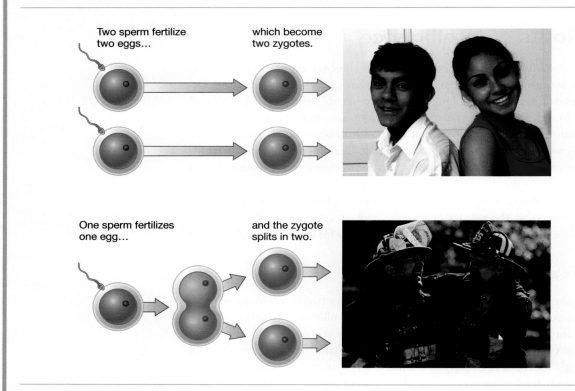

Two sperm fertilize two eggs...

which become two zygotes.

One sperm fertilizes one egg...

and the zygote splits in two.

Sometimes a woman releases a single egg that is fertilized and then splits into two. This sequence results in monozygotic (identical) twins with 100% overlap in their genetic pattern. Sometimes a woman releases two eggs in the same month, and both are fertilized. The result is dizygotic twins—conceived at the same time, born on the same day, but with only 50% overlap in their genetic pattern (the same overlap as ordinary siblings).

though, see Nisbett, 2009; for an exploration of the specific genes shaping intelligence, see Payton, 2009; Rizzi & Posthuma, 2012.)

Environment and Individual IQ

We can easily demonstrate, though, that environmental factors also matter for intelligence. For example, one study examined the intelligence scores for pairs of brothers and found that the correlation between the brothers' scores was *smaller* for brothers who were widely separated in age (Sundet, Eriksen, & Tambs, 2008). This result is difficult to explain genetically, because the genetic resemblance is the same for a pair of brothers born, say, one year apart as it is for a pair born five years apart. In both cases, the brothers share 50% of their genetic material. However, this result makes sense on environmental grounds. The greater the age difference between the brothers, the more likely it is that the family circumstances

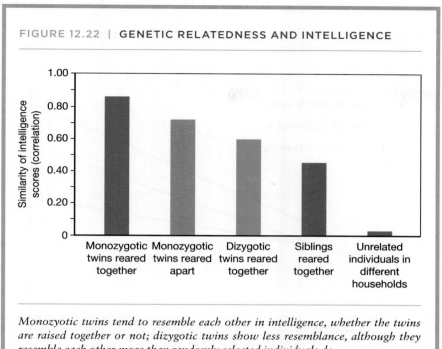

FIGURE 12.22 | GENETIC RELATEDNESS AND INTELLIGENCE

Monozyotic twins tend to resemble each other in intelligence, whether the twins are raised together or not; dizygotic twins show less resemblance, although they resemble each other more than randomly selected individuals do.

changed between the years of one brother's childhood and the years of the other's. Thus, a greater age difference would increase the probability that the brothers grew up in different environments, and to the degree that these environments shape intelligence, we would expect the more widely spaced brothers to resemble each other less than the closely spaced siblings—just as the data show.

We've also known for years that impoverished environments impede intellectual development, and these effects are cumulative: The longer the child remains in such an environment, the greater the harm. This point emerges in the data as a negative correlation between IQ and age. That is, the older the child (the longer she had been in the impoverished environment), the lower her IQ (Asher, 1935; Gordon, 1923; also see Heckman, 2006). Related results come from communities where schools have closed. These closings typically lead to a decline in intelligence test scores—with a drop of roughly 6 points for every year of school missed (Green, Hoffman, Morse, Hayes, & Morgan, 1964; see also Ceci & Williams, 1997; Neisser et al., 1996).

Let's also emphasize, however, the optimistic finding that *improving* the environment can *increase* IQ. In one study, researchers focused on cases in which the government had removed children from their biological parents because of abuse or neglect (Duyme, Dumaret, & Tomkiewicz, 1999). The researchers compared the children's "pre-adoption IQ" (when the children were living in a high-risk environment) with their IQ in adolescence—after years of living with their adoptive families. The data showed substantial improvements in the children's scores,

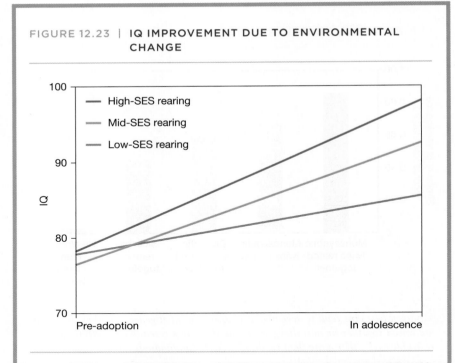

FIGURE 12.23 | IQ IMPROVEMENT DUE TO ENVIRONMENTAL CHANGE

Researchers examined the IQ scores of children who were adopted out of horrible environments in which the children had been abused or neglected. After the adoption (when the children were in better environments), the children's IQ scores were markedly higher—and all the more so if the children were adopted into a family with the higher socioeconomic status (SES). (After Duyme, Dumaret, & Tomkiewicz, 1999)

thanks to this environmental change (see Figure 12.23). (Also see Diamond & Lee, 2011; Grotzer & Perkins, 2000; Martinez, 2000; Nisbett, 2009; for evidence indicating an improvement in intelligence from short-term *music* training, see Moreno et al., 2011.)

The impact of environmental factors is also undeniable in another fact. Around the globe, scores on intelligence tests have been increasing over the last few decades, at a rate of approximately 3 points per decade. This pattern is known as the **Flynn effect**, after James R. Flynn (1984, 1987, 1999, 2009; see also Daley, Whaley, Sigman, Espinosa, & Neumann, 2003; Kanaya, Scullin, & Ceci, 2003), one of the first researchers to note this effect. This improvement has been documented in relatively affluent nations and also in impoverished third-world nations (see Figure 12.24). Moreover, this effect is stronger in measures of fluid intelligence—such as the Raven's Matrices—so it seems to be a genuine change in how quickly and flexibly people can think, and not just a worldwide increase in how much information people have.

There's disagreement about the causes of the Flynn effect (Daley et al., 2003; Dickens & Flynn, 2001; Flynn, 2009; Greenfield, 2009; Nisbett, 2009), and it's

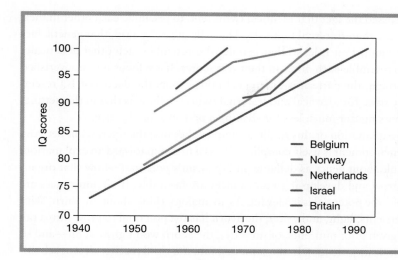

FIGURE 12.24 | **THE FLYNN EFFECT**

IQ scores have been improving worldwide, in developed nations (like those shown here) and also in third-world nations. There's debate over the cause of this improvement, but there's no question that the improvement must be explained largely in environmental (not genetic) terms.

likely that several factors contribute: In third-world nations, improvements in nutrition and health care are surely relevant. In affluent nations, some scholars propose, intelligence is promoted by the "information complexity" of our world: Whether we're browsing the Internet or reading the back of a cereal box, we often encounter complicated displays containing many bits of information, and it's plausible that our experience with this complexity is what's helping us all to grow smarter. Whatever the explanation, though, the Flynn effect cannot be explained genetically. While the human genome does change, it doesn't change at a pace commensurate with this effect. Therefore, this worldwide improvement becomes part of the package of evidence documenting that intelligence can indeed be improved by suitable environmental conditions.

The Interaction Among Genetic Factors, Environment, and IQ

Let's be clear, though, that genetic and environmental effects don't just "add" together. Instead, these influences interact with each other in crucial ways. This point is especially clear when we take a closer look at the impact of *poverty*.

Poverty interferes with intellectual development (Hackman & Farah, 2009; Lubinski, 2004; Raizada & Kishiyama, 2010), and children who live in poverty during their preschool years are more at risk than children who live in poverty in middle or late childhood (Duncan, Yeung, Brooks-Gunn, & Smith, 1998; Farah et al., 2006). Apparently, then, the harmful effects of poverty aren't due only to inferior education. Instead, the effects derive from many factors, including exposure to toxins found in lower-quality housing, lack of stimulation, poor nutrition, and inferior health care. All of these factors interfere with the normal development of the brain, with tragic consequences for intellectual functioning.

Living in poverty is a fact about the environment, but its effects *interact with* genetic influences (Turkheimer, Haley, Waldron, D'Onofrio, & Gottesman, 2003; Tucker-Drob, Rhemtulla, Harden, Turkheimer & Fask, 2011). Specifically, we've already discussed the fact that identical twins tend to resemble each other in their IQ scores more than fraternal twins do. This tells us, we've said, that genetic factors play an important role, so that people who resemble each other genetically are likely to resemble each other in their test scores. If we focus on impoverished families, though, the pattern is different. In this group, the degree of IQ resemblance is the *same* for identical and fraternal twins—telling us that in this setting, genetic factors matter much less for shaping a person's intelligence.

The full explanation of this result is complex, because the interaction between genes and environment is itself complicated. As a first step toward an explanation, though, think about genes as defining an organism's *potential*—how that organism might grow and develop if circumstances are favorable. If circumstances are *not* favorable, the potential is irrelevant. As an analogy, think about an acorn. With the right nutrients, light, and water, the acorn has the potential to grow into a tall tree. But if given poor nutrients, or no water, the acorn won't grow at all—and so will never show its potential. In the same fashion, if a child receives decent schooling, good health care, and adequate nutrition, he'll develop the potential specified in his genes, and so, as the years go by, he'll make the most of the predisposition he was born with. But if a child grows up in an impoverished environment, it matters much less whether he has a fine potential—because the environment doesn't allow the potential to emerge. Hence, in impoverished environments, genetic factors—the source of the potential—count for relatively little. (For different examples of how environmental factors interact with genes, and for richer [and more sophisticated] accounts of this interaction, see Davis et al., 2009; Taylor, Roehrig, Hensler, Connor, & Schatschneider, 2010; also Vinkhuyzen et al., 2011.)

Comparisons Between Men and Women

So far, our focus has been on the roots of IQ for individuals—a particular person who grows up in poverty, or a particular person whose fraternal twin happens to have a high IQ. The ferocious controversy attached to IQ scores, however, concerns a different issue—namely, the differences in measured intelligence that are found between *groups*. Specifically, debate has focused on the comparison between men and women, and the comparison between American Whites and American Blacks.

Before we tackle these issues, though, we need to address an important methodological point. We've discussed evidence showing that genetic patterns matter a lot for intelligence, but we need to be clear that the evidence presented so far applies only to comparisons from one person to the next and is entirely irrelevant to comparisons among groups. The reason, quite simply, is that sometimes individual-to-individual differences are caused by the same factors as group-to-group differences, and sometimes they're caused by different factors. Hence, we can't draw claims about group differences based on studies comparing individuals, or claims about comparisons among individuals based on studies comparing groups. Each needs to be examined in its own right.

With this point in place, what can we say about alleged differences between men's and women's mental capacities? Overall, the data are clear that neither sex is more intelligent than the other, and there's no reliable difference between

HUMAN DIVERSITY

It is important that the comparisons between men and women, or the comparisons between American Blacks and American Whites, are between the averages for each group. This point is crucial, because—of course—men differ from each other in their intellectual prowess, and so do women. Likewise, the scores of European American test takers vary enormously, as do the scores of African American test takers. Indeed, the variation within each group (within each sex, or within a racially defined group) is much, much larger than any between-group variations researchers have detected. We therefore learn little about any individual's abilities simply by knowing his or her group membership, and it would be wrong (and in most settings, illegal) to use group membership as a basis for making decisions about that individual.

men and women in their IQ scores. The data suggest that men's scores are more *variable* than women's, but there are no reliable differences between the averages (e.g., Blinkhorn, 2005; Deary, 2012; Johnson, Segal & Bouchard, 2008). We do detect differences, though, when we consider more specialized abilities. On average, women do better on many verbal tasks—especially tasks that require clear and fluent writing (Halpern, 2011; Halpern et al., 2007). Men, for their part, tend (on average) to do better on tests designed to measure spatial abilities, such as tests requiring mental rotation (see Chapter 10). Men also do better on tasks that require them to navigate through a virtual (computerized) three-dimensional environment (like the fictional worlds you must "travel through" in many computer games; Halpern et al., 2007).

These differences, documented in the lab, are often cited as the source of the so-called gender gap in academic achievement. One study examined the test scores for 15-year-olds in 41 countries (Machin & Pekkarinen, 2008). In every country, girls outscored boys in tests of reading; in most countries, boys out-scored girls in tests of mathematics. The scores for boys were also (as in other data sets) more variable than scores for girls, with more boys than girls ending up with scores distant from (above or below) the average for their sex (Johnson, Carothers, & Deary, 2008).

Another study compared the SAT scores of 40,000 American high school students. The study showed that men (on average) did better than women on the math portion of the test, even when the investigators limited their comparison to men and women who had taken the same high-school math courses (Benbow, 1988; Benbow, Lubinski, Shea, & Eftekhari-Sanjani, 2000; for related data, see Halpern et al., 2007).

Other studies, however, tell a different story. For example, men and women are equally likely to take calculus in high school, and it's the women who get better grades (Gallagher & Kaufman, 2005). In other studies, the gender gap is quite small and inconsistent from one country to the next (Else-Quest, Shibley & Linn, 2010). In fact, one recent study, reporting on a 2008 U.S. assessment, found no difference between male and female high school students in their math achievement (Hyde, Lindberg, Linn, Ellis, & Williams, 2008; Johnson et al., 2008). In college, men and women get equal math grades (Bridgeman & Lewis, 1996), and there's no difference between the sexes in their understanding of mathematical concepts (Hyde & Linn, 2006).

What lies behind all of these findings? For those studies that do detect gender differences in educational performance, what's the cause? Some authors suggest biological explanations, pointing to a possible link between spatial abilities and the male hormone testosterone (Cherrier et al., 2001; Janowsky, Oviatt, & Orwoll, 1994; Hier & Crowley, 1982; Van Goozen, Cohen-Kettenis, Gooren, Frijda, & Can de Poll, 1995). But the findings linking hormones and intellectual performance are mixed, so conclusions about this point must be tentative (e.g., Fine, 2010; Halari et al., 2005; Halpern, 2011; Hines et al., 2003; Vuoksimaa et al., 2010; also see Ceci & Williams, 2010; Halpern, 2000; Newcombe, 2007; Spelke, 2005).

The data are quite clear, though, about a different influence: Many people (including parents and teachers) believe that women are ill-suited for math, so they provide women with little encouragement for learning mathematics (Halpern, 2011). Likewise, parents expect their sons to do better than their daughters in math courses (Frome & Eccles, 1998) and often attribute their sons' success in math to ability while attributing their daughter's success in math to hard work (Parsons, Adler, & Kaczala, 1982; also Stake & Nickens, 2005; Steele, 2003).

In these (and other) ways, women get less support than men for learning math, and this has a strong effect on their progress. In addition, women are exposed to influences that actually *undermine* their math performance; we'll return to this issue in a moment. It's also important that women's performance in spatial tasks can be markedly improved through practice (Feng, Spence, & Pratt, 2007; Halpern et al., 2007; Spence & Feng, 2010), so it's plain that we're not looking at a permanent and irremediable difference between the sexes!

Indeed, in light of the positive effects of practice and instruction, we may want to put less emphasis on the ultimate causes of the apparent sex differences in achievement and put our emphasis instead on efforts toward eradicating these differences, to make sure that all of us—male and female—reach our full potential. Otherwise, as one author put it, we may "waste a most valuable resource: the abilities and efforts of more than half the world's population" (Shaffer, 2004, p. 237).

Comparisons Between American Whites and American Blacks

Furious debate has also swirled around another comparison—between American (and European) Whites and African Americans, and many studies suggest the average intelligence score of the White population is higher by 10 to 15 points (Jencks & Phillips, 1998; Jensen, 1985; Loehlin, Lindzey, & Spuhler, 1975; Reynolds, Chastain, Kaufman, & McLean, 1987). There's uncertainty over whether the gap between the racial groups has been shrinking (e.g., Dickens & Flynn, 2006a, 2006b; Rushton & Jensen, 2006), but, even so, the difference in average scores between Blacks and Whites is well documented, making it important for us to ask what the difference is, and what it might or might not tell us.

Let's start with the hypothesis that has been most controversial: Could it be that genes of African ancestry somehow lead to lower IQ scores than do genes of European ancestry? This hypothesis is problematic from the start, because it assumes the groups we're comparing (modern American Whites and modern African Americans) really are distinct genetically. This assumption is questionable, because the genetic overlap between these two groups is enormous (e.g., Cavalli-Sforza, Menozzi, & Piazza, 1994; Krimsky & Sloan, 2011; Tattersall & Desalle, 2011). More directly, though, researchers have used various methods to determine what proportion of someone's ancestors were Black Africans and what proportion were Europeans. (This can be done, for example, through biochemical markers in the blood.) The evidence shows no linkage between IQ and this assessment of ancestry, powerfully arguing against a genetic account of the evidence (Scarr & Carter-Saltzman, 1983).

How, therefore, should we explain the race difference in test scores? Part of the answer is economic, because Blacks and Whites in the United States do not have the same opportunities or the same resources. On average, African Americans have lower incomes than Whites and live in less-affluent neighborhoods. A higher proportion of Blacks than Whites are exposed to poor nutrition, low-quality educational resources, and poor health care (Neisser et al., 1996), and, as we've already mentioned, these environmental factors have an impact on IQ. On this basis, some of the difference between Blacks and Whites isn't a "race difference" at all, but instead an "economic status difference" (Scarr & Carter-Saltzman, 1982; Scarr & Weinberg, 1983; also see Jencks & Phillips, 1998).

In addition, we cannot lose track of the fact that, in America, Blacks are often treated differently than Whites by the people they encounter. They also grow up with different role models than Whites, and they typically make different assumptions about what life paths will be open to them. Do these facts matter for intelligence scores? Consider studies of **stereotype threat**, a term that describes the negative impact that social stereotypes, once activated, can have on task performance. Concretely, imagine an African American taking an intelligence test.

She might well become anxious because she knows this is a test on which she's expected to do poorly. This anxiety might be compounded by the thought that her poor performance will only serve to confirm others' prejudices. These feelings, in turn, could erode performance by making it more difficult for her to pay attention and do her best work. Moreover, given the thought that poor performance is inevitable, she might well decide not to expend enormous effort—if she's likely to do poorly, why struggle against the tide?

Evidence for effects like these comes from various studies, including some in which two groups of African Americans are given exactly the same test. One group is told at the start that the test is designed to assess their intelligence; the other group is led to believe that the test is simply composed of challenges and is not designed to assess them in any way. The first group, for which the instructions trigger stereotype threat, does markedly worse (Steele, 2010; Steele & Aronson, 1995).

Dozens of studies confirm this role for stereotype threat (Steele, 2010; Walton & Spencer, 2009), and, indeed, related data have been reported for groups other than African Americans. In other words, we're all influenced by the expectations that our culture creates for us, and in many cases those expectations can undermine performance. In one study, for example, male and female college students all took a math test. Half of the students were told that this test had shown gender differences in the past; in this group, male students outperformed the females. The other half of the students were told that the test had been shown in the past to be gender neutral; in this group, there was no gender difference in performance (Ambady, Shih, Kim, & Pittinsky, 2001; Blascovich, Spencer, Quinn, & Steele, 2001; Brown & Josephs, 1999; Cheryan & Bodenhausen, 2000; Crawford & Chaffin, 1997; Dar-Nimrod & Heine, 2006; Halpern et al., 2007).

Returning to African Americans, it's also possible to *improve* performance by shifting expectations and motivation. One group of researchers asked middle-school students to write brief essays—just a few sentences—about things they valued, and they were given a list of possible values to choose from: "athletic ability, being good at art, being smart, creativity" and so on (Cohen, Garcia, Apfel, & Master, 2006; Cohen, Garcia, Purdie-Vaughns, Apfel, & Brzustoski, 2009). This brief exercise, repeated periodically during the school year, was enough to shift students' perspective, getting them to focus on things they valued rather than school-based anxieties. In fact, this intervention improved the grades of African American seventh-graders by a striking 40%, markedly reducing the difference between White students' and Black students' grades. Remarkably, effects of the intervention were still detectable in a follow-up study with the same students two years later. (For a similar study, examining the gender difference in college-age students, see Miyake, Kost-Smith, Finkelstein, Pollock, Cohen, & Ito, 2010.)

These results draw our attention back to the question of what intelligence is— or, more broadly, what it is that "intellectual tasks" require. One requirement, of course, is a set of cognitive skills and capacities (e.g., mental speed, or executive control). A different requirement, however, is the proper attitude toward testing— and a bad attitude (anxiety about failing, fear of confirming other's negative expectations) can hurt performance. These attitudes, in turn, are influenced by social pressures and prejudice, and, through this mechanism, these external forces can powerfully shape each person's achievements—and can, in particular, contribute to the differences between IQ scores for Whites and Blacks.

What, therefore, is our path forward? The answer has many parts. As we have seen, intelligence is far from a perfect predictor of success—in the academic world, in the workplace—and surely we can do more to foster other capacities that can help people flourish. In addition, the links between poverty and intelligence add to the (already enormous) urgency of making sure that everyone receives adequate nutrition and health care and appropriate educational opportunities. It's also possible that we can improve intelligence directly—perhaps with targeted training of executive function, or with careful instruction to help people develop crystallized intelligence (cf. Nisbett, 2009). But, in addition, we can move forward by shifting people's expectations, because, as we've seen, these too are an important influence on intellectual performance. The shift in expectations won't be easy, because the expectations are held—and reinforced—by teachers, parents, and even young children; the expectations are built into many social institutions. Nonetheless, given what we know about the linkage between intelligence and success in the workplace, or that between intelligence and health, efforts on all of these fronts must be a high priority for all of us.

CHAPTER SUMMARY

- Problem solving is often likened to a process of search in which you seek a path leading from a starting point to the goal. In many problems, though, there are too many paths to allow examination of each, and this is why problem-solving heuristics are crucial. Heuristics applicable to a wide range of problems include hill climbing and means-end analysis.

- Problem solving is also aided by visual images or diagrams. For some purposes, these work equally well, but each has its own advantages. Visual images are easily adjusted if one wishes to change the size or position of some element. Diagrams, in contrast, have the advantage of standing independent of interpretation of them and thus they can facilitate reinterpretation.

- Analogies to earlier-solved problems are often helpful. Nonetheless, analogies seem to be underused by many problem solvers, plausibly because problem solvers search memory with an emphasis on a problem's superficial features, rather than its underlying dynamic. Analogy use can be promoted, therefore, by instructions or contexts that encourage people to focus on a problem's deeper structure.

- Experts in an area generally pay more attention to a problem's underlying structure rather than its surface form, and this helps the experts find and use analogies. Focusing on the problem's underlying structure also helps the experts to break the problem into subproblems.

- The likelihood of solving a problem is enormously influenced by how someone perceives or defines the problem. The problem definition can include unnoticed assumptions about the form the solution must take, assumptions about the use or function of elements contained within the problem, and assumptions about what types of procedures one should try in solving the problem. These various forms of problem-solving sets are usually helpful, because they guide the problem solver away from pointless lines of attack on the problem. But the problem-solving set can also be an obstacle to problem solving—if, for example, the solution requires a change in the set. Thus, problem solving sets in the form of functional fixedness or Einstellung can be significant obstacles to problem solution.

- Investigators interested in creativity have often relied on detailed case studies of famous creative individuals. These case studies have identified certain shared traits that seem to be "prerequisites" for great creativity. The case studies also suggest a need for a sociocultural approach to creativity.

- Some scholars suggest that creative problem solving proceeds through four stages: preparation, incubation, illumination, and verification. However, researchers are skeptical about these four stages, and careful studies of creativity have provided little evidence to suggest that creativity involves special or exotic processes. For example, incubation is often mentioned as a form of unconscious problem solving, but studies indicate that the benefits of incubation, when they occur, can be understood in simpler terms: recovery from fatigue or the forgetting of unfruitful earlier approaches. In the same way, the moment of illumination seems to indicate only that the problem solver has located a new approach to a problem; in many cases, this new approach ends up leading to a dead end.

- In light of these data, many authors have suggested that creativity may simply be the extraordinary product that results from an assembly of ordinary elements—elements that include cognitive processes (memory search through spreading activation, heuristics, etc.), and also emotional and personality characteristics that foster the processes and circumstances needed for creativity.

- Research on intelligence has been controversial. However, the commonly used measures of intelligence seem to be both reliable and valid. The validity is indicated by correlations often observed between IQ scores and performance in tasks that seem to require intelligence. These correlations are far from perfect (that is, well below 1.00), but this simply reminds us that other factors beyond intelligence matter for performance in most domains.

- Most intelligence tests involve numerous subtests, but people who do well on one portion of the test tend to do well across the board. This is the sort of evidence that persuades researchers that there is such a thing as intelligence in general—usually referred to as *g*. However, we can also distinguish various forms of more specialized intelligence, and so performance on many tasks depends both on someone's level of *g* and also on that person's profile of more specific strengths and weaknesses. This pattern is often summarized in hierarchical models of intelligence.

- We also need to distinguish between fluid and crystallized intelligence. Fluid intelligence refers to the ability to deal with new and unusual problems; crystallized intelligence refers to your acquired knowledge and skills.

- General intelligence, or *g*, can be understood in part in terms of mental speed, on the idea that people we call smart are literally faster in their intellectual functioning. A different proposal centers on the notion of *working-memory capacity* and *executive control*, with the suggestion that people who are intelligent are literally better able to monitor and direct their own thought processes. This notion of executive control fits well with the parieto-frontal integration theory, which emphasizes the coordination of several brain areas in creating intelligent behavior.

- Intellectual performance also depends on someone's attitude and motivation. As a result, it is convenient and often useful to measure intelligence with a single number (like an IQ score), but, if we want to understand and improve intelligence, we need to look past this single measure.

- IQ scores tell us a lot about an individual, but they don't assess all of the person's mental capacities. Researchers have also emphasized the importance of practical intelligence, rationality, and emotional intelligence. The theory of multiple intelligences goes further, proposing eight different types of intelligence.

- There is no question that genes influence intelligence. This is evident in the fact that people who resemble each other more closely (e.g., identical twins) also tend to resemble each other closely in their IQ scores; this remains true even if the twins were separated at birth and raised separately. It is also true, however, that environmental factors influence intelligence. This is reflected in the fact that various aspects of poverty can undermine intelligence, and various forms of enrichment in the environment can improve it. The impact of environment is also evident in the worldwide improvement in IQ scores known as the Flynn effect.

- Crucially, we must understand the interaction between genetic and environmental forces in determining someone's IQ. As a crude summary, we can think of the genes as specifying someone's potential, but how that potential will unfold is heavily shaped by the person's environment.

- There has been debate about differences between men and women in their mental abilities. Data show no difference between the sexes in overall IQ, although men's scores are more variable than women's. There are differences, however, on more specific tests, with women (on average) having an advantage on some verbal tests, and men (on average) having an advantage on some spatial tests.

- Some authors suggest these differences in ability are the cause of the so-called gender gap in academic achievement. However, this gap is inconsistent—showing up in some data and not in others. In all cases, though, the gap is likely to be attributable to the different types of expectations and encouragement men and women are exposed to, and, indeed, the expectations that many men and women have for themselves.

- Debate has been even more heated concerning the comparison between the IQ scores of African Americans and of White Americans. The gap that has been documented can be understood in part in terms of the lower levels of nutrition, medical care, and education available for many American Blacks. In addition, a large role is played by stereotype threat—a term referring to the negative impact that social stereotypes, once activated, can have on task performance.

The Workbook Connection

See the *Cognition Workbook* for further exploration of intelligence:

- Demonstration 12.1: Analogies
- Demonstration 12.2: Incubation
- Demonstration 12.3: Verbalization and Problem Solving
- Demonstration 12.4: Remote Associates
- Demonstration 12.5: IQ Testing
- Research Methods: Defining the Dependent Variable
- Research Methods: Correlations
- Cognitive Psychology and Education: Improving Intellectual Performance
- Cognitive Psychology and the Law: Problem Solving in the Courts
- Cognitive Psychology and the Law: Intelligence and the Legal System

NEED HELP STUDYING?

 wwnorton.com/studyspace

Visit StudySpace to access free review material such as

- Chapter study plans
- Quizzes
- Flashcards, and more

Go to **wwnorton.com/zaps** for these online labs:

- Gestalt Problem Solving
- Missionaries and Cannibals

The solutions to the puzzles on page 468 are "reading between the lines," "split second timing," "search high and low," "hole in one," "Jack in the box," and "double or nothing."

CHAPTER THIRTEEN

Conscious Thought, Unconscious Thought

The field of psychology emerged as a separate discipline, distinct from philosophy and biology, in the late 1800s, and, in those early years of our field, the topic of consciousness was a central concern: In Wilhelm Wundt's laboratory in Germany, researchers sought to understand the "elements" of consciousness; William James, in America, sought to understand the "stream" of consciousness.

However, the young field of psychology soon rejected this focus on consciousness, arguing that this research was subjective and unscientific. By the early 20th century, therefore, the topic of consciousness was largely gone from mainstream psychological research (although theorizing about consciousness, without much experimentation, continued, particularly among clinical psychologists).

Over the last few decades, though, it has become clear that a scientific investigation of consciousness is possible, and armed with new tools and new conceptualizations, researchers have made enormous advances in their understanding of what consciousness is, how it functions, and how the brain makes consciousness possible. Ironically, much of this progress has come not from examining consciousness directly,

PREVIEW OF CHAPTER THEMES

- Throughout this text, we have discussed processes that provide an unnoticed support structure for cognition. We begin, therefore, by reviewing themes from earlier chapters, in order to ask what sorts of things are accomplished within the "cognitive unconscious."

- Overall, it appears that you can perform a task unconsciously if you arrive at the task with a routine that can be guided by strong habits or powerful cues within the situation. With this constraint, unconscious processes can be remarkably sophisticated.

- Unconscious operations are fast and efficient, but are also inflexible and difficult to control. They free you to pay attention to higher-order aspects of a task but leave you ignorant about the sources of your ideas, beliefs, and memories.

- From a biological perspective, we know that most operations of the brain are made possible by highly specialized modules. These modules can be interrelated by means of workspace neurons, literally connecting one area of the brain to another and allowing the integration of different processing streams.

- The workspace neurons create a "global workspace," and this is what makes consciousness possible; the operations of this workspace fit well with many things we know to be true about consciousness.

- However, profound questions remain about how (or whether) the global workspace makes possible the subjective experience that for many theorists is the defining element of consciousness.

but from studying what happens in the *absence of* conscious awareness. This strategy has allowed us to detail the sorts of circumstances in which consciousness seems not to be needed; this, in turn, has allowed valuable insights into when consciousness *is* needed and, with that, just what it is that consciousness contributes to our mental lives. This understanding of what consciousness is *for* has in turn illuminated questions about what consciousness *is*.

Let's acknowledge at the start, though, that there's still much about consciousness that we don't understand and, indeed, still disagreement about how consciousness should be defined and studied. With that, there is still disagreement about whether we should distinguish different types of consciousness or, at least, different sorts of things that might be included under the broad label of "consciousness."

We'll return to these conceptual issues later in the chapter. For now, we'll proceed with this rough definition: Consciousness is a state of awareness of sensations or ideas, such that you can reflect on those sensations and ideas, know what it "feels like" to experience these sensations and ideas, and can, in many cases, report to others that you are aware of the sensations and ideas. As we'll see later, this broad definition has certain problems, but it will serve us well enough as an initial guide for our discussion.

The Cognitive Unconscious

Activities like thinking, remembering, and categorizing all feel quick and effortless. You instantly recognize the words on this page; you easily remember where you were this morning; you have no trouble deciding to have cheddar on your sandwich, not Swiss. As we've seen throughout this book, however, these (and other) intellectual activities are possible only because of an elaborate "support structure"—processes and mechanisms working "behind the scenes." Indeed, describing this behind-the-scenes action has been one of the main concerns of this text.

Psychologists refer to this behind-the-scenes activity as the **cognitive unconscious**—mental activity that you're not aware of but that makes possible your ordinary interactions with the world. The processes that unfold in the cognitive unconscious are sophisticated and powerful, and, as we'll see, it's actually quite *helpful* that a lot of mental work can take place without conscious supervision. At the same time, we also need to discuss the ways in which the *absence* of supervision can, in some cases, be a problem for you.

Unconscious Processes, Conscious Products

For many purposes, it is useful to distinguish the *products* created within your mind (beliefs you have formed, conclusions you have reached) from the *processes* that led to these products. This distinction isn't always clear cut and so, in some cases, we can quibble about whether a particular mental step counts as "product" or "process" (see, for early discussion, Miller, 1962; Neisser, 1967; Nisbett & Wilson, 1977; Smith & Miller, 1978; White, 1988). Even so, this distinction allows an important rule of thumb—namely, that you're generally aware of your mental products, but unaware of your mental processes.

For example, we saw in Chapter 7 that your memories of the past seamlessly combine genuine recall with some amount of after-the-fact reconstruction. Thus, when you "remember" your restaurant dinner last month, you're probably weaving together elements that were actually recorded into memory at the time of the dinner, with other elements that are just inferences or assumptions. These other elements, in turn, draw on your general knowledge about how restaurant meals usually unfold; this knowledge allows you to make reasonable suppositions about the specific dinner you're trying to recall.

We've argued that this weaving together is a good thing, because (among its other benefits) it allows you to fill in bits that you've forgotten, or bits you didn't notice in the first place. But this weaving together also creates a risk of error: If, for example, the dinner you're trying to recall was somehow unusual, then assumptions based on the more typical pattern may be misleading.

Let's be clear, though, about what's conscious here and what's not. Your recollection of the dinner is a mental *product* and is surely something you're aware of. Thus, you can reflect on the dinner if you wish and can describe the dinner if someone asks you. You're unaware, though, of the *process* that brought you this knowledge, so you have no way of telling which bits are supplied by memory retrieval and which bits rest on inference or assumption. Likewise, you cannot tell which bits have been inadvertently "imported" from other (but related) episodes. And, of course, if you can't determine which bits are which, there's no way for you to reject the inferences or to avoid the (entirely unnoticed) assumptions. That's why memory errors, when they occur, are undetectable: Since the process that brings you a "memory" is unconscious, you can't distinguish genuine recall from (potentially misguided) assumption.

Here's a different example: In Chapter 3, we considered a case in which people were briefly shown the stimulus "CORN"; we also considered a case in which people were shown "CQRN." Despite the different stimuli, both groups of people perceived the input to be "CORN"—a correct perception for the first group, but an error for the second.

For reasons we described in that earlier chapter, though, people won't be able to tell whether they're in the first group or the second, so they won't be able to tell whether they're perceiving correctly or *mis*-perceiving. Both groups are aware of the product created by their minds, and so both groups have the conscious experience of "seeing" the word CORN. But they're unaware of the processes and, specifically, clueless about whether the stimulus was actually perceived or merely inferred. These processes unfold in (what we're now calling) the cognitive unconscious, and, as such, are entirely hidden from view.

The Influence of Unconscious Attributions

The role of the cognitive unconscious is also evident in other settings, and, in those settings, we meet another layer of complexity—because, in many cases, participants seem to be engaging in a process of unconscious *reasoning*.

In Chapter 6, for example, we discussed a study in which participants convinced themselves that several utterly fictitious names actually were the names of famous people. In this procedure, participants were apparently aware of the fact that some of the names they were reading were distinctive; their conscious experience told them that these names somehow "stood out" from other names on the list. But, to make sense of the data from this study, we need to take a further step and argue that thoughts roughly like these were going through the participants' minds: "That name rings a bell, and I'm not sure why. But the experimenter is asking me about famous names, and there are other famous names on this list in front of me. I guess, therefore, that this one must also be the name of some famous person." This surely sounds like something that we want to count as "thinking," but it's thinking, the evidence suggests, of which the participants were entirely unaware, thinking that took place in their cognitive unconscious.

Similarly, let's consider an eyewitness who's pondering a police lineup. In this case, the witness may reason this way: "Face Number Two looks familiar to me, and the police think it's likely that one of these guys is the man who robbed me. I guess, therefore, that Number Two is familiar because I saw him at the robbery." Once again, however, the person isn't aware of this reasoning, and, indeed, is likely to deny thinking anything along these lines! Instead, the witness simply (and sometimes falsely) "remembers" seeing the face at the robbery and so can end up, in some circumstances, an unwitting victim of a mistaken inference.

In Chapter 7, we described another situation involving eyewitnesses, noting in particular what happens if a witness gets feedback after making an identification. Imagine, for example, that the witness has chosen Number Two from the lineup, and the police say something like, "Good; the person you've chosen is our suspect." In one study, witnesses who received no feedback said that their confidence in their lineup selection was (on average) 47%; witnesses who got the feedback, though, expressed much greater confidence: 71%. Of course, this leap in confidence makes no sense, because there's no way for the feedback to have "strengthened" the witnesses' memory, or to have influenced their selection. (Bear in mind that the feedback arrived only after the witness had made the selection!) So why did the feedback elevate confidence? It seems that the witnesses must have been thinking something like, "The police say I got the right answer, so I guess I can set aside my doubts." Of course, witnesses aren't aware of making this adjustment—and so the thought process here is again unconscious.

But the effects of feedback don't stop there. Witnesses who receive this sort of feedback also end up "remembering" that they got a closer, longer, clearer view of the perpetrator, that the lighting was good, and so on (see Figure 13.1). Here the witnesses seem to be thinking something like, "I chose the right person, so I guess I must have gotten a good view after all." Once more, however, these aren't conscious thoughts, and in this case the witness is being misled by some after-the-fact reconstruction.

These examples should make it plain that unconscious processes can sometimes involve *interpretation* and *inference*. And, in some settings, this unconscious thinking can be rather sophisticated. In an early experiment by Nisbett and Schachter (1966), participants were asked to endure a series of electric shocks, with each shock slightly more severe than the one before. The question of interest was how far into the series the participants would go. What was the maximum shock they would voluntarily accept?

Before beginning the series of shocks, some of the participants were given a pill that, they were told, would diminish the pain but would also have several side effects: It would cause their hands to shake, butterflies in the stomach, irregular breathing, and the like. Of course, none of this was true. The pill was a placebo and had no analgesic properties, nor did it produce any of these side effects. Even so, this inert pill was remarkably effective: Participants given the pill were willing to accept four times as much amperage as control participants.

Why was the placebo so effective? Nisbett and Schachter proposed that their control participants noticed that their hands were shaking, that their stomachs were upset, and so on. (These are, of course, common manifestations of fear—including the fearful anticipation of electric shock.) The participants then used these self-observations as evidence in judging their own states, drawing on what (in Chapter 11) we called "somatic markers." It is as if participants said to

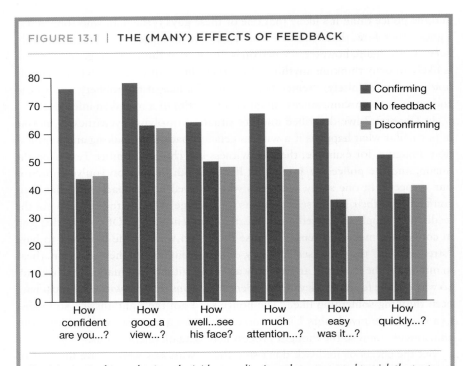

FIGURE 13.1 | THE (MANY) EFFECTS OF FEEDBACK

Participants in this study viewed a (videotaped) crime, then attempted to pick the perpetrator's picture out of a lineup. Later, participants were either given confirming feedback for their choice ("Good, you identified the actual suspect"), disconfirming feedback ("Actually, the suspect was . . .") or no feedback. Then participants were asked further questions about the video. The feedback arrived well after participants had viewed the crime (and after they'd made their ID selection), but the feedback altered participants' memory for what they had seen: Those who had received confirming feedback now recalled that they'd gotten a better view of the crime, including a better view of the face, even though all participants got the same view! Participants who received confirming feedback also recalled that their ID had been fast and easy, even though in truth their IDs had been no easier, no faster, than anyone else's. (After Wells, Olson, & Charman, 2003)

themselves, "Oh look, I'm trembling! I guess I must be scared. Therefore, these shocks must really be bothering me." This led them to terminate the shock series relatively early. Placebo participants, in contrast, attributed the same physical symptoms to the pill. "Oh look, I'm trembling! That's just what the experimenter said the pill would do. I guess I can stop worrying, therefore, about the trembling. Let me look for some other indication of whether the shock is bothering me." As a consequence, these participants were less influenced by their own physical symptoms. They detected these symptoms but discounted them, attributing them to the pill and not to the shock. In essence, then, they overruled the evidence of their own anxiety and so misread their own internal state. (For related studies, see Nisbett & Wilson, 1977; Wilson, 2002; Wilson & Dunn, 2004.)

Let's be clear, though, that this reasoning about the pill was entirely unconscious for the participants. In fact, the participants in this study were specifically asked why they had accepted so much shock, and, in response, they never mentioned the pill. When asked directly, "While you were taking the shock, did you think about the pill at all?," participants consistently said things like, "No, I was too worried about the shock to think of anything else."

Notice, then, that participants were observing "symptoms," generating hypotheses about those symptoms, drawing conclusions, and then making decisions based on these conclusions; they were, however, aware of none of these steps. As it turns out, these participants reached erroneous conclusions, because they'd been misled about the pill by the experimenter. But that takes nothing away from what they are doing intellectually—and unconsciously.

Mistaken Introspections

It does seem useful, then, to distinguish between the (unconscious) processes involved in thought and the (conscious) products that result from these processes. As we've said, this distinction isn't always clearcut, but even so, it does support a useful rule of thumb about what you're aware of in your mental life and what you're not. Thus, you arrive at a conclusion, but the steps leading to the conclusion are hidden from view. You reach a decision, but, again, are unable to introspect about the processes leading to that decision.

Sometimes, however, the processes of thought do seem to be conscious. Sometimes you reason carefully and deliberately, weighing each step and scrutinizing each bit of logic. You feel like you can voice the reasons for your decision, or the basis for your conclusion, if anyone asks. These surely sound like cases in which your thoughts *are* conscious. Remarkably, though, this sense of knowing your own thoughts may, in such cases, be an *illusion*. You feel like the relevant thought processes were conscious, but you may be mistaken!

We've just discussed one example of this pattern: In the Nisbett and Schachter (1966) study, participants steadfastly denied that their willingness to accept shock was influenced by the pill they'd taken. Instead, they offered other explanations—explanations that had nothing to do with the pill. Apparently, then, the participants had some beliefs about why they had acted as they did, but their beliefs were *wrong*—systematically ruling out a factor (the pill) that, in truth, was having an enormous impact.

Related examples are easy to find. Participants in one study read a brief excerpt from John Updike's novel *Rabbit Run*. They were then asked to describe what emotional impact the excerpt had on them, and they were also asked *why* the excerpt had the impact it did: Which sentences or which images, within the excerpt, led to the emotional "kick"? The participants were impressively consistent in their judgments, with 86% pointing to a particular passage (describing the messiness of a baby's crib) as playing an important role in creating the emotional tone of the passage. However, it appears that the participants' judgments were simply wrong. Another group of participants read the same excerpt, but minus the bit about the crib. These participants reacted to the overall excerpt in exactly the same way as the earlier group. Apparently, the bit about the crib wasn't crucial at all (Nisbett & Wilson, 1977; for other, more recent data, see Bargh, 2005; Custers & Aarts, 2010).

DO WE KNOW WHY WE DO WHAT WE DO?

For years, there has been debate over whether the government should regulate (and limit) cigarette advertising, based on the idea that we don't want to lure people into this unhealthy habit. In response, the tobacco industry has sometimes offered survey data, asking people "Why did you start smoking?" The industry notes that, in some of these surveys, people do not attribute their start to the ads; therefore the ads do no harm; therefore the ads should not be regulated. Let's be clear, though, that this argument assumes that people know why they do what they do, and this assumption is often mistaken!

In studies like these, participants think they know why they acted as they did, but they're mistaken. Their self-reports are offered with full confidence, and in many cases the participants report that they carefully and deliberately thought about their actions, so that the various causes and influences were, it seems, out in plain view. Nonetheless, from our perspective as researchers, we can see that these introspective reports are wrong—ignoring factors we know to be crucial, highlighting factors we know to be irrelevant.

How could these introspections get so far off track? The answer starts with the fact that we've already showcased—namely, that the processes of thought are often unconscious. People seeking to introspect, therefore, have no way to inspect these processes, and so, if they're going to explain their own behavior, they need some other source of information, and in most cases that other source is likely to be an *after-the-fact reconstruction*. Roughly put, people reason in this fashion: "Why did I act that way? I have no direct information, but perhaps I can draw on my broad knowledge about why, in general, people might act in certain ways in this situation. From that base, I can make some plausible inferences about why I acted as I did." Thus, for example: "I know that, in general, passages about babies or passages about squalor can be emotionally moving; I bet that's what moved me in reading this passage."

These after-the-fact reconstructions will often be correct, because your beliefs about why people act as they do are generally sensible: "Why am I angry at Gail? She just insulted me, and I know that, in general, people tend to get angry when they've been insulted. I bet, therefore, that I'm angry because she insulted me." In cases such as this one, an inference based on generic knowledge is likely to be accurate.

However, in other cases these reconstructions will be totally wrong (as in the experiments we've mentioned). They will go off track, for example, if your beliefs about a specific setting happen to be mistaken; in that case, inferences based on those beliefs will obviously be problematic. Likewise, the reconstructions will go off track if you didn't notice some relevant factor in the setting; here, too, inferences not taking that factor into account will likely yield mistaken interpretations.

But let's also be clear that these after-the-fact reconstructions don't "feel like" inferences. When research participants (or people in general) explain their own behaviors, they're usually convinced that they're simply *remembering* their own mental processes based on some sort of direct inspection of what went on in their own minds. These reconstructions, in other words, feel like genuine "introspections." The evidence we've reviewed, however, suggests that these subjective feelings are mistaken, and so, ironically, this is one more case in which people are conscious of the product and not the process. They are aware of the conclusion ("I acted as I did because . . .") but not aware of the process that led them to the conclusion. Hence, they continue to believe (falsely) that the conclusion rests on an introspection, when, in truth, it rests on an after-the-fact reconstruction. Hand in hand with this, they continue to believe confidently that they know themselves, even though, in reality, their self-perception is (in these cases at least) focusing on the wrong factors. (For more on this process of "self-interpretation," see Cooney & Gazzaniga, 2003.)

Unconscious Guides to Conscious Thinking

Many people find these claims to be troubling. Each of us likes to believe we know ourselves reasonably well. Each of us likes to believe that we typically know why we've acted as we have, or why we believe what we do. The research we're considering, though, challenges these ideas. Often we don't know where our beliefs, or emotions, or actions came from. We don't know which of our "memories" are based on actual recall, and which are inferences. We don't know which of our "perceptions" are mistaken. And even when we insist that we do know why we acted in a certain way, and are sure we remember the reasoning that led to our actions, we can be wrong!

Sometimes, though, you surely are aware of your own thoughts. Sometimes you make decisions based on a clear, well-articulated "inner dialogue" with yourself. Sometimes you make discoveries based on a visual image that you carefully (and consciously!) scrutinized. Even here, though, there's a role for the cognitive unconscious, because even here a support structure is needed—a support structure that exists at (what philosophers have called) the "fringe" or the "horizon" of your conscious thoughts (Husserl, 1931; James, 1890).

Evidence for this unnoticed fringe comes from a wide variety of cases in which your thoughts are influenced by an "unseen hand." For example, in our description of problem solving (Chapter 12), we emphasized the role of *set*—unnoticed assumptions and definitions that guide your search for the problem's solution. Even when the problem solving is conscious and deliberate, even when you "think out loud" about the steps of the problem solution, you are guided by a set. For the most part this is a good thing, because (as we argued in the earlier chapter) the set keeps you focused, protecting you from distracting and unproductive lines of thought. But the set can sometimes be an obstacle to problem solving, and the fact that the set is unconscious makes it all the more difficult to overcome the obstacle: A problem solver cannot easily pause and reflect on the set, and so she cannot alter the problematic beliefs or abandon the misleading assumptions.

Similarly, in our discussion of decision-making (Chapter 11), we emphasized the importance of a decision's *frame*. You might be completely focused on the decision and fully aware of your options. Nonetheless, you'll be heavily influenced by the (unnoticed) framing of the decision—the way the options are described and the way the question itself is posed. You don't think about the framing itself, but the framing unmistakably colors your thoughts about the decision and plays a large role in determining which option you'll choose.

In these ways, then, your deliberate, conscious thinking—about problems, decisions, and more—is guided by an unnoticed framework. Thus, you're aware that you're working on a problem, but not aware of how your set guides your approach to the problem. You're consciously thinking about your options in a decision, but not conscious of how the decision frame guides your assessment of your options. In each case, the unconscious mental framework protects you from uncertainty and ambiguity, but it also governs the content and the sequence of your thoughts.

Blind Sight and Amnesia

One last line of evidence for unconscious processes comes primarily from patients who have suffered brain damage. Consider, for example, the discussion of Korsakoff's syndrome in Chapter 6. Patients suffering from this syndrome seem to have no conscious memory of events they've witnessed or things they've done. If asked directly about these events, the patients will insist that they have no recollection. If asked to perform tasks that require recollection—like navigating to the store, based on a memory of the store's location—the patients will fail.

Even so, it's false to claim that these patients have "no memories," because, on tests of *implicit* memory, amnesic patients seem quite normal. In other words,

CONSCIOUSNESS IS GUIDED BY UNCONSCIOUS FRAMEWORKS

You often fail to detect the ambiguity you encounter—such as the two ways to interpret "Out of order." This is because you (unconsciously) supply a framework that guides your interpretation.

they do seem to "remember" if we probe their memories indirectly—not asking them explicitly what they recall, but instead looking for evidence that their current behavior is shaped by specific prior experiences. In these indirect tests, the patients are plainly influenced by memories they don't know they have! Clearly, therefore, some aspects of remembering—and some influences of experience—can go smoothly forward even in the absence of a conscious memory.

Of course, it's not just patients with amnesia who show this distinction between implicit and explicit memory: As we saw in Chapter 6, people with intact, healthy brains also show the effects of implicit memory, even when they have no conscious recollection of the event that gave rise to this memory. This pattern explains why Jacoby and Witherspoon (1982) referred to implicit memory as "memory without awareness," and so, in both healthy populations and cases of brain damage, we see that (at least one type of) memory does not depend on consciousness.

Parallel claims can be made for *perception*. Consider, for example, the phenomenon of **blind sight**. This is a pattern observed in patients who have suffered damage to the visual cortex, and, as a result, they are, for all practical purposes, blind: If asked what they see, they insist they see nothing. They do not react to flashes of bright light. They hesitate to walk down a corridor, convinced they will collide with whatever obstacles lie in their path. In one experiment, however, visual stimuli were presented to these patients, and they were forced to guess whether the stimuli were (for example) X's or O's, circles or squares. Quite reliably, these patients "guessed" correctly (Rees, Kreiman, & Koch, 2002; Weiskrantz, 1986, 1997; de Gelder, 2010). Similarly, if the patients are forced to guess where various objects are placed and to reach toward those objects, they tend to reach in the right direction with the appropriate hand position (given the shape and size of the target object). Indeed, one patient was able to identify the emotional expression (sad versus happy versus afraid) on faces in front of him (de Gelder, 2010). In all cases, though, the patients insist they can not see the targets, and can offer no explanation when asked why their "guesses" are consistently accurate. Apparently, therefore, these patients are not aware of seeing, but, even so, can in some ways "see."

How is this possible? The answer lies in the fact that there are several neural pathways carrying information from the eyeball to the brain. Damage to one of these pathways is the reason that these patients seem (on many measures) to be blind. However, information flow is still possible along some of the other pathways (including a pathway through a brain area called the superior colliculus, in the midbrain; Tamietto et al., 2010), and this is what allows these patients to use visual information that they cannot (consciously) see. One way or the other, though, it's clear that we need again to distinguish between "perception" and "conscious perception," because unmistakably it is possible to perceive in the absence of consciousness. (For more data, also showing a sharp distinction between a patient's conscious perception of the world and her ability to gather and use visual information, see Goodale & Milner, 2004; Logie & Della Salla, 2005 and also Figure 13.2. For more on unconscious perception in people with intact brains, see Chapter 4.)

FIGURE 13.2 | CONSCIOUS SEEING; UNCONSCIOUS SEEING

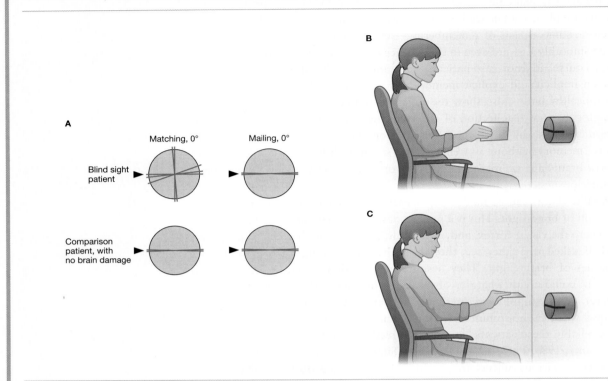

In one condition (Panel B), a blind-sight patient was instructed to hold a piece of cardboard so that its orientation "matched" the orientation of the slot. As can be seen in Panel A, she had considerable difficulty in this task, and often held the card at an angle far from the correct angle. This performance confirms the blind-sight diagnosis. In another condition, though, the patient was asked to imagine that she was "mailing" the card, placing it into a "mailslot" (Panel C). In this condition, her performance was perfect, and she consistently matched the card's orientation to the orientation of the slot. It would seem, then, that the patient is (consciously) blind, but is able to see, and to use the information that she sees in guiding her own actions. (After Goodale, Milner, Jakobson, & Carey, 1991)

Consciousness and Executive Control

Where, then, does all of this leave us? Clearly, a huge range of activities, including complex activities, can be accomplished unconsciously. You can see, you can remember, you can decide, you can interpret, you can infer—all without any awareness of these activities. So why do you need consciousness at all? What function does it serve? And related to this, what things *can't* you do unconsciously?

The Limits of Unconscious Performance

In tackling these questions, let's start with the fact that your unconscious steps seem, in each of the cases we've discussed, quite sensible. If, for example, the police tell you that the guy you selected from a lineup is indeed their suspect, this suggests that you did, in fact, get a good look at him during the crime. (Otherwise, how were you able to recognize him?) It's not crazy, therefore, that you'd "adjust" your memory for what you saw, because you now know that your view must have been decent. Likewise, imagine that you're making judgments about how famous various people are, and you're looking at a list that includes some unmistakably famous names. If, in this setting, one of the other names seems somehow familiar, it again seems entirely sensible that you'd (unconsciously) infer that this name, too, belongs to someone famous.

Over and over, therefore, your unconscious judgments and inferences tend to be fast, efficient, and also *reasonable*. In other words, your unconscious judgments and inferences are well-tuned to, and appropriately guided by, cues in the situation, and also in tune with your prior habits and inclinations. This pattern is obviously a good thing, because it means that your unconscious processing won't be foolish or capricious. But the pattern also provides an important clue about the nature of—and possible limitations on—unconscious processing.

Here's a proposal: Unconscious reasoning can be complex and sophisticated, but it is strongly guided either by the situation you're in or by prior habit. Thus, when you (unconsciously) draw a conclusion or make a selection, these steps are likely to be the ones favored by familiarity or by the setting itself. Similarly, when you unconsciously make some response—whether it's an overt action, like reaching for an object that you cannot consciously see, or a mental response, like noting the meaning of a word you did not consciously perceive—you're likely to make a familiar response, a response that's "normal" and perhaps well practiced in that situation.

This proposal obviously suggests that unconscious reasoning will typically be appropriate for the circumstances, but it also suggests that unconscious processing will generally be inflexible—relying on habitual or stimulus-governed actions, and hence not subject to control. This inflexibility is, in fact, easy to demonstrate: Consider, for example, the observation that it's difficult for you to "turn off" your unconscious steps even when you want to. As an illustration, think about the inferences you use to fill gaps in memory (both during encoding and during retrieval). These inferences are, we've said, often helpful, but we've discussed how these processes can lead to error—and, in some cases, to large and consequential errors. Knowing these facts about memory, however, is no protection at all. Just as you cannot choose to avoid a perceptual illusion, you also cannot choose to avoid memory error. The process of making inferences is automatic and effortless, and it's also irresistible (see Figure 13.3).

In the same way, the inferences and assumptions that are built into object recognition (Chapter 3) are usually helpful—helping you identify objects even if your view is brief and incomplete. Sometimes, though, you want to shut off these inferences, but you can't. Thus, for example, if you're proofreading something you've written, you want to be alert to what's actually on the page and not be fooled by your ideas about what *should* be there. Plainly, though, proofreading is very hard—and you (unconsciously) "correct" what's on the page whether you want to or not, and so you often fail to see the misspelling or the missing word. (To see how this works, you might look back at CWB Demonstration 3.4.)

FIGURE 13.3 | **OUT OF CONTROL**

A   Müller-Lyer illusion

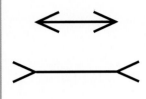

B   Poggendorff illusion

C   Ponzo illusion

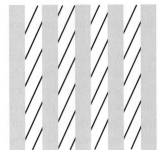

The inferences you make in perception and memory are automatic and unconscious—and so not something you can "turn off" when you want to. Hence the errors produced by these inferences are akin to perceptual illusions—shaping your reality whether you like it or not. In (A), the two horizontals are the same length. In (B), the black segments are perfectly aligned, and so, if you could remove the yellow bars, you'd see perfectly straight black lines. In (C), the two yellow horizontals are the same length. Knowing these facts, however, does not in any way protect you from the illusions. (These illusions are named, by the way, in honor of the people who created them.)

Similarly, the inflexibility in routine makes it all too easy for you to become a victim of habit, relying on your customary thought patterns even when you hope to avoid them. This is one of the reasons that problem-solving sets (Chapter 12) are so powerful and so difficult to break out of. It is also the reason that **action slips**—doing something different from what you intend—take the form that they do. In most cases, these slips involve doing what's *normal* or *habitual* in a situation, rather than what you want to do on that occasion. For example, you're in the car, driving to the store. You intend to turn left at the corner, but, distracted for a moment, you turn right, taking the route that you usually take on your way to school. Action slips like this one almost invariably involve the intrusion of a strong and familiar habit, slipping into what's "normal" even if it's not, at that moment, what you intend (Norman, 1981; Reason, 1990; also see Langer, 1989). All of this is just as we'd expect if routine is forceful, automatic, and uncontrolled.

The Role for Control

Roughly put, therefore, the idea is that unconscious processes—in perception, in memory, in reasoning—serve as a sophisticated and often-useful set of "mental reflexes," guided by the circumstances and therefore generally appropriate for the circumstances—but also guided by the circumstances *and therefore inflexible.*

Let's be clear, though, about the *advantages* produced by the fact that unconscious processes are largely uncontrolled. Because they're uncontrolled, unconscious processes can proceed without any sort of "supervision," and this allows you to run many of these processes at the same time—increasing the speed and efficiency of your mental life. In addition, since you're not supervising these unconscious processes, you're free to devote your attention to other, more pressing matters.

But how could it be that these often-complex processes can run without supervision? Part of the answer is straightforwardly biological, and the sequence of events for some unconscious processing (e.g., the steps needed for perception) is likely built into the essential structure of the nervous system. Hence, no supervision, no attention, was ever required for these steps! For other sorts of unconscious processing, though, the answer is different, and it's an answer we first met in Chapter 4. There we argued that, when you're learning a new task, you need to monitor each step, so that you'll know when it's time to start the next step. Then you need to *choose* the next step and get it started. Obviously, this combination of monitoring, choosing, and launching gives you close control over how things proceed, but this need for supervision of the task makes the performance quite demanding.

After some practice, however, things are different. The steps needed for the task are still there, but you don't think about them one by one. That's because you have stored in memory a complete routine that specifies what all the steps should be and when each step should be initiated. All you need to do, therefore, is launch the routine, and from that point forward you let the familiar sequence unfold. Thus, with no need for monitoring or decisions, you can do the task without paying close attention to it.

WORKBOOK
DEMONSTRATION 13.1

In short, practice allows you to perform a task while allocating your resources elsewhere, and, as we described in Chapter 4, this has important benefits. When you're in the midst of a conversation, for example, you need, again and again, to search through memory to find suitable words for expressing your intended meaning. In this setting, you'd be distracted and slowed if you had to think through the mechanics of this memory search, as you hunted for each word. It's crucial, therefore, that you can rely on well-practiced routine for this search, so you can instead focus on other issues (like choosing what ideas you want to convey in the conversation).

For our present discussion, though, the key idea is that practice diminishes the need for supervision and control of a task. This allows you to cease paying attention to the task and thus allows you to perform the task outside of awareness, unconsciously. In Chapter 4, we described these changes, made possible by practice, in terms of *executive control*, and that notion is still important here: Unconscious actions go forward without executive control. When you need to direct your own mental processes—to rise above habit, or to avoid responding to salient cues in your surrounding—you need executive control, so you need conscious processing. (For some complications, though, and a potential distinction between executive control and conscious experience, see Feldman, Barrett, Tugade, & Engle, 2004.)

The Prerequisites for Control

Sometimes, therefore, you don't want control of your own mental steps, because *absence* of control (and absence of supervision) buys you certain gains. But sometimes you do want control, and that leads us to ask: What makes control possible? In order to perform its function, executive control has certain straightforward needs. First, the executive needs some means of launching desired actions, and overriding unwanted actions. In other words, the executive needs an "output" side—things it can do, actions it can initiate. Second, the executive needs some means of representing its goals and subgoals so that they can serve as guides to action; related, the executive probably needs some means of representing its plan or "agenda." (In Chapter 12, we referred to this plan as a *task model*.) Then, third, on the "input" side, the executive needs somehow to know what's going on in the mind: What bits of information are coming in? How can these bits of information be integrated with each other? Is there any conflict among the arriving information, or conflict between the information and the current goals? Fourth, it also seems plausible that the executive needs to know how easily, and how smoothly, current processes are unfolding. If the processes are proceeding without difficulties, there's no need to make adjustments, but if the processes are somehow stymied, the executive would probably seek an alternative path toward the goal.

As it turns out, these claims about the *prerequisites for control* fit well with the *traits of conscious experience* and with current claims about the biological basis for consciousness. Let's look at some of those biological claims, so that we can then work through how all these perspectives on consciousness might be woven together.

The Cognitive Neuroscience of Consciousness

In the last decade or so, there has been an avalanche of intriguing research on the relationship between consciousness and brain function. Some of this research has focused on cases of brain damage, including the cases of amnesia or blind sight mentioned earlier in this chapter. Other research scrutinizes people with normal brains and has asked, roughly, what changes we can observe in the brain when someone becomes conscious of a stimulus. In other words, what are the **neural correlates** of consciousness (Atkinson, Thomas, & Cleeremans, 2000; Baars & Franklin, 2003; Bogen, 1995; Chalmers, 1998; Crick & Koch, 1995; Dehaene & Naccache, 2001; Kim & Blake, 2005; Rees et al., 2002)? As we'll see, consideration of these neural correlates will lead us directly back to the questions we've just been pondering.

The Many Brain Areas Needed for Consciousness

To explore the neural correlates of consciousness, researchers rely on the various recording techniques we described in Chapter 2. Thus, some studies use neuro-imaging (PET or fMRI) to assess activity at specific brain locations. Other studies use EEG to track the brain's electrical activity. Using these methods, several studies have asked how the pattern of brain activity changes when someone shifts attention from one idea to another. Other studies have tracked the changes that occur in brain activity when someone first becomes aware of a stimulus that's been in front of their eyes all along.

Research in this arena makes it clear that many different brain areas are crucial for consciousness, so we can't expect to locate some group of neurons or some place in the brain that's the "consciousness center" and functions as if it's a bulb that lights up when you're conscious, and then changes its brightness when your mental state changes. Overall, though, the evidence suggests we'll need to distinguish two broad categories of brain sites, corresponding to two aspects of consciousness (see Figure 13.4).

First, there is the level of alertness or sensitivity, independent of what you are currently alert or sensitive *to*. We can think of this as the difference between being dimly aware of a stimulus (or an idea, or a memory), and being highly alert and totally focused on that stimulus. This aspect of consciousness is compromised when someone suffers damage to certain sites in either the thalamus or the *reticular activating system* in the brainstem—a system that controls the overall arousal level of the forebrain and that also helps control the cycling between sleep and wakefulness (e.g., Koch, 2008).

Second, consciousness obviously varies in its content. Sometimes you're thinking about your immediate environment; sometimes you're thinking about past events. Sometimes you're focused on some current task, and sometimes you're dreaming about the future. These various contents for consciousness require different brain sites, and so cortical structures in the visual system are especially active when you're consciously aware of sights in front of your eyes (or aware of a visual image that you have created); cortical structures in the forebrain are essential when you're thinking about some stimulus that is no longer present in your environment; and so on.

This broad distinction between the *degree of awareness* and the *content of consciousness* therefore helps us understand the diversity of brain areas involved

FIGURE 13.4 | **TWO SEPARATE ASPECTS OF CONSCIOUSNESS**

At any given moment, a radio might be receiving a particular station either dimly or with a clear signal. Likewise, at any given moment the radio might be receiving a rock station, or a jazz station, or the news. These two dimensions—the clarity of the signal and the station choice—correspond roughly to the two aspects of consciousness described in the text.

in supporting consciousness. The distinction is also useful for us in thinking about *variations* in consciousness, as suggested by Figure 13.5 (after Laureys, 2005; also Koch, 2008). In dreaming, for example, you are conscious of a richly detailed scene, with its various sights and sounds and events, and so there's a well-defined content, but your sensitivity to the environment is low. In contrast, in the peculiar state associated with sleepwalking, you're sensitive to certain aspects of the world so that you can, for example, navigate through the environment, but you seem to have no particular thoughts in mind, and so the content of your consciousness is not well defined.

The Neuronal Workspace

But what is it in the brain that makes consciousness possible at all? Researchers have offered a variety of proposals, but many investigators endorse one version or another of the **neuronal workspace hypothesis**. In broad outline, here is the proposal: As we first discussed in Chapter 2, different areas within the brain seem highly specialized in their function. The brain areas that make vision possible, for example, are separate from the brain areas that support hearing. Even within vision, the various aspects of perception each depend on their own brain sites, with one area specialized for the perception of color, another for the perception of movement, another for the perception of faces, and so on.

As we described in Chapters 2 and 4, though, these diverse elements need to be reassembled so that we don't perceive round + red + moving; we instead perceive *falling apple*. We don't perceive rectangular + white + still; we instead perceive *book page*. In the earlier chapters, we referred to this as the *binding problem*—the task of linking together the different aspects of experience in order to create a coherent whole.

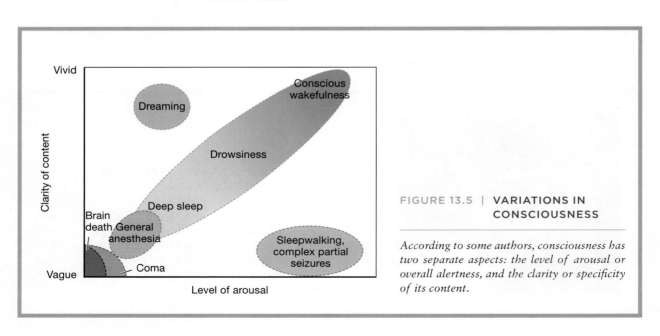

FIGURE 13.5 | **VARIATIONS IN CONSCIOUSNESS**

According to some authors, consciousness has two separate aspects: the level of arousal or overall alertness, and the clarity or specificity of its content.

We have already argued that *attention* plays a key role in this integration—that is, in solving the binding problem. Thus, for example, a moving stimulus in front of your eyes will trigger a response in one brain area; a red stimulus will trigger a response in another area. In the absence of attention, these two neural responses will be independent of each other. However, if you're paying attention to a single stimulus that is red and moving, the neurons in these two systems fire in synchrony (see Chapter 2), and when neurons fire in this coordinated fashion, the brain seems to register this as a linkage among the different processing areas. As a result, these attributes are bound together, so that you end up correctly perceiving the stimulus as a unified whole.

This integration requires communication, so that neurons in one brain area can send signals to (and receive signals from) other, perhaps distant, brain areas. This communication is made possible by "workspace neurons," neurons that literally connect one area of the brain to another. However, the process of carrying information back and forth via the workspace neurons is selective, so it's certainly not the case that every bit of neural activity gets linked to every other bit. Instead, various mechanisms create a *competition* among different brain processes, and the "winner" in this competition (typically, the most active process) is communicated to other brain areas, while other information is not.

Which elements will "win" in this competition? Again, attention is crucial: When you pay attention to a stimulus, this involves (among other neural steps) activity in the prefrontal cortex that can *sustain* and *amplify* the activity in other neural systems (Maia & Cleeremans, 2005). This will obviously shape how the competition plays out: By increasing the activity in one area or another, attention ensures that this area wins the competition—and thus ensures that information from this area is broadcast to other brain sites.

As a result of all of this, the information flow from each brain area to all the others is *limited*; this point is guaranteed by the competition. At the same time, the information flow is also *controllable,* by virtue of what you choose to pay attention to.

With this backdrop, we're ready for our hypothesis: The integrated activity, made possible by the workspace neurons, literally provides the biological basis for consciousness. The workspace neurons themselves don't carry the *content* of consciousness; the content—the sense of seeing something red, the sense of seeing something moving—is presumably represented in the same neurons, the same processing modules, that analyzed the perceptual information in the first place. But what the workspace neurons do is glue these bits together, creating a unified experience and allowing the exchange of information from one module to the next. (For some of the specific versions of this hypothesis, see Baars, 2005; Baars & Franklin, 2003; Cooney & Gazzaniga, 2003; Crick & Koch, 2003; Dehaene & Changeux, 2011; Dehaene & Naccache, 2001; Engel & Singer, 2001; Maia & Cleeremans, 2005; Roser & Gazzaniga, 2004. We should mention, though, that some researchers have offered alternatives to this conception, although most of these alternatives also emphasize the role of consciousness in coordinating and integrating distinct processing modules; see, for example, Morsella & Bargh, 2011; Morsella, Krieger & Bargh, 2010.)

The Function of the Neuronal Workspace

Again, let's pause to outline the proposal that's before us: Any idea—whether it's an idea about a stimulus in front of your eyes, or an idea drawn from memory—is represented in the brain by means of a widespread pattern of activity, with different parts of the brain each representing just one of the idea's elements. You become *aware of* that idea, though, when these various elements are linked to each other in a single overarching representation made possible by the workspace.

What does this linkage do for you? What does it make possible? And how is all of this related to our earlier comments about executive control? Let's start with some basic facts about conscious experience: It's important, first, that your experience feels unitary and coherent: As we've noted in several contexts, you're not aware of red and also aware of movement, and of roundness, and of closeness. Instead, you are aware of a single experience in which the apple rolls slowly by you. This integrated coherence, of course, is just what the workspace allows: one representation, constructed from the coordinated activity of many processing components (Roser & Gazzaniga, 2004).

Likewise, we emphasized in Chapter 4 that conscious experience is *selective*. In other words, you're conscious of only a narrow slice of the objects and events in your world, so that you might focus on the rose's color but fail to notice its thorns, or a driver might be so absorbed in a phone call that he misses his exit. Moreover, you can typically *choose* what you're going to focus on (so that you might, when picking up the rose, decide to pay attention to those thorns!). These observations, too, are easily accommodated by the workspace model: The information carried by the workspace neurons is, we've said, governed by a competition (and so is limited) and also shaped by how you focus attention. In this way, the properties of the workspace readily map onto the properties of your experience.

Let's also note that attention both amplifies *and sustains* neural activity. As a result, the workspace, supported by attention, allows you to maintain mental representations in an active state for an extended period of time. Thus, the workspace makes it possible for you to continue thinking about a stimulus or idea even after the specific trigger for that idea is removed. This point allows us to link the workspace proposal to claims about working memory (Chapter 5) and to the brain areas associated with working memory's function—specifically, the prefrontal cortex (or PFC; Goldman-Rakic, 1987). (For other evidence linking activation in the PFC to conscious awareness, see McIntosh, Rajah, & Lobaugh, 1999; Miller & Cohen, 2001.) This seems appropriate, since working memory is, of course, the memory that holds materials you're currently *working on*, and this presumably means materials currently within your conscious awareness.

The Neuronal Workspace and Executive Control

What is the connection between the neuronal workspace and executive control? Bear in mind that the workspace allows you to combine what's going on in one neural system with what's going on in others. This allows you to reflect on relationships and combinations among various inputs or ideas, and this in turn allows you to produce new combinations of ideas or new combinations of operations. Thus, the neural mechanisms underlying consciousness are just the right sort to allow you to produce novel thoughts, thoughts that allow you to rise above habit or routine. In this way, the workspace provides a plausible neural basis for executive functioning, and, with this, allows you to escape the limits that characterize unconscious processing.

The workspace also provides another crucial function. We said earlier that unconscious processes are generally guided by prior habits, and, if there's a conflict between habit and current goals, this has little influence on the unconscious process. In contrast, conscious thought *is* guided by a sense of your goals, and it can launch exactly the behavior that will lead to those goals.

How might the workspace support this sensitivity to current goals? By linking the various processing modules, the workspace makes it possible to compare what's going on in one module with what's going on elsewhere in the brain, and this allows you to detect conflict—if, for example, two simultaneous stimuli are triggering incompatible responses, or if a stimulus is triggering a response incompatible with your goals. This, in turn, makes it possible for you to shift processing in one system (again, by adjusting how you pay attention) in light of what is going on in other systems.

In fact, this capacity to detect conflict among various mental operations is itself supported by specific mechanisms that seem to function largely as "conflict detectors." Several brain sites support this function, including the **anterior cingulate cortex** (ACC), a structure linked to (and slightly behind) the frontal cortex, and also connected to structures (including the amygdala, nucleus accumbens, and hypothalamus) that play pivotal roles in emotion, motivation, and feelings of reward (Botvinick, Cohen, & Carter, 2004; van Veen & Carter, 2006). (For more on connecting the functioning of the ACC to conscious awareness, see Dehaene et al., 2003; but for some complications, see Mayr, 2004.)

The neuronal workspace idea also helps us with another puzzle—a shift in consciousness that everyone experiences virtually every day: specifically, the difference between being *awake* and being *asleep*. When you're asleep (and not dreaming), you're not conscious of the passing of time, not conscious of any ongoing stream of thought, and not conscious of many events taking place in your vicinity. This is not, however, because the brain is less active during sleep than it is when you're awake; brain activity during sleep is, in fact, quite intense. What, then, is the difference between the "sleeping brain" and the "awake brain"? When you're asleep (and not dreaming), evidence suggests that communication breaks down between different parts of the cortex, so that the brain's various activities are not coordinated with each other. The obvious suggestion, then, is that this communication (mediated by the neuronal workspace) is crucial for consciousness, so it makes sense that sleeping people, having temporarily lost this communication, are not conscious of their state or their circumstances (Massimini et al., 2005). (For a similar account of the loss of consciousness during surgical anesthesia, see Alkire, Hudetz & Tononi, 2008; for more on other "states" of consciousness, see Gleitman, Gross, & Reisberg, 2011.)

The Role of Phenomenal Experience

In several ways, therefore, we can draw parallels between the functioning of the neuronal workspace and the traits and capacities of consciousness. We can also link our claims about the workspace to the needs of executive control: The workspace, for example, supports the comparisons among processing streams that allow the executive to monitor mental processes; the workspace also supports the sustained neural activity that makes it possible for the executive to keep its goals and plans in view. The mechanisms involved in the workspace can also amplify certain types of activity, and this allows the executive to take control of mental events—ramping up desired activities, and allowing distractions to languish.

Qualia

Let's emphasize, though, that these suggestions still leave a substantial puzzle untouched, and, in fact, some authors argue that the workspace proposal dodges what philosophers call the "hard problem" of consciousness (e.g., Chalmers, 1996, 1998). Specifically, several theorists have claimed that we need to distinguish between "access consciousness" and "phenomenal consciousness" (e.g., Block, 1997, 2005; Koulder, Gardelle, Sackur & Dupoux, 2010; but also see Cohen & Dennett, 2011; Lau & Rosenthal, 2011). Access consciousness can be defined as your sensitivity to certain types of information (and thus your *access* to that information), and discussions of this aspect of consciousness (like our discussion so far) generally emphasize the function of this access—that is, what you can do if you have this access, and what you can't do *without* this access.

Phenomenal consciousness, in contrast, isn't about the use or function of information. Instead, this sort of consciousness centers on what it actually *feels like* to have certain experiences—that is, the subjective experience that distinguishes a conscious being from a "zombie" (or robot or computer) that might have access to the same information, but with no "inner experience."

Philosophers use the term **qualia** to refer to these subjective experiences. (Qualia is the plural form of the word; the singular is *quale*.) As an example, imagine meeting some unfortunate soul who has never tasted chocolate. You could offer this person a detailed and vivid description of what chocolate tastes like. You could compare chocolate's flavor to various other flavors. You might even provide this person with a full account of chocolate's impact on the nervous system (which receptors on the tongue are activated, and so on). What you could not do, however, is convey the subjective first-person experience of just what chocolate tastes like. In other words, you could provide this person with lots of information, but not the *quale* of chocolate taste. (For a different example, see Figure 13.6.)

There are many questions to ask about qualia: Philosophers, for example, might ask whether any one of us can ever understand the qualia experienced by other people—a question, in essence, about whether you experience the world in the same way I do. Neuroscientists might ask how the nervous system produces qualia—how does biological tissue give rise to subjective states? But a cognitive psychologist might ask: How do qualia matter in shaping mental processes?

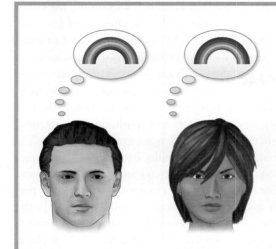

FIGURE 13.6 | THE INVERTED SPECTRUM

Does each of us experience the world in the same way? Philosophers sometimes cast this question in terms of the "inverted spectrum" problem. Imagine that your nervous system is somehow "wired differently" than mine. When you perceive red, *the color you're experiencing is the color I call* violet. *When you perceive* blue, *the color you're experiencing is the color I call* yellow. *Of course, you and I have both learned to call the color of stop lights "red," even though we have very different experiences when looking at a stop light. We've both learned that mixing yellow and red paints creates orange, even though we have different experiences of this "orange." How, then, would we ever find out if your color experience differs from mine?*

Fluency

In truth, we know relatively little about how people are influenced by the subjective experience of consciousness. We've argued in this chapter that the *information content* of consciousness is crucial, but does it matter how this content "feels" from a first-person perspective?

Research provides some intriguing hints about these issues—but let's be clear that these are *hints*, and claims here must be somewhat speculative. Surely, though, this is no surprise: Qualia are, by their nature, undetectable by anyone other than the person who experiences them, so they are obviously difficult to study. It is also possible that some qualia matter deeply in shaping your thoughts and actions, while others do not; as a result, research in this arena has to pursue leads wherever we can find them!

Consider, as an illustration, the experience of *processing fluency*. In Chapter 6, we discussed the fact that the steps of perception sometimes proceed swiftly and with little effort but other times proceed more slowly and only with a lot of effort. The same is true for the steps of remembering, or deciding, or any other mental process. Thus, overall, mental processing is sometimes more fluent and sometimes less so, and people seem sensitive to this degree of fluency: They know when their steps have gone easily, and when not.

As we discussed earlier, though, people don't detect the fluency *as* fluency. They do not have the experience of "Boy, that object sure was easy to perceive." Instead, people simply have a broad sense that their processing was, on this occasion, somehow special—and then they generally try to figure out *why* the processing was special. Hence, they might decide that the input is one they've met recently (and so the fluency leads to a subjective sense of *familiarity*). Or they might conclude that the name they're considering belongs to someone famous. And so on.

Fluency effects can be demonstrated in many arenas. For example, the confidence expressed in a particular memory is influenced by the fluency of retrieval, apparently based on reasoning along the lines of "That memory came to mind easily; I guess it must be a strong memory and therefore an *accurate* memory, so I can be confident that the memory is right." This reasoning is often sensible—but can be misleading. For example, if you retrieve a memory over and over, the retrieval becomes more fluent because of this "practice," quite independent of how firmly established the memory was at the start. As a result, repeated retrieval increases memory confidence—whether the memory is accurate or not.

Likewise, in Chapter 11, we discussed the availability heuristic—the strategy of judging how frequent something is in the world by relying on how easily you can think of relevant examples. For example, are you in general an assertive person? People seem to answer such questions by trying to think of events in the past in which they've been assertive, and, if the examples come easily to mind, they decide that, yes, they are frequently assertive (Schwarz et al., 1991). So here, too, fluency of retrieval guides your thoughts. (For still other examples of fluency effects, see Alter & Oppenheimer, 2006; Kahneman, 2011; Oppenheimer, 2005, 2008; Oppenheimer & Frank, 2007.)

Fluency is certainly different from the more commonly discussed examples of qualia: the raw experience of tasting chocolate, or the experience of itch, or red. Even so, you do notice and react to your own fluency—and so this does seem to be an element of your mental life that you're conscious of. And, just as with other qualia, you can experience your own fluency but no one else can, and you can't experience anyone else's fluency. It's also important that we can describe the subjective experience of fluency only in rough terms—talking about someone "resonating" to an input, or suggesting that a visual stimulus somehow "rings a bell." To go beyond these descriptions, we need to rely on the fact that each of us knows what fluency feels like, because we've all experienced fluent processing, and we've all experienced processing that's not fluent. Each of these points is a central trait of qualia, and so research on fluency may provide important insights about how and when people are influenced by this entirely personal, entirely subjective, aspect of conscious experience.

Consciousness as Justification for Action

Other evidence hints at a different role for the actual experience of consciousness—a role in promoting, and perhaps allowing, *spontaneous* and *intentional* behavior (Dehaene and Naccache, 2001). To understand this point, consider the blindsight patients. We've so far emphasized the fact that these patients are sensitive to visual information, and this tells us something important: Apparently, some aspects of vision can go forward with no conscious awareness and with no conscious supervision. But it's also striking that these patients insist that they are blind, and their behaviors are consistent with this self-assessment: They are fearful of walking across a room (lest they bump into something), they fail to react to many stimuli, and so on.

Note the puzzle here: If, as it seems, these patients can see (at least to some extent), why don't they *use* the information that they gain by vision—for example, to guide their reaching or to navigate across the room? The evidence suggests that these patients see enough so that they reach correctly when they do reach. Why, then, don't they reach out on their own? Why do they reach (in the right direction, with the right hand shape) only when the experimenter insists that they try? Or, to put this more generally, why don't they use their (unconscious) perception of the visual world to guide their actions? Is it possible that perceptual information has to be *conscious* before someone puts that information to use? (For further discussion of this puzzle, see Dennett, 1992; Goodale & Milner, 2004; Weiskrantz, 1997.)

Roughly the same questions can be asked about people who suffer from amnesia. We've emphasized how much amnesic patients do remember, when properly tested (i.e., with tests of implicit memory). But it's also important that people with amnesia do not use this (implicitly) remembered information. Thus, for example, amnesic patients will insist that they don't know the route to the hospital cafeteria, so they won't go to the cafeteria on their own. However, if we demand that they *guess* which way to turn to get to the cafeteria, they typically guess correctly. Once again, therefore, we might ask: Why don't the amnesic patients spontaneously use their (implicit) memories? Why do they reveal their knowledge only when we insist that they guess? Is it possible that remembered information has to be conscious before it is put to use?

Similar questions arise when we consider data from people with no brain damage—such as ordinary college students. Participants in one study were shown a list of words and then, later, tested in either of two ways (Graf, Mandler, & Haden, 1982). Some were explicitly asked to recall the earlier list and were given word stems as cues: "What word on the prior list began 'CLE'?" Other participants were tested indirectly: "Tell me the first word that comes to mind beginning 'CLE.'"

The results show rather poor memory in the explicit test but much better performance in the implicit test. This observation echoes many findings we have reviewed: You often have implicit memories for episodes you have explicitly forgotten. But note that there's something peculiar in this result: In the explicit test, participants could, in principle, have proceeded this way: "I don't recall any words from the list beginning with 'CLE.' Perhaps I'll just guess. Let's see: What words come to mind that begin with 'CLE'?" In this way, participants could use their implicit memory to supplement what they remember explicitly. If they did this, the performance difference between the two conditions would be erased; performance on the explicit test would be just as good as performance on the implicit test. Given the results, however, participants are obviously not using this strategy. For some reason, participants in this situation seem unable or unwilling to use their implicit memories to guide explicit responding.

What is going on in all of these cases? Here is one plausible answer: In many situations, you need to take action based on remembered or perceived information. In some settings, the action is overt (walking across the room or making a verbal response); at other times, the action is mental (reaching a decision or drawing a conclusion). In all cases, though, it seems not enough merely to have access to the relevant information. In addition, you also seem to need some justification, some reason, to take the information seriously.

By analogy, imagine that you're trying to remember some prior event, and some misty thoughts about that event come to mind. You vaguely recall that friends were present on the target occasion; you have a dim idea that food was served. You might hesitate to voice these thoughts, though, because you're not convinced that these thoughts are *memories*. (Perhaps they're chance associations or dreams you once had.) Thus, you will report your memory only if you're satisfied that you are, in fact, remembering. In other words, in order to report on your recollection, you need more than the remembered information. You also need some reason to believe that the remembered information is credible.

What convinces you that the remembered information is credible? The answer, perhaps, is conscious experience. The idea, in other words, is that you'll take action based on some information only if the information "feels right"—that is, only if it has the right qualia. If the experience has these qualities, this convinces you that the presented information is more than a passing fantasy, more than a chance association, and so you take the information seriously and take action based on the information. However, when the conscious presentation is impoverished, as it seems to be in blind sight or in amnesia, you fail to take seriously the information provided by your own eyes or your own memory, so you're paralyzed into inactivity. (For related discussion, see Johnson, 1988; Johnson, Hashtroudi, & Lindsay, 1993.)

In fact, these points can be linked to our earlier claims about the neuronal workspace. Bear in mind that the workspace allows an integration from multiple brain areas, and it's plausible that this integration is essential when you're trying to decide whether or not to take a memory (or a perception) seriously. The integration allows you to see, among other points, that the information provided by vision is confirmed by touch, that the information gained from your senses is consistent with your other beliefs, and so on. This convergence of cues plays a key role in persuading you that the perception or memory is real, and not just a passing thought.

In Shakespeare's play, Macbeth asks himself whether the dagger he sees is real or "a dagger of the mind, a false creation proceeding from a heat-oppressed brain" (Act 2, Scene 1). He tries to decide by checking the visual information against other cues, asking whether the dagger is "sensible to feeling as to sight." The idea we're discussing here is the same: The confluence of inputs provided by the neuronal workspace helps provide the richness—and, plausibly, the conscious experience itself—that is used in deciding whether your ideas and perceptions and memories are "false creations" or true to reality. And it's only after you decide that they're real that you use them as a basis for action.

Consciousness: What Is Left Unsaid

The cognitive unconscious is remarkably sophisticated—able to recognize objects in the world, to reason, to draw conclusions, to retrieve information from

A DAGGER OF THE MIND?

In Act 2, Scene 1, Macbeth asks himself whether he sees a real dagger, or "a dagger of the mind, a false creation . . . (of) a heat-oppressed brain." He tries to decide by checking the visual information against other cues. The proposal we're considering is that this is a common pattern—in which you check the credibility of your own thoughts by considering the qualia associated with those thoughts.

memory. As a result, you often have no direct information about why you decided what you did, or acted as you did. We've seen throughout this book, however, that careful research can reveal these processes, leaving us with an understanding of these processes that is both theoretically rich and pragmatically useful.

The fact remains, though, that you *are* aware of some things in your mind, and, as we've now seen, researchers have also made progress in describing the function of this awareness, and also its biological underpinnings. Let's be clear, however, that there's a great deal we still don't know about consciousness. Our remarks about qualia have been speculative, and debate continues about the completeness (or accuracy) of theorizing about the neuronal workspace. In this chapter, we've also held other issues to the side: Can we specify what it is that changes in conscious experience during dreams, or during religious meditation, or when someone is taking drugs? And how should we think about an issue of consciousness that emerged in Chapter 10, in our discussion of visual imagery? There we saw that individuals may *differ* in their conscious experience, with some people apparently enjoying rich, detailed visual images, so that their conscious experience often includes "mental pictures," but with other people insisting they have no mental imagery at all. This is plainly a point in need of investigation—aimed

WORKBOOK
DEMONSTRATION 13.2

at an understanding of the functional consequences of these differences, and their biological roots.

A different—and immensely difficult—puzzle centers on how the three pounds of the human brain make consciousness possible. The brain, after all, is a physical object, with a certain mass, a certain temperature (a degree or two warmer than the rest of the body) and a certain volume (a bit less than a half gallon). It occupies a specific position in space. Our conscious thoughts and experiences, on the other hand, aren't physical objects and have none of these properties. An idea, for example, doesn't have mass or a specific temperature; a feeling of sadness or fear has neither volume nor a location in space.

How, therefore, is it possible for a physical entity like the brain to give rise to nonphysical thoughts and feelings? Conversely, how can your thoughts and feelings *influence* your brain or your body? Imagine that you want to wave to a friend, and so you do. Your arm, of course, is a physical object with an identifiable mass. To move your arm, therefore, you need some physical force. But your initial idea ("I want to wave to Dan") is not a physical thing with a mass or a position in space. How, then, could this (nonphysical) idea produce a (physical) force to move your arm?

The puzzles in play here all stem from a quandary that philosophers refer to as the **mind-body problem**. The term refers to the fact that the mind (and the ideas, thoughts, and feelings it contains) is an entirely different sort of entity from the physical body, and yet the two, somehow, can influence each other. How can this be? The mind-body problem remains a mystery. In this chapter, we've discussed the *correlation* between brain states and conscious states, but we've left untouched the much harder question of how either of these states *causes* changes in the other.

Thus we leave this chapter acknowledging that our discussion has only tackled *part of* the problem of consciousness and left other parts untouched. Indeed, it's possible that only some aspects of consciousness can be studied by means of scientific research, while other aspects require other forms of inquiry (e.g., philosophical analysis—see, for example, Dehaene & Changeux, 2004). Nonetheless, the data we have reviewed in this chapter, and the conclusions that flow from these data, do provide powerful insights into the nature of consciousness, and these data will certainly inform any future discussions of this profound and complex issue. This by itself—the mere fact that research can address these extraordinarily difficult issues—has to be a source of enormous satisfaction for investigators working on these intriguing problems.

CHAPTER SUMMARY

- An enormous amount of cognitive processing happens "behind the scenes," in the cognitive unconscious. In many cases, you are conscious only of the products that result from your mental processes; the processes themselves are unconscious. This is reflected in the fact that you are not conscious of searching through memory; you are aware only of the results produced by that search. Similarly, you cannot tell when you have truly perceived a word and when you have merely inferred the word's presence.

- Unconscious processing can be rather sophisticated. For example, implicit memory influences you without your being aware that you are remembering at all, and this influence is typically mediated by a complex process through which you attribute a feeling of familiarity to a particular cause. Unconscious attributions can also shape how you interpret and react to your own bodily states.

- Even when your thinking is conscious, you are still influenced by unconscious guides that shape and direct your thought. This is evident in the effects of framing in decision making and the effects of sets in guiding your problem-solving efforts.

- Still further evidence for unconscious achievements comes from the study of blind sight and amnesia; in both cases, patients seem to have knowledge (gained from perception or from memory) but no conscious awareness of that knowledge.

- The cognitive unconscious allows enormous efficiency, but at the cost of flexibility or control. Likewise, the cognitive unconscious keeps you from being distracted by the details of your mental processes, but in some cases there is a cost to your ignorance about how your mental processes unfolded and how you arrived at a particular memory or a particular perception. These trade-offs point the way toward the function of consciousness: Conscious thinking is less efficient but more controllable, and it is also better informed by information about process.

- The neuronal workspace hypothesis begins with the fact that most of the processing in the brain is carried out by separate, specialized modules. When you pay attention to a stimulus, however, the neurons in the various modules are linked by means of workspace neurons. This linkage amplifies and sustains the processing within individual modules, and it allows integration and comparison of the various modules. This integration, it is proposed, is what makes consciousness possible. The integration provides the basis for the unity in your experience; it also allows flexibility and the detection of conflict.

- Consciousness may also give you a sense that you have adequate justification for taking an action. This may be why amnesic patients seem unable to take action based on what they (unconsciously) recall and why blind-sight patients seem unable to respond to what they (unconsciously) see.

- Several theorists have argued that we must distinguish types of conscious experience. The considerations in this chapter bear more directly on "access consciousness," which is a matter of how information is accessed and used within the mind. The chapter has had less to say about "phenomenal consciousness," which is concerned with the subjective experience of being conscious. Even so, research on mental *fluency* provides an intriguing hint both of how you are guided by qualia, and how we can do research on the effects of qualia.

The Workbook Connection

See the *Cognition Workbook* for further exploration of conscious and unconscious thought:

- Demonstration 13.1: Practice and the Cognitive Unconscious
- Demonstration 13.2: The Quality of Consciousness
- Research Methods: Introspection
- Cognitive Psychology and Education: Mindfulness
- Cognitive Psychology and the Law: Unconscious Thinking

NEED HELP STUDYING?

 wwnorton.com/studyspace

Visit StudySpace to access free review material such as

- Chapter study plans
- Quizzes
- Flashcards, and more

Go to **wwnorton.com/zaps** for these online labs:

- Implicit Learning
- Ponzo Illusion

Glossary

ACC See *anterior cingulate cortex*.

acquisition The process of placing new information into *long-term memory*.

action potential A brief change in the electrical potential of an *axon*. The action potential is the physical basis of the signal sent from one end of a neuron to the other and usually triggers a further (chemical) signal to other neurons.

action slip An error in which someone performs some behavior, or makes some response, that is different from the behavior or response intended.

activation level A measure of the current status for a *node* or *detector*. Activation level is increased if the node or detector receives the appropriate input from its associated nodes or detectors; activation level will be high if input has been received frequently or recently.

acuity The ability to discern fine detail. See also *visual acuity*.

ad hoc category A mental category made up on the spot in response to a specific question.

affective forecasting The process of predicting how you will feel at some future point about an object or state of affairs. It turns out that people are surprisingly inaccurate in these predictions and (for example) understate their own capacity to adapt to changes.

affirming the consequent An error often made in logical reasoning. The error begins with these two premises: (a) "If A then B," and (b) "B is true." The error consists of drawing the false conclusion that (c) "A must therefore be true." Compare with *denying the antecedent*.

agnosia A disturbance in a person's ability to identify familiar objects.

all-or-none law The principle stating that a *neuron* or *detector* either *fires* completely or does not fire at all; no intermediate responses are possible. (Graded responses are possible, however, by virtue of the fact that a neuron or detector can fire more or less frequently, and for a longer or shorter time.)

ambiguous figure A drawing that can be readily perceived in more than one way.

amnesia A disruption of memory, often due to brain damage.

amygdala An almond-shaped structure in the *limbic system* that plays a central role in emotion and in the evaluation of stimuli.

anarthria A disorder characterized by an inability to control the muscles needed for ordinary speech. Anarthric individuals cannot speak, although other aspects of language functioning are unimpaired.

anchoring A tendency to use the first available estimate for some fact as a reference point for that fact, and then perhaps to make some (small) adjustment from that reference point in determining your final estimate. As a result of anchoring, the first-available estimate often has a powerful influence on you, even if that estimate comes from a source that gives it little credibility.

anecdotal evidence Data or results collected casually, without documentation, and without any steps that might help you determine if the report is accurate or representative of a broader pattern. This evidence is often presented as an informal report or narrative (i.e., an anecdote) relayed in conversation.

anomia A disruption of language abilities, usually resulting from specific brain damage, in which the individual loses the ability to name objects, including highly familiar objects.

antecedent The formal name for the "if . . ." clause in an "if . . . then . . ." statement. See also *consequent*.

anterior cingulate cortex (ACC) A brain structure known to play a crucial role in detecting and resolving conflicts among different brain systems.

anterograde amnesia An inability to remember experiences that occurred *after* the event that triggered the memory disruption.

A1

Often contrasted with *retrograde amnesia*.

aphasia A disruption to language capacities, often caused by brain damage.

apraxia A disturbance in the capacity to initiate or organize voluntary action, often caused by brain damage.

Area V1 The site on the *occipital lobe* where axons from the *lateral geniculate nucleus* first reach the cerebral *cortex*. This site is (for one neural pathway) the location at which information about the visual world first reaches the brain.

articulatory rehearsal loop One of the low-level assistants hypothesized as part of the *working-memory system*. This loop draws on *subvocalized* (covert) speech, which serves to create a record in the *phonological buffer*. Materials in this buffer then fade, but they can be refreshed by another cycle of covert speech.

association cortex The traditional name for the portion of the human *cortex* outside of the *motor* and *sensory projection areas*.

associations Functional connections that are hypothesized to link *nodes* within a mental network or *detectors* within a detector network; these associations are often hypothesized as the "carriers" of activation, from one node or detector to the next.

associative links See *associations*.

attended channel In *selective attention* experiments, research participants are exposed to simultaneous inputs and instructed to ignore all of these except one. The attended channel is the input to which participants are instructed to pay attention. Often contrasted with *unattended channel*.

attribute substitution A commonly used strategy in which someone needs one type of information but relies instead on a more-accessible form of information. This strategy works well if the more-accessible form of information is, in fact, well correlated with the desired information. An example is the

case in which someone needs information about how frequent an event is in the world and relies instead on how easily he or she can think of examples of the event.

attribution The step of explaining a feeling or event, usually by identifying the factors (or an earlier event) that are the cause of the current feeling or event. Hence this term is often elaborated with the more specific term: *causal attribution*.

autobiographical memory The aspect of memory that records the episodes and events in a person's life.

automatic tasks Tasks that are well practiced and that do not require flexibility; these tasks usually require little or no attention, and they can be carried out if the person is also busy with some other task. Usually contrasted with *controlled tasks*.

automaticity A state achieved by some tasks and some forms of processing, in which the task can be performed with little or no attention. Automatized actions can, in many cases, be combined with other activities without interference. Automatized actions are also often difficult to control, leading many to refer to them as "mental reflexes."

availability heuristic A strategy used to judge the frequency of a certain type of object or the likelihood of a certain type of event. The first step is to assess the ease with which examples of the object or event come to mind; this "availability" of examples is then used as an index of frequency or likelihood.

axon The part of a *neuron* that typically transmits a signal away from the neuron's cell body and carries the signal to another location.

back propagation A learning procedure, common in *connectionist networks*, in which an *error signal* is used to adjust the inputs to a *node* within the network (so that the node will

be less responsive in the future to the inputs that led it to the inappropriate response). The error signal is then transmitted to those same inputs, so that they can make their own similar adjustments. In this way, the error signal is transmitted backward through the network, starting with the nodes that immediately triggered the incorrect response, but with each node then passing the error signal back to the nodes that caused it to *fire*.

base-rate information Information about the broad likelihood of a particular type of event (also referred to as "prior probability"). Often contrasted with *diagnostic information*.

baseline level A standard or basis for comparison, often assessed by some measurement before a manipulation takes place, or with a group that never receives the experimental manipulation.

basic-level categorization A level of categorization hypothesized as the "natural" and most informative level, neither too specific nor too general. People tend to use basic-level terms (such as "chair," rather than the more general "furniture" or the more specific "armchair") in their ordinary conversation and in their reasoning.

behaviorist theory Broad principles concerned with how behavior changes in response to different configurations of stimuli (including stimuli often called "rewards" and "punishments"). In its early days, behaviorist theory sought to avoid mentalistic terms.

belief bias A tendency, within logical reasoning, to endorse a conclusion if the conclusion happens to be something one believes is true anyhow. In displaying this tendency, people seem to ignore both the premises of the logical argument and logic itself, and they rely instead on their broader pattern of beliefs about what is true and what is not.

belief perseverance A tendency to continue endorsing some assertion or claim, even when the clearly available evidence completely undermines that claim.

bigram A pair of letters. For example, the word "FLAT" contains the bigrams *FL*, *LA*, and *AT*.

binding problem The problem of reuniting the various elements of a scene, given the fact that these elements are initially dealt with by different systems in the brain.

binocular rivalry A pattern that arises when the input to one eye cannot be integrated with the input to the other eye. In this circumstance, the person tends to be aware of only one eye's input at a time.

bipolar cell A type of *neuron* in the eye. Bipolar cells receive their input from the *photoreceptors* and transmit their output to the retinal *ganglion cells*.

blind sight A pattern resulting from brain damage, in which the person seems unable to see in part of his or her field of vision but can often correctly respond to visual inputs when required to by an experimenter.

Boaz The author's exceedingly crazy German short-haired pointer, and arguably the prototype for the category *dog*.

BOLD (blood oxygenation level dependent) A measure of how much oxygen the brain's hemoglobin is carrying in specific parts of the brain; this provides a quantitative basis for comparing activity levels in different brain areas.

bottom-up influences The term given to effects governed by the stimulus input itself and that shape the processing of that input. Often contrasted with *top-down influences*.

bottom-up processing See *data-driven processing* and *bottom-up influences*.

boundary extension A tendency for people to remember pictures as being less "zoomed in" (and thus having wider boundaries) than they actually were.

Broca's area An area in the left *frontal lobe* of the brain; damage here typically causes *nonfluent aphasia*.

Capgras syndrome A relatively rare disorder, resulting from specific forms of brain damage, in which the afflicted person recognizes the people in his or her world but denies that they are who they appear to be. Instead, the person insists, these familiar individuals are well-disguised impostors.

catch trials Presentations within a research procedure in which the target stimulus is absent or in which a stimulus requires a "no" response. Catch trials are included within a study to guarantee that the participant is taking the task seriously, and not just responding in the same fashion on every trial.

categorical perception The tendency to hear speech sounds "merely" as members of a category—the category of "z" sounds, the category of "p" sounds, and so on. As a consequence, one tends to hear sounds *within* the category as being rather similar to each other; sounds from different categories, however, are perceived as quite different.

categorical syllogism A logical argument containing two *premises* and a conclusion, and concerned with the properties of, and relations between, categories. An example is, "All trees are plants. All plants require nourishment. Therefore, all trees require nourishment." This is a valid syllogism, since the truth of the premises guarantees the truth of the conclusion.

causal attribution An interpretation of a thought or behavior in which one decides what caused the behavior.

ceiling level A level of performance in a task that is near the maximum level possible. (In many tasks, this is performance near 100%.)

cell body The area of a biological cell containing the nucleus and the metabolic machinery that sustains the cell.

center-surround cell A *neuron* in the visual system that has a "donut-shaped" *receptive field*; stimulation in the center of the receptive field has one effect on the cell; stimulation in the surrounding ring has the opposite effect.

central executive The hypothesized director of the *working-memory system*. This is the component of the system needed for any interpretation or analysis; in contrast, mere storage of materials can be provided by *working memory*'s assistants, which work under the control of the central executive. Also see *executive control*.

central fissure The separation dividing the *frontal lobes* on each side of the brain from the *parietal lobes*.

cerebellum The largest area of the *hindbrain*, crucial for the coordination of bodily movements and balance.

cerebral hemisphere One of the two hemispherical brain structures— one on the left side, one on the right—that constitute the major part of the *forebrain* in mammals.

change blindness A pattern in which perceivers do not see, or take a long time to see, large-scale changes in a visual stimulus. This pattern reveals how little people perceive, even from stimuli in plain view, if they are not specifically attending to the target information.

childhood amnesia The pattern of not remembering the first 3 or 4 years of life. This pattern is very common; a century ago, it was explained in terms of repression of anxious events in those years; more recent accounts focus on the psychological and biological immaturity of 3- and 4-year-olds, which makes them less able to form new episodic memories.

chronometric study Literally "time measurement" study; generally, a study that measures the amount of time a task takes, often used as a means of examining the task's components or used as a means of examining which brain events are simultaneous with specific mental events.

chunk The hypothetical storage unit in *working memory*; it is estimated that working memory can hold 7 *plus-or-minus 2* chunks. An unspecified quantity of information can be contained within each chunk, since the content of each chunk depends on how the memorizer has organized the materials to be remembered.

coarticulation A trait of speech production in which the way a sound is produced is altered slightly by the immediately previous and immediately following sounds. Because of this "overlap" in speech production, the acoustic properties of each speech sound vary according to the context in which that sound appears.

cocktail party effect A term often used to describe a pattern in which a person seems to "tune out" all conversations reaching his or her ears *except for* the conversation he or she wishes to pay attention to; however, if some salient stimulus (such as the person's name) appears in one of the other conversations, the person is reasonably likely to detect this stimulus.

cognitive neuroscience The study of the biological basis for cognitive functioning.

cognitive unconscious The broad set of mental activities of which people are completely unaware but that make possible ordinary thinking, remembering, reasoning, and so on.

commissure One of the thick bundles of fibers via which information is sent back and forth between the two *cerebral hemispheres*.

competence The pattern of skills and knowledge that might be revealed under optimal circumstances. Often contrasted with *performance*.

computerized axial tomography (**CT scanning**) A *neuroimaging technique* that uses X-rays to construct a precise three-dimensional image of the brain's anatomy.

concept-driven processing A type of processing in which the sequence of mental events is influenced by a broad pattern of knowledge and expectations (sometimes referred to as *top-down processing*). Often contrasted with *data-driven processing*.

concurrent articulation task A requirement that someone speak or mime speech while doing some other task. In many cases, the person is required to say "Tah-Tah-Tah" over and over, or "one, two, three, one, two, three." These procedures occupy the muscles and control mechanisms needed for speech, and so they prevent the person from using these resources for *subvocalization*.

conditional statement A statement of the format "If X then Y," with the first part (the "if" clause, or *antecedent*) provides a condition under which the second part (the "then" clause, or *consequent*) is guaranteed to be true.

cone A *photoreceptor* that is able to discriminate hues and that has high *acuity*. Cones are concentrated in the *retina*'s *fovea* and become less frequent in the visual periphery. Often contrasted with *rod*.

confirmation bias A family of effects in which people seem more sensitive to evidence that confirms their beliefs than they are to evidence that challenges their beliefs. Thus, if people are given a choice about what sort of information they would like in order to evaluate their beliefs, they request information that is likely to confirm their beliefs. Likewise, if they are presented with both confirming and disconfirming evidence, they are more likely to pay attention to, be influenced by, and remember the confirming evidence, rather than the disconfirming.

confound A variable other than the independent variable that could potentially explain the pattern of observed results. For example, if participants always serve in the *control condition* first and the *experimental condition* second, then any differences between these conditions might be due either to the *independent variable* or to an effect of practice (favoring the experimental condition, which came second). In this case, practice would be a confound.

conjunction error An error in perception in which someone correctly perceives what features are present but misperceives how the features are joined, so that (for example) a red circle and a green square might be misperceived as a red square and a green circle.

connection weight The strength of a connection between two *nodes* in a network. The greater the connection weight, the more efficiently activation will flow from one node to the other.

connectionism An approach to theorizing about the mind that relies on *parallel distributed processing* among elements that provide a *distributed representation* of the information being considered.

connectionist networks See *connectionism*.

consequent The ". . . then" clause in an "if . . . then . . ." statement. Also see *antecedent* and *conditional statement*.

consequentiality The perceived importance of an event, or the perception of how widespread and long-lasting the event's effects will be.

consolidation The biological process through which new memories are "cemented in place," acquiring some degree of permanence through the creation of new (or altered) neural connections.

content morpheme A *morpheme* that carries meaning. Often contrasted with *function morpheme*.

context reinstatement A procedure in which someone is led to the same mental and emotional state he or she was in during a previous event; context reinstatement can often promote accurate recollection of that event.

context-dependent learning A pattern of data in which materials learned in one setting are well remembered when the person returns to that setting, but less well remembered in other settings.

contralateral control A pattern in which the left half of the brain controls the right half of the body, and the right half of the brain controls the left half of the body.

control condition A condition in which research participants are not exposed to the experimental manipulation, thereby serving as a basis for comparison with participants in the *experimental condition* (who are exposed to the experimental manipulation).

controlled tasks Tasks that are novel or that require flexibility in one's approach; these tasks usually require attention, so they cannot be carried out if the person is also busy with some other task. Usually contrasted with *automatic tasks*.

convergent data A pattern in which different experimental procedures all yield results pointing toward the same conclusion, so that the results "converge" on that conclusion.

convolutions The wrinkles visible in the *cortex* that allow the enormous surface area of the human brain to be stuffed into the relatively small volume of the skull.

cornea The transparent tissue at the front of each eye that plays an important role in focusing the incoming light.

corpus callosum The largest of the *commissures* linking the left and right *cerebral hemispheres*.

cortex The outermost surface of an organ in the body; psychologists are most commonly interested in the brain's cortex.

counterbalance A procedure used to ensure that any potential *confound* will have an equal effect on all the experimental conditions, with the goal of ensuring that any difference between the conditions could not possibly be due to the confound. Thus, an experimenter might expose half the participants to the *control condition* first and half to the *experimental condition* first. In this case, practice favors

the experimental condition for half of the participants and favors the control condition for the other half. Therefore, practice should have an equal impact on the two conditions and so cannot be a source of difference between them, because the experimenter has counterbalanced the effect of practice.

covariation A relationship between two variables such that the presence (or magnitude) of one variable can be predicted from the presence (or magnitude) of the other. Covariation can be positive or negative. If positive, then increases in one variable occur when increases in the other occur. If negative, then decreases in one variable occur when decreases in the other occur.

crystallized intelligence Someone's acquired knowledge, including the person's repertoire of verbal knowledge and cognitive skills. See also *fluid intelligence*.

CT scanning See *computerized axial tomography*.

data-driven processing A type of processing in which the sequence of mental events is determined largely by the pattern of incoming information (sometimes referred to as *bottom-up processing*). Often contrasted with *concept-driven processing*.

decay theory of forgetting The hypothesis that with the passage of time, memories may fade or erode.

deduction A process through which you start with claims, or general assertions, and ask what further claims necessarily follow from these *premises*. Often contrasted with *induction*.

deep processing A mode of thinking in which you pay attention to the meaning and implications of the material; deep processing typically leads to excellent memory retention. Often contrasted with *shallow processing*.

Deese-Roediger-McDermott procedure See *DRM procedure*.

demand character Cues within an experiment that signal to the

participant how he or she is "supposed to" respond.

dendrites The part of a *neuron* that usually detects the incoming signal.

denying the antecedent An error often made in logical reasoning. The error begins with these two premises: (a) "If A then B," and (b) "A is false." The error consists of drawing the false conclusion that (c) "B must therefore also be false." Often contrasted with *affirming the consequent*.

dependent variable The variable that the researcher observes or measures to determine if the *independent variable* has an effect or influence. The dependent variable can take many forms (e.g., speed of responding, number of errors, type of errors, a biological measure such as brain activation at a certain site).

descriptive account An account that tells us how things are, as opposed to how they should be. Often contrasted with *normative account*.

descriptive rules Rules that simply describe the regularities in a pattern of observations, with no commentary on whether the pattern is "proper," "correct," or "desirable."

destructive updating The hypothesized mechanism through which new learning or new information on a topic replaces old knowledge or information in memory, so that the old information is erased or destroyed by the newer input.

detector A *node* within a processing network that *fires* primarily in response to a specific target contained within the incoming perceptual information.

diagnostic information Information about an individual case indicating whether the case belongs in one category or another. Often contrasted with *base-rate information*.

dichotic listening A task in which research participants hear two simultaneous verbal messages— one presented via headphones to the left ear, a second presented to the right ear. In typical experiments, participants are asked to pay attention to one of these inputs (the *attended channel*) and urged to ignore the other.

digit-span task A task often used for measuring *working memory*'s storage capacity. Research participants are read a series of digits (e.g., "8 3 4") and must immediately repeat them back. If they do this successfully, they are given a slightly longer list (e.g., "9 2 4 0"), and so forth. The length of the longest list a person can remember in this fashion is that person's digit span. Also see *operation span*.

direct memory testing A form of memory testing in which people are asked explicitly to remember some previous event. *Recall* and standard *recognition* testing are both forms of direct memory testing. Often contrasted with *indirect memory testing*.

distributed knowledge Information stored via a *distributed representation*.

distributed representation A mode of representing ideas or contents in which there is no one *node* (or specific group of nodes) representing the content and no one place where the content is stored. Instead, the content is represented via a pattern of simultaneous activity across many nodes. Those same nodes will also participate in other patterns, and so those same nodes will also be part of other distributed representations. Often contrasted with *local representation*.

divided attention The skill of performing multiple tasks simultaneously.

dizygotic twins See *fraternal twins*.

doctrine of formal disciplines In educational philosophy, the notion that the best way to train the mind is to provide education in disciplines such as logic, math, and linguistics (i.e., disciplines that hinge on formal structures).

double dissociation An argument used by researchers to show that two processes or two structures are truly distinct. To make this argument, one must show that each of the processes or structures can be disrupted without in any way interfering with the other.

double-blind procedure A procedure in which neither the research participant nor the person administering the study knows which condition of the study the participant is in (e.g., receiving medication or a placebo; being in the experimental group or in the control group). In this case, there is no risk that the person administering the study can convey to the participant how the participant is "supposed to" behave in the study.

DRM procedure A commonly used experimental procedure for eliciting and studying memory errors. In this procedure, a person sees or hears a list of words that are all related to a single theme; however, the word that names the theme is not itself included. Nonetheless, people are very likely to remember later that the theme word was presented.

dual-coding theory A theory that imaginable materials, such as high-imagery words, will be doubly represented in memory: The word itself will be remembered, and so will the corresponding mental image.

dual-process model Any model of thinking that claims people have two distinct means of making judgments—one of which is fast, efficient, but prone to error, and one that is slower, more effortful, but also more accurate.

early selection A proposal that *selective attention* operates at an early stage of processing, so that the unattended inputs receive little analysis.

edge enhancement A process created by *lateral inhibition* in which the *neurons* in the visual system give exaggerated responses to edges of surfaces.

Einstellung The phenomenon in *problem solving* in which people develop a certain attitude or perspective on a problem and then approach all subsequent problems with the same rigid attitude.

elaborative rehearsal A way of engaging materials to be remembered, such that you pay attention to what the materials mean and how they are related to each other, or to other things in the surroundings, or to other things you already know. Often contrasted with *maintenance rehearsal*.

electroencephalography A recording of voltage changes occurring at the scalp that reflect activity in the brain underneath.

emotional intelligence The ability to understand your own and others' emotions and to control your emotions appropriately.

encoding specificity The tendency, when memorizing, to place in memory both the materials to be learned and also some amount of the context of those materials. As a result, these materials will be recognized as familiar, later on, only if the materials appear again in a similar context.

error signal Feedback given to a network to indicate that the network's response was not the desired one. Often the magnitude of the error signal is proportional to the difference between the response produced and the response that should have been produced. The signal can then be used to adjust the network or system (often via *back propagation*) so that the error will be smaller in the future.

event-related potential Changes in an EEG in the brief period just before, during, and after an explicitly defined event, usually measured by averaging together many trials in which this event has occurred.

excitatory connection A link from one *node*, or one *detector*, to another, such that activation of one node activates the other.

Often contrasted with *inhibitory connection*.

executive control The mental resources and processes used to set goals, choose task priorities, and avoid conflict among competing habits or responses.

exemplar-based reasoning Reasoning that draws on knowledge about specific category members, rather than drawing on more-general information about the overall category.

expected value An estimate of the subjective gain that will result from choosing a particular option. Expected value is calculated as the likely value of the consequences of that option, if these are obtained, multiplied by the probability of gaining those consequences. (Also referred to as "expected utility.")

experimental condition A condition in which research participants are exposed to an experimental manipulation, thereby serving as a basis for comparison with participants in the *control condition* so that the researcher can learn whether the experimental manipulation changes the participants' thoughts, feelings, or behavior.

explicit memory A memory revealed by *direct memory testing* and typically accompanied by the conviction that one is, in fact, remembering—that is, drawing on some sort of knowledge (perhaps knowledge about a specific prior episode, or perhaps more general knowledge). Often contrasted with *implicit memory*.

external validity The quality of a research design that ensures that the data accurately reflect the circumstances outside of the study that the researcher hopes to understand. External validity requires that the research participants, the research task, and the research stimuli are all appropriately representative of the people, tasks, and stimuli to which the researcher wants to *generalize* the results.

extralinguistic context The social and physical setting in which an utterance is encountered; usually, cues within this setting guide the interpretation of the utterance.

factor analysis A statistical method for studying the interrelations among various tests. The goal is to discover the extent to which the tests are influenced by the same factors.

false alarm A response in which someone indicates that he or she has detected a target even though the specified target is actually absent.

false memory A memory, sincerely reported, that misrepresents how an event actually unfolded. In some cases, a false memory can be wholly false and can report an event that never happened at all.

familiarity In some circumstances, the subjective feeling that you have encountered a stimulus before; in other circumstances, the objective fact that you have indeed encountered a stimulus before and are now in some way influenced by that encounter, whether or not you recall that encounter or feel that the stimulus is familiar.

family resemblance The notion that members of a category (e.g., all dogs, all games) resemble each other. In general, family resemblance relies on some number of *features* being shared by any group of category members, even though these features may not be shared by all members of the category. Therefore, the basis for family resemblance may shift from one subset of the category to another.

feature One of the small set of elements out of which more-complicated patterns are composed.

feature net A system for recognizing patterns that involves a network of *detectors*, with detectors for features as the initial layer in the system.

figure/ground organization The processing step in which the perceiver determines which aspects of the stimulus belong to the central object (or "figure") and which aspects belong to the background (or "ground").

file-drawer problem The concern that *null findings* or disappointing findings are not published and are, so to speak, placed in a file drawer and forgotten. This problem can create a situation in which the published research is not representative of the full pattern of evidence.

filter A hypothetical mechanism that would block potential distractors from further processing.

fire To respond in a discrete and specific way—as when a *neuron*, after receiving a strong enough stimulus, sends a signal down its *axon*, which in turn causes a release of *neurotransmitter* from the membrane at the end of the axon.

fixation target A visual mark (such as a dot or a plus sign) at which one points one's eyes (or "fixates"). Fixation targets are used to help people control their eye position.

flashbulb memory A memory of extraordinary clarity, typically for some highly emotional event, retained despite the passage of many years.

fluent aphasia A disruption of language, caused by brain damage, in which afflicted individuals are able to produce speech but the speech is not meaningful, and the individuals are not able to understand what is said to them. Often contrasted with *nonfluent aphasia*.

fluid intelligence The ability to deal with new and unusual problems. See also *crystallized intelligence*.

Flynn effect A worldwide increase in IQ scores over the last several decades, occurring in both third-world and developed nations, and proceeding at a rate of roughly 3 points per decade.

fMRI scanning See *functional magnetic resonance imaging*.

forebrain One of the three main structures (along with the *hindbrain* and the *midbrain*) of the brain; the forebrain plays a crucial role in supporting intellectual functioning.

form perception The process through which people see the basic shape, size, and position of an object.

four-card task See *selection task*.

fovea The center of the *retina* and the region on the eye in which acuity is best; when you look at an object, you are lining up that object with the fovea.

frame Aspects of how a decision is phrased that are, in fact, irrelevant to the decision but that influence people's choices nonetheless.

fraternal (dizygotic) twins Twins that develop from two different eggs that are simultaneously fertilized by two sperm. Like ordinary siblings, they share 50% of their genes. See also *identical twins*.

free recall A method of assessing memory. The person being tested is asked to come up with as many items as possible from a particular source (such as "the list you heard earlier" or "things you saw yesterday"), in any sequence.

frequency estimate People's assessment of how often they have encountered examples of a particular category and how likely they are to encounter new examples of that category.

frontal lobe The lobe of the brain in each *cerebral hemisphere* that includes the *prefrontal area* and the *primary motor projection area*.

function morpheme A *morpheme* that signals a relation between words within a sentence, such as the morpheme "s" indicating a plural in English, or the morpheme "ed" indicating past tense. Often contrasted with *content morpheme*.

functional equivalence A series of close parallels in how two systems work—how they respond to inputs, what errors they make, and so on. An example is the functional equivalence between vision and visual imagery.

functional fixedness A tendency to be rigid in how you think about an object's function. This generally involves a strong tendency to think of an object only in terms of its *typical* function.

functional magnetic resonance imaging (fMRI) A neuroimaging technique that uses magnetic fields to construct a detailed three-dimensional representation of the activity levels in different areas of the brain at a particular moment in time.

fusiform face area (FFA) A brain area apparently specialized for the perception of faces.

fuzzy boundary A distinction between categories that identifies each instance only as "more or less likely" to be in a category, rather than specifying whether each instance is or is not included in the category.

gamma-band oscillation A particular rhythm of *firing* that seems to signal in the nervous system when different parts of the visual system are all responding to the same stimulus.

ganglion cell A type of *neuron* in the eye. The ganglion cells receive their input from the *bipolar cells*, and then the *axons* of the ganglion cells gather together to form the *optic nerve*, carrying information back to the *lateral geniculate nucleus*.

garden-path sentence A sentence that initially leads the reader to one understanding of how the sentence's words are related but then requires a change in this understanding in order to comprehend the sentence. Examples are "The old man ships" and "The horse raced past the barn fell."

general intelligence (g) A mental capacity that is hypothesized as contributing to the performance of virtually any intellectual task. The existence of g is documented by the statistical overlap among diverse forms of mental testing.

generalization The step of making claims about people, tasks, and stimuli other than those scrutinized within a research study. This step is legitimate only if the study has *external validity*.

generativity The idea that you can combine and recombine basic units to create (or "generate") new and more-complex entities. Linguistic rules, for example, are generative, because they govern how a limited number of words can be combined and recombined to produce a vast number of sentences.

generic knowledge Knowledge of a general sort, as opposed to knowledge about specific episodes.

geon One of the basic shapes proposed as the building blocks of all complex three-dimensional forms. Geons take the form of cylinders, cones, blocks, and the like, and they are combined to form "geon assemblies." These are then combined to produce entire objects.

glia A type of cell found (along with neurons) in the central nervous system. Glial cells have many functions, including the support of neurons, the repair of neural connections in case of damage, and a key role in guiding the initial development of neural connections. A specialized type of glia also provide electrical insulation for some neurons, allowing much faster transmission of neural signals.

goal neglect A pattern of behavior in which you fail to keep your goal in mind, so that (for example) you rely on habitual responses even if those responses will not move you toward the goal.

goal state The state you are working toward in trying to solve a problem. Often contrasted with *initial state*.

graded membership The idea that some members of a category are "better" members and therefore are more firmly in the category than other members.

grammatical Conforming to the rules that govern the sequence of words acceptable within the language.

heuristic A strategy that is reasonably efficient and works most of the time. In using a heuristic, you are in effect choosing to accept some risk of error in order to gain efficiency.

hill-climbing strategy A commonly used strategy in *problem solving*. If people use this strategy, then whenever their efforts toward solving a problem give them a choice, they will choose the option that carries them closer to the goal.

hindbrain One of the three main structures (along with the *forebrain* and the *midbrain*) of the brain; the hindbrain sits atop the spinal cord and includes several structures crucial for controlling key life functions.

hippocampus A structure in the *temporal lobe* that is involved in the creation of *long-term memories* and spatial memory.

hypothalamus A small structure at the base of the *forebrain* that plays a vital role in the control of motivated behaviors such as eating, drinking, and sexual activity.

identical (monozygotic) twins Twins that develop from a single fertilized egg that then splits in half. These twins are genetically identical. See also *fraternal twins*.

ill-defined problem A problem for which the goal state is specified only in general terms and the operators available for reaching the goal state are not obvious at the start. Often contrasted with *well-defined problem*.

illumination The third in a series of stages often hypothesized as crucial for creativity. The first stage is *preparation*; the second, *incubation*. Illumination is the stage in which some new key insight or new idea suddenly comes to mind, and is then (on this hypothesis) followed by *verification*.

illusion of truth An effect of *implicit memory* in which claims that are familiar end up seeming more plausible.

illusory covariation A pattern that people "perceive" in data, leading them to believe that the presence of one factor allows them to predict the presence of another factor. However, this perception occurs even in the absence of any genuine relationship between these two factors. As an example, people perceive that a child's willingness to cheat in an academic setting is an indicator that the child will also be willing to cheat in athletic contests. However, this perception is incorrect, and so the covariation that people perceive is "illusory."

image file Visual information stored in *long-term memory*, specifying what a particular object or shape looks like. Information within the image file can then be used as a "recipe" or set of instructions for how to construct an active image of this object or shape.

image-scanning procedure An experimental procedure in which participants are asked to form a specific mental image and then are asked to scan, with their "mind's eye," from one point in the image to another. By timing these scans, the experimenter can determine how long "travel" takes across a mental image.

implicit memory A memory revealed by *indirect memory testing* and usually manifested as a *priming* effect in which current performance is guided or facilitated by previous experiences. Implicit memories are often accompanied by no conscious realization that one is, in fact, being influenced by specific past experiences. Often contrasted with *explicit memory*.

inattentional blindness A pattern in which perceivers seem literally not to see stimuli right in front of their eyes; this pattern is caused by the participants' attending to some other stimulus and not expecting the target to appear.

incidental learning Learning that takes place in the absence of any intention to learn and, correspondingly, in the absence of any expectation of a subsequent memory test. Often contrasted with *intentional learning*.

incubation The second in a series of stages often hypothesized as crucial for creativity. The first stage is *preparation*; the third, *illumination,* and the fourth, *verification*. Incubation is hypothesized to involve events that occur when you put a problem out of your conscious thoughts but continue nonetheless to work on the problem unconsciously. Many current psychologists are skeptical about this process, and propose alternative accounts for data ostensibly documenting incubation.

independent variable In an experimental study, the variable that the researcher deliberately manipulates to ask whether it has an impact on the target (*dependent*) variable. Outside of experimental studies, the independent variable can involve some preexisting difference (e.g., the participants' age or sex), allowing the researcher to ask if this preexisting difference influences the target variable. Sometimes called the "predictor variable."

indirect memory testing A form of memory testing in which research participants are not told that their memories are being tested. Instead, they are tested in a fashion in which previous experiences can influence current behavior. Examples of indirect tests include *word-stem completion*, the *lexical-decision task*, and *tachistoscopic recognition*. Often contrasted with *direct memory testing*.

induction A pattern of reasoning in which you seek to draw general claims from specific bits of evidence. Often contrasted with *deduction*.

information processing A particular approach to theorizing in which complex mental events, such as learning, remembering, and deciding, are understood as being built up out of a large number of discrete steps. These steps occur one by one, with each providing as its "output" the input to the next step in the sequence.

inhibitory connection A link from one *node*, or one *detector*, to another, such that activation of one node decreases the *activation level* of the other. Often contrasted with *excitatory connection*.

initial state The state you are in at the start of your efforts toward solving a problem. *Problem solving* can be understood as the attempt to move, with various operations, from the initial state to the *goal state*.

input node A *node*, within a network, that receives at least part of its activation from *detectors* sensitive to events in the external world.

insensitivity A property of an experiment that makes the experiment unable to detect differences. An experiment can be insensitive, for example, if the procedure is too easy, so that *performance* is at *ceiling levels*.

inspection time The time someone needs to make a simple discrimination between two stimuli; used in some settings as a measure of mental speed, and then used as a way to test the claim that intelligent people literally have faster processing in their brains.

integrative agnosia A disorder caused by a specific form of damage to the *parietal lobe*; people with this disorder appear relatively normal in tasks requiring them to detect whether specific *features* are present in a display, but they are impaired in tasks that require them to judge how the features are bound together to form complex objects.

intentional learning The acquisition of memories in a setting in which people know that their memory for the information will be tested later. Often contrasted with *incidental learning*.

interactive model A model of cognitive processing that relies on an ongoing interplay between *data-driven* and *concept-driven* processing.

interference theory of forgetting The hypothesis that materials are lost from memory because of interference from other materials also in memory. Interference that is caused by materials learned prior to the learning episode is

called "proactive interference;" interference that is caused by materials learned after the learning episode is called "retroactive interference."

internal validity A trait of a research study that reflects the study's ability to measure what it intends to measure. A study is internally valid if the *dependent variables* measure what they are intended to measure, and if the pattern of results in the dependent variables can be attributed to the *independent variables* (and not to some *confound*).

interrater reliability The degree of agreement between two or more individuals who have each independently assessed some target quality. Thus, two individuals might judge how beautiful various faces are, and then the agreement between the two raters can be calculated.

introspection The process through which you "look within," to observe and record the contents of your own mental life.

intrusion error A memory error in which you recall elements not part of the original episode that you are trying to remember (and so other knowledge "intrudes" into your recall).

invalid In the context of research design, the determination that a study does not measure what it intends to measure (in which case the study lacks *internal validity*) or does not reflect the circumstances outside of the lab that the researcher hoped to explore (in which case the study lacks *external validity*).

invalid syllogism A syllogism (such as a *categorical syllogism*, or a syllogism built on a conditional) in which the conclusion is not logically demanded by the premises.

Korsakoff's syndrome A clinical syndrome characterized primarily by dense *anterograde amnesia*. Korsakoff's syndrome is caused by damage to specific brain regions, and it is often precipitated by a

form of malnutrition common among long-term alcoholics.

late selection A proposal that *selective attention* operates at a late stage of processing, so that the unattended inputs receive considerable analysis.

lateral fissure The separation dividing the *frontal lobes* on each side of the brain from the *temporal lobes*.

lateral geniculate nucleus (LGN) An important way station in the *thalamus* that is the first destination for visual information sent from the eyeball to the brain.

lateral inhibition A pattern in which cells, when stimulated, inhibit the activity of neighboring cells. In the visual system, lateral inhibition in the *optic nerve* creates *edge enhancement*.

lens The transparent tissue located near the front of each eye that (together with the *cornea*) plays an important role in focusing the incoming light. Muscles control the degree of curvature of the lens, allowing the eye to form a sharp image on the *retina*.

lesion A specific area of tissue damage.

level of processing An assessment of how "deeply" newly learned materials are engaged; *shallow processing* involves thinking only about the material's superficial traits; *deep processing* involves thinking about what the material means. Deep processing is typically associated with a greater probability of remembering the now-processed information.

lexical-decision task A test in which participants are shown strings of letters and must indicate, as quickly as possible, whether each string of letters is a word in English or not. It is supposed that people perform this task by "looking up" these strings in their "mental dictionary."

LGN See *lateral geniculate nucleus*.

limbic system A set of brain structures including the *amygdala*, *hippocampus*, and parts of the *thalamus*. The limbic system is believed to be involved in the control of emotional behavior and motivation, and it also plays a key role in learning and memory.

limited-capacity system A group of processes in which resources are limited so that extra resources supplied to one process must be balanced by a withdrawal of resources somewhere else, with the result that the total resources expended do not exceed some limit.

linguistic relativity The proposal that the language that we speak shapes our thought, because the structure and vocabulary of our language create certain ways of thinking about the world.

linguistic universal A rule that appears to apply to every human language.

local representation A representation in which information is encoded in some small number of identifiable *nodes*. Local representations are sometimes spoken of as "one idea per node" or "one content per location." Often contrasted with *distributed representation*.

localization of function The research endeavor of determining what specific job is performed by a particular region of the brain.

long-term memory (LTM) The storage system in which we hold all of our knowledge and all of our memories. Long-term memory contains memories that are not currently activated; those that are activated are represented in *working memory*.

longitudinal fissure The separation dividing the brain's left *cerebral hemisphere* from the right.

M cells Specialized cells within the *optic nerve* that provide the input for the *magnocellular cells* in the *lateral geniculate nucleus*. Often contrasted with *P cells*.

magnetic resonance imaging (MRI) A *neuroimaging technique* that uses magnetic fields (created by radio waves) to construct a detailed three-dimensional representation of brain tissue. Like *CT scans*, MRI scans reveal the brain's anatomy, but they are much more precise than CT scans.

magnocellular cells Cells in the *lateral geniculate nucleus* specialized for the perception of motion and depth. Often contrasted with *parvocellular cells*.

maintenance rehearsal A rote, mechanical process in which items are continually cycled through *working memory*, merely by being repeated over and over. Also called "item-specific rehearsal," and often contrasted with *elaborative rehearsal*.

manner of production The way in which a speaker momentarily obstructs the flow of air out of the lungs to produce a speech sound. For example, the airflow can be fully stopped for a moment, as it is in the [t] or [b] sound; or the air can continue to flow, as it does in the pronunciation of [f] or [v].

mapping The process of figuring out how aspects of one situation or argument correspond to aspects of some other situation or argument; this process is crucial for a problem solver's ability to find and use analogies.

mask A visual presentation used to interrupt the processing of another visual stimulus.

massed learning A memorization strategy in which someone works on memorizing for a solid block of time. Often contrasted with *spaced learning*; akin to "cramming."

matching strategy A shortcut apparently used in reasoning tasks; to use this strategy, the person selects a conclusion that contains the same words (e.g., "not," "some," "all") as the *premises*.

means-end analysis A strategy used in *problem solving* in which the person is guided, step-by-step, by a comparison of the difference, at that moment, between the current state and the *goal state*, and a consideration of the *operators* available for reducing that difference.

memory rehearsal Any mental activity that has the effect of maintaining information in *working memory*. Two types of rehearsal are often distinguished: *maintenance rehearsal* and *elaborative rehearsal*.

mental accounting A process that seems to guide decision making, in which different choices and different resources are kept separate, so that gains in one "account" (for example) do not influence choices about a different account.

mental model An internal representation in which an abstract description is translated into a relatively concrete representation, with that representation serving to illustrate how that abstract state of affairs might be realized.

mental rotation A process that participants seem to use in comparing one imagined form to another. To make the comparison, participants seem to imagine one form rotating into alignment with the other, so that the forms can be compared.

metacognitive judgment A judgment in which you stand back from a particular mental activity and comment on the activity, rather than using it or participating in it.

metalinguistic judgment A particular type of *metacognitive judgment* in which you stand back from your ordinary language use and comment on language or linguistic processes. An example would be a judgment about whether a particular sentence is grammatical or not.

midbrain One of the three main structures (along with the *forebrain* and the *hindbrain*) of the brain; the midbrain plays an important role in coordinating movements, and it contains structures that serve as "relay" stations for information arriving from the sensory organs.

mind-body problem The difficulty in understanding how the mind (a nonphysical entity) and the body (a physical entity) can influence each other, so that physical events can cause mental events, and mental events can cause physical ones.

minimal attachment A *heuristic* used in *sentence parsing*. The listener or reader proceeds through the sentence seeking the simplest possible *phrase structure* that will accommodate the words heard so far.

misinformation effect An effect in which reports about an earlier event are influenced by misinformation someone received after experiencing the event. In the extreme, misinformation can be used to create *false memories* concerning an entire event that, in truth, never occurred.

mnemonic strategy A technique designed to improve memory accuracy and to make learning easier; in general, mnemonic strategies seek in one fashion or another to help memory by imposing an organization on the materials to be learned.

modal model A nickname for a specific conception of the "architecture" of memory. In this model, *working memory* serves both as the storage site for material now being contemplated and as the "loading platform" for *long-term memory*. Information can reach working memory through the processes of perception, or it can be drawn from long-term memory. Once in working memory, material can be further processed, or it can simply be recycled for subsequent use. This model encouraged a large quantity of valuable research, but has now largely been set aside, with modern theorizing offering a very different conception of working memory.

modus ponens A logical rule stipulating that from the two premises "If P then Q" and "P is true," you can draw the conclusion "Therefore, Q is true." Often contrasted with *modus tollens*.

modus tollens A logical rule stipulating that from the two premises "If P then Q" and "Q is false," you can draw the conclusion "Therefore, P is false." Often contrasted with *modus ponens*.

monozygotic twins See *identical twins*.

morpheme The smallest language unit that carries meaning.

Psycholinguists distinguish *content morphemes* (the primary carriers of meaning) from *function morphemes* (which specify the relations among words).

MRI See *magnetic resonance imaging*.

multiple intelligences A proposal put forward by Gardner that there are many forms of intelligence, including linguistic, spatial, musical, bodily-kinesthetic, and personal.

necessary condition A condition that *must* be fulfilled in order for a certain consequence to occur. However, necessary conditions may not guarantee that the consequence will occur, since other conditions may also be necessary. Often contrasted with *sufficient condition*.

Necker cube One of the classic *ambiguous figures*; the figure is a two-dimensional drawing that can be perceived as a cube viewed from above or as a cube viewed from below.

neglect syndrome See *unilateral neglect syndrome*.

neural correlate An event in the nervous system that occurs at the same time as, and may be the biological basis of, a specific mental event or state.

neural net model An alternative term for connectionist models. This term is used to emphasize the hypothesized parallels between this sort of computer model and the functioning of the nervous system.

neural synchrony A pattern of *firing* by *neurons* in which neurons in one brain area fire at the same time as neurons in another area; the brain seems to use this pattern as an indication that the neurons in different areas are firing in response to the same stimulus.

neuroimaging technique A method for examining either the structure or the activation pattern within a living brain.

neuron An individual cell within the nervous system.

neuronal workspace hypothesis A specific claim about how the brain makes conscious experience possible; the proposal is that

"workspace neurons" link together the activity of various specialized brain areas, and this linkage makes possible integration and comparison of different types of information.

neuropsychology The branch of psychology concerned with the relation between various forms of brain dysfunction and various aspects of mental functioning. Neuropsychologists study, for example, *amnesia*, *agnosia*, and *aphasia*.

neurotransmitter One of the chemicals released by *neurons* in order to stimulate adjacent neurons. See also *synapse*.

neutral depiction A representation that directly reflects the layout and appearance of an object or scene (and so is, on this basis, a "depiction"), but without adding any specifications about how that depiction is to be understood (and so is, on this basis, "neutral"). Often contrasted with *organized depiction*.

node An individual unit within an associative network. In a scheme using *local representations*, nodes represent single ideas or concepts. In a scheme using *distributed representations*, ideas or contents are represented by a pattern of activation across a wide number of nodes; the same nodes may also participate in other patterns and therefore in other representations.

nonfluent aphasia A disruption of language, caused by brain damage, in which someone loses the ability to speak or write with any fluency. Often contrasted with *fluent aphasia*.

normative account An account that tells how things ought to be, as opposed to how they are. Also referred to as "prescriptive account"; often contrasted with *descriptive account*.

noun phrase (NP) One of the constituents of a *phrase structure* that defines a *sentence*.

null finding A result showing no difference between groups or between conditions. A null finding is generally ambiguous, because it may indicate either that there is no difference, or that the study was simply not sensitive enough to detect a difference.

object recognition The steps or processes through which people identify the objects they encounter in the world around them.

occipital lobe The rearmost lobe in each *cerebral hemisphere*, and which includes the primary visual projection area.

operation span A measure of *working memory*'s capacity. This measure turns out to be predictive of performance in many other tasks, presumably because these tasks all rely on working memory. This measure is also the modern replacement for the (less useful) measure obtained from the *digit-span task*.

operator In *problem solving*, a tool or action one can use to move from the problem's *initial state* to the *goal state*.

optic nerve The bundle of nerve fibers, formed from the *retina*'s *ganglion cells*, that carries information from the eyeball to the brain.

organized depiction A representation that directly reflects the layout and appearance of an object or scene (and so is, on this basis, a "depiction") but that also adds some specifications about how the depiction is to be understood (e.g., where the form's top is, what the form's *figure/ground organization* is). Often contrasted with a *neutral depiction*.

overregularization error An error in which someone perceives or remembers a word or event as being closer to the "norm" than it really is. For example, misspelled words are read as though they were spelled correctly; atypical events are misremembered in a fashion that brings them closer to more-typical events; words with an irregular past tense (such as "ran") are replaced with a regular past tense ("runned").

P cells Specialized cells within the *optic nerve* that provide the input

for the *parvocellular cells* in the *lateral geniculate nucleus*. Often contrasted with *M cells*.

parahippocampal place area (PPA) A brain area apparently specialized for the perception of places.

parallel distributed processing A system of handling information in which many steps happen at once (i.e., in parallel) and in which various aspects of the problem or task are represented only in a distributed fashion.

parallel processing A system in which many steps are going on at the same time. Usually contrasted with *serial processing*.

parietal lobe The lobe in each *cerebral hemisphere* that lies between the *occipital* and *frontal lobes* and includes some of the *primary sensory projection areas*, as well as circuits that are crucial for the control of attention.

parieto-frontal integration theory (P-FIT) A proposal that emphasizes the close coordination among several brain areas (including areas in the *parietal lobe* and areas in the *frontal lobe*) in making intelligence possible.

parsing The process through which an input is divided into its appropriate elements—for example, dividing the stream of incoming speech into its constituent words—or in which a sequence of words is divided into its constituent phrases.

parvocellular cells Cells in the *lateral geniculate nucleus* specialized for the perception of patterns. Often contrasted with *magnocellular cells*.

path constraint A limit that rules out some operation in *problem solving*. Path constraints might take the form of resource limitations (limited time to spend on the problem, or limited money) or limits of other sorts (perhaps ethical limits on what one can do).

peer-review process The process through which scientific papers are evaluated before they are judged to be of high enough quality to be published in the field's scholarly journals. The papers are reviewed

by individuals who are experts on the topic—in essence, peers of the authors of the papers being reviewed.

peg-word systems A type of *mnemonic strategy* using words or locations as "pegs" on which to "hang" the materials to be remembered.

percept An internal representation of the world that results from perceiving; percepts are *organized depictions*.

perceptual reference frame The set of specifications about how a form is to be understood and that provides the organization in an *organized depiction*.

performance The actual behavior someone produces (including the errors he or she makes) under ordinary circumstances. Often contrasted with *competence*.

permastore A hypothesized state in which individual memories seem to be held in storage forever (hence, the state can be considered "permanent storage").

perseveration error A pattern of responding in which you produce the same response over and over, even though you know that the task requires a change in response. This pattern is often observed in patients with brain damage in the *frontal lobe*.

PET scanning See *positron emission tomography*.

P-FIT See *parieto-frontal integration theory*.

phonemes The basic categories of sound used to convey language. For example, the words "peg" and "beg" differ in their initial phoneme—[p] in one case, [b] in the other.

phonemic restoration effect A pattern in which people "hear" *phonemes* that actually are not presented but that are highly likely in that context. Thus, if one is presented with the word "legislature" but with the [s] sound replaced by a cough, one is likely to hear the [s] sound anyhow.

phonological buffer A passive storage device that serves as part of the *articulatory rehearsal loop*. The phonological buffer serves as part of the mechanisms ordinarily needed for hearing. In memory rehearsal, however, the buffer is loaded by means of *subvocalization*. Materials within the buffer then fade, but they can be refreshed by new covert speech under the control of the *central executive*.

phonology The study of the sounds that are used to convey language.

photoreceptor A cell on the *retina* that responds directly to the incoming light; photoreceptors are of two kinds: *rods* and *cones*.

phrase structure The pattern of requirements and relationships, governed by *phrase structure rules*, that defines the structure of a *sentence* (e.g., dividing the sentence into a *noun phrase* and a *verb phrase*, and then specifying the required contents of each phrase).

phrase structure ambiguity Ambiguity in how a *sentence* should be interpreted, resulting from the fact that more than one phrase structure is compatible with the sentence. An example of such ambiguity is, "I saw the bird with my binoculars."

phrase structure rule A constraint that governs the pattern of branching in a phrase structure. Equivalently, phrase structure rules govern what the constituents must be for any syntactic element of a *sentence*.

place of articulation The position at which a speaker momentarily obstructs the flow of air out of the lungs to produce a speech sound. For example, the place of articulation for the [b] sound is the lips; the place of articulation for the [d] sound is created by the tongue briefly touching the roof of the mouth.

positron emission tomography (PET scanning) A *neuroimaging technique* that determines how much glucose (the brain's fuel) is being used by specific areas of the brain at a particular moment in time.

postsynaptic membrane The cell membrane of the *neuron* "receiving" information across the *synapse*. Often contrasted with *presynaptic membrane*.

practical intelligence The ability to solve everyday problems through skilled reasoning that relies on tacit knowledge acquired through experience.

pragmatic reasoning schema A collection of rules, derived from ordinary practical experience, that defines what inferences are appropriate in a specific situation. These reasoning schemata are usually defined in terms of a goal or theme, so one schema defines the rules appropriate for reasoning about situations involving "permission," and a different schema defines the rules appropriate for thinking about situations involving cause-and-effect relations.

pragmatics A term referring to knowledge of how language is ordinarily used, knowledge (for example) that tells most English speakers that "Can you pass me the salt?" is actually a request for the salt, not an inquiry about someone's arm strength.

predictive validity As assessment of whether a test measures what it is intended to measure, based on whether the test scores correlate with (that is, can predict) some other relevant criterion.

prefrontal cortex The outer surface (*cortex*) of the frontmost part of the brain (i.e., the frontmost part of the *frontal lobe*). This brain area has many functions but is crucial for the planning of complex or novel behaviors, so this brain area is often mentioned as one of the main sites underlying the brain's executive functions.

premise A *proposition* that is assumed to be true in a logic problem; the problem asks what conclusion follows from its premises.

preparation The first in a series of stages often hypothesized as crucial for creativity. The second stage is *incubation*; the

third, *illumination*; the fourth, *verification*. Preparation is the stage in which you commence effortful work on the problem, often with little progress.

prescriptive rules Rules describing how things are supposed to be instead of how they are. Often called *normative* rules and contrasted with *descriptive rules*.

presynaptic membrane The cell membrane of the *neuron* "sending" information across the *synapse*. Often contrasted with *postsynaptic membrane*.

primacy effect An often-observed advantage in remembering the early-presented materials within a sequence of materials. This advantage is generally attributed to the fact that you can focus attention on these items, simply because, at the beginning of a sequence, you are obviously not trying to divide attention between these items and other items in the series. Often contrasted with *recency effect*.

primary motor projection areas The strip of tissue, located at the rear of the *frontal lobe*, that is the departure point for nerve cells that send their signals to lower portions of the brain and spinal cord, and which ultimately result in muscle movement.

primary projection areas Regions of the *cortex* that serve as the brain's receiving station for sensory information (sensory projection areas) or as a dispatching station for motor commands (motor projection areas).

primary sensory projection areas The main points of arrival in the *cortex* for information arriving from the eyes, ears, and other sense organs.

priming A process through which one input or cue prepares a person for an upcoming input or cue.

problem solving A process in which you begin with a goal and seek some steps that will lead toward that goal.

problem-solving protocol A record of how someone seeks to solve a problem; the record is created by simply asking the person to think aloud while working on the problem. The written record of this thinking-aloud is the protocol.

problem-solving set The starting assumptions that a person uses when trying to solve a new problem. These assumptions are often helpful, because they guide the person away from pointless strategies. But these assumptions can sometimes steer the person away from worthwhile strategies, so they can be an obstacle to problem solving.

problem space The set of all states that can be reached in solving a problem, as you move, by means of the problem's *operators*, from the problem's *initial state* toward the problem's *goal state*.

process-pure task A task that relies on only a single mental process. If tasks are "process-pure," then we can interpret the properties of task performance as revealing the properties of the underlying process. If tasks are not process-pure, however, we cannot interpret performance as revealing the properties of a specific process.

processing fluency An improvement in the speed or ease of processing that results from prior practice in using those same processing steps.

processing pathway The sequence of *detectors* and *nodes*, and the connections among these various units, that activation flows through in dealing with (recognizing or thinking about) a specific stimulus.

production task An experimental procedure used in studying concepts, in which the person is asked to name as many examples (e.g., as many fruits) as possible.

proposition The smallest unit of knowledge that can be either true or false. Propositions are often expressed via simple sentences, but this is merely a convenience, and other modes of representation are available.

prosody The pattern of pauses and pitch changes that characterize speech production. Prosody can be used (among other functions) to emphasize elements of a spoken *sentence*, to highlight the sentence's intended structure, or to signal the difference between a question and an assertion.

prosopagnosia A syndrome in which patients lose their ability to recognize faces and to make other fine-grained discriminations within a highly familiar category, even though their other visual abilities seem relatively intact.

prototype theory The claim that mental categories are represented by means of a single "best example," or prototype, identifying the "center" of the category. In this view, decisions about category membership, and inferences about the category, are made with reference to this best example, often an average of the examples of that category that you have actually encountered.

pseudoword A letter string designed to resemble an actual word, even though it is not. Examples include "blar," "plome," and "tuke."

qualia (singular: *quale*) The subjective conscious experiences or "raw feels" of awareness. Examples include the pain of a headache and the exact way chocolate tastes.

random assignment A procedure in which participants are assigned on a random basis to one condition or another. This ensures that there will be no systematic differences, at the start of the experiment, between the participants in the various conditions. If differences are then observed at the end of the experiment, the researcher knows that the differences were caused by something inside of the experiment itself. Random assignment is required because participants inevitably differ from each other in various ways; random assignment ensures, however, that these differences are equally represented in all conditions (i.e., that all conditions have a mix of early-arrived participants and late-arrivals, a mix of motivated participants and less-motivated ones, etc.).

rating task A task in which research participants must evaluate some item or category with reference to some dimension, usually expressing their response in terms of some number. For example, participants might be asked to evaluate birds for how *typical* they are within the category of "birds," using a "1" response to indicate "very typical" and a "7" response to indicate "very atypical."

reason-based choice A proposal for how people make decisions. The central idea is that people make a choice when—and only when—they detect what they believe to be a persuasive reason for making that choice.

recall The task of memory *retrieval* in which the rememberer must come up with the desired materials, sometimes in response to a cue that names the context in which these materials were earlier encountered ("Name the pictures you saw earlier"), sometimes in response to a question that requires the sought-after information ("Name a fruit" or "What is the capital of California?"). Often contrasted with *recognition*.

recency effect The tendency to remember materials that occur late in a series. If the series was just presented, the recency effect can be attributed to the fact that these late-arriving items are still in working memory (simply because nothing else has arrived after these items, to bump them out of working memory).

receptive field The portion of the visual field to which a cell within the visual system responds. If the appropriately shaped stimulus appears in the appropriate position, the cell's *firing* rate will change. The firing rate will not change if the stimulus is of the wrong form or is in the wrong position.

recognition The task of memory *retrieval* in which the items to be remembered are presented and the person must decide whether or not the item was encountered in some earlier circumstance. Thus, for example, one might be asked, "Have you ever seen this person before?" or "Is this the poster you saw in the office yesterday?" Often contrasted with *recall*.

recognition by components model A model (often referred to by its initials, RBC) of *object recognition*. In this model, a crucial role is played by *geons*, the (hypothesized) basic building blocks out of which all the objects we recognize are constructed.

recognition threshold The briefest exposure to a stimulus that still allows accurate recognition of that stimulus. For words, the recognition threshold typically lies between 10 and 40 ms. Words shown for longer durations are usually easily perceived; words shown for briefer durations are typically difficult to perceive.

reconstruction A process in which one draws on broad patterns of knowledge in order to figure out how a prior event actually unfolded. In some circumstances, people rely on reconstruction to fill gaps in what they recall; in other circumstances, people rely on reconstruction because it requires less effort than actual *recall*.

recursion A property of rule systems that allows a symbol to appear both on the left side of a definition (the part being defined) and on the right side (the part providing the definition). Recursive rules within *syntax*, for example, allow a *sentence* to include another sentence as one of its constituents, as in the following example: "Solomon says that Jacob is a great singer."

referent The actual object, action, or event in the world that a word or phrase refers to.

rehearsal loop See *articulatory rehearsal loop*.

relational rehearsal A form of mental processing in which you think about the relations, or connections, among ideas. The connections created (or strengthened) in this way will later guide memory search.

reliability The degree of consistency with which a test measures a trait or attribute. See also *test-retest reliability*.

"remember/know" A distinction between two experiences you can have in recalling a past event. If you "remember" having encountered a stimulus before, then you usually can offer information about that encounter, including when, where, and how it occurred. If you merely "know" that you encountered a stimulus before, then you are likely to have a sense of familiarity with the stimulus but may have no idea when or where the stimulus was last encountered.

repetition priming A pattern of *priming* that occurs simply because a stimulus is presented a second time; processing is more efficient on the second presentation.

replication A procedure of repeating an experiment (often with small variations) to ensure that the result is reliable.

research literature The term scientists use to describe the papers published on a particular topic in *peer-reviewed* technical journals. These papers are usually referred to via citations of a particular format, such as "Monk, 2012," referring perhaps to a paper published in a technical journal by Peter Monk.

representativeness heuristic A strategy often used in making judgments about categories. This strategy is broadly equivalent to making the assumption that in general, the instances of a category will resemble the prototype for that category and, likewise, that the prototype resembles each instance.

response selector A (hypothesized) mental resource needed for the selection and initiation of a wide range of responses, including overt responses (e.g., moving in a particular way) and covert responses (e.g., initiating a memory search).

response threshold The quantity of information, or quantity of

activation, needed in order to trigger a response.

response time The amount of time (usually measured in milliseconds) needed for a person to respond to a particular event (such as a question or a cue to press a specific button).

retention interval The amount of time that passes between the initial learning of some material and the subsequent memory *retrieval* of that material.

retina The light-sensitive tissue that lines the back of the eyeball.

retrieval The process of locating information in memory and activating that information for use.

retrieval block A circumstance in which a person seems unable to retrieve a bit of information that he or she knows reasonably well.

retrieval cue An instruction or stimulus input, provided at the time of recall, that can potentially guide recall and help the person to retrieve the target memory.

retrieval failure A mechanism that probably contributes to a great deal of forgetting. Retrieval failure occurs when a memory is, in fact, in long-term storage, but you are unable to locate that memory when trying to retrieve it.

retrieval path A connection (or series of connections) that can lead to a sought-after memory in long-term storage.

retrograde amnesia An inability to remember experiences that occurred *before* the event that triggered the memory disruption. Often contrasted with *anterograde amnesia*.

review article A scholarly report that summarizes the results of many different research papers, seeking to synthesize those results into a coherent pattern.

risk aversion A tendency toward avoiding risk. People tend to be risk averse when contemplating gains, choosing instead to hold tight to what they already have. Often contrasted with *risk seeking*.

risk seeking A tendency toward seeking out risk. People tend to be risk seeking when contemplating losses, because they are willing to gamble in hopes of avoiding (or diminishing) their losses. Often contrasted with *risk aversion*.

rod A *photoreceptor* that is sensitive to very low light levels but that is unable to discriminate hues and that has relatively poor *acuity*. Often contrasted with *cone*.

savant syndrome A pattern of traits in a developmentally disabled person such that the person has some remarkable talent that contrasts with his or her very low level of general intelligence.

schema (pl. schemata) Knowledge describing what is typical or frequent in a particular situation. For example, a "kitchen schema" would stipulate that a stove and refrigerator are likely to be present, whereas a coffeemaker may be or may not be present, and a piano is likely not to be present.

selection task An experimental procedure, commonly used to study reasoning, in which a person is presented with four cards with certain information on either side of the card. The person is also given a rule that may describe the cards, and the person's task is to decide which cards must be turned over to find out if the rule describes the cards or not. Also called the "four-card task."

selective attention The skill through which one focuses on one input or one task while ignoring other stimuli that are also on the scene.

self-reference effect The tendency to have better memory for information relevant to oneself than for other sorts of material.

self-report data A form of evidence in which the person is asked directly about his or her own thoughts or experiences.

self-schema The set of interwoven beliefs and memories that constitute your knowledge about yourself.

self-selected group A group of participants who are in a particular condition within a study because they put

themselves in that condition. In some cases, participants choose which condition to be in. In other cases, they have some trait (e.g., showing up late; arriving only in the evening) that causes them to be put into a particular condition. In all cases, there is a risk that these participants are, from the start of the experiment, different from those in the other conditions. If so, then any differences observed within the experiment are ambiguous: These differences might be the result of the experimental manipulation but could also be the lingering effect of some preexisting difference.

semantic bootstrapping An important process in language learning in which someone (usually a child) uses knowledge of semantic relationships as a basis for figuring out the *syntax* of the language.

semantic priming A process in which activation of an idea in memory causes activation to spread to other ideas related to the first in meaning.

sentence A sequence of words that conforms to the rules of *syntax* (and so has the right constituents in the right sequence).

sentence verification task An experimental procedure used for studying memory in which participants are given simple sentences (e.g., "Cats are animals") and must respond as quickly as possible whether the sentence is true or false.

sequential lineup A procedure used for eyewitness identification in which the witness sees faces one by one and cannot see the next face until he has made a yes or no decision about the face now in view.

serial position A data pattern summarizing the relationship between some performance measure (often, likelihood of *recall*) and the order in which the test materials were presented. In memory studies, the serial position curve tends to be U-shaped, with people best able to recall the

first-presented items (the *primacy effect*) and also the last-presented items (the *recency effect*).

serial processing A system in which only one step happens at a time (and so the steps go on in a series). Usually contrasted with *parallel processing*.

7 plus-or-minus 2 A number often offered as an estimate of the holding capacity of *working memory*.

shadowing A task in which research participants are required to repeat back a verbal input, word for word, as they hear it.

shallow processing A mode of thinking about material in which you pay attention only to appearances and other superficial aspects of the material; shallow processing typically leads to poor memory retention. Often contrasted with *deep processing*.

short-term memory An older term for what is now called *working memory*.

simultaneous multiple constraint satisfaction An attribute of much of our thinking, in which we seem able to find solutions to problems, or answers to questions, that satisfy several requirements ("multiple constraints"), by using a search process that seems to be guided by all of these requirements at the same time.

single-cell recording A technique for recording the moment-by-moment *activation level* of an individual *neuron* within a healthy, normally functioning brain.

somatic markers States of the body used in decision making. For example, a tight stomach and an accelerated heart rate when someone is thinking about an option can signal to the person that the option has risk associated with it.

source confusion A memory error in which you misremember where a bit of information was learned or where a particular stimulus was last encountered.

source memory A form of memory that allows you to recollect the episode in which learning took place or the time and place in which a particular stimulus was encountered.

source monitoring The process of keeping track of when and where you encountered some bit of information (i.e., keeping track of the source of that information).

spaced learning A memorization strategy in which someone works on memorizing for a while, then does something else, then returns to memorizing, then does something else, and so on. Often contrasted with *massed learning*.

span test A procedure used for measuring *working memory*'s holding capacity. In newer studies, the *operation span* test is used.

spatial attention The mechanism through which you allocate processing resources to particular positions in space, so that you more efficiently process any inputs from that region in space.

specific language impairment A syndrome in which individuals seem to have normal intelligence but problems in learning the rules of language.

speech segmentation The process through which a stream of speech is "sliced" into its constituent words and, within words, into the constituent *phonemes*.

spreading activation A process through which activation travels from one *node* to another, via *associative links*. As each node becomes activated, it serves as a source for further activation, spreading onward through the network.

stereotype threat A mechanism through which a person's performance is influenced by the perception that his or her score will confirm stereotypes about his or her group.

storage The state in which a memory, once acquired, remains until it is retrieved. Many people understand storage to be a "dormant" process, so that the memory remains unchanged while it is in storage. Modern theories, however,

describe a more dynamic form of storage, in which older memories are integrated with (and sometimes replaced by) newer knowledge.

Stroop interference A classic demonstration of *automaticity* in which people are asked to name the color of ink used to print a word, and the word itself is a different color name. For example, research participants might see the word "yellow" printed in blue ink and be required to say "blue." Considerable interference is observed in this task, with participants apparently unable to ignore the word's content, even though it is irrelevant to their task.

subcortical Beneath the surface (i.e., beneath the cortex).

subjective utility A measure of how valuable a state of affairs would be for you. This notion is central to "utility theory" accounts of decision making, on the idea that you try to select the option that will lead to the greatest subjective utility.

subliminal prime A *prime* that is presented so quickly that it is not consciously detected; such primes nonetheless can have an impact on subsequent perceptions or thoughts.

subproblem A subdivision of a problem being solved. Subproblems are produced when a person tries to solve a problem by breaking it into components or steps, each with its own goal, but so that solving all the subproblems results in solution of the overall problem.

subthreshold activation Activation levels below *response threshold*. Subthreshold activation, by definition, will not trigger a response; nonetheless, this activation is important because it can accumulate, leading eventually to an *activation level* that exceeds the response threshold.

subvocalization Covert speech, in which you go through the motions of speaking, or perhaps form a detailed motor plan for speech movements, but without making any sound.

sufficient condition A condition that, if satisfied, guarantees that a certain consequence will occur. However, sufficient conditions may not be necessary for that consequence (since the same consequence might occur for some other reasons). Often contrasted with *necessary condition*.

summation The addition of two or more separate inputs so that the effect of these combined inputs is greater than the effect of any one of the inputs by itself.

surface structure The representation of a *sentence* that is actually expressed in speech. In some treatments, this structure is referred to as "s-structure." Often contrasted with *underlying structure*.

synapse The area that includes the *presynaptic membrane* of one *neuron*, the *postsynaptic membrane* of another neuron, and the tiny gap between them. The presynaptic membrane releases a small amount of *neurotransmitter* that drifts across the gap and stimulates the postsynaptic membrane.

syntax Rules governing the sequences and combinations of words in the formation of phrases and *sentences*.

System 1 A commonly used name for judgment and reasoning strategies that are fast and effortless, but prone to error.

System 2 A commonly used name for judgment and reasoning strategies that are slower and require more effort than System 1 strategies, but are less prone to error.

tachistoscope A device that allows the presentation of stimuli for precisely controlled amounts of time, including very brief presentations.

temporal lobe The lobe of the *cortex* lying inward and down from the temples. The temporal lobe in each *cerebral hemisphere* includes the primary auditory projection area, *Wernicke's area*, and, subcortically, the *amygdala* and *hippocampus*.

test-retest reliability An assessment of whether a test is consistent in what it measures, determined by asking whether the test's results on one occasion are correlated with the results from the same test (or a close variant on it) on another occasion.

thalamus A part of the lower portion of the *forebrain* that serves as a major relay and integration center for sensory information.

threshold The activity level at which a cell or *detector* responds, or *fires*.

TMS See *transcranial magnetic stimulation*.

token node A *node* that represents a specific example or instance of a category and therefore is used in propositions concerned with specific events and individuals. Often contrasted with *type node*.

top-down influences The term given to factors arising from your knowledge and expectations, and shaping your processing of the stimulus input.

top-down processing See *concept-driven processing*.

TOT phenomenon An often-observed effect in which people are unable to remember a particular word, even though they are certain that the word (typically identified via its definition) is in their vocabulary. People in this state often can remember the starting letter for the word and its number of syllables, and they insist that the word is on the "tip of their tongue" (hence the "TOT" label).

transcendental method A type of theorizing first proposed by the philosopher Immanuel Kant. To use this method, you first observe the effects or consequences of a process and then ask, What must the process have been in order to bring about these effects?

transcranial magnetic stimulation (TMS) A technique in which a series of strong magnetic pulses at a specific location on the scalp causes temporary disruption in the brain region directly underneath this scalp area.

tree structure A style of depiction often used to indicate hierarchical relationships, such as the relationships (specified by phrase structure rules) among the words in a phrase or *sentence*.

type node A *node* that represents a general category and therefore is embedded in propositions that are true for the entire category. Often contrasted with *token node*.

typicality The degree to which a particular case (an object, or a situation, or an event) is typical for its kind.

unattended channel A stimulus (or group of stimuli) that a person is not trying to perceive. Ordinarily, little information is understood or remembered from the unattended channel. Often contrasted with *attended channel*.

underlying structure An abstract representation of the *sentence* to be expressed; sometimes called "deep structure" (or "d-structure"). Often contrasted with *surface structure*.

unilateral neglect syndrome A pattern of symptoms in which patients ignore all inputs coming from one side of space. Patients with this syndrome put only one of their arms into their jackets, eat food from only half of their plates, read only half of words (e.g., they might read "blouse" as "use"), and so on.

utility A measure of the subjective value that an individual puts on a particular outcome; this measure can then be used to compare various outcomes, allowing choices to be based on these comparisons.

utility maximization The proposal that people make decisions by selecting the option that has the greatest *utility*.

V1 See *Area V1*.

valid syllogism A syllogism for which the conclusion follows from the *premise*, in accord with the rules of logic.

validity The extent to which a method or procedure measures what it is supposed to measure. Validity is assessed in a variety of ways, including *predictive validity*.

verb phrase (VP) One of the constituents of a phrase structure that defines a *sentence*.

verification One of the four steps commonly hypothesized as part of creative *problem solving*; in this step, you confirm that a new idea really does lead to a problem solution, and you work out the details. (The other steps are *preparation, incubation,* and *illumination.*)

viewpoint-dependent recognition A process in which the ease or success of *recognition* depends on the perceiver's particular viewing angle or distance with regard to the target object.

viewpoint-independent recognition A process in which the ease or success of *recognition* does *not* depend on the perceiver's particular viewing angle or distance with regard to the target object.

visual acuity A measure of your ability to see fine detail.

visual features The constituents of a visual pattern—vertical lines, curves, diagonals and so on—that, together, form the overall pattern.

visual search task A commonly used laboratory task in which research participants are asked to search for a specific target (e.g., a shape, or a shape of a certain color) within a field of other stimuli; usually the researcher is interested in how quickly the participants can locate the target.

visuospatial buffer One of the low-level assistants used as part of the *working-memory system*. This buffer plays an important role in storing visual or spatial representations, including visual images.

voice-onset time (VOT) The time that elapses between the start of a speech sound and the onset of *voicing*. VOT is the main feature distinguishing "voiced" consonants (such as [b], with a near-zero VOT) and "unvoiced" consonants (such as [p], with a VOT of approximately 60 ms).

voicing One of the properties that distinguishes different categories of speech sounds. A sound is considered "voiced" if the vocal folds are vibrating while the sound is produced. If the vocal folds start vibrating sometime after the sound begins (i.e., with a long *voice-onset time*), the sound is considered "unvoiced."

weapon-focus effect A pattern, often alleged for witnesses to violent crimes, in which one pays close attention to some crucial detail (such as the weapon within a crime scene) to the exclusion of much else.

well-defined problem A problem for which the *goal state* is clearly specified at the start and the operators available for reaching that goal are clearly identified. Often contrasted with *ill-defined problem*.

Wernicke's area An area in the left *frontal lobe* of the brain; damage here typically causes *fluent aphasia*.

***what* system** The system of visual circuits and pathways leading from the visual *cortex* to the *temporal lobe* and especially involved in object recognition. Often contrasted with the *where system*.

***where* system** The system of visual circuits and pathways leading from the visual *cortex* to the *parietal lobe* and especially involved in the spatial localization of objects and in the coordination of movements. Often contrasted with the *what system*.

winner-takes-all system A process in which a node that is more strongly activated inhibits nodes that are more weakly activated, so that the stronger node comes more and more to dominate the weaker nodes.

word-stem completion A task in which people are given the beginning of a word (e.g., "TOM") and must provide a word that starts with the letters provided. In some versions of the task, only one solution is possible, and so performance is measured by counting the number of words completed. In other versions of the task, several solutions are possible for each stem, and performance is assessed by determining which of the responses fulfill some other criterion.

word-superiority effect The data pattern in which research participants are more accurate and more efficient in recognizing words (and wordlike letter strings) than they are in recognizing individual letters.

working memory The storage system in which information is held while that information is being worked on. All indications are that working memory is a system, not a single entity, and that information is held here via active processes, not via some sort of passive storage. Formerly called "short-term memory."

working-memory system A system of mental resources used for holding information in an easily accessible form. The *central executive* is at the heart of this system, and the executive then relies on a number of low-level assistants, including the *visuospatial buffer* and the *articulatory rehearsal loop*.

References

Ackerman, P. L., Beier, M. E., & Boyle, M. O. (2002). Individual differences in working memory within a nomological network of cognitive and perceptual speed abilities. *Journal of Experimental Psychology: General, 131*, 567–589.

Aggleton, J. P., & Brown, M. W. (2006). Interleaving brain systems for episodic and recognition memory. *Trends in Cognitive Sciences, 10*, 455–463.

Ajzen, I. (1977). Intuitive theories of events and the effects of base-rate information on prediction. *Journal of Personality & Social Psychology, 35*, 303–314.

Alexander, K. W., Quas, J. A., Goodman, G. S., Ghetti, S., Edelstein, R. S., Redlich, A. D., et al. (2005). Traumatic impact predicts long-term memory for documented child sexual abuse. *Psychological Science, 16*, 33–40.

Alkire, M., Hudetz, A. & Tononi, G. (2008). Consciousness and anesthesia. *Science, 322*, 876–880.

Allport, A. (1989). Visual attention. In M. Posner (Ed.), *Foundations of cognitive science* (pp. 631–682). Cambridge, MA: MIT Press.

Allport, D., Antonis, B., & Reynolds, P. (1972). On the division of attention: A disproof of the single channel hypothesis. *Quarterly Journal of Experimental Psychology, 24*, 225–235.

Almor, A., & Sloman, S. A. (2000). Reasoning versus text processing in the Wason selection task: A non-deontic perspective on perspective effects. *Memory & Cognition, 28*, 1060–1070.

Alter, A. L., & Oppenheimer, D. M. (2006). Predicting stock price fluctuations using processing fluency. *Proceedings of the National Academy of Sciences, 103*(24), 9369–9372.

Altmann, E. M., & Gray, W. D. (2002). Forgetting to remember: The functional relationship of decay and interference. *Psychological Science, 13*, 27–33.

Ambady, N., Shih, M., Kim, A., & Pittinsky, T. L. (2001). Stereotype susceptibility in children: Effects of identity activation on quantitative performance. *Psychological Science, 12*, 385–390.

Amishav, R., & Kimchi, R. (2010). Perceptual integrality of componential and configural information in faces. *Psychonomic Bulletin & Review, 17*, 743–748.

Anderson, J. R. (1976). *Language, memory, and thought*. Hillsdale, NJ: Erlbaum.

Anderson, J. R. (1980). *Cognitive psychology and its implications*. San Francisco: Freeman.

Anderson, J. R. (1993). Problem solving and learning. *American Psychologist, 48*, 35–44.

Anderson, J. R., & Bower, G. H. (1972). Recognition and retrieval processes in free recall. *Psychological Review, 79*, 97–123.

Anderson, J. R., & Bower, G. H. (1973). *Human associative memory*. Washington, DC: Winston.

Anderson, R., & Helstrup, T. (1993). Visual discovery in mind and on paper. *Memory & Cognition, 21*, 283–293.

Ansburg, P. I., & Hill, K. (2003). Creative and analytic thinkers differ in their use of attentional resources. *Personality and Individual Differences, 34*, 1141–1152.

Ariely, D. (2009). *Predictably irrational*. New York, NY: Harper.

Ariely, D., & Norton, M. (2007). How actions create—not just reveal—preferences. *Trends in Cognitive Sciences, 12*, 13–16.

Arkes, H. (1991). Costs and benefits of judgment errors: Implications for debiasing. *Psychological Bulletin, 110*, 486–498.

Arkes, H., & Harkness, A. (1983). Estimates of contingency between two dichotomous variables. *Journal of Experimental Psychology: General, 112*, 117–135.

Armstrong, S. L., Gleitman, L. R., & Gleitman, H. (1983). What some concepts might not be. *Cognition, 13*, 263–308.

Arneson, J., Sackett, P., & Beatty, A. (2011). Ability-performance relationships in education and employment settings: Critical tests of the more-is-better and good-enough hypotheses. *Psychological Science, 22*, 1336–1342.

Arnau, R. C., & Thompson, B. (2000). Second order confirmatory factor analysis of the Wais-III. *Assessment, 7,* 237–246.

Aron, A. (2008). Progress in executive-function research. *Current Direct-ions in Psychological Science, 17,* 124–129.

Arrigo, J. M., & Pezdek, K. (1997). Lessons from the study of psychogenic amnesia. *Current Directions in Psychological Science, 6,* 148–152.

Ash, I. K., & Wiley, J. (2006). The nature of restructuring in insight: An individual-differences approach. *Psychonomic Bulletin & Review, 13,* 66–73.

Asher, E. J. (1935). The inadequacy of current intelligence tests for testing Kentucky Mountain children. *Journal of Genetic Psychology, 46,* 480–486.

Aslin, R. N., Saffran, J. R., & Newport, E. L. (1998). Computation of conditional probability statistics by 8-month-old infants. *Psychological Science, 9,* 321–324.

Atkinson, A. P., Thomas, M. S. C., & Cleeremans, A. (2000). Consciousness: Mapping the theoretical landscape. *Trends in Cognitive Sciences, 4,* 372–382.

Atkinson, R. C., & Shiffrin, R. M. (1968). Human memory: A proposed system and its control processes. In K. W. S. Spence &. J. T. Spence (Eds.), *The psychology of learning and motivation* (pp. 89–105). New York, NY: Academic Press.

Atran, S. (1990). *Cognitive foundations of natural history.* New York, NY: Cambridge University Press.

Attneave, F. (1953). Psychological probability as a function of experienced frequency. *Journal of Experimental Psychology, 46,* 81–86.

Baars, B. J. (1988). Momentary forgetting as a "resetting" of a conscious global workspace due to competition between incompatible contexts. In M. J. Horowitz (Ed.), *Psychodynamics and cognition* (pp. 269–293). Chicago, IL: University of Chicago Press.

Baars, B. J. (2005). Global workspace theory of consciousness: Toward a cognitive neuroscience of human experience. *Progress in Brain Research, 150,* 45–53.

Baars, B. J., & Franklin, S. (2003). How conscious experience and working memory interact. *Trends in Cognitive Sciences, 7,* 166–172.

Baddeley, A. D. (1986). *Working memory.* Oxford, England: Clarendon.

Baddeley, A. D. (1992). Is working memory working? The fifteenth Bartlett lecture. *Quarterly Journal of Experimental Psychology, 44A,* 1–31.

Baddeley, A. D. (1996). Exploring the central executive. *Quarterly Journal of Experimental Psychology: Human Experimental Psychology, 49A,* 5–28.

Baddeley, A. D. (1999). *Essentials of human memory.* Hove, England: Psychology Press.

Baddeley, A. D. (2012). Working memory: Theories, models, and controversies. *Annual Review of Psychology, 63,* 1–12.

Baddeley, A. D., & Hitch, G. (1974). Working memory. In G. Bower (Ed.), *Recent advances in learning and motivation* (pp. 47–90). New York, NY: Academic Press.

Baddeley, A. D., & Hitch, G. (1977). Recency re-examined. In S. Dornic (Ed.), *Attention and performance VI* (pp. 646–667). Hillsdale, NJ: Erlbaum.

Baddeley, A. D., Aggleton, J. P., & Conway, M. A. (Eds.). (2002). *Episodic memory: New directions in research.* New York, NY: Oxford University Press.

Baddeley, A. D., Gathercole, S., & Papagno, C. (1998). The phonological loop as a language learning device. *Psychological Review, 105,* 158–173.

Baddeley, A. D., Logie, R. H., Nimmo-Smith, I., & Brereton, J. (1985). Components of fluent reading. *Journal of Memory and Language, 24,* 119–131.

Bahrick, H. (1984). Semantic memory content in permastore: 50 years of memory for Spanish learned in school. *Journal of Experimental Psychology: General, 113,* 1–29.

Bahrick, H., Bahrick, P. O., & Wittlinger, R. P. (1975). Fifty years of memory for names and faces: A cross-sectional approach. *Journal of Experimental Psychology: General, 104,* 54–75.

Bahrick, H., & Hall, L. (1991). Lifetime maintenance of high school mathematics content. *Journal of Experimental Psychology: General, 120,* 20–33.

Bahrick, H., Hall, L. K., & Berger, S. A. (1996). Accuracy and distortion in memory for high school grades. *Psychological Science, 7,* 265–271.

Balch, W., Bowman, K., & Mohler, L. (1992). Music-dependent memory in immediate and delayed word recall. *Memory & Cognition, 20,* 21–28.

Bang, M., Medin, D., & Atran, S. (2007). Cultural mosaics and mental models of nature. *Proceedings of the National Academy of Sciences. 104,* 13868–13874.

Baratgin, J., & Noveck, I. A. (2000). Not only base rates are neglected in the engineer-lawyer problem: An investigation of reasoners' underutilization of complementarity. *Memory & Cognition, 28,* 79–91.

Barclay, J., Bransford, J., Franks, J., McCarrell, N., & Nitsch, K. (1974). Comprehension and semantic flexibility. *Journal of Verbal Learning & Verbal Behavior, 13,* 471–481.

Bargh, J. B. (2005). Toward demystifying the nonconscious control of social behavior. In R. Hasslin, J. Uleman, & J. A. Bargh, (Eds.), *The new unconscious* (pp. 37–58). New York, NY: Oxford University Press.

Baron, J. (1988). *Thinking and reasoning.* Cambridge, England: Cambridge University Press.

Baron, J. (1998). *Judgment misguided: Intuition and error in public decision making.* New York, NY: Oxford University Press.

Barsalou, L. (1988). The content and organization of autobiographical memories. In U. Neisser & E. Winograd (Eds.), *Remembering reconsidered* (pp. 193–243). Cambridge, England: Cambridge University Press.

Barsalou, L., & Sewell, D. R. (1985). Contrasting the representation of scripts and categories. *Journal of Memory and Language, 24,* 646–665.

Bartlett, F. C. (1932). *Remembering: A study in experimental and social psychology.* Cambridge, England: Cambridge University Press.

Bartolomeo, P., Bachoud-Levi, A-C., De Gelder, B., Denes, G., Barba, G. D., Brugieres, P., et al. (1998). Multiple-domain dissociation between impaired visual perception and preserved mental imagery in a patient with bilateral extrastriate lesions. *Neuropsychologia, 36*(3), 239–249.

Bassok, M. (1996). Using content to interpret structure: Effects on analogical transfer. *Current Directions in Psychological Science, 5*, 54–57.

Bassok, M., & Novick, L. R. (2012). Problem solving. In Holyoak, K. J., & Morrison, R. G. (Eds.), *The Oxford Handbook of Thinking and Reasoning* (pp. 413–432). New York, NY: Oxford University Press.

Bates, E., Devescovi, A., & Wulfeck, B. (2001). Psycholinguistics: A cross-language perspective. *Annual Review of Psychology, 52*, 369–398

Bates, T. C., & Shieles, A. (2003). Crystallized intelligence as a product of speed and drive for experience: The relationship of inspection time and openness to g and Gc. *Intelligence, 31*, 275–287.

Bauer, P. J. (2007). *Remembering the times of our lives: Memory in infancy and beyond.* Mahwah, NJ: Erlbaum.

Beach, C. M. (1991). The interpretation of prosodic patterns at points of syntactic structural ambiguity: Evidence for cue trading relations. *Journal of Memory and Language, 30*, 644–663.

Bechara, A., Damasio, H., & Damasio, A. R. (2003). Role of the amygdala in decision-making. *Annals of the New York Academy of Sciences, 985*, 356–369.

Bechara, A., Damasio, H., Tranel, D., & Damasio, A. R. (2005). The Iowa Gambling Task and the somatic marker hypothesis: Some questions and answers. *Trends in Cognitive Sciences, 9*, 159–162.

Bechara, A., Tranel, D., Damasio, H., Adolphs, R., Rockland, C., & Damasio, A. (1995). Double dissociation of conditioning and declarative knowledge relative to the amygdala and hippocampus in humans. *Science, 269*, 1115–1118.

Bédard, J., & Chi, M. (1992). Expertise. *Current Directions in Psychological Science, 1*, 135–139.

Begg, I., Anas, A., & Farinacci, S. (1992). Dissociation of processes in belief: Source recollection, statement familiarity, and the illusion of truth. *Journal of Experimental Psychology: General, 121*, 446–458.

Begg, I., Armour, V., & Kerr, T. (1985). On believing what we remember. *Canadian Journal of Behavioral Science, 17*, 199–214.

Behrmann, M. (2000). The mind's eye mapped onto the brain's matter. *Current Directions in Psychological Science, 9*, 50–54.

Behrmann, M., & Avidan, G. (2005). Congenital prosopagnosia: Face-blind from birth. *Trends in Cognitive Sciences, 9*, 180–187.

Behrmann, M., Peterson, M. A., Moscovitch, M., & Suzuki, S. (2006). Independent representation of parts and relations between them: Evidence from integrative agnosia. *Journal of Experimental Psychology: Human Perception and Performance, 32*, 1169–1184.

Behrmann, M., & Tipper, S. (1999). Attention accesses multiple reference frames: Evidence from visual neglect. *Journal of Experimental Psychology: Human Perception and Performance, 25*, 83–101.

Bekerian, D. A., & Baddeley, A. D. (1980). Saturation advertising and the repetition effect. *Journal of Verbal Learning & Verbal Behavior, 19*, 17–25.

Bellugi, U. (1971). Simplification in children's language. In R. Huxley & E. Ingram (Eds.), *Language acquisition: Models and methods.* New York, NY: Academic Press.

Benbow, C. P. (1988). Sex differences in mathematical reasoning ability in intellectually talented preadolescents: Their nature, effects, and possible causes. *Behavior and Brain Sciences, 11*, 169–232.

Benbow, C. P., Lubinski, D., Shea, D. L., & Eftekhari-Sanjani, H. (2000). Sex differences in mathematical reasoning ability at age 13: Their status 20 years later. *Psychological Science, 11*, 474–480.

Berko, J. (1958). The child's learning of English morphology. *Word, 14*, 150–177.

Besner, D., & Stolz, J. A. (1999a). Unconsciously controlled processing: The Stroop effect reconsidered. *Psychonomic Bulletin & Review, 6*, 449–455.

Besner, D., & Stolz, J. A. (1999b). What kind of attention modulates the Stroop effect? *Psychonomic Bulletin & Review, 6*, 99–104.

Bever, T. (1970). The cognitive basis for linguistic structures. In J. R. Hayes (Ed.), *Cognition and the development of language* (pp. 279–362). New York, NY: Wiley.

Bialystok, E., Craik, F., Green, D., & Gollan, T. (2009). Bilingual minds. *Psychological Science in the Public Interest, 10*, 89–129.

Biederman, I. (1985). Human vision understanding: Recent research and a theory. *Computer Vision, Graphics, and Image Processing, 32*, 29–73.

Biederman, I. (1987). Recognition by components: A theory of human image understanding. *Psychological Review, 94*, 115–147.

Biederman, I. (1990). Higher-level vision. In D. Osherson, S. Kosslyn, & J. Hollerbach (Eds.), *An invitation to cognitive science: Visual cognition and action, Vol. 2* (pp. 41–72). Cambridge, MA: MIT Press.

Bilalić, M., McLeod, P., & Gobet, F. (2010). The mechanism of the Einstellung (set) effect: A pervasive source of cognitive bias. *Current Directions in Psychological Science, 19*, 111–115.

Binder, J., & Desai, R. (2011). The neurobiology of semantic memory. *Trends in Cognitive Sciences, 15*, 527–536.

Bishop, D. Pine, S. Scott, J. Stevenson, E. Taylor, & A. Thapar (Eds.). *Rutter's Child and Adolescent Psychiatry* (pp. 782–801). Oxford, England: Blackwell.

Bishop, D., & Norbury, C. F. (2008). Speech and language disorders. In M. Rutter D.

Bisiach, E., & Luzzatti, C. (1978). Unilateral neglect of representational space. *Cortex, 14*, 129–133.

Bisiach, E., Luzzatti, C., & Perani, D. (1979). Unilateral neglect, representational schema, and consciousness. *Brain, 102,* 609–618.

Blascovich, J., Spencer, S. J., Quinn, D., Steele, C. (2001). African Americans and high blood pressure: The role of stereotype threat. *Psychological Science, 12,* 225–229.

Blinkhorn, S. (2005). A gender bender. *Nature, 438,* 31–32.

Block, N. (1997). Biology vs. computation in the study of consciousness. *Behavioral and Brain Sciences, 20,* 1.

Block, N. (2005). Two neural correlates of consciousness. *Trends in Cognitive Sciences, 9,* 46–52.

Bloom, P. (Ed.). (1994). *Language acquisition.* Cambridge, MA: MIT Press.

Blount, G. (1986). Dangerousness of patients with Capgras Syndrome. *Nebraska Medical Journal, 71,* 207.

Bobrow, S., & Bower, G. H. (1969). Comprehension and recall of sentences. *Journal of Experimental Psychology, 80,* 455–461.

Bogen, J. E. (1995). On the neurophysiology of consciousness: I. An overview. *Consciousness & Cognition: An International Journal, 4,* 52–62.

Boole, G. (1854). *An investigation of the laws of thought, on which are founded the mathematical theories of logic and probabilities.* London, England: Maberly.

Bornstein, B. (1963). Prosopagnosia. In L. Halpern (Ed.), *Problems of dynamic neurology* (pp. 283–318). Jerusalem: Hadassah Medical Organization.

Bornstein, B., Sroka, H., & Munitz, H. (1969). Prosopagnosia with animal face agnosia. *Cortex, 5,* 164–169.

Boroditsky, L. (2001). Does language shape thought? Mandarin and English speakers' conceptions of time. *Cognitive Psychology, 43,* 1–22.

Boroditsky, L. (2011, February). How language shapes thought. *Scientific American,* 63–65.

Borst, G., Thompson, W., & Kosslyn, S. (2011). Understanding the dorsal and ventral systems of the human cerebral cortex. *American Psychologist, 66,* 624–632.

Botvinick, M. M., Cohen, J. D., & Carter, C. S. (2004). Conflict monitoring and anterior cingulate cortex: An update. *Trends in Cognitive Sciences, 8,* 539–546.

Bouchard, T. J., Jr., Lykken, D. T., McGue, M., Segal, N. L., & Tellegen, A. (1990). Sources of human psychological differences: The Minnesota study of twins reared apart. *Science, 250,* 223–250.

Bouchard, T. J., Jr., & McGue, M. (1981). Familial studies of intelligence: A review. *Science, 212,* 1055–1059.

Bourke, P. A., & Duncan, J. (2005). Effect of template complexity on visual search and dual-task performance. *Psychological Science, 16,* 208–213.

Bowden, E., Jung-Beeman, M., Fleck, J., & Kounios, J. (2005). New approaches to demystifying insight. *Trends in Cognitive Sciences, 9,* 322–328.

Bower, G. H. (1970). Analysis of a mnemonic device. *American Scientist, 58,* 496–510.

Bower, G. H. (1972). Mental imagery and associative learning. In L. W. Gregg (Ed.), *Cognition in learning and memory* (pp. 51–88). New York, NY: Wiley.

Bower, G. H., Karlin, M. B., & Dueck, A. (1975). Comprehension and memory for pictures. *Memory & Cognition, 3,* 216–220.

Bower, G. H., & Reitman, J. S. (1972). Mnemonic elaboration in multilist learning. *Journal of Verbal Learning and Verbal Behavior, 11,* 478–485.

Bower, G. H., & Winzenz, D. (1970). Comparison of associative learning strategies. *Psychonomic Science, 20,* 119–120.

Bower, J. M., & Parsons, L. M. (2003). Rethinking the "lesser brain." *Scientific American, 289*(August), 50–57.

Bowers, J. (2009). On the biological plausibility of grandmother cells: Implications for neural network theories in psychology and neuroscience. *Psychological Review, 116,* 220–251.

Brackett, M. A., & Mayer, J. D. (2003). Convergent, discriminant, and incremental validity of competing measures of emotional intelligence. *Personality and Social Psychology Bulletin, 29,* 1147–1158.

Brackett, M. A., Rivers, S. E., Shiffman, S., Lerner, N., & Salovey, P. (2006). Relating emotional abilities to social functioning: A comparison of self-report and performance measures of emotional intelligence. *Journal of Personality and Social Psychology, 91,* 780–795.

Bransford, J. (1979). *Human cognition: Learning, understanding and remembering.* Belmont, CA: Wadsworth.

Bransford, J., & Franks, J. J. (1971). The abstraction of linguistic ideas. *Cognitive Psychology, 2,* 331–350.

Bransford, J., & Johnson, M. K. (1972). Contextual prerequisites for understanding: Some investigations of comprehension and recall. *Journal of Verbal Learning and Verbal Behavior, 11,* 717–726.

Brase, G. (2008). Frequency interpretation of ambiguous statistical information facilitates Bayesian reasoning. *Psychonomic Bulletin & Review, 15,* 284–289.

Brewer, J., Zhao, Z., Desmond, J., Glover, G., & Gabrieli, J. (1998). Making memories: Brain activity that predicts how well visual experience will be remembered. *Science, 281,* 1185–1187.

Brewer, N., & Wells, G. L. (2006). The confidence-accuracy relationship in eyewitness identification: Effects of lineup instructions, foil similarity, and target-absent base rates. *Journal of Experimental Psychology: Applied, 12,* 11–30.

Brewer, W., & Treyens, J. C. (1981). Role of schemata in memory for places. *Cognitive Psychology, 13,* 207–230.

Bridgeman, B., & Lewis, C. (1996). Gender differences in college mathematics grades and SAT-M scores: A reanalysis of Wainer & Steinberg. *Journal of Educational Measurement, 33,* 257–270.

Brigham, J., & Cairns, D. L. (1988). The effect of mugshot inspections on eyewitness identification accuracy. *Journal of Applied Social Psychology, 18,* 1394–1410.

Brigham, J., & Wolfskiel, M. P. (1983). Opinions of attorneys and law enforcement personnel on the accuracy of eyewitness identification. *Law and Human Behavior, 7,* 337–349.

Broadbent, D. E. (1958). *Perception and communication.* London, England: Pergamon.

Brooks, L., Norman, G., & Allen, S. (1991). Role of specific similarity in a medical diagnostic task. *Journal of Experimental Psychology: General, 120,* 278–287.

Brown, A. L. (1979). Theories of memory and the problems of development: Activity, growth, and knowledge. In L. S. Cermak & F. I. M. Craik (Eds.), *Levels of processing in human memory* (pp. 225–258). Hillsdale, NJ: Erlbaum.

Brown, A. S. (1991). A review of the tip-of-the-tongue experience. *Psychological Bulletin, 109,* 204–223.

Brown, A. S. (2002). Consolidation theory and retrograde amnesia in humans. *Psychonomic Bulletin & Review, 9,* 403–425.

Brown, A. S., & Halliday, H. E. (1990, November). *Multiple-choice tests: Pondering incorrect alternatives can be hazardous to your knowledge.* Paper presented at the meeting of the Psychonomic Society, New Orleans, LA.

Brown, A. S., & Marsh, E. (2008). Evoking false beliefs about autobiographical experience. *Psychonomic Bulletin & Review, 15,* 186–190.

Brown, E., Deffenbacher, K., & Sturgill, W. (1977). Memory for faces and the circumstances of encounter. *Journal of Applied Psychology, 62,* 311–318.

Brown, J., Reynolds, J. & Braver, T. (2007). A computational model of fractionated conflict-control mechanisms in task-switching. *Cognitive Psychology, 55,* 37–85.

Brown, R., & Kulik, J. (1977). Flashbulb memories. *Cognition, 5,* 73–99.

Brown, R., & McNeill, D. (1966). The "tip of the tongue" phenomenon. *Journal of Verbal Learning and Verbal Behavior, 5,* 325–337.

Brown, R. P., & Josephs, R. A. (1999). A burden of proof: Stereotype relevance and gender differences in math performance. *Journal of Personality and Social Psychology, 76,* 246–257.

Bruck, M., & Ceci, S. J. (1999). The suggestibility of children's memory. *Annual Review of Psychology, 50,* 419–440.

Bruck, M., & Ceci, S. J. (2009). Developmental science in the courtroom. In S. Lilienfeld and J. Skeem (Eds.), *Psychological science in the courtroom: Controversies and consensus.* New York, NY: Guilford.

Bruner, J. S. (1973). *Beyond the information given.* New York, NY: Norton.

Buchanan, T. W. (2007). Retrieval of emotional memories. *Psychological Bulletin, 133,* 761–779.

Buchanan, T. W., & Adolphs, R. (2004). The neuroanatomy of emotional memory in humans. In D. Reisberg & P. Hertel (Eds.), *Memory and emotion* (pp. 42–75). New York, NY: Oxford University Press.

Bukach, C., Gauthier, I., & Tarr, M. J. (2006). Beyond faces and modularity: The power of an expertise framework. *Trends in Cognitive Sciences, 10,* 159–166.

Bundesen, C., Kyllingsbaek, S., & Larsen, A. (2003). Independent encoding of colors and shapes from two stimuli. *Psychonomic Bulletin & Review, 10,* 474–479.

Burgess, G. C., Braver, T. S., Conway, A. R. A., & Gray, J. R. (2011). Neural mechanisms of interference control underlie the relationship between fluid intelligence and working memory span. *Journal of Experimental Psychology: General, 140,* 674–692.

Burton, A. M., Young, A., Bruce, V., Johnston, R., & Ellis, A. (1991). Understanding covert recognition. *Cognition, 39,* 129–166.

Buschman, T. J., & Miller, E. K. (2007). Top-down and bottom-up control of attention in the prefrontal and posterior parietal cortices. *Science, 315,* 1860.

Busey, T. A., Tunnicliff, J., Loftus, G. R., & Loftus, E. F. (2000). Accounts of the confidence-accuracy relation in recognition memory. *Memory & Cognition, 7,* 26–48.

Butler, K., Arrington, C., & Weywadt, C. (2011). Working memory capacity modulates task performance but has little influence on task choice. *Memory & Cognition, 39,* 708–724.

Buzsáki, G., & Draguhn, A. (2004). Neuronal oscillations in cortical networks. *Science, 304,* 1926–1929.

Cabeza, R., Ciaramelli, E., Olson, I. R., & Moscovitch, M. (2008). The parietal cortex and episodic memory: An attentional account. *Nature Reviews Neuroscience, 9*(8), 613–625.

Cabeza, R., & Nyberg, L. (2000). Imaging cognition II: An empirical review of 275 PET and fMRI studies. *Journal of Cognitive Neuroscience, 12,* 1–47.

Cabeza, R., & St. Jacques, P. (2007). Functional neuroimaging of autobiographical memory. *Trends in Cognitive Sciences, 11,* 219–227.

Campitelli, G., & Gobet, F. (2011). Deliberate practice: Necessary but not sufficient. *Current Directions in Psychological Science. 20,* 280–285.

Cann, D. R., & Katz, A. N. (2005). Habitual acceptance of misinformation: Examination of individual differences and source attributions. *Memory & Cognition, 33,* 405–417.

Capgras, J., & Reboul-Lachaux, J. (1923). L'illusion des "sosies" dans un delire systematise chronique. *Bulletine de Societe Clinique de Medicine Mentale, 11,* 6–16.

Caramazza, A., & Shelton, J. (1998). Domain-specific knowledge systems in the brain: The animate-inanimate distinction. *Journal of Cognitive Neuroscience, 10,* 1–34.

Carmichael, L. C., Hogan, H. P., & Walters, A. A. (1932). An experimental study of the effect of language on the reproduction of visually perceived form. *Journal of Experimental Psychology, 15,* 73–86.

Carpenter, P., & Eisenberg, P. (1978). Mental rotation and the frame of reference in blind and sighted individuals. *Perception & Psychophysics, 23,* 117–124.

Carpenter, S., Pashler, H., & Cepeda, N. (2009). Using tests to enhance 8th grade students' retention of U.S. history facts. *Applied Cognitive Psychology, 23,* 760–771.

Carrasco, M., Ling, S., & Read, S. (2004). Attention alters appearance. *Nature Neuroscience, 7,* 308–313.

Carrasco, M., Penpeci-Talgar, C., & Eckstein, M. (2000). Spatial covert attention increases contrast sensitivity across the CSF: Support for signal enhancement. *Vision Research, 40,* 1203–1215.

Carroll, J. B. (1993). *Human cognitive abilities: A survey of factor-analytic studies.* New York: Cambridge University Press.

Carroll, J. B. (2005). The three-stratum theory of cognitive abilities. In D. P. Flanagan & P. L. Harrison (Eds.), *Contemporary intellectual assessment: Theories, tests, and issues* (2nd ed., pp. 69–76). New York: Guilford.

Carson, S., Peterson, J. B., & Higgins, D. M. (2005). Reliability, validity, and factor structure of the Creative Achievement Questionnaire. *Creativity Research Journal, 17,* 37–50

Catrambone, R. (1998). The subgoal learning model: Creating better examples so that students can solve novel problems. *Journal of Experimental Psychology: General, 127,* 355–376.

Catrambone, R., Craig, D., & Nersessian, N. (2006). The role of perceptually represented structure in analogical problem solving. *Memory & Cognition, 34,* 1126–1132.

Cattell, J. M. (1885). Über die Zeit der Erkennung and Benennung von Schriftzeichen, Bildern and Farben. *Philosophische Studien, 2,* 635–650.

Cave, K. R. (2012). Spatial attention. In D. Reisberg (Ed.), *The Oxford handbook of cognitive psychology.* New York, NY: Oxford University Press.

Cavalli-Sforza, L., Menozzi, P., & Piazza, A. (1994). *The history and geography of human genes.* Princeton, NJ: Princeton University Press.

Ceci, S., & Bruck, M. (1995). *Jeopardy in the courtroom: A scientific analysis of children's testimony.* Washington, DC: American Psychological Association.

Ceci, S. J., & Williams, W. M. (1997). Schooling, intelligence, and income. *American Psychologist, 52,* 1051–1058.

Ceci, S., & Williams, W. (2010). Sex differences in math-intensive fields. *Current Directions in Psychological Science, 19,* 275–279.

Chabris, C., & Simons, D. (2010). *The invisible gorilla: How our intuitions deceive us.* New York, NY: Crown Archetype.

Chalmers, D. (1996). *The conscious mind.* New York, NY: Oxford University Press.

Chalmers, D. (1998). What is a neural correlate of consciousness? In T. Metzinger (Ed.), *Neural correlates of consciousness: Empirical and conceptual issues* (pp. 17–39). Cambridge, MA: MIT Press.

Chambers, D., & Reisberg, D. (1985). Can mental images be ambiguous? *Journal of Experimental Psychology: Human Perception and Performance, 11,* 317–328.

Chan, J., Thomas, A., & Bulevich, J. (2009). Recalling a witnessed event increases eyewitness suggestibility: The reversed testing effect. *Psychological Science, 20,* 66–73.

Chao, L., Weisberg, J., & Martin, A. (2002). Experience-dependent modulation of category related cortical activity. *Cerebral Cortex, 12,* 545–551.

Chapman, J., & Chapman, L. J. (1959). Atmosphere effect re-examined. *Journal of Experimental Psychology, 58,* 220–226.

Chapman, L. J., & Chapman, J. (1971). Test results are what you think they are. *Psychology Today, 5,* 106–110.

Charniak, E. (1972). *Toward a model of children's story comprehension.* Unpublished doctoral dissertation, Massachusetts Institute of Technology, Cambridge, MA.

Chase, W., & Ericsson, K. A. (1982). Skill and working memory. In G. H. Bower (Ed.), *The psychology of learning and motivation* (pp. 1–58). New York, NY: Academic Press.

Chase, W., & Simon, H. (1973). Perception in chess. *Cognitive Psychology, 4,* 55–81.

Chen, J.-Y. (2007). Do Chinese and English speakers think about time differently? Failure of replicating Boroditsky (2001). *Cognition, 104,* 427–436.

Chen, Z., & Cave, K. R. (2006). Reinstating object-based attention under positional certainty: The importance of subjective parsing. *Perception and Psychophysics, 68,* 992–1003.

Cheng, P., & Holyoak, K. J. (1985). Pragmatic reasoning schemas. *Cognitive Psychology, 17,* 391–416.

Cheng, P., Holyoak, K. J., Nisbett, R. E., & Oliver, L. M. (1986). Pragmatic versus syntactic approaches to training deductive reasoning. *Cognitive Psychology, 18,* 293–328.

Cherrier, M. M., Asthana, S., Plymate, S., Baker, L., Matsumoto, A. M., Peskind, E., et al. (2001). Testosterone supplementation improves spatial and verbal memory in healthy older men. *Neurology, 57,* 80–88.

Cherry, E. C. (1953). Some experiments on the recognition of speech with one and with two ears. *Journal of the Acoustical Society of America, 25,* 975–979.

Cheryan, S., & Bodenhausen, G. V. (2000). When positive stereotypes threaten intellectual performance: The psychological hazards of "model minority" status. *Psychological Science, 11,* 399–402.

Chi, M. (1976). Short-term memory limitations in children: Capacity or processing deficits? *Memory & Cognition, 4,* 559–572.

Chi, M., Feltovich, P., & Glaser, R. (1981). Categorization and representation of physics problems by experts and novices. *Cognitive Science, 5,* 121–152.

Chincotta, D., & Underwood, G. (1997). Digit span and articulatory suppression: A cross-linguistic comparison. *European Journal of Cognitive Psychology, 9,* 89–96.

Chomsky, N. (1957). *Syntactic structures.* The Hague, Netherlands: Mouton.

Chomsky, N. (1965). *Aspects of a theory of syntax.* Cambridge, MA: MIT Press.

Chomsky, N. (1975). *Reflections on language.* London, England: Temple-Smith.

Chomsky, N. (1986). *Knowledge of language: Its nature, origin and use.* New York, NY: Praeger.

Chomsky, N., & Halle, M. (1968). *The sound pattern of English*. New York, NY: Harper & Row.

Christen, F., & Bjork, R. A. (1976). *On updating the loci in the method of loci*. Paper presented at the meeting of the Psychonomic Society, St. Louis, MO.

Christensen, B. T., & Schunn, C. D. (2005). Spontaneous access and analogical incubation effects. *Creativity Research Journal, 17*, 207–220.

Christensen, B. T., & Schunn, C. (2007). The role of analogical distance to analogical function and pre-inventive structure: The case of engineering design. *Memory & Cognition, 35*, 29–38.

Christiaansen, R., Sweeney, J., & Ochalek, K. (1983). Influencing eyewitness descriptions. *Law and Human Behavior, 7*, 59–65.

Chroback, Q. M., & Zaragoza, M. S. (2008). Inventing stories: Forcing witnesses to fabricate entire fictitious events leads to freely reported false memories. *Psychonomics Bulletin and Review, 15*, 1190–1195.

Chronicle, E. P., MacGregor, J. N., & Ormerod, T. C. (2004). What makes an insight problem? The roles of heuristics, goal conception, and solution recoding in knowledge-lean problems. *Journal of Experimental Psychology: Learning, Memory, & Cognition, 30*, 14–27.

Chun, W. Y., & Kruglanski, A. W. (2006). The role of task demands and processing resources in the use of base-rate and individuating information. *Journal of Personality and Social Psychology, 91*, 205–217.

Claparède, E. (1951). Reconnaissance et moiité. In D. Rapaport (Ed.), *Organization and pathology of thought* (pp. 58–75). New York, NY: Columbia University Press. (Original work published in 1911.)

Coates, S. L., Butler, L. T., & Berry, D. C. (2006). Implicit memory and consumer choice: The mediating role of brand familiarity. *Applied Cognitive Psychology 20*(8), 1101–1116.

Cohen, G. L., Garcia, J., Apfel, N., & Master, A. (2006). Reducing the racial achievement gap: A social-psychological intervention. *Science, 313*, 1307–1310.

Cohen, G. L., Garcia, J., Purdie-Vaughns, V., Apfel, N., & Brzustoski, P. (2009). Recursive processes in self-affirmation: Intervening to close the minority achievement gap. *Science, 324*, 400–403.

Cohen, M., & Dennett, D. (2011). Consciousness cannot be separated from function. *Trends in Cognitive Sciences, 15*, 358–364.

Cohen, M. A., Alvarez, G. A., & Nakayama, K. (2011). Natural-scene perception requires attention. *Psychological Science, 22*, 1165–1172.

Cohen, N. J., & Squire, L. R. (1980). Preserved learning and retention of pattern analyzing skill in amnesics: Dissociation of knowing how and knowing that. *Science, 210*, 207–210.

Coley, J. D., Medin, D. L., & Atran, S. (1997). Does rank have its privilege? Inductive inferences within folkbiological taxonomies. *Cognition, 64*, 73–112.

Collins, A. M., & Loftus, E. F. (1975). A spreading activation theory of semantic processing. *Psychological Review, 82*, 407–428.

Collins, A. M., & Quillian, M. R. (1969). Retrieval time from semantic memory. *Journal of Verbal Learning and Verbal Behavior, 8*, 240–247.

Colom, R., Haier, R. J., Head, K., Alvarez-Linera, J., Quiroga, M. A., Shih, P. C., et al. (2009). Gray matter correlates of fluid, crystallized, and spatial intelligence: Testing the P-FIT model. *Intelligence, 37*, 124–135.

Combs, B., & Slovic, P. (1979). Causes of death: Biased newspaper coverage and biased judgments. *Journalism Quarterly, 56*, 837–843, 849.

Comrie, B. (1981). *Language universals and linguistic typology*. Chicago, IL: University of Chicago Press.

Connolly, T., & Zeelenberg, M. (2002). Regret in decision making. *Current Directions in Psychological Science, 11*, 212–216.

Conrad, C. (1972). Cognitive economy in semantic memory. *Journal of Experimental Psychology, 92*, 149–154.

Conway, A. R. A., Kane, M. J., Bunting, M., Hambrick, D., Wilhelm, O., and Engle, R. (2005). Working memory span tasks: A methodological review and user's guide. *Psychonomic Bulletin & Review, 12*, 769–786.

Conway, A. R. A., Kane, M. J., & Engle, R. W. (2003). Working memory capacity and its relation to general intelligence. *Trends in Cognitive Sciences, 7*, 547–552.

Conway, M., Anderson, S., Larsen, S., Donnelly, C., McDaniel, M., McClelland, A. G. R., et al. (1994). The formation of flashbulb memories. *Memory & Cognition, 22*, 326–343.

Conway, M., Cohen, G., & Stanhope, N. (1991). On the very long-term retention of knowledge acquired through formal education: Twelve years of cognitive psychology. *Journal of Experimental Psychology: General, 120*, 395–409.

Conway, M., Cohen, G., & Stanhope, N. (1992). Why is it that university grades do not predict very long term retention? *Journal of Experimental Psychology: General, 121*, 382–384.

Conway, M., Collins, A. F., Gathercole, S., & Anderson, S. J. (1996). Recollections of true and false autobiographical memories. *Journal of Experimental Psychology: General, 125*, 69–98.

Conway, M., & Fthenaki, K. (1999). Disruption and loss of autobiographical memory. In L. S. Cermak (Ed.), *Handbook of neuropsychology: Memory*. Amsterdam: Elsevier.

Conway, M., & Haque, S. (1999). Overshadowing the reminiscence bump: Memories of a struggle for independence. *Journal of Adult Development, 6*, 35–43.

Conway, M., & Holmes, A. (2004). Psychosocial stages and the accessibility of autobiographical memories across the life cycle. *Journal of Personality, 72*, 461–480.

Conway, M., & Pleydell-Pearce, C. W. (2000). The construction of autobiographical memories in the self-memory system. *Psychological Review, 107*, 261–288.

Conway, M., & Ross, M. (1984). Getting what you want by revising what you had. *Journal of Personality and Social Psychology, 39,* 406–415.

Cook, V. J. (1988). *Chomsky's universal grammar: An introduction.* Cambridge, MA: Basil Blackwell.

Cooney, J. W., & Gazzaniga, M. S. (2003). Neurological disorders and the structure of human consciousness. *Trends in Cognitive Sciences, 7,* 161–165.

Cooper, L., & Shepard, R. N. (1973). Chronometric studies of the rotation of mental images. In W. G. Chase (Ed.), *Visual information processing* (pp. 75–176). New York, NY: Academic Press.

Corbetta, M., & Shulman, G. L. (2002). Control of goal-directed and stimulus-driven attention in the brain. *Nature Reviews Neuroscience, 3*(3), 201–215.

Coricelli, G., Dolan, R., & Sirigu, A. (2007). Brain, emotion and decision making: The paradigmatic example of regret. *Trends in Cognitive Sciences, 11,* 258–265.

Corter, J., & Gluck, M. (1992). Explaining basic categories: Feature predictability and information. *Psychological Bulletin, 111,* 291–303.

Cosmides, L. (1989). The logic of social exchange: Has natural selection shaped how humans reason? Studies with the Wason selection task. *Cognition, 31,* 187–276.

Cosmides, L., & Tooby, J. (1996). Are humans good intuitive statisticians after all? Rethinking some conclusions from the literature on judgment. *Cognition, 58,* 1–73.

Courtney, S. M., Petit, L., Maisog, J. M., Ungerleider, L. G., & Haxby, J. V. (1998). An area specialized for spatial working memory in human frontal cortex. *Science, 279,* 1347–1351.

Cowan, N. (2010). The magical mystery four: How is working memory capacity limited, and why? *Current Directions in Psychological Science, 19,* 51–57.

Cowan, R., & Carney, D. (2006). Calendrical savants: Exceptionality and practice. *Cognition, 100,* B1–B9.

Coyle, T., Pillow, D., Snyder, A., & Kochunov, P. (2011). Processing speed mediates the development of general intelligence (g) in adolescence. *Psychological Science, 22,* 1265–1269.

Craik, F. I. M., & Lockhart, R. S. (1972). Levels of processing: A framework for memory research. *Journal of Verbal Learning and Verbal Behavior, 11,* 671–684.

Craik, F. I. M., & Tulving, E. (1975). Depth of processing and the retention of words in episodic memory. *Journal of Experimental Psychology: General, 104,* 269–294.

Craik, F. I. M., & Watkins, M. J. (1973). The role of rehearsal in short-term memory. *Journal of Verbal Learning and Verbal Behavior, 12,* 599–607.

Crawford, M., & Chaffin, R. (1997). The meanings of difference: Cognition in social and cultural context. In P. J. Caplan, M. Crawford, J. S. Hyde, & J. T. E. Richardson (Eds.), *Gender differences in human cognition* (pp. 81–130). New York: Oxford University Press.

Crick, F., & Koch, C. (1995). Are we aware of neural activity in primary visual cortex? *Nature, 375,* 121–123.

Crick, F., & Koch, C. (2003). A framework for consciousness. *Nature Neuroscience, 6,* 119–126.

Crombag, H. F. M., Wagenaar, W. A., & van Koppen, P. J. (1996). Crashing memories and the problem of "source monitoring." *Applied Cognitive Psychology, 10,* 95–104.

Crystal, D. (1987). *The Cambridge encyclopedia of language.* Cambridge, England: Cambridge University Press.

Csibra, G., Davis, G., Spratling, M. W., & Johnson, M. H. (2000). Gamma oscillations and object processing in the infant brain. *Science, 290,* 1582–1585.

Cui, X., Jeter, C., Yang, D., Montague, P. R., & Eagleman, D. M. (2006). Vividness of mental imagery: Individual variability can be measured objectively. *Vision Research, 47,* 474–478.

Cummins, D. (1992). Role of analogical reasoning in induction of problem categories. *Journal of Experimental Psychology: Learning, Memory and Cognition, 18,* 1103–1124.

Cummins, D. (2004). The evolution of reasoning. In J. P. Leighton & R. J. Sternberg (Eds.), *The nature of reasoning* (pp. 339–374). New York, NY: Cambridge University Press.

Cummins, D., & Allen, C. (Eds.). (1998). *The evolution of mind.* New York, NY: Oxford University Press.

Custers, R., & Aarts, H. (2010). The unconscious will: How the pursuit of goals operates outside of conscious awareness. *Science, 329,* 47–50.

Cutler, B. L., Penrod, S. D., & Dexter, H. R. (1990). Juror sensitivity to eyewitness identification evidence. *Law and Human Behavior, 14,* 185–191.

Daley, T. C., Whaley, S. E., Sigman, M. D., Espinosa, M. P., & Neumann, C. (2003). IQ on the rise: The Flynn effect in rural Kenyan children. *Psychological Science, 14,* 215–219.

Damasio, A. R. (1985). Disorders of complex visual processing. In M.-M. Mesulam (Ed.), *Principles of Behavioral Neurology.* Philadelphia, PA: Davis.

Damasio, A. R. (1994). *Descartes' error: Emotion, reason, and the human brain.* New York, NY: Putnam.

Damasio, A. R. (1999). *The feeling of what happens: Body and emotion in the making of consciousness* (1st ed.). New York, NY: Harcourt Brace.

Damasio, A. R., Damasio, H., & Van Hoesen, G. W. (1982). Prosopagnosia: Anatomic basis and behavioral mechanisms. *Neurology, 32,* 331–341.

Damasio, A. R., Tranel, D., & Damasio, H. (1989). Disorders of visual recognition. In H. Goodglass & A. R. Damasio (Eds.), *Handbook of neuropsychology,* Vol. 2 (pp. 317–332). New York, NY: Elsevier.

Damasio, A. R., Tranel, D., & Damasio, H. (1990). Face agnosia and the neural substrates of memory. *Annual Review of Neuroscience, 13,* 89–109.

Damasio, H., Grabowski, T., Tranel, D., Hichwa, R. D., & Damasio, A. R. (1996). A neural basis for lexical retrieval. *Nature, 380,* 499–505.

Daneman, M., & Carpenter, P. (1980). Individual differences in working memory and reading. *Journal of Verbal Learning and Verbal Behavior, 19*, 450–466.

Daneman, M., & Hannon, B. (2001). Using working memory theory to investigate the construct validity of multiple-choice reading comprehension tests such as the SAT. *Journal of Experimental Psychology: General, 130*, 208–223.

Daniloff, R., & Hammarberg, R. (1973). On defining coarticulation. *Journal of Phonetics, 1*, 185–194.

Danthiir, V., Roberts, R. D., Schulze, R., & Wilhelm, O. (2005). Mental speed: On frameworks, paradigms, and a platform for the future. In O. Wilhelm & R. W. Engle (Eds.), *Handbook of understanding and measuring intelligence* (pp. 27–46). Thousand Oaks, CA: Sage.

Dar-Nimrod, I., & Heine, S. (2006). Exposure to scientific theories affects women's math performance. *Science, 314*, 435.

Davachi, L., & Dobbins, I. (2008). Declarative memory. *Current Directions in Psychological Science, 17*, 112–118.

Davachi, L., Mitchell, J., & Wagner, A. (2003). Multiple routes to memory: Distinct medial temporal lobe processes build item and source memories. *Proceedings of the National Academy of Science, 100*, 2157–2162.

Davis, D., Loftus, E., Vanous, S., & Cucciare, M. (2008). "Unconscious transference" can be an instance of "change blindness." *Applied Cognitive Psychology, 22*, 605–623.

Davis, O. S. P., Haworth, C. M. A., & Plomin, R. (2009). Dramatic increase in heritability of cognitive development from early to middle childhood: An 8-year longitudinal study of 8,700 pairs of twins. *Psychological Science, 20*, 1301–1308.

Dawes, R. M. (1988). *Rational choice in an uncertain world*. San Diego, CA: Harcourt Brace Jovanovich.

De Gelder, B. (2010, May). Uncanny sight in the blind. *Scientific American*, 60–64.

De Groot, A. (1965). *Thought and choice in chess*. The Hague, Netherlands: Mouton.

De Groot, A. (1966). Perception and memory versus thought: Some old ideas and recent findings. In B. Kleinmuntz (Ed.), *Problem solving* (pp. 19–50). New York, NY: Wiley.

de Haan, E., & Cowey, A. (2011). On the usefulness of "what" and "where" pathways in vision. *Trends in Cognitive Sciences, 15*, 460–466.

De Neys, W. (2006). Dual processing in reasoning: Two systems but one reasoner. *Psychological Science, 17*, 428–433.

De Neys, W., Vartanian, O., & Goel, V. (2008). Smarter than we think: When our brains detect that we are biased. *Psychological Science, 19*, 483–489.

De Renzi, E., Faglioni, P., Grossi, D., & Nichelli, P. (1991). Apperceptive and associative forms of prosopagnosia. *Cortex, 27*, 213–221.

Deary, I. J. (2001a). Human intelligence differences: A recent history. *Trends in Cognitive Science, 5*, 127–130.

Deary, I. J. (2001b). Human intelligence differences: Toward a combined experimental-differential approach. *Trends in Cognitive Science, 5*, 164–170.

Deary, I. J. (2012). Intelligence. *Annual Review of Psychology, 63*, 453–482.

Deary, I. J., & Derr, G. (2005). Reaction time explains IQ's association with death. *Psychological Science, 16*, 64–69.

Deary, I. J., Weiss, A., & Batty, G. D. (2010). Intelligence and personality as predictors of illness and death: How researchers in differential psychology and chronic disease epidemiology are collaborating to understand and address health inequalities. *Psychological Science in the Public Interest, 11*, 53–79.

Deary, I. J., Whiteman, M. C., Starr, J. M., Whalley, L. J. & Fox, H. C. (2004). The impact of childhood intelligence on later life: Following up the Scottish Mental Surveys of 1932 and 1947. *Journal of Personality and Social Psychology, 86*, 130–147.

Deese, J. (1957). Serial organization in the recall of disconnected items. *Psychological Reports, 3*, 577–582.

Deese, J., & Kaufman, R. A. (1957). Serial effects in recall of unorganized and sequentially organized verbal material. *Journal of Experimental Psychology, 54*, 180–187.

DeHaan, R. L. (2011). Teaching creative science thinking. *Science, 334*, 1499–1500.

Dehaene, S., Artiges, E., Naccache, L., Martelli, C., Viard, A., Schurhoff, F., et al. (2003). Conscious and subliminal conflicts in normal subjects and patients with schizophrenia: The role of the anterior cingulate. *Proceedings of the National Academy of Sciences, USA, 100*, 13722–13727.

Dehaene, S., & Changeux, J. (2004). Neural mechanisms for access consciousness. In M. Gazzaniga (Ed.), *The cognitive neurosciences III*. Cambridge, MA: MIT Press.

Dehaene S., & Changeux, J. (2011). Experimental and theoretical approaches to conscious processing. *Neuron, 70*, 200–227.

Dehaene, S., & Naccache, L. (2001). Toward a cognitive neuroscience of consciousness: Basic evidence and a workspace framework. *Cognition, 79*, 1–37.

Dehaene, S., Sergent, C., & Changeux, J. (2003). A neuronal network model linking subjective reports and objective physiological data during conscious perception. *Proceedings of the National Academy of Science, USA, 100*, 8520–8525.

Demonet, J. F., Wise, R. A., & Frackowiak, R. S. J. (1993). Language functions explored in normal subjects by positron emission tomography: A critical review. *Human Brain Mapping, 1*, 39–47.

Dempster, F. N. (1981). Memory span: Sources of individual and developmental differences. *Psychological Bulletin, 89*, 63–100.

Dennett, D. (1992). *Consciousness explained*. Boston, MA: Little, Brown.

Dennett, D. (2001). Are we explaining consciousness yet? *Cognition, 79,* 221–237.

Diamond, A., & Lee, K. (2011). Interventions shown to aid executive function development in children from 4 to 12 years old. *Science, 333,* 959–964.

Diamond, R., & Carey, S. (1986). Why faces are and are not special: An effect of expertise. *Journal of Experimental Psychology: General, 115,* 107–117.

Diana, R., Yonelinas, A., & Ranganath, C. (2007). Imaging recollection and familiarity in the medial temporal lobe: A three-component model. *Trends in Cognitive Sciences, 11,* 379–386.

Dickens, W. T., & Flynn, J. R. (2001). Heritability estimates versus large environmental effects: The IQ paradox resolved. *Psychological Review, 108(2),* 346–369.

Dickens, W. T., & Flynn, J. R. (2006a). Black Americans reduce the racial IQ gap: Evidence from standardization samples. *Psychological Science, 17,* 913–920.

Dickens, W. T., & Flynn, J. R. (2006b). Common ground and differences. *Psychological Science, 17,* 923–924.

Dickson, R., Pillemer, D., & Bruehl, E. (2011). The reminiscence bump for salient personal memories: Is a cultural life script required? *Memory & Cognition, 39,* 977–991.

Dobbins, I. G., Foley, H., Wagner, A. D., & Schacter, D. L. (2002). Executive control during episodic retrieval: Multiple prefrontal processes subserve source memory. *Neuron, 35,* 989–996.

Dodds, R., Ward, T., & Smith, S. (2007). A review of the experimental literature on incubation in problem solving and creativity. In M. Runco (Ed.), *Creative research handbook,* 3rd ed. Cresskill, NJ: Hampton.

Donnelly, C. M., & McDaniel, M. A. (1993). Use of analogy in learning scientific concepts. *Journal of Experimental Psychology: Learning, Memory and Cognition, 19,* 975–986.

Donnelly, C. M., & McDaniel, M. A. (2000). Analogy with knowledgeable learners: When analogy confers benefits and exacts costs. *Psychonomic Bulletin & Review, 7,* 537–543.

Douglas, A., Neuschatz, J., Imrich, J., & Wilkinson, M. (2010). Does post identification feedback affect evaluations of eyewitness testimony and identification procedures? *Law & Human Behavior, 34,* 282–294.

Douglass, A. B., & Steblay, N. (2006). Memory distortion in eyewitnesses: A meta-analysis of the post-identification feedback effect. *Applied Cognitive Psychology, 20,* 859–870.

Downs, J., & Shafir, E. (1999). Why some are perceived as more confident and more insecure, more reckless and more cautious, more trusting and more suspicious, than others: Enriched and impoverished options in social judgment. *Psychonomic Bulletin & Review, 6,* 598–610.

Drews, F. A., Pasupathi, M., & Strayer, D. L. (2008). Passenger and cell phone conversations in simulated driv-

ing. *Journal of Experimental Psychology: Applied, 14,* 392–400.

Dronkers, N., Wilkins, D., Van Valin, R., Redefern, B., and Jaeger, J. (2004). Lesion analysis of the brain areas involved in language comprehension. *Cognition, 92,* 145–177.

Dudai, Y. (2004). The neurobiology of consolidations, or, how stable is the engram. *Annual Review of Psychology, 55,* 51–86.

Duncan, G. J., Yeung, W. J., Brooks-Gunn, J., & Smith, J. R. (1998). How much does childhood poverty affect the life chances of children? *American Sociological Review, 63,* 406–423.

Duncan, J. (1994). Attention, intelligence, and the frontal lobes. In M. Gazzaniga (Ed.), *The cognitive neurosciences.* Cambridge, MA: MIT Press.

Duncan, J., Parr, A., Woolgar, A., Thompson, R., Bright, P., Cox, S., Bishop, S. & Nimmo-Smith, I. (2008) Goal neglect and Spearman's g: Competing parts of a complex task. *Journal of Experimental Psychology: General, 137,* 131–148.

Duncker, K. (1945). *On problem-solving* (Psychological Monographs: General and Applied, Vol. 58, No. 5 [whole no. 270]). Washington, DC: American Psychological Association.

Dunn, B., Galton, H., Morgan, R., Evans, D., Oliver, C., Meyer, M., et al. (2010). Listening to your heart: How interoception shapes emotion experience and intuitive decision making. *Psychological Science, 21,* 1835–1844.

Dunning, D., & Parpal, M. (1989). Mental addition versus subtraction in counterfactual reasoning. *Journal of Personality and Social Psychology, 57,* 5–15.

Dunning, D., & Perretta, S. (2002). Automaticity and eyewitness accuracy: A 10- to 12-second rule for distinguishing accurate from inaccurate positive identifications. *Journal of Applied Psychology, 87,* 951–962.

Durgin, F. H. (2000). The reverse Stroop effect. *Psychonomic Bulletin & Review, 7,* 121–125.

Duyme, M., Dumaret, A. C., & Tomkiewicz, S. (1999). How can we boost IQs of "dull children"? A late adoption study. *Proceedings of the National Academy of Sciences, 96,* 8790–8794.

Easterbrook, J. A. (1959). The effect of emotion on cue utilization and the organization of behavior. *Psychological Review, 66,* 183–201.

Eberhard, K. M., Spivey-Knowlton, M. J., Sedivy, J. C., & Tanenhaus, M. K. (1995). Eye movements as a window into real-time spoken language comprehension in natural contexts. *Journal of Psycholinguistic Research, 24,* 409–436.

Eddy, D. M. (1982). Probabilistic reasoning in clinical medicine: Problems and opportunities. In D. Kahneman, P. Slovic, & A. Tversky (Eds.), *Judgment under uncertainty: Heuristics and biases* (pp. 249–267). Cambridge, England: Cambridge University Press.

Edelson, M., Sharon, T., Dolan, R., & Dudai, Y. (2011). Following the crowd: Brain substrates of long-term memory conformity. *Science, 333*, 108–111.

Edelstyn, N. M. J., & Oyebode, F. (1999). A review of the phenomenology and cognitive neuropsychological origins of the Capgras Syndrome. *International Journal of Geriatric Psychiatry, 14*, 48–59.

Egan, D., & Schwartz, B. (1979). Chunking in the recall of symbolic drawings. *Memory & Cognition, 7*, 149–158.

Egly, R., Driver, J., & Rafal, R. D. (1994). Shifting visual attention between objects and locations: Evidence from normal and parietal lesion subjects. *Journal of Experimental Psychology: General, 123*, 161–177.

Egner, T. (2008). Multiple conflict-driven control mechanisms in the human brain. *Trends in Cognitive Sciences, 12*, 374–380.

Eich, J. E. (1980). The cue-dependent nature of state dependent retrieval. *Memory & Cognition, 8*, 157–173.

Einstein, G. O., McDaniel, M. A., & Lackey, S. (1989). Bizarre imagery, interference, and distinctiveness. *Journal of Experimental Psychology: Learning, Memory, and Cognition, 15*, 137–146.

Elliott, M. A., & Müller, H. J. (2000). Evidence for 40-Hz oscillatory short-term visual memory revealed by human reaction-time measurements. *Journal of Experimental Psychology: Learning, Memory and Cognition, 26*, 7093–7718.

Ellis, H. D., & De Pauw, K. W. (1994). The cognitive neuropsychiatric origins of the Capgras delusion. In A. S. David & J. C. Cutting (Eds.), *The neuropsychology of schizophrenia* (pp. 317–335). Hillsdale, NJ: Erlbaum.

Ellis, H. D., & Lewis, M. B. (2001). Capgras delusion: A window on face recognition. *Trends in Cognitive Sciences, 5*, 149–156.

Ellis, H. D., & Young, A. (1990). Accounting for delusional misidentifications. *British Journal of Psychiatry, 157*, 239–248.

Else-Quest, N., Hyde, J., & Linn, M. (2010). Cross-national patterns of gender differences in mathematics: A meta-analysis. *Psychological Bulletin, 136*, 103–127.

Elstein, A., Holzman, G., Ravitch, M., Metheny, W., Holmes, M., Hoppe, R., et al. (1986). Comparison of physicians' decisions regarding estrogen replacement therapy for menopausal women and decisions derived from a decision analytic model. *American Journal of Medicine, 80*, 246–258.

Engel, A. K., & Singer, W. (2001). Temporal binding and the neural correlates of sensory awareness. *Trends in Cognitive Sciences, 5*, 16–25.

Engle, R. W., & Kane, M. J. (2004). Executive attention, working memory capacity, and a two-factor theory of cognitive control. In B. Ross (Ed.), *The psychology of learning and motivation 44* (pp. 145–199). New York, NY: Elsevier.

Epstein, W. (1961). The influence of syntactical structure on learning. *American Journal of Psychology, 74*, 80–85.

Ericsson, K. A. (2003). Exceptional memorizers: Made, not born. *Trends in Cognitive Sciences, 7*, 233–235.

Ericsson, K. A. (2005). Recent advances in expertise research: A commentary on the contributions to the special issue. *Applied Cognitive Psychology, 19*, 233–241.

Ericsson, K. A., Krampe, R. T. & Tesch-Römer, C. (1993). The role of deliberate practice in the acquisition of expert performance. *Psychological Review, 10*, 363–406.

Ericsson, K. A. & Towne, T. J. (2012). Experts and their superior performance. In D. Reisberg (Ed.), *The Oxford handbook of cognitive psychology*. New York, NY: Oxford University Press.

Ericsson, K. A., & Ward, P. (2007). Capturing the naturally occurring superior performance of experts in the laboratory: Toward a science of expert and exceptional performance. *Current Directions in Psychological Science, 16*, 346–350.

Ernest, C. (1977). Imagery ability and cognition: A critical review. *Journal of Mental Imagery, 2*, 181–216.

Ervin-Tripp, S. (1993). Conversational discourse. In J. B. Gleason & N. B. Ratner (Eds.), *Psycholinguistics* (pp. 237–270). New York, NY: Harcourt Brace Jovanovich.

Estes, Z. (2003). Domain differences in the structure of artifactual and natural categories. *Memory & Cognition, 31*, 199–214.

Evans, J. S. B. T. (1982). *The psychology of deductive reasoning*. London, England: Routledge & Kegan Paul.

Evans, J. S. B. T. (1989). *Bias in human reasoning*. Hillsdale, NJ: Erlbaum.

Evans, J. S. B. T. (1993). The mental model theory of conditional reasoning: Critical appraisal and revision. *Cognition, 48*, 1–20.

Evans, J. S. B. T. (2003). In two minds: Dual-process accounts of reasoning. *Trends in Cognitive Sciences, 7*, 454–459.

Evans, J. S. B. T. (2006). The heuristic-analytic theory of reasoning: Extension and evaluation. *Psychonomics Bulletin & Review, 13*, 378–395.

Evans, J. S. B. T. (2008). Dual-processing accounts of reasoning, judgment, and social cognition. *Annual Review of Psychology, 59*, 255–278.

Evans, J.S.B.T. (2012a). Dual-process theories of deductive reasoning: Facts and fallacies. In Holyoak, K. J., & Morrison, R. G. (Eds.), *The Oxford Handbook of Thinking and Reasoning* (pp. 115–133). New York, NY: Oxford University Press.

Evans, J. S. B. T. (2012b). Reasoning. In D. Reisberg (Ed.), *The Oxford handbook of cognitive psychology*. New York, NY: Oxford University Press.

Evans, J. S. B. T., & Feeney, A. (2004). The role of prior belief in reasoning. In J. P. Leighton & R. J. Sternberg (Eds.), *The nature of reasoning* (pp. 78–102). New York, NY: Cambridge University Press.

Evans, J. S. B. T., Handley, S., Neilens, H., & Over, D. (2007). Thinking about conditions: A study of individual differences. *Memory & Cognition, 35*, 1772–1784.

Evans, J. S. B. T., Handley, S. J., Perham, N., Over, D. E., & Thompson, V. A. (2000). Frequency versus probability formats in statistical word problems. *Cognition, 77*, 197–213.

Evans, J. S. B. T., Newstead, S. E., & Byrne, R. M. J. (1993). *Human reasoning: The psychology of deduction.* London, England: Erlbaum.

Evans, J. S. B. T., Over, D., & Manktelow, K. (1993). Reasoning, decision making and rationality. *Cognition, 49*, 165–187.

Eysenck, M. W. (1982). *Attention and arousal: Cognition and performance.* Berlin, Germany: Springer.

Eysenck, H. J. (1986). Toward a new model of intelligence. *Personality and Individual Differences, 7(5),* 731–736.

Farah, M. J. (1985). Psychophysical evidence for a shared representational medium for mental images and percepts. *Journal of Experimental Psychology: General, 114,* 91–103.

Farah, M. J. (1990). *Visual agnosia: Disorders of object recognition and what they tell us about normal vision.* Cambridge, MA: MIT Press.

Farah, M. J., & Smith, A. (1983). Perceptual interference and facilitation with auditory imagery. *Perception & Psychophysics, 33,* 475–478.

Farah, M. J., Hammond, K. M., Levine, D. N., & Calvanio, R. (1988). Visual and spatial mental imagery: Dissociable systems of representation. *Cognitive Psychology, 20,* 439–462.

Farah, M. J., Soso, M., & Dasheiff, R. (1992). Visual angle of the mind's eye before and after unilateral occipital lobectomy. *Journal of Experimental Psychology: Human Perception and Performance, 18,* 241–246.

Feldman, H., Goldin-Meadow, S., & Gleitman, L. (1978). Beyond Herodotus: The creation of language by linguistically deprived deaf children. In A. Lock (Ed.), *Action, gesture and symbol: The emergence of language* (pp. 351–414). New York, NY: Academic Press.

Feldman Barrett, L., Tugade, M. M., & Engle, R. W. (2004). Individual differences in working memory capacity and dual-process theories of the mind. *Psychological Bulletin, 130,* 553–573.

Feng, J., Spence, I., & Pratt, J. (2007). Playing an action video game reduces gender differences in spatial cognition. *Psychological Science, 18, 850*–855.

Fenske, M. J., Raymond, J. E., Kessler, K., Westoby, N., & Tipper, S. P. (2005). Attentional inhibition has social-emotional consequences for unfamiliar faces. *Psychological Science, 16,* 753–758.

Ferreira, M. B., Garcia-Marques, L., Sherman, S. J., & Sherman, J. W. (2006). Automatic and controlled components of judgment and decision. *Journal of Personality & Social Psychology, 91,* 797–813.

Fiedler, K., Brinkmann, B., Betsch, T., & Wild, B. (2000). A sampling approach to biases in conditional probability judgments: Beyond base rate neglect and statistical format. *Journal of Experimental Psychology: General, 129,* 399–418.

Fiedler, K., Walther, E., Armbruster, T., Fay, D., & Naumann, U. (1996). Do you really know what you have seen? Intrusion errors and presuppositions effects on constructive memory. *Journal of Experimental Social Psychology, 2,* 484–511.

Fine, C. (2010). *Delusions of gender.* New York, NY: Norton.

Finke, R. (1990). *Creative imagery: Discoveries and inventions in visualization.* Hillsdale, NJ: Erlbaum.

Finke, R. A. (1993). Mental imagery and creative discovery. In B. Roskos-Ewoldsen, M. J. Intons-Peterson, & R. Anderson (Eds.), *Imagery, creativity, and discovery* (pp. 255–285). New York, NY: North-Holland.

Finke, R. A., Ward, T. B., & Smith, S. M. (1992). *Creative cognition: Theory, research, applications.* Cambridge, MA: MIT Press.

Finke, R., & Kosslyn, S. M. (1980). Mental imagery acuity in the peripheral visual field. *Journal of Experimental Psychology: Human Perception and Performance, 6,* 126–139.

Finke, R., & Pinker, S. (1982). Spontaneous imagery scanning in mental extrapolation. *Journal of Experimental Psychology: Learning, Memory, & Cognition, 8,* 142–147.

Finke, R., & Slayton, K. (1988). Explorations of creative visual synthesis in mental imagery. *Memory & Cognition, 16,* 252–257.

Fischhoff, B., Slovic, P., & Lichtenstein, S. (1978). Fault trees: Sensitivity of estimated failure probabilities to problem representation. *Journal of Experimental Psychology: Human Perception & Performance, 4,* 330–344.

Fisher, R., & Craik, F. I. M. (1977). The interaction between encoding and retrieval operations in cued recall. *Journal of Experimental Psychology: Human Learning and Memory, 3,* 701–711.

Fisher, R., & Schreiber, N. (2007). Interview protocols to improve eyewitness memory. In M. P. Toglia et al. (Eds.), *Handbook of eyewitness psychology.* Mahwah, NJ: Erlbaum.

Flanagan, D. P., McGrew, K. S., & Ortiz, S. (2000). *The Wechsler Intelligence Scales and Gf-Gc Theory: A contemporary approach to interpretation.* Boston: Allyn & Bacon.

Fleck, J. I., Beeman, M., & Kounios, J. (2012) Insight. In D. Reisberg (Ed.), *The Oxford handbook of cognitive psychology.* New York, NY: Oxford University Press.

Fleck, J. I., & Weisberg, R. W. (2004). The use of verbal protocols as data: An analysis of insight in the candle problem. *Memory & Cognition, 32,* 990–1006.

Fong, G., Krantz, D., & Nisbett, R. (1986). The effects of statistical training on thinking about everyday problems. *Cognitive Psychology, 18,* 253–292.

Fong, G., & Nisbett, R. (1991). Immediate and delayed transfer of training effects in statistical reasoning. *Journal of Experimental Psychology: General, 120,* 34–45.

Forgas, J., & East, R. (2003). Affective influences on social judgments and decisions: Implicit and explicit processes.

In J. P. Forgas and K. D. Williams (Eds.), *Social judgments: Implicit and explicit processes* (pp. 198–226). New York, NY: Cambridge University Press.

Franconeri, S. (2012). The nature and status of visual resources. In D. Reisberg (Ed.), *The Oxford handbook of cognitive psychology*. New York, NY: Oxford University Press.

Fredrickson, B. L. (2000). Extracting meaning from past affective experiences: The importance of peaks, ends, and specific emotions. *Cognition & Emotion, 14*(4), 577–606.

Frenda, S. J., Nichols, R. M., & Loftus, E. F. (2011). Current issues and advances in misinformation research. *Current Directions in Psychological Science, 20*, 20–23.

Freyd, J. J. (1996). *Betrayal trauma: The logic of forgetting childhood abuse.* Cambridge, MA: Harvard University Press.

Freyd, J. J. (1998). Science in the memory debate. *Ethics & Behavior, 8*, 101–113.

Friedman, A. (1979). Framing pictures: The role of knowledge in automatized encoding and memory for gist. *Journal of Experimental Psychology: General, 108*, 316–355.

Friedman, A., & Brown, N. R. (2000a). Reasoning about geography. *Journal of Experimental Psychology: General, 129*, 193–219.

Friedman, A., & Brown, N. R. (2000b). Updating geographical knowledge: Principles of coherence and inertia. *Journal of Experimental Psychology: Learning, Memory and Cognition, 26*, 900–914.

Fries, P., Reynolds, J. H., Rorie, A. E., & Desimone, R. (2001). Modulation of oscillatory neural synchronization by selective visual attention. *Science, 291*, 1560–1563.

Frome, P. M., & Eccles, J. S. (1998). Parents' influence on children's achievement-related perceptions. *Journal of Personality and Social Psychology, 74*(2), 435–452.

Frost, P. (2000). The quality of false memory over time: Is memory for misinformation "remembered" or "known"? *Psychonomic Bulletin & Review, 7*, 531–536.

Fukuda, K., Vogel, E., Mayr, U., & Awh, E. (2011). Quantity, not quality: The relationship between fluid intelligence and working memory capacity. *Psychonomic Bulletin & Review, 17*, 673–679.

Gable, P. A., & Harmon-Jones, E. (2008). Approach-motivated positive affect reduces breadth of attention. *Psychological Science, 19*, 476–482.

Gallagher, A. M., & Kaufman, J. C. (2005). Gender differences in mathematics: What we know and what we need to know. In A. M. Gallagher & J. C. Kaufman (Eds.), *Gender differences in mathematics: An integrative psychological approach* (pp. 316–331). New York: Cambridge University Press.

Gallo, D. A. (2010). False memories and fantastic beliefs: 15 years of the DRM illusion. *Memory & Cognition, 38*, 833–848.

Gallo, D. A., Roberts, M. J., & Seamon, J. G. (1997). Remembering words not presented in lists: Can we avoid creating false memories? *Psychonomic Bulletin & Review, 4*, 271–276.

Galton, F. (1883). *Inquiries into human faculty.* London, England: Dent.

Gardiner, J. M. (1988). Functional aspects of recollective experience. *Memory & Cognition, 16*, 309–313.

Gardner, H. (2006). *Multiple intelligences: New horizons in theory and practice.* New York, NY: Basic Books.

Garrett, B. (2011). *Convicting the innocent: Where criminal prosecutions go wrong.* Cambridge, MA: Harvard University Press.

Garry, M., Manning, C. G., Loftus, E. F., & Sherman, S. J. (1996). Imagination inflation: Imagining a childhood event inflates confidence that it occurred. *Psychonomic Bulletin & Review, 3*, 208–214.

Gathercole, S. E., & Pickering, S. J. (2000). Assessment of working memory in six- and seven-year-old children. *Journal of Educational Psychology, 92*, 377–390.

Gauthier, I. L., & Bukach, C. (2007). Should we reject the expertise hypothesis? *Cognition, 103*, 322–330.

Gauthier, I. L., Skudlarski, P., Gore, J. C., & Anderson, A. W. (2000). Expertise for cars and birds recruits brain areas involved in face recognition. *Nature Neuroscience, 3*, 191–197.

Gazzaniga, M. S., Ivry, R. B., & Mangun, G. R. (2002). *Cognitive neuroscience: The biology of the mind* (2nd ed.). New York, NY: Norton.

Gelman, S., & Wellman, H. (1991). Insides and essences: Early understandings of the non-obvious. *Cognition, 38*, 213–244.

Gentner, D., & Jeziorski, M. (1989). Historical shifts in the use of analogy in science. In B. Gholson, W. Shadish, R. Neimeyer, & A. Houts (Eds.), *Psychology of science: Contributions to metascience* (pp. 296–325). Cambridge, England: Cambridge University Press.

Gentner, D., & Smith, L. A. (2012). Analogical learning and reasoning. In D. Reisberg (Ed.), *The Oxford handbook of cognitive psychology*. New York, NY: Oxford University Press.

Geraerts, E., Bernstein, D., Merckelbach, H., Linders, C., Raymaekers, L., & Loftus, E. F. (2008). Lasting false beliefs and their behavioral consequences. *Psychological Science, 19*, 749–753.

Geraerts, E., Lindsay, D. S., Merckelbach, H., Jelicic, M., Raymaekers, L., Arnold, M. M., et al. (2009). Cognitive mechanisms underlying recovered-memory experiences of childhood sexual abuse. *Psychological Science, 20*, 92–99.

Geraerts, E., Schooler, J. W., Merckelbach, H., Jelicic, M., Hauer, B., & Ambadar, Z. (2007). The reality of recovered memories: Corroborating continuous and discontinuous memories of child sexual abuse. *Psychological Science, 18*, 564–568.

German, T., & Barrett, H. C. (2005). Functional fixedness in a technologically sparse culture. *Psychological Science, 16*, 1–5.

Geschwind, N. (1970). The organization of language and the brain. *Science, 170,* 940–944.

Ghetti, S., Edelstein, R. S., Goodman, G. S., Cordon, I. M., Quas, J. A., Alexander, K. W., et al. (2006). What can subjective forgetting tell us about memory for childhood trauma? *Memory & Cognition, 34,* 1011–1025.

Gibson, E. (2006). The interaction of top-down and bottom-up statistics in the resolution of syntactic category ambiguity. *Journal of Memory & Language, 54,* 363–388.

Gibson, E., Bishop, C., Schiff, W., & Smith, J. (1964). Comparison of meaningfulness and pronounceability as grouping principles in the perception and retention of verbal material. *Journal of Experimental Psychology, 67,* 173–182.

Gick, M., & Holyoak, K. J. (1980). Analogical problem solving. *Cognitive Psychology, 12,* 306–355.

Giesbrecht, T., Lynn, S. J., Lilienfeld, S., & Merckelbach, H. (2008). Cognitive processes in dissociation: An analysis of core theoretical assumptions. *Psychological Bulletin, 134,* 617–647.

Gigerenzer, G. (1991). From tools to theories: A heuristic of discovery in cognitive psychology. *Psychological Review, 98,* 254–267.

Gigerenzer, G., Gaissmaier, W., Kurz-Milcke, E., Schwartz, L. M., & Woloshin, S. (2008). Helping doctors and patients make sense of health statistics. *Psychological Science in the Public Interest, 8,* 53–96.

Gigerenzer, G., Hell, W., & Blank, H. (1988). Presentation and content: The use of base rates as a continuous variable. *Journal of Experimental Psychology: Human Perception and Performance, 14,* 513–525.

Gigerenzer, G., & Hoffrage, U. (1995). How to improve Bayesian reasoning without instruction: Frequency formats. *Psychological Review, 102,* 684–704.

Gigerenzer, G., & Hug, K. (1992). Domain-specific reasoning: Social contracts, cheating and perspective change. *Cognition, 43,* 127–172.

Gilbert, D. T. (1989). Thinking lightly about others: Automatic components of the social inference process. In J. S. Uleman & J. A. Bargh (Eds.), *Unintended thought* (pp. 189–211). New York, NY: Guilford.

Gilbert, D. T. (2006). *Stumbling on happiness.* New York, NY: Random House.

Gilbert, D. T., & Ebert, J. E. J. (2002). Decisions and revisions: The affective forecasting of changeable outcomes. *Journal of Personality and Social Psychology, 82,* 503–514.

Gilbert, D. T., Morewedge, C. K., Risen, J. L., & Wilson, T. D. (2004). Looking forward to looking backward. *Psychological Science, 15,* 346–350.

Gilbert, S. J., & Shallice, T. (2002). Task switching: A PDP model. *Cognitive Psychology, 44,* 297–337.

Gilhooly, K. J. (1988). *Thinking: Direct, undirected and creative* (2nd ed.). New York, NY: Academic Press.

Gilhooly, K. J., Logie, R. H., Wetherick, N., & Wynn, V. (1993). Working memory and strategies in syllogistic-reasoning tasks. *Memory & Cognition, 21,* 115–124.

Gilovich, T. (1983). Biased evaluation and persistence in gambling. *Journal of Personality & Social Psychology, 44,* 1110–1126.

Gilovich, T. (1991). *How we know what isn't so.* New York, NY: Free Press.

Gilovich, T., & Douglas, C. (1986). Biased evaluations of randomly determined gambling outcomes. *Journal of Experimental Social Psychology, 22,* 228–241.

Gilovich, T., & Medvec, V. H. (1995). The experience of regret: What, when and why. *Psychological Review, 102,* 379–395.

Gilovich, T., Medvec, V. H., & Kahneman, D. (1998). Varieties of regret: A debate and partial resolution. *Psychological Review, 105,* 602–605.

Girotto, V. (2004). Task understanding. In J. P. Leighton & R. J. Sternberg (Eds.), *The nature of reasoning* (pp. 103–128). New York, NY: Cambridge University Press.

Girotto, V., & Gonzalez, M. (2001). Solving probabilistic and statistical problems: A matter of information structure and question form. *Cognition, 78,* 247–276.

Giudice, N. A., Betty, M. R., & Loomis, J. M. (2011). Functional equivalence of spatial images from touch and vision: Evidence from spatial updating in blind and sighted individuals. *Journal of Experimental Psychology: Learning Memory & Cognition, 37,* 621–634.S.

Glanzer, M., & Cunitz, A. R. (1966). Two storage mechanisms in free recall. *Journal of Verbal Learning and Verbal Behavior, 5,* 351–360.

Gläscher, J., Daw, N., Dayan, P., O'Doherty, J. P. (2010). States versus rewards: Dissociable neural prediction error signals underlying model-based and model-free reinforcement learning. *Neuron, 66,* 585–595.

Gleitman, H., Gross, J., & Reisberg, D. *Psychology* (8th ed.). New York, NY: Norton.

Gleitman, L., & Papafragou, A. (2012). Relations between language and thought. In Reisberg, D. (Ed.), *The Oxford Handbook of Cognitive Psychology.* New York, NY: Oxford University Press.

Glisky, E. L., Polster, M. R., & Routhieaux, B. C. (1995). Double dissociation between item and source memory. *Neuropsychology, 9,* 229–235.

Godden, D. R., & Baddeley, A. D. (1975). Context-dependent memory in two natural environments: On land and underwater. *British Journal of Psychology, 66,* 325–332.

Goebel, R., Khorram-Sefat, D., Muckli, L., Hacker, H., & Singer, W. (1998). The constructive nature of vision: Direct evidence from functional magnetic resonance imaging studies of apparent motion and motion imagery. *European Journal of Neuroscience, 10,* 1563–1573.

Goldenberg, G., Müllbacher, W., & Nowak, A. (1995). Imagery without perception—A case study of anosognosia for cortical blindness. *Neuropsychologia, 33,* 1373–1382.

Goldenberg, J., Mazursky, D., & Solomon, S. (1999). Creative sparks. *Science, 285,* 1495–1496.

Goldin-Meadow, S. (2003). The resilience of language: What gesture creation in deaf children can tell us about how all children learn language. New York, NY: Psychology Press.

Goldman-Rakic, P. S. (1987). Development of cortical circuitry and cognitive function. *Child Development, 58,* 601–622.

Goldman-Rakic, P. S. (1995). Architecture of the prefrontal cortex and the central executive. In J. Grafman & K. J. Holyoak (Eds.), *Structure and functions of the human prefrontal cortex* (Annals of the New York Academy of Sciences, Vol. 769, pp. 71–83). New York, NY: New York Academy of Sciences.

Goldman-Rakic, P. S. (1998). The prefrontal landscape: Implications of functional architecture for understanding human mentation and the central executive. In A. C. Roberts & T. W. Robbins (Eds.), *The prefrontal cortex: Executive and cognitive functions* (pp. 87–102). New York, NY: Oxford University Press.

Goldstone, R. (1996). Alignment-based nonmonotonicities in similarity. *Journal of Experimental Psychology: Learning, Memory and Cognition, 22,* 988–1001.

Goldstone, R. L, & Son, J. Y. (2012). Similarity. In Holyoak, K. J. & Morrison, R. G. (Eds.), *The Oxford Handbook of Thinking and Reasoning* (pp. 155–176). New York, NY: Oxford University Press.

Goodale, M. A. (1995). The cortical organization of visual perception and visuomotor control. In S. M. Kosslyn & D. Osherson (Eds.), *Visual cognition: An invitation to cognitive science* (2nd ed., pp. 167–213). Cambridge, MA: MIT Press.

Goodale, M. A., & Milner, A. D. (2004). *Sight unseen.* New York, NY: Oxford University Press.

Goodale, M. A., Milner, A. D., Jacobson, L. S., & Carey, D. P. (1991). A neurological dissociation between perceiving objects and grasping them. *Nature, 349,* 154–156.

Goodman, G. S., Ghetti, S., Quas, J. A., Edelstein, R. S., Alexander, K. W., Redlich, A., D., et al. (2003). A prospective study of memory for child sexual abuse: New findings relevant to the repressed-memory controversy. *Psychological Science, 14,* 113–118.

Goodman, N. (1972). Seven strictures on similarity. In N. Goodman (Ed.), *Problems and projects* (pp. 437–446). New York, NY: Bobbs-Merrill.

Gopie, N., Craik, F., & Hasher, L. (2011). A double dissociation of implicit and explicit memory in younger and older adults. *Psychological Science, 22,* 634–640.

Gordon, H. (1923). Mental and scholastic tests among retarded children. *Educational pamphlet, no. 44.* London: Board of Education.

Gordon, R. D. (2006). Selective attention during scene perception: Evidence from negative priming. *Memory & Cognition, 34,* 1484–1494.

Gottfredson, L. S. (1997a). Mainstream science on intelligence: An editorial with 52 signatories, history, and bibliography. *Intelligence, 24,* 13–23.

Gottfredson, L. S. (1997b). Why g matters: The complexity of everyday life. *Intelligence, 24,* 79–132.

Gottfredson, L. S. (2004). Intelligence: Is it the epidemiologists' elusive "fundamental cause" of social class inequalities in health? *Journal of Personality and Social Psychology, 86,* 174–199.

Gould, S. J. (1981). *The mismeasure of man.* New York, NY: Norton.

Graesser, A. C., Millis, K. K., & Zwaan, R. A. (1997). Discourse comprehension. *Annual Review of Psychology, 48,* 163–189.

Graf, P., & Schacter, D. L. (1985). Implicit and explicit memory for new associations in normal and amnesic subjects. *Journal of Experimental Psychology: Learning, Memory and Cognition, 11,* 501–518.

Graf, P., Mandler, G., & Haden, P. E. (1982). Simulating amnesic symptoms in normals. *Science, 218,* 1243–1244.

Grainger, J., Rey, A., & Dufau, S. (2008). Letter perception: from pixels to pandemonium. *Trends in Cognitive Sciences, 12,* 381–387.

Grainger, J., & Whitney, C. (2004). Does the huamn mnid raed wrods as a wlohe? *Trends in Cognitive Sciences, 8,* 58–59.

Grant, H. M., Bredahl, L. C., Clay, J., Ferrie, J., Groves, J. E., McDorman, T. A., et al. (1998). Context-dependent memory for meaningful material: Information for students. *Applied Cognitive Psychology, 12,* 617–623.

Gray, J. R., Chabris, C. F., & Braver, T. S. (2003). Neural mechanisms of general fluid intelligence. *Nature Neuroscience, 6,* 316–322.

Green, R. L., Hoffman, L. T., Morse, R., Hayes, M. E. B., & Morgan, R. F. (1964). *The educational status of children in a district without public schools.* Cooperative Research Project No. 23211. Washington, DC: Office of Education. U.S. Department of Health, Education, and Welfare.

Greenberg, J., Ferguson, C., & Morav-csik, E. (Eds.). (1978). *Universals of human language.* Stanford, CA: Stanford University Press.

Greenfield, P. M. (2009). Technology and informal education: What is taught, what is learned. *Science, 323,* 69–71.

Gregg, M. K., & Samuel, A. G. (2008). Change deafness and the organizational properties of sounds. *Journal of Experimental Psychology: Human Perception & Performance, 34,* 974–991.

Grewal, D., & Salovey, P. (2005). Feeling smart: The science of emotional intelligence. *American Scientist, 93,* 330–339.

Griffin, D. W., Gonzalez, R., Koehler, D. J., & Gilovich, T. (2012). Judgmental heuristics: A historical overview. In Holyoak, K. J., & Morrison, R.G. (Eds.), *The Oxford Handbook of Thinking and Reasoning* (pp. 322–345). NY: Oxford University Press.

Griggs, R., & Cox, J. R. (1982). The elusive thematic-materials effect in Wason's selection task. *British Journal of Psychology, 73,* 407–420.

Grill-Spector, K., & Sayres, R. (2008). Object recognition: Insights from advances in fMRI methods. *Current Directions in Psychological Science, 17,* 73–79.

Grodner, D., & Gibson, E. (2005). Consequences of the serial nature of linguistic input. *Cognitive Science, 29,* 261–291.

Grotzer, T. A., & Perkins, D. N. (2000). Teaching intelligence: A performance conception. In R. J. Sternberg (Ed.), *Handbook of intelligence* (pp. 492–515). Cambridge: Cambridge University Press.

Gruber, H. E. (1981). *Darwin on man: A psychological study of scientific creativity* (2nd ed.). Chicago, IL: University of Chicago Press.

Guilford, J. (1967). *The nature of human intelligence.* New York, NY: Scribner.

Guilford, J. (1979). Some incubated thoughts on incubation. *Journal of Creative Behavior, 13,* 1–8.

Gupta, N., Jang, Y., Mednick, S., & Huber, D. (2012). The road not taken: Creative solutions require avoidance of high-frequency responses. *Psychological Science, 23,* 288–294.

Haber, R. N. (1969). Eidetic images. *Scientific American, 220,* 36–44.

Haber, R. N., & Haber, L. (1988). The characteristics of eidetic imagery. In D. Fein & L. Obler (Eds.), *The exceptional brain* (pp. 218–241). New York, NY: Guilford.

Hackman, D., & Farah, M. (2009). Socioeconomic status and the developing brain. *Trends in Cognitive Sciences, 13,* 65–73.

Hafstad, G. S., Memon, A., & Logie, R. H. (2004). Post-identification feedback, confidence, and recollections of witnessing conditions in child witnesses. *Applied Cognitive Psychology, 18,* 901–912.

Hahn, U., Prat-Sala, M., Pothos, E. M., & Brumby, D. P. (2010) Exemplar similarity and rule application. *Cognition, 114,* 1–18.

Haier, R. J. (2011). Biological basis of intelligence: What does brain imaging show? In R. J. Sternberg & S. B. Kaufman (Eds.), *The Cambridge Handbook of Intelligence* (pp. 351–368). New York, NY: Cambridge University Press.

Halamish, V., & Bjork, R. (2011). When does testing enhance retention? A distribution-based interpretation of retrieval as a memory modifier. *Journal of Experimental Psychology: Learning Memory & Cognition, 37,* 801–812.

Halari, R., Hines, M., Kumari, V., Mehrotra, R., Wheeler, M., Ng, V., et al. (2005). Sex differences and individual differences in cognitive performance and their relationship to endogenous gonadal hormones and gonadotrophins. *Behavioral Neuroscience, 119,* 104–117.

Halberstadt, J. & Rhodes, G. (2003). It's not just average faces that are attractive: Computer-manipulated averageness makes birds, fish, and automobiles attractive. *Psychonomic Bulletin & Review, 10,* 149–156.

Halle, M. (1990). Phonology. In D. Osherson & H. Lasnik (Eds.), *Language: An invitation to cognitive science* (pp. 43–68). Cambridge, MA: MIT Press.

Halpern, D. (1984). *Thought and knowledge: An introduction to critical thinking.* Hillsdale, NJ: Erlbaum.

Halpern, D. (2010). How neuromythologies support sex role stereotypes. *Science, 330,* 1320–1321.

Halpern, D. (2011). *Sex differences in cognitive abilities, 4th edition.* Florence, KY: Psychology Press.

Halpern, D., Benbow, C., Geary, D., Gur, R. C., Hyde, J., & Gernsbacher, M. (2007). The science of sex differences in science and mathematics. *Psychological Science in the Public Interest, 8,* 1–51.

Hamann, S. (2001). Cognitive and neural mechanisms of emotional memory. *Trends in Cognitive Sciences, 5,* 394–400.

Hamill, R., Wilson, T. D., & Nisbett, R. E. (1980). Insensitivity to sample bias: Generalizing from atypical cases. *Journal of Personality and Social Psychology, 39,* 578–589.

Hampshire, A., Duncan, J., & Owen, A. M. (2007). Selective tuning of the blood oxygenation level-dependent response during simple target detection dissociates human frontoparietal subregions. *Journal of Neuroscience, 27*(23), 6219–6223.

Hanako, Y., & Smith, L. B. (2005). Linguistic cues enhance the learning of perceptual cues. *Psychological Science, 16,* 90–95.

Handel, S. (1989). *Listening: An introduction to the perception of auditory events.* Cambridge, MA: MIT Press.

Handley, S. J., Newstead, S. E., & Trippas, D. (2011). Logic, beliefs, and instruction: A test of the default interventionist account of belief bias. *Journal of Experimental Psychology: Learning, Memory & Cognition, 37,* 28–43.

Hanley, J. R., & Chapman, E. (2008). Partial knowledge in a tip-of-the-tongue state about two- and three-word proper names. *Psychonomic Bulletin & Review, 15,* 156–160.

Hannon, B., & McNaughton-Cassill, M. (2011). SAT performance: Understanding the contributions of cognitive/learning and social/personality factors. *Applied Cognitive Psychology, 25,* 528–535.

Hardt, O., Einarsson, E., & Nader, K. (2010). A bridge over troubled water: Reconsolidation as a link between cognitive and neuroscientific memory research traditions. *Annual Review of Psychology, 61,* 141–168.

Harinck, F., Van Dijk, E., Van Beest, I., & Mersmann, P. (2007). When gains loom larger than losses: Reversed loss aversion for small amounts of money. *Psychological Science, 18,* 1099–1105.

Harley, T. A., & Bown, H. E. (1998). What causes a tip-of-the-tongue state? Evidence for lexical neighbourhood effects in speech production. *British Journal of Psychology, 89*(1), 151–174.

Harwood, D. G., Barker, W. W., Ownby, R. L., & Duara, R. (1999). Prevalence and correlates of Capgras syndrome in Alzheimer's disease. *International Journal of Geriatric Psychiatry, 14,* 415–420.

Hasselmo, M. E. (1999). Neuromodulation: Acetylcholine and memory consolidation. *Trends in Cognitive Science, 6,* 351–359.

Hawkins, J. (Ed.). (1988). *Explaining language universals.* London, England: Basil Blackwell.

Hayes, J. (1985). Three problems in teaching general skills. In S. Chipman, J. Segal, & R. Glaser (Eds.), *Thinking and learning skills* (pp. 391–406). Hillsdale, NJ: Erlbaum.

Hayes, J., & Simon, H. (1977). Psychological differences among problem solving isomorphs. In N. Castellan, D. Pisoni, & G. Potts (Eds.), *Cognitive theory* (pp. 21–42). Hillsdale, NJ: Erlbaum.

Hayne, H. (2004). Infant memory development: Implications for childhood amnesia. *Developmental Review 24*, 33–73.

Hayward, W., & Williams, P. (2000). Viewpoint dependence and object discriminability. *Psychological Science, 11*, 7–12.

Heathcote, A., Freeman, E., Etherington, J., Tonkin, J., & Bora, B. (2009). A dissociation between similarity effects in episodic face recognition. *Psychonomic Bulletin & Review, 16*, 824–831.

Heckman, J. J. (2006). Skill formation and the economics of investing in disadvantaged children. *Science, 312*, 1900–1902.

Hegarty, M. (2004). Mechanical reasoning by mental simulation. *Trends in Cognitive Sciences, 8*, 280–285.

Hegarty, M., & Stull, A. T. (2012). Visuospatial thinking. In Holyoak, K. J., & Morrison, R. G. (Eds.), *The Oxford Handbook of Thinking and Reasoning* (pp. 606–630). New York, NY: Oxford University Press.

Heil, M., Rösler, F., & Hennighausen, E. (1993). Imagery-perception interaction depends on the shape of the image: A reply to Farah. *Journal of Experimental Psychology: Human Perception and Performance, 19*, 1313–1319.

Heil, M., Rösler, F., & Hennighausen, E. (1994). Dynamics of activation in long-term memory: The retrieval of verbal, pictorial, spatial and color information. *Journal of Experimental Psychology: Learning, Memory and Cognition, 20*, 169–184.

Heit, E. (2000). Properties of inductive reasoning. *Psychonomic Bulletin & Review, 7*, 569–592.

Heit, E., & Bott, L. (2000). Knowledge selection in category learning. In D. L. Medin (Ed.), *The psychology of learning and motivation: Advances in research and theory*, Vol. 39 (pp. 163–199). San Diego, CA: Academic Press.

Heit, E., & Feeney, A. (2005). Relations between premise similarity and inductive strength. *Psychonomic Bulletin & Review, 12*, 340–344.

Heller, J., & Reif, F. (1984). Prescribing effective human problem-solving processes: Problem description in physics. *Cognition and Instruction, 1*, 177–216.

Helmuth, L. (2001). Boosting brain activity from the outside in. *Science, 292*, 1284–1286.

Henderson, J. M. (2011). Eye movements and scene perception. In I. D. Gilchrist and S. Liversedge (Eds.), *Oxford handbook of eye movements* (pp. 593–606). Oxford, England: Oxford University Press.

Henderson, J. M. & Hollingworth, A. (2003). Global transsaccadic change blindness during scene perception. *Psychological Science, 14*, 493–497.

Henle, M. (1962). On the relation between logic and thinking. *Psychological Review, 69*, 366–378.

Henle, M. (1978). Foreword. In R. Revlin & R. Mayer (Eds.), *Human reasoning* (pp. xiii–xviii). New York, NY: Wiley.

Hennessey, B., & Amabile, A. (2010). Creativity. *Annual Review of Psychology, 61*, 569–598.

Henry, P. J., Sternberg, R. J., & Grigorenko, E. (2005). Capturing successful intelligence through measures of analytic, creative, and practical skills. In O. Willhelm & R. Engle (Eds.), *Understanding and measuring intelligence* (pp. 295–311). Thousand Oaks, CA: Sage.

Hermer-Vasquez, L., Spelke, E. S., & Katsnelson, A. S. (1999). Sources of flexibility in human cognition: Dual-task studies of space and language. *Cognitive Psychology, 39*, 3–36.

Hernández, M., Costa, A., & Humphreys, G. (2012). Escaping caption: Bilingualism modulates distraction from working memory. *Cognition, 122*, 37–50.

Hertwig, R., Herzog, S. M., Schooler, L. J., & Reimer, T. (2008). Fluency heuristic: A model of how the mind exploits a by-product of information retrieval. *Journal of Experimental Psychology: Learning, Memory & Cognition, 34*, 1191–1206.

Hertwig, R., & Ortmann, A. (2003). Economists' and psychologists' experimental practices: How they differ, why they differ, and how they could converge. In I. Brocas & J. D. Carrillo (Eds.), *The psychology of economic decisions: Rationality and well-being*, Vol. 1 (pp. 253–272). New York, NY: Oxford University Press.

Hicks, J. L., & Marsh, R. L. (1999). Remember-Know judgments can depend on how memory is tested. *Psychonomic Bulletin & Review, 6*, 117–122.

Hier, D. B., & Crowley, W. F. (1982). Spatial ability in androgen-deficient men. *New England Journal of Medicine, 306*, 1202–1205.

Higbee, K. L. (1977). *Your memory: How it works and how to improve it.* Englewood Cliffs, NJ: Prentice-Hall.

Hilchey, M., & Klein, R. (2011). Are there bilingual advantages on nonlinguistic interference tasks? Implications for the plasticity of executive control processes. *Psychonomic Bulletin & Review, 18*, 625–658.

Hill, A. L. (1978). Savants: mentally retarded individuals with specific skills. In N. R. Ellis (Ed.), *International review of research in mental retardation: Vol. 9*. New York: Academic Press.

Hillyard, S. A., Vogel, E. K., & Luck, S. J. (1998). Sensory gain control (amplification) as a mechanism of selective attention: Electrophysiological and neuroimaging evidence. *Philosophical Transactions of the Royal Society: Biological Sciences, 353*, 1257–1270.

Hilton, D. J. (1995). The social context of reasoning: Conversational inference and rational judgment. *Psychological Bulletin, 118*, 248–271.

Hilton, D. J. (2003). Psychology and the financial markets: Applications to understanding and remedying irrational decision-making. In I. Brocas & J. D. Carrillo (Eds.),

The psychology of economic decisions: Rationality and well-being, Vol. 1 (pp. 273–297). New York, NY: Oxford University Press.

Hilts, P. J. (1995). *Memory's ghost: The strange tale of Mr. M and the nature of memory*. New York, NY: Simon & Schuster.

Hirst, W., Phelps, E., Buckner, R., Budson, A., Cuc, A., et al. (2009). Long-term memory for the terrorist attack of September 11: Flashbulb memories, event memories, and the factors that influence their retention. *Journal of Experimental Psychology: General, 138,* 161–176.

Hirst, W., Spelke, E., Reaves, C., Caharack, G., & Neisser, U. (1980). Dividing attention without alternation or automaticity. *Journal of Experimental Psychology: General, 109,* 98–117.

Hitch, G. J., Towse, J. N., & Hutton, U. (2001). What limits children's working memory span? Theoretical accounts and applications for scholastic development. *Journal of Experimental Psychology: General, 130,* 184–198.

Hodges, J. R., & Graham, K. S. (2001). Episodic memory: Insights from semantic dementia. In A. D. Baddeley, J. P. Aggleton, & M. A. Conway (Eds.), *Episodic memory: New directions in research* (pp. 132–152). New York, NY: Oxford University Press.

Holland, J. H., Holyoak, K. F., Nisbett, R. E., & Thagard, P. R. (1986). *Induction*. Cambridge, MA: MIT Press.

Holmberg, D., & Homes, J. G. (1994). Reconstruction of relationship memories: A mental models approach. In N. Schwarz & S. Sudman (Eds.), *Autobiographical memory and the validity of retrospective reports* (pp. 267–288). New York, NY: Springer.

Holmes, J. B., Waters, H. S., & Rajaram, S. (1998). The phenomenology of false memories: Episodic content and confidence. *Journal of Experimental Psychology: Learning, Memory and Cognition, 24,* 1026–1040.

Holyoak, K. (2012). Analogy and relational reasoning. In Holyoak, K. J., & Morrison, R. G. (Eds.), *The Oxford Handbook of Thinking and Reasoning* (pp. 234–259). New York, NY: Oxford University Press.

Homa, D., Dunbar, S., & Nohre, L. (1991). Instance frequency, categorization, and the modulating effect of experience. *Journal of Experimental Psychology: Learning, Memory and Cognition, 17,* 444–458.

Homa, D., Sterling, S., & Trepel, L. (1981). Limitation of exemplar-based generalization and the abstraction of categorical information. *Journal of Experimental Psychology: Human Learning and Memory, 7,* 418–439.

Hon, N., Epstein, R. A., Owen, A. M., & Duncan, J. (2006). Frontoparietal activity with minimal decision and control. *Journal of Neuroscience, 26*(38), 9805–9809.

Horn, J. L. (1985). Remodeling old models of intelligence. In B. B. Wolman (Ed.), Handbook of intelligence: Theories, measurements, and applications (pp. 267–300). New York: Wiley.

Horn, J. L., & Blankson, N. (2005). Foundations for better understanding of cognitive abilities. In D. Flanagan & P. Harrison (Eds.), *Contemporary intellectual assessment: Theories, tests, and issues* (2nd ed., pp. 41-68). New York: Guilford.

Horn, J. L., & Noll, J. (1994). A system for understanding cognitive capabilities: A theory and the evidence on which it is based. In D. K. Detterman (Ed.), *Current topics in human intelligence: Vol. 4. Theories of intelligence.* Norwood, NJ: Ablex.

Hornby, P. (1974). Surface structure and presupposition. *Journal of Verbal Learning and Verbal Behavior, 13,* 530–538.

Hoschedidt, S. M., Dongaonkar, B., Payne, J., & Nadel, L. (2012). Emotion, stress and memory. In D. Reisberg (Ed.), *The Oxford handbook of cognitive psychology.* New York, NY: Oxford University Press.

Howe, M. L. (2011). The adaptive nature of memory and its illusions. *Current Directions in Psychological Science, 20,* 312–315.

Howe, M. L., Courage M. L., and Rooksby, M. (2009). The genesis and development of autobiographical memory. In M. L. Courage & N. Cowan (Eds.), *The development of memory in infancy and childhood* (pp. 177–196). Hove, England: Psychology Press.

Hsee, C. K., & Hastie, R. (2005). Decision and experience: Why don't we choose what makes us happy? *Trends in Cognitive Sciences, 10,* 31–37.

Hsee, C. K., Hastie, R., & Chen, J. (2008). Hedonomics: Briding decision research with happiness research. *Perspectives on Psychological Science, 3,* 224–243.

Hubel, D. (1963). The visual cortex of the brain. *Scientific American, 209*(November), 54–62.

Hubel, D., & Wiesel, T. (1959). Receptive fields of single neurones in the cat's visual cortex. *Journal of Physiology, 148,* 574–591.

Hubel, D., & Wiesel, T. (1968). Receptive fields and functional architecture of monkey striate cortex. *Journal of Physiology, 195,* 215–243.

Huey, E. D., Krueger, F., & Grafman, J. (2006). Representations in the human prefrontal cortex. *Current Directions in Psychological Science, 5,* 167–171.

Hummel, J. E. (2012). Object recognition. In D. Reisberg (Ed.), *The Oxford handbook of cognitive psychology.* New York, NY: Oxford University Press.

Hummel, J. E., & Biederman, I. (1992). Dynamic binding in a neural network for shape recognition. *Psychological Review, 99,* 480–517.

Hummel, J. E., & Stankiewicz, B. J. (1998). Two roles for attention in shape perception: A structural description model of visual scrutiny. *Visual Cognition, 5,* 49–79.

Hung, J., Driver, J., & Walsh, V. (2005). Visual selection and posterior parietal cortex: Effects of repetitive transcranial magnetic stimulation on partial report analyzed by Bundesen's theory of visual attention. *Journal of Neuroscience, 25*(42), 9602–9612.

Hunt, E. (1995). *Will we be smart enough? A cognitive analysis of the coming workforce.* New York: Russell Sage Foundation.

Hunt, R., & Ellis, H. D. (1974). Recognition memory and degree of semantic contextual change. *Journal of Experimental Psychology, 103,* 1153–1159.

Husserl, E. (1931). *Ideas.* New York, NY: Collier.

Hutchison, K. A. (2003). Is semantic priming due to association strength or feature overlap? A *micro* analytic review. *Psychonomic Bulletin & Review, 10,* 785–813.

Hyde, J., Lindberg, S., Linn, M., Ellis, A., & Williams, C. (2008). Gender similarities characterize math performance. *Science, 321,* 494–495.

Hyde, T. S., & Jenkins, J. J. (1969). Differential effects of incidental tasks on the organization of recall of a list of highly associated words. *Journal of Experimental Psychology, 82,* 472–481.

Hyman, I. E., Jr. (2000). Creating false autobiographical memories: Why people believe their memory errors. In E. Winograd, R. Fivush, & W. Hirst (Eds.), *Ecological approaches to cognition: Essays in honor of Ulric Neisser.* Hillsdale, NJ: Erlbaum.

Hyman, I., Boss, M., Wise, B., McKenzie, K. & Caggiano, J. (2010). Did you see the unicycling clown? Inattentional blindness while walking and talking on a cell phone. *Applied Cognitive Psychology, 24,* 597–607.

Intons-Peterson, M. J. (1983). Imagery paradigms: How vulnerable are they to experimenters' expectations? *Journal of Experimental Psychology: Human Perception & Performance, 9,* 394–412.

Intons-Peterson, M. J. (1999). Comments and caveats about "scanning visual mental images." *Cahiers de Psychologie Cognitive, 18,* 534–540.

Intons-Peterson, M. J., & White, A. (1981). Experimenter naiveté and imaginal judgments. *Journal of Experimental Psychology: Human Perception and Performance, 7,* 833–843.

Intraub, H., & Bodamer, J. (1993). Boundary extension: Fundamental aspect of pictorial representation or encoding artifact? *Journal of Experimental Psychology: Learning, Memory and Cognition, 19,* 1387–1397.

Intraub, H., & Dickinson, C. A. (2008). False memory 1/20th of a second later. *Psychological Science, 19,* 1007–1014.

Intraub, H., & Richardson, M. (1989). Wide-angle memories of close-up scenes. *Journal of Experimental Psychology: Learning, Memory and Cognition, 15,* 179–187.

Intraub, H., Gottesman, C. V., & Bills, A. J. (1998). Effects of perceiving and imagining scenes on memory for pictures. *Journal of Experimental Psychology: Learning, Memory and Cognition, 24,* 1–16.

Intraub, H., Hoffman, J. E., Wetherhold, C. J., & Stoehs, S.-A. (2006). More than meets the eye: The effect of planned fixations on scene representation. *Perception and Psychophysics, 68,* 759–769.

Isha, A., & Sagi, D. (1995). Common mechanisms of visual imagery and perception. *Science, 268,* 1772–1774.

Jackendoff, R. (1972). *Semantic interpretation in generative grammar.* Cambridge, MA: MIT Press.

Jackendoff, R. (1987). *Consciousness and the computational mind.* Cambridge, MA: MIT Press.

Jacoby, L. L. (1978). On interpreting the effects of repetition: Solving a problem versus remembering a solution. *Journal of Verbal Learning and Verbal Behavior, 17,* 649–667.

Jacoby, L. L. (1983). Remembering the data: Analyzing interactive processes in reading. *Journal of Verbal Learning and Verbal Behavior, 22,* 485–508.

Jacoby, L. L., Allan, L., Collins, J., & Larwill, L. (1988). Memory influences subjective experience: Noise judgments. *Journal of Experimental Psychology: Learning, Memory and Cognition, 14,* 240–247.

Jacoby, L. L., & Dallas, M. (1981). On the relationship between autobiographical memory and perceptual learning. *Journal of Experimental Psychology: General, 3,* 306–340.

Jacoby, L. L., & Hollingshead, A. (1990). Reading student essays may be hazardous to your spelling: Effects of reading incorrectly and correctly spelled words. *Canadian Journal of Psychology, 44,* 345–358.

Jacoby, L. L., Jones, T. C., & Dolan, P. O. (1998). Two effects of repetition: Support for a dual process model of know judgments and exclusion errors. *Psychonomic Bulletin & Review, 5,* 705–509.

Jacoby, L. L., Kelley, C. M., Brown, J., & Jasechko, J. (1989). Becoming famous overnight: Limits on the ability to avoid unconscious influences of the past. *Journal of Personality and Social Psychology, 56,* 326–338.

Jacoby, L. L., Lindsay, D. S., & Hessels, S. (2003). Item-specific control of automatic processes: Stroop process dissociations. *Psychonomic Bulletin & Review, 10,* 638–644.

Jacoby, L. L., & Whitehouse, K. (1989). An illusion of memory: False recognition influenced by unconscious perception. *Journal of Experimental Psychology: General, 118,* 126–135.

Jacoby, L. L., & Witherspoon, D. (1982). Remembering without awareness. *Canadian Journal of Psychology, 36,* 300–324.

James, L. E., & Burke, D. M. (2000). Phonological priming effects on word retrieval and Tip-of-the-Tongue experiences in young and older adults. *Journal of Experimental Psychology: Learning, Memory and Cognition, 26,* 1378–1391.

James, W. (1890). *The principles of psychology,* Vol. 2. New York, NY: Dover.

Janiszewski, C., & Uy, D. (2008). Precision of the anchor influences the amount of adjustment. *Psychological Science, 19,* 121–127.

Janowsky, J. S., Oviatt, S. K., & Orwoll, E. S. (1994). Testosterone influences spatial cognition in older men. *Behavioral Neuroscience, 108,* 325–332.

January, D., & Kako, E. (2007). Re-evaluating evidence for linguistic relativity: Reply to Boroditsky (2001). *Cognition, 104,* 417–426.

Jeffries, R., Polson, P., Razran, L., & Atwood, M. (1977). A process model for missionaries-cannibals and other river-crossing problems. *Cognitive Psychology, 9*, 412–440.

Jelicic, M., Smeets, T., Peters, M., Candel, I., Horselenberg, R., & Merckelbach, H. (2006). Assassination of a controversial politician: Remembering details from another non-existent film. *Applied Cognitive Psychology, 20*, 591–596.

Jencks, C., & Phillips, M. (Eds). (1998). *The Black-White test score gap*. Washington DC: Brookings Institution.

Jenkins, R., Lavie, N., & Driver, J. (2005). Recognition memory for distractor faces depends on attentional load at exposure. *Psychological Bulletin & Review, 12*, 314–320.

Jennings, D. L., Amabile, T. M., & Ross, L. (1982). Informal covariation assessment: Data-based versus theory-based judgments. In D. Kahneman, P. Slovic, & A. Tversky (Eds.), *Judgments under uncertainty: Heuristics and biases* (pp. 211–230). Cambridge, England: Cambridge University Press.

Jensen, A. R. (1985). The nature of the black-white difference on various psychometric tests: Spearman's hypothesis. *Behavioral and Brain Sciences, 8*, 193–263.

Jepson, D., Krantz, D., & Nisbett, R. (1983). Inductive reasoning: Competence or skill? *Behavioral and Brain Sciences, 6*, 494–501.

Joels, M., Fernandez, G., & Roosendaal, B. (2011). Stress and emotional memory: A matter of timing. *Trends in Cognitive Sciences*, 15, 280–288.

Johnson, H., & Seifert, C. (1994). Sources of the continued influence effect: When misinformation affects later inferences. *Journal of Experimental Psychology: Learning, Memory and Cognition, 20*, 1420–1436.

Johnson, M. K. (1988). Reality monitoring: An experimental phenomenological approach. *Journal of Experimental Psychology: General, 117*, 390–394.

Johnson, M. K., Hashtroudi, S., & Lindsay, S. (1993). Source monitoring. *Psychological Bulletin, 114*, 3–28.

Johnson, W., Carothers, A., & Deary, I. J. (2008). Sex differences in variability in general intelligence. *Perspectives on Psychological Science, 3*, 518–531.

Johnson, W., Nijenhuis, J., & Bouchard, T. (2007). Replication of the hierarchical visual-perceptual-image rotation model in de Wolff and Buiten's (1963) battery of 46 tests of mental ability. *Intelligence, 35*, 69–81.

Johnson, W., Segal, N. L., & Bouchard, T. J., Jr., (2008). Heritability of fluctuating asymmetry in a human twin sample: The effect of trait aggregation. *American Journal of Human Biology, 20*, 651–658.

Johnson-Laird, P. N. (1983). *Mental models*. Cambridge, MA: Harvard University Press.

Johnson-Laird, P. N. (1988). A computational analysis of consciousness. In A. Marcel & E. Bisiach (Eds.), *Consciousness in contemporary science* (pp. 357–368). Oxford, England: Oxford University Press.

Johnston, J. & McClelland, J. (1973). Visual factors in word perception. *Perception & Psychophysics, 14*, 365–370.

Jones, G. (2003). Testing two cognitive theories of insight. *Journal of Experimental Psychology: Learning, Memory and Cognition, 29*, 1017–1027.

Jones, T. C., & Bartlett, J. C. (2009). When false recognition is out of control: The case of facial conjunctions. *Memory & Cognition, 37*, 143–157.

Jonides, J., Kahn, R., & Rozin, P. (1975). Imagery instructions improve memory in blind subjects. *Bulletin of the Psychonomic Society, 5*, 424–426.

Jonides, J., Lacey, S. C., & Nee, D. E. (2005). Processes of working memory in mind and brain. *Current Directions in Psychological Science, 14*, 2–5.

Jonides, J., Lewis, R., Nee, D. E., Lustig, C. A., Berman, M. G., & Moore, K. S. (2008). The mind and brain of short-term memory. *Annual Review of Psychology, 59*, 193–224.

Jung, R., & Haier, R. (2007). The parieto-frontal integration theory (P-FIT) of intelligence: Converging neuroimaging evidence. *Behavioral and Brain Sciences, 30*, 135–154.

Just, M., Carpenter, P. A., & Hemphill, D. D. (1996). Constraints on processing capacity: Architectural or implementational? In D. Steier & T. Mitchell (Eds.), *Mind matters: A tribute to Allen Newell* (pp. 141–178). Mahwah, NJ: Erlbaum.

Kahneman, D. (1973). *Attention and effort*. Englewood Cliffs, NJ: Prentice-Hall.

Kahneman, D. (2003). A perspective on judgment and choice: Mapping bounded rationality. *American Psychologist, 58*, 697–720.

Kahneman, D. (2011). *Thinking, fast and slow*. New York, NY: Farrar, Straus and Giroux.

Kahneman, D., & Snell, J. (1992). Predicting a changing taste: Do people know what they will like? *Journal of Behavioral Decision Making, 5*, 187–200.

Kahneman, D., & Tversky, A. (1973). On the psychology of prediction. *Psychological Review, 80*, 237–251.

Kahney, H. (1986). *Problem solving: A cognitive approach*. Milton Keynes, England: Open University Press.

Kamin, L. (1974). *The science and politics of IQ*. Potomac, MD: Erlbaum.

Kanaya, T., Scullin, M. H., & Ceci, S. (2003). The Flynn effect and U.S. policies: The impact of rising IQ scores on American society via mental retardation diagnoses. *American Psychologist, 58*, 778–790.

Kane, M. J., Brown, L. H., McVay, J. C., Silvia, P. J., Myin-Germeys, I., & Kwapil, T. R. (2007). For whom the mind wanders, and when: An experience-sampling study of working memory and executive control in daily life. *Psychological Science, 18*, 614–621.

Kane, M. J., Conway, A., Hambrick, D., & Engle, R. (2007). Variation in working memory capacity as variation in executive attention and control. In A. Conway, K. Jarrold, M. Kane, A. Miyake, & J. Towse, (Eds.), *Variation in working memory* (pp. 21–46). New York, NY: Oxford University Press.

Kane, M. J., & Engle, R. W. (2003). Working-memory capacity and the control of attention: The contributions of goal neglect, response competition, and task set to Stroop interference. *Journal of Experimental Psychology: General, 132,* 47–70.

Kanwisher, N. (2006). What's in a face? *Science, 311,* 617–618.

Kaplan, A. S., & Murphy, G. L. (2000). Category learning with minimal prior knowledge. *Journal of Experimental Psychology: Learning, Memory, & Cognition, 26,* 829–846.

Karpicke, J., & Blunt, J. (2011). Retrieval practice produces more learning than elaborative studying with concept mapping. *Science, 331,* 772–775.

Karpicke, J., & Roediger, H. (2010). Is expanding retrieval a superior method for learning text materials? *Memory & Cognition, 38,* 116–124.

Kassin, S., Bogart, D., & Kerner, J. (2012). Confessions that corrupt: Evidence from the DNA exoneration cases. *Psychological Science, 23,* 1–5.

Kassin, S., Drizin, S., Grisso, T., Gudjonsson, G., Leo, R., & Redlich, A. (2010). Police-induced confessions: Risk factors and recommendations. *Law & Human Behavior, 34,* 3–38.

Katona, G. (1940). *Organizing and memorizing.* New York, NY: Columbia University Press.

Katz, A. (1983). What does it mean to be a high imager? In J. Yuille (Ed.), *Imagery, memory and cognition* (pp. 39–63). Hillsdale, NJ: Erlbaum.

Katz, B. (1952, November). The nerve impulse. *Scientific American, 187,* 55–64.

Kaufman, A. S., & Kaufman, N. L. (2004). *Manual for Kaufman Assessment Battery for Children—Second Edition (KABC-II)—Comprehensive Form.* Circle Pines, MN: American Guidance Service.

Kaufman, J. C., Kaufman, S. B., & Plucker, J. (2012). Contemporary theories of intelligence. In D. Reisberg (Ed.), *The Oxford handbook of cognitive psychology.* New York, NY: Oxford University Press.

Kay, P., & Regier, T. (2007). Color naming universals: The case of Berinmo. *Cognition, 102,* 289–298.

Keil, F. C. (1986). The acquisition of natural-kind and artifact terms. In W. Demopoulos & A. Marras (Eds.), *Language, learning, and concept acquisition* (pp. 133–153). Norwood, NJ: Ablex.

Keil, F. C. (1989). *Concepts, kinds, and cognitive development.* Cambridge, MA: MIT Press.

Keil, F. C. (2003). Folkscience: Coarse interpretations of a complex reality. *Trends in Cognitive Sciences, 7,* 368–373.

Keil, F. C., Smith, W. C., Simons, D. J., & Levin, D. T. (1998). Two dogmas of conceptual empiricism: Implications for hybrid models of the structure of knowledge. *Cognition, 65,* 103–135.

Kelly, S. W., Burton, A. M., Kato, T., & Akamatsu, S. (2001). Incidental learning of real-world regularities. *Psychological Science, 12,* 86–89.

Kensinger, E. (2007). Negative emotion enhances memory accuracy. *Current Directions in Psychological Science, 16,* 213–218.

Kermer, D., Driver-Linn, E., Wilson, T., & Gilbert, D. (2006). Loss aversion is an effective forecasting error. *Psychological Science, 17,* 649–653.

Kerr, N. H. (1983). The role of vision in "visual imagery" experiments: Evidence from the congenitally blind. *Journal of Experimental Psychology: General, 112,* 265–277.

Kershaw, T. C., & Ohlsson, S. (2004). Multiple causes of difficulty in insight: The case of the nine-dot problem. *Journal of Experimental Psychology: Learning, Memory, & Cognition, 30,* 3–13.

Keys, D., & Schwartz, B. (2007). "Leaky" rationality: How research on behavioral decision making challenges normative standards of rationality. *Perspectives on Psychological Science, 2,* 162–180.

Keysers, C., Cohen, J., Donald, M., Guth, W., John, E., et al. (2008). Explicit and implicit strategies in decision making. In C. Engel & W. Singer (Eds.), *Better than conscious? Decision making, the human mind, and implications for institutions* (pp. 225–258). Cambridge, MA: MIT Press.

Khlemani, S., & Johnson-Laird, P. N. (2012). Theories of the syllogism: A meta-analysis. *Psychological Bulletin, 138,* 427–457.

Kihlstrom, J. F. (2006). Trauma and memory revisited. In B. Uttl, N. Ohta, & A. Siegenthaler (Eds.), *Memory and emotion: Interdisciplinary perspectives* (pp. 259–291). Malden, MA: Blackwell.

Kihlstrom, J. F., & Schacter, D. L. (2000). Functional amnesia. In F. Boller & J. Grafman (Eds.), *Handbook of neuropsychology* (2nd ed., Vol. 2, pp. 409–427). Amsterdam, Netherlands: Elsevier.

Kim, C.-Y., & Blake, R. (2005). Psychophysical magic: Rendering the visible "invisible." *Trends in Cognitive Sciences, 9,* 381–388.

Kim, S., & Murphy, G. (2011). Ideals and category typicality. *Journal of Experimental Psychology: Learning, Memory & Cognition, 37,* 1092–1112.

Kimberg, D. Y., D'Esposito, M., & Farah, M. J. (1998). Cognitive functions in the prefrontal cortex in working memory and executive control. *Current Directions in Psychological Science, 6,* 185–192.

King, R. N., & Koehler, D. J. (2000). Illusory correlations in graphological inference. *Journal of Experimental Psychology: Applied, 6,* 336–348.

Klahr, D., & Simon, H. A. (2001). What have psychologists (and others) discovered about the process of scientific discovery? *Current Directions in Psychological Science, 10,* 75–79.

Klauer, K. C., Musch, J., & Naumer, B. (2000). On belief bias in syllogistic reasoning. *Psychological Review, 107,* 852–884.

Klauer, K. C., & Zhao, Z. (2004). Double dissociations in visual and spatial short-term memory. *Journal of Experimental Psychology: General, 133,* 355–381.

Klayman, J., & Brown, K. (1993). Debias the environment instead of the judge: An alternative approach to reducing error in diagnostic (and other) judgment. *Cognition, 49,* 97–122.

Knoblich, G., Ohlsson, S., & Raney, G. E. (2001). An eye movement study of insight problem solving. *Memory & Cognition, 29,* 1000–1009.

Knowlton, B., & Foerde, K. (2008). Neural representations of nondeclarative memories. *Current Directions in Psychological Science, 17,* 107–111.

Koch, C. (2008). The neuroscience of consciousness. In L. R. Squire, F. E. Bloom, N. C. Spiter, S. du Lac, A. Ghosh, & Berg, D. (Eds.), *Fundamental neuroscience* (3rd ed.), (pp. 1223–1236). Burlington, MA: Academic Press.

Koch, C., & Tsuchiya, N. (2007). Attention and consciousness: Two distinct brain processes. *Trends in Cognitive Sciences, 11,* 16–22.

Kohler, W. (1969). *The task of Gestalt psychology.* Princeton, NJ: Princeton University Press.

Kopelman, M. D., & Kapur, N. (2001). The loss of episodic memories in retrograde amnesia: Single-case and group studies. In A. D. Baddeley, J. P. Aggleton, & M. A. Conway (Eds.), *Episodic memory: New directions in research* (pp. 110–131). New York, NY: Oxford University Press.

Kosslyn, S. M. (1976). Can imagery be distinguished from other forms of internal representation? Evidence from studies of information retrieval times. *Memory & Cognition, 4,* 291–297.

Kosslyn, S. M. (1980). *Image and mind.* Cambridge, MA: Harvard University Press.

Kosslyn, S. M. (1983). *Ghosts in the mind's machine.* New York, NY: Norton.

Kosslyn, S. M. (1994). *Image and brain: The resolution of the imagery debate.* Cambridge, MA: MIT Press.

Kosslyn, S. M., Ball, T. M., & Reiser, B. J. (1978). Visual images preserve metric spatial information: Evidence from studies of image scanning. *Journal of Experimental Psychology: Human Perception and Performance, 4,* 1–20.

Kosslyn, S. M., Pascual-Leone, A., Felician, O., Camposano, S., Keenan, J. P., Thompson, W. L., et al. (1999). The role of area 17 in visual imagery: Convergent evidence from PET and rTMS. *Science, 284,* 167–170.

Kosslyn, S. M., & Thompson, W. L. (1999). Shared mechanisms in visual imagery and visual perception: Insights from cognitive neuroscience. In M. S. Gazzaniga (Ed.), *The new cognitive neurosciences* (pp. 975–986). Cambridge, MA: MIT Press.

Kosslyn, S. M., & Thompson, W. L. (2003). When is early visual cortex activated during mental imagery? *Psychological Bulletin, 129,* 723–746.

Koulder, S., deGardelle, V., Sackur, J., & Dupoux, E. (2010). How rich is consciousness? The partial awareness hypothesis. *Trends in Cognitive Science, 14,* 301–307.

Kounios, J., & Beeman, M. (2009). The *Aha!* moment: The cognitive neuroscience of insight. *Current Directions in Psychological Science, 18,* 210–216.

Kovelman, I., Shalinsky, M. H., Berens, M. S., & Petito, L. (2008). Shining new light on the brain's "bilingual signature": A functional Near Infrared Spectroscopy investigation of semantic processing. *Neuroimage, 39,* 1457–1471.

Kozhevnikov, M., Kosslyn, S., & Shephard, J. (2005). Spatial versus object visualizers: A new characterization of visual cognitive style. *Memory & Cognition, 33,* 710–726.

Krimsky, S., & Sloan, K. (Eds.). (2011). *Race and the genetic revolution: Science, myth, and culture.* New York, NY: Columbia University Press.

Kroll, J. F., & Potter, M. C. (1984). Recognizing words, pictures, and concepts: A comparison of lexical, object, and reality decisions. *Journal of Verbal Learning and Verbal Behavior, 23,* 39–66.

Kruglanski, A., & Orehek, E. (2007). Partitioning the domain of social inference: Dual mode and systems models and their alternatives. *Annual Review of Psychology, 58,* 291–316.

Krynski, T., & Tenenbaum, J. (2007). The role of causality in judgment under uncertainty. *Journal of Experimental Psychology: General, 136,* 430–450.

Kulatunga-Moruzi, C., Brooks, L., & Norman, G. (2011). Teaching posttraining: Influencing diagnostic strategy with instructions at test. *Journal of Experimental Psychology: Applied, 17,* 195–209.

Kumon-Nakamura, S., Glucksberg, S., & Brown, M. (1995). How about another piece of pie: The allusional pretense theory of discourse irony. *Journal of Experimental Psychology: General, 124,* 3–21.

Kunar, M., Carter, R., Cohen, M., & Horowitz, T. (2008). Telephone conversation impairs sustained visual attention via a central bottleneck. *Psychonomic Bulletin & Review, 15,* 1135–1140.

Kunda, Z. (1990). The case for motivated reasoning. *Psychological Bulletin, 108,* 480–498.

Kunda, Z., & Nisbett, R. E. (1986). The psychometrics of everyday life. *Cognitive Psychology, 18,* 195–224.

Kuncel, N. R., Hezlett, S. A., & Ones, D. S. (2004). Academic performance, career potential, creativity, and job performance: Can one construct predict them all? *Journal of Personality and Social Psychology, 86,* 148–161.

Kurtz, K., & Loewenstein, J. (2007). Converging on a new role for analogy in problem solving and retrieval: When two problems are better than one. *Memory & Cognition, 35,* 334–341.

LaBar, K. (2007). Beyond fear: Emotional memory mechanisms in the human brain. *Current Directions in Psychological Science, 16,* 173–177.

LaBar, K., & Cabeza, R. (2006). Cognitive neuroscience of emotional memory. *Nature Reviews Neuroscience, 7,* 54–64.

Labov, B. (2007). Transmission and diffusion. *Language, 83,* 344–387.

Lai, C. S., Fisher, S. E., Hurst, J. A., Vargha-Khadem, F., & Monaco, A. P. (2001). A forkhead-domain gene is mutated in a severe speech and language disorder. *Nature, 413,* 519–522.

Lakoff, G. (1987). Cognitive models and prototype theory. In U. Neisser (Ed.), *Concepts and conceptual development* (pp. 63–100). Cambridge, England: Cambridge University Press.

Lamble, D., Kauranen, T., Laakso, M., & Summala, H. (1999). Cognitive load and detection thresholds in car following situations: Safety implications for using mobile (cellular) telephones while driving. *Accident Analysis & Prevention, 31,* 617–623.

Lampinen, J., Meier, C., Arnal, J., & Leding, J. (2005). Compelling untruths: Content borrowing and vivid false memories. *Journal of Experimental Psychology: Learning, Memory & Cognition, 31,* 954–963.

Lane, S., & Zaragoza, M. (1995). The recollective experience of cross-modality confusion errors. *Memory & Cognition, 23,* 607–610.

Lane, S. M., & Schooler, J. W. (2004). Skimming the surface: Verbal overshadowing of analogical retrieval. *Psychological Science, 15,* 715–719.

Laney, C. (2012). The sources of memory errors. In D. Reisberg (Ed.), *The Oxford handbook of cognitive psychology.* New York, NY: Oxford University Press.

Laney, C., & Loftus, E. F. (2010). False memory. In J. Brown & E. Campbell (Eds.), *The Cambridge handbook of forensic psychology* (pp. 187–194). Cambridge: Cambridge University Press.

Laney, C., Morris, E., Bernstein, D., Wakefield, B., & Loftus, E.,F. (2008). Asparagus: A love story: Healthier eating could be just a false memory away. *Experimental Psychology, 55,* 291–300.

Langer, E. (1989). *Mindfulness.* Reading, MA: Addison-Wesley.

Lassiter, G. D. & Meissner, C. (2010). Police interrogations and false confessions. Washington, DC: American Psychological Assocation.

Lau, H., & Rosenthal, D. (2011). Empirical support for higher-order theories of conscious awareness. *Trends in Cognitive Science, 15,* 365–373.

Laureys, S. (2005). The neural correlate of (un)awareness: lessons from the vegetative state. *Trends in Cognitive Sciences, 9,* 556–559.

Lavie, N. (2001). Capacity limits in selective attention: Behavioral evidence and implications for neural activity. In J. Braun, C. Koch, & J. L. Davis (Eds.), *Visual attention and cortical circuits* (pp. 49–68). Cambridge, MA: MIT Press.

Lavie, N. (2005). Distracted and confused? Selective attention under load. *Trends in Cognitive Sciences, 9,* 75–82.

Lavie, N., Lin, Z., Zokaei, N., & Thoma, V. (2009). The role of perceptual load in object recognition. *Journal of Experimental Psychology: Human Perception & Performance, 35,* 1346–1358.

Layard, R. (2010). Measuring subjective well being. *Science, 327,* 534–535.

LeBoeuf, R. A., & Shafir, E. (2012). Decision making. In Holyoak, K. J., & Morrison, R. G. (Eds.), *The Oxford Handbook of Thinking and Reasoning* (pp. 301–321). New York, NY: Oxford University Press.

Lehman, D. R., & Nisbett, R. (1990). A longitudinal study of the effects of undergraduate education on reasoning. *Developmental Psychology, 26,* 952–960.

Leo, R. (2008). *Police interrogations and American justice.* Cambridge, MA: Harvard.

Levin, D., Takarae, Y., Miner, A., & Keil, F. (2001). Efficient visual search by category: Specifying the features that mark the difference between artifacts and animals in preattentive vision. *Perception and Psychophysics, 63,* 676–697.

Levin, I., & Gaeth, G. (1988). How consumers are affected by the framing of attribute information before and after consuming the product. *Journal of Consumer Research, 15,* 374–378.

Levin, I., Schnittjer, S., & Thee, S. (1988). Information framing effects in social and personal decisions. *Journal of Experimental Social Psychology, 24,* 520–529.

Levine, L. J. (1997). Reconstructing memory for emotions. *Journal of Experimental Psychology: General, 126,* 165–177.

Levine, L. J., & Bluck S. (2004). Painting with broad strokes: Happiness and the malleability of event memory. *Cognition and Emotion, 18,* 559–574.

Levine, L. J., & Edelstein, R. S. (2009). Emotion and memory narrowing: A review and goal relevance approach. *Cognition and Emotion, 23,* 833–875

Levy, J., & Pashler, H. (2008). Task prioritisation in multitasking duringn driving: Opportunity to abort a concurrent task does not insulate braking responses from dual-task slowing. *Applied Cognitive Psychology, 22,* 507–525.

Li, P., Abarbanell, L., Gleitman, L., & Papafragou, A. (2011). Spatial reasoning in Tenejapan Mayans. *Cognition, 120,* 33–53.

Li, P., & Gleitman, L. R. (2002). Turning the tables: Language and spatial reasoning. *Cognition, 83,* 265–294.

Liberman, A. (1970). The grammars of speech and language. *Cognitive Psychology, 1,* 301–323.

Liberman, A., Harris, K., Hoffman, H., & Griffith, B. (1957). The discrimination of speech sounds within and across phoneme boundaries. *Journal of Experimental Psychology, 54,* 358–368.

Lichtenstein, S., & Slovic, P. (2006). *The construction of preference.* New York, NY: Cambridge University Press.

Lichtenstein, S., Slovic, P., Fischhoff, B., Layman, M., & Combs, B. (1978). Judged frequency of lethal events. *Journal of Experimental Psychology: Human Learning and Memory, 4,* 551–578.

Lidz, J., Waxman, S., & Freedman, J. (2003). What infants know about syntax but couldn't have learned: Experimental evidence for syntactic structure at 18 months. *Cognition, 89,* B65–B73.

Light, L. L., & Carter-Sobell, L. (1970). Effects of changed semantic context on recognition memory. *Journal of Verbal Learning and Verbal Behavior, 9,* 1–11.

Lindsay, D. S., Hagen, L., Read, J. D., Wade, K. A., & Garry, M. (2004). True photographs and false memories. *Psychological Science, 15*, 149–154.

Lisker, L., & Abramson, A. (1970). *The voicing dimension: Some experiments in comparative phonetics*. Paper presented at the Proceedings of the Sixth International Congress of Phonetic Sciences, Prague.

Lockhart, R. S., Craik, F. I. M., & Jacoby, L. (1976). Depth of processing, recall, and recognition. In J. Brown (Ed.), *Recall and recognition* (pp. 75–102). New York, NY: Wiley.

Loehlin, J. C., Lindzey, G., & Spuhler, J. N. (1975). *Race difference in intelligence*. San Francisco: Freeman.

Loewenstein, G., & Schkade, D. (1999). Wouldn't it be nice? Predicting future feelings. In D. Kahneman, E. Diener, & N. Schwarz (Eds.), *Well-being: The foundations of hedonic psychology* (pp. 85–105). New York, NY: Russell Sage Foundation.

Loewenstein, G., Weber, E. U., Hsee, C. K., & Welch, N. (2001). Risk as feelings. *Psychological Bulletin, 127*, 267–286.

Loewenstein, J., Thompson, L., & Gentner, D. (1999). Analogical encoding facilitates knowledge transfer in negotiation. *Psychonomic Bulletin & Review, 6*, 586–597.

Loftus, E. F. (1979). *Eyewitness testimony*. Cambridge, MA: Harvard University Press.

Loftus, E. F. (1997). Memory for a past that never was. *Current Directions in Psychological Science, 6*, 60–64.

Loftus, E. F. (2003). Make-believe memories. *American Psychologist, 58*, 867–873.

Loftus, E. F. (2004). Memories of things unseen. *Current Directions in Psychological Science, 13*, 145–147.

Loftus, E. F., & Greene, E. (1980). Warning: Even memory for faces may be contagious. *Law and Human Behavior, 4*, 323–334.

Loftus, E. F., & Guyer, M. J. (2002). Who abused Jane Doe? The hazards of the single case history. *Skeptical Inquirer, 26*, 24–32.

Loftus, E. F., & Palmer, J. C. (1974). Reconstruction of automobile destruction: An example of the interaction between language and memory. *Journal of Verbal Learning and Verbal Behavior, 13*, 585–589.

Logie, R. H. (2012). Disorders of attention. In D. Reisberg (Ed.), *The Oxford handbook of cognitive psychology*. New York, NY: Oxford University Press.

Logie, R. H., & Della Salla, S. (2005). Disorders of visuospatial working memory. In P. Shah & A. Miyake (Eds.), *The Cambridge handbook of visuospatial thinking* (pp. 81–120). New York, NY: Cambridge University Press.

Lopes, P. N., Salovey, P., Cote, S., & Beers, M. (2005). Emotion regulation ability and the quality of social interaction. *Emotion, 5*, 113–118.

Lubinski, D. (2004). Introduction to the special section on cognitive abilities: 100 years after Spearman's (1904) "'General intelligence,' objectively determined and measured." *Journal of Personality and Social Psychology, 86*, 96–111.

Lucas, M. (2000). Semantic priming without association: A meta-analytic review. *Psychonomic Bulletin & Review, 7*, 618–630.

Luchins, A. (1942). *Mechanization in problem solving: The effect of Einstellung*. (Psychological Monographs, Vol. 54, No. 6 [whole no. 248]). Evanston, IL: American Psychological Association.

Luchins, A., & Luchins, E. (1950). New experimental attempts at preventing mechanization in problem solving. *Journal of General Psychology, 42*, 279–297.

Luchins, A., & Luchins, E. (1959). *Rigidity of behavior: A variational approach to the effects of Einstellung*. Eugene: University of Oregon Books.

Luminet, O., & Curci, A. (Eds.). (2009). *Flashbulb memories: New issues and new perspectives*. New York, NY: Psychology Press.

Luria, A. R. (1966). *Higher cortical functions in man*. New York, NY: Basic Books.

Lynn, S., Neuschatz, J., Fite, R., & Rhue. J. (2001) Hypnosis and memory: Implications for the courtroom and psychotherapy. In M. Eisen & G. Goodman (Eds.), *Memory, suggestion, and the forensic interview*. New York, NY: Guilford Press.

MacDonald, J., & Lavie, N. (2008). Load induced blindness. *Journal of Experimental Psychology: Human Perception & Performance, 34*, 1078–1091.

MacDonald, M., Pearlmutter, N., & Seidenberg, M. (1994). The lexical nature of syntactic ambiguity. *Psychological Review, 101*, 676–703.

MacGregor, J. N., Ormerod, T. C., & Chronicle, E. P. (2001). Information processing and insight: A process model of performance on the 9-dot and related problems. *Journal of Experimental Psychology: Learning, Memory and Cognition, 27*, 176–201.

Machin, S., & Pekkarinen, T. (2008). Global sex differences in test score variability. *Science, 322*, 1331–1332.

Mack, A. (2003). Inattentional blindness: Looking without seeing. *Current Directions in Psychological Science, 12*, 180–184.

Mack, A., & Rock, I. (1998). *Inattentional blindness*. Cambridge, MA: MIT Press.

Mahon, B., & Caramazza, A. (2009). Concepts and categories: A cogniive neuropsychological perspective. *Annual Review of Psychology, 60*, 27–51.

Mahoney, M., & DeMonbreun, B. (1978). Problem-solving bias in scientists. *Cognitive Therapy and Research, 1*, 229–238.

Maia, T. V., & Cleeremans, A. (2005). Consciousness: Converging insights from connectionist modeling and neuroscience. *Trends in Cognitive Sciences, 9*, 397–404.

Maia, T. V., & McClelland, J. L. (2005). The somatic marker hypothesis: Still many questions but no answers. *Trends in Cognitive Sciences, 9*, 162–164.

Majid, A., Bowerman, M., Kita, S., Haun, D. B. M., & Levinson, S. (2004). Can language restructure cognition? The case for space. *Trends in Cognitive Sciences, 8*, 108–114.

Malt, B. C., & Smith, E. E. (1984). Correlated properties in natural categories. *Journal of Verbal Learning and Verbal Behavior, 23,* 250–269.

Mandler, G. (2008). Familiarity breeds attempts: A critical review of dual-process theories of recognition. *Perspectives on Psychological Science, 3,* 390–399.

Mandler, J. M., & Ritchey, G. H. (1977). Long-term memory for pictures. *Journal of Experimental Psychology: Human Learning and Memory, 3,* 386–396.

Marcus, G. B. (1986). Stability and change in political attitudes: Observe, recall, and "explain." *Political Behavior, 8,* 21–44.

Marcus, G. F. (2001). The algebraic mind: Integrating connectionism and cognitive science. Cambridge, MA: MIT Press.

Marcus, G. F., Pinker, S., Ullman, M., Hollander, M., Rosen, T., & Xu, F. (1992). *Overregularization in language acquisition* (Monographs of the Society for Research in Child Development, Vol. 57, No. 4 [serial no. 228]). Chicago, IL: University of Chicago Press.

Marcus, G. F., Vijayan, S., Rao, S. B., & Vishton, P. M. (1999). Rule learning by seven-month-old infants. *Science, 283,* 77–80.

Marino, A., & Scholl, B. (2005). The role of closure in defining the "objects" of object-based attention. *Perception & Psychophysics, 67,* 1140–1149.

Markman, A. B., & Gentner, D. (2001). Thinking. *Annual Review of Psychology, 52,* 223–247.

Marks, D. (1983). Mental imagery and consciousness: A theoretical review. In A. Sheikh (Ed.), *Imagery: Current theory, research and application* (pp. 96–130). New York, NY: Wiley.

Marmor, G. S., & Zabeck, L. A. (1976). Mental rotation by the blind: Does mental rotation depend on visual imagery? *Journal of Experimental Psychology: Human Perception and Performance, 2,* 515–521.

Marslen-Wilson, W. D. (1987). Functional parallelism in spoken word recognition. *Cognition, 25,* 71–102.

Marslen-Wilson, W. D. (1990). Activation, competition, and frequency in lexical access. In G. T. Altmann (Ed.), *Cognitive models of speech processing: Psycholinguistic and computational perspectives* (pp. 148–172). Cambridge, MA: MIT Press.

Marslen-Wilson, W. D., & Teuber, H. L. (1975). Memory for remote events in anterograde amnesia: Recognition of public figures from news photographs. *Neuropsychologia, 13,* 353–364.

Martin, M., & Jones, G. V. (2006). Visual sharpness contingency in recognition memory for orientation: Mnemonic illusion suppressed by sensory signature. *Journal of Experimental Psychology: General, 135,* 542–552.

Martin, R. C. (2003). Language processing: Functional organization and neuroanatomical basis. *Annual Review of Psychology, 54,* 55–89.

Maritnez, M. E. (2000). *Education as the cultivation of intelligence.* Mahwah, NJ: Erlbaum.

Massaro, D. (1994). Psychological aspects of speech perception. In M. A. Gernsbacher (Ed.), *Handbook of psycholinguistics* (pp. 219–263). New York, NY: Academic Press.

Massimini, M., Ferrarelli, F., Huber, R., Esser, S., Singh, H., & Tononi, G. (2005). Breakdown of cortical effective connectivity during sleep. *Science, 309,* 2228–2232.

Mather, M., Shafir, E., & Johnson, M. K. (2000). Misremembrance of options past: Source monitoring and choice. *Psychological Science, 11,* 132–138.

Matsuki, K., Chow, T., Hare, M., Elman, J., Scheepers, C., & McRae, K. (2011). Event- based plausibility influences on-line language comprehension. *Journal of Experimental Psychology: Learning, Memory & Cognition, 37,* 913–934.

Mattys, S. (2012). Speech perception. In D. Reisberg, (Ed.), *The Oxford handbook of cognitive psychology.* N.Y.: Oxford University Press.

Mayer, J. D., Roberts, R. D., & Barsade, S. G. (2008a). Human abilities: Emotional intelligence. *Annual Review of Psychology, 59,* 507–536.

Mayer, R. E. (2012). Problem solving. In D. Reisberg (Ed.), *The Oxford handbook of cognitive psychology.* New York, NY: Oxford University Press.

Mayr, U. (2004). Conflict, consciousness, and control. *Trends in Cognitive Sciences, 8,* 145–148.

Mazzoni, G., & Lynn, S. (2007). Using hypnosis in eyewitness memory. In D. Ross, M. Toglia, R. Lindsay, & D. Read (Eds.), *Handbook of eyewitness memory: Vol. 1. Memory for events.* Mahwah, NJ: Erlbaum.

Mazzoni, G., Loftus, E. F., & Kirsch, I. (2001). Changing beliefs about implausible autobiographical events. *Journal of Experimental Psychology: Applied, 7,* 51–59.

Mazzoni, G., & Memon, A. (2003). Imagination can create false autobiographical memories. *Psychological Science, 14,* 186–188.

McAdams, C., & Reid, R. (2005). Attention modulates the responses of simple cells in the monkey visual cortex. *Journal of Neuroscience, 25,* 11022–11033.

McCaffrey, T. (2012). Innovation relies on the obscure: A key to overcoming the classic problem of functional fixedness. *Psychological Science, 23,* 215–218.

McCann, R., & Johnston, J. (1992). Locus of the single-channel bottleneck in dual-task interference. *Journal of Experimental Psychology: Human Perception and Performance, 18,* 471–484.

McClelland, J. L., & Rumelhart, D. E. (1981). An interactive model of context effects in letter perception. Part 1. An account of basic findings. *Psychological Review, 88,* 375–407.

McCllelland, J. L., Mirman, D., & Holt, L. (2006). Are there interactive processes in speech perception? *Trends in Cognitive Sciences, 10,* 363–369.

McCloskey, M., & Glucksberg, S. (1978). Natural categories. Well-defined or fuzzy sets? *Memory & Cognition, 6,* 462–472.

McDaniel, M., Anderson, J., Derbish, M., & Morrisette, N. (2007). Testing the testing effect in the classroom. *European Journal of Cognitive Psychology, 19,* 494–513.

McDaniel, M., & Einstein, G. (1986). Bizarre imagery as an effective mnemonic aid: The importance of distinctiveness. *Journal of Experimental Psychology: Learning, Memory and Cognition, 12*, 54–65.

McDaniel, M., & Einstein, G. (1990). Bizarre imagery: Mnemonic benefits and theoretical implications. In R. Logie & M. Denis (Eds.), *Mental images in human cognition* (pp. 183–192). New York, NY: North Holland.

McDermott, K. B., & Roediger, H. (1994). Effects of imagery on perceptual implicit memory tests. *Journal of Experimental Psychology: Learning, Memory and Cognition, 20*, 1379–1390.

McDermott, K. B., & Roediger, H. (1998). False recognition of associates can be resistant to an explicit warning to subjects and an immediate recognition probe. *Journal of Memory & Language, 39*, 508–520.

McFarland, C., & Buehler, R. (2012). Negative moods and the motivated remembering of past selves: The role of implicit theories of personal stability. *Journal of Personality and Social Psychology, 102*, 242–263.

McGaugh, J. L. (2000). Memory—A century of consolidation. *Science, 287*, 248–251.

McGrew, K. (2009). CHC theory and the human cognitive abilities project: Standing on the shoulders of the giants of psychometric intelligence research. *Intelligence, 37*, 1–10.

McGue, M., Bouchard, T. J., Jr., Iacono, W. G., & Lykken, D. T. (1993). Behavioral genetics of cognitive ability: A life span perspective. In R. Plomin & G. E. McClearn (Eds.), *Nature, nurture and psychology* (pp. 59–76). Washington, DC: American Psychological Association.

McGuire, M. J., & Maki, R. H. (2001). When knowing more means less: The effect of fan on metamemory judgment. *Journal of Experimental Psychology: Learning, Memory and Cognition, 27*, 1172–1179.

McIntosh, A. R., Rajah, M. N., & Lobaugh, N. J. (1999). Interactions of prefrontal cortex in relation to awareness in sensory learning. *Science, 284*, 1531–1533.

McKelvie, S. (1995). The VVIQ as a psychometric test of individual differences in visual imagery vividness: A critical quantitative review and plea for direction. *Journal of Mental Imagery, 19*(3&4), 1–106.

McKone, E., & Robbins, R. (2007). The evidence rejects the expertise hypothesis: Reply to Gauthier & Bukach. *Cognition, 103*(2), 331–336.

McKone, E., & Robbins, R. (2010). Are faces special? In A. W. Calder, G. Rhodes, M. Johnston, & J. C. Haxby (Eds.). *Handbook of face perception.* Oxford, England: Oxford University Press.

McNally, R. J. (2003). Recovering memories of trauma: A view from the laboratory. *Current Directions in Psychological Science, 12*, 32–35.

McNally, R. J., Lasko, N., Clancy, S. A., Macklin, M. L., Pitman, R. K., & Orr, S. P. (2004). Psychophysiological responding during script-driven imagery in people reporting abduction by space aliens. *Psychological Science, 15*, 493–497.

McRae, K., & Jones, M. (2012). Semantic memory. In D. Reisberg (Ed.), *The Oxford handbook of cognitive psychology.* New York, NY: Oxford University Press.

Meadows, J. C. (1974). Disturbed perception of colours associated with localized cerebral lesions. *Brain, 97*, 615–632.

Medin, D. L. (1989). Concepts and conceptual structure. *American Psychologist, 44*, 1469–1481.

Medin, D. L., Coley, J. D., Storms, G., & Hayes, B. K. (2003). A relevance theory of induction. *Psychonomic Bulletin & Review, 10*, 517–532.

Medin, D. L., Goldstone, R., & Gentner, D. (1993). Respects for similarity. *Psychological Review, 100*, 254–278.

Medin, D. L., & Ortony, A. (1989). Psychological essentialism. In S. Vosniadou & A. Ortony (Eds.), *Similarity and analogical reasoning* (pp. 179–195). New York, NY: Cambridge University Press.

Medin, D. L., Schwartz, H., Blok, S. V., & Birnbaum, L. A. (1999). The semantic side of decision making. *Psychonomic Bulletin & Review, 6*, 562–569.

Mednick, S. (1962). The associative basis of the creative process. *Psychological Review, 69*, 220–232.

Mednick, S., & Mednick, M. (1967). *Examiner's manual, Remote Associates Test.* Boston, MA: Houghton Mifflin.

Mellers, B., Chang, S.-J., Birnbaum, M., & Ordóñez, L. (1992). Preferences, prices, and ratings in risky decision making. *Journal of Experimental Psychology: Human Perception and Performance, 18*, 347–361.

Mellers, B., Schwartz, A., & Ritov, I. (1999). Emotion-based choice. *Journal of Experimental Psychology: General, 128*, 332–345.

Mervis, C. B., Catlin, J., & Rosch, E. (1976). Relationships among goodness-of-example, category norms and word frequency. *Bulletin of the Psychonomic Society, 7*, 268–284.

Metcalfe, J. (1986). Premonitions of insight predict impending error. *Journal of Experimental Psychology: Learning, Memory and Cognition, 12*, 623–634.

Metcalfe, J., & Weibe, D. (1987). Intuition in insight and noninsight problem solving. *Memory & Cognition, 15*, 238–246.

Meyer, D. E., & Schvaneveldt, R. W. (1971). Facilitation in recognizing pairs of words: Evidence of a dependence between retrieval operations. *Journal of Experimental Psychology, 90*, 227–234.

Meyer, D. E., Schvaneveldt, R. W., & Ruddy, M. G. (1974). Functions of graphemic and phonemic codes in visual word recognition. *Memory & Cognition, 2*, 309–321.

Michel, C., Rossion, B., Han, J., Chung, C.-S., & Caldara, R. (2006). Holistic processing is finely tuned for faces of one's own race. *Psychological Science, 17*, 608–615.

Mill, J. S. (1874). *A system of logic* (8th ed.). New York, NY: Harper.

Miller, A. (1986). *Imagery in scientific thought.* Cambridge, MA: MIT Press.

Miller, E. K., & Cohen, J. D. (2001). An integrative theory of prefrontal cortex function. *Annual Review of Neuroscience, 24*, 167–202.

Miller, E. K., & Cohen, J. D. (2001). An integrative theory of prefrontal cortex function. *Annual Review of Neuroscience, 24*, 167–202.

Miller, E. M. (1994). Intelligence and brain myelination: A hypothesis. *Personality and Individual Differences, 17*, 803–832.

Miller, G. A. (1951). *Language and communication.* New York, NY: McGraw-Hill.

Miller, G. A. (1956). The magical number seven plus or minus two: Some limits on our capacity for processing information. *Psychological Review, 63*, 81–97.

Miller, G. A. (1962). *Psychology: The science of mental life.* New York, NY: Harper & Row.

Miller, G. A. (1991). *The science of words.* New York, NY: Freeman.

Miller, G. A., Bruner, J. S., & Postman, L. (1954). Familiarity of letter sequences and tachistoscopic identification. *Journal of General Psychology, 50*, 129–139.

Miller, G. A., Galanter, E., & Pribram, K. (1960). *Plans and the structure of behavior.* New York, NY: Holt, Rinehart and Winston.

Miller, G. A., & Nicely, P. (1955). An analysis of perceptual confusions among some English consonants. *Journal of the Acoustical Society of America, 27*, 338–352.

Milner, B. (1966). Amnesia following operation on the temporal lobes. In C. W. M. Whitty & O. L. Zangwill (Eds.), *Amnesia* (pp. 109–133). London, England: Butterworths.

Milner, B. (1970). Memory and the medial temporal regions of the brain. In K. H. Pribram & D. E. Broadbent (Eds.), *Biology of memory* (pp. 29–48). New York, NY: Academic Press.

Minda, J. P., & Smith, J. D. (2001). Prototypes in category learning: The effects of category size, category structure and stimulus complexity. *Journal of Experimental Psychology: Learning, Memory and Cognition, 27*, 775–799.

Mitroff, I. (1981). Scientists and confirmation bias. In R. Tweney, M. Doherty, & C. Mynatt (Eds.), *On scientific thinking* (pp. 170–175). New York, NY: Columbia University Press.

Miyake, A., & Friedman, N. (2012). The nature and organization of individual differences in executive functions: Four general conclusions. *Current Directions in Psychological Science, 21*, 8–14.

Miyake, A., Kost-Smith, L., Finkelstein, N., Pollock, S., Cohen, G., & Ito, T. (2010). Reducing the gender achievement gap in college science: A classroom study of values affirmation. *Science, 330*, 1234–1237.

Miyashita, Y. (1995). How the brain creates imagery: Projection to primary visual cortex. *Science, 268*, 1719–1720.

Moons, W. G., Mackie, D. M., & Garcia-Marques, T. (2009). The impact of repetition-induced familarity on agreement with weak and strong arguments. *Journal of Personality & Social Psychology, 96*, 32–44.

Moore, C. M., & Egeth, H. (1997). Perception without attention: Evidence of grouping under conditions of inattention. *Journal of Experimental Psychology: Human Perception and Performance, 23*, 339–352.

Moray, N. (1959). Attention in dichotic listening: Affective cues and the influence of instructions. *Quarterly Journal of Experimental Psychology, 11*, 56–60.

Moreno, S., Bialystok, E., Barac, R., Schellenberg, G., Cepeda, N., & Chau, T. (2011). Short-term music training enhances verbal intelligence and executive function. *Psychological Science, 22*, 1425–1433.

Morewedge, C., & Kahneman, D. (2010). Associative processes in intuitive judgment. *Trends in Cognitive Sciences, 14*, 435–440.

Morrison, C., & Conway, M. (2010). First words and first memories. *Cognition, 116*, 23–32.

Morsella, E., & Bargh, J. (2011). Unconscious action tendencies: Sources of "unintegrated" action. In Caciopo, J. & Decety, J. (Eds.), *The handbook of social neuroscience* (pp. 335–347). New York, NY: Oxford.

Morsella, E., Krieger, S., & Bargh, J. (2010). Minimal neuroanatomy for a conscious brain: Homing in on the networks constituting consciousness. *Neural Networks, 23*, 14–15.

Moscovitch, M. (1982). Multiple dissociations of function in amnesia. In L. S. Cermak (Ed.), *Human memory and amnesia* (pp. 337–370). Hillsdale, NJ: Erlbaum.

Moss, J., Kotovsky, K., & Cagan, J. (2011). The effect of incidental hints when problems are suspended before, during, or after an impasse. *Journal of Experimental Psychology: Learning, Memory & Cognition, 37*, 140–148.

Most, S. B., Simons, D. J., Scholl, B. J., Jimenez, R., Clifford, E., & Chabris, C. F. (2001). How not to be seen: The contribution of similarity and selective ignoring to sustained inattentional blindness. *Psychological Science, 12*, 9–17.

Mulligan, N. W., & Besken, M. (2012). Implicit memory. In D. Reisberg (Ed.), *The Oxford handbook of cognitive psychology.* New York, NY: Oxford University Press.

Mumford, M., & Antes, A. (2007). Debates about the "general" picture: Cognition and creative achievement. *Creativity Research Journal, 19*, 367–374.

Murdock, B. B., Jr. (1962). The serial position effect of free recall. *Journal of Experimental Psychology, 64*, 482–488.

Murphy, G. L. (2003). *The big book of concepts.* Cambridge, MA: MIT Press.

Murphy, G. L., & Medin, D. L. (1985). The role of theories in conceptual coherence. *Psychological Review, 92*, 289–316.

Murphy, G. L., & Ross, B. H. (2005). The two faces of typicality in category-based induction. *Cognition, 95*, 175–200.

Murphy, S. T. (2001). Feeling without thinking: Affective primacy and the nonconscious processing of emotion. In J. A. Bargh & D. K. Apsley (Eds.), *Unraveling the complexities of social life: A festschrift in honor of Robert B. Zajonc* (pp. 39–53). Washington, DC: American Psychological Association.

Mynatt, C., Doherty, M., & Tweney, R. (1977). Confirmation bias in a simulated research environment: An experimental study of scientific inference. *Quarterly Journal of Experimental Psychology, 29,* 85–95.

Mynatt, C., Doherty, M., & Tweney, R. (1978). Consequences of confirmation and disconfirmation in a simulated research environment. *Quarterly Journal of Experimental Psychology, 30,* 395–406.

Nadel, L., & Moscovitch, M. (2001). The hippocampal complex and long-term memory revisited. *Trends in Cognitive Sciences, 5,* 228–230.

Nakamura, J., & Csikszentmihalyi, M. (2001). Catalytic creativity: The case of Linus Pauling. *American Psychologist, 56,* 337–341.

Naqvi, N., Shiv, B., & Bechara, A. (2006). The role of emotion in decision making. *Current Directions in Psychological Science, 15,* 260–264.

Nasar, J., Hecht, P., & Wener, R. (2008). Mobile telephones, distracted attention, and pedestrian safety. *Accident Analysis and Prevention, 4,* 69–75.

Nee, D., Berman, M., Moore, K., & Jonides, J. (2008). Neuroscientific evidence about the distinction between short- and long-term memory. *Current Directions in Psycholkogical Science, 17,* 102–106.

Needham, D., & Begg, I. (1991). Problem-oriented training promotes spontaneous analogical transfer: Memory-oriented training promotes memory for training. *Memory & Cognition, 19,* 543–557.

Neely, J. H. (1977). Semantic priming and retrieval from lexical memory: Role of inhibitionless spreading activation and limited capacity attention. *Journal of Experimental Psychology: General, 106,* 226–254.

Neisser, U. (1967). *Cognitive psychology.* New York, NY: Appleton-Century-Crofts.

Neisser, U., & Becklen, R. (1975). Selective looking: Attending to visually significant events. *Cognitive Psychology, 7,* 480–494.

Neisser, U., Boodoo, G., Bouchard, T. J., Jr., Boykin, A. W., Brody, N., Ceci, S. J., et al. (1996). Intelligence: Knowns and unknowns. *American Psychologist, 51(2),* 77–101.

Neisser, U., & Harsch, N. (1992). Phantom flashbulbs: False recollections of hearing the news about *Challenger.* In E. Winograd & U. Neisser (Eds.), *Affect and accuracy in recall: Studies of "flashbulb" memories* (pp. 9–31). Cambridge, England: Cambridge University Press.

Neisser, U., Winograd, E., & Weldon, M. S. (1991, November). *Remembering the earthquake: "What I experienced" vs. "How I heard the news."* Paper presented at the meeting of the Psychonomic Society, San Francisco, CA.

Nettelbeck, T. (2003). Inspection time and g. In H. Nyborg (Ed.), *The scientific study of general intelligence: A tribute to Arthur Jensen* (pp. 77–92). New York: Elsevier.

Newcombe, N. S. (2007). Taking science seriously: Straight thinking about spatial sex differences. In S. Ceci & W. Williams (Eds.), *Why aren't more women in science?* (pp. 69–77). Washington, DC: American Psychological Association.

Newcombe, F., Ratcliff, G., & Damasio, H. (1987). Dissociable visual and spatial impairments following right posterior cerebral lesions: Clinical, neuropsychological and anatomical evidence. *Neuropsychologia, 25,* 149–161.

Newell, A., & Simon, H. (1972). *Human problem solving.* Englewood Cliffs, NJ: Prentice-Hall.

Nickerson, R. S., & Adams, M. J. (1979). Long-term memory for a common object. *Cognitive Psychology, 11,* 287–307.

Nisbett, R. (Ed.). (1993). *Rules for reasoning.* Hillsdale, NJ: Erlbaum.

Nisbett, R., Krantz, D. H., Jepson, C., & Kunda, Z. (1983). The use of statistical heuristics in everyday inductive reasoning. *Psychological Review, 90,* 339–363.

Nisbett, R., & Ross, L. (1980). *Human inference: Strategies and shortcomings of social judgment.* Englewood Cliffs, NJ: Prentice-Hall.

Nisbett, R., & Schachter, S. (1966). Cognitive manipulation of pain. *Journal of Experimental Social Psychology, 2,* 277–236.

Nisbett, R., & Wilson, T. (1977). Telling more than we can know: Verbal reports on mental processes. *Psychological Review, 84,* 231–259.

Nisbett, R. E., & Miyamoto, Y. (2005). The influence of culture: Holistic versus analytic perception. *Trends in Cognitive Science, 9,* 467–473.

Norman, D. (1981). Categorization of action slips. *Psychological Review, 88,* 1–15.

Norman, D., & Shallice, T. (1986). Attention to action: Willed and automatic control of behavior. In R. Davidson, G. Schwartz, & D. Shapiro (Eds.), *Consciousness and self-regulation* (pp. 1–18). New York, NY: Plenum.

Norman, D., Rumelhart, D. E., & Group, T. L. R. (1975). *Explorations in cognition.* San Francisco: Freeman.

Noveck, I., & Reboul, A. (2008). Experimental pragmatics: A Gricean turn in the study of language. *Trends in Cognitive Sciences, 12,* 425–431.

Noveck, J., & Sperber, D. (2005). *Experimental pragmatics.* New York, NY: Oxford University Press.

Novick, L., & Holyoak, K. (1991). Mathematical problem solving by analogy. *Journal of Experimental Psychology: Learning, Memory and Cognition, 17,* 398–415.

O'Connor, D., Fukui, M., Pinsk, M., & Kastner, S. (2002). Attention modulates responses in the human lateral geniculate nucleus. *Nature Neuroscience, 5,* 1203–1209.

O'Connor, M., Walbridge, M., Sandson, T., & Alexander, M. (1996). A neuropsychological analysis of Capgras syndrome. *Neuropsychiatry, Neuropsychology, and Behavioral Neurology, 9,* 265–271.

O'Craven, K. M., & Kanwisher, N. (2000). Mental imagery of faces and places activates corresponding stimulus-specific brain regions. *Journal of Cognitive Neuroscience, 12,* 1013–1023.

O'Kane, G., Kensinger, E. A., & Corkin, S. (2004). Evidence for semantic learning in profound amnesia: An investigation with patient H.M. *Hippocampus, 14(4),* 417–425.

Oaksford, M., & Chater, N. (1995). Information gain explains relevance which explains the selection task. *Cognition, 57,* 97–108.

Obrecht, N., Chapman, G., & Gelman, R. (2009). An encounter frequency account of how experience affects likelihood estimation. *Memory & Cognition, 37,* 632–643.

Ochsner, K. N., & Schacter, D. L. (2000). A social cognitive neuroscience approach to emotion and memory. In J. C. Borod (Ed.), *The neuropsychology of emotion* (pp. 163–193). New York, NY: Oxford University Press.

Öhman, A. (2002). Automaticity and the amygdala: Nonconscious responses to emotional faces. *Current Directions in Psychological Science, 11,* 62–66.

Oldfield, R. (1963). Individual vocabulary and semantic currency: A preliminary study. *British Journal of Social and Clinical Psychology, 2,* 122–130.

Oliphant, G. W. (1983). Repetition and recency effects in word recognition. *Australian Journal of Psychology, 35,* 393–403.

Oppenheimer, D. M. (2004). Spontaneous discounting of availability in frequency judgment tasks. *Psychological Science, 15,* 100–105.

Oppenheimer, D. M. (2005). Consequences of erudite vernacular utilized irrespective of necessity: Problems with using long words needlessly. *Applied Cognitive Psychology, 20*(2), 139–156.

Oppenheimer, D. M. (2008). The secret life of fluency. *Trends in Cognitive Sciences, 12,* 237–241.

Oppenheimer, D. M. (2008). The secret life of fluency. *Trends in Cognitive Sciences, 12,* 237–241.

Oppenheimer, D. M., & Frank, M. C. (2007). A rose in any other font wouldn't smell as sweet: Fluency effects in categorization. *Cognition, 106,* 1178–1194.

Osman, M. (2004). An evaluation of dual-process theories of reasoning. *Psychonomic Bulletin & Review, 11,* 988–1010.

Ost, J., Vrij, A., Costall, A., & Bull, R. (2002). Crashing memories and reality monitoring: Distinguishing between perceptions, imaginations and "false memories." *Applied Cognitive Psychology, 16,* 125–134.

Overton, D. (1985). Contextual stimulus effects of drugs and internal states. In P. D. Balsam & A. Tomie (Eds.), *Context and learning* (pp. 357–384). Hillsdale, NJ: Erlbaum.

Owens, J., Bower, G. H., & Black, J. B. (1979). The "soap opera" effect in story recall. *Memory & Cognition, 7,* 185–191.

Özgen, E. (2004). Language, learning, and color perception. *Current Directions in Psychological Science, 13,* 95–98.

Özgen, E., & Davies, I. R. L. (2002). Acquisition of categorical color perception: A perceptual learning approach to the linguistic relativity hypothesis. *Journal of Experimental Psychology: General, 131,* 477–493.

Paivio, A. (1969). Mental imagery in associative learning and memory. *Psychological Review, 76,* 241–263.

Paivio, A. (1971). *Imagery and verbal processes.* New York, NY: Holt, Rinehart & Winston.

Paivio, A., & Csapo, K. (1969). Concrete image and verbal memory codes. *Journal of Experimental Psychology, 80,* 279–285.

Paivio, A., & Okovita, H. W. (1971). Word imagery modalities and associative learning in blind and sighted subjects. *Journal of Verbal Learning and Verbal Behavior, 10,* 506–510.

Paivio, A., Smythe, P. C., & Yuille, J. C. (1968). Imagery versus meaningfulness of nouns in paired-associate learning. *Canadian Journal of Psychology, 22,* 427–441.

Paivio, A., Yuille, J. C., & Madigan, S. (1968). *Concreteness, imagery, and meaningfulness values for 925 nouns.* Journal of Experimental Psychology Monograph Supplement, Vol. 76, No. 1, Pt. 2. Washington, DC: American Psychological Association.

Palmer, S., Schreiber, C., & Fox, C. (1991, November). *Remembering the earthquake: "Flashbulb" memory for experienced vs. reported events.* Paper presented at the meeting of the Psychonomic Society, San Francisco, CA.

Pansky, A., & Koriat, A. (2004). The basic-level convergence effect in memory distortions. *Psychological Science, 15,* 52–59.

Papafragou, A., Li, P., Choi, Y., & Han, C-h. (2007). Evidentiality in language and cognition. *Cognition, 103,* 253–299.

Parker, E., Cahill, L., & McGaugh, J. (2006). A case of unusual autobiographical remembering. *Neurocase, 121,* 35–49.

Parkin, A. J. (1984). Levels of processing, context, and facilitation of pronunciation. *Acta Psychologia, 55,* 19–29.

Parsons, J. E., Adler, T. F., & Kaczala, C. M. (1982). Socialization of achievement attitudes and beliefs: Parental influences. *Child Development, 53*(2), 310–321.

Pashler, H. (1991). Dual-task interference and elementary mental mechanisms. In D. E. Meyer & S. Kornblum (Eds.), *Attention and performance XIV* (pp. 245–264). Hillsdale, NJ: Erlbaum.

Pashler, H. (1992). Attentional limitations in doing two tasks at the same time. *Current Directions in Psychological Science, 1,* 44–47.

Pashler, H. (1996). Structures, processes and the flow of information. In E. Bjork & R. Bjork (Eds.), *Handbook of perception and cognition,* 2nd ed., Vol. 10: *Memory* (pp. 3–29). San Diego, CA: Academic Press.

Pashler, H., & Johnston, J. (1989). Interference between temporally overlapping tasks: Chronometric evidence for central postponement with or without response grouping. *Quarterly Journal of Experimental Psychology, 41A,* 19–45.

Pashler, H., Rohrer, D., Cepeda, N., & Carpenter, S. (2007). Enhancing learning and retarding forgetting: Choices and consequences. *Psychonomic Bulletin & Review, 14,* 187–193.

Payne, J. D., Nadel, L., Britton, W. B., & Jacobs, W. J. (2004). The bio-psychology of trauma and memory. In D. Reisberg & P. Hertel (Eds.), *Memory and emotion* (pp. 76–128). New York, NY: Oxford University Press.

Payton, A. (2009). The impact of genetic research on our understanding of normal cognitive aging: 1995 to 2009. *Neuropsychology Review, 19*, 451–477.

Paz-Alonso, P., & Goodman, G. (2008). Trauma and memory: Effects of post-event misinformation, retrieval order, and retention interval. *Memory, 16*, 58–75.

Peace, K. A., & Porter, S. (2004). A longitudinal investigation of the reliability of memories for trauma and other emotional experiences. *Applied Cognitive Psychology, 18*, 143–1159.

Pearson, J., Rademaker, R. L., & Tong, F. (2011). Evaluating the mind's eye: The metacognition of visual imagery. *Psychological Science, 22*, 1535–1542.

Pederson, E., Danziger, E., Wilkins, D., Levinson, S., Kita, S., & Senft, G. (1998). Semantic typology and spatial conceptualization. *Language, 74*, 557–589.

Pedrone, R., Hummel, J. E., & Holyoak, K. J. (2001). The use of diagrams in analogical problem solving. *Memory & Cognition, 29*, 214–221.

Peissig, J., & Tarr, M. J. (2007). Visual object recognition: Do we know more now than we did 20 years ago? *Annual Review of Psychology, 58*, 75–96.

Penfield, W., & Roberts, L. (1959). *Speech and brain mechanisms.* Prince-ton, NJ: Princeton University Press.

Penn, D. C., & Povinelli, D. J. (2012). The human enigma. In Holyoak, K. J., & Morrison, R. G. (Eds.), *The Oxford Handbook of Thinking and Reasoning* (pp. 529–542). New York, NY: Oxford University Press.

Peterson, M., Kihlstrom, J. F., Rose, P., & Glisky, M. (1992). Mental images can be ambiguous: Reconstruals and reference-frame reversals. *Memory & Cognition, 20*, 107–123.

Pezdek, K., Blandon-Gitlin, I., & Gabbay, P. (2006). Imagination and memory: Does imagining implausible events lead to false autobiographical memories? *Psychonomic Bulletin & Review, 13*, 764–769.

Phelps, E. (2004). Human emotion and memory: Interactions of the amygdala and hippocampal complex. *Current Opinion in Neurobiology, 14*, 198–202.

Phillips, J., KIein, G., & Sieck, W. (2004). Expertise in judgment and decision making: A case for training intuitive decision skills. In D. Koeh-ler & N. Harvey (Eds.), *Blackwell handbook of judgment and decision making* (pp. 297–315). Malden, MA: Blackwell.

Piaget, J. (1952). *The origins of intelligence in children.* New York, NY: International Universities Press.

Pillemer, D. B. (1984). Flashbulb memories of the assassination attempt on President Reagan. *Cognition, 16*, 63–80.

Pinker, S (1994). The language instinct: How the mind creates language. New York, NY: Harper Perennial.

Pinker, S. (1987). The bootstrapping problem in language acquisition. In B. MacWhinney (Ed.), *Mechanisms of language acquisition* (pp. 339–441). Hillsdale, NJ: Erlbaum.

Pinker, S. (1991). Rules of language. *Science, 253*, 530–535.

Pinker, S. (1994). *The language instinct.* New York, NY: Penguin.

Plomin, R., Corley, R., DeFries, J. C., & Fulker, D. W. (1990). Individual differences in television viewing in early childhood: Nature as well as nurture. *Psychological Science, 1*, 371–377.

Plomin, R., & Spinath, F. M. (2004). Intelligence: Genetics, genes, and genomics. *Journal of Personality and Social Psychology, 86*, 112–129.

Poeppel, D., & Hickok, G. (2004). Towards a new functional anatomy of language. *Cognition, 92*, 1–12.

Polk, T., & Newell, A. (1995). Deduction as verbal reasoning. *Psychological Review, 102*, 533–566.

Pollack, I., & Pickett, J. (1964). Intelligibility of excerpts from fluent speech: Auditory versus structural context. *Journal of Verbal Learning and Verbal Behavior, 3*, 79–84.

Poole, D. A., & Lindsay, D. S. (2001). Children's eyewitness reports after exposure to misinformation from parents. *Journal of Experimental Psychology: Applied, 7*, 27–50.

Popper, K. (1934). *The logic of scientific discovery.* London, England: Routledge.

Porter, S., & Peace, K. A. (2007). The scars of memory: A prospective, longitudinal investigation of the consistency of traumatic and positive emotional memories in adulthood. *Psychological Science, 18*(5), 435–441.

Posner, M., & Rothbart, M., (2007). Research on attention networks as a model for the integration of psychological science. *Annual Review of Psychology, 58*, 1–23.

Posner, M., & Snyder, C. (1975). Facilitation and inhibition in the processing of signals. In P. Rabbitt & S. Dornic (Eds.), *Attention and performance V* (pp. 669–682). New York, NY: Academic Press.

Posner, M., Snyder, C., & Davidson, B. (1980). Attention and the detection of signals. *Journal of Experimental Psychology: General, 109*, 160–174.

Postman, L., & Phillips, L. W. (1965). Short-term temporal changes in free recall. *Quarterly Journal of Experimental Psychology, 17*, 132–138.

Pretz, J. (2008). Intuition versus analysis: Strategy and experience in complex everyday problem solving. *Memory & Cognition, 36*, 554–566.

Pylyshyn, Z. (1981). The imagery debate: Analogue media versus tacit knowledge. In N. Block (Ed.), *Imagery* (pp. 151–206). Cambridge, MA: MIT Press.

Qiu, J., Li, H., Yang, D., Luo, Y., Li, Y., Wu, Z., & Zhang, Q. (2008). The neural basis of insight problem solving: An event-related potential study. *Brain and Cognition, 68*, 100–106.

Quinlan, P. T. (2003). Visual feature integration theory: Past, present and future. *Psychological Bulletin, 129*, 643–673.

Rae, C., Digney, A. L., McEwan, S. R., & Bates, T. C. (2003). Oral creatine monohydrate supplementation improves brain performance: A double-blind, placebo-controlled, cross-over trial. *Proceedings of the Royal Society of London, Series B: Biological Sciences, 270*, 2147–2150.

Raghubir, P., & Menon, G. (2005). When and why is ease of retrieval informative? *Memory & Cognition, 33*, 821–832.

Raizada, R., & Kishiyama, M. (2010). Effects of socioeconomic status on brain development. *Frontiers in Human Neuroscience, 5*, 1–18.

Ramachandran, V. S., & Blakeslee, S. (1998). *Phantoms in the brain.* New York, NY: Morrow.

Ramsden, S., Richdson, F., Josse, G., Thomas, M., Ellis, C., Shakeshaft, C. Seghier, M. & Price, C. (2011). Verbal and nonverbal intelligence changes in the teenage brain. *Nature, 479*, 113–116.

Ranganath, C., & Blumenfeld, R. S. (2005). Doubts about double dissociations between short- and long-term memory. *Trends in Cognitive Sciences, 9*, 374–380.

Ranganath, C., Yonelinas, A. P., Cohen, M. X., Dy, C. J., Tom, S., & D'Esposito, M. (2003). Dissociable correlates for familiarity and recollection within the medial temporal lobes. *Neuropsychologia, 42*, 2–13.

Rao, G. A., Larkin, E. C., & Derr, R. F. (1986). Biologic effects of chronic ethanol consumption related to a deficient intake of carbohydrates. *Alcohol and Alcoholism, 21*, 369–373.

Rathbone, C. J., Moulin, C. J. A., & Conway, M. A. (2008). Self-centered memories: The reminiscence bump and the self. *Memory & Cognition, 36*, 1403–1414.

Ravenzwaaij, D. V., Brown, S., & Wagenmakers, E.-J. (2011). An integrated perspective on the relation between response speed and intelligence. *Cognition, 119*, 381–393.

Rayner, K., & Pollatsek, A. (2011). Basic processes in reading. In D. Reisberg (Ed.), *Handbook of cognitive psychology.* New York, NY: Oxford University Press.

Read, J. D. (1999). The recovered/false memory debate: Three steps forward, two steps back? *Expert Evidence, 7*, 1–24.

Reason, J. T. (1990). *Human error.* Cambridge, England: Cambridge University Press.

Redelmeier, D., & Shafir, E. (1995). Medical decision making in situations that offer multiple alternatives. *Journal of the American Medical Association, 273*, 4, 302–305.

Redelmeier, D. A., & Tversky, A. (1996). On the belief that arthritis pain is related to the weather. *Proceedings of the National Academic of Sciences, USA, 93*, 2895–2896.

Reed, S. (1993). Imagery and discovery. In B. Roskos-Ewoldsen, M. J. Intons-Peterson, & R. Anderson (Eds.), *Imagery, creativity, and discovery: A cognitive perspective* (pp. 287–312). New York, NY: North-Holland.

Rees, G., Kreiman, G., & Koch, C. (2002). Neural correlates of consciousness in humans. *Nature Reviews Neuroscience, 3*, 261–270.

Reeves, L., & Weisberg, R. (1994). The role of content and abstract information in analogical transfer. *Psychological Bulletin, 115*, 381–400.

Rehder, B., & Hastie, R. (2001). Causal knowledge and categories: The effects of causal beliefs on categorization, induction, and similarity. *Journal of Experimental Psychology: General, 130*, 323–360.

Rehder, B., & Hastie, R. (2004). Category coherence and category-based property induction. *Cognition, 91*, 113–153.

Rehder, B., & Ross, B. H. (2001). Abstract coherent categories. *Journal of Experimental Psychology: Learning, Memory, & Cognition, 27*, 1261–1275.

Reicher, G. M. (1969). Perceptual recognition as a function of meaningfulness of stimulus material. *Journal of Experimental Psychology, 81*, 275–280.

Reisberg, D. (1996). The non-ambiguity of mental images. In C. Cornold, R. H. Logie, M. Brandimonte, G. Kaufmann & D. Reisberg (Eds.), *Stretching the imagination: Representation and transformation in mental imagery* (pp. 119–171). New York, NY: Oxford University Press.

Reisberg, D. (2000). The detachment gain: The advantage of thinking out loud. In B. Landau, J. Sabini, E. Newport, & J. Jonides (Eds.), *Perception, cognition and language: Essays in honor of Henry and Lila Gleitman* (pp. 139–156). Cambridge, MA: MIT Press.

Reisberg, D., & Heuer, F. (2004). Memory for emotional events. In D. Reisberg & P. Hertel (Eds.), *Memory and emotion* (pp. 3–41). New York, NY: Oxford University Press.

Reitman, W. (1964). Heuristic decision procedures, open constraints, and the structure of ill-defined problems. In M. Shelley & G. Bryan (Eds.), *Human judgments and optimality* (pp. 282–315). New York, NY: Wiley.

Rensink, R. A. (2012). Perception and attention. In D. Reisberg (Ed.), *Handbook of cognitive psychology.* New York, NY: Oxford University Press.

Rensink, R. A. (2002). Change detection. *Annual Review of Psychology, 53*, 245–277.

Rensink, R. A., O'Regan, J. K., & Clark, J. J. (1997). To see or not to see: The need for attention to perceive changes in scenes. *Psychological Science, 8*, 368–373.

Repp, B. (1992). Perceptual restoration of a "missing" speech sound: Auditory induction or illusion? *Perception & Psychophysics, 51*, 14–32.

Reynolds, C. R., Chastain, R. L., Kaufman, A. S., & McLean, J. E. (1987). Demographic characteristics and IQ among adults: Analysis of the WAIS-R standardization sample as a function of the stratification variables. *Journal of School Psychology, 25(4)*, 323–342.

Reynolds, J. H., Pasternak, T., & Desimone, R. (2000). Attention increases sensitivity of V4 neurons. *Neuron, 26*, 703–714.

Rhodes, G. (2012). Face recognition. In D. Reisberg (Ed.), *Handbook of cognitive psychology.* New York, NY: Oxford University Press.

Rhodes, G., Brake, S., & Atkinson, A. (1993). What's lost in inverted faces? *Cognition, 47*, 25–57.

Riccio, D. C., Millin, P. M., & Gisquet-Verrier, P. (2003). Retrograde amnesia: Forgetting back. *Current Directions in Psychological Science, 12*, 41–44.

Richard, A. M., Lee, H., & Vecera, S. P. (2008). Attentional spreading in object-based attention. *Journal of Experimental Psychology: Human Perception & Performance, 34*, 842–853.

Richardson, J. (1980). *Mental imagery and human memory.* New York, NY: St. Martin's.

Richler, J. J., Cheung, O. S., & Gauthier, I. (2011). Holistic processing predicts face recognition. *Psychological Science, 22,* 464–471.

Richler, J. J., Wong, Y. K., & Gauthier, I. (2011). Perceptual expertise as a shift from strategic interference to automatic holistic processing. *Current Directions in Psychological Science, 20,* 129–134.

Riesenhuber, M., & Poggio, T. (1999). Hierarchical models of object recognition in cortex. *Nature Neuroscience, 2,* 1019–1025.

Riesenhuber, M., & Poggio, T. (2002). Neural mechanisms of object recognition. *Current Opinion in Neurobiology, 12,* 162–168.

Rinck, M. (1999). Memory for everyday objects: Where are the digits on numerical keypads? *Applied Cognitive Psychology, 13,* 329–350.

Rips, L. (1975). Inductive judgements about natural categories. *Journal of Verbal Learning and Verbal Behavior, 14,* 665–681.

Rips, L. (1989). Similarity, typicality, and categorization. In S. Vosniadou & A. Ortony (Eds.), *Similarity and analogical reasoning* (pp. 21–59). Cambridge, England: Cambridge University Press.

Rips, L. (1990). Reasoning. *Annual Review of Psychology, 41,* 321–353.

Rips, L., & Collins, A. (1993). Categories and resemblance. *Journal of Experimental Psychology: General, 122,* 468–489.

Rips, L. J., Smith, E. E., & Medin, D. L. (2012). Concepts and categories: Memory, meaning, and metaphysics. In Holyoak, K. J. & Morrison, R. G. (Eds.), *The Oxford Handbook of Thinking and Reasoning* (pp. 177–209). New York, NY: Oxford University Press.

Ritchie, J. M. (1985). The aliphatic alcohols. In A. G. Gilman, L. S. Goodman, T. W. Rall, & F. Murad (Eds.), *The pharmacological basis of therapeutics* (pp. 372–386). New York, NY: Macmillan.

Rizzi, T., & Posthuma, D. (2012). Genes and intelligence. In D. Reisberg (Ed.), *The Oxford handbook of cognitive psychology.* New York, NY: Oxford University Press.

Robbins, S., Schwartz, B., & Wasserman, E. (2001). *Psychology of learning and behavior* (5th ed.). New York, NY: Norton.

Roberson, D., Davies, I., & Davidoff, J. (2000). Color categories are not universal: Replications and new evidence from a stone-age culture. *Journal of Experimental Psychology: General, 129,* 369–398.

Robertson, L., Treisman, A., Friedman-Hill, S., & Grabowecky, M. (1997). The interaction of spatial and object pathways: Evidence from Balint's syndrome. *Journal of Cognitive Neuroscience, 9,* 295–317.

Roediger, H. L. (1980). The effectiveness of four mnemonics in ordering recall. *Journal of Experimental Psychology: Human Learning and Memory, 6,* 558–567.

Roediger, H. L., & Marsh, E. (2005). The positive and negative consequences of multiple-choice testing. *Journal of Experimental Psychology: Learning, Memory & Cognition, 31,* 1155–1159.

Roediger, H. L., & McDermott, K. (1995). Creating false memories: Remembering words not presented in lists. *Journal of Experimental Psychology: Learning, Memory and Cognition, 21,* 803–814.

Roediger, H. L., & McDermott, K. (2000). Tricks of memory. *Current Directions in Psychological Science, 9,* 123–127.

Rogers, T., & Patterson, K. (2007). Object categorization: Reversals and explanations of the basic-level advantage. *Journal of Experimental Psychology: General, 136,* 451–469.

Roid, G. (2003). *Stanford-Binet Fifth Edition.* Itasca, IL: Riverside.

Rosch, E. (1973). On the internal structure of perceptual and semantic categories. In T. E. Moore (Ed.), *Cognitive development and the acquisition of language* (pp. 111–144). New York, NY: Academic Press.

Rosch, E. (1975). Cognitive representations of semantic categories. *Journal of Experimental Psychology: General, 104,* 192–233.

Rosch, E. (1977a). Human categorization. In N. Warren (Ed.), *Advances in cross-cultural psychology* (pp. 1–49). London, England: Academic Press.

Rosch, E. (1977b). Linguistic relativity. In P. Johnson-Laird & P. Wason (Eds.), *Thinking: Readings in cognitive science* (pp. 501–519). New York, NY: Cambridge University Press.

Rosch, E. (1978). Principles of categorization. In E. Rosch & B. B. Lloyd (Eds.), *Cognition and categorization* (pp. 27–48). Hillsdale, NJ: Erlbaum.

Rosch, E., & Mervis, C. B. (1975). Family resemblances. Studies in the internal structure of categories. *Cognitive Psychology, 7,* 573–605.

Rosch, E., Mervis, C. B., Gray, W., Johnson, D., & Boyes-Braem, P. (1976). Basic objects in natural categories. *Cognitive Psychology, 3,* 382–439.

Rosenbaum, R., Köhler, S., Schacter, D., Moscovitch, M. Westmacott, R., Black, S., Gao, F. & Tulving, E. (2005). The case of K.C.: Contributions of a memory–impaired person to memory theory. *Neuropsychologia, 43,* 989–1021.

Roser, M., & Gazzaniga, M. S. (2004). Automatic brains—Interpretive minds. *Current Directions in Psychological Science, 13,* 56–59.

Ross, B. (1984). Remindings and their effects in learning a cognitive skill. *Cognitive Psychology, 16,* 371–416.

Ross, B. (1987). This is like that: The use of earlier problems and the separation and similarity effects. *Journal of Experimental Psychology: Learning, Memory and Cognition, 13,* 629–639.

Ross, B. (1989). Distinguishing types of superficial similarities: Different effects on the access and use of earlier problems. *Journal of Experimental Psychology: Learning, Memory and Cognition, 15,* 456–468.

Ross, J., & Lawrence, K. A. (1968). Some observations on memory artifice. *Psychonomic Science, 13*, 107–108.

Ross, L., & Anderson, C. (1982). Shortcomings in the attribution process: On the origins and maintenance of erroneous social assessments. In D. Kahneman, P. Slovic, & A. Tversky (Eds.), *Judgment under uncertainty: Heuristics and biases* (pp. 129–152). New York, NY: Cambridge University Press.

Ross, L., Lepper, M., & Hubbard, M. (1975). Perseverance in self perception and social perception: Biased attributional processes in the debriefing paradigm. *Journal of Personality and Social Psychology, 32*, 880–892.

Ross, M., & Wilson, A. E. (2003). Autobiographical memory and conceptions of self: Getting better all the time. *Current Directions in Psychological Science, 12*, 66–69.

Rouder, J. N., & Ratcliff, R. (2006). Comparing exemplar- and rule-based theories of categorization. *Current Directions in Psychological Science, 5*, 9–13.

Rubin, D. C., & Kontis, T. S. (1983). A schema for common cents. *Memory & Cognition, 11*, 335–341.

Rubin, D. C., & Kozin, M. (1984). Vivid memories. *Cognition, 16*, 81–95.

Rubin, D., C. & Talarico, J. (2007). Flashbulb memories are special after all; in phenomology, not accuracy.. *Applied Cognitive Psychology, 21*, 557–558.

Rubin, E. (1915). *Synoplevede figuren*. Copenhagen, Denmark: Gyldendalske.

Rubin, E. (1921). *Visuell wahrgenommene figuren*. Copenhagen, Denmark: Gyldendalske.

Rueckl, J. G., & Oden, G. C. (1986). The integration of contextual and featural information during word identification. *Journal of Memory and Language, 25*, 445–460.

Rugg, M. D., & Curran, T. (2007). Event-related potentials and recognition memory. *Trends in Cognitive Sciences, 11*, 251–257.

Rugg, M. D., & Yonelinas, A. P. (2003). Human recognition memory: A cognitive neuroscience perspective. *Trends in Cognitive Sciences, 7*, 313–319.

Rumelhart, D. E. (1997). The architecture of mind: A connectionist approach. In J. Haugeland (Ed.), *Mind design 2: Philosophy, psychology, artificial intelligence* (2nd rev. & enlarged ed.). Cambridge, MA: MIT Press.

Rumelhart, D. E., & Siple, P. (1974). Process of recognizing tachistoscopically presented words. *Psychological Review, 81*, 99–118.

Rundus, D. (1971). Analysis of rehearsal processes in free recall. *Journal of Experimental Psychology, 89*, 63–77.

Rushton, J. P., & Jensen, A. R. (2006). The totality of available evidence shows the race IQ gap still remains. *Psychological Science, 17*, 921–922.

Russell, C., & Driver, J. (2005). New indirect measures of "inattentive" visual grouping in a change-detection task. *Perception & Psychophysics, 67*, 606–623.

Ruthruff, E., Johnston, J. C., & Remington, R. W. (2009). How strategic is the central bottleneck: Can it be overcome by trying harder? *Journal of Experimental Psychology: Human Perception & Performance, 35*, 1368–1384.

Saalmann, Y., Pigarev, I., & Vidyasagar, T. (2007). Neural mechanisms of visual attention: How top-down feedback highlights relevant locations. *Science, 316*, 1612–1615.

Saffran, J. R. (2003). Statistical language learning: Mechanisms and constraints. *Current Directions in Psychological Science, 12*, 110–114.

Salame, P., & Baddeley, A. D. (1982). Disruption of short-term memory by unattended speech: Implications for the structure of working memory. *Journal of Verbal Learning and Verbal Behavior, 21*, 150–164.

Salthouse, T. A. (2004). What and when of cognitive aging. *Current Directions in Psychological Science, 13*, 140–144.

Salthouse, T. A. (2012). Consequences of age-related cognitive declines. *Annual Review of Psychology, 63*, 201–226.

Salthouse, T., & Pink, J. (2008). Why is working memory related to fluid intelligence? *Psychonomic Bulletin & Review, 15*, 364–371.

Sampaio, C., & Brewer, W. (2009). The role of unconscious memory errors in judgments of confidence for sentence recognition. *Memory & Cognition, 37*, 158–163.

Samuel, A. G. (1987). Lexical uniqueness effects on phonemic restoration. *Journal of Memory and Language, 26*, 36–56.

Samuel, A. G. (1991). A further examination of attentional effects in the phonemic restoration illusion. *Quarterly Journal of Experimental Psychology: Human Experimental Psychology, 43*, 679–699.

Savova, V., Roy, D., Schmidt, L. & Tenenbaum, J. (2007). Discovering syntactic hierarchies. Proceedings of the Twenty-Ninth Annual Conference of the Cognitive Science Society, Nashville, TN.

Sawyer, R. K. (2006). *Explaining creativity: The science of human innovation*. New York, NY: Oxford University Press.

Scarr, S., & Carter-Saltzman, L. (1982). Genetics and intelligence. In R. J. Sternberg (Ed.), *Handbook of human intelligence* (pp. 792–896). New York: Cambridge University Press.

Scarr, S., & Weinberg, R. A. (1983). The Minnesota adoption studies genetic differences and malleability. *Child Development, 54*, 260–267.

Schab, F. (1990). Odors and the remembrance of things past. *Journal of Experimental Psychology: Learning, Memory and Cognition, 16*, 648–655.

Schacter, D. (1996). *Searching for memory: The brain, the mind and the past*. New York, NY: Basic Books.

Schacter, D. (1996). *Searching for memory: The brain, the mind, and the past*. New York, NY: Basic Books.

Schacter, D. (1999). The seven sins of memory. *American Psychologist, 54*, 182–203.

Schacter, D., Guerin, S., & St. Jacques, P. (2011). Memory distortion: an adaptive perspective. *Trends in Cognitive Sciences, 15*, 467–474.

Schacter, D., & Tulving, E. (1982). Amnesia and memory research. In L. S. Cermak (Ed.), *Human memory and amnesia* (pp. 1–32). Hillsdale, NJ: Erlbaum.

Schacter, D., Tulving, E., & Wang, P. (1981). *Source amnesia: New methods and illustrative data*. Paper presented at the meeting of the International Neuropsychological Society, Atlanta, GA.

Schmithorst, V. J. (2009). Developmental sex differences in relation of neuroanatomical connectivity to intelligence. *Intelligence, 37*, 164–173.

Schneider, S. (1992). Framing and conflict: Aspiration level contingency, the status quo, and current theories of risky choice. *Journal of Experimental Psychology: Learning, Memory and Cognition, 18*, 1040–1057.

Schooler, J., Ohlsson, S., & Brooks, K. (1993). Thoughts beyond words: When language overshadows insight. *Journal of Experimental Psychology: General, 122*, 166–183.

Schraw, G., Dunkle, M., & Bendixen, L. (1995). Cognitive processes in well-defined and ill-defined problem solving. *Applied Cognitive Psychology, 9*, 523–538.

Schreiber, C. A., & Kahneman, D. (2000). Determinants of the remembered utility of aversive sounds. *Journal of Experimental Psychology: General, 129*, 27–42.

Schulz-Hardt, S., Frey, D., Lüthgens, C., & Moscovici, S. (2000). Biased information search in group decision making. *Journal of Personality and Social Psychology, 78*, 655–669.

Schunn, C. D., & Anderson, J. R. (1999). The generality/specificity of expertise in scientific reasoning. *Cognitive Science, 23*, 337–370.

Schustack, M., & Sternberg, R. (1981). Evaluation of evidence in causal inference. *Journal of Experimental Psychology: General, 110*, 101–120.

Schwartz, B. (2003). *The paradox of choice*. New York, NY: Ecco.

Schwartz, B. L. (1999). Sparkling at the end of the tongue: The etiology of tip-of-the-tongue phenomenology. *Psychonomic Bulletin & Review, 5*, 379–393.

Schwartz, B. L., & Metcalfe, J. (2011). Tip-of-the-tongue (TOT) states: retrieval, behavior, and experience. *Memory & Cognition 39*, 737–749.

Schwartz, J., Chapman, G., & Brewer, N. (2004). The effects of accountability on bias in physician decision making: Going from bad to worse. *Psychonomic Bulletin & Review, 11*, 173–178.

Schwarz, N. (1998). Accessible content and accessibility experiences: The interplay of declarative and experiential information in judgments. *Personality and Social Psychology Review, 2*, 87–99.

Schwarz, N. (1999). Self-reports: How the questions shape the answers. *American Psychologist, 54*, 93–105.

Schwarz, N., Bless, H., Strack, F., Klumpp, G., Rittenauer-Schatka, H., & Simons, A. (1991). Ease of retrieval as information: Another look at the availability heuristic. *Journal of Personality & Social Psychology, 61*, 195–202.

Scoboria, A., Mazzoni, G., Kirsch, I., & Jimenez, S. (2006). The effects of prevalence and script information on plausibility, belief, and memory of autobiographical events. *Applied Cognitive Psychology, 20*, 1049–1064.

Seamon, J. G., Philbin, M. M., & Harrison, L. G. (2006). Do you remember proposing marriage to the Pepsi machine? False recollections from a campus walk. *Psychonomic Bulletin & Review, 13*, 752–755.

Sedivy, J. C., Tanenhaus, M. K., Chambers, C. G., & Carlson, G. N. (1999). Achieving incremental semantic interpretation through contextual representation. *Cognition, 71*, 109–147.

Seegmiller, J. K., Watson, J. M., & Strayer, D. L. (2011). Individual differences in susceptibility to inattentional blindness. *Journal of Experimental Psychology: Learning, Memory & Cognition, 37*, 785–791.

Segal, E. (2004). Incubation in insight problem solving. *Creative Research Journal, 16*, 141–148.

Segal, S., & Fusella, V. (1970). Influence of imaged pictures and sounds in detection of visual and auditory signals. *Journal of Experimental Psychology, 83*, 458–474.

Segal, S., & Fusella, V. (1971). Effect of images in six sense modalities on detection of visual signal from noise. *Psychonomic Science, 24*, 55–56.

Selfridge, O. (1955). *Pattern recognition and modern computers*. Proceedings of the Western Joint Computer Conference, Los Angeles, CA.

Selfridge, O. (1959). Pandemonium: A paradigm for learning. In D. Blake & A. Uttley (Eds.), *The mechanisation of thought processes: Proceedings of a symposium held at the National Physics Laboratory* (pp. 511–529). London, England: H. M. Stationery Office.

Seltzer, B., & Benson, D. F. (1974). The temporal pattern of retrograde amnesia in Korsakoff's Disease. *Neurology, 24*, 527–530.

Semmler, C., & Brewer, N. (2006). Postidentification feedback effects on face recognition confidence: Evidence for metacognitive influences. *Applied Cognitive Psychology, 20*, 895–916.

Senghas, A., Román, D., & Mavillapalli, S. (2006). *Simply unique*. London: Leonard Cheshire International.

Servos, P., & Goodale, M. A. (1995). Preserved visual imagery in visual form agnosia. *Neuropsychologia, 33*, 1383–1394.

Sevdalis, N., & Harvey, N. (2007). Biased forecasting of postdecisional affect. *Psychological Science, 18*, 678–681.

Shaffer, D. (2004). *Social and personality development* (5th ed.). New York: Wadsworth.

Shafir, E. (1993). Choosing versus rejecting: Why some options are both better and worse than others. *Memory & Cognition, 21*, 546–556.

Shafir, E., & LeBoeuf, R. A. (2002). Rationality. *Annual Review of Psychology, 53*, 491–517.

Shafir, E., Simonson, I., & Tversky, A. (1993). Reason-based choice. *Cognition, 49*, 11–36.

Shaklee, H., & Mims, M. (1982). Sources of error in judging event covariations. *Journal of Experimental Psychology: Learning, Memory and Cognition, 8*, 208–224.

Sharman, S. J., & Barnier, A. J. (2008). Imagining nice and nasty events in the distant or recent past: Recent positive events show the most imagination inflation. *Acta Psychologica, 129*, 228–233.

Sharman, S. J., Manning, C., & Garry, M. (2005). Explain this: Explaining childhood events inflates confidence for those events. *Applied Cognitive Psychology, 19*, 67–74.

Shepard, R. N. (1988). The imagination of the scientist. In K. Egan & D. Nadaner (Eds.), *Imagination and education* (pp. 153–185). New York, NY: Teachers College Press.

Shepard, R. N., & Cooper, L. A. (1982). *Mental images and their transformations*. Cambridge, MA: MIT Press.

Shepard, R. N., & Metzler, J. (1971).Mental rotation of three-dimensional objects. *Science, 171*, 701–703.

Sheppard, L. D. (2008). Intelligence and speed information-processing: A review of 50 years of research. *Personality and Individual Differences, 44*, 535–551.

Shin, H., & Kominski, R. (2010). *Language use in the United States, 2007*. Washington, DC: U.S. Dept. of Commerce Economics and Statistics Administration, US Census Bureau.

Silbersweig, D. A., Stern, E., Frith, C., Cahill, C., Holmes, A., Grootoonk, S., et al. (1995). A functional neuroanatomy of hallucinations in schizophrenia. *Nature, 378*, 176–179.

Simon, H. (1973). The structure of ill-defined problems. *Artificial Intelligence, 4*, 181–201.

Simons, D. J., & Ambinder, M. S. (2005). Change blindness: Theory and consequences. *Current Directions in Psychological Science, 14*, 44–48.

Simons, D. J., & Chabris, C. F. (1999). Gorillas in our midst: Sustained inattentional blindness for dynamic events. *Perception, 28*, 1059–1074.

Simonton, D. K. (2003). Scientific creativity as constrained stochastic behavior: The integration of product, person, and process perspectives. *Psychological Bulletin, 129*, 475–494.

Simonton, D. K. (2009). Creativity as a Darwinian phenomenon: The blind-variation and selective-retention model. In M. Krausz, D. Dutton, & K. Bardsley (Eds.), *The idea of creativity* (2nd ed., pp. 63–81). Leiden, Netherlands: Brill.

Simonton, D. K., & Damian, R. D. (2012). Creativity. In D. Reisberg (Ed.), *The Oxford handbook of cognitive psychology*. New York, NY: Oxford University Press.

Sio, U. N., & Ormerod, T. C. (2009). Does incubation enhance problem solving? A meta-analytic review. *Psychological Bulletin, 135*, 94–120.

Skotko, B. G., Kensinger, E. A., Locascio, J. J., Einstein, G., Rubin, D. C., Tupler, L. A., et al. (2004). Puzzling thoughts for H.M.: Can new semantic information be anchored to old semantic memories? *Neuropsychology, 18*(4), 756–769.

Skotko, B. G., Rubin, D., & Tupler, L. (2008). H.M.'s personal crossword puzzles. *Memory, 16*, 89–96.

Slamecka, N. J., & Graf, P. (1978). The generation effect: Delineation of a phenomenon. *Journal of Experimental Psychology: Human Learning and Memory, 4*, 592–604.

Slobin, D. (1966). Grammatical transformations and sentence comprehension in childhood and adulthood. *Journal of Verbal Learning and Verbal Behavior, 5*, 219–227.

Slovic, P., Finucane, M., Peters, E., & MacGregor, D. G. (2002). The affect heuristic. In T. Gilovich, D. Griffin, & D. Kahneman (Eds.), *Heuristics and biases* (pp. 397–420). New York, NY: Cambridge University Press.

Slovic, P., Fischhoff, B., & Lichtenstein, S. (1982). Facts versus fears: Understanding perceived risk. In D. Kahneman, P. Slovic, & A. Tversky (Eds.), *Judgment under uncertainty: Heuristics and biases* (pp. 463–489). Cambridge, England: Cambridge University Press.

Smedslund, J. (1963). The concept of correlation in adults. *Scandinavian Journal of Psychology, 4*, 165–173.

Smeets, T., Jelicic, M., Peters, M. J. V., Candel, I., Horselenberg, R., & Merckelbach, H. (2006). "Of course I remember seeing that film"—How ambiguous questions generate crashing memories. *Applied Cognitive Psychology, 20*, 779–789.

Smith, E. E. (1988). Concepts and thought. In R. J. Sternberg & E. E. Smith (Eds.), *The psychology of human thought* (pp. 19–49). Cambridge, England: Cambridge University Press.

Smith, E. E., Balzano, G. J., & Walker, J. H. (1978). Nominal, perceptual, and semantic codes in picture categorization. In J. W. Cotton & R. L. Klatzky (Eds.), *Semantic factors in cognition*. Hillsdale, NJ: Erlbaum.

Smith, E. E., Jonides, J., & Koeppe, R. (1996). Dissociating verbal and spatial working memory using PET. *Cerebral Cortex, 6*, 11–20.

Smith, E. E., Rips, L. J., & Shoben, E. J. (1974). Structure and process in semantic memory: A featural model for semantic decisions. *Psychological Review, 81*, 214–241.

Smith, E. R., & Miller, F. (1978). Limits on perception of cognitive processes: A reply to Nisbett & Wilson. *Psychological Review, 85*, 355–362.

Smith, J. D. (2002). Exemplar theory's predicted typicality gradient can be tested and disconfirmed. *Psychological Science, 13*, 437–442.

Smith, M. (1982). *Hypnotic memory enhancement of witnesses: Does it work?* Paper presented at the meeting of the Psychonomic Society, Minneapolis, MN.

Smith, S. M. (1979). Remembering in and out of context. *Journal of Experimental Psychology: Human Learning and Memory, 5*, 460–471.

Smith, S. M. (1985). Background music and context-dependent memory. *American Journal of Psychology, 6*, 591–603.

Smith, S. M., & Blankenship, S. (1991). Incubation and the persistence of fixation in problem solving. *American Journal of Psychology, 104*, 61–87.

Smith, S. M., & Blankenship, S. E. (1989). Incubation effects. *Bulletin of the Psychonomic Society, 27*, 311–314.

Smith, S. M., Glenberg, A., & Bjork, R. A. (1978). Environmental context and human memory. *Memory & Cognition, 6*, 342–353.

Smith, S. M., & Vela, E. (2001). Environmental context-dependent memory: A review and meta-analysis. *Psychonomic Bulletin & Review, 8*, 203–220.

Smith, S. M., & Ward, T.B. (2012). Cognition and the creation of ideas. In Holyoak, K. J., & Morrison, R. G. (Eds.), *The Oxford Handbook of Thinking and Reasoning* (pp. 456–474). New York, NY: Oxford University Press.

Snow, R. E. (1994). Abilities in academic tasks. In R. J. Sternberg & R. K. Wagner (Eds.), *Mind in context: Interactionist perspectives on human intelligence* (pp. 3–37). Cambridge, England: Cambridge University Press.

Snow, R. E. (1996). Aptitude development and education. *Psychology, Public Policy, and Law, 2*, 536–560.

Speekenbrink, M., & Shanks, D. (2012). Decision making. In D. Reisberg (Ed.), *The Oxford handbook of cognitive psychology*. New York, NY: Oxford University Press.

Spelke, E., Hirst, W., & Neisser, U. (1976). Skills of divided attention. *Cognition, 4*, 215–230.

Spelke, E. S. (2005). Sex differences in intrinsic aptitude for mathematics and science? A critical review. *American Psychologist, 60(9)*, 950–958.

Spellman, B. A., Holyoak, K. J., & Morrison, R. G. (2001). Analogical priming via semantic relations. *Memory & Cognition, 29*, 383–393.

Spence, C., & Read, L. (2003). Speech shadowing while driving: On the difficulty of splitting attention between eye and ear. *Psychological Science, 14*, 251–256.

Spence, I., & Feng, J. (2010). Video games and spatial cognition. *Review of General Psychology, 14*, 92–104.

Sperber, D., Cara, F., & Girotto, V. (1995). Relevance theory explains the selection task. *Cognition, 57*, 31–95.

Sperber, D., & Wilson, D. (1986). *Relevance: Communication and cognition*. Cambridge, MA: Harvard University Press.

Spiegel, D. (1995). Hypnosis and suggestion. In D. L. Schacter, J. T. Coyle, G. D. Fischbach, M.-M. Mesulam, & L. E. Sullivan (Eds.), *Memory distortion: How minds, brains and societies reconstruct the past* (pp. 129–149). Cambridge, MA: Harvard University Press.

Sporer, S. (1988). Long-term improvement of facial recognition through visual rehearsal. In M. Gruneberg, P. Morris, & R. Sykes (Eds.), *Practical aspects of memory: Current research and issues* (pp. 182–188). New York, NY: Wiley.

Sporer, S., Penrod, S., Read, D., & Cutler, B. (1995). Choosing, confidence, and accuracy: A meta-analysis of the confidence-accuracy relation in eyewitness identification studies. *Psychological Bulletin, 118*, 315–327.

Squire, L., & McKee, R. (1993). Declarative and nondeclarative memory in opposition: When prior events influence amnesic patients more than normal subjects. *Memory & Cognition, 21*, 424–430.

Stake, J., & Nickens, S. (2005). Adolescent girls' and boys' science peer relationships and perceptions of the possible self as scientist. *Sex Roles, 52*, 1–11.

Stangor, C., & McMillan, D. (1992). Memory for expectancy-congruent and expectancy-incongruent information: A review of the social and social developmental literatures. *Psychological Bulletin, 111*, 42–61.

Stanovich, K. E. (2009). *What intelligence tests miss: The psychology of rational thought*. New Haven, CT: Yale University Press.

Stanovich, K. E. (2012). On the distinction between rationality and intelligence: Implications for understanding individual differences in reasoning. In Holyoak, K. J., & Morrison, R. G. (Eds.), *The Oxford Handbook of Thinking and Reasoning* (pp. 433–455). New York, NY: Oxford University Press.

Stanovich, K. E., & West, R. F. (1998). Who uses base rates and P(Du,H)? An analysis of individual differences. *Memory & Cognition, 26*, 161–179.

Stanovich, K. E., & West, R. F. (2000). Individual differences in reasoning: Implications for the rationality debate. *Behavioral and Brain Sciences, 23*, 645–665.

Stapel, D., & Semin, G. (2007). The magic spell of language: Linguistic categories and their perceptual consequences. *Journal of Personality and Social Psychology, 93*, 23–33.

Steblay, N. J. (1992). A meta-analytic review of the weapon focus effect. *Law and Human Behavior, 16*, 413–424.

Steele, C. (2010). *Whistling Vivaldi: And other clues to how stereotypes affect us*. New York, NY: Norton.

Steele, C. M. & Aronson, J. (1995). Stereotype threat and the intellectual test performance of African Americans. *Journal of Personality and Social Psychology, 69(5)*, 797–811.

Sternberg, R. J. (1985). General intellectual ability. In R. Sternberg (Ed.), *Human abilities: An information processing approach*. New York: Freeman.

Sternberg, R. J. (1988). A three-facet model of creativity. In R. J. Sternberg (Ed.), *The nature of creativity* (pp. 125–147). Cambridge, England: Cambridge University Press.

Sternberg, R. J., Kaufman, J. C., & Grigorenko, E. L. (2008). *Applied intelligence*. New York, NY: Cambridge University Press.

Stevens, A., & Coupe, P. (1978). Distortions in judged spatial relations. *Cognitive Psychology, 10*, 422–437.

Storm, B. (2011). The benefit of forgetting in thinking and remembering. *Current Directions in Psychological Science, 20*, 291–295.

Storm, B., Angello, G., & Bjork, E. (2011). Thinking can cause forgetting: Memory dynamics in creative problem solving. *Journal of Experimental Psychology: Learning Memory & Cognition, 37*, 1287–1293.

Strayer, D. L., & Drews, F. A. (2007). Cell-phone-induced driver distraction. *Current Directions in Psychological Science, 16*, 128–131.

Strayer, D. L., Drews, F. A., & Johnston, W. A. (2003). Cell phone induced failures of visual attention during simulated driving. *Journal of Experimental Psychology: Applied, 9*, 23–32.

Strayer, D. L., & Johnston, W. A. (2001). Driven to distraction: Dual-task studies of simulated driving and conversing on a cellular phone. *Psychological Science, 12*, 462–466.

Strenze, T. (2007). Intelligence and socioeconomic success: A meta-analytic review of longitudinal research. *Intelligence, 35*, 401–426.

Stromeyer, C. (1982). *An adult eidetiker*. In U. Neisser (Ed.), *Memory observed* (pp. 399–404). New York, NY: Freeman.

Stromeyer, C., & Psotka, J. (1970). The detailed texture of eidetic images, *Nature, 225,* 346–349.

Stroop, J. R. (1935). Studies of interference in serial verbal reaction. *Journal of Experimental Psychology, 18,* 643–662.

Stuss, D. T., & Knight, R. T. (Eds.). (2002). *Principles of frontal lobe function*. New York, NY: Oxford University Press.

Stuss, D. T., & Levine, B. (2002). Adult clinical neuropsychology: Lessons from studies of the frontal lobes. *Annual Review of Psychology, 53,* 401–433.

Sulin, R. A., & Dooling, D. J. (1974). Intrusion of a thematic idea in retention of prose. *Journal of Experimental Psychology, 103,* 255–262.

Sumby, W. H. (1963). Word frequency and serial position effects. *Journal of Verbal Learning and Verbal Behavior, 1,* 443–450.

Sundet, J., Eriksen, W., & Tambs, K. (2008). Intelligence correlations between brothers decrease with increasing age difference: Evidence for shared environmental effects in young adults. *Psychological Science, 19,* 843–847.

Svartik, J. (1966). *On voice in the English verb*. The Hague, Netherlands: Mouton.

Symons, C. S., & Johnson, B. T. (1997). The self-reference effect in memory: A meta-analysis. *Psychological Bulletin, 121,* 371–394.

Tabachnick, B., & Brotsky, S. (1976). Free recall and complexity of pictorial stimuli. *Memory & Cognition, 4,* 466–470.

Talarico, J. M., & Rubin, D. C. (2003). Confidence, not consistency, characterizes flashbulb memories. *Psychological Science, 14,* 455–461.

Talmi, D., Grady, C. L., Goshen-Gottstein, Y., & Moscovitch, M. (2005). Neuroimaging the serial position curve: A test of single-store versus dual-store models. *Psychological Science, 16,* 716–723.

Tamietto, M., et al. (2010). Collicular vision guides nonconscious behavior. *Journal of Cognitive Neuroscience, 22,* 888–902.

Tanenhaus, M. K., & Spivey-Knowlton, M. J. (1996). Eyetracking. *Language & Cognitive Processes, 11,* 583–588.

Tanenhaus, M. K., & Trueswell, J. C. (2006). Eye movements and spoken language comprehension. In M. J. Traxler & M. A. Gernsbacher (Eds.), *Handbook of psycholinguistics* (2nd ed.). Amsterdam, Netherlands: Elsevier.

Tarr, M. (1995). Rotating objects to recognize them: A case study on the role of viewpoint dependency in the recognition of three-dimensional objects. *Psychonomic Bulletin & Review, 2,* 55–82.

Tarr, M. (1999). News on views: Pandemonium revisited. *Nature Neuroscience, 2,* 932–935.

Tarr, M., & Bülthoff, H. (1998). Image-based object recognition in man, monkey and machine. *Cognition, 67,* 1–208.

Tattersall, I., & DeSalle, R. (2011). *Race? Debunking a scientific myth*. College Station, TX: Texas A&M University Press.

Taylor, J., Roehrig, A., Hensler, B., Connor, C. & Schatschneider, C. (2010). Teacher quality moderates the genetic effects on early reading. *Science, 328,* 512–514.

Terr, L. C. (1991). Acute responses to external events and posttraumatic stress disorders. In M. Lewis (Ed.), *Child and adolescent psychiatry: A comprehensive textbook* (pp. 755–763). Baltimore, MD: Williams & Wilkins.

Terr, L. C. (1994). *Unchained memories: The stories of traumatic memories, lost and found*. New York, NY: Basic Books.

Thaler, R. & Sunstein, C. (2009). Nudge: Improving decisions about health, wealth, and happiness. New York, NY: Penguin.

Thioux, M., Stark, D. E., Klaiman, C., & Shultz, R. T. (2006). The day of the week when you were born in 700 ms: Calendar computation in an autistic savant. *Journal of Experimental Psychology: Human Perception and Performance, 32,* 1155–1168.

Thomas, A. K., & Loftus, E. F. (2002). Creating bizarre false memories through imagination. *Memory & Cognition, 30,* 423–431.

Thomas, J. (1974). An analysis of behavior in the Hobbits-Orcs problem. *Cognitive Psychology, 6,* 257–269.

Thompson, P. (1980). Margaret Thatcher: A new illusion. *Perception, 9,* 483–484.

Thompson, W. L., & Kosslyn, S. M. (2000). Neural systems activated during visual mental imagery: A review and meta-analyses. In J. Mazziotta & A. Toga (Eds.), *Brain mapping II: The applications* (pp. 535–560). New York, NY: Academic Press.

Thompson, W. L., Kosslyn, S. M., Hoffman, M. S., & Kooij, K. v. d. (2008). Inspecting visual mental images: Can people "see" implicit properties as easily in imagery and perception? *Memory & Cognition, 36,* 1024–1032.

Thompson, W. L., Slotnick, S., Burrage, M., & Kosslyn, S. (2009). Two forms of spatial imagery: Neuroimaging evidence. *Psychological Science, 20,* 1245–1253.

Thomsen, D. K., & Berntsen, D. (2009). The long-term impact of emotionally stressful events on memory characteristics and life story. *Applied Cognitive Psychology, 23,* 579–598.

Thomson, D., Milliken, B., & Smilek, D. (2010). Long-term conceptual implicit memory: A decade of evidence. *Memory & Cognition, 38,* 42–46.

Tinti, C., Schmidt, S., Sotgiu, I., Testa, S., & Curci, A. (2009). The role of importance/consequentiality appraisal in flashbulb memory formation: The case of the death of Pope John Paul II. *Applied Cognitive Psychology, 23,* 236–253.

Todd, P. M., & Gigerenzer, G. (2007). Environments that make us smart. *Current Directions in Psychological Science, 16,* 167–171.

Tombu, M., & Jolicoeur, P. (2003). A central capacity sharing model of dual-task performance. *Journal of*

Experimental Psychology: Human Perception & Performance, 29, 3–18.

Tong, F., Nakayama, K., Vaughan, J. T., & Kanwisher, N. (1998). Binocular rivalry and visual awareness in human extrastriate cortex. *Neuron, 21,* 753–759.

Topolinski, S., & Reber, R. (2010). Gaining insight into the "Aha" experience. *Current Directions in Psychological Science, 19,* 402–405.

Treisman, A. (1964). Verbal cues, language, and meaning in selective attention. *American Journal of Psychology, 77,* 206–219.

Treisman, A., & Gelade, G. (1980). A feature-integration theory of attention. *Cognitive Psychology, 12,* 97–136.

Treisman, A., Sykes, M., & Gelade, G. (1977). Selective attention and stimulus integration. In S. Dornic (Ed.), *Attention and performance VI* (pp. 333–361). Hillsdale, NJ: Erlbaum.

Trucker-Drob, E., Rhemtulla, M., Harden, K., Turkheimer, E. & Fask, D. (2011). Emergence of a gene x socioeconomic status interaction on infant mental ability between 10 months and 2 years. *Psychological Science, 22,* 125–133.

Trueswell, J. C., Tanenhaus, M.K., & Garnsey, S. M. (1994). Semantic influences on parsing: Use of thematic role information in syntactic ambiguity resolution. *Journal of Memory and Language, 33,* 285–318.

Tsai, C. & Thomas, M. (2011). When does feeling of fluency matter? How abstract and concrete thinking influence fluency effects? *Psychological Science, 22,* 348–354.

Tsushima, Y., Sasaki, Y., & Watanabe, T. (2006). Greater disruption due to failure of inhibitory control on an ambiguous distractor. *Science, 314,* 1786–1788.

Tucker-Drob, E. M., Rhemtulla, M., Harden, K. P., Turkheimer, E., & Fask, D. (2011). Emergence of a gene x socioeconomic status interaction on infant mental ability between 10 months and 2 years. *Psychological science, 22,* 125–133.

Tuffiash, M., Roring, R., & Ericsson, K. A. (2007). Expert performance in SCRABBLE: Implications for the study of the structure and acquisition of complex skills. *Journal of Experimental Psychology: Applied, 13,* 124–134.

Tulving, E. (1983). *Elements of episodic memory.* Oxford, England: Oxford University Press.

Tulving, E. (1993). What is episodic memory? *Current Directions in Psychological Science, 2,* 67–70.

Tulving, E. (2002). Episodic memory: From mind to brain. *Annual Review of Psychology, 53,* 1–25.

Tulving, E., & Gold, C. (1963). Stimulus information and contextual information as determinants of tachistoscopic recognition of words. *Journal of Experimental Psychology, 92,* 319–327.

Tulving, E., Mandler, G., & Baumal, R. (1964). Interaction of two sources of information in tachistoscopic word recognition. *Canadian Journal of Psychology, 18,* 62–71.

Turkheimer, E., Haley, A., Waldron, M., D'Onofrio, B., & Gottesman, I. I. (2003). Socioeconomic status modifies heritability of IQ in young children. *Psychological Science, 14,* 623–628.

Tversky, A., & Kahneman, D. (1973). Availability: A heuristic for judging frequency and probability. *Cognitive Psychology, 5,* 207–232.

Tversky, A., & Kahneman, D. (1974). Judgments under uncertainty: Heuristics and biases. *Science, 185,* 1124–1131.

Tversky, A., & Kahneman, D. (1982). Evidential impact of base rates. In D. Kahneman, P. Slovic, & A. Tversky (Eds.), *Judgment under uncertainty: Heuristics and biases* (pp. 153–160). New York, NY: Cambridge University Press.

Tversky, A., & Kahneman, D. (1987). Rational choice and the framing of decisions. In R. Hogarth & M. Reder (Eds.), *Rational choice: The contrast between economics and psychology* (pp. 67–94). Chicago, IL: University of Chicago Press.

Tweney, R. D., Doherty, M. E., & Mynatt, C. R. (1981). *On scientific thinking.* New York, NY: Columbia University Press.

Ullman, S. (2007). Object recognition and segmentation by a fragment-based hierarchy. *Trends in Cognitive Science, 11,* 58–64.

Ungerleider, L. G., & Haxby, J. V. (1994). "What" and "where" in the human brain. *Current Opinions in Neurobiology, 4,* 157–165.

Ungerleider, L. G., & Mishkin, M. (1982). Two cortical visual systems. In D. J. Ingle, M. A. Goodale, & R. J. W. Mansfield (Eds.), *Analysis of visual behavior* (pp. 549–586). Cambridge, MA: MIT Press.

Unkelbach, C. (2007). Reversing the truth effect: Learning the interpretation of processing fluency in judgments of truth. *Journal of Experimental Psychology: Learning, Memory and Cognition, 33,* 219–230.

Unsworth, N., & Engle, R. (2007). The nature of individual differences in working memory capacity: Active maintenance in primary memory and controlled search in secondary memory. *Psychological Review, 114,* 104–132.

Valentine, T. (1988). Upside-down faces: A review of the effects of inversion upon face recognition. *British Journal of Psychology, 79,* 471–491.

Van der Lely, H. (2005). Domain-specific cognitive systems: Insight from grammatical-SLI. *Trends in Cognitive Science, 9,* 53–59.

Van Essen, D. C., & DeYoe, E. A. (1995). Concurrent processing in the primate visual cortex. In M. S. Gazzaniga (Ed.), *The cognitive neurosciences* (pp. 383–400). Cambridge, MA: MIT Press.

Van Goozen, S., Cohen-Kettenis, P., Gooren, L., Frijda, N., & Van de Poll, N. (1995). Gender differences in behavior: Activating cross-sex hormones. *Psychoneuroendocrinology, 20,* 343–363.

Van Steenburgh, J. J., Fleck, J. I., Beeman, M., & Kounios, J. (2012). Insight. In Holyoak, K. J., & Morrison, R. G. (Eds.), *The Oxford Handbook of Thinking and Reasoning* (pp. 475–491). NY: Oxford University Press.

Vandierendonck, A., Liefooghe, B., & Verbruggen, F. (2010). Task switching: Interplay of reconfiguration and interference control. *Psychological Bulletin, 136,* 601–626.

Vanpaemel, W., & Storms, G. (2008). In search of abstraction: The varying abstraction model of categorization, *Psychonomic Bulletin & Review, 15,* 732–749.

Vartanian, O., Martindale, C., & Matthews, J. (2009). Divergent thinking ability is related to faster relatedness judgments. *Psychology of Aesthetics, Creativity, and the Arts, 3,* 99–103.

Vergaujwe, E., Barrouillet, P., & Camos, V. (2010). Do mental processes share a domain-general resource? *Psychological Science, 21,* 384–390.

Vernon, P. A. (Ed.). (1987). *Speed of information processing and intelligence.* Canada: Ablex.

Verstijnen, I. M., Hennessey, J. M., van Leeuwen, C., Hamel, R., & Goldschmidt, G. (1998). Sketching and creative discovery. *Design Studies, 19,* 519–546.

Verstijnen, I. M., van Leeuwen, C., Goldschmidt, G., Hamel, R., & Hennessey, J. M. (1998). Creative discovery in imagery and perception: Combining is relatively easy, restructuring takes a sketch. *Acta Psychologica, 99,* 177–200.

Vinkhuyzen, A. A., van der Sluis, S., & Posthuma, D. (2011). Life events moderate variation in cognitive ability (g) in adults. *Molecular Psychiatry, 16*(1), 4–6.

Visser, B., Ashton, M., & Vernon, P. (2006). Beyond "g": Putting multiple intelligences theory to the test. *Intelligence, 34,* 487–502.

Vitevitch, M. S. (2003). Change deafness: The inability to detect changes between two voices. *Journal of Experimental Psychology: Human Perception and Performance, 29,* 333–342.

Vo, M. L. H., & Henderson, J. M. (2009) Does gravity matter? Effects of semantic and syntactic inconsistencies on the allocation of attention during scene perception. *Journal of Vision, 9*(3): 24, 1–15.

von Neumann, J., & Morgenstern, O. (1947). *Theory of games and economic behavior.* Princeton, NJ: Princeton University Press.

Vul, E., & Pashler, H. (2007). Incubation benefits only after people have been misdirected. *Memory & Cognition, 35,* 701–710.

Vuoksimaa, E., et al. (2010). Having a male co-twin masculinizes mental rotation performance in females. *Psychological Science, 21,* 1069–1071.

Vuong, Q. C., & Tarr, M. (2004). Rotation direction affects object recognition. *Vision Research, 44,* 1717–1730.

Wade, C. (2006). Some cautions about jumping on the brain-scan bandwagon. *The APS Observer, 19,* 23–24.

Wade, K. A., Garry, M., Read, J. D., & Lindsay, D. S. (2002). A picture is worth a thousand lies: Using false photographs to create false childhood memories. *Psychononic Bulletin & Review, 9,* 597–603.

Wagenaar, W. A., & Groeneweg, J. (1990). The memory of concentration camp survivors. *Applied Cognitive Psychology, 4,* 77–88.

Wagner, A. D., Koutstaal, W., & Schacter, D. L. (1999). When encoding yields remembering: Insights from event-related neuroimaging. *Philosophical Transactions of the Royal Society of London, Biology, 354,* 1307–1324.

Wagner, A. D., Schacter, D. L., Rotte, M., Koutstaal, W., Maril, A., Dale, A., et al. (1998). Building memories: Remembering and forgetting of verbal experiences as predicted by brain activity. *Science, 281,* 1188–1191.

Wagner, A. D., Shannon, B., Kahn, I., & Buckner, R. (2005). Parietal lobe contributions to episodic memory retrieval. *Trends in Cognitive Sciences, 9,* 445–453.

Wagner, R. K. (2000). Practical intelligence. In R. J. Sternberg (Ed.), *Handbook of human intelligence* (pp. 380–395). New York: Cambridge University Press.

Walker, S. (1993). Supernatural beliefs, natural kinds, and conceptual structure. *Memory & Cognition, 20,* 655–662.

Wallas, G. (1926). *The art of thought.* New York, NY: Harcourt, Brace.

Wallis, G., & Bülthoff, H. (1999). Learning to recognize objects. *Trends in Cognitive Sciences, 3,* 22–31.

Walton, G. & Spencer, S. (2009). Latent ability: Grades and test scores systematically underestimate the intellectual ability of negatively stereotyped students. *Psychological Science, 20,* 1132–1139.

Wang, M., & Bilger, R. (1973). Consonant confusion in noise: A study of perceptual features. *Journal of the Acoustical Society of America, 54,* 1248–1266.

Wang, R., Li, J., Fang, H., Tian, M., & Liu, J. (2012). Individual differences in holistic processing predict face recognition ability. *Psychological Science, 23,* 169–177.

Wang, S. H., and Morris, R. G. (2010). Hippocampal-neocortical interactions in memory formation, consolidation, and reconsolidation. *Annual Review of Psychology, 61,* 49–79.

Wason, P. (1966). Reasoning. In B. Foss (Ed.), *New horizons in psychology* (pp. 135–151). Middlesex, England: Penguin.

Wason, P. (1968). Reasoning about a rule. *Quarterly Journal of Experimental Psychology, 20,* 273–281.

Wason, P., & Johnson-Laird, P. (1972). *Psychology of reasoning: Structure and content.* Cambridge, MA: Harvard University Press.

Watkins, M., Wilson, S., Kotz, K., Carbone, M., & Babula, T. (2006). Factor structure of the Wechsler Intelligence Scale for Children—Fourth edition among referred students. *Educational and Psychological Measurement, 66,* 975–983.

Watkins, M. J. (1977). The intricacy of memory span. *Memory & Cognition, 5,* 529–534.

Wattenmaker, W. D., Dewey, G. I., Murphy, T. D., & Medin, D. L. (1986). Linear separability and concept learning: Context, relational properties, and concept naturalness. *Cognitive Psychology, 18,* 158–194.

Waugh, N. C., & Norman, D. A. (1965). Primary memory. *Psychological Review, 72,* 89–104.

Wearing, D. (2011). *Forever today: A memoir of love and amnesia*. New York, NY: Doubleday.

Weaver, C. (1993). Do you need a "flash" to form a flashbulb memory? *Journal of Experimental Psychology: General, 122,* 39–46.

Weber, E., & Johnson, E. (2009). Mindful judgment and decision making. *Annual Review of Psychology, 60,* 53–85.

Weber, N., Brewer, N., Wells, G., Semmler, C., & Keast, A. (2004). Eyewitness identification accuracy and response latency: The unruly 10–12-second rule. *Journal of Experimental Psychology: Applied, 10,* 139–147.

Wechsler, D. (2003). *Wechsler intelligence scale for children—Fourth edition*. San Antonio, TX: Psychological Corporation.

Wegner, D., Wenzlaff, R., Kerker, R., & Beattie, A. (1981). Incrimination through innuendo: Can media questions become public answers? *Journal of Personality and Social Psychology, 40,* 822–832.

Weisberg, R. (1986). *Creativity: Genius and other myths*. New York, NY: Freeman.

Weisberg, R., & Alba, J. (1981). An examination of the alleged role of "fixation" in the solution of several "insight" problems. *Journal of Experimental Psychology: General, 110,* 169–192.

Weisberg, R., DiCamillo, M., & Phillips, D. (1978). Transferring old associations to new problems: A nonautomatic process. *Journal of Verbal Learning and Verbal Behavior, 17,* 219–228.

Weiskrantz, L. (1986). *Blindsight: A case study and implications*. New York, NY: Oxford University Press.

Weiskrantz, L. (1997). *Consciousness lost and found*. New York, NY: Oxford University Press.

Wells, G. L., & Bradfield, A. L. (1998). "Good, you identified the suspect": Feedback to eyewitnesses distorts their reports of the witnessed experience. *Journal of Applied Psychology, 83,* 360–376.

Wells, G. L., Lindsay, R. C. L., & Ferguson, T. J. (1979). Accuracy, confidence, and juror perceptions in eyewitness identification. *Journal of Applied Psychology, 64,* 440–448.

Wells, G. L., Luus, C. A. E., & Windschitl, P. (1994). Maximizing the utility of eyewitness identification evidence. *Current Directions in Psychological Science, 3,* 194–197.

Wells, G. L., Olson, E. A., & Charman, S. D. (2002). The confidence of eyewitnesses in their identifications from lineups. *Current Directions in Psychological Science, 11,* 151–154.

Wells, G. L., Olson, E. A., & Charman, S. D. (2003). Distorted retrospective eyewitness reports as functions of feedback and delay. *Journal of Experimental Psychology: Applied, 9,* 42–51.

Wells, G. L., & Quinlivan, D. S. (2009). Suggestive eyewitness identification procedures and the Supreme Court's reliability test in light of eyewitness science: 30 years later. *Law and Human Behavior, 33,* 1–24.

Westmacott, R., & Moscovitch, M. (2003). The contribution of autobiographical significance to semantic memory. *Memory & Cognition, 31,* 761–774.

Wetherick, N. (1989). Psychology and syllogistic reasoning. *Philosophical Psychology, 2,* 111–124.

Wharton, C., Holyoak, K., Downing, P., & Lange, T. (1994). Below the surface: Analogical similarity and retrieval competition in reminding. *Cognitive Psychology, 26,* 64–101.

Wheeler, D. (1970). Processes in word recognition. *Cognitive Psychology, 1,* 59–85.

White, J. (2008). Illusory intelligences? *Journal of Philosophy of Education, 42,* 611–630.

White, P. (1988). Knowing more than we can tell: "Introspective access" and causal report accuracy 10 years later. *British Journal of Psychology, 79,* 13–45.

Whitney, C. (2001). How the brain encodes the order of letters in a printed word: The SERIOL model and selective literature review. *Psychonomic Bulletin & Review, 8,* 221–243.

Whittlesea, B. W. A. (2002). False memory and the discrepancy-attribution hypothesis: The prototype-familiarity illusion. *Journal of Experimental Psychology: General, 131,* 96–115.

Whittlesea, B. W. A., Jacoby, L., & Girard, K. (1990). Illusions of immediate memory: Evidence of an attributional basis for feelings of familiarity and perceptual quality. *Journal of Memory and Language, 29,* 716–732.

Whorf, B. L. (1956). *Language, thought, and reality*. Cambridge, England: Technology Press.

Wilkins, M. (1928). The effect of changed material on ability to do formal syllogistic reasoning. *Archives of Psychology, 16,* 83.

Willemsen, M., Böckenholt, U., & Johnson, E. (2011). Choice by value encoding and value construction: Processes of loss aversion. *Journal of Experimental Psychology: General, 140,* 303–324.

Williams, L. M., Liddell, B. J., Kemp, A. H., Bryant, R. A., Meares, R. A., Peduto, A S., & Gordon, E. (2006). Amygdala-prefrontal dissociation of subliminal and supraliminal fear. *Human Brain Mapping 27*(8), 652–661.

Wilson, T. D. (2002). *Strangers to ourselves: Discovering the adaptive unconscious*. Cambridge, MA: Harvard University Press.

Wilson, T. D., & Dunn, E. W. (2004). Self-knowledge: Its limits, value, and potential for improvement. *Annual Review of Psychology, 55,* 493–518.

Wilson, T. D., Wheatley, T., Meyers, J. M., Gilbert, D., & Axsom, D. (2000). Focalism: A source of durability bias in affective forecasting. *Journal of Personality and Social Psychology, 78,* 821–836.

Winkielman, P., & Schwarz, N. (2001). How pleasant was your childhood? Beliefs about memory shape inferences from experienced difficulty of recall. *Psychological Science, 12,* 176–179.

Winnick, W., & Daniel, S. (1970). Two kinds of response priming in tachistoscopic recognition. *Journal of Experimental Psychology, 84*, 74–81.

Winograd, E., & Neisser, U. (Eds.). (1993). *Affect and accuracy in recall: Studies of "flashbulb" memories.* New York, NY: Cambridge University Press.

Wiseman, S., & Neisser, U. (1974). Perceptual organization as a determinant of visual recognition memory. *American Journal of Psychology, 87*, 675–681.

Wittgenstein, L. (1953). *Philosophical investigations* (G. E. M. Anscombe, Trans.). Oxford, England: Blackwell.

Wixted, J. (1991). Conditions and consequences of maintenance rehearsal. *Journal of Experimental Psychology: Learning, Memory and Cognition, 17*, 963–973.

Wixted, J. (2004). The psychology and neuroscience of forgetting. *Annual Review of Psychology, 55*, 235–269.

Wollen, K. A., Weber, A., & Lowry, D. (1972). Bizarreness versus interaction of mental images as determinants of learning. *Cognitive Psychology, 3*, 518–523.

Womelsdorf, T., Schoffelen, J.-M., Oostenveld, R., Singer, W., Desimone, R., Engel, A., & Fries, P. (2007). Modulation of neuronal interactions through neuronal synchronization. *Science, 316*, 1609–1612.

Wong, A. C.-N., Palmeri, T. J., & Gauthier, I. (2009). Conditions for facelike expertise with objects. *Psychological Science, 20*, 1108–1117.

Wood, N., & Cowan, N. (1995). The cocktail party phenomenon revisited: How frequent are attention shifts to one's name in an irrelevant auditory channel? *Journal of Experimental Psychology: Learning, Memory and Cognition, 21*, 255–260.

Woodworth, R., & Sells, S. (1935). An atmosphere effect in formal syllogistic reasoning. *Journal of Experimental Psychology, 18*, 451–460.

Wright, D., & Skagerberg, E. (2007). Postidentification feedback affects real eyewitnesses. *Psychological Science, 18*, 172–177.

Xu, F., & Garcia, V. (2008). Intuitive statistics by 8-month-old infants. *Proceedings of the National Academy of Sciences, 105*, 5012–5015.

Yamaguchi, M., & Proctor, R. (2011). Automaticity without extensive training: The role of memory retrieval in implementation of task-defined rules. *Psychonomic Bulletin and Review, 18*, 347–354.

Yantis, S. (2008). The neural basis of selective attention: Cortical sources and targets of attentional modulation. *Current Directions in Psychological Science, 17*, 86–90.

Yates, F. A. (1966). *The art of memory.* London, England: Routledge and Kegan Paul.

Yeni-Komshian, G. (1993). Speech perception. In J. B. Gleason & N. B. Ratner (Eds.), *Psycholinguistics* (pp. 90–133). New York, NY: Harcourt Brace Jovanovich.

Yin, R. (1969). Looking at upside-down faces. *Journal of Experimental Psychology, 81*, 141–145.

Young, A. W., Hellawell, D., & Hay, D. C. (1987). Configurational information in face perception. *Perception, 16*, 747–759

Yuille, J. (Ed.). (1983). *Imagery, memory, and cognition.* Hillsdale, NJ: Erlbaum.

Zaragoza, M. S., Payment, K. E., Ackil, J. K., Drivdahl, S. B., & Beck, M. (2001). Interviewing witnesses: Forced confabulation and confirmatory feedback increases false memories. *Psychological Science, 12*, 473–477.

Zelazo, P. D. (2006). The dimensional change card sort (DCCS): A method of assessing executive function in children. *Nature Protocols, 1*, 297–301.

Zihl, J., Von Cramon, D., & Mai, N. (1983). Selective disturbance of movement vision after bilateral brain damage. *Brain, 106*, 313–340.

Zimler, J., & Keenan, J. M. (1983). Imagery in the congenitally blind: How visual are visual images? *Journal of Experimental Psychology: Learning, Memory and Cognition, 9*, 269–282.

Credits

Photographs

p. 3: © Steve Prezant/Corbis; **p. 5:** J. Carlee Adams/Bullshotz Photography; **p. 6:** © Image Source/SuperStock; **p. 7:** Brooks Kraft/Corbis; **p. 8:** Dr. Jacopo AnneseDirector, The Brain Observatory, University of California San Diego; **p. 9:** Center for the History of Psychology/University of Akron; **p. 12:** Ferdinand Hamburger Archives, Sheridan Libraries, Johns Hopkins University; **p. 13:** Tracey Lind, 2011; **p. 15:** Lebrecht Music and Arts Photo Library/Alamy; **p. 24:** From J. Jonides; **p. 25** AP Photo; **p. 29:** Cary Wolinksy/Aurora Photos; **p. 32:** SPL/Photo Researchers; **p. 33:** (right) Children's Hospital and Medical Center/Corbis; **p. 36:** (left) Courtesy Warren Museum, Harvard Medical School; (center and right) Damasio, H., Grabowski, T., Frank, R., Galaburda, A. M., & Damasio, A. R. (1994), The return of Phineas Gage: Clues about the brain from the skull of a famous patient, *Science,* 264; courtesy Hanna Damasio; **p. 41:** Dr. M. Phelps and Dr. J. Mazziotta et al./Neurology/Photo Researchers, Inc.; **p. 42:** (left) James Cavallini/Photo Researchers, Inc.; (center) G. Tompkinson/Photo Researchers, Inc.; (right) Scott Camazine/Photo Researchers, Inc.; **p. 44:** Jack Liu; **p. 45:** Courtesy of Tong, F., Kakayma, K., Vaughen, J. T., & Kanwisher, N. Binocular rivalry and visual awareness in human estrastriate cortex, *Neuron* 21, 735–759; **p. 50:** © The Natural History Museum, London; **p. 53:** (B) SPL/ Photo Researchers, Inc.; (C) CNRI/SPL/Photo Researchers, Inc.; (D) Guigoz/ Dr. A Privat/Petit Format/Science Source/ Photo Researchers, Inc.; **p. 58:** Omikron/ Photo Researchers, Inc.; **p. 75:** © Cat Gwynn/Corbis; **p. 81:** Photograph by Jeffery Grosscup; **p. 85:** Russell Glenister/Corbis; **p. 110:** Thompson, Peter (1980), Margaret Thatcher: A new illusion, *Perception,* Vol. 9, pages 483–484; **p. 111:** Gauthier, I., Skudlarski, P., Gore, J., & Anderson, A. (2000), Expertise for cars and birds recruits brain areas involved in face recognition, *Nature Neuroscience, 3,* 191–197, Fig. 3; **p. 112:** (left) Kevin Winter/Getty Images; (right) Stephen Lovekin/Getty Images; **p. 117:** Paul Bradbury/Getty Images; **p. 120:** Courtesy of Daniel J. Simons;

p. 123: iStockphoto; **p. 126:** (top) Galina Barskaya | Dreamstime .com; (bottom) Titania1980 | Dreamstime.com; **p. 127:** Levin, D. T., & Simons, D. J. (1997), Failure to detect changes to attended objects in motion pictures, *Psychonomic Bulletin and Review, 4(4),* 501–506 ; **p. 136:** Rykoff Collection/Corbis; **p. 145:** The Granger Collection; **p. 148:** AP Photo/Marshall Gorby, Springfield News-Sun; **p. 163:** Digital Vision/Getty Images; **p. 172:** Talmi, Grady, Goshen-Gottstein, & Moscovitch, 2005; **p. 186:** (left) © Imagic Chicago/Alamy; (right) © Stuart Black / Alamy; **p. 188:** © Delaware Art Museum, Samuel and Mary R. Bancroft Memorial, 1935; **p. 189:** © Sidney Harris/ScienceCartoonsPlus.com; **p.194:** After Wiseman and Neisser, 1974; **p. 199:** Tim Macpherson/Cultura/Getty Images; **p. 213:** (top left) Jason LaVeris/FimMagic/Getty Images; (top center) Jason DeCrow/AP Photo; (top right) Jordan Strauss/Wire Image/Getty Images; (bottom left) Chris Pizzello/AP Photo; (bottom center) Theo Wargo/Getty Images; (bottom right) Stephen Shugerman/Getty Images; **p. 222:** Courtesy of Daniel Reisberg; **p. 225:** Junko Kimura/Getty Images; **p. 229:** (top) © Ros Drinkwater / Alamy; (bottom) Polaris; **p. 237:** Ryan McVay/Getty Images; **p. 240:** Photograph from "Role of schemata in memory for places," by W. F. Brewer and J. C. Treyens, *Cognitive Psychology, 13,* 207–230; **p. 248:** Eric Kayne/*Houston Chronicle*; **p. 252:** Les Stone/Sygma/Corbis; **p. 253:** Lindsay, D. S., et al., True photographs and false memories, *Psychological Science* 15 (149–154); **p. 254:** Robyn Mackenzie/Shutterstock; **p. 263:** AP Photo/Jim Cooper; **p. 266:** Dolan, R. J., et al. (2000), Dissociable temporal lobe activations during emotional episodic memory retrieval, *NeuroImage, 11,* 203–209; **p. 268:** (left) Bettmann/Corbis; (center) Reuters; (right) Joel Ryan/AP Photo; **p. 283:** Gozooma/Gallery Stock; **p. 285:** Tierfotoagentur/Alamy; **p. 288:** (top left) Getty Images; (all others) Eric Isselée | Dreamstime.com; **p. 291:** © Adrian Lewart/Dreams time.com; **p. 293:** (top) Rick & Nora Bowers/Alamy; (bottom left) Photoshot Holdings Ltd/Alamy; (bottom right) Hiroya Minakuchi/Getty Images; **p. 295:** Emilio Ereza/AgeFotostock;

p. 296: EPA European PressPhoto Agency B.V./Alamy; p. 299: © Look and Learn/the Bridgeman Art Library International; p. 301: © Sidney Harris/ScienceCartoonsPlus.com; p. 303: © age fotostock/Superstock; p. 306: Courtesy of Robert Malseed; p. 308: Courtesy of Daniel Reisberg; p. 323: J. Meric/ Getty Images; p. 330: © Courtney Leigh Rubin/Creators Syndicate, Inc.; p. 332: iStockphoto; p. 338: © Lebrecht Music & Arts/Corbis; p. 340: Hulton-Deutsch Collection/Corbis; p. 343: © Sidney Harris; p. 356: ColsTravel/Alamy; p. 363: Photomontage by Friderike Heuer; p. 369: Claus Fritzmann/ dieKleinert/Alamy; p. 373: Comstock/Getty Images; p. 376: Atlantide Phototravel/Corbis; p. 381: Tenniel, John (1820– 1914) / Private Collection / The Bridgeman Art Library; p. 382: Creative Commons; p. 384: © Kellydt/Dreamstime .com; p. 392: Intraub, H., and Richardson, M., Boundary extension in picture memory, *Journal of Experimental Psychology, 15,* 179–87, reprinted by permission; p. 399: Sean Justice/Getty Images; p. 408: © Yungshu Chao/iStockPhoto; p. 412: (left) National Pictures; p. 420: © Sidney Harris/ ScienceCartoonsPlus.com; p. 425: © Sidney Harris/Science CartoonsPlus.com; p. 439: Mark Parisi/offthemark.com; p. 445: Lucidio Studio, Inc. / Getty Images; p. 463: © Sam Gross / The New Yorker Collection / www.cartoonbank.com; p. 480: From Jung, R. E., & Haier, R. J. (2007), The parieto-frontal integration theory (P-FIT) of intelligence: Converging neuroimaging evidence, *Behavioral and Brain Sciences, 30,* 135–187, courtesy Brain and Behavioral Associates, PC; p. 482: Selfe, S. Nadia, A Case of Extraordinary Drawing Ability in an Autistic Child, New York: Academic Press, 1977, reproduced by permission of Academic Press and Lorna Selfe; p. 484: (top) Tony Freeman / PhotoEdit; p. 484: (bottom) © Bob Sacha; p. 489: Robert Churchill/Getty Images; p. 497: Sarah Wilmer /Gallery Stock; p. 504: Joel W. Rogers/Corbis; p. 506: © John Caldwell; p. 513: Alamy; p. 523: © John Springer Collection/Corbis.

Figures

p. 61, Figure 2.15: Figure 4.30 A and B from Coren, Porac, & Ward, *Sensation and Perception, 3rd Edition* (1989), p. 155. Reprinted with permission of John Wiley & Sons, Inc.; p. 86, Figure 3.8: Selfridge, Oliver, Context influences perception (pattern recognition), *Proceedings of the Western Computer Conference,* copyright © 1955 by IEEE [We have made diligent efforts to contact the copyright holder to obtain permission to reprint this selection. If you have information that would help us, please write to Permissions Department, W. W. Norton & Company, Inc., 500 Fifth Avenue, New York, NY 10110]; p. 103, Figure 3.16: From Rumelhat & McClelland, An inter-active model of context effects in letter perception, *Psychological Review, 88.5:* 375–407, copyright © 1981 by the American Psychological Association; p. 107, Figure 3.18: Reprinted from Irving Biederman, Human image understanding: Recent research and a theory, *Computer Vision, Graphics and Image Processing, 32,* 29–73, copyright © 1985, published by Elsevier Inc., with permission from Elsevier; p. 151, Figure 4.16: Kimberg, D'Esposito, & Farah, Fig. 1 from Cognitive functions in the prefrontal cortex—Working memory and executive control, *Current Directions in Psychological Science,* Vol. 6, No. 6 (Dec. 1997), p. 186, copyright © 1998 American Psychological Society, reprinted by permission of Blackwell Publishing Ltd.; p. 174, Figure 5.6: From Cabeza, R., & Nyberg, L., Imaging cognition II: An empirical review of 275 PET and fMRI studies, *Journal of Cognitive Neuroscience, 12,* 1–47, Fig. 7, p. 17, copyright © 2000 by the Massachusetts Institute of Technology, reprinted by permission; p. 194, Figure 5.15: From Wiseman & Neisser, Perceptual organization as a determinant of visual recognition memory, *American Journal of Psychology* 87:4 (December 1974), copyright © 1974 by the Board of Trustees of the University of Illinois, used with permission of the author and the University of Illinois Press; p. 274, Figure 7.12: From Conway, Cohen, & Stanhope, On the very long-term retention of knowledge acquired through formal education: Twelve years of cognitive psychology, *Journal of Experimental Psychology 120,* 395–409, reprinted by permission of the American Psychological Association; p. 370, Figure 10.3: From Shepard & Metzler (1971), Mental rotation of three-dimensional objects, *Science 171:* 701–703, copyright © 1971, The American Association for the Advancement of Science, reprinted with permission from AAAS; p. 417, Figure 11.2: From Nisbett, Krantz, Jepson, & Kunda, The use of statistical heuristics in everyday reasoning, *Psychological Review, 90,* 339–363, reprinted by permission of the American Psychological Association; p. 418, Figure 11.3: From Fong & Nisbett, Immediate and delayed transfer of training effects in statistical reasoning, *Journal of Experimental Psychology, 120,* Fig. 2, pp. 34–45, reprinted by permission of the American Psychological Association; p. 431, Figure 11.10: Tversky, A., & Kahneman, D., Rational choice and the framing of decisions, *Journal of Business,* 59:4, part 2, copyright © 1986 by the University of Chicago Press, reprinted by permission; p. 440, Figure 11.16: From Kermer et al., *Cognitive Psychology, 3rd Edition,* Figure 13.10, p. 378, copyright © 2006 Cengage Learning, reprinted with permission; p. 456, Figure 12.8: R. Bootzin, Fig. 8.15 from *Psychology Today: An Introduction, 4th Edition,* copyright © The McGraw-Hill Companies, Inc., reprinted with permission.

Author Index

Friedman-Hill, S. R., 70, 88
Fries, P., 69
Frijda, N., 490
Frome, P. M., 490
Frost, P., 256
Fthenaki, K., 230
Fukuda, K., 479
Fukui, M., 128
Fulker, D. W., 483
Fusella, V., 373, 374

Gabbay, P., 250
Gable, P. A., 267
Gabrieli, J., 180
Gaeth, G., 435
Gage, P., 35, 36, 150
Gaissmaier, W., 418
Galanter, E., 16
Gallagher, A. M., 490
Gallo, D. A., 244
Galton, F., 365, 379
Garcia, J., 492
Garcia-Marques, L., 413
Garcia-Marques, T, 219
Gardelle, V., 518
Gardiner, J. M., 213
Gardner, H., 481–82
Garnsey, S. M., 347
Garrett, B., 248
Garry, M., 250, 256
Gathercole, S., 26, 175, 256
Gauthier, I., 110, 111, 112
Gazzaniga, M. S., 68, 505, 515, 516
Gelade, G., 69, 143
Gelman, R., 403
Gelman, S., 300
Gentner, D., 303, 305, 452
Geraerts, E., 251, 253, 254, 271, 272
German, T., 300, 459
Geschwind, N., 351
Ghetti, S., 272
Gibson, E., 92, 345, 346
Gick, M., 452, 454
Giesbrecht,T., 272
Gigerenzer, G., 414, 415, 418, 419, 428
Gilbert, C. A., 136
Gilbert, D., 440
Gilbert, D. T., 414, 439, 440, 441
Gilbert, S. J., 149
Gilhooly, K. J., 424, 426

Gilovich, T., 402, 409, 411, 412, 420, 422, 437
Girard, K., 226
Girotto, V., 414, 428
Gisquet-Verrier, P., 230
Giudice, N. A., 377
Glanzer, M., 167, 169
Gläscher, J., 480
Glaser, R., 455
Gleitman, H., 298, 517
Gleitman, L., 359
Gleitman, L. R., 298, 352, 359
Glenberg, A., 202
Glisky, E. L., 32
Glisky, M., 384
Glover, G., 180
Gluck, M., 292
Glucksberg, S., 299, 350
Gobet, F., 420, 457
Godden, D. R., 201
Goebel, R., 375
Goel, V., 413
Gold, C., 113
Goldenberg, G., 378
Goldenberg, J., 470
Goldin-Meadow, S., 352
Goldman-Rakic, P. S., 150, 516
Goldschmidt, G., 384, 451
Goldstone, R., 303
Gollan, T., 360
Gonzalez, C., 402, 414
Goodale, M. A., 67, 378, 507, 508, 521
Goodman, G., 271
Goodman, G. S., 270
Goodman, N., 303
Gooren, L., 490
Gordon, H., 485
Gordon, R. D., 263
Gore, J. C., 110
Goshen-Gottstein, Y., 171, 172
Gottesman, I. I., 487
Gottesman, C. V., 391
Gottfredson, L. S., 472, 475
Gould, S. J., 471
Grabowecky, M., 70, 88
Grabowski, T., 310
Grady, C. L., 171, 172
Graesser, A. C., 350
Graf, P., 182, 216, 232, 521
Grafman, J., 150

Graham, K. S., 264
Grainger, J., 95
Grant, H. M., 202
Gray, J. R., 175, 479
Gray, W. D., 258, 287
Green, R. L., 485
Green, D., 360
Green, M. A., 248
Greenberg, J., 342
Greenfield, P. M., 486
Gregg, M. K., 128
Grewal, D., 481
Griffin, D. W., 402, 411, 413
Griffith, B., 332
Griggs, R., 428
Grigorenko, E. L., 481
Grisso, T., 253
Grodner, D., 345
Groeneweg, J., 269
Gross, J., 517
Grossi, D., 109
Grotzer, T. A., 486
Group, T. L. R., 314
Gruber, H. E., 469
Gudjonsson, G., 253
Guerin, S., 264
Guilford, J., 469
Gupta, N., 469
Guyer, M. J., 272

Haber, R. N., 381
Hacker, H., 375
Hackman, D., 487
Haden, P., 216
Haden, P. E., 521
Hafstad, G. S., 256
Hahn, U., 453
Haier, R., 479, 480
Halamish, V., 262
Halari, R., 490
Halberstadt, J., 293
Haley, A., 487
Hall, L., 265, 275
Halle, M., 328, 334
Halliday, H. E., 219
Halpern, D., 458, 489, 490, 492
Hamann, S., 266, 271
Hambrick, D., 149, 175
Hamel, R., 384, 451
Hamill, R., 405
Hammarberg, R., 329
Han, C-H., 359
Han, J., 112

Hanako, Y., 359
Handel, S., 332
Handley, S. J., 414, 425
Hannon, B., 175, 480
Hanye, H., 275
Harden, K. P., 487
Hardt, O., 266
Harinck, F., 433
Harkness, A., 409
Harley, T. A., 258
Harmon-Jones, E., 267
Harris, K., 332
Harrison, L. G., 250
Harsch, N., 268, 269
Harvey, N., 439
Harwood, D. G., 30
Hashtroudi, S., 522
Hasselmo, M. E., 271
Hastie, R., 308, 309, 439, 440
Haun, D. B. M., 358
Hawkins, J., 342
Haxby, J. V., 67, 150
Hayes, M. E. B., 485
Hayes, B. K., 308
Hayes, J., 453
Hayward, W., 106
Heathcote, A., 256
Hebb, D., 318
Hecht, P., 148
Heckman, J. J., 485
Hegarty, M., 378, 450
Heil, M., 374, 390
Heine, S., 492
Heit, E., 307, 308
Hell, W., 415
Heller, J., 457
Helmuth, L., 46
Helstrup, T., 450
Hemphill, R., 148
Henderson, J. M., 247, 391
Henle, G., 423
Henner, M., 263
Hennessey, B., 464, 465
Hennessey, J. M., 384, 451
Hennighausen, E., 374, 390
Henry, P. J., 481
Hensler, B. S., 488
Hermer-Vazquez, L., 359
Hernández, M., 360
Hertwig, R., 226, 411, 414
Herzog, S. M., 226
Hessels, S., 121
Heuer, F., 267
Hezlett, S. A., 474
Hichwa, R. D., 31

A68   **Author Index**

Singer, W., 375, 515
Sio, U. N., 467
Siple, P., 90, 98
Sirigu, A., 438
Skagerberg, E., 255
Skotko, B. G., 230
Skudlarski, P., 110
Slamecka, N. J., 182
Sloan, K., 491
Slobin, D., 346
Sloman, S. A., 428
Slotnick, S., 378
Slovic, P., 403, 404, 414, 435, 437, 438
Smedslund, J., 409
Smeets, T., 239
Smilek, D., 227
Smith, J. R., 487
Smith, A., 373
Smith, E., 499
Smith, E. E., 289
Smith, J., 92
Smith, J. D., 297
Smith, L. A., 452
Smith, L. B., 359
Smith, S., 202, 203, 467, 468
Smith, S. M., 202, 468, 469
Smith, W. C., 300
Smythe, P. C., 389
Snell, J., 439
Snow, R. E., 476
Snyder, A., 479
Snyder, C., 131, 132, 134
Solomon, S., 470
Sotgiu, I., 270
Spearman, C., 476
Speekenbrink, M., 431
Spelke, E. S., 490
Spelke, E., 157
Spelke, E. S., 359
Spellman, B., 113
Spence, I., 490
Spence, C., 148
Spence, I., 490
Spencer, S. J., 492
Spencer, S., 492
Sperber, D., 350, 428
Spiegel, D., 260
Spinath, F. M., 474, 483
Spivey-Knowlton, M. J., 349
Sporer, S., 255
Spratling, M. N., 69
Spuhler, J. N., 491
Squire, L. R., 232

Sroka, H., 109
St. Jacques, P., 264
Stake, J., 490
Stangor, C., 420
Stanhope, N., 192, 274, 275
Stankiewicz, B. J., 104
Stanovich, K. E., 413, 481
Stapel, D., 359
Starr, J. M., 474
Steblay, N. J., 267
Steele, C. M., 490, 492
Steele, C., 492
Sternberg, R. J., 409, 481
Stevens, A., 388
Stoehs, S.-A., 391
Stolz, J. A., 155
Storm, B., 260, 469
Storms, G., 297, 308
Strayer, D. L., 128, 148, 149
Strenze, T., 474
Stromeyer, C., 381
Stroop, J. R., 155
Stull, A. T., 378, 450
Sturgill, W., 221, 393
Stuss, D., 150
Sulin, R. A., 193
Summala, H., 148
Sundet, J., 484
Sunstein, C., 441
Suzuki, S., 88
Svartik, J., 346
Sweeney, J., 251
Sykes, M., 69
Symons, C. S., 265

Tabachnick, B., 393
Takarae, Y., 300
Talarico, J. M., 269
Talmi, D., 171, 172
Tambs, K., 484
Tamietto, M., 507
Tanenhaus, M. K., 344, 346, 347, 349
Tarr, M., 106, 108
Tarr, M. J., 111
Tattersall, I., 491
Taylor, J., 488
Tellegen, A., 483
Tenenbaum, J., 417
Terr, L. C., 271
Testa, S., 270
Teuber, H. L., 231
Thagard, P. R., 415
Thaler, R., 441
Thatcher, M., 109, 270

Thee, S., 435
Thioux, M., 482
Thomas, A., 250
Thomas, A. K., 250
Thomas, J., 449
Thomas, M., 227
Thomas, M. S. C., 512
Thompsen, D. K., 270
Thompson, B., 476
Thompson, P., 109, 110
Thompson, V. A., 414
Thompson, W., 67
Thompson, W. L., 375, 378, 384
Thomson, D., 227
Tian, M., 112
Tinti, C., 270
Tipper, S., 121, 139
Titchener, E. B., 9, 10
Todd, P. M., 419
Tom, S., 214
Tomkiewicz, S., 485, 486
Tong, F., 45, 380
Tononi, G., 517
Tooby, J., 414
Topolinski, S., 467
Towne, T. J., 154, 455, 457
Towse, J. N., 173
Tranel, D., 67, 109, 310, 438
Treisman, A., 69, 70, 88, 119, 143
Treyens, J. C., 239, 240
Trueswell, J. C., 344, 347
Tsai, C., 227
Tsushima, Y., 121
Tucker-Drob, E. M., 487
Tuffiash, M., 457
Tugade, M. M., 511
Tulving, E., 113, 182, 183, 186, 205, 231, 264
Tunnicliff, J., 255
Tupler, L., 230
Turkheimer, E., 487
Tversky, A., 401, 402, 409, 410, 415, 417, 431, 432, 435
Tweney, R. D., 409, 421

Ullman, S., 108
Underwood, G., 21
Ungerleider, L. G., 67, 150
Unkelbach, C., 219
Unsworth, N., 150
Updike, J., 503

Valentine, T., 109
Van Beest, I., 433
Vandierendonck, A., 149
Van de Poll, N., 490
Van Dijk, E., 433
Van Essen, D. C., 66
Van Goozen, S., 490
Van Hoesen, G. W., 110
van Koppen, P. J., 239
van Leeuwen, C., 384, 451
Vanous, S., 221
Vanpaemel, W., 297
van Steenburgh, J. J., 467
van Veen, V., 517
Vartanian, O., 413, 469
Vaughan, J. T., 45
Vecera, S. P., 139, 140
Vela, E., 202
Verbruggen, F., 149
Vergaujwe, E., 148
Vernon, P. A., 479, 482
Verstijnen, I. M., 384, 451
Vidyasagar, T., 70
Vijayan, S., 355
Vinkhuyzen, 488
Vishton, P. M., 355
Visser, B., 482
Vitevitch, M. S., 128
Vo, M. L. H., 247, 391
Vogel, E., 479
Vogel, E. K., 128
Von Cramon, D., 68
von Neumann, J., 430, 431
Vrij, A., 239
Vul, E., 469
Vuoksimaa, E., 490
Vuong, Q. C., 106

Wade, K. A., 251
Wagenaar, W. A., 239, 269
Wagenmakers, E.-J., 479
Wagner, R. K., 481
Wagner, A., 214
Wagner, A. D., 180, 214
Walbridge, M., 31
Waldron, M., 487
Walker, S., 300
Wallas, G., 465
Wallis, G., 106
Walsh, V., 88, 137
Walters, A. A., 386, 387
Walton, G., 492
Wang, M., 328
Wang, P., 232

Subject Index

Note: Italicized page locators indicate figures; notes and tables are denoted with *n* and *t*.

incubation in, 465, 467–69, *468*, 494

moment of illumination in, 465, *466*, 467

nature of, 469–70, *470*, *471*

crystallized intelligence, 477–78, *478*, *495*

CT (computerized axial tomography) scans, 40, 41, 43

data, codable, 415–16, *416*

data format, importance of, 414

deaf children, language learning in, 352

deaf community, *25*

decay, forgetting and, 257, 259

decision-making, 429–41, 443

amygdala and, 34

emotional factors in, 437–41, *439*, *440*, 443

framing in

of outcomes, *431*, 431–34, *432*, *433*

of questions and evidence, *434*, 434–35

maximizing utility vs. seeing reasons, 435–37, *436*, *437*

reason-based choice and, 435

regret and, 437, 438

risk aversion in, 433

risk seeking in, 433

utility theory in, 430–31

deduction, 419

deep processing, 182–83, *183*, 184, *187*, 197

Deese-Roediger-McDermott (DRM) procedure, *243*, 243–44, 277

definitions, 284–87, *286*, 319

degraded pictures, recognizing, *107*

demand character, avoiding concerns about, 372–73

dendrites, 52, *53*

depictions, 366, 383

descriptive rules, 339–40

detectors

bigram, 94, *95*

feature, 87, 97

letter, 97

networks of, 115, 207

diagnostic information, 411

diagrams in problem-solving, 450–51, *452*, 493

dichotic listening, 119–20, *120*

digits, memory for, 193, *193*

digit-span task, 172–74

direct memory tests, 216

disconfirmation and confirmation, 419–23, *420*, *421*

distributed knowledge, 100–101

distributed processing, 315–17

distributed representations, 315–17, 320

divergent thinking, creativity as, *470*

diversity of knowledge, 393–94

divided attention, 117, *145*, 145–52, 151–52, 154, 158

executive control and, 149–51, *151*

general resources identification and, 147–49, *148*, *149*

specificity of resources and, 146–47, *147*

dizygotic twins, intelligence and, 483–84, *484*, *485*

dogs chase cats proposition, network representation of, 314–15, *315*

dot detectors, 61

double dissociation, 230

dreaming, consciousness and, 514

DRM (Deese-Roediger-McDermott) procedure, *243*, 243–44, 277

dual coding, 390, 395

dual-process models, 411–19

background knowledge and, 416–18, *418*

data format in, 414–15

evidence and, 418–19

more sophisticated strategies in, 412–13

System 1 and System 2 in, 413–14

duck/rabbit figure, 383, *383*

early selection hypothesis, 128–29

echoic memory, 165

edge detectors, 62

edge enhancement, lateral inhibition and, 60, *61*

EEG (electroencephalogram), 43

efficiency vs. accuracy, 101–2, 304

eidetic imagery, 380–82, *381*, 395

Einstellung, 459–62, *461*, 494

elaborative (or relational) rehearsal, 179, 197

El Al plane crash, 239

electrical activity of brain, recording, 42–43, *44*

electric shock treatment, 501–3, *502*, 503

electroencephalogram (EEG), 43

emotion

decision-making and, 437–41, *439*, *440*, 443

memory and, *266*, 266–67, 278–79

emotional intelligence, 481, 495

encoding specificity, 204–6, 234

environment and intelligence, 484–87, *486*, *487*

interaction among genetics, IQ, and, 487–88, 495

episodic memories, 227, *227*, 229

errors

affirming the consequent, *426*

conjunction, 70

denying the antecedent, *426*

heuristics and, 442

in logic, 400, *425*, 425–26, *426*

memory, *see* memory errors

over-regularization, 354

word recognition, 92, 98–100, *99*

error signals, 318

event-related potential, 43, *44*

evidence

conclusions drawn from, *see* judgment

framing of, *434*, 434–35

for working-memory system, 19–22, *20*, *21*, 27

excitatory connections, 103, *103*

executive control, 149–51, *151*, 177, 479

consciousness and, 508–12, *510*

neuronal workspace and, 516–17

exemplars, 292–97, 319, 320

analogies from, 292–94

prototypes and, 295–97, *296*, 319–20

typicality and, 292, *293*, 294–95, *295*

exoneration of the innocent, 248

expectation-based priming, 134, 143

expected value, 430

experts as problem-solvers, 455–56, 494

explanatory theories, 305–7, *306*

explicit memory, 216, 235, 277

amnesia and, 232-33, *233*

implicit memory and, *217*, 227, *227*

extralinguistic context, 348–49, *349*

eyes, 56–58, *57*, *58*

see also visual system

eyewitnesses, memory of, 248, 500–501, *502*

faces

brain activity and awareness of, 43

recognition of, 31, 34–35, 76, 108–12, *109*, *110*, *111*, *112*, 116

factor analysis, 476

false fame test, 218–19

perception and, 364, 373–76, *374*
as stimulation, 373
vivid, 380
images
auditory, 373, *374*
chronometric studies of, 366–70, *367, 368, 369, 394*
demand character and, 372–73
dual coding and, 390, 395
individual differences and, 379–80
introspections about, 365–66
in long-term memory, 364, 385–86, *386*
as a memory aid, 389
mental rotation and, *370*, 370–72, *371*
perception and, 364, 373–76, *374*
pictures vs., *382*, 382–85, *383, 384*, 395
self-report data on, 365–66
sensory effects in, 376–77
spatial vs. visual, 377–79, 394–95
verbal coding of, 386–88, *387, 388*
vividness of, 380
image-scanning experiments, map of fictional island used in, *367*, 367
image-scanning procedure, 368, *368*
implicit memory, 215–27, 235, 277
attribution to wrong source, 221, *222*
attribution to wrong stimulus, 220–21
cognitive unconscious and, 506–7
consciousness and, *525*
explicit memory and, *217*, 227, *227*
false fame test and, 218–19
familiarity and, 224–27, *226*
hypothesis about, 223–25, 224n, *225*
illusion of truth and, 219–20
theoretical treatments of, 221–27, *224, 226*
without awareness, 215–17, *217, 219*
inattentional blindness, *122*, 122–24, *123*
incidental learning, 182, 184
incubation
creativity and, 465, 467–69, *468*, 494
indirect memory tests, 216, *219*
induction, 419, *420*, 441
inferences based on theories, 307–8, *308*
information processing
memory acquisition and, 165
modal model of, 165–67, *166*
view of memory, 165, *166*
inhibitory connections, 102, 103, *103*

initial state, 447
inner ear, 22, 23
inner hand, *25*
inner speech, 23
inner voice, *20*, 22, 23
insight problems, studies of, *466*
inspection time and intelligence, 479
integrative agnosia, 88
intelligence, 470–93, *494, 495*
beyond IQ tests, 481–83, *485*
building blocks of, 478–80, *480*
defining and measuring, 472–73, *473*
emotional, 481, *495*
fluid and crystallized, 477–78, *478, 495*
general vs. specialized, 475–76, *495*
hierarchical model of, 476–77, *477*
intellectual functioning and, 480–81
multiple, 481–82
practical, 481, *495*
roots of, 483–93
comparisons of groups in
American Whites and African Americans, 491–93, *496*
men and women, 488–91, *489, 495–96*
environment and, 484–87, *486, 487*
genetics and, 483–84, *484, 485, 495*
interaction among genetics, environment, and IQ, 487–88, *495*
tests, *see* IQ tests
intentional behavior, consciousness and, 520
intentional learning, 182, *183*, 184
interference and forgetting, 257, 259, 263–64
interpolated activity, recency effect and, 169, *170*
introspection, 10–11, 26–27, 365–66, 503–5, *504*
intrusion errors, 242
invalid syllogisms, 424
inversion effect, faces and, *109*
IQ tests, 472–73, *473*, 494–95
comparisons of scores
between American Whites and African Americans, 491–93, 496
between men and women, 488–91, *489*, 495–96
intelligence beyond, 481–83, *485*

poverty and, 485–88, *487*
reliability and validity in, 473–75, 475t
usefulness of, 480–81
see also intelligence
iris, 57

judgment, 400–406, 441
covariation and, 407–11
base-rate neglect in, 411, 417
base rates in, 409–11, 410t, 442
illusory, 407–9, *408*, 411, 442
dual-process models and, 411–19
background knowledge and, 417–18, *418*
codable data and, 415–16, *416*
data format in, 414–15
evidence and, 418–19
more sophisticated strategies in, 412–13
System 1 and System 2 in, 413–14
heuristics, 400, 441
attribute substitution, 401–2, 401t
availability, 401–4
reasoning from single case to entire population and, 405–6, *406*
representativeness, 402, 404–5, 441
justification for action, consciousness and, 520–23, *523*

KABC (Kaufman Assessment Battery for Children), 472
Kantian logic, 16, 20
Kaufman Assessment Battery for Children (KABC), 472
Kennedy assassination, 267
knowledge, 281, 318–20
about animals, *312*, 312–13
background, 5–6, 417–18, *418*
distributed, 100–101
diversity of, 393–94
generic, 265
locally represented, 101
schematic, 244–45, 277
evidence for, 245, *246*, 247
reliance on, 263
scientific study of, 4
spatial, 388
visual, 363–95
Korsakoff's syndrome, 231–32, 233, 506

reasoning, 442–43
about conditional statements, *426, 426–27, 427*
about syllogisms, 423–24, *424*
cognitive unconscious and, 500
confirmation and disconfirmation and, 419–23, *420*
belief perseverance in, 422–23
confirmation bias, 420–21, *421,* 442
reinterpreting disconfirming evidence, 422
in decision-making, 429–41, 443
emotional factors in, 437–41, *439, 440,* 443
framing of
outcomes in, *431,* 431–34, *432, 433*
questions and evidence in, *434,* 434–35
maximizing utility vs. seeing reasons, 435–37, *436, 437*
reason-based choice and, 435
utility theory in, 430–31, 443
logic and, 423–29, 442
conditional statements and, *426, 426–27, 427*
errors in, 400, *425,* 425–26, *426*
four-card task and, *426,* 426–29, *427, 428, 429,* 443
from single case to entire population, 405–6, *406*
recall, free, 167, *168*
recency effect, 167, *168,* 169, *170*
receptive fields, 61–63, *62, 63,* 71
recognition
by components, 104–6, *105, 107*
of degraded pictures, *107*
errors, 98–100, *99*
of faces, 31, 34–35, 76, 108–12, *109, 110, 111, 112,* 116
holistic, 111–12, *112*
memory tests and, 211
object, *see* object recognition
pattern, 111, *112*
via multiple views, 106, 108
viewpoint-dependent, 108
viewpoint-independent, 106
word, *see* word recognition
reconstruction, after-the-fact, 499, 504–5
recovered memories, 271, 272
recovery from confusion, 95–97, *96*
reference frame, *384*
referents, 335, 336

regret, decision-making and, 437, 438
rehearsal
articulatory, 26
memory and, 168–69, 178–79, *180,* 197
relational (elaborative), 179
types of, 178–79, *180*
working memory, *24*
rehearsal loop, 18, *25, 26, 27,* 177
relational (or elaborative) rehearsal, 179
reliability and validity, 473–75, 475t
remembering, long, long-term, 272–75, *273, 274*
"remember/know" distinction, 256–57
reminiscence bump, 275, *276*
Remote Associates Test, *471*
repetition priming, 89, 94, 131, 210, 216
representativeness heuristic, 402, 404–5, 441
repressed memories, 271
research
in cognitive psychology: an example, 16–26
on happiness, 440–41
resemblance, categorization via, 297–303, 298t, *299,* 304
response selector, 149
response threshold, 93, 206
response times, 130–32
retention intervals, 257, *258, 259,* 272, 275
reticular activating system, 513
retina, 56, *57,* 71
retrieval, *see* memory retrieval
retrieval cues, 203–4, 207, *208,* 271
retrieval failure, 257, *258*–59, 271, 278
retrieval paths, 187, 197, 200–201, 211, 234, 241
retrograde amnesia, 228–30, *228*
right prefrontal cortex, 32
risk-aversion, 433
risk-seeking, 433
rods of eye, 56, *58, 58,* 71
Rorschach tests, 407–8, *408, 409,* 411

sample bias, 442
sample size, *416*
San Francisco earthquake (1989), 269
SAT scores, 490
savant syndrome, 482, *482*
schemata, 244–45, 263, 392–93
schematic knowledge, 244–45, 277
evidence for, 245, *246,* 247
reliance on, 263

schizophrenia, 32
scientific study of knowledge, 4
segmentation, speech, 328, *330*
selection task, *see* four-card task
selective attention, 118–45
change blindness and, 125–28, *126, 127*
chronometric studies and, 134–35, *135*
conscious and unconscious perception in, 124–25, *125*
costs and benefits in, 133–34, *144*
dichotic listening and, 119–20, *120*
early vs. late selection and, 128–29
feature binding and, 142–43, *144*
inattentional blindness and, *122,* 122–24, *123*
and limits on cognitive capacity, 121, 144–45
object-based vs. space-based, *138,* 138–42, *139, 141*
priming and, 130–33, 131t, *132*
selective priming and, 129–30
spatial attention and, 134–38, *135, 136, 137*
unattended inputs and, 120–21
selective priming, 129–30
self, memory and, 265–66
self-reference effect, 265, 278
self-report data, 365–66
self-schema, 265
semantic bootstrapping, 355
semantic facts, time needed in confirming of, *313*
semantic priming, 208–10, *211*
sensory effects in imagery, 376–77
sensory memory, 165
sentences, *325, 325*–26, 337
active, 346
in extralinguistic context, 348–49, *349*
garden-path, 344–45, *350*
parsing of, 344–50, *347, 349,* 361
passive, 346
syntax of, 337–44
linguistic rules and competence, 338–40, *340*
linguistic universals, 338–40, *340*
phrase structure of, 338, *339*
sentence verification, 289, 311–14, *312, 313,* 319
September 11 attack (2001), 270
serial-position curve, 167, *168*
serial-position effect, rate of list presentation and, *171*

visual perception, 75, 115, 374, 394
visual processing pathways, 65, *65*
visual search tasks, 142
visual shapes, memory span and, 22
visual system, *56–70*, 71
   lateral inhibition, 58–60, *59, 61*
   optic nerve, 58, 59–60, 71
   parallel processing in, *64,* 64–68, *65, 67,* 71, 72
   photoreceptors, 56–58, *57, 58*
   receptive fields, 61–63, *62, 63*
   single neurons and single-cell recording, 60–61, 71
   visual maps and firing synchrony, 69–70
visuo-spatial buffer, 177
vivid imagery, 380
vocal folds (vocal cords), *327*
voicing, 326

WAIS (Wechsler Adult Intelligence Scale), 472
water-jar problem, 460–61, *461*
Wechsler Adult Intelligence Scale (WAIS), 472
Wechsler Intelligence Scale for Children (WISC), 472
well-defined problems, 458
well-formedness

feature nets and, 94–95, *95*
   in word recognition, 90–92
Wernicke's area, 351, *351*
what system, 66–67, *67, 68,* 71
where system, 67, *67, 68,* 71
White Americans, IQ scores of, 491–93, 496
WISC (Wechsler Intelligence Scale for Children), 472
witnesses, memory of, 500–501, *502*
WMC, *see* working-memory capacity (WMC)
women, academic achievement and, 488–91, *489,* 495–96
word recognition, 88–92, 115
   errors in, 92, 98–100, *99*
   factors in, 88–89, *89*
   feature nets and, 92–102
   McClelland and Rumelhart model of, 102–4, *103*
   repetition priming in, 89, 94
   well-formedness in, 90–92
   word-superiority effect in, 90, *91,* 115
words
   building, 336–37, 361
   linguistic rules and, *325*
   meaning and, 335–36
word-stem completion, 216
word-superiority effect, 90, *91,* 115

working memory, 16–26, 166–67, 171–78, 196–97
   active nature of, *174,* 174–76, *176*
   brain damage and, *24*
   in broader context, 25–26
   function of, 171–72
   holding capacity of, 172–74
   initial observations on, 16–15
   long-term memory vs., 165–71, *168, 170, 171, 172*
   nature of, 22–25
   neuronal workspace and, 516
   proposal in, 17–19, *19*
   short-term memory as, 165
   span test of, 17, 21, *21*
working-memory capacity (WMC), 175–76, 479, 495
working-memory system, 17, 176–77
   central executive in, 17–18, *19, 20,* 27, 176–78
   evidence for, 19–22, *20, 21,* 27
   low-level assistants in, 18, *19,* 27
   phonological buffer in, 18–19, *19, 20*
   rehearsal loop in, 18, *25, 26,* 27, 177
   visuospatial buffer in, 177
World Trade Center attack (2001), 267, *268*

z-scores, 478